INTRODUCTION

Since 1982, when *Test Cricket Lists* was first published, there has been a dramatic increase in the number of Test matches: 263 were played between August 1982 and October 1992, while only 933 were played between March 1877 and August 1982.

These past ten years have produced many outstanding contests. New record partnerships have been established, and outstanding bowling figures returned. There have also been several fine wicketkeeping and fielding performances. While descriptions of the most impressive games may be found in the 'Famous Test Matches' section, the complete records are detailed in the updated and extended 'Test Match Records' section. And, to this end, statistician Charlie Wat has been magnificent. His attention to detail and presentation of the statistics are matched only by his great knowledge, understanding and love of the game, all of which have proved to be a constant source of strength.

In compiling this book, I am indebted to the works of some far more erudite students of the game than me. In particular, I acknowledge my debt to the *Wisden Book of Test Cricket* and the *Wisden Book of Cricket Records,* both compiled by Bill Frindall, the *Wisden Cricketers' Almanack,* edited by Graeme Wright, and the *Complete Who's Who of Test Cricketers* by Christopher Martin-Jenkins.

It should be noted that in order to meet publication deadlines it was not possible to include details of Zimbabwe's first Test match or India's first Test against South Africa, but all other figures are current.

GRAHAM DAWSON
Melbourne, September 1992

TEST

CRICKET

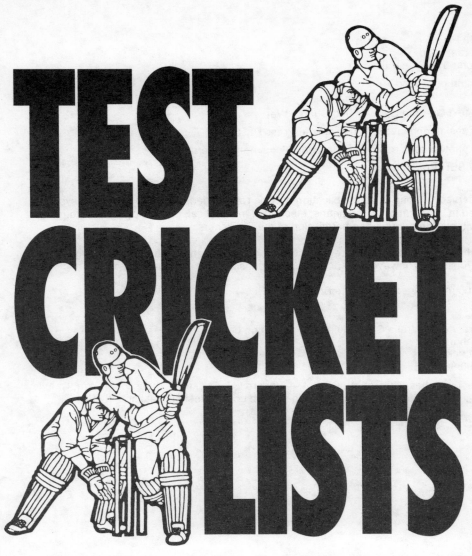

LISTS

Compiled by Graham Dawson — Statistics by Charlie Wat

The Five Mile Press

The Five Mile Press
351 Whitehorse Road
Balwyn Victoria 3103 Australia

This edition first published 1992

Designed by SBR Productions

Printed and bound in Australia by The Book Printer.

National Library of Australia Cataloguing-in-Publication data
Dawson, Graham.
Test cricket lists.
ISBN 0 86788 554 8

1. Test matches (Cricket). 2. Cricket — Records. 3. Cricket — Statistics. I. Wat, Charlie. II. Atkinson, Graeme, 1945- . Nissan-Datsun book of test cricket lists. III. Title.

796.35865

COVER PHOTOGRAPHS:

Front:

i England batsman Robin Smith is bowled by Bruce Reid, to the delight of the Australian slips fieldsmen. (Australia v England, Brisbane, 1990-91.)
(Courtesy PBL Marketing.)

ii Terry Alderman (centre) is congratulated by fellow Australians Geoff Marsh (left) and Dean Jones (right) after an early bowling success against England at the 'Gabba. (Australia v England, Brisbane, 1990-91.)
(Courtesy PBL Marketing.)

Back:

Three great cricketers from three eras of Test cricket: W.G. Grace played for England from 1880 to 1899; Sir Donald Bradman played for Australia from 1928 to 1948; Craig McDermott, who began his Test career in 1984, continues to play fine cricket for Australia.
(Courtesy the Melbourne Herald and Weekly Times*, and PBL Marketing.)*

CONTENTS

PART 1
FAMOUS TEST MATCHES

A Guide to the Symbols

Throughout this book we have used asterisks (*) alongside individual scores to indicate the player was not out.

In the score cards we have also used an asterisk after a player's name to indicate the captain of the team, and a dagger (†) to indicate the wicketkeeper.

All other symbols are explained where they occur.

AUSTRALIA v ENGLAND 1876–77

The Melbourne Cricket Ground, Melbourne
15, 16, 17, 19 March 1877
Australia won by 45 runs

Australia 245 (C. Bannerman 165 retired hurt) and 104; England 196 (H. Jupp 63, W.E. Midwinter 5 for 78) and 108 (T. Kendall 7 for 55)

This is regarded as the first official Test match. England was represented by professional players who had been touring Australia during the 1876–77 season, but it would have been a stronger team had it included the leading amateur cricketers of the day.

Australia won the toss and batted first. Charles Bannerman dominated the innings and, after receiving the first ball in Test cricket, went on to score the first Test century. He eventually retired hurt after making 165 in an Australian total of 245.

Surrey opener Harry Jupp top-scored in England's first innings with a patient knock of 63.

Shaw and Ulyett combined to bowl Australia out for 104, but the target of 154 proved too much for the England batsmen. The Victorian Kendall captured 7 wickets for 55 as England was dismissed for 208; Australia won by 45 runs.

A collection at the ground for the injured Bannerman raised £165.

See page 14 for the complete scoreboard.

AUSTRALIA v ENGLAND 1878–79

The Melbourne Cricket Ground, Melbourne
2, 3, 4 January 1879
Australia won by 10 wickets

England 113 (C.A. Absolom 52, F.R. Spofforth 6 for 48) and 160 (F.R. Spofforth 7 for 62); Australia 256 (A.C. Bannerman 73, T. Emmet 7 for 68) and 0 for 19

This was the only Test match played on this tour by the England team led by Lord Harris. Unlike Lillywhite's combination in the first Test, it was composed chiefly of amateurs and was not as strong a team. The Australians, however, formed a more formidable outfit than their earlier counterparts. W.L. Murdoch and A.C. Bannerman strengthened the batting, while the bowling of Spofforth ('The Demon') proved too much for the England batsmen. He claimed the first hat-trick in Test cricket, his victims being Royle, Mackinnon and Emmett, and bowled Australia to a convincing victory. He finished the match with the fine figures of 13 for 110.

ENGLAND v AUSTRALIA 1880

The Oval, London
6, 7, 8 September 1880
England won by 5 wickets

England 420 (W.G. Grace 152, A.P. Lucas 55, Lord Harris 52) and 5 for 57; Australia 149 (F. Morley 5 for 56) and 327 (W.L. Murdoch 153 not out)

This was the first Test match to be played on English soil, and the Australian team was weakened by the absence of its greatest bowler of the time, Spofforth.

The England team, led by Lord Harris, included for the first time three brothers, E.M., W.G., and G.F. Grace. E.M. Grace opened the England innings with W.G. Grace, whose 152 was the first Test century scored by an Englishman. The third and youngest brother, G.F. Grace, made the first 'pair' of ducks in Test cricket, but his oufield catch to dismiss the Australian Bonnor was also long remembered. The batsmen were on their way back for the third run when he held the catch.

He died less than a month later after catching a severe cold in a club game. The cold developed into congestion of the lungs, and he was dead within three days.

ENGLAND v AUSTRALIA 1882

The Ashes Match
The Oval, London
28, 29 August 1882
Australia won by 7 runs

Australia 63 (R.G. Barlow 5 for 19) and 122 (H.H. Massie 55); England 101 (F.R. Spofforth 7 for 46) and 77 (F.R. Spofforth 7 for 44)

This most remarkable and exciting match will be remembered for as long as cricket history exists. The Ashes match was Australia's first Test victory in England. The win was set up by Spofforth's magnificent bowling, and his figures of 14 for 90 enhanced his reputation as the finest bowler in the world.

Australia was bundled out for 63 after winning the toss. England's reply was not much better, and the team was dismissed for 101. Australia's second innings was an improvement on the first, and Massie led the way with 55 in an opening stand of 66 with Bannerman. But the rest struggled. By mid-afternoon on the second day, Australia had been dismissed for 122, with a lead of just 84 runs.

AUSTRALIA v ENGLAND 1876-77 (First Test)

Melbourne Cricket Ground, 15, 16, 17, 19 March.

Australia won by 45 runs

AUSTRALIA

C.Bannerman	retired hurt	165		b Ulyett	4
N.Thompson	b Hill	1		c Emmett b Shaw	7
T.P.Horan	c Hill b Shaw	12		c Selby b Hill	20
D.W.Gregory*	run out	1	(9)	b Shaw	3
B.B.Cooper	b Southerton	15		b Shaw	3
W.E.Midwinter	c Ulyett b Southerton	5		c Southerton b Ulyett	17
E.J.Gregory	c Greenwood b Lillywhite	0		c Emmett b Ulyett	11
J.M.Blackham†	b Southerton	17		lbw b Shaw	6
T.W.Garrett	not out	18	(4)	c Emmett b Shaw	0
T.K.Kendall	c Southerton b Shaw	3		not out	17
J.Hodges	b Shaw	0		b Lillywhite	8
Extras	(B 4, LB 2, W 2)	8		(B 5, LB 3)	8
Total		245			104

ENGLAND

H.Jupp	lbw b Garrett	63	(3)	lbw b Midwinter	4
J.Selby†	c Cooper b Hodges	7	(5)	c Horan b Hodges	38
H.R.J.Charlwood	c Blackham b Midwinter	36	(4)	b Kendall	13
G.Ulyett	lbw b Thompson	10	(6)	b Kendall	24
A.Greenwood	c E.J.Gregory b Midwinter	1	(2)	c Midwinter b Kendall	5
T.Armitage	c Blackham b Midwinter	9	(8)	c Blackham b Kendall	3
A.Shaw	b Midwinter	10		st Blackham b Kendall	2
T.Emmett	b Midwinter	8	(9)	b Kendall	9
A.Hill	not out	35	(1)	c Thompson b Kendall	0
J.Lillywhite*	c and b Kendall	10		b Hodges	4
J.Southerton	c Cooper b Garrett	6		not out	1
Extras	(LB 1)	1		(B 4, LB 1)	5
Total		196			108

ENGLAND	O	M	R	W		O	M	R	W
Shaw	55.3	34	51	3	Shaw	34	16	38	5
Hill	23	10	42	1	Ulyett	19	7	39	3
Ulyett	25	12	36	0	Hill	14	6	18	1
Southerton	37	17	61	3	Lillywhite	1	0	1	1
Armitage	3	0	15	0					
Lillywhite	14	5	19	1					
Emmett	12	7	13	0					
AUSTRALIA	O	M	R	W		O	M	R	W
Hodges	9	0	27	1	Kendall	33.1	12	55	7
Garrett	18.1	10	22	2	Midwinter	19	7	23	1
Kendall	38	16	54	1	D.W.Gregory	5	1	9	0
Midwinter	54	23	78	5	Garrett	2	0	9	0
Thompson	17	10	14	1	Hodges	7	5	7	2

FALL OF WICKETS

Wkt	A 1st	E 1st	A 2nd	E 2nd
1st	2	23	7	0
2nd	40	79	27	7
3rd	41	98	31	20
4th	118	109	31	22
5th	142	121	35	62
6th	143	135	58	68
7th	197	145	71	92
8th	243	145	75	93
9th	245	168	75	100
10th	245	196	104	108

Umpires: C.A.Reid and R.B.Terry

England looked comfortable in the second innings when W.G. Grace and Ulyett took the score to 51 after the early loss of Hornby and Barlow, but inspired bowling by the 'The Demon' (Spofforth) and Boyle, supported by magnificent fielding, carried Australia to a thrilling victory. See page 16 for the complete scoreboard.

The day after the match, *The Sporting Times* carried an 'In Memoriam' announcement as follows:

'IN AFFECTIONATE REMEMBRANCE
OF
ENGLISH CRICKET
which died at the Oval
on
29th August 1882.
Deeply lamented by a large
circle of sorrowing friends and
acquaintances.
R.I.P.
N.B. — The body will be cremated and
the ashes taken to Australia.'

ENGLAND v AUSTRALIA 1884

The Oval, London
11, 12, 13 August 1884
Drawn

Australia 551 (W.L. Murdoch 211, P.S. McDonnell 103, H.J.H. Scott 102); England 346 (W.W. Read 117, W.H. Scotton 90) and 2 for 85

Murdoch won the toss for Australia and the team piled on the runs — 2 for 363 on the first day before being dismissed for 551 (the first score of over 500 in a Test innings). Murdoch's 211 was the first double-century in Test cricket, and his partnership with Scott realised a then record 207 for the third wicket.

During Australia's record-breaking innings every member of the England team had a bowl. The most successful was the wicketkeeper, Hon. A. Lyttelton, who took the last four wickets with lobs.

England was in trouble in the first innings at 8 for 181, but was saved by the partnership of the opener, Scotton, and Read, who added 151 for the ninth wicket. (Scotton batted for 340 minutes and was at the wicket for 332 of England's 346 runs.)

AUSTRALIA v ENGLAND 1886–87

Sydney Cricket Ground, Sydney
28, 29, 31 January 1887
England won by 13 runs

England 45 (C.T.B. Turner 6 for 15, J.J. Ferris 4 for 27) and 184 (J.J. Ferris 5 for 76); Australia 119 and 97 (W. Barnes 6 for 28)

After being sent in to bat, England was bundled out for its lowest score against Australia (45). Turner and Ferris, both on debut, bowled unchanged in England's innings.

Australia gained a first-innings lead of 74 after being dismissed for 119. Moses and Jones top-scored with 31 each.

After two days' play, England's lead was only 29 with just 3 wickets in hand. On the final day, England's Briggs compiled the top score for the game, 33, to set Australia 111 runs for victory. Moses, 24, and Jones, 18, again batted well, but it was Barnes and Lohmann who triumphed and bowled England to a great win.

ENGLAND v AUSTRALIA 1890

The Oval, London
11, 12 August 1890
England won by 2 wickets

Australia 92 (F. Martin 6 for 50) and 102 (F. Martin 6 for 52); England 100 and 8 for 95 (J.J. Ferris 5 for 49)

Played on a slow wicket soaked by heavy rain, this was a match dominated by the ball. In his only Test against Australia, the Kent bowler Martin spearheaded England's victory with match figures of 12 for 102.

In a nerve-tingling finish with England needing 1 run to tie and 2 to win, Sharpe joined MacGregor at the wicket. The Australian bowler Ferris continually beat Sharpe, but wasn't able to claim the wicket Australia desperately needed. At last, Sharpe put bat to ball; he and his partner MacGregor ran for a suicidal single, but Barrett's return was too high for Ferris to reach. England won the match on the overthrow.

AUSTRALIA v ENGLAND 1894-95

Sydney Cricket Ground, Sydney
14, 15, 17, 18, 19, 20 December 1895
England won by 10 runs

Australia 586 (S.E. Gregory 201, G. Giffen 161, F.A. Iredale 81, J. McBlackham 74, T. Richardson 5 for 181) and 166 (J. Darling 53, R. Peel 6 for 67); England 325 (A. Ward 75, J. Briggs 57) and 437 (A. Ward 117, J.T. Brown 53)

ENGLAND v AUSTRALIA 1882 (Only Test)

Kennington Oval, London, 28, 29 August.

Australia won by 7 runs

AUSTRALIA

A.C.Bannerman	c Grace b Peate	9		c Studd b Barnes	13
H.H.Massie	b Ulyett	1		b Steel	55
W.L.Murdoch*	b Peate	13	(4)	run out	29
G.J.Bonnor	b Barlow	1	(3)	b Ulyett	2
T.P.Horan	b Barlow	3		c Grace b Peate	2
G.Giffen	b Peate	2		c Grace b Peate	0
J.M.Blackham†	c Grace b Barlow	17		c Lyttelton b Peate	7
T.W.Garrett	c Read b Peate	10	(10)	not out	2
H.F.Boyle	b Barlow	2	(11)	b Steel	0
S.P.Jones	c Barnes b Barlow	0	(8)	run out	6
F.R.Spofforth	not out	4	(9)	b Peate	0
Extras	(B 1)	1		(B 6)	6
Total		63			122

ENGLAND

R.G.Barlow	c Bannerman b Spofforth	11	(3)	b Spofforth	0
W.G.Grace	b Spofforth	4	(1)	c Bannerman b Boyle	32
G.Ulyett	st Blackham b Spofforth	26	(4)	c Blackham b Spofforth	11
A.P.Lucas	c Blackham b Boyle	9	(5)	b Spofforth	5
Hon.A.Lyttelton†	c Blackham b Spofforth	2	(6)	b Spofforth	12
C.T.Studd	b Spofforth	0	(10)	not out	0
J.M.Read	not out	19	(8)	b Spofforth	0
W.Barnes	b Boyle	5	(9)	c Murdoch b Boyle	2
A.G.Steel	b Garrett	14	(7)	c and b Spofforth	0
A.N.Hornby*	b Spofforth	2	(2)	b Spofforth	9
E.Peate	c Boyle b Spofforth	0		b Boyle	2
Extras	(B 6, LB 2, NB 1)	1		(B 3, LB 1)	4
Total		101			77

ENGLAND	O	M	R	W		O	M	R	W
Peate	38	24	31	4	Peate	21	9	40	4
Ulyett	9	5	11	1	Ulyett	6	2	10	1
Barlow	31	22	19	5	Barlow	13	5	27	0
Steel	2	1	1	0	Steel	7	0	15	2
					Barnes	12	5	15	1
					Studd	4	1	9	0

AUSTRALIA	O	M	R	W		O	M	R	W
Spofforth	36.3	18	46	7	Spofforth	28	15	44	7
Garrett	16	7	22	1	Garrett	7	2	10	0
Boyle	19	7	24	2	Boyle	20	11	19	3

FALL OF WICKETS

Wkt	A 1st	E 1st	A 2nd	E 2nd
1st	6	13	66	15
2nd	21	18	70	15
3rd	22	57	70	51
4th	26	59	79	53
5th	30	60	79	66
6th	30	63	99	70
7th	48	70	114	70
8th	53	96	117	75
9th	59	101	122	75
10th	63	101	122	77

Umpires: L.Greenwood and R.Thoms

This high-scoring match was one of many highlights and records: The aggregate of 1514 runs was a new mark, Australia's score of 586 remained an Australian record for 30 years, the ninth-wicket partnership of 154 by Gregory and Blackham still remains Australia's best, and, for the first time, a team won after following-on.

Giffen produced an outstanding all-round performance for Australia: 161 and 41 with the bat, and 8 for 238 from 118 overs with the ball. But luck went against the Australians. First, Blackham sustained a severe thumb injury and couldn't keep wicket in England's second innings. Then, after five days' play, with Australia needing just 64 runs with 8 wickets in hand to win, the heavens opened and the rain tumbled down. The next day followed with blazing sunshine, and Australia was caught on a classic 'sticky' wicket. Briggs and Peel took full advantage of the conditions to bowl England to a memorable victory. The details of this absorbing Test are set out on page 18.

ENGLAND v AUSTRALIA 1896

Old Trafford, Manchester
16, 17, 18 July 1896
Australia won by 3 wickets

Australia 412 (F.A. Iredale 108, G. Giffen 80, G.H.S. Trott 53, T. Richardson 7 for 168) and 7 for 125 (T. Richardson 6 for 76); England 231 (A.A. Lilley 65 not out, K.S. Ranjitsinhji 62) and 305 (K.S. Ranjitsinhji 154 not out)

In this classic match, the two outstanding performers were on the defeated England team. Richardson returned match figures of 13 for 239 from 110 overs, and Ranjitsinhji, playing in his first Test, scored 62 and a masterly 154 not out.

Australia's victory was set up by the top-order batsmen. Iredale, 108, Giffen, 80, and Trott, 53, led the way to the Australian first-innings total of 412. In England's first innings, Lilley and the 'Prince' (Ranjitsinhji) both compiled half-centuries, but it was not enough to avoid the follow-on. In their second innings, Ranjitsinhji played one of the great Test innings. He scored 154 not out in his three hours and ten minutes at the crease, but the team was all out for 305.

What should have been a formality for Australia almost turned into a nightmare. Richardson bowled superbly. He had Australia on the brink at 7 for 100 before Trumble and Kelly were able to scramble for the last 25 runs needed to record Australia's first Test win in England for eight years.

ENGLAND v AUSTRALIA 1902

Old Trafford, Manchester
24, 25, 26 July 1902
Australia won by 3 runs

Australia 299 (V.T. Trumper 104, C. Hill 65, R.A. Duff 54, J. Darling 51, W.H. Lockwood 6 for 48) and 86 (W.H. Lockwood 5 for 28); England 262 (Hon. F.S. Jackson 128, L.C. Braund 65) and 120 (H. Trumble 6 for 53)

Australia went into this vital Test one up with two matches to play, and England had made four changes to the team that had lost the previous Test at Sheffield. Significantly, Jessop and Hirst were left out of the team, and F.W. Tate, a bowler with no batting ability, was included for his first Test.

Trumper played a magnificent innings for Australia and posted his century before lunch. With Hill, 65, Duff, 54, and Darling, 51, making useful contributions, Australia posted 299, a somewhat disappointing total after the opening stand of 135.

England's reply was dominated by Jackson, 128, and Braund, 65, who scored 193 out of 262. With a lead of 37, Australia collapsed in its second innings and was dismissed for a paltry 86. Only Darling, 37, and Gregory, 24, reached double figures. Tate dropped Darling early in his innings; if the catch had been taken, Australia would have struggled to reach 50.

With light rain falling, England needed 124 to square the series. After a steady start, the wickets began to tumble — 15 runs were needed with two wickets to fall when Rhodes joined Lilley. Lilley fell to a magnificent outfield catch by Hill. With 8 runs required, Tate was the last man, and the rain was coming down in torrents. After a delay of 45 minutes, play resumed. Rhodes calmly played three balls from Trumble, then Tate faced Saunders. The first ball was snicked for four; Tate survived the next two and was then clean-bowled by the fourth ball of the over. Australia had snatched victory by 3 runs.

Both Lockwood and Trumble bowled superbly: Lockwood claimed 11 wickets and Trumble 10.

AUSTRALIA v ENGLAND 1894-95 (First Test)

Sydney Cricket Ground, 14, 15, 17, 18, 19, 20 December. England won by 10 runs

AUSTRALIA

J.J.Lyons	b Richardson	1		b Richardson	25
G.H.S.Trott	b Richardson	12		c Gay b Peel	8
G.Giffen	c Ford b Brockwell	161		lbw b Briggs	41
J.Darling	b Richardson	0		c Brockwell b Peel	53
F.A.Iredale	c Stoddart b Ford	81	(6)	c and b Briggs	5
S.E.Gregory	c Peel b Stoddart	201	(5)	c Gay b Peel	16
J.C.Reedman	c Ford b Peel	17		st Gay b Peel	4
C.E.McLeod	b Richardson	15		not out	2
C.T.B.Turner	c Gay b Peel	1		c Briggs b Peel	2
J.M.Blackham*†	b Richardson	74	(11)	c and b Peel	2
E.Jones	not out	11	(10)	c MacLaren b Briggs	1
Extras	(B 8, LB 3, W 1)	12		(B 2, LB 1, NB 4)	7
Total		586			166

ENGLAND

A.C.MacLaren	c Reedman b Turner	4	b Giffen	20
A.Ward	c Iredale b Turner	75	b Giffen	117
A.E.Stoddart*	c Jones b Giffen	12	c Giffen b Turner	36
J.T.Brown	run out	22	c Jones b Giffen	53
W.Brockwell	c Blackham b Jones	49	b Jones	37
R.Peel	c Gregory b Giffen	4	b Giffen	17
F.G.J.Ford	st Blackham b Giffen	30	c and b McLeod	48
J.Briggs	b Giffen	57	b McLeod	42
W.H.Lockwood	c Giffen b Trott	18	b Trott	29
L.H.Gay†	c Gregory b Reedman	33	b Trott	4
T.Richardson	not out	0	not out	12
Extras	(B 17, LB 3, W 1)	21	(B 14, LB 8)	22
Total		325		437

ENGLAND	O	M	R	W		O	M	R	W
Richardson	55.3	13	181	5	Richardson	11	3	27	1
Peel	53	14	140	2	Peel	30	9	67	6
Briggs	25	4	96	0	Lockwood	16	3	40	0
Brockwell	22	7	78	1	Briggs	11	2	25	3
Ford	11	2	47	1					
Stoddart	3	0	31	1					
Lockwood	3	2	1	0					

AUSTRALIA	O	M	R	W		O	M	R	W
Jones	19	7	44	1	Jones	19	0	57	1
Turner	44	16	89	2	Turner	35	14	78	1
Giffen	43	17	75	4	Giffen	75	25	164	4
Trott	15	4	59	1	Trott	12.4	2	22	2
McLeod	14	2	25	0	McLeod	30	7	67	2
Reedman	3.3	1	12	1	Reedman	6	1	12	0
Lyons	2	2	0	0	Lyons	2	0	12	0
					Iredale	2	1	3	0

FALL OF WICKETS

Wkt	A 1st	E 1st	E 2nd	A 2nd
1st	10	14	44	26
2nd	21	43	115	45
3rd	21	78	217	130
4th	192	149	245	135
5th	331	155	290	147
6th	379	211	296	158
7th	400	211	385	159
8th	409	252	398	161
9th	563	325	420	162
10th	586	325	437	166

Umpires: C.Bannerman and J.Phillips

ENGLAND v AUSTRALIA 1902

The Oval, London
11, 12, 13 August 1902
England won by 1 wicket

Australia 324 (H. Trumble 64 not out, M.A. Noble 52, G.H. Hirst 5 for 77) and 121 (W.H. Lockwood 5 for 45); England 183 (H. Trumble 8 for 65) and 9 wickets for 263 (G.L. Jessop 104, G.H. Hirst 58 not out)

This classic contest is referred to as 'Jessop's match' for it was he ('The Croucher') who won the game for England.

Darling called correctly, and Australia took advantage of the good weather and pitch to compile 324. Trumble's 64 not out proved his all-round ability.

England made a modest reply, scoring 183 with Trumble claiming 8 for 65.

Australia's second innings started disastrously with Trumper being run out for 2. After this early setback, the Australia batsmen struggled and only Hill, 34, and Armstrong, 21, were able to score more than 20. Australia was all out for 121, for a lead of 262.

England collapsed, and was at one point only 5 for 48. The match looked to be over. Then 'The Croucher' joined Jackson, and the pair turned the game around for the home team. In 75 minutes, Jessop smashed 104 runs with 17 boundaries and a five. But 15 runs were still required when the last man, Rhodes, joined Hirst. Legend says Hirst said to Rhodes, 'We'll get them in singles.' However, although these men of Yorkshire did score the runs needed to record a famous victory, they did not do it in singles.

AUSTRALIA v ENGLAND 1903–04

Sydney Cricket Ground, Sydney
11, 12, 14, 15, 16, 17 December 1903
England won by 5 wickets

Australia 285 (M.A. Noble 133) and 485 (V.T. Trumper 185 not out, R.A. Duff 84, C. Hill 51, W. Rhodes 5 for 94); England 577 (R.E. Foster 287, L.C. Braund 102, J.T. Tyldesley 53) and 5 for 194 (T.W. Hayward 91, G.H. Hirst 60 not out)

Under the leadership of Pelham Warner, this touring party was the first to come to Australia under the MCC's banner. Previous tours to Australia had been privately sponsored, and team selection had been undertaken by individuals.

Noble was Australia's new captain, and he started well by winning the toss and making the top score, 133, in a respectable total of 285.

England struggled at first, but Foster and Braund turned the tide. After two days' play, the visitors trailed by 42 runs with 6 wickets in hand. On the third day, Foster's innings blossomed. He struck 38 boundaries in a new Test record score of 287.

England's total of 577 was a new innings high for Test cricket.

Foster shared century partnerships with Braund, 192, Relf, 115, and Rhodes, 130. The Foster–Rhodes last-wicket partnership still stands as an England record.

A superb, unbeaten century from Trumper, with valuable contributions from Duff and Hill, carried Australia's second innings to 485. Rhodes was once more the pick of England's bowlers. He finished with 5 for 94 from a marathon spell of 40 overs.

England's target was 194. The team was in trouble at 4 for 82, then Hirst was missed by Laver after just 1 run had been added. After the let-off, the Yorkshireman assisted Hayward to wipe off the deficit. They saw England home by 5 wickets, with Hayward, 91, being dismissed near the end of the match.

SOUTH AFRICA v ENGLAND 1905–06

Old Wanderers, Johannesburg
2, 3, 4 January 1906
South Africa won by 1 wicket

England 184 and 190 (P.F. Warner 51); South Africa 91 (W. Lees 5 for 34) and 9 wickets for 287 (A.W. Nourse 93 not out, G.C. White 81)

In this low-scoring match, England gained a first-innings lead of 93. Faulkner bowled superbly to capture 4 for 26 and restrict England's second innings to 190. Crawford batted well in both innings, scoring 44 and 43.

When Nourse joined White, the home team was struggling at 6 for 105 and England appeared likely to win. Nourse played with remarkable maturity as he and White carried the score to 226. After White's departure, Vogler and Schwarz fell at 230 and 239 respectively. The last man in was South Africa's captain Sherwell; when he arrived at the crease, 45 runs were still required for victory. Amid great excitement, Nourse and Sherwell hit the runs needed to win. It was South Africa's first Test victory.

AUSTRALIA v ENGLAND 1907–08

Sydney Cricket Ground, Sydney
13, 14, 16, 17, 18, 19 December 1907
Australia won by 2 wickets

England 273 (G. Gunn 119, A. Cotter 6 for 101) and 300 (G. Gunn 74, J. Hardstaff Sr 63); Australia 300 (C. Hill 87, A. Fielder 6 for 82) and 8 for 275 (H. Carter 61)

With A.O. Jones indisposed, Fane took over the captaincy of England. He called correctly, and took first use of a good pitch. George Gunn was called up to take Jones's place in the team and, on debut, made 119 and 74 to top-score in both of England's innings.

Australia gained a lead of 27 runs after compiling a first-innings total of 300. Hill top-scored with 87, while Fielder was best with the ball, claiming 6 for 82.

England matched Australia's 300, so the home team needed to score 274 to win the first match of the series.

Trumper, Hill and Macartney fell cheaply, and the innings continued to stutter. With just 3 wickets remaining, 89 runs were still needed; however, wicketkeeper Carter, 61 (the top score), Cotter, 34 not out, and Hazlitt, 33 not out, steered Australia to an exciting win. The ninth-wicket partnership between Cotter and Hazlitt realised 56 in just 39 minutes.

AUSTRALIA v ENGLAND 1907–08

Melbourne Cricket Ground, Melbourne
1, 2, 3, 4, 6, 7 January 1908
England won by one wicket

Australia 266 (M.A. Noble 61, J.N. Crawford 5 for 79) and 397 (W.W. Armstrong 77, M.A. Noble 64, V.T. Trumper 63, C.G. Macartney 54, H. Carter 53, S.F. Barnes 5 for 72); England 382 (K.L. Hutchings 126, J.B. Hobbs 83, A. Cotter 5 for 142) and 9 wickets for 282 (F.L. Fane 50).

The first Test in Sydney was close, but this one was even closer.

Australia's 266 was a modest effort after an 84-run opening stand by Trumper and Macartney. The skipper, Noble, top-scored with 61.

This match saw the Test debut of J.B. Hobbs. He made 83 and paved the way for Hutchings to smash 126 with 25 fours and a six. England finished with 382 for a lead of 116.

Five batsmen scored half-centuries as Australia compiled a second-innings total of 397, despite the untiring effort of S.F. Barnes who captured 5 for 72 from 27.4 overs.

England needed to score 282 to win the match and level the series. After the fifth day, it was 4 for 159 and anyone's game. When Rhodes was run out, it was 8 for 209 with 73 runs still required. Barnes and Humphries added 34, but 39 were still needed when the last pair was at the crease. Finally, with one run needed, the batsmen went for a suicidal single. But Hazlitt's throw was wild and England scored a thrilling victory.

SOUTH AFRICA v ENGLAND 1922–23

Newlands, Cape Town
1, 2, 3, 4 January 1923
England won by one wicket

South Africa 113 and 242 (R.H. Catterall 76, H.W. Taylor 68, G.G. Macaulay 5 for 64); England 183 (J.M. Blanckenberg 5 for 61) and 9 for 173 (A.E. Hall 7 for 63)

England gained the ascendancy on the first day, dismissing South Africa for 113 and being 4 for 128 in reply. Fender was the best of England's bowlers and finished with 4 for 29. Carr, 42, and Russell, 39, batted well for the visitors.

The second day saw a complete turn-around in fortunes. Blanckenberg and Hall demolished the middle- and lower-order England batsmen and the lead was restricted to just 70 runs.

After Hearne went out at 2 for his second 'duck' in the match, Catterall and Taylor dominated the batting and, at the close, they had taken South Africa's second-innings score to 134.

Macaulay and Kennedy bowled England back into the match on the third day. South Africa's lead was 172. Inspired by Hall's fine bowling, the home team struck back. England finished the day at 6 for 86.

The England captain, Mann, and Jupp added 68 for the seventh wicket to give the visitors a glimmer of hope. When the last man, Macaulay, joined Kennedy, 5 runs were still needed for victory. Kennedy hit a four before a single by Macaulay finished the match.

As well as the exciting finish, it was a memorable game for a number of reasons: Macaulay took the wicket of Hearne with his first ball in Test cricket, and also made the winning run; Hall, the other debutant in the match, took 11 wickets for 112 and almost bowled South Africa to victory.

AUSTRALIA v ENGLAND 1924–25

Adelaide Oval, Adelaide
16, 17, 19, 20, 21, 22, 23 January 1925
Australia won by 11 runs

Australia 489 (J. Ryder 201 not out, T.J.E. Andrews 72, A.J. Richardson 69) and 250 (J. Ryder 88); England 365 (J.B. Hobbs 119, E.H. Hendren 92) and 363 (W.W. Whysall 75, H. Sutcliffe 59, A.P.F. Chapman 58)

England went into the game, the third of the series, two matches down. Gilligan called incorrectly for the third time, so Australia again had the advantage of batting first.

Luck was against the visitors, for their two top bowlers were injured: the spearhead Tate broke down with Australia 3 for 22, and then Gilligan's strained thigh sent him away from the field as well. At this point, Australia was struggling at 6 for 119, but the last 4 wickets added 370 to carry the home team out of danger. Ryder's 201 not out was scored in six and a half hours.

England's batting order was shuffled with the innings starting late on the second day. Hobbs, at No.5, played beautifully for 119; Hendren was also in fine form and scored 92. The deficit was 124.

In its second innings, Australia was caught on a sticky wicket. After Ryder, 88, Ponsford, 43, and Taylor, 34, had laid the foundations for another big total, the England bowlers Kilner and Woolley captured the last 7 wickets for 35.

England's target was 375 to keep the series alive. Hobbs and Sutcliffe were superb on the difficult wicket, and then Whysall and Chapman gave the visitors a glimmer of hope. On the seventh morning, 27 runs were needed with 2 wickets in hand. Gilligan holed out to V.Y. Richardson off Gregory and, when Mailey had Freeman caught by Oldfield, Australia was home by 11 runs.

ENGLAND v AUSTRALIA 1926

The Oval, London
14, 16, 17, 18 August 1926
England won by 289 runs

England 280 (H. Sutcliffe 76, A.A. Mailey 6 for 138) and 436 (H. Sutcliffe 161, J.B. Hobbs 100); Australia 302 (J.M. Gregory 73, H.L. Collins 61) and 125

It was decided this match should be played to a result because the previous matches in the series had been drawn.

England appointed Percy Chapman as captain, recalled Rhodes at the age of 48-years-and-10-months, and selected the 21-year-old fast bowler Larwood for his second Test match.

Hobbs and Sutcliffe opened with a 53-run partnership for England, but the rest struggled against Mailey's spin and the result was a modest 280.

Australia fared little better before Collins and Gregory added 107 for the seventh wicket. Oldfield and Grimmett then posted 67 for the ninth to establish a meagre 22-run lead.

Hobbs and Sutcliffe produced the batting of the match on a rain-affected pitch, scoring 172 for the first wicket. The openers both made centuries and laid the foundations for an England victory. The visitors needed to score 415 to retain the Ashes on a difficult pitch.

With pace and hostility, Larwood made the early break before the 'Old Master' took over. Rhodes justified the selectors gamble by capturing 4 for 44 in Australia's second innings and 6 for 79 for the match. England regained the Ashes that were lost in Australia in 1920–21.

ENGLAND v AUSTRALIA 1928–29

Exhibition Ground, Brisbane
30 November, 1, 3, 4, 5 December 1928
England won by 675 runs

England 521 (E.H. Hendren 169, H. Larwood 70, A.P.F. Chapman 50) and 8 for 342 dec. (C.P. Mead 72, D.R. Jardine 65 not out, C.V. Grimmett 6 for 131); Australia 122 (H. Larwood 6 for 32) and 66

This was Brisbane's first Test match and one of only two to be played at the Exhibition Ground. The 675-run winning margin is the largest Test match victory, by runs, ever recorded.

Under Chapman, who had regained the Ashes at The Oval in 1926, England had one of its strongest teams. But many of the Australian stalwarts, including Collins, Bardsley, Macartney, Andrews, Taylor and Mailey, had retired after the last tour of England.

Hendren, playing perhaps his finest innings against Australia, scored a masterly 169 as England reached 521. Towards the end of the innings, Gregory injured his knee attempting to take a return catch and was told by the doctor that he would never play again.

It was in this match that Bradman made his debut, although he failed, scoring only 18 and 1. He was subsequently left out of the team for the second Test.

Larwood crashed through Australia's batting. He captured 6 for 32, and, with Tate claiming 3 for 50, the home team was bundled out for 122.

With Kellaway indisposed with food poisoning and Gregory out of the match, Chapman decided to bat again. He eventually made the first declaration in a Test in Australia at 8 for 342.

Australia's target: just 742 runs! On a difficult pitch, the effort put up by the home team was abysmal: all out for 66 in just 25.3 overs. Woodfull carried his bat in making 30.

Larwood had an outstanding match: He scored 70 and 37, and took 6 for 32 and 2 for 30. And, to round it off, he took 4 catches in Australia's second innings.

AUSTRALIA v ENGLAND 1928–29

Adelaide Oval, Adelaide
1, 2, 4, 5, 6, 7, 8 February 1929
England won by 12 runs

England 334 (W.R. Hammond 119 not out, J.B. Hobbs 74, H. Sutcliffe 64, C.V. Grimmett 5 for 102) and 383 (W.R. Hammond 177, D.R. Jardine 98); Australia 369 (A. Jackson 164, J. Ryder 63, J.C. White 5 for 130) and 336 (J. Ryder 87, D.G. Bradman 58, A.F. Kippax 51, J.C. White 8 for 126)

The tension in this match is indicated by the scores: 334, 369, 383, and 336. England came home in a thriller by 12 runs.

Hammond, whose three previous innings had been 251, 200 and 32 run out, was once again England's premier batsman. After Hobbs and Sutcliffe had provided their customary century opening partnership, Hammond held the innings together, scoring 72 of the last 88 runs to finish with 119 not out.

This was Jackson's first Test. He opened the innings for Australia with Woodfull, but soon his three partners, Woodfull, Hendry, and Kippax, were back in the pavilion for just 19. He, however, reached his century with a slashing square cut off Larwood, and was eventually dismissed for 164.

Although Hobbs and Sutcliffe fell cheaply this time, Hammond and Jardine ground out a 262-run partnership for the third wicket. England finished with 383, and Australia required 349 to win.

The home team was in with a real chance until Hobbs, one of the finest fieldsmen, ran Bradman out for 58. It was then 8 for 320 before 'Farmer' White snared the last 2 wickets to win the match for England.

Despite the batting deeds of Hammond and Jackson, White's effort in the match cannot be overlooked. With 5 for 130 in Australia's first innings and 8 for 126 in the second, he had match figures of 13 for 256 from 124.5 overs.

WEST INDIES v ENGLAND 1929–30

Sabina Park, Kingston, Jamaica
3, 4, 5, 7, 8 , 9, 10, 11,12 April 1930
Drawn

England 849 (A. Sandham 325, L.E.G. Ames 149, G. Gunn 85, E.H. Hendren 61, R.E.S. Wyatt 58, J.O'Connor 51, O.C. Scott 5 for 266) and 9 for 272 dec. (E.H. Hendren 55, A. Sandham 50); West Indies 286 (R.K. Nunes 66) and 5 for 408 (G.A. Headley 223, R.K. Nunes 92)

This was the final Test of the first series played between these teams in the Caribbean. England had won at Port-of-Spain by 167 runs, and then the West Indies won at Georgetown by 289. With the series level, it was decided to play the Test in Kingston to a finish.

Sandham, who batted for more than 10 hours, posted the first triple-century in Test cricket. His innings was the backbone of the massive England total of 849. (This is still the second-highest innings total in Test history.) The West Indies trailed by 563, but the England captain, the Hon. F.S.G. Calthorpe, did not enforce the follow-on. Sandham scored 50 in the second innings to give himself a match aggregate of 375.

The West Indies was set 836 to win and posted a highly respectable 5 for 408 before rain and a waiting ship ended the match. The 20-year-old George Headley made his debut in the series, scoring 703 runs with 4 centuries at an average of 87.87.

ENGLAND v AUSTRALIA 1930

Lord's Cricket Ground, London
27, 28, 30 June, 1 July 1930
Australia won by 7 wickets

England 425 (K.S. Duleepsinhji 173, M.W. Tate 54) and 375 (A.P.F. Chapman 121, G.O.B. Allen 57, C.V. Grimmett 6 for 167); Australia 6 wickets for 729 dec. (D.G. Bradman 254, W.M. Woodfull 155, A.F. Kippax 83, W.H. Ponsford 81) and 3 for 72

This was the match in which Bradman played the innings he considered to be (technically) the best in his life.

Australia had gone to Lord's one down, but determined to square the series. Duleepsinhji emulated his famous uncle Ranjisinhji by contributing a century, 173, in his first Test against Australia to England's total of 425.

Woodfull and Ponsford gave Australia a flying start and posted 162 for the first wicket. With Bradman's arrival, the scoring rate increased. At stumps, 'The Don' was 155 not out, with Australia 2 for 404 — 829 runs had been scored in two days' play. On the third day, Bradman and Kippax continued on to post a 192-run partnership. Woodfull declared at tea with a new record score for Australia of 729 (since broken). Bradman's chanceless 254 had taken just five and a half hours to compile.

Grimmett struck early in England's second innings, dismissing Hobbs and Woolley. And when he removed Hammond just after play resumed on the final day, Australia knew victory was a distinct possibility. Chapman scored a fine century, but it wasn't enough to save the match. Australia's target was 72, and they had plenty of time to polish off the runs. The Bradman era had dawned!

AUSTRALIA v WEST INDIES 1930–31

Sydney Cricket Ground, Sydney
27, 28 February, 2, 3, 4 March 1931
West Indies won by 30 runs

West Indies 6 wickets for 350 dec. (F.R. Martin 123 not out, G. Headley 105, G.C. Grant 62) and 5 wickets for 124 dec.; Australia 224 (A. Fairfax 54) and 220 (A.G. Fairfax 60 not out)

This match was the first Test win for the West Indies against Australia. It was a fine achievement, for they had been soundly beaten in the first four matches of the series.

Grant won the toss, and the West Indies went in to bat. Centuries by the opener, Martin, and Headley, plus 62 by the skipper took the visitors to 6 for 350 on the second day.

Overnight rain followed by hot morning sunshine produced a classic sticky wicket. The West Indies collapsed from an overnight 2 for 298 to 6 for 350 when Grant declared. Considering the state of the pitch, Australia did well to score 224. And, when the West Indies batted again, wicket conditions had deteriorated further.

Grant on 27 not out decided to declare with a lead of just 250. The gamble came off, for Australia was bowled out for 220 to give the West Indies a memorable win. Bradman went for a duck in Australia's second innings.

AUSTRALIA v ENGLAND 1932–33

Adelaide Oval, Adelaide
13, 14, 16, 17, 18, 19 January 1933
England won by 338 runs

England 341 (M. Leyland 83, R.E.S. Wyatt 78, E. Paynter 77, T.W. Wall 5 for 72) and 412 (W.R. Hammond 85, L.E.G. Ames 69, D.R. Jardine 56); Australia 222 (W. H. Ponsford 85) and 193 (W.M. Woodfull 73 not out, D.G. Bradman 66)

This must have been one of the most unpleasant Test matches ever played. The 'Bodyline' controversy had reached its ugliest; in fact, ill-feeling was so great that Jardine had to persuade local officials to close the ground to spectators while the England team had its final practice session the day before the match.

Jardine elected to bat first, but his team was soon in desperate trouble with the score at 4 for 30. Leyland, 83, and Wyatt, 78, added 156 for the fifth wicket before Verity helped Paynter carry the total beyond 300.

The crowd became hostile early in Australia's innings when Woodfull was struck a painful blow above the heart by a Larwood thunderbolt. Later in the innings, Oldfield went down after misjudging a Larwood delivery. This incident stirred the crowd to fever pitch, and they began to count the England team 'out' — 'one, two, three, four, five, six, seven, eight, nine, ten, out!'. Australia was dismissed for 222, with Ponsford, 85, top-scoring.

England produced an even team performance in its second innings. With six batsmen reaching 40, the total climbed to 412. Australia's target was 532, which proved far too difficult a task. Only Bradman, 66, and Woodfull, who carried his bat for 73, offered any resistance.

It was during this match that the Australian captain, Woodfull, made his famous utterance to the MCC tour management, Sir Pelham Warner and Lionel Palairet: 'There are two teams out there and one of them is trying to play cricket.'

ENGLAND v AUSTRALIA 1934

Lord's Cricket Ground, London
22, 23, 25 June 1934
England won by an innings and 38 runs

England 440 (L.E.G. Ames 120, M. Leyland 109, C.F. Walters 82); Australia 284 (W.A. Brown 105, H. Verity 7 for 61) and 118 (H. Verity 8 for 43)

This Test became known as 'Verity's Match'. Batting first, England compiled 440, with Leyland and the wicketkeeper, Ames, both scoring centuries. Walters, who was relieved of the captaincy after the first Test, returned to form with 82.

By the close of play on the second day (Saturday), Australia had reached 2 for 192, but rain over the weekend drenched the pitch. The England left-arm spinner Verity was able to exploit the conditions perfectly when play resumed.

Australia lost its last 8 wickets for 81, with Verity claiming 6 for 37. Forced to follow-on, the visitors were demolished by this Yorkshireman. Australia was all-out for 118 — Verity taking 8 for 43. On the final day, he took 14 wickets for 80 runs and so equalled Rhodes's earlier record of 15 wickets in Anglo-Australian Tests.

Footnote: It was England's first win against Australia at Lord's since 1896, and they have not won against Australia at the 'home' of cricket since.

WEST INDIES v ENGLAND 1934–35

Kensington Oval, Bridgetown, Barbados
8, 9, 10 January 1935
England won by 4 wickets
West Indies 102 and 6 for 51 dec. (C.I.J. Smith 5 for 16); England 7 for 81 dec. and 6 for 75 (E.A. Martindale 5 for 22)

This was a low-scoring match played on a rain-affected pitch where the respective captains, Grant and Wyatt, became involved in an absorbing tactical battle.

England sent the West Indies in to bat and they were all out for a miserable 102. The visitors hardly did any better, reaching 5 for 81 at the end of the first day's play.

More rain delayed the start of the second day until after tea. Hammond and Holmes went out in the first over, so Wyatt immediately declared, 21 runs behind.

Grant changed the batting order to protect his best batsmen, but by stumps the West Indies were 3 for 33. More rain fell overnight and delayed the resumption until mid-afternoon. Before tea, 3 wickets fell for 18. Grant declared at 6 for 51, leaving England 73 to win.

Wyatt reversed his batting order but the move backfired — 6 wickets fell for 48 before Hammond and Wyatt managed to score the runs needed for victory. This is the only Test at Bridgetown which the West Indies has lost.

SOUTH AFRICA v AUSTRALIA 1935–36

Old Wanderers, Johannesburg
24, 26, 27, 28 December 1935
Drawn
South Africa 157 and 491 (A.D. Nourse 231); Australia 250 (J.H.W. Fingleton 62, W.A. Brown 51) and 2 wickets for 274 (S.J. McCabe 189 not out)

Australia gained a 93-run lead on the first innings. In the second, Dudley Nourse hammered the Australian spinners, Grimmett, O'Reilly and Fleetwood-Smith, to score 231 in under five hours and give South Africa a lead of 398. But then McCabe played an innings to be compared with his 187 not out at Sydney in the 'Bodyline' series. He joined Fingleton after Brown fell cheaply, and reached 50 in 40 minutes before a light appeal was granted. The next morning, he raced to his century in 90 minutes, and scored 100 in the pre-lunch session (59-159) — with 20 boundaries.

Australia's 250 was posted in 199 minutes, but when the score reached 2 for 274 there was an appeal against the light — from the fielding captain. Herbie Wade felt his fieldsmen were in danger of being hit by McCabe's aggressive strokes. Shortly after the players left the ground, the pitch was under water.

ENGLAND v AUSTRALIA 1938

The Oval, London
20, 22, 23, 24 August 1938
England won by an innings and 579 runs
England 7 wickets for 903 dec. (L. Hutton 364, M. Leyland 187, J. Hardstaff Jnr 169 not out, W.R. Hammond 59, A. Wood 53); Australia 201 (W.A. Brown 69, W.E. Bowes 5 for 49) and 123

This will always be remembered as 'Hutton's match'. On a belter of a pitch, he and Leyland added 318 on the first day after Edrich had become O'Reilly's 100th wicket against England. The second-wicket partnership was broken with the run out of Leyland, but not before 382 had been added to the score.

By stumps on the second day, England had reached 5 for 634 with Hutton 300 not out. Australia's fielding was outstanding as the team attempted to defend Bradman's record Test score for Anglo-Australian tests. Hutton eventually was dismissed for 364, the highest Test innings at the time. He played the then longest innings in first-class cricket, batting for more than 13 hours.

Hammond finally declared at 7 for 903, which is still the highest total in Test cricket. With both Bradman (who injured an ankle bowling) and Fingleton unable to bat, Australia's reply was a moderate 201. Brown, who opened, was last man out for 69. The second innings was even worse — all out for 123 — and England had inflicted the heaviest defeat in Test history. The margin was an innings and 579 runs.

SOUTH AFRICA v ENGLAND 1938–39

Kingsmead, Durban
3, 4, 6, 7, 8, 9, 10, 11 ,13, 14 March 1939
Drawn

South Africa 530 (P.G.V. Van der Bijl 125, A.D. Nourse 103, A. Melville 78, R.E. Grieveson 75, E.L. Dalton 57, R.T.D. Perks 5 for 100) and 481 (A. Melville 103, P.G.V. Van der Bijl 97, B. Mitchell 89, K.G. Viljoen 74); England 316 (L.E.G. Ames 84, E. Paynter 62) and 5 for 654 (W.J. Edrich 219, W.R. Hammond 140, P.A. Gibb 120, E. Paynter 75, L. Hutton 55)

This was the famous 'timeless' Test. There was play on nine out of ten possible days, and the game only ended because the ship that was to take the England team home could wait no longer.

After the tenth day, England was just 40 runs away from achieving an amazing victory.

Details of the close-of-play scores on each day were as follows:

Day 1: South Africa 2 for 229

Day 2: South Africa 6 for 423

Day 3: South Africa all out 530
England 1 for 35 (rain stopped play)

Day 4: England 7 for 268 (bad light stopped play)

Day 5: England all out 316
South Africa 3 for 193

Day 6: South Africa all out 481
England 0 for 0 (bad light stopped play)

Day 7: England 1 for 253 (bad light)

Day 8: Rain

Day 9: England 3 for 496 (bad light)

Day 10: England 5 for 654 (interruptions because of rain)

ENGLAND v AUSTRALIA 1948

Headingley, Leeds
22, 23, 24, 26, 27 July 1948
Australia won by 7 wickets

England 496 (C. Washbrook 143, W.J. Edrich 111, L. Hutton 81, A.V. Bedser 79) and 8 for 365 dec. (D.C.S. Compton 66, C. Washbrook 65, L. Hutton 57, W.J. Edrich 54); Australia 458 (R.N. Harvey 112, S.J.E. Loxton 93, R.R. Lindwall 77, K.R. Miller 58) and 3 for 404 (A.R. Morris 182, D.G. Bradman 173 not out)

This was a memorable match with many highlights. England batted better than at any other stage in the series, and was content to have scored 496. But it should have been better, for at one stage on the second day they were 2 for 423.

Australia started poorly and lost Morris, Hassett and Bradman cheaply (3 for 68). Then Harvey, in his first Test against England, joined Miller, and they proceeded to hit themselves out of trouble. After Miller departed, Loxton took over and he smashed 5 sixes and 8 fours in an innings of 93. The 19-year-old Harvey reached his century; then Lindwall added 77 and Australia trailed by only 38 runs.

England again batted soundly in the second innings and, by the end of the fourth day, was 8 for 362 (a lead of 400). Yardley batted on for 5 minutes the following morning, so he could use the heavy roller in the hope that it would further break up the pitch.

Australia only needed to draw the match to retain the Ashes, but when Bradman joined Morris they went for victory. They got there with less than 15 minutes remaining. Bradman fed the strike to Harvey to allow him to hit the winning runs.

It was 'The Don's' last innings at Leeds. In four Tests at the ground, he scored 963 runs with an average of 192.6.

SOUTH AFRICA v AUSTRALIA 1949–50

Kingsmead, Durban
20, 21, 23, 24 January 1950
Australia won by 5 wickets

South Africa 311 (E.A.B. Rowan 143, A.D. Nourse 66) and 99 (I.W. Johnson 5 for 34); Australia 75 (H.J. Tayfield 7 for 23) and 5 for 336 (R.N. Harvey 151 not out, S.J.E. Loxton 54)

This was a truly remarkable victory by Australia after South Africa gained a first-innings lead of 236 runs. Rowan's patient knock of 143 was the backbone of the Springboks' innings which carried on well into the second day. It is contended that Hassett, the Australian captain, in conjunction with his bowlers, Miller and Johnston, did not attempt to take South African wickets on the second day.

The South Africa innings eventually finished on 311. By stumps, Australia was dismissed for a paltry 75, with 10 wickets falling for 44. Tayfield, the off-spinner, claimed 7 for 23.

Nourse, South Africa's skipper, had the weekend to decide whether he should enforce the follow-on. With rain threatening, he decided to bat again. South Africa's collapse was worse than Australia's, with the last 8 wickets falling for just 14 runs. South Africa was dismissed for 99 — and Australia needed 336 to win.

On a wearing, turning pitch, Harvey proceeded to play possibly his finest Test innings. He finished on 151 not out and was involved in match-winning partnerships with Loxton (135 for the fifth wicket), and McCool (106 unbroken for the sixth). Australia got home by 5 wickets to be 2-0 up in the series.

ENGLAND v WEST INDIES 1950

Lord's Cricket Ground, London
24, 26, 27, 28, 29 June 1950
West Indies won by 326 runs

West Indies 326 (A.F. Rae 106, E.D. Weekes 63, F.M.M. Worrell 52, R.O. Jenkins 5 for 116) and 6 for 425 dec. (C.L. Walcott 168 not out, G.E. Gomez 70, E.D. Weekes 63); England 151 (S. Ramadhin 5 for 66) and 274 (C. Washbrook 114, S. Ramadhin 6 for 86)

In this match, the West Indies scored its first Test win in England, and at the 'home' of cricket. No pace attack here! It was the 'spin twins', Ramadhin and Valentine, who bowled their team to victory.

Rae scored a century in the visitors' first innings total of 326. England replied with only 151; the opening stand realised 62, and the last wicket added 29 — with not much in between.

Walcott, who was dropped at 9, went on to remain 168 not out. With Gomez, he added 211 for the sixth wicket. England's task was to score 601 to win, or to bat for two days to save the game.

It was all over early on the final morning. Washbrook offered the most resistance, and scored 114 in a determined five and a half hours at the crease.

The 'spin twins' bowling figures were as follows:

England's first innings:
Valentine 45-28-48-4
Ramadhin 43-27-66-5

England's second innings:
Valentine 71-47-79-3
Ramadhin 72-43-86-6.

AUSTRALIA v WEST INDIES 1951–52

Melbourne Cricket Ground, Melbourne
31 December 1951, 1, 2, 3 January 1952
Australia won by one wicket

West Indies 272 (F.M.M. Worrell 108, K.R. Miller 5 for 60) and 203 (J.B. Stollmeyer 54, G.E. Gomez 52); Australia 216 (R.N. Harvey 83, J. Trim 5 for 34) and 9 for 260 (A.L. Hassett 102, A.L. Valentine 5 for 88)

The injured Worrell scored a superb century in the first innings to carry the West Indies to 272, but Miller captured 5 for 60 to spearhead Australia's attack. The visitors, however, gained a first-innings lead of 56 after a disappointing reply from Australia. Only Harvey, 83, mastered the attack of which Trim, 5 for 34, was the star.

Despite half-centuries by Stollmeyer and Gomez, the West Indies could only manage 203 in the second innings for a lead of 259. The captain, Hassett, scored a superb 102, but, despite his efforts, Australia looked beaten when the ninth wicket fell at 222. With 38 runs needed, Johnston joined Ring at the crease. As they crept closer to the target, confusion became evident in the West Indies's team: Ring and Johnson took 13 off a Valentine over, and 7 off the next by Ramadhin. Then, Ramadhin limped off and nearly everyone was trying to set the field.

Johnston deflected Worrell to fine leg for the single that won an unlikely victory.

Later, Johnston was reported to have said: 'I was never worried. I knew we couldn't make the runs!'.

ENGLAND v AUSTRALIA 1953

The Oval, London
15, 17, 18, 19 August 1953
England won by 8 wickets

Australia 275 (R.R. Lindwall 62, A.L. Hassett 53) and 162 (G.A.R. Lock 5 for 45); England 306 (L. Hutton 82, T.E. Bailey 64) and 2 for 132 (W.J. Edrich 55 not out)

In this match, England regained the Ashes which had been in Australia's possession for 19 years.

The first four Tests in this damp summer had been drawn. The final match began with Hassett giving Australia a solid start after calling correctly for the fifth time in the series. A shower of rain during the luncheon break freshened-up the wicket, and the England bowler Trueman (playing his only Test of the summer) took full advantage of the lively strip. Australia slumped from 2 for 107 to 5 for 118. Only aggressive late-order batting by Lindwall gave Australia's innings respectability.

Hutton, 82, played a fine captain's knock for England. Bailey and Bedser added 44 for the last wicket, and England gained a first-innings lead of 31.

After Hassett's dismissal, Morris and Hole (promoted to No.3) carried Australia's first-innings score to 59. Then followed a sensational 15 minutes when the Ashes were lost: Hole was lbw to Laker, then Lock's first ball to Harvey bowled him. Miller was caught at short leg off Laker for a duck, and Morris was trapped in front from the first ball of Lock's next over. Four wickets had fallen for 2 runs.

Archer scored 49 with some strong hitting before Australia was all out for 162.

England, needing just 132 to regain the Ashes, acquired the runs with little difficulty. Compton made the winning hit off Morris; this was the signal for thousands of delighted fans to stream on to the ground to acknowledge their heroes.

AUSTRALIA v ENGLAND 1954–55

Melbourne Cricket Ground, Melbourne
31 December 1954, 1, 3, 4, 5 January 1955
England won by 128 runs
England 191 (M.C. Cowdrey 102) and 279 (P.B.H. May 91, W.A. Johnston 5 for 25); Australia 231(J.B. Statham 5 for 60) and 111 (F.H. Tyson 7 for 27)

More than 300 000 people attended this New Year Test. It has been remembered as the 'watering of the wicket' match. The respected Melbourne *Age* cricket writer Percy Beames saw the MCG curator watering the pitch on the Sunday rest day! Fortunately, this watering helped England more than Australia.

Cowdrey rescued England with one of his great innings. After the magnificent bowling of Miller had England reeling at 4 for 41, Cowdrey's century carried the visitors to 191. Australia's reply was not much better, but the tail wagged sufficiently to give the home team a 40-run lead.

The pitch was at its best the Monday following the Sunday watering. Johnston bowled superbly for Australia, but England's 279 (including 91 runs from May) set Australia a target of 240.

With Morris and Favell out, Australia was 2 for 75 at the end of the fourth day, needing only a further 165 to win. When Harvey fell to a brilliant leg side catch by Evans off Tyson, England's danger-man was gone. Australia crashed, losing 8 wickets for 36 in only 80 minutes on the final morning. A 'typhoon' had wrecked Australia: Tyson returned 7 for 27 as England went 2-1 up in the series.

ENGLAND v AUSTRALIA 1956

Old Trafford, Manchester
26, 27, 28, 30, 31 July 1956
England won by an innings and 170 runs
England 459 (Rev. D.S. Sheppard 113, P.E. Richardson 104, M.C. Cowdrey 80); Australia 84 (J.C. Laker 9 for 37) and 205 (C.C. McDonald 89, J.C. Laker 10 for 53)

This was 'Laker's Match' on a dust bowl of an Old Trafford pitch. Groundsman Bert Stack as good as admitted he was instructed to prepare the wicket to suit the England spinners, Laker and Lock.

There were no problems for Richardson and Cowdrey. They compiled 174 for the first wicket and, with Sheppard scoring a century, England posted a daunting 459. McDonald and Burke started Australia's innings steadily, scoring 48 for the first wicket. But after McDonald's dismissal, the rest capitulated, and Australia was all out for 84. After tea on the second day, Laker had taken 7 wickets for 8 runs from 22 balls. Laker's first 9 overs had yielded 0 for 21; his next 7.4 returned 9 for 16.

Australia followed-on, 375 runs behind. McDonald was soon to retire hurt, and out came Harvey who was dismissed on his first ball, a full toss from Laker to Cowdrey (the great left-hander made a pair on the same day!). Rain permitted only 49 minutes play on the third day (Saturday) when Burke was dismissed. On Monday, there was more rain, and only 19 overs of play were possible, but McDonald and Craig survived on the soft, rain-affected pitch. On the final day, they continued until lunch to give the visitors some hope of survival.

Sunshine ended Australia's hopes. Laker utilised the sticky wicket to spin a web over the batsmen. Craig went just after lunch after almost four and a half hours of defiant defence. Mackay, Miller and Archer followed in quick succession. When McDonald went for 89 after more than five and a half resolute hours at the crease, it was all but over. Maddocks was trapped in front to give Laker 'all ten'. All hell erupted, the result and retention of the Ashes forgotten in the thrill of Laker's historic achievement.

His figures were 16.4-4-39-9 and 51.2-23-53-10.

PAKISTAN v AUSTRALIA 1956–57

National Stadium, Karachi
11, 12, 13, 15, 17 October 1956
Pakistan won by 9 wickets

Australia 80 (Fazal Mahmood 6 for 34) and 187 (R. Benaud 56, Fazal Mahmood 7 for 80); Pakistan 199 (A.H. Kardar 69, Wazir Mohammad 67) and 1 for 69.

This Test match, the first between Pakistan and Australia, was played on a matting wicket. Fazal Mahmood, the 'Bedser of Pakistan', and Khan Mohammad bowled unchanged to rout Australia. The visitors were bundled out for just 80. The match featured some of the slowest scoring in the game's history — only 95 in five and a half hours on the first day and 112 on the fourth.

There was little joy for the Australians. Ray Lindwall, however, captured his 200th Test wicket (the second Australian, after Grimmett, to do so). Australia dismissed the leading Pakistan batsman, Hanif Mohammad, cheaply in both innings.

Fazal ripped through Australia's second innings to set up the historic victory. The great bowler finished with 13 for 114 from 75 overs.

INDIA v AUSTRALIA 1959–60

Green Park (Modi Stadium), Kanpur
19, 20, 21, 23, 24 December 1959
India won by 119 runs

India 152 (A.K. Davidson 5 for 31) and 291 (N.J. Contractor 74, R.B. Kenny 51, A.K. Davidson 7 for 93); Australia 219 (C.C. McDonald 53, R.N. Harvey 51, J.M. Patel 9 for 69) and 105 (J.M. Patel 5 for 55)

The pitch at Green Park had recently been relaid, and Davidson and Benaud took full advantage of the conditions to bundle India out for 152. McDonald and Harvey scored half-centuries as Australia replied with 219. Jasu Patel, a 35-year-old off-spinner, played the fifth of his seven Tests and wrecked Australia with 9 for 69.

India batted with more application in the second innings and, despite a magnificent effort by Davidson (7 for 93 from 57 overs), reached 291. Contractor and Kenny compiled half-centuries.

The task of scoring 225 proved too great for Australia, and the team was bowled out for a disappointing 105. Patel again exploited the conditions superbly to finish with 5 for 55, giving him 14 wickets for the match.

AUSTRALIA v WEST INDIES 1960–61

Woolloongabba, Brisbane
9, 10, 12, 13, 14 December 1960
Match tied

West Indies 453 (G.S. Sobers 132, F.M.M. Worrell 65, J.S. Solomon 65, F.C.M. Alexander 60, W.W. Hall 50, A.K. Davidson 5 for 135) and 284 (F.M.M. Worrell 65, R.B. Kanhai 54, A.K. Davidson 6 for 87); Australia 505 (N.C. O'Neill 181, R.B. Simpson 92, C.C. McDonald 57) and 232 (A.K. Davidson 80, R. Benaud 52, W.W. Hall 5 for 63)

This Test will live forever in cricket history. It was the first tie in almost 500 matches, and was truly one of the great games highlighted by many outstanding individual efforts.

Sobers, 132 with 21 fours, played one of the greatest innings ever, according to the Australian captain, Benaud. The grace of Worrell (who scored 65 in each innings), the 181 runs scored by O'Neill, the fast bowling of Hall, and the magnificent all-round performance of Davidson (who scored 44 and 80 and captured 5 for 135 and 6 for 87) also contributed to the memorable impact of this match.

So to the final day: Hall and Valentine added 25 valuable runs to the West Indies's tally, leaving Australia 233 to win in just over five hours. Midway through the afternoon session, all looked lost as Simpson, Harvey, McDonald, O'Neill, Favell and Mackay were back in the pavilion with only 92 on the board. But Davidson and Benaud staged a tremendous fight-back, adding 134 for the seventh wicket before Solomon threw Davidson out.

Grout joined his captain with 7 runs needed to win. He took a single and faced the last over which was to be bowled by Hall (remember: they were 8-ball overs). The first ball took Grout on the thigh for 1 leg-bye (5 needed). The next delivery was a bouncer; Benaud swung, got a faint edge, and was caught behind by Alexander.

Meckiff was the new batsman. He played his first ball defensively, then Grout called him for a bye from the next. Four were now needed to win from four balls, with 2 wickets in hand. Grout skied the next ball towards square leg; Kanhai was waiting to take the catch, but Hall charged towards the ball, causing his teammates to scatter. The big fast bowler, however, muffed the chance, and the batsmen ran a single.

Three balls to go, 3 runs to win. Meckett swung the next ball towards the mid-wicket boundary, and the game looked over as the batsmen turned to complete the third run. But Conrad Hunte returned fast and flat to Alexander beside the bails, with Grout just short of his crease.

The scores were tied as the last man, Kline, joined Meckitt with two balls left. He pushed the first ball to square leg, and Meckitt called for the single. Joe Solomon gathered, and from 20 metres and with one stump at which to aim, ran Meckitt out — a thrilling finish to a magnificent game of cricket and the first tie in Test match history. See the final scoreboard below:

AUSTRALIA v WEST INDIES 1960-61 (First Test)

Woolloongabba, Brisbane, 9, 10, 12, 13, 14 December. Match tied

WEST INDIES

C.C.Hunte	c Benaud b Davidson	24	c Simpson b Mackay	39
C.W.Smith	c Grout b Davidson	7	c O'Neill b Davidson	6
R.B.Kanhai	c Grout b Davidson	15	c Grout b Davidson	54
G.S.Sobers	c Kline b Meckiff	132	b Davidson	14
F.M.M.Worrell*	c Grout b Davidson	65	c Grout b Davidson	65
J.S.Solomon	hit wkt b Simpson	65	lbw b Simpson	47
P.D.Lashley	c Grout b Kline	19	b Davidson	0
F.C.M.Alexander†	c Davidson b Kline	60	b Benaud	5
S.Ramadhin	c Harvey b Davidson	12	c Harvey b Simpson	6
W.W.Hall	st Grout b Kline	50	b Davidson	18
A.L.Valentine	not out	0	not out	7
Extras	(LB 3, W 1)	4	(B 14, LB 7, W 2)	23
Total		453		284

AUSTRALIA

C.C.McDonald	c Hunte b Sobers	57	b Worrell	16
R.B.Simpson	b Ramadhin	92	c sub (L.R.Gibbs) b Hall	0
R.N.Harvey	b Valentine	15	c Sobers b Hall	5
N.C.O'Neill	c Valentine b Hall	181	c Alexander b Hall	26
L.E.Favell	run out	45	c Solomon b Hall	7
K.D.Mackay	b Sobers	35	b Ramadhin	28
A.K.Davidson	c Alexander b Hall	44	run out	80
R.Benaud*	lbw b Hall	10	c Alexander b Hall	52
A.T.W.Grout†	lbw b Hall	4	run out	2
I.Meckiff	run out	4	run out	2
L.F.Kline	not out	3	not out	0
Extras	(B 2, LB 8, NB 4, W 1)	15	(B 2, LB 9, NB 3)	14
Total		505		232

AUSTRALIA	O	M	R	W		O	M	R	W
Davidson	30	2	135	5	Davidson	24.6	4	87	6
Meckiff	18	0	129	1	Meckiff	4	1	19	0
Mackay	3	0	15	0	Benaud	31	6	69	1
Benaud	24	3	93	0	Mackay	21	7	52	1
Simpson	8	0	25	1	Kline	4	0	14	0
Kline	17.6	6	52	3	Simpson	7	2	18	2
					O'Neill	1	0	2	0

WEST INDIES	O	M	R	W		O	M	R	W
Hall	29.3	1	140	4	Hall	17.7	3	63	5
Worrell	30	0	93	0	Worrell	16	3	41	1
Sobers	32	0	115	2	Sobers	8	0	30	0
Valentine	24	6	82	1	Valentine	10	4	27	0
Ramadhin	15	1	60	1	Ramadhin	17	3	57	1

FALL OF WICKETS

	W	A	W	A
Wkt	1st	1st	2nd	2nd
1st	23	84	13	1
2nd	42	138	88	7
3rd	65	194	114	49
4th	239	278	127	49
5th	243	381	210	57
6th	283	469	210	92
7th	347	484	241	226
8th	366	489	250	228
9th	452	496	253	232
10th	453	505	284	232

Umpires: C.J.Egar and C.Hoy

AUSTRALIA v WEST INDIES 1960–61

Adelaide Oval, Adelaide
27, 28, 30, 31 January, 1 February 1961
Drawn

West Indies 393 (R.B. Kanhai 117, F.M.M. Worrell 71, F.C.M. Alexander 63 not out, R. Benaud 5 for 96) and 6 for 432 dec. (R.B. Kanhai 115, F.C.M. Alexander 87 not out, C.C. Hunte 79, F.M.M. Worrell 53); Australia 366 (R.B. Simpson 85, R. Benaud 77, C.C. McDonald 71, L.R. Gibbs 5 for 97) and 9 for 273 (N.C. O'Neill 65, K.D. Mackay 62 not out)

This match produced an even longer period of suspense than did the tied Test in Brisbane.

Kanhai produced his best batting of the series, ripping a century off Australia's attack in each innings. The West Indian wicketkeeper, Alexander, added great depth to his team's batting, scoring 63 not out and 87 not out from the lower order. Worrell was again among the run-scorers with 71 and 53. Australia sorely missed the injured Davidson on a belter of an Adelaide pitch.

The highlight of Australia's first innings was the hat-trick taken by Gibbs. The victims were Mackay, Grout and Misson. It was the first hat-trick in Australia–West Indies Tests, and the first to be taken in Australia for 57 years.

Worrell's declaration left Australia 460 to score in about six and a half hours. When McDonald, Favell and Simpson fell before stumps on the fourth day, things were serious.

O'Neill, 65, Burge, 49, and Grout, 42, batted well. But the match seemed over just after tea when Australia was 9 for 207 with 110 minutes still to play. The last man, Kline (who had been dismissed repeatedly in the nets), walked out to join Mackay. The pair remained calm in the crisis as Worrell continually changed his bowlers. The new ball was seen off and the spinners kept out. Mackay faced the last over from Hall and was so determined to save the game that he took several deliveries on the body. His courage was rewarded! The last pair saved the day for Australia.

ENGLAND v AUSTRALIA 1961

Old Trafford, Manchester
27, 28, 29, 31 July, 1 August 1961
Australia won by 54 runs

Australia 190 (W.M. Lawry 74, J.B. Statham 5 for 53) and 432 (W.M. Lawry 102, A.K. Davidson 77 not out, N.C. O'Neill 67, R.B. Simpson 51); England 367 (P.B.H. May 95, K.F. Barrington 78, G. Pullar 63) and 201 (E.R. Dexter 76, R. Benaud 6 for 70).

It was one Test apiece when the teams arrived in Manchester for the fourth match of the series. The pitch was the complete opposite to the 'dust bowl' of 1956. Once again, Australia's innings was held together by Lawry, who scored 74 in a disappointing total of 190. Statham exploited the conditions superbly, returning 5 for 53 from 21 overs.

England reached 6 for 358 before Simpson crashed through the lower order, capturing 4 for 2 in 26 balls. Simpson was bowling because Benaud was still struggling with the shoulder injury which caused him to miss the second Test at Lord's.

The Ashes were at stake, and Australia's batsmen put their heads down. Lawry scored his second century of the series, and with O'Neill, 67, and Simpson, 51, gave Australia a lead of 154 with 4 wickets in hand at the start of the final day.

Mackay, Benaud and Grout fell for the addition of 3 runs when the No. 11 batsman, McKenzie, joined Davidson. The pair produced one of the finest last-wicket partnerships seen, so that when Flavell bowled the 19-year-old McKenzie, 98 runs had been added. The home team was left with 256 to score at 67 per hour.

After a steady start by Pullar and Subba Row that realised 40, 'Lord Ted' Dexter accepted the challenge. He hammered the Australian attack to score 76 in 84 minutes, before Benaud switched to bowl around the wicket. The change worked! Dexter was caught behind, with England 2 for 150. Two balls later, May was bowled around his legs and the tide had turned.

From 1 for 150, England crashed to 9 for 193, with Australia's captain producing a match-winning spell. Benaud's return, injured shoulder and all, was 6 for 70 from 32 overs. When Davidson captured the last wicket, Australia had won by 54 runs to retain the Ashes.

ENGLAND v WEST INDIES 1963

Lord's Cricket Ground, London
20, 21, 22, 24, 25 June 1963
Drawn

West Indies 301 (R.B. Kanhai 73, J.S. Solomon 56, F.S. Trueman 6 for 100) and 229 (B.F. Butcher 133, F.S. Trueman 5 for 52); England 297 (K.F. Barrington 80, E.R. Dexter 70, F.J. Titmus 52 not out, C.C. Griffith 5 for 91) and 9 for 228 (D.B. Close 70, K.F. Barrington 60)

This Test did much for cricket in England. Fortunes

fluctuated over five days before the game ended in a thrilling draw.

The West Indies opened proceedings with 301. 'Fiery Fred' (F.S. Trueman) took 6 for 100 before Shackleton, with 3 wickets in four balls, finished off the innings. Dexter savaged the attack for 70 and, with Barrington's 80, England's deficit was only 4 runs. The West Indies started the second innings poorly: 2 for 15 became 5 for 104 before Butcher rescued the side with a superb 133. There was another late-order collapse when 5 wickets fell for 15 runs on the fourth morning, leaving England 234 runs to win and almost two days' play to make them.

England slumped to 3 for 31, and lost Cowdrey with a broken arm. At the close of play on the fourth day, England needed 118 with 6 wickets in hand. The pre-lunch session on the final day was washed out, and England had 200 minutes to score the 118 required. At tea, the score had advanced to 5 for 171, with 63 needed in 85 minutes. Close continued to score freely and seemed likely to take England to victory. When the 200 was posted, 34 runs were needed in 45 minutes, with 5 wickets still in hand. Then the drama started — Hall had Titmus and Trueman out in one over, and then Griffiths dismissed Close.

Now 15 runs were needed in 20 minutes, with 2 wickets in hand, including the injured Cowdrey. Allen and Shackleton reduced the margin to 6 runs from three balls. Shackleton was run out! Cowdrey came out with his broken left arm in plaster (fortunately for England, he went to the non-striker's end). Allen blocked the last two balls for the game to end in a nail-biting draw.

AUSTRALIA v SOUTH AFRICA 1963–64

Adelaide Oval, Adelaide
24, 25, 27, 28, 29 January 1964
South Africa won by 10 wickets

Australia 345 (P.J.P. Burge 91, R.B. Simpson 78, B.K. Shepherd 70, B.C. Booth 58, T.L. Goddard 5 for 60) and 331 (B.K. Shepherd 78, N.C. O'Neill 66); South Africa 595 (E.J. Barlow 201, R.G. Pollock 175, N.J.N. Hawke 6 for 139) and 0 for 82

This match is best-remembered for producing South Africa's highest partnership in Test matches. Barlow and Pollock blasted the Australian attack to score 341 in only 283 minutes.

Pollock raced to his century in just over two hours, and his 175 was compiled in 283 minutes with 18 fours and 3 sixes. Barlow was not quite as aggressive, his 201 coming in six and a half hours with 27 fours.

South Africa's 595 was its record total against Australia, and lasted until the first match of the next series. Barlow dismissed Shepherd, Benaud and McKenzie on the final morning to finish with 3 for 6 from 5 overs, then proceeded to score 47 not out. He and Goddard scored the 82 needed for victory.

INDIA v AUSTRALIA 1964–65

Brabourne Stadium, Bombay
10, 11, 12, 14, 15 October 1964
India won by 2 wickets

Australia 320 (P.J.P. Burge 80, B.N. Jarman 78, T.R. Veivers 67) and 274 (R.M. Cowper 81, B.C. Booth 74, W.M. Lawry 68); India 341 (Nawab of Pataudi Jnr 86, M.L. Jaisimha 66, V.L. Manjrekar 59) and 8 for 256 (D.N. Sardesai 56, Nawab of Pataudi Jnr 53)

This was a Test that could have gone either way. Australia was unfortunate to lose its No.3 batsman, O'Neill, who went down with 'Delhi belly' and couldn't bat in either innings.

The game appeared likely to finish in a draw until Australia lost 6 for 28 in its second innings, crashing from 3 for 246 to be all out for 274. Steady batting carried India to 8 for 224 shortly after tea on the final day. The experienced Borde with the wicketkeeper, Indrajitsinhji, managed to score the 32 runs needed for victory in what was a great game. It was India's second Test win over Australia.

ENGLAND v AUSTRALIA 1972

Lord's Cricket Ground, London
22, 23, 24, 26 June 1972
Australia won by 8 wickets

England 272 (A.W. Greig 54, R.A.L. Massie 8 for 84) and 116 (R.A.L. Massie 8 for 53); Australia 308 (G.S. Chappell 131, I.M. Chappell 56, R.W. Marsh 50, J.A. Snow 5 for 57) and 2 for 81 (K.R. Stackpole 57 not out).

This was 'Massie's Match'. In his Test debut, the 25-year-old West Australian returned figures of 32.5-7-84-8 and 27.2-9-53-8 — a total of 16 wickets for 137. Only Laker with 19 and Barnes with 17 have taken more wickets than Massie in a Test. He was supported in the attack by the fast and fiery Lillee, who captured just 4 wickets for 140.

Because of Massie's outstanding bowling, Greg Chappell's innings tends to be overlooked. He, however, played one of his greatest innings, scoring 131 after Australia had lost 2 for 7.

Massie bowled unchanged from the nursery end in England's second innings to cut a swathe through the line-up (as he had done in the first). Australia continued its great record at the 'home' of cricket and won by 8 wickets.

WEST INDIES v AUSTRALIA 1973

Queen's Park Oval, Port-of-Spain, Trinidad
23, 24, 25, 27, 28 March 1973
Australia won by 44 runs

Australia 332 (K.D. Walters 112, I.R. Redpath 66, G.S. Chappell 56) and 281 (I.M. Chappell 97, L.R. Gibbs 5 for 102); West Indies 280 (R.B. Kanhai 56, A.I. Kallicharran 53) and 289 (A.I. Kallicharran 91, R.C. Fredericks 76).

Australia pulled off a fighting victory on a turning pitch in Trinidad.

Walters played one of his great Test innings. He scored 100 between lunch and tea on the first day. (Later, in December 1974 in Perth, he was to score 100 between tea and stumps against England.)

The West Indies replied with 280 to trail by 52 on the first innings. They were disadvantaged by the fact that their No.3 batsman, Rowe, tore the ligaments in his right ankle on the first day and was unable to bat in either innings.

Ian Chappell's gutsy 97 was the foundation of Australia's second effort with the bat. He was seventh out at 231, and then some strange bowling by Gibbs allowed the last 3 wickets to add 50 (including 33 for the last wicket between Walker and Hammond).

The home team's target was 334. At lunch on the final day, an improbable victory seemed likely when Kallicharran and Foster were together with the score at 4 for 268. The tireless Walker snared 'Kalli' on the first ball after lunch, and then O'Keeffe removed Foster. The rout continued with O'Keefe picking up one of his best returns in the Test arena, taking 4 for 57 from 24.1 overs.

ENGLAND v AUSTRALIA 1975

Headingley, Leeds
14, 15, 16, 18, 19 (no play) August 1975
Drawn

England 288 (D.S. Steele 73, J.H. Edrich 62, A.W. Greig 51, G.J. Gilmour 6 for 85) and 291 (D.S. Steele 92); Australia 135 (P.H. Edmonds 5 for 28) and 3 for 220 (R.B. McCosker 95 not out, I.M. Chappell 62).

This game at Headingley was the third Test of a four-match series. Australia, holding the Ashes, was leading 1-0.

England collapsed from 5 for 268 to be all out for 288. Gilmour was the wrecker, capturing a career-best 6 for 85 from 31 overs. Australia was bundled out for 135 in reply. Edmonds, on debut, was the destroyer with 5 for 28 from 20 overs. Steele with 92 (after 73 in the first innings) and Greig, 49 (after his 51 in the first 'dig'), carried the home team to 291. The lead was 444 as Australia chased an improbable victory. By the end of the fourth day, they were in with a chance at 3 for 220.

When the ground staff arrived the next morning, they discovered to their horror that the pitch had been vandalised. The wicket had been dug up and oil poured onto it. Play was impossible so the game was abandoned. Ironically, it started raining at about midday, so little play would have been possible anyway.

WEST INDIES v INDIA 1975–76

Queen's Park Oval, Port-of-Spain, Trinidad
7, 8, 10, 11, 12 April 1976
India won by 6 wickets

West Indies 359 (I.V.A. Richards 177, C.H. Lloyd 68, B.S. Chandrasekhar 6 for 120) and 6 for 271 dec. (A.I. Kallicharran 103 not out); India 228 (M.A. Holding 6 for 65) and 4 for 406 (G.R. Viswanath 112, S.M. Gavaskar 102, M. Amarnath 85).

In this match, India scored over 400 in the fourth innings to win. The only previous occasion had been at Headingley in 1948 (see page 25).

Richards with 177 mastered the Indian spinners, and made nearly half of the West Indies first-innings total of 359. The youthful Holding ripped through the visitors, who were bowled out for 228, leaving a deficit of 131. The home team built on that first-innings lead and, after Kallicharran reached his century, Lloyd declared. India needed to score 403 in a day and a half. (Australia's target at Leeds had been 404.)

Gavaskar, at his best, smashed 86 with 12 fours before stumps were drawn at 1 for 134. India needed 269 runs in six hours. After Gavaskar's early departure, Viswanath took over and, with Amarnath as the sheet anchor, they progressed steadily towards an improbable victory. The West Indian spinners bowled poorly and without the skill of their opposite numbers. Even though 'Vishy' and Amarnath were run out, Patel took over and India was home with 7 overs to spare.

Lord Harris at the crease as captain of the England team which toured Australia in 1878-79.

W.G. Grace played for England from 1880 to 1899 and is regarded as the father of the modern game.

WEST INDIES v INDIA 1975–76

Sabina Park, Kingston, Jamaica
21, 22, 24, 25 April 1976
West Indies won by 10 wickets
India 6 for 306 dec. (A.D. Gaekwad 81 retired hurt, S.M. Gavaskar 66) and 97 (M. Amarnath 60); West Indies 391 (R.C. Fredericks 82, D.L. Murray 71, I.V.A. Richards 64, M.A. Holding 55, B.S. Chandrasekhar 5 for 135) and 0 for 13.

This match was the one that followed India's great victory at Port-of-Spain. The pitch at Sabina Park had been relaid, and played with an unpredictable and uneven bounce.

Lloyd sent the Indians in on winning the toss. Before bad light stopped play on the first day, they had scored 1 for 175. On the second morning, however, everything went wrong for India. Viswanath, on being caught off the glove, suffered a fractured finger. Gaekwad, who had batted through the first day, was struck above the left ear and retired hurt on 81. Patel top-edged Holding, and was also forced off the field. Bedi declared just before tea at 6 for 306.

India struck back strongly, with Julien the sixth batsman out at 217. With the bowlers tiring, Murray and Holding added 107 for the seventh wicket.

With a first innings lead of 85, the West Indies struck early with Holding trapping Gavaskar. At 5 for 97, India's second innings closed as five batsmen were absent hurt. In addition to Viswanath, Gaekwad and Patel, Bedi and Chandrasekhar sustained finger injuries while fielding. At first it was thought that Bedi had declared again, but after the West Indies won the match, India's captian issued a statement that the second innings should be recorded as completed.

AUSTRALIA v ENGLAND 1976–77

The Centenary Test
Melbourne Cricket Ground, Melbourne
12, 13, 14, 16, 17 March 1977
Australia won by 45 runs
Australia 138 and 9 for 419 dec. (R.W. Marsh 110 not out, I.C. Davis 68, K.D. Walters 66, D.W. Hookes 56); England 95 (D.K. Lillee 6 for 26) and 417 (D.W. Randall 174, D.L. Amiss 64, D.K. Lillee 5 for 139)

The Centenary of Test cricket was celebrated with a special match at Melbourne 100 years after that first match in March 1877.

Australia, sent in on a lively pitch, was bundled out for just 138. The big Sunday crowd roared as Lillee and Walker crashed through England's batting. England was all out for 95 as a result of the onslaught — Lillee 6 for 26, Walker 4 for 54.

Officials were concerned; the match seemed certain to be over by the fourth day, and the Queen and Duke of Edinburgh were not due to attend until the afternoon of the fifth.

The pitch was now favouring the batsmen. Although the home side was in trouble at 3 for 53 in the second innings, they were able to turn that situation around. Marsh reached his first Test century against England, and the 21-year-old Hookes, on debut, hit Greig for 5 successive fours. The gutsy McCosker (who had his jaw fractured in the first innings) batted at No.10 and scored 25 in an invaluable partnership of 54 with Marsh. Chappell declared with Australia leading by 462.

Randall and Amiss gave England a glimmer of hope with a third-wicket stand of 166. But O'Keeffe had both Randall and Greig caught at short leg by Cosier, then Lillee trapped Knott in front. The result was an Australian victory by 45 runs — the same margin by which they had won the first match 100 years earlier. See page 34 for the final scoreboard.

NEW ZEALAND v ENGLAND 1977–78

Basin Reserve, Wellington
10, 11, 12, 14, 15 February 1978
New Zealand won by 72 runs
New Zealand 228 (J.G. Wright 55, C.M. Old 6 for 54) and 123 (R.G.D. Willis 5 for 32; England 215 (G. Boycott 77) and 64 (R.J. Hadlee 6 for 26).

This was the forty-eighth match in 48 years between the two countries

Wright, playing his first Test, laid the foundation for New Zealand's innings. His 55 was scored in almost six hours and, with Congdon, 44, the home team reached a modest 228. Old bowled into the howling gale and finished with 6 for 54 from 30 overs. If Wright was laborious, then Boycott was, too. His 77 took almost seven and a half hours to compile. England lost its last 6 wickets for 32 to trail by 13 runs on the first innings.

New Zealand's second-innings collapse was just as dramatic. The home team went from 1 for 82 to be all out for 123, with the last 9 wickets falling for 41. Willis was the destroyer, taking 5 for 32. England's target was 137, but by the end of the fourth day the innings was in tatters: 8 wickets had fallen for 53. Rain delayed the inevitable on the

AUSTRALIA v ENGLAND 1976-77 (Centenary Test)

Melbourne Cricket Ground, 12, 13, 14, 16, 17 March. Australia won by 45 runs

AUSTRALIA

I.C.Davis	lbw b Lever	5		c Knott b Greig	68
R.B.McCosker	b Willis	4	(10)	c Greig b Old	25
G.J.Cosier	c Fletcher b Lever	10	(4)	c Knott b Lever	4
G.S.Chappell*	b Underwood	40	(3)	b Old	2
D.W.Hookes	c Greig b Old	17	(6)	c Fletcher b Underwood	56
K.D.Walters	c Greig b Willis	4	(5)	c Knott b Greig	66
R.W.Marsh†	c Knott b Old	28		not out	110
G.J.Gilmour	c Greig b Old	4		b Lever	16
K.J.O'Keeffe	c Brearley b Underwood	0	(2)	c Willis b Old	14
D.K.Lillee	not out	10	(9)	c Amiss b Old	25
M.H.N.Walker	b Underwood	2		not out	8
Extras	(B 4, LB 2, NB 8)	14		(LB 10, NB 15)	25
Total		138		(9 wkts dec.)	419

ENGLAND

R.A.Woolmer	c Chappell b Lillee	9		lbw b Walker	12
J.M.Brearley	c Hookes b Lillee	12		lbw b Lillee	43
D.L.Underwood	c Chappell b Walker	7	(10)	b Lillee	7
D.W.Randall	c Marsh b Lillee	4	(3)	c Cosier b O'Keeffe	174
D.L.Amiss	c O'Keeffe b Walker	4	(4)	b Chappell	64
K.W.R.Fletcher	c Marsh b Walker	4	(5)	c Marsh b Lillee	1
A.W.Greig*	b Walker	18	(6)	c Cosier b O'Keeffe	41
A.P.E.Knott†	lbw b Lillee	15	(7)	lbw b Lillee	42
C.M.Old	c Marsh b Lillee	3	(8)	c Chappell b Lillee	2
J.K.Lever	c Marsh b Lillee	11	(9)	lbw b O'Keeffe	4
R.G.D.Willis	not out	1		not out	5
Extras	(B 2, LB 2, NB 2, W 1)	7		(B 8, LB 4, NB 7, W 3)	22
Total		95			417

ENGLAND	O	M	R	W		O	M	R	W
Lever	12	1	36	2	Lever	21	1	95	2
Willis	8	0	33	2	Willis	22	0	91	0
Old	12	4	39	3	Old	27.6	2	104	4
Underwood	11.6	2	16	3	Greig	14	3	66	2
					Underwood	12	2	38	1

AUSTRALIA	O	M	R	W		O	M	R	W
Lillee	13.3	2	26	6	Lillee	34.4	7	139	5
Walker	15	3	54	4	Walker	22	4	83	1
O'Keeffe	1	0	4	0	Gilmour	4	0	29	0
Gilmour	5	3	4	0	Chappell	16	7	29	1
					O'Keeffe	33	6	108	3
					Walters	3	2	7	0

FALL OF WICKETS

	A	E	A	E
Wkt	1st	1st	2nd	2nd
1st	11	19	33	28
2nd	13	30	40	113
3rd	23	34	53	279
4th	45	40	132	290
5th	51	40	187	346
6th	102	61	244	369
7th	114	65	277	380
8th	117	78	353	385
9th	136	86	407	410
10th	138	95	-	417

Umpires: T.F.Brooks and M.G.O'Connell

final morning for 40 minutes. It then took the Kiwis 49 minutes to claim the last 2 wickets, both falling to Richard Hadlee, who finished with 6 for 26. England was all out for 64.

New Zealand defeated England for the first time amid chaotic scenes at The Basin Reserve.

NEW ZEALAND v WEST INDIES 1979–80

Carisbrook, Dunedin
8, 9, 10, 12, 13 February 1980
New Zealand won by 1 wicket

West Indies 140 (D.L. Haynes 55, R.J. Hadlee 5 for 34) and 212 (D.L. Haynes 105, R.J. Hadlee 6 for 68); New Zealand 249 (B.A. Edgar 65, R.J. Hadlee 51) and 9 for 104

After Lloyd called correctly, Hadlee tore the heart out of the visitors' innings. They were were 3 for 4 after Hadlee had bowled 13 deliveries. Haynes with 55 played a lone hand, as the West Indies were bowled out for 140.

Against hostile fast bowling, Edgar and Howarth played with great courage and determination for New Zealand, with Edgar taking almost five hours to score 65. After a middle-order collapse, Hadlee and Cairns added 64 in 34 minutes for the eighth wicket. Cairns hit Parry for 3 sixes in one over, and Hadlee's 51 runs included 9 fours.

New Zealand's lead was a valuable 109 runs. Again it was Haynes who held the visitors' innings together. He scored 105 out of 212, and added 88 for the fifth wicket with King and 63 for the sixth with Murray to save the side.

New Zealand needed 104 to win. By lunch on the final day they had reached 2 for 33. Under intense pressure from the pace battery (Holding, Croft and Garner), they crashed to be 7 for 54 and appeared to be beaten.

Again Hadlee and Cairns came to the rescue. They added 19 for eighth wicket before Cairns and Troup put on 27 for the ninth. At tea it was 8 for 95. With 1 run added, Holding hit Cairns off-stump without dislodging the bail. Cairns went when the score reached 100. Boock, the No.11 batsman, joined Troup. He survived the last five balls of Holding's over. Garner continued the attack. The first ball produced a bye. On the second ball, Boock survived an appeal for lbw. He defended the next two before pushing the fifth ball behind point for 2. With scores level, the batsmen scampered a leg bye to produce a thrilling New Zealand victory.

Hadlee's 11 wickets included a Test record of 7 lbw decisions (of the total 12 lbw decisions made in the match).

AUSTRALIA v INDIA 1980–81

Melbourne Cricket Ground, Melbourne
7, 8, 9, 10, 11 February 1981
India won by 59 runs

India 237 (G.R. Viswanath 114) and 324 (C.P.S. Chauhan 85, S.M. Gavaskar 70); Australia 419 (A.R. Border 124, K.D. Walters 78, G.S. Chappell 76) and 83 (Kapil Dev 5 for 28).

This was a sensational match — not only because of Australia's amazing second-innings collapse on the final day, but because India had come near to forfeiting the match on the previous day when the captain, Gavaskar, disagreed with an lbw decision and wanted to call off the game. When Gavaskar was given out, he indicated he had hit the ball on to his pad; then, as he walked past his partner, Chauhan, he urged him to leave the field with him. Fortunately, the Indian team manager, Wing Commander Durrani, intervened and ordered Chauhan to continue his innings.

Chappell sent India in on an MCG pitch that had been criticised all summer. The decision was vindicated when India slumped to 6 for 115. They were kept in the match by Viswanath, who went in at 2 for 22, and was ninth man out after making 114. In reply, Australia struggled early before Chappell and Border added 108 for the fourth wicket. Border reached his century on the third morning, and then Walters and Marsh held the lower order together.

Australia had a significant lead of 182, although resolute batting by Gavaskar and Chauhan had reduced this to 74 at the end of the third day. Then, 35 minutes before lunch, the 'Gavaskar incident' occurred. When Chauhan was dismissed shortly after, Lillee became Australia's leading Test wicket-taker.

Vengsarkar, Viswanath and Patil helped rebuild India's innings, but a late-order collapse left Australia needing only 143 to win.

India's attack was seriously depleted. Kapil Dev had pulled a thigh muscle and didn't bowl on the fourth evening. Yadav suffered a fractured toe batting in the first innings when he was struck by a Pascoe yorker, and Doshi had a fractured instep and was greatly distressed. Nevertheless, Australia was reeling at 3 for 24 at the end of the day, with

Dyson, Wood, and Chappell all back in the pavilion.

The injured Kapil Dev joined the fray on the final morning and, despite the disability, bowled unchanged to capture 5 of the last 7 wickets to fall. India managed an unlikely victory by 59 runs.

ENGLAND v AUSTRALIA 1981

Headingley, Leeds
16, 17, 18, 20, 21 July 1981
England won by 18 runs

Australia 9 for 401 dec. (J. Dyson 102, K.J. Hughes 89, G.N. Yallop 58, I.T. Botham 6 for 95) and 111 (R.G.D. Willis 8 for 43); England 174 (I.T. Botham 50) and 356 (I.T. Botham 149 not out, G.R. Dilley 56, T.M. Alderman 6 for 135).

For this third Test of the series, Brearley replaced Botham as England's captain. Hughes won the toss for the third time in succession for Australia, and batted first. Dyson's solid century and the skipper's 89 steered Australia to the relative safety of 401 before declaring.

Australia's pace bowlers, Lillee, Alderman and Lawson, bundled England out for 174. The deposed Botham, who had taken 6 wickets in Australia's innings, top-scored with 50.

England followed-on, 227 runs behind, but the second innings went along similar lines to the first. When Taylor became Alderman's fourth victim for the innings, the score was 7 for 135.

Botham proceeded to play one of the great Test hands and, with admirable support from the tail, at least avoided the innings defeat and gave his team a glimmer of hope. With Dilley (56), he added 117 for the eighth wicket in 80 minutes; with Old (29), it was 67 for the ninth; and with Willis (2), it was 37 for the last. Botham finished with 149 not out and posted his century from 87 balls. (Jessop had taken just 75 at The Oval in 1902—see page 19.)

Australia had almost the entire final day to score 130 to win. With the score at 1 for 56, Willis changed ends to bowl with the wind. He proceeded to take 8 of the last 9 wickets to fall and, in a career-best peformance, returned 8 for 43 from 15.1 overs as England snatched a dramatic 18-run victory.

This was only the second time that a team following-on had won a Test match. The previous occasion was in Sydney in December 1894 (see page 15). Early in England's second innings, odds of 500 to 1 for an England victory were posted in the betting tents at Headingley.

AUSTRALIA v ENGLAND 1982–83

Melbourne Cricket Ground, Melbourne
26, 27, 28, 29, 30 December 1982
England won by 3 runs

England 284 (C.J. Tavare 89, A.J. Lamb 83) and 294 (G. Fowler 65); Australia 287 (K.J. Hughes 66, D.W. Hookes 53, R.W. Marsh 53) and 288 (D.W. Hookes 68, A.R. Border 62 not out, N.G. Cowans 6 for 77)

This was one of the great Test matches. In terms of runs, the only closer Tests were the two tied between Australia and the West Indies at Brisbane in 1960-61 (see page 28) and India and Australia at Madras in 1986-87 (see page 41).

Chappell sent England in on a slightly damp pitch. The visitors were soon struggling at 3 for 56 before Tavare and Lamb added 161 for the fourth wicket in sparkling fashion. England's tail failed to wag, and the innings ended at 284.

On the second day, Australia was bowled out for 287. After Cowans dismissed Dyson and Chappell with successive deliveries, Hughes grafted a patient 66 to hold the innings together. Hookes and Marsh, with a mixture of aggression and good fortune, scored half-centuries.

The pattern continued on the third day with England being dismissed for 294. This time, it was the lower order that held the innings together. Botham scored his 46 at a run a ball before Pringle and Taylor realised 61 for the eighth wicket.

Australia's target was 292. An occasional ball was keeping low on the relaid pitch, but the outfield was unusually fast (the result of a prolonged drought that had restricted the watering of the ground).

Fortunes fluctuated throughout Australia's innings. Early on, England was on top. Chappell fell cheaply, again to Cowans, and when Dyson was brilliantly caught by Tavare at slip it was 3 for 71. Australia regained the initiative when Hughes and Hookes posted a century partnership for the fourth wicket. Then an inspired spell from Cowans tipped the scales England's way. He captured 4 for 19 in 7 overs to have the home team in desperate trouble at 9 for 218. Thomson joined Border with 74 runs still required. By stumps, the last pair had taken the score to 255; they were half-way there.

On the final morning 18 000 spectators turned up for the climax to what had been the most enthralling Test since the tie at the 'Gabba 22 years earlier.

Willis kept the field back for Border to enable him to take singles. The pugnacious left-hander had been out of touch, and the lack of pressure helped play him back to form.

The new ball had been taken early on the final morning with the score at 259, but still the last pair defied the English team. Botham started the eighteenth over of the day with 4 runs needed for an improbable victory. Thomson fended at the first ball, edging it to Tavare at second slip. The straightforward catch bounced out, but within reach of Miller at first slip. He completed the catch, and England had won the titanic struggle by 3 runs.

With that final wicket, Botham became the second England player (Rhodes being the other) to score 1000 runs and take 100 wickets against Australia.

PAKISTAN v INDIA 1982–83

Niaz Stadium, Hyderbad
14, 15, 16, 18, 19 January 1983
Pakistan won by an innings and 119 runs
Pakistan 3 for 581 dec. (Javed Miandad 280 not out, Mudassar Nazar 231); India 189 (B.S. Sandhu 71, M. Amarnath 61, Imran Khan 6 for 35), 273 (M. Amarnath 64, S.M. Gavaskar 60, D.B. Vengsarkar 58 not out)

The feature of this match was the third-wicket partnership between Mudassar Nazar and Javed Miandad. Their stand realised 451 runs which equalled the then world Test record for any wicket (Ponsford and Bradman had added 451 for the second wicket at The Oval in 1934). Mudassar and Miandad both made their highest Test score.

Pakistan out-classed India for the third successive match to record its most emphatic series victory over its subcontinent neighbour.

In this game, Viswanath played his eighty-fifth consecutive Test to equal the then record of G.S. Sobers. In the series, Pakistan's captain, Imran Khan, was outstanding. He captured 40 wickets.

ENGLAND v NEW ZEALAND 1983

Headingley, Leeds
28, 29, 30 July, 1 August 1983
New Zealand won by 5 wickets
England 225 (C.J. Tavare 69, A.J. Lamb 58, B.L. Cairns 7 for 74) and 252 (D.I. Gower 112 not out, E.J. Chatfield 5 for 95); New Zealand 377 (J.G. Wright 93, B.A. Edgar 84, R.J. Hadlee 75) and 5 for 103 (R.G.D. Willis 5 for 35)

After 17 defeats and 11 draws, this was New Zealand's first Test victory in England.

Howarth sent the home team in on a seamer's pitch. It was a successful opening day for the visitors, and England was bowled out for 225. Just before tea, only 2 wickets had fallen when Martin Crowe took a brilliant diving catch at square leg to remove Lamb. Cairns, with 7 for 74, became the first New Zealand bowler to capture 7 wickets in a Test innings against England.

Edgar was forced to retire hurt early on the second day, but his opening partner, Wright, became New Zealand's sheet anchor. On his way to scoring 93 in almost five hours, he was involved in two tragic run outs — both Howarth and Jeff Crowe were victims of his indecision. Later, Edgar returned and, with the hard-hitting Hadlee, carried New Zealand's first-innings total to 377.

England's second effort was only a slight improvement on the first. But Gower, in scoring his first century at home in four years, held the innings together.

New Zealand required 101 to win, but, with Willis in full flight, Kiwi hearts were fluttering as Coney walked to the crease with the score at 4 for 61. Jeff Crowe went at 83, then Hadlee joined Coney, and they proceeded to wipe off the deficit with more than a day to spare.

NEW ZEALAND v ENGLAND 1983–84

Lancaster Park, Christchurch
3, 4, 5, February 1984
New Zealand won by an innings and 132 runs
New Zealand 307 (R.J. Hadlee 99); England 82 and 93 (R.J. Hadlee 5 for 28)

This match, played on a suspect pitch at Lancaster Park, was completed in just under 12 hours' playing time. New Zealand recorded its largest ever victory in a Test match.

The England touring party had been hit by injuries, but that was no excuse for the wayward bowling on the first day. Hadlee took full advantage of the erratic attack to blast 99 from 81 balls in less than two hours.

When Fowler was bowled in the last over of the opening day, England was in trouble. On the second day, the team was in deeper trouble when play resumed after tea. Hadlee and Chatfield exploited the conditions perfectly as the visitors tumbled to 7 for 53.

The follow-on was not avoided as Chatfield and Cairns cleaned up the tail. Starting the second innings 225 runs behind, England was soon in desperate trouble at 6 for 33. (The lowest score for

England against New Zealand was 64 at Wellington in 1977-78.) Randall and Taylor added 39 before Taylor was run out. Fittingly, Hadlee captured the last 3 wickets to finish with match figures of 8 for 44 from 35 overs — and with his 99 he was undoubtedly the Man of the Match.

PAKISTAN v ENGLAND 1983–84

National Stadium, Karachi
2, 3, 4, 6 March 1984
Pakistan won by 3 wickets

England 182 (D.I. Gower 58, Abdul Qadir 5 for 74) and 159 (D.I. Gower 57); Pakistan 277 (Salim Malik 74, Mohsin Khan 54, N.G.B. Cook 6 for 65) and 7 for 66 (N.G.B. Cook 5 for 18)

This was Pakistan's first victory over England in 13 home Tests. England arrived on the subcontinent after the tour of New Zealand and, with no time to acclimatize to the different conditions, went straight into the first match of the series.

Gower called correctly, and England reached 1 for 90 in the afternoon session before the Pakistani bowlers Sarfraz and Qadir took over. Only Gower's patient 58 prevented a complete rout.

Pakistan's innings followed a similar pattern. Cook ripped through the middle order to have the home team struggling at 6 for 138. Qadir, who was dropped on 1, showed his all-round capabilities to add 75 with Salim Malik for the seventh wicket. Salim finished with 74, and, when the last pair, Tauseef and Azeem, added 37 runs, Pakistan's lead had stretched to 95.

England's second innings followed a similar pattern to the first with only Gower providing stout resistance.

Pakistan, with a target of just 65, was quickly in trouble. Cook was on for the fourth over of the innings: 3 for 26 soon became 6 for 40 before the 20-year-old wicketkeeper, Anil Dalpat, steadied the innings. Cook finished the match with 11 wickets for 83, while Abdul Qadir claimed 8 for 133.

ENGLAND v WEST INDIES 1984

Lord's Cricket Ground, London
28, 29, 30 June, 2, 3 July 1984
West Indies won by 9 wickets

England 286 (G. Fowler 106, B.C. Broad 55, M.D. Marshall 6 for 85) and 9 for 300 dec. (A.J. Lamb 110, I.T. Botham 81); West Indies 245 (I.V.A. Richards 72, I.T. Botham 8 for 103) and 1 for 344 (C.G. Greenidge 214 not out, H.A. Gomes 92 not out)

England controlled the match for four of the five days, only to be convincingly defeated at the end. Fowler and Broad, on debut, scored a rare century opening stand against the West Indies pace battery. Fowler applied himself for over six hours to post his second Test century. The last 6 England wickets fell for only 43 as Marshall cleaned up the tail to finish with 6 for 70.

Botham knocked over the top order to have the West Indies in trouble at 3 for 35. Richards and Lloyd dug in until Botham trapped Richards in front for 72. Umpire Barry Meyer later admitted that he had considered recalling Richards, fearing he may have made a mistake. Botham was magnificent, and finished with 8 for 103 as England gained a first innings lead of 41 runs.

This advantage was quickly lost as the home team slumped to 3 for 36. Lamb, with support from Gatting and Botham, turned the innings around. The irrepressible Botham hammered 81, while Lamb finished with 110. When Gower declared early on the final morning, the West Indies required 342 to win in five and a half hours.

Greenidge proceeded to play a superb innings. He made the England attack look pedestrian as he plundered 29 boundaries in compiling a brilliant double-century. Greenidge and Gomes added an unbroken 287 for the second wicket to bring the West Indies home with almost 12 overs to spare.

For the first time a Man of the Match award was shared — Botham joined Greenidge for the honour.

Finally, of the 30 dismissals in the match, 12 were lbw, thereby equalling the record set at Dunedin in 1979-80.

AUSTRALIA v WEST INDIES 1984–85

Sydney Cricket Ground, Sydney
30, 31 December 1984, 1, 2 January 1985
Australia won by an innings and 55 runs

Australia 9 for 471 dec. (K.C. Wessels 173, A.R. Border 69); West Indies 163 (R.G. Holland 6 for 54) and 253 (C.H. Lloyd 72, I.V.A. Richards 58)

This was the 110th and final Test for the West Indian captain, Lloyd. It was his seventy-fourth match as skipper. The Sydney pitch had favoured the spinners all season, so it came as a surprise when the visitors left out their only slow bowler, Harper, to include Holding, who was returning after injury.

Two days of rain had left the pitch and outfield damp, but Border decided to bat first. Wood and Wessels were both missed early in their innings.

These missed chances were to cost the West Indies dearly. Wessels was the sheet anchor of Australia's innings. He occupied the crease for more than eight hours in compiling his fourth Test century. The home team batted on for an hour on the third day, and before stumps the West Indies was following on.

Australia's leg spinner, Holland, was the destroyer. He returned career-best figures of 6 for 54.

The visitors performed only slightly better in the second innings. Although Richards and Lloyd threatened to play the big innings required by the West Indies, Australia held all the aces. Lloyd top-scored with 72 and received a standing ovation from the crowd of 25 000 as he returned to the pavilion. It was the first time in 27 matches that the West Indies had been defeated (since Melbourne in 1981-82), and its first loss by an innings since 1968-69 (also in Melbourne).

NEW ZEALAND v PAKISTAN 1984–85

Carisbrook, Dunedin
9, 10, 11, 13, 14 February 1985
New Zealand won by 2 wickets

Pakistan 274 (Qasim Omar 96, Javed Miandad 79, R.J. Hadlee 6 for 51) and 223 (Qasim Omar 89); New Zealand 220 (M.C. Crowe 57, Wasim Akram 5 for 56) and 8 for 278 (J.V. Coney 111 not out, M.D. Crowe 84, Wasim Akram 5 for 72)

On a seamer's pitch, both teams went into the match without a spinner! Howarth won the toss and, not surprisingly, decided to bowl first.

Coming together at 2 for 100, Qasim Omar and Javed Miandad added 141 in a brilliant batting display. Along the way, Javed Miandad, at 27, became the youngest player to reach 5000 Test runs. A dramatic collapse — 5 wickets falling for 10 in the last 30 minutes of play on the first day — tipped the scales in favour of New Zealand. Hadlee, as was normally the case, did the damage. The final return for the Kiwi champion was 6 for 51.

New Zealand struggled against the Pakistan pace quartet, particularly the 18-year-old Wasim Akram (who was playing in only his second Test).

Qasim Omar was again the dominant Pakistan batsman. He followed his first innings 96 with 89. Rashid and Akram added 42 for the last wicket to lift the overall lead to 277.

New Zealand was soon in desperate trouble at 4 for 23. Akram had 3 wickets when Coney joined Martin Crowe at the crease. They survived for the remainder of the afternoon, and in the process carried the score to 114. The pair continued to bat patiently on the final morning until Crowe was out for 84 just before lunch. His stand with Coney had realised 157.

Pakistan then regained the upper hand, taking the seventh wicket at 216. Cairns, who was not wearing a helmet, was struck on the head by Akram and retired hurt. Chatfield joined Coney after Bracewell was dismissed at 228. The last pair was required to make 50, as Cairns was severely concussed and was to spend three days in hospital. By tea the score had advanced to 235. Coney, on 97, was dropped by the keeper from the first ball of the final session. The excitement was intense as the final pair carried New Zealand to a thrilling victory.

With the field set deep for Coney, he faced 48 balls in the partnership, while Chatfield, in compiling his highest Test score, received 84 deliveries.

ENGLAND v AUSTRALIA 1985

Lord's Cricket Ground, London
27, 28, 29 June, 1, 2 July 1985
Australia won by 4 wickets

England 290 (D.I. Gower 86, C.J. McDermott 6 for 70) and 261 (I.T. Botham 85, M.W. Gatting 75 not out, R.G. Holland 5 for 68); Australia 425 (A.R. Border 196, G.M. Ritchie 94, I.T. Botham 5 for 109) and 6 for 127.

Australia kept its great record at the 'home' of cricket intact in a game that was dominated by its captain, Border. He scored 196 and 41 not out, which was 43 per cent of his team's runs.

Border sent England in to bat. Inspired fast bowling by McDermott soon had the home side in trouble, and only another brilliant knock by Gower saved his team from total collapse.

Australia was struggling at 4 for 101 when Ritchie joined Border. They added 216 for the fifth wicket before Botham returned to restrict the visitors' lead to 135. He picked up 5 wickets in a Test innings for the twenty-fifth time.

Gower used two night watchmen on the third evening. But when they went early on Monday morning, together with Lamb and the skipper himself, England was on the ropes at 6 for 98. Enter Botham who, with Gatting, put on 131 for the seventh wicket. Australia's leg spinner, Holland, decided to bowl around the wicket. He finely lured Botham into going for a big hit; 'Beefy' holed out to Border at deep point.

Australia, needing 127 to win, slumped to 3 for 46 by the close of play on the fourth day. It was soon 5 for 65 on the final morning before Border and Phillips carried the score to 116 and relative safety.

Australia won by 4 wickets. It was Australia's fifth victory at Lord's since Verity's match in 1934 (see page 23).

SRI LANKA v INDIA 1985–86

P. Saravanamutta Stadium, Colombo
6, 7, 8, 10, 11 September 1985
Sri Lanka won by 149 runs

Sri Lanka 385 (S.A.R. Silva 111, R.L. Dias 95, R.S. Madugalle 54, L.R.D. Mendis 51, Chetan Sharma 5 for 118) and 3 for 206 dec. (P.A. De Silva 75, R.L. Dias 60 not out); India 244 (K. Srikkanth 64, M. Amarnath 60, S.M. Gavaskar 52) and 198 (Kapil Dev 78, R.J. Ratnayake 5 for 49).

This was Sri Lanka's first Test win in only their fourteenth Test match.

After slow batting on the opening day, Silva's century and Dias's polished 95 provided the nucleus for the home team's total of 385. This score was achieved even though the last 6 wickets fell for 17 runs.

India never recovered from a catastrophic start to its first innings. Half-centuries to Srikkanth, Gavaskar, and Amarnath helped after it was 3 for 3, but the team still trailed by 141 runs.

Quick scoring by Aravinda de Silva and Dias enabled Sri Lanka to declare 347 ahead. Only a hard-hitting 78 by the skipper, Kapil Dev, saved India from complete humiliation. Ratnayake was the chief wrecker. He completed a fine double with the ball and followed 4 for 76 with 5 for 49. Silva's century and nine dismissals were an unprecedented feat by a wicketkeeper in a Test match.

AUSTRALIA v NEW ZEALAND 1985–86

Woolloongabba, Brisbane
8, 9, 10, 11, 12 November 1985
New Zealand won by an innings and 41 runs

Australia 179 (K.C. Wessels 70, R.J. Hadlee 9 for 52) and 333 (A.R. Border 152 not out, G.R.J. Matthews 115, R.J. Hadlee 6 for 71); New Zealand 7 for 553 dec. (M.D. Crowe 188, J.F. Reid 108, R.J. Hadlee 54)

In this match, New Zealand scored its most overwhelming Test victory away from home. The win was set up by the champion fast bowler, Richard Hadlee, who cut through Australia's batting line-up like a warm knife slicing butter.

Hadlee captured the first 8 wickets before taking a well-judged outfield catch off Brown's bowling to dismiss Lawson. Brown returned the favour, catching Holland for a duck.

Australia was all out for 179. Hadlee finished with 9 for 52. Only Laker (twice at Manchester in 1956) and Lohmann (in Johannesburg in 1895-96) had recorded better figures in Test cricket.

Centuries to Reid and Martin Crowe placed the visitors in an impregnable position. Coney declared on the fourth morning with a lead of 374.

In just over two hours, Hadlee, Chatfield and Snedden had reduced Australia to 5 for 67. Then Border and Matthews added 197 for the sixth wicket to offer Australia a glimmer of hope. But the tail failed to offer Border enough assistance to make New Zealand bat again.

Hadlee captured 6 for 71 to finish with match figures of 52.3-13-123-15, the best by a New Zealand bowler.

WEST INDIES v ENGLAND 1985–86

Recreation Ground, St John's, Antigua
11, 12, 13, 15, 16 April 1986
West Indies won by 240 runs

West Indies 474 (D.L. Haynes 131, M.D. Marshall 76, M.A. Holding 73, R.A. Harper 60) and 2 for 246 dec. (I.V.A. Richards 110 not out, D.L. Haynes 70); England 310 (D.I. Gower 90, W.N. Slack 52, G.A. Gooch 51) and 170 (G.A. Gooch 51)

This was the final Test of a five-match series, and was historic on two counts. First, the West Indies emulated Australia's achievement in winning all five home Tests on more than one occasion. They had defeated India 5-0 in the 1961-62 series. Second, and more significantly, Richards, in scoring 110 not out in the West Indies second innings, recorded the fastest Test century ever in terms of balls faced — 56 to reach three figures, 58 in all. The previous best had been J.M. Gregory's 67 against South Africa at Johannesburg in 1921-22.

Richard's innings was played without blemish while England was trying to make run-scoring as difficult as possible. For the most part, there were six men on the boundary and sometimes as many as nine.

His innings occupied 83 minutes, and he scored 110 of the 146 runs made in that time. The details were as follows:

..36126141 (24 off 10)
.211.412.1 (36 off 20)
112.2111.. (45 off 30)
.1.1624441 (68 off 40)
12..664612 (96 off 50)
..21.461 (110 off 58).

INDIA v AUSTRALIA 1986–87

Chepauk (Chidambaram Stadium), Madras
18, 19, 20, 21, 22 September 1986
Match tied

Australia 7 for 574 dec. (D.M. Jones 210, D.C. Boon 122, A.R. Border 106) and 5 for 170 dec.; India 397 (Kapil Dev 119, R.J. Shastri 62, K.R. Srikkanth 53, M. Azharuddin 50, G.R.J. Matthews 5 for 103) and 347 (S.M. Gavaskar 90, M. Amarnath 51, G.R.J. Matthews 5 for 146, R.J. Bright 5 for 94)

This match resulted in the second tie in Test history. (Australia was also involved in the first tie — against the West Indies — in 1960-61. See page 28.) At the finish, it was Australia who managed to avoid defeat, even though they had dominated proceedings for the first four days' play. Australia declared both its innings, and lost only 12 wickets in the match.

Australia's first innings continued until early on the third day. Jones' double-century was the cornerstone of the visitors' highest Test score in India, and Boon and Border were the other centurions; However, the Indian skipper, Kapil Dev, made sure that Australia batted again by blasting a century off 109 balls with 21 fours.

The off-spinner Matthews picked up 5 wickets in an innings for the first time. From the 49 overs remaining on the fourth day, Australia scored 170. This allowed Border to declare on the final morning, setting India 348 to win from a minimum of 87 overs.

After a steady start, Gavaskar and Amarnath picked up the tempo and, when they went to tea at 2 for 190, India had a realistic chance of winning. The target for the final session was 158 runs from 30 overs. At the start of the final 20 overs, 118 runs were needed with 7 wickets in hand.

Gavaskar, 90, went out at 251; when Kapil Dev was out 2 runs later, Australia again had a chance. Shastri, Pandit and Chetan Sharma turned the game India's way until only 18 runs were needed from 30 balls. The situation changed again when Sharma and More were dismissed in an over by Bright. Yadav, who had hit Matthews for six, was ninth out at 344, bowled by Bright. With eight balls remaining, Maninder Singh joined Shastri and defended two balls from Bright, giving Shastri the strike for the last over from Matthews. The first ball was blocked. He went for a big hit off the second, mistimed the stroke, but after a misfield was able to take 2 runs.

The third ball was pushed to mid-wicket for a single, and the scores were tied. Maninder defended the fourth, but from the fifth delivery he was trapped lbw. The match ended in a thrilling tie before 30 000 excited fans. Matthews picked up his second 5-wicket haul, and the left-armer Bright gained the other 5. All 10 wickets in India's second innings had fallen to spin. See page 42 for the final scoreboard.

PAKISTAN v WEST INDIES 1986–87

Iqbal Stadium, Faisalabad
24, 26, 27, 28, 29 October 1986
Pakistan won by 186 runs

Pakistan 159 (Imran Khan 61) and 328 (Wasim Akram 66, Salim Yousuf 61); West Indies 248 (R.B. Richardson 54, Wasim Akram 6 for 91) and West Indies 53 (Abdul Qadir 6 for 16)

This was an amazing match in which fortunes fluctuated continually until the fourth afternoon when the wily Qadir destroyed the West Indies. The second-innings total of 53 was the visitors' lowest score in a Test match.

Imran decided to bat first, but it wasn't long before the innings was in tatters at 5 for 37. He rescued the sinking ship with a hard-hitting 61, and had support from Salim Malik, until a lifting delivery broke Malik's arm just above the wrist.

With Richards ill and forced to bat down the order, the West Indies failed to establish its first innings. Wasim Akram ran through the tail to

INDIA v AUSTRALIA 1986-87 (First Test)

Chidambaram Stadium, Chepauk, Madras, 18, 19, 20, 21, 22 September. A tie

AUSTRALIA

D.C.Boon	c Kapil Dev b Sharma	122	(2)	lbw b Maninder Singh	49
G.R.Marsh	c Kapil Dev b Yadav	22	(1)	b Shastri	11
D.M.Jones	b Yadav	210		c Azharuddin b Maninder Singh	24
R.J.Bright	c Shastri b Yadav	30			
A.R.Border*	c Gavaskar b Shastri	106	(4)	b Maninder Singh	27
G.M.Ritchie	run out	13	(5)	c Pandit b Shastri	28
G.R.J.Matthews	c Pandit b Yadav	44	(6)	not out	27
S.R.Waugh	not out	12	(7)	not out	2
T.J.Zoehrer†					
C.J.McDermott					
B.A.Reid					
Extras	(B 1, LB 7, NB 6, W 1)	15		(LB 1, NB 1)	2
Total	(7 wkts dec.)	574		(5 wkts dec.)	170

INDIA

S.M.Gavaskar	c and b Matthews	8		c Jones b Bright	90
K.Srikkanth	c Ritchie b Matthews	53		c Waugh b Matthews	39
M.Amarnath	run out	1		c Boon b Matthews	51
M.Azharuddin	c and b Bright	50		c Ritchie b Bright	42
R.J.Shastri	c Zoehrer b Matthews	62	(7)	not out	48
C.S.Pandit	c Waugh b Matthews	35	(5)	b Matthews	39
Kapil Dev*	c Border b Matthews	119	(6)	c Bright b Matthews	1
K.S.More†	c Zoehrer b Waugh	4	(9)	lbw b Bright	0
C.Sharma	c Zoehrer b Reid	30	(8)	c McDermott b Bright	23
N.S.Yadav	c Border b Bright	19		b Bright	8
Maninder Singh	not out	0		lbw b Matthews	0
Extras	(B 1, LB 9, NB 6)	16		(B 1, LB 3, NB 2)	6
Total		397			347

INDIA	O	M	R	W		O	M	R	W
Kapil Dev	18	5	52	0	Sharma	6	0	19	0
Sharma	16	1	70	1	Kapil Dev	1	0	5	0
Maninder Singh	39	8	135	0	Shastri	14	2	50	2
Yadav	49.5	9	142	4	Maninder Singh	19	2	60	3
Shastri	47	8	161	1	Yadav	9	0	35	0
Srikkanth	1	0	6	0					

AUSTRALIA	O	M	R	W		O	M	R	W
McDermott	14	2	59	0	McDermott	5	0	27	0
Reid	18	4	93	1	Reid	10	2	48	0
Matthews	28.2	3	103	5	Matthews	39.5	7	146	5
Bright	23	3	88	2	Bright	25	3	94	5
Waugh	11	2	44	1	Border	3	0	12	0
					Waugh	4	1	16	0

FALL OF WICKETS

	A	I	A	I
Wkt	1st	1st	2nd	2nd
1st	48	62	31	55
2nd	206	65	81	158
3rd	282	65	94	204
4th	460	142	125	251
5th	481	206	165	253
6th	544	220	-	291
7th	573	245	-	331
8th	-	330	-	334
9th	-	334	-	344
10th	-	397	-	347

Umpires: D.N.Dotiwalla and V.Vikramraju

restrict the visitors' lead to 89 runs.

Resolute batting by Mohsin, Qasim Omar and the wicketkeeper, Salim Yousuf (who had been sent in as night-watchman), gave Pakistan some hope. The lead was 135 when Akram joined Imran. Akram proceeded to punish the West Indies attack to post his first Test half-century. The Pakistan fightback was epitomised by Salim Malik, who came out to bat with his arm in plaster, and helped Akram add 32 for the last wicket.

The West Indies required 240 to win in four sessions; after one, their innings was destroyed by Imran and Qadir. Qadir picked up the final wicket next morning to finish with 6 for 16. Pakistan had won easily after an absorbing battle.

INDIA v PAKISTAN 1986–87

Karnataka State Cricket Association Stadium (Chinnaswamy Stadium), Bangalore
13, 14, 15, 17 March 1987
Pakistan won by 16 runs

Pakistan 116 (Maninder Singh 7 for 27) and 249; India 145 (D. B. Vengsarkar 50, Iqbal Qasim 5 for 48, Tauseef Ahmed 5 for 54) and 204 (S.M. Gavaskar 96)

This was the fifth and final match in a series in which the first four games had been drawn. The Test was played on a pitch that encouraged the spinners, although both teams thought the conditions would be helpful to the seamers.

Imran batted first after winning the toss. It wasn't long before the visitors were in deep trouble. Maninder Singh produced career-best figures of 7 for 27 as he spun Pakistan out for their lowest score against India of 116.

Vengsarkar played resolutely in scoring 50, placing the home team in a position to establish a sizeable first-innings lead. But Tauseef and Iqbal captured the last 6 wickets for 19. India's lead was thus restricted to 29 — unlikely to be enough, as they would be batting last on a pitch that was deteriorating rapidly.

Imran shuffled his batting order in the second innings and sent Miandad in first with Ramiz. It was a titanic struggle with first one team, then the other, gaining the ascendancy until Yousuf and Tauseef added 51 for the ninth wicket. Pakistan's lead was 220.

Gavaskar played one of his great innings on a pitch that enabled the off-spinner to bowl bouncers. Unfortunately for India, their master batsman didn't get enough support, with only Vengsarkar, Azharuddin and Binny reaching double figures.

The Test victory gave Pakistan its first series win in India, and only its third victory in any Test series outside Pakistan.

PAKISTAN v ENGLAND 1987–88

Iqbal Stadium, Faisalbad
7, 8, 9, 11, 12 December 1987
Drawn

England 292 (B.C. Broad 116, M.W. Gatting 79, Iqbal Qasim 5 for 83) and 6 for 137 dec. (G.A. Gooch 65); Pakistan 191 (Salim Malik 60) and 1 for 51

This was one of the most acrimonious Test matches in history. The bitter row between the England captain, Gatting, and the umpire Shakoor Rana almost brought about the cancellation of the tour. The loss of a whole day's play and 30 minutes from another may have cost England the chance to level the series.

Gatting won the toss, and, on a pitch that had been prepared for the spinners, batted first. Broad occupied the crease for seven hours in compiling 116.

Gatting's innings was exactly the opposite. Sparked by anger at the standard of umpiring, he smashed 79 off just 81 deliveries.

With three balls remaining to complete the second day's play, Pakistan was struggling at 5 for 106 in reply to England's 292.

Gatting moved Capel from deep square leg to save the single. As Hemmings came in to bowl, Gatting signalled to Capel that he had come in close enough, whereupon Shakoor Rana, at square leg, stopped play to inform the batsman, Salim Malik, of Capel's position. The umpire claimed that Gatting had unfairly moved the fieldsman behind the batsman's back. Gatting objected, suggesting that Shakoor Rana had overstepped his bounds.

The umpire refused to play on until he received an apology from the England skipper. By the time Gatting's enforced apology had restored an uneasy truce, six hours' playing time had been lost. A further three and a half were then lost to rain and bad light on the fourth day.

The Pakistan officials refused to make up for the lost third day, and so the game petered out to a tame draw. The home team thereby retained their one match lead in the series.

AUSTRALIA v NEW ZEALAND 1987–88

Melbourne Cricket Ground, Melbourne
26, 27, 28, 29, 30 December 1987
Drawn

New Zealand 317 (J.G. Wright 99, M.D. Crowe 82, C.J. McDermott 5 for 97) and 286 (M D Crowe 79, A I C Dodemaide 6 for 58); Australia 357 (P R Sleep 90, S R Waugh 55, A I C Dodemaide 50, R J Hadlee 5 for 109) and 9 for 230 (D C Boon 54, R J Hadlee 5 for 67)

This final Test of the three-match series was a classic contest that developed into a nail-biting finish. New Zealand was put in to bat and had reached 1 for 119 when Jones deflected McDermott; Australia's wicketkeeper, Dyer, rolled over, then held the ball aloft claiming the catch. The umpires conferred, and the decision was given against the batsman. The television replays, however, showed the ball leaving the 'keeper's gloves and rolling on the ground.

With that controversy behind them, the visitors went on to score 317. Wright became the third New Zealand batsman to be dismissed for 99 in a Test innings.

Australia's middle and lower order staged a grand recovery to give the home team a 40-run first innings lead. Sleep, 90, Waugh, 55, and the Victorian Dodemaide, 50 on debut, led the fightback after Australia had slumped to 5 for 121.

Martin Crowe again played beautifully in New Zealand's second innings and struck 12 majestic boundaries in an innings of 79. The all-rounder Dodemaide followed his first innings half-century with 6 for 58 from 28.3 overs in the second — and in doing so made a fine start to his Test career.

With the New Zealand second innings ending on the third ball of the final day, Australia required 247 for victory from a minimum of 92 overs. At 4 for 176, the target was only 71 from 28 overs when Hadlee was recalled to the attack. He bowled superbly until the end of the match, and almost pulled off an improbable victory for the visitors. McDermott and Whitney, the last pair, had to survive for 4.5 overs to save the match and give Australia the Trans-Tasman Trophy for the first time. Hadlee had taken 10 wickets in a Test match for a record eighth time, and had joined Botham on 373 wickets.

INDIA v WEST INDIES 1987–88

Chepauk (Chidambaram Stadium), Madras
11, 12, 14, 15 January 1988
India won by 255 runs

India 382 (Kapil Dev 109, Arun Lal 69) and 8 for 217 dec. (W.V. Raman 83); West Indies 184 (I.V.A. Richards 68, N.D.Hirwani 8 for 61) and 160 (A.L.Logie 67, N.D. Hirwani 8 for 75)

In this match India recorded the most convincing of its six victories against the West Indies. The player mainly responsible was a new cap, the 19-year-old leg spinner Hirwani. He captured 8 wickets in each innings to equal the performance of Australia's Massie at Lord's in 1972. Coincidentally, Hirwani returned match figures of 16 for 136, for Massie's were an almost indentical 16 for 137.

Shastri, captaining India for the first time, won the toss and batted first on an under-prepared pitch. The home team was struggling at 5 for 156 when the former captain, Kapil Dev, joined another new cap, Ajay Sharma. The pair added 113 for the sixth wicket, and Kapil Dev's contribution was a match-winning 109 from 119 balls. In difficult batting conditions, 382 was a most respectable score.

The West Indies struggled from the start of its innings, and certainly missed the experienced opener Greenidge. Richardson batted for two hours for 36, and Richards produced some amazing strokes in compiling 68. The follow-on was avoided on the third morning as Hirwani, on debut, finished with 8 for 61 from 18.3 overs.

With time on its side, India steadily increased its lead. Raman, yet another new cap, showed considerable maturity in making 83. Walsh was again the pick of the West Indies bowlers, toiling manfully to finish with 4 for 55.

The West Indies required 416 to win, or more realistically, to bat for one and a half days to save the game. Their batsmen played as if it were a limited overs match, and the Test was over on the fourth day. This time, Hirwani finished with 8 for 75 from 15.2 overs, and India's wicketkeeper, More, excelled in the difficult conditions. He stumped six batsmen in the match, five of them in the second innings, and in doing so made two Test records.

WEST INDIES v PAKISTAN 1987–88

Queen's Park Oval, Port-of-Spain, Trinidad
14, 15, 16, 17, 19 April 1988
Drawn

West Indies 174 and 391 (I.V.A. Richards 123, P.J.L. Dujon 106 not out, Imran Khan 5 for 115); Pakistan 194 (Salim Malik 66) and 9 for 341 (Javed Miandad 102)

Pakistan had won the first Test of the three-match series by 9 wickets, so this second game was vital. The West Indies's captain, Richards, and the team's No.1 fast bowler, Marshall, returned after missing the first match through illness and injury.

It was Richards who top-scored with 49 in a disappointing first-innings total of 174. Richardson was next best with 42, and the home team was out by tea on the first day. Worse was to follow for Pakistan as they slumped to 5 for 50, then 7 for 68 early on the second morning.

Salim Malik and Salim Yousuf saved the side with a 94-run partnership for the eighth wicket. The tail wagged sufficiently for Pakistan to gain a 20-run lead on the first innings, and Marshall celebrated his return by claiming 4 for 55.

Early on the third day, the West Indies was struggling at 4 for 81 until Richards took over. He added 94 with Hooper for the fifth wicket, and 97 with Dujon for the sixth, and scored his twenty-second Test century off 134 balls. Dujon went on to complete his fifth Test century, and along the way added 90 runs for the last two wickets with Benjamin and Walsh.

Pakistan's target was 372. When Javed Miandad was seventh out after scoring a flawless 102, only 84 runs were needed for victory. Marshall tipped the scales in favour of the home team when he dismissed Wasim Akram, but then Salim Yousuf and Ijaz Faqih defended stoutly. In the last over, Yousuf was trapped in front by Richards. Abdul Qadir survived the final five balls with the fieldsman clustered around the bat. Pakistan retained their lead in the series.

WEST INDIES v PAKISTAN 1987–88

Kensington Oval, Bridgetown, Barbados
22, 23, 24, 26, 27 April 1988
West Indies won by 2 wickets

Pakistan 309 (Ramiz Raja 54, Shoaib Mohammad 54) and 262 (Shoaib Mohammad 64, M.D. Marshall 5 for 65); West Indies 306 (I.V.A. Richards 67, C.L. Hooper 54) and 8 for 268 dec. (R.B. Richardson 64)

The West Indies went into this last match of the series one down and needing to win. They had not lost a home series since 1972-73 when Ian Chappell's Australian team was successful, and they had not lost a match at Bridgetown since 1935.

Richards won the toss and sent the visitors in to bat. Pakistan's innings was a mixed bag. Shoaib Mohammad and Ramiz Raja scored half-centuries, and Aamer Malik played well for 32. But with the score at 7 for 218, the team was in trouble.

Then Salim Yousuf and Wasim Akram added 67 for the eighth wicket, with the 50-run partnership coming in only 5 overs. Yousuf then deflected a ball from Marshall on to his face. His nose was broken in two places, and Aamer Malik had to keep wicket in both innings for Pakistan.

The West Indies's reply followed a similar pattern to Pakistan's innings. Haynes grafted for almost five hours to score 48, while Richards attacked the bowling and reached 67 from 80 balls. The home team's tail wagged; Marshall and Benjamin put on 58 for the ninth wicket and the last pair, Benjamin and Walsh, added 23 to bring the West Indies to within 3 runs of Pakistan's total.

By the end of the third day the West Indies had struck back and Pakistan was 6 for 177. Shoaib scored his second half-century of the match, while Mudassar, 41, and Javed Miandad, 34, made useful contributions.

On the fourth morning, Imran held the tail together. The Pakistan skipper scored 43 not out as the visitors gained a lead of 265. Marshall finished with 5 for 65 to complete a 9-wicket haul for the month.

Throughout the final innings, fortunes fluctuated. First one team, then the other, gained the ascendancy. When Richards and Ambrose fell early on the final day, to be followed shortly afterwards by Marshall, the West Indies still required 59 runs to win with 2 wickets in hand. Careful batting by Dujon, and some lusty hitting by Benjamin, saw the West Indies through to victory just after lunch. Benjamin, batting at No.10, had a fine double, scoring 31 run out and 40 not out. The victory levelled the series for the West Indies.

But Pakistan had done well! It was the first time since 1973-74 that a visiting team had squared a rubber in the Caribbean.

PAKISTAN v AUSTRALIA 1988–89

National Stadium, Karachi
15, 16, 17, 19, 20 September 1988
Pakistan won by an innings and 188 runs
Pakistan 9 for 469 dec. (Javed Miandad 211, Shoaib Mohammad 94); Australia 165 (P.L. Taylor 54 not out, Iqbal Qasim 5 for 35) and 116

This match will be remembered more for what happened off the field than on it.

When Waugh was given out lbw to the left-arm spinner Iqbal Qasim, to leave Australia 5 for 54, all hell broke lose. Manager Egan, a former Test umpire, and coach Simpson went to the Pakistan Board officials' room to lodge their protest in no uncertain terms. Then, during the tea interval, they called the Australian journalists to a press conference at which they criticised the pitch and umpire Mahboob Shah's decisions. After the match, the Australian captain, Border, described the Karachi pitch as the worst he had seen anywhere and hinted that the tourists might return home and not complete the tour.

Back to the cricket! Javed Miandad scored his fifth test double-century in steering his team to a formidable total of 469. Reid, Dodemaide and May toiled manfully for Australia with poor support from the field. Several chances were missed.

Australia's batsmen had no answer to Pakistan's spinners, Iqbal Qasim, Abdul Qadir and Tauseef Ahmed. Only Peter Taylor, batting at No.7, reached 50. The match was over early on the final day with the home team scoring a resounding victory.

ENGLAND v AUSTRALIA 1989

Old Trafford, Manchester
27, 28, 29, 31 July, 1 August 1989
Australia won by 9 wickets
England 260 (R.A. Smith 143, G.F. Lawson 6 for 72) and 264 (R.C. Russell 128 not out, J.E. Emburey 64, T.M.Alderman 5 for 66); Australia 447 (S.R.Waugh 92, M.A. Taylor 85, A.R. Border 80, D.M.Jones 69) and 1 for 81

This was the fourth Test of a six-match series. Australia had won the first two Tests and the third was drawn.

Gower decided to bat first after winning the toss. This time Lawson made the early breakthrough and England was soon in trouble at 3 for 57. Smith played superbly to score his maiden Test century, but only Gower and Foster offered any support. Foster contributed 39 in an eighth-wicket partnership of 74.

Taylor and Marsh put on 135 for the first wicket as Australia set about building a sizeable first-innings advantage. When the innings ended early on the fourth morning, the visitors' lead had reached 187. Just after lunch, the match was all but over. England had crashed, losing 6 for 59, with Lawson and Alderman claiming 3 wickets apiece. Rain delayed the inevitable — after all, the match was being played in Manchester!

On the final day, Russell and Emburey batted through the first session. Emburey finally went for 64 after adding 142 with the gritty wicketkeeper Russell for the seventh wicket. Russell became the fourth England player to score his maiden first-class century in a Test match. Alderman, who was surprisingly wicketless in the first innings, picked up 5 in the second, while Lawson claimed 3 to finish with 9 for the match.

The target of 78 presented no problems for Australia and, when Boon hit Cook to the boundary, there was great rejoicing in the visitors' camp. The Ashes had been regained in England for the first time since 1934.

ENGLAND v INDIA 1990

Lord's Cricket Ground, London
26, 27, 28, 30, 31 July 1990
England won by 247 runs
England 4 for 653 dec. (G. A .Gooch 333, A .J. Lamb 139, R.A. Smith 100 not out) and 4 for 272 dec. (G. A. Gooch 123, M.A .Atherton 72): India 451 (M. Azharuddin 121, R.J. Shastri 100, Kapil Dev 77 not out, D.B. Vengsarkar 52, A.R.C. Fraser 5 for 104) and 224

This high-scoring Test was a match of many records. The aggregate number of runs, 1603, was two more than the previous record for Lord's (established in 1930 when England played Australia).

Azharuddin sent England in to bat. Late on the second day, Gooch was able to declare at 4 for 653. The skipper was dropped behind by More on 36, and then went on to record the highest Test score at Lord's. Gooch's 333 included 3 sixes and 43 fours; it was the third-highest Test score made by an England cricketer and the sixth-highest overall. Lamb and Smith also compiled centuries, while the partnership of 308 by Gooch and Lamb was the best for any wicket for England against India.

The visitors replied in a positive manner: Azharuddin scored his century off just 88 balls; Shastri, in a new role as opener, also reached three figures. It was 9 for 430 when the last man, Hirwani, joined Kapil Dev, and India needed 24 runs to avoid the follow-on.

Hirwani survived one ball from Fraser; then Hemmings bowled to Kapil Dev. The champion all-rounder blocked the first two balls before launching an unbelievable assault on the hapless off-spinner. Four successive deliveries were smashed down the ground for 6. Fraser dismissed Hirwani with the next ball.

Gooch continued on from his first-innings massacre of the Indian attack. His 123 came off only 113 balls, and included 4 sixes and 13 fours. His match aggregate of 456 was 76 more than the previous record held by Greg Chappell.

India was left with seven hours to bat to save the match, or score 472 to win. On a wearing pitch, the task was always going to prove too difficult, and it was Gooch who ended the game by throwing out Sharma. England won handsomely by 247 runs.

NEW ZEALAND v SRI LANKA 1990–91

Basin Reserve, Wellington
31 January, 1, 2, 3, 4 February 1991
Drawn

New Zealand 174 and 4 for 671 (M.D. Crowe 299, A.H. Jones 186, J.G. Wright 88); Sri Lanka 497 (P.A. de Silva 267, A.P. Gurusinha 70, A. Ranatunga 55, D.K. Morrison 5 for 153)

This match will be remembered forever as the Test in which a new world Test record partnership for any wicket was established.

Sri Lanka dominated the first half of the match and had played itself into a winning position before New Zealand produced a superb fightback to save the game. Ratnayake and Labrooy, with 4 wickets apiece, combined on the opening day to bowl the home team out for 174. Aravinda de Silva then hammered the New Zealand bowlers to all parts of the ground as he posted his country's highest Test score. His 267 contained 40 fours, and was scored from 376 balls. Sri Lanka declared on the third day with a lead of 323. New Zealand had the task of batting for 15 hours to save the game.

Wright and Franklin posted 134 for the opening stand, but then both batsmen were out within 14 runs. This set the stage for the highest partnership in Test history. The New Zealand captain, Martin Crowe, joined Jones and in just over nine hours together they added 467, surpassing the previous best of 451. (Ponsford and Bradman scored 451 for the second wicket against England in 1934, and Mudassar Nazar and Javed Miandad made their partnership of 451 against India in 1982-83.)

Jones was out for 186, and Crowe was dismissed in the final over of the match for 299.

WEST INDIES v SOUTH AFRICA 1991–92

Kensington Oval, Bridgetown, Barbados
18, 19, 20, 22, 23 April 1992
West Indies won by 52 runs

West Indies 262 (K L T Arthurton 59, D L Haynes 58) and 283 (J C Adams 79 not out, B C Lara 64); South Africa 345 (A C Hudson 163, K C Wessels 59) and 148 (K C Wessels 74, P N Kirsten 52, C E L Ambrose 6 for 34, C A Walsh 4 for 31)

It was an historic occasion when Wessels led his teammates out at the Kensington Oval in Barbados. It was South Africa's first Test for 22 years and its first ever clash against the West Indies. The West Indies Board selected Bridgetown as the venue for the only Test match; the home team had not lost there since 1935 when England won by 4 wickets.

Wessels followed the accepted procedure for Kensington Oval and sent the West Indies in to bat. Haynes and Simmons added 99 before lunch, but then both openers fell in the space of nine balls from Snell. Richardson and Athurton put on 82 for the fourth wicket before the middle and lower order collapsed. The last 6 wickets fell for only 22 runs.

South Africa gained a first-innings lead of 83. Opener Hudson scored 163 on debut to become the first South African cricketer to score a century in his first Test match. It was his country's 173rd Test. Only Wessels, 59, and Kuiper, 34, offered any worthwhile contributions apart from the century-maker. Adams was the most successful bowler with 4 for 43. By stumps on the third day, South Africa had a firm grip on the match. The West Indies's lead was only 101 with just 3 wickets in hand. Donald and Snell had ripped the heart out of the home team's batting, taking 3 wickets apiece. After the rest day, however, the tail wagged and 99 runs were added on the fourth day, including

62 for the last wicket by Adams and Patterson. Adams, on debut, completed a fine double. He held the middle and lower order together with 79 not out.

South Africa's target was 201. By the end of the fourth day's play, they were just 79 runs away from victory with 8 wickets in hand. Wessels had played magnificently and was 74 at the close (he and Kristen had added 95 for the third wicket after the openers Hudson and Rushmere had gone cheaply).

On the final day, the visitors were routed by sustained hostile fast bowling from Ambrose and Walsh. Both bowlers claimed 4 wickets apiece as South Africa lost 8 for 26. Only Wessels and Kristen reached double figures. Extras was third top score on 11. Pringle was next best with 4.

The West Indies won a memorable match by 52 runs.

ENGLAND v PAKISTAN 1992

Lord's Cricket Ground, London
18, 19, 20, 21 June 1992
Pakistan won by 2 wickets

England 255 (A.J. Stewart 74, G.A. Gooch 69, Waqar Younis 5 for 91) and 175 (A.J. Stewart 69 not out); Pakistan 293 (Aamir Sohail 73, Asif Mujtaba 59, Salim Malik 55) and 8 for 141

This was the most tense and exciting end to a Test Match at Lord's since England drew with the West Indies in 1963 (see page 30). England has not defeated Pakistan at Lord's since 1978, and since then has won only four Tests at the 'home' of cricket against seven defeats.

Gooch decided to bat first on a pitch that was noticeably cracked from the outset. The skipper, with Stewart, gave the home team the best possible start, putting on 123 for the first wicket. From the moment Wasim Akram bowled Gooch for 69, England's innings lost momentum and only Lamb, 30, and Russell, 22 not out, played with authority. Stewart had been the sheet anchor, taking 4 hours to score 74, and Waqaar Younis was at his destructive best. He ripped the heart out of England's middle order to finish with 5 for 91.

The fact that Pakistan failed to sew up the match in the first innings was a result of fast and hostile bowling by Malcolm on the third afternoon. He claimed 4 for 70 as the visitors crashed from 3 for 228, to be all out for 293 with a lead of just 38. Before Malcolm's blitz, Aamir Sohail, 73, Asif Mujtaba, 59, and Salim Malik, 55, had laid the foundation for a sizeable Pakistani total.

England, however, failed to capitilize on the fightback, and its second innings never gained momentum. Stewart played a lone hand as he became the first Englishman to carry his bat in a Test match at Lord's. Wasim Akram was the chief destroyer, this time taking 4 for 66. The leg spinner Mushtaq Ahmed picked up a further three wickets, to give him 5 for the match.

Against the apparent ease of Pakistan's task (138 to win), England fought back magnificently to grab the balance of power. With DeFreitas and Botham injured and unable to bowl, the burden was left to Lewis and the new cap Salisbury. The leg spinner, operating around the wicket to the left-handers, almost achieved the impossible.

In the end, it was the bowlers Wasim and Waqar who guided Pakistan to victory. They came together with their side in desperate trouble at 8 for 95 with 43 runs still required. In the space of an hour, they won the match, Wasim driving Salisbury to the cover boundary after the extra half hour of play had been claimed by the umpires.

SRI LANKA v AUSTRALIA 1992–93

Sinhalese Sports Club, Colombo, Sri Lanka
17, 18, 19, 21, 22 August 1992.
Australia won by 16 runs.

Australia 256 (I. A. Healy 66 not out) and 471 (D.C. Boon 68, G.R.J. Matthews 64, D.M. Jones 57, M.E. Waugh 56); Sri Lanka 8 dec. 547 (A. P. Gurusinha 137, R.S. Kaluwitharana 132 not out, A. Ranatunga 127, R.S. Mahanama 78) and 164.

Because of the civil unrest in Sri Lanka, this was the first time a Test match had been played there in six years.

Australia was sent in to bat on a pitch that was expected to assist the seam bowlers. It did, to the extent that the Australians lost 7 wickets in the afternoon session after Taylor and Boon had added 76 for the second wicket. The unlikely destroyer was the opening batsman Hathurusingha, bowling gentle medium pace. He finished with 4 for 66. The innings was rescued by the wicketkeeper Healy, who, together with Warne and Whitney, added 94 runs for the last 2 wickets. Still, 256 was a disappointing total.

The home team then batted for the best part of two days to gain a lead of 291 runs. Gurusinha was the sheet anchor of the innings. He was at the crease for nearly nine hours in compiling 137 runs. With Ranatunga, he added 230 for the fourth wicket; this was only 10 runs short of their own all-time partnership record for Sri Lanka.

The coup-de-grace was delivered by the pint-sized Sri Lankan wicketkeeper, Kaluwitharana. On debut, he smashed the bowling to score 132 not out from only 158 balls with 26 boundaries. With Kaluwitharana in full flight, the declaration made by Ranatunga with just over one hour's play remaining on the third day was surprising.

Moody was dismissed early on the fourth morning, but from then on the Australians fought hard in a desperate attempt to save the match. Nearly all the recognised batsmen started well, but failed to go on and make the big score that was needed. Over 360 runs were added on the fourth day, for the loss of 7 wickets. Once again, the Australian tail wagged, with Matthews holding the innings together while the bowlers McDermott, 40, Warne, 35, and Whitney, 10 not out, all made useful contributions.

Sri Lanka needed 181 runs to win from a minimum of 58 overs. When Mahanama and Hathurusingha opened with a stand of 76 it appeared almost certain that the home team would record its first Test victory over Australia.

Mahanama, 39, was first out in the second last over before tea. In the next over, Hathurusingha, 36, was run out by Moody, who threw the stumps down at the wicketkeeper's end. Then came the turning point. Border, after running more than 25 metres, caught de Silva for 37, and it was 3 for 127. When Ranatunga, Atapattu and Kaluwitharana went cheaply, it was 6 for 137. With 15 overs remaining, Sri Lanka needed 36 runs to win; Australia 4 wickets.

Matthews trapped Ramanayake, and then Warne proceeded to clean up the tail. The leg-spinner captured 3 for 0 from his last 11 balls. Australia had scored an amazing victory by 16 runs after trailing by 291 on the first innings. Only once before had Australia won a Test after trailing by more than 200 on the first innings. That was against South Africa at Durban in 1949-50 (see page 25).

PART 2
TEST CRICKET LISTS

33 NOTABLE DEBUTS

1 G. Gunn (England), on holidays in Australia for health reasons in 1907-08, was called into the injury-hit England side for the Sydney Test. Playing his first innings on Australian soil — and his first Test match innings — Gunn hit a brilliant 119 in two and a half hours and followed up with 74 in the second innings.

2 H.L. Collins (Australia) began his Test career with consecutive scores of 70 and 104 (Sydney), 64 (Melbourne), and 162 (Adelaide) against England in 1920-21.

3 A.L. Valentine (West Indies) made his debut in the match against England at Manchester in 1950 and took the first 8 wickets to fall.

4 L.G. Rowe (West Indies) made history by scoring 214 and 100* in his first Test match, which was against New Zealand at Kingston in 1971-72. Rowe is the only batsman to have made 100 in each innings on his Test debut, and only one of three players — R.E. Foster (England) and D.S.B.P. Kuruppu (Sri Lanka) being the others — to make a double-century on debut.

5 R.E. Foster (England) made his debut against Australia at Sydney in 1903-04 and, after an uncertain start, helped himself to a glorious 287 with 38 boundaries in 420 minutes. Foster added 192 for the fifth wicket with G.H. Hirst, 115 for the ninth with R.E. Relf, and 130 for the tenth with W. Rhodes, the latter being scored in an amazing 66 minutes.

6 D.S.B.P. Kuruppu (Sri Lanka) achieved the rare feat of being on the field throughout his maiden Test. He took 776 minutes to reach his double-century — the slowest 200 in first-class cricket — and batted for 777 minutes for 201* against New Zealand at Colombo in 1986-87.

7 R.A.L. Massie (Australia) confounded the opposition batsmen with an astonishing display of swing-bowling in overcast conditions during the match against England at Lord's in 1972. He took 8 for 53 and 8 for 84 for an Australian record Test match 'bag' of 16 wickets.

8 N.D. Hirwani (India), exacting great turn on an under-prepared pitch, exploited the weakness of the West Indies batsmen to take 8 for 61 and 8 for 75 at Madras in 1987-88, thereby establishing an Indian record for wickets in a Test.

9 H.B. Taber (Australia), playing against South Africa at Johannesburg in 1966-67, caught 7 and stumped 1, a 'bag' never equalled by a wicketkeeper in a first Test.
Note: A.T.W. Grout of Australia caught 6 in an innings in his first Test, against South Africa in 1957-58.)

10 J.E. Barrett became the first Australian player to carry his bat through a completed innings in a Test against England. Barrett scored 67* in Australia's second innings at Lord's in 1890 — his first Test match.

11 F. Martin (England) took 12 wickets in his first Test appearance, against Australia at The Oval in 1890. His figures were 6 for 50 and 6 for 52.

12 A.E. Trott (Australia), playing his first Test against England at the Adelaide Oval in January 1895, scored 110 runs (38* and 72*) without being dismissed, and bowled unchanged throughout the second innings, to take 8 wickets for 43 runs.

13 E.G. Arnold (England) took the wicket of the great Victor Trumper with his first delivery in a Test match at Sydney in December 1903.

14 A. Warren (England) in his only Test match took 5 wickets for 57 in the first innings against Australia at Leeds in 1905.

15 G.M. Parker, a South African cricketer playing Bradford League cricket during the South African tour of England in 1924, was called up to play for his country in the first Test at Birmingham, although he was not a member of the touring party. He took 6 wickets for 152 in England's only innings.

16 W.R. Hammond (England) scored 51 runs and took 5 wickets in his first Test, which was against South Africa at Johannesburg in 1927-28.

17 **M.J.C. Allom (England), playing against New Zealand in Christchurch in 1930, took 4 wickets in five balls, including a hat-trick.**

18 H.D. Smith (New Zealand) bowled E. Paynter (England) with his first ball in Test cricket at Christchurch in 1932-33. It was his only wicket in his only Test.

19 C.S. Marriott (England) took 11 wickets in his first and only Test, against the West Indies at the Oval in 1933.

20 J.C. Laker (England), playing against the West Indies at Bridgetown during the 1947-48 season, took 7 for 103 in his first Test innings.

21 H.H.H. Johnson (West Indies) played in his first Test at the age of 37 when he appeared against England at Kingston during 1947-48. He took 5 for 41 in his first innings, and 5 for 55 in his second.

22 A.T.W. Grout (Australia) kept wickets against South Africa in his first Test which was at Johannesburg in 1957-58, and set a then-World Test record of six catches in an innings.

23 C.A. Milton (England) played his first Test against New Zealand at Leeds in 1958. He scored 104* in England's only innings, and became the first England player to be on the ground throughout an entire Test match (although there was no play on the first two days).

24 J.D.F. Larter (England) took 9 wickets in his first Test, against Pakistan at The Oval in 1962.

25 P.J. Petherick (New Zealand) took a hat-trick in his first Test, played against Pakistan at Lahore in October 1976. In the same match, Javed Miandad scored 163 and 25* in his first Test.

26 Yajurvindra Singh (India) equalled two Test records in his first Test. Playing against England at Bangalore in the fourth Test of the 1976-77 season, he took five catches in the first innings and a total of seven for the match — both records for non-wicketkeepers.

27 R.A. Duff (Australia) played against England at Melbourne in his first Test in 1901-02. He top-scored in the first innings with 32, and again in the second with 104. He also shared in the first hundred partnership for the tenth wicket with W.W. Armstrong (who was also playing in his first Test).

28 C.V. Grimmett (Australia) took 11 wickets in his first Test. Playing against England in Sydney during the 1924-25 season, he captured 5 for 45 in the first innings and 6 for 37 in the second.

29 B.R. Taylor (New Zealand) is the only Test cricketer to have made 100 and to have taken 5 wickets in an innings on debut. He scored 105 and took 5 for 86 in the match against India at Calcutta in 1964-65.

30 A.V. Bedser (England) took 11 wickets in each of his first two Test matches. In his first, against India at Lord's in June 1946, he took 7 for 49 and 4 for 96. In his second, the following month at Manchester, he captured 4 for 41 and 7 for 52.

31 J.K. Lever (England), playing against India at Delhi in 1976-77, scored 53 and took 7 for 46 and 3 for 24. It was his first Test match.

32 M. Azharuddin (India) began his Test career with 110 at Calcutta, 48 and 105 at Madras, and 122 and 54* at Kanpur — all against England in 1984-85.

33 A.I.C. Dodemaide (Australia) was brought in as a replacement for the injured B.A. Reid, and scored 50 in his first innings and took 6 for 58 in the second against New Zealand at Melbourne in 1987-88.

6 INGLORIOUS DEBUTS

1 M. Leyland was dismissed for a 'duck' during England's only innings in the third Test against the West Indies at The Oval in 1928 — his first appearance for his country.

2 D.G. Bradman scored only 18 and 1 in his debut in the first Test against England at Brisbane in the 1928-29 season. He was subsequently dropped from the team for the second Test, but was reinstated for the third, in which he scored 79 and 112.

3 L. Hutton (England) scored a 'duck' and 1 in his debut Test match against New Zealand at Lord's in 1937. In his second match, he made 100 and 14.

4 I.M. Chappell (Australia) made a modest 11 runs and bowled 26 overs without a wicket in his debut Test against Pakistan at Melbourne in 1964-65.

5 New Zealand batsman J.M. Parker fractured a bone in his hand while fielding against Pakistan at Wellington in 1973, and was unable to bat in his debut match.

6 G.A. Gooch (England) recorded a pair of 'ducks' in his first Test, which was against Australia at Birmingham in 1975.

A NOTABLE UMPIRING DEBUT

Umpire W.E. Alley, standing in his first Test match (England v India at Birmingham in 1974), was given little time to settle in, being required to make a decision about the first ball of the match. His verdict? S.M. Gavaskar, out, caught behind by Knott, bowled Arnold.

13 RAPID RISES

1 Joseph Emile Patrick McMaster (England) deserves his spot in the record books. His Test appearance for England against South Africa at Cape Town in 1888-89 was his only match in first-class cricket. As he scored a 'duck', McMaster must be the only cricketer of Test match status who never scored a run in his entire first-class career.

2 L. Hone, of Ireland, kept wicket for England against Australia at Melbourne in 1878-79. Hone never appeared in English county cricket.

3 B.A.F. Grieve (England) appeared in only three first-class matches, of which two, against South Africa in 1888-89 at Port Elizabeth and Cape Town, were Test matches.

4 Edric Leadbeater (England) was flown to India as a replacement for A.E.G. Rhodes during the 1951-52 season. He played in his first Test before being capped for his county.

5 G.M. Parker (South Africa) came into the South African Test side from the Bradford League to play against England at Birmingham in 1924. It was only his second first-class match. His entire first-class career comprised three games, two of which were Tests.

6 D.W. Carr (England) played his first first-class game for Kent at The Oval on 27 May 1909, aged 37. He was chosen for the Gentlemen v Players match on 8 July, made his debut in county cricket on 29 July, and appeared for England against Australia on 9 August. It was his sixth first-class game, and he had risen to Test honours within 10 weeks of his first-class debut.

7 A.L. Valentine and S. Ramadhin (West Indies) were selected to tour England in 1950 after each had played in only two first-class games.

8 S.F. Barnes (England) was selected to tour Australia in 1901-02 after only six first-class games and 13 first-class wickets.

9 I.A.R. Peebles (England) played for his country against South Africa before he had made his debut in county cricket.

10 A.G. Chipperfield (Australia) was selected to tour England in 1934 after playing only three first-class games.

11 T.R. McKibbin (Australia) played against England in 1894-95 in what was his sixth first-class match. (A.G. Fairfax, E.L. A'Beckett, D.G. Bradman, W.J. O'Reilly, J.R. Thomson and I.C. Davis were other Australians to make their Test debuts within 10 matches of their first-class debut.)

12 G.J. Bonnor (Australia) was selected to tour England in 1880 without ever having played a first-class game.

13 G.E. Vivian (New Zealand) was selected to tour India, Pakistan and England in 1965 without having appeared in a first-class match. He made his first-class debut in the Test against India at Calcutta in 1964-65.

5 GREAT CRICKETING FAMILIES

1 Gregory (Australia). The family produced four Test cricketers, two (Dave and Syd) of whom captained Australia. The father of the clan was Edward William who played in Sydney in the 1820s. Four of his children played cricket for NSW — Dave (Australia's first captain), Ned, Charlie and Arthur. Ned's sons were Syd and Charles (who scored the first triple-century in a first-class game in Australia). Jack, who arrived on the scene in the 1920s, was the grandson of Edward William, and so became a cricket star a century after his grandfather.

2 Mohammad (Pakistan). At least one Mohammad brother represented Pakistan in 100 of that country's first 101 Tests in 27 years of Test cricket between 1952-80. A fifth brother, Raees, was once Pakistan's twelth man against India (1954-55). Three brothers — Hanif, Mushtaq and Sadiq — all played together in one Test against New Zealand in 1969, and all batted and bowled during the match. Between them, Hanif, Mushtaq, Sadiq and Wazir aggregated almost 11 000 Test runs with 29 centuries. They have also held 115 catches and taken 80 wickets.

3 Amarnath (India). Father 'Lala' and son Surinder are the only father-son combination to record 100s on debut. The second son, Mohinder, narrowly missed becoming one of the few to score a century in each innings when he made 90 and 100 against Australia in Perth in 1977-78.

4 Bannerman (Australia). Elder brother Charles faced the first ball bowled in Test cricket, scored the first run, the first 50, and the first 100. He was also the first Australian to make a century in England, New Zealand and Canada. Younger brother Alec scored the first run in a Test on English soil.

5 Chappell (Australia). The grandsons of Victor Richardson, Ian, Greg and Trevor represent only the fourth set of three brothers to appear in Test cricket. Ian and Greg captained Australia more than 50 times between them, and are the only brothers to have scored centuries in each innings of a Test, and were the first brothers to score a century in the same Test. They are the only brothers who have each scored over 5000 Test runs.

NICKNAMES OF TEST CRICKETERS

Governor-General	C.G. Macartney	(Australia)
The Demon	F.R. Spofforth	(Australia)
The Terror	C.T.B. Turner	(Australia)
Jonah	E. Jones	(Australia)
Horseshoe	A.L. Collins	(Australia)
Tibby	A. Cotter	(Australia)
Barney	W.A. S. Oldfield	(Australia)
Bacchus	R.W. Marsh	(Australia)
Sam	J.B. Gannon	(Australia)
Wallaby	R.M. Cowper	(Australia)
Rowdy	A.A. Mallett	(Australia)
Tangles	M.H.N. Walker	(Australia)
Garth	G.D. McKenzie	(Australia)
The Phantom	W.M. Lawry	(Australia)
Slasher	K.D. Mackay	(Australia)
Big Ship	W.W. Armstrong	(Australia)
Tappy	D. Tallon	(Australia)
Nugget	K.R. Miller	(Australia)
Stumpy	B.M. Laird	(Australia)
Nip	C.E. Pellew	(Australia)
Stork	H.S.T.L. Hendry	(Australia)
Gus	G.J. Gilmour	(Australia)
Tiger	W.J. O'Reilly	(Australia)
Percy	P.I. Philpott	(Australia)
Roo	B. Yardley	(Australia)
Fot	D.K. Lillee	(Australia)
Hammy	H.S.B. Love	(Australia)
Pud	H.M. Thurlow	(Australia)
Dainty	H. Ironmonger	(Australia)
Ranji	H.V. Horden	(Australia)
Tich	S.E. Gregory	(Australia)
Alf	M.A. Noble	(Australia)
Froggy	A.L. Thomson	(Australia)
Chuck	L.O.B. Fleetwood-Smith	(Australia)
Old Man	W.G. Grace	(England)
The Baron	Lord Hawke	(England)
Mr. Smith	K.S. Ranjitsinjhi	(England)
&	K.S. Duleepsinjhi	(England)
Tavish	A.C. Maclaren	(England)
Nab	A.G. Steel	(England)
Coo or Stork	L.C.H. Palairet	(England)
Bunny	A.P. Lucas	(England)

The Croucher	G.L. Jessop	(England)
Jonah	A.P. Jones	(England)
Tip	R.E. Foster	(England)
Monkey	A.N. Hornby	(England)
Patsy	E. Hendren	(England)
Lol	H. Larwood	(England)
Dick	A.A. Lilley	(England)
Razor	W.C. Smith	(England)
Boot	W. Flowers	(England)
The Coroner	E.M. Grace	(England)
Farmer	J.C. White	(England)
The Guvnor	R. Abel	(England)
Charlie	C. Blythe	(England)
Dusty	W. Rhodes	(England)
Tangy	W. Voce	(England)
Hotstuff	J. Hardstaff Sr	(England)
Quack Quack	G. Duckworth	(England)
Lord Ted	E.R. Dexter	(England)
Barnacle	T.E. Bailey	(England)
Plum	P.F. Warner	(England)
Arkle	D.W. Randall	(England)
Typhoon	F.H. Tyson	(England)
Fiery Fred	F.A. Trueman	(England)
The Iron Duke	D.R. Jardine	(England)
George	J.B. Statham	(England)
Stork	F.G.J. Ford	(England)
Deadly	D.L. Underwood	(England)
Kipper	M.C. Cowdrey	(England)
Round the Corner	C.A. Smith	(England)
Tich	A.P. Freeman	(England)
'Orse	G.G. Arnold	(England)
Johnny Won't Hit Today	J.W.H.T. Douglas	(England)
Gnome	K.W.R. Fletcher	(England)
Plank	P. Lever	(England)
Beau	G.A.R. Lock	(England)
Ollie	C. Milburn	(England)
Noddy	G. Pullar	(England)
Toey	H.J. Tayfield	(South Africa)
Nummy	H.G. Deane	(South Africa)
Bonnor	J. Middleton	(South Africa)
Doodles	L.E. Tapscott	(South Africa)
Dusty	G.L. Tapscott	(South Africa)
Buster	W.S. Farrer	(South Africa)
Big Bird	J. Garner	(West Indies)
Puss	E. Achong	(West Indies)
Snuffy	C.R. Brown	(West Indies)
Joey	M.C. Carey	(West Indies)
Collie	O.G. Smith	(West Indies)
Bogo	J.R. Reid	(New Zealand)
Polly	P.R. Umrigar	(India)

107 TEST CRICKETERS WHO BATTED RIGHT-HANDED AND BOWLED LEFT-ARM

Australia

M.J. Bennett
R.J. Bright
H.L. Collins
A.R. Dell
L.O. Fleetwood-Smith
J.B. Gannon
T.G. Hogan
R.J. Inverarity
C.G. Macartney
I. Meckiff
D.J. Sincock
E.R.H. Toshack
M.R. Whitney
W.J. Whitty

England

J.C. Balderstone
R.G. Barlow
C. Blythe
J.B. Bolus
J. Briggs
H.R. Bromley-Davenport
D.B. Carr
D.C.S. Compton
C. Cook
G. Cook
N.G.B. Cook
P.H. Edmonds
P.R. Foster
M.J. Hilton
G.H. Hirst
J.L. Hopwood
J. Iddon
R. K. Illingworth
I.J. Jones
J.K. Lever
G.A.R. Lock
B.W. Luckhurst
G.A.E. Paine
C.W.L. Parker
W. Rhodes
F.E. Rumsey
D.S. Steele
P.C.R. Tufnell

D.L. Underwood
H. Verity
W. Voce
A. Waddington
P.M. Walker
J.C. White
H.I. Young
J.A. Young

South Africa

W.H. Ashley
C.P. Carter
G.A. Chevalier
M.K. Elgie
A.E. Hall
G.A. Kempis
M.J. Macaulay
A.H. McKinnon
Q. McMillan
J.B. Plimsoll
N.A. Quinn
A. Rose-Innes
G.A. Rowe
P.L van der Merwe

West Indies

M.R. Bynoe
G.M. Carew
B.D. Julien
R.R. Jumadeen
C.B. Lambert
S. Shivnarine
A.L. Valentine
F.M.M. Worrell

New Zealand

S.L. Boock
T.B. Burtt
M.E. Chapple
R.O. Collinge
F.E. Fisher
N. Gallichan
E.J. Gray
A.F. Lissette
J.F.M. Morrison
D.R. O'Sullivan
M.W. Priest
G.B. Troup
B.W. Yuile

India

B.S. Bedi
R.J.D. Jamshedji
Maninder Singh
M.H. Mankad
Mushtaq Ali
R.G. Patel
A.K. Sharma
R.J. Shastri
K.K. Tarapore
S.L. Venkatapathy Raju

Pakistan

Inzamamul Haq
Liaqat Ali
Mufasir-ul-Haq
Nadeem Ghauri
Pervez Sajjad
Saleem Jaffer
Shujauddin

Sri Lanka

S.D. Anurasiri
S. Jeganathan
A.K. Kuruppuarachchi
A.N. Ranasinghe
R.G.C.E. Wijesuriya

98 TEST CRICKETERS WHO BATTED LEFT-HANDED AND BOWLED RIGHT-ARM

Australia

D.D. Blackie
I.W. Callen
R.M. Cowper
L.S. Darling
R.A. Gaunt
J.M. Gregory
R.N. Harvey
T.V. Hohns
W.P. Howell
T.J. Laughlin
E.L. McCormick
K.D. Mackay
T.R. McKibbin
R.W. McLeod
A.L. Mann

R.W. Marsh
R.L.A. Massie
G.R.J. Matthews
L.C. Mayne
J.D.A. O'Connor
W.J. O'Reilly
G.F. Rorke
B.K. Shepherd
P.L. Taylor
T.R. Veivers
K.C. Wessels

England
R.W. Barber
J. Birkenshaw
B.C. Broad
D.B. Close
G.R. Dilley
J.H. Edrich
R.M. Ellison
J.A. Flavell
G. Fowler
D.I. Gower
K. Higgs
J.T. Ikin
H. Morris
M.S. Nichols
C.M. Old
P.H. Parfitt
R.T.D. Perks
J.S.E. Price
G. Pullar
P.E. Richardson
T.F. Smailes
J.B. Statham
R. Subba Row
R. Tattersall
C.L. Townsend
D.W. White

South Africa
J.F.W. Nicolson
A.W. Nourse
R.G. Pollock
K.C. Wessels

West Indies
C.E.L. Ambrose
M.C. Carew
J.D.C. Goddard
H.A. Gomes
A.B. Howard
A.I. Kallicharran
B.C. Lara
P.D. Lashley
C.H. Lloyd
C.A. McWatt
G.C. Shillingford

New Zealand
V.R. Brown
D.C. Cleverley
G.F. Cresswell
B.A. Edgar
R.J. Hadlee
E.G. McLeod
L.S.M. Miller
B.D. Morrison
G.W.F. Overton
J.F. Reid
I.M. Sinclair
M.C. Snedden
B.R. Taylor
G.E. Vivian
J.G. Wright

India
S. Amarnath
N.J. Contractor
A.G. Milka Singh
S.V. Nayak
A.M. Pai

Pakistan
Sadiq Mohammad
Wasim Raja

Sri Lanka
F.S. Ahangama
E.A.R. de Silva
A.P. Gurusinha
M.A.W.R. Madurasinghe
A. Ranatunga
J.R. Ratnayeke
C.P. Senanayake
H.P. Tillekeratne
K.P.J. Warnaweera

14 TEST CRICKETERS WHO HAVE BEEN KNIGHTED

Australia

Sir Donald George Bradman

England

Sir George Oswald Browning Allen
Sir Michael Colin Cowdrey
Sir John Berry Hobbs
Sir Leonard Hutton
Sir Francis Stanley Jackson
Sir Henry Dudley Gresham Leveson Gower
Sir Charles Aubrey Smith
Sir Pelham Francis Warner

West Indies

Sir Learie Nicholas Constantine
Sir Garfield St Auburn Sobers
Sir Frank Mortimor Maglinne Worrell

New Zealand

Sir Richard John Hadlee
Sir Jack Newman

SOME OF CRICKET'S DOUBLE INTERNATIONALS

E = England — A = Australia
SA = South Africa — NZ = New Zealand
W = Wales — WI = West Indies
Sc = Scotland — An = Antigua

	Cricket	*Rugby*	*Soccer*
A.N. Hornby	E	E	-
S.M.J. Woods	A/E	E	-
G. McGregor	E	Sc	-
A.E. Stoddard	E	E	-
C.B. Fry	E	-	E
(Missed at rugby due to injury)			
F. Mitchell	E/SA	E	-
L.B. Fishlock	E	-	E
J.H. Sinclair	SA	SA/E	-
R.O. Schwarz	SA	E	-
L.H. Gay	E	-	E
R.H. Spooner	E	E	-
R.E. Foster	E	-	E
(Only man to captain England at cricket and soccer)			
A. Ducat	E	-	E
H.T.W. Hardinge	E	-	E
J.W.H. Makepeace	E	-	E
K.W. Hough	NZ	-	NZ/A
A.E. Knight	E	-	E
M.J. Turnbull	E	W	-
(Also played Hockey for Wales)			

J. Arnold	E	-	E
W. Gunn	E	-	E
G.C. White	SA	-	SA
J. Sharp	E	-	E
R.S. Grant	WI	-	E
J.M.M. Commaille	SA	-	SA
M.K. Elgie	SA	Sc	-
S. O'Linn	SA	-	SA
C.A. Smith	E	-	E
Hon A. Lyttelton	E	-	E
G.F. Vernon	E	E	-
H.G. Owen-Smith	SA	E	-
D.C.S. Compton	E	-	E
J.H. Anderson	SA	SA	-
G.R.P. Dickinson	NZ	NZ	-
M.P. Donnelly	NZ	E	-
M.K. Elgie	SA	Sc	-
T.A. Harris	SA	SA	-
R.H.M. Hands	SA	E	-
P.S.T. Jones	SA	SA	-
W. Watson	E	-	E
W.H. Milton	SA	E	-
C.A. Milton	E	-	E
O.E. Nothling	A	A	-
M.L. Page	NZ	NZ	-
A.W. Powell	SA	SA	-
A. Richards	SA	SA	-
M.J.K. Smith	E	E	-
E.W.T. Tindill	NZ	NZ	-
C.B. Van Ryneveld	SA	E	-
F.C.M. Alexander	WI	-	E
(Amateur International)			
I.V.A. Richards	WI	-	An

The following Test Cricketers won F.A. Cup Winners Medals:

E.G. Wynyard — with Old Carthusians 1880-81
J. Sharp — with Everton 1905-06
H. Makepeace — with Everton 1905-06
A. Ducat — with Aston Villa 1919-20
D.C.S. Compton — with Arsenal 1949-50

Other Test cricketers who were well-known soccer players in England include:

I.T. Botham **(Skunthorpe United)**
D.B. Close (Leeds United, Bradford City, Arsenal)
J. Dewes (Middlesborough, Plymouth Argyle, Walsall)
S. O'Linn (Charlton Athletic)
C.J. Poole (Gillingham, Mansfield Town)
D.R. Smith (Bristol City, Milwall)
F. Sugg (Sheffield Wed, Derby County, Burnley)
K. Taylor (Huddersfield Town, Bradford P.A.)
F.J. Titmus (Watford)

A.J. Watkins (Plymouth Argyle, Cardiff City)
E.G. Wynyard (Old Carthusians)
D.L. Bairstow (Bradford City)
R.W.V. Robins (Nottingham Forest)
M. Sherwin (Notts County)
M.J. Stewart (Charlton Athletic)
L.E.G. Ames (Clapton Orient, Gillingham)
J.C. Balderstone (Huddersfield Town, Carlisle United, Doncaster Rovers)
H.E. Dollery (Reading)
W.J. Edrich (Tottenham Hotspurs)
J.A. Flavell (Walsall)
W.Gunn (Notts County)
W.R. Hammond (Bristol Rovers)
J. Hardstaff Sr. (Nottingham Forest)
E.H. Hendren (Manchester City, Brentford
H. Howell (Wolverhampton Wanderers, Accrington Stanley)
W.W. Keeton (Sunderland, Nottingham Forest)
J.W. Sharpe (Notts County)
A. Sidebottom (Manchester United, Huddersfield Town, Halifax)
W. Storer (Derby County)
A. Waddington (Halifax Town)
F. Barratt (Aston Villa, Sheffield Wed)

SOME TEST CRICKETERS WHO PLAYED OTHER SPORTS AT INTERNATIONAL LEVEL:

B.C. Booth (Australia) (1956 Olympics)	Hockey
B. Dooland (Australia)	Baseball
V.Y. Richardson (Australia)	Baseball
W.R. Endean (South Africa)	Hockey
P.W. Sherwell (South Africa)	Tennis
K. Thomson (New Zealand)	Hockey
C.B. Fry (England) (Fry held the World long jump record for 21 years)	Athletics
D.C. Cleverley (New Zealand)	Amateur boxing
J.W.H.T. Douglas (England) (Douglas won the gold medal in the middleweight boxing division in the 1908 London Olympics, and also represented England in amateur soccer)	Boxing

CRICKETERS ROLL OF HONOUR: TEST CRICKETERS KILLED IN THE BOER WAR, WORLD WAR I AND WORLD WAR II

Boer War

J.J. Ferris (Australia/England)

World War I

A. Cotter (Australia)
C. Blythe (England)
K.L. Hutchings (England)
R.M.H. Hands (South Africa)
E.B. Lundie (South Africa)
R.O. Schwarz (South Africa)
G.C. White (South Africa)

World War II

R.G. Gregory (Australia)
K. Farnes (England)

TEST CAREERS WHICH ENDED IN TRAGEDY

1 K.J. Wadsworth (New Zealand). One of his country's finest wicketkeepers, Ken Wadsworth died of cancer at the peak of his career, aged 29, on 19 August 1976.

2 O.G. Smith (West Indies). 'Collie' Smith, a versatile allrounder, died from injuries received in a car accident in England in 1959. He was 26-years-old.

3 G.B. Street (England). A good county wicketkeeper and useful tail-end batsman. He played one Test for England against South Africa in 1922-23, but was tragically killed at the age of 24 years in a motorcycle accident just before the 1924 season.

4 F. Morley (England). A left-arm fast bowler, Morley was a member of Hon. Ivo Bligh's team which sailed to Australia for the 1882-83 season. Morley was apparently hurt in a collision at sea, but carried on throughout the tour with an injured hip. Upon his return to England, his health deteriorated, and he died the following year, aged 33.

7 TEST CRICKETERS WHO WERE RHODES SCHOLARS

C.B. Van Ryneveld	South Africa
J.P. Duminy	South Africa
P.A.M. Hands	South Africa
R.H.M. Hands	South Africa
H.G. Owen-Smith	South Africa
D.B. Pithey	South Africa
J.A. Dunning	New Zealand

TEST CRICKET CAPTAINS BORN ABROAD

Australia

P.S. McDonnell	England
T.P. Horan	Ireland

England

Lord Harris	West Indies
P.F. Warner	West Indies
F.L. Fane	Ireland
D.R. Jardine	India
G.O.B. Allen	Australia
F.R. Brown	Peru
M.C. Cowdrey	India
E.R. Dexter	Italy
A.R. Lewis	Wales
M.H. Denness	Scotland
A.W. Greig	South Africa
A.J. Lamb	South Africa

South Africa

E.A. Halliwell	England

Pakistan

A.H. Kardar	India
Fazal Mahmood	India
Asif Iqbal	India
Majid J. Khan	India

10 CRICKETERS WHO RETIRED HURT

1 J.J. Kelly (Australia). A useful batsman and outstanding wicketkeeper, Kelly played 36 Tests for Australia around the turn of the century. He retired from first-class cricket after his last tour of England because of the effects of a damaged finger and a blow over the the heart from a ball received in a Test at Manchester.

2 C. Milburn (England). One of the most punishing batsmen seen on the Test arena for many years, Colin Milburn was involved in a car accident in 1969 which cost him his left eye. He attempted a county comeback in 1973, but to all intents and purposes his career was finished by the crash.

3 R.K. Oxenham (Australia). An excellent all-rounder, Oxenham represented his country in seven Tests in the late 1920s and 1930s. He was seriously injured in a car accident in 1937 and never fully recovered. He died in 1939.

4 N.J. Contractor (India). An opening bat and occasional medium-pace bowler, Contractor captained India on 12 occasions. During a match against Barbados, on the 1961-62 tour of the West Indies, he was hit on the head by a ball from C.C. Griffith. His skull was fractured and he remained gravely ill for some days. Fortunately, he recovered, but never again played international cricket.

5 G.F. Rorke (Australia). A big man, Gordon Rorke played four Tests for Australia and was a very effective fast bowler in Sheffield Shield cricket. His Test career was unfortunately cut short in 1959-60 when he contracted hepatitis while on tour in India.

6 G.B. Stevens (Australia). An opening batsman, Gavin Stevens played four Tests for Australia in 1959-60. He dehydrated badly from the same strain of hepatitis that G.F. Rorke picked up. He lost 13 kilograms and was sent home early from the subcontinent. He never played first-class cricket again.

7 I.J. Jones (England). A Welshman, Jones represented England on 15 occasions, taking 44 wickets as a fast bowler. In May 1968, yet to reach his peak, he tore the ligaments in his elbow. From then on, he was a spent force in top cricket.

8 W. Bates (England). In a short but brilliant career, Billy Bates represented England 15 times, scoring 656 runs and taking 50 wickets in the late 1880s. His career came to an abrupt end in Melbourne in 1887 when he was struck in the eye at net practice. He suffered permanent damage to his sight and was forced to retire.

9 J.B. Briggs (England). A regular member of the England team during the late 1880s, Briggs scored over 800 runs and took 118 wickets. During a Test against Australia in 1899, he was struck over the heart by a ball while fielding, and suffered what was believed to be an epileptic fit. He retired from the game and, although he attempted a first-class comeback the following year, his Test career was over.

10 R. C. Motz (New Zealand). One of New Zealand's most successful Test bowlers, Motz took 100 Test wickets but was forced to retire from first class cricket when it was discovered he had been bowling for some time with a displaced vertebra.

37 TEST CRICKETERS WHO WERE TEST UMPIRES

Australia

C. Bannerman
G. Coulthard
T.W. Garrett*
F.G. McShane#
H.H. Massie¶
A.J. Richardson
J.P.F. Travers

* T.W. Garrett, who was playing in the game, replaced umpire Hodges after tea on the last day in the match between England and Australia at Melbourne in 1884-85.

F.G. McShane played and umpired in the same series between Australia and England in Australia in 1884-85.

¶ Massie substituted for E.H. Elliott in the match between Australia and England at Sydney in 1884-85.

England

R.G. Barlow
J. Birkenshaw
L.C. Braund
H.R. Butt
J.F. Crapp
A. Dolphin
H. Elliott
A.E. Fagg
W.Gunn
J.H. Hampshire
J. Hardstaff Sr
F. Hearne
A. Hill
J.W. Hitch
J. Lillywhite
A.S.M. Oakman §
N. Oldfield
K.E. Palmer
W.F.F. Price
M. Sherwin
E.J. Smith
G.J. Thompson
H. Young

W. Gunn replaced the injured umpire Swift during the match between Australia and England at Sydney in 1886-87. He had been playing in the Test.

§ A.S.M. Oakman deputised for H.D. Bird (who had an injured back) after tea on the third day of the first Test between England and Australia at Birmingham in 1975.

West Indies

E.E. Achong
G.E. Gomez

South Africa

W.W. Wade

New Zealand

J.A. Cowie
E.W.T. Tindill

Pakistan

Javed Akhtar
Mohammad Aslam

SOME PLAYERS WHO HAVE OPENED THE BATTING AND BOWLING IN THE SAME MATCH*

* First innings only apply in this record

Australia

G. Giffen	v England, Sydney, 1882-83
G.E. Palmer	v England, Sydney, 1884-85
W. Bruce	v England, Melbourne, 1884-85
C.T.B. Turner	v England, Lord's, 1890
C.T.B. Turner	v England, The Oval, 1890
J.J. Lyons	v England, Sydney, 1894-95
G.H.S. Trott	v England, Sydney, 1894-95
G.H.S. Trott	v England, Melbourne, 1894-95
W.W. Armstrong	v South Africa, Johannesburg, 1902-03
V.T. Trumper	v South Africa, Johannesburg, 1902-03
M.A. Noble	v England, Sydney, 1907-08
F.J. Laver	v England, Lord's, 1909
C. Kelleway	v England, Melbourne, 1911-12
C. Kelleway	v England, Sydney, 1920-21
J.M. Gregory	v South Africa, Durban, 1921-22

England

A. Shaw	v Australia, Melbourne, 1876-77
G. Ulyett	v Australia, Melbourne, 1878-79

C.T. Studd	v Australia, Melbourne, 1882-83
R.B. Barlow	v Australia, Sydney, 1882-83
G. Ulyett	v Australia, Sydney, 1884-85
G.A. Lohmann	v South Africa, Port Elizabeth, 1895-96
G.A. Lohmann	v South Africa, Johannesburg, 1895-96
G.L. Jessop	v Australia, Melbourne, 1901-02
J.B. Hobbs	v South Africa, Johannesburg, 1909-10
J.B. Hobbs	v South Africa, Durban, 1909-1910
J.B. Hobbs	v South Africa, Cape Town, 1909-1910
M.W. Tate	v Australia, Adelaide, 1924-25
W.R. Hammond	v South Africa, Cape Town, 1930-31
W.R. Hammond	v South Africa, Durban, 1930-31
R.E.S. Wyatt	v West Indies, Port-of-Spain, 1934-35
R.E.S. Wyatt	v West Indies, Georgetown, 1934-35
R.E.S. Wyatt	v South Africa, Lord's, 1935
W.J. Edrich	v South Africa, Johannesburg, 1938-39
T.E. Bailey	v West Indies, Kingston, 1953-54
T.E. Bailey	v Australia, Sydney, 1954-55
T.E. Bailey	v South Africa, Port Elizabeth, 1956-57

South Africa

A. Rose-Innes	v England, Cape Town, 1888-89
J.H. Sinclair	v England, Johannesburg, 1895-96
G.A. Faulkner	v England, The Oval, 1907
D.J. Meintjes	v England, Johannesburg, 1922-23
T.L. Goddard	v England, Nottingham, 1955
T.L. Goddard	v England, The Oval, 1955
T.L. Goddard	v Australia, Cape Town, 1957-58

West Indies

F.M.M. Worrell	v England, Nottingham, 1957
F.M.M. Worrell	v England, Leeds, 1957
F.M.M. Worrell	v England, The Oval, 1957

India

Pankaj Roy	v West Indies, Delhi, 1958-59
M.L. Jaisimha	v England, Delhi, 1961-62
M.L. Jaisimha	v England, Madras, 1961-62
M.L. Jaisimha	v West Indies, Port-of-Spain, 1961-62
M.L. Jaisimha	v England, Delhi, 1963-64
M.L. Jaisimha	v England, Kanpur, 1963-64
M.L. Jaisimha	v Australia, Madras, 1964-65
M.L. Jaisimha	v Australia, Bombay, 1964-65
M.L. Jaisimha	v Australia, Calcutta, 1964-65
M.L. Jaisimha	v New Zealand, Calcutta, 1964-65
M.L. Jaisimha	v New Zealand, Bombay, 1964-65
M.L. Jaisimha	v New Zealand, Madras, 1964-65
M.L. Jaisimha	v New Zealand, Delhi, 1964-65
M.L. Jaisimha	v West Indies, Bombay, 1966-67
B.K. Kunderan	v England, Birmingham, 1967
S. Abid Ali	v New Zealand, Wellington, 1967-68.
S. Abid Ali	v New Zealand, Bombay, 1969-70
S. Abid Ali	v New Zealand, Nagpur, 1969-70
S. Abid Ali	v New Zealand, Hyderabad, 1969-70
S. Abid Ali	v West Indies, Kingston, 1970-71
S. Abid Ali	v West Indies, Port-of-Spain, 1970-71
S.M. Gavaskar	v England, Madras, 1972-73
E.D. Solkar	v England, Manchester, 1974
M. Amarnath	v England, Madras, 1976-77
S.M. Gavaskar	v England, Bombay, 1976-77
S.M. Gavaskar	v Australia, Melbourne, 1977-78
S.M. Gavaskar	v Pakistan, Lahore, 1978-79
M. Prabhakar	v New Zealand, Napier, 1989-90
M. Prabhakar	v New Zealand, Auckland, 1989-90
M. Prabhakar	v Sri Lanka, Chandigarh, 1990-91

Pakistan

Mudassar Nazar	v New Zealand, Lahore, 1984-85
Mudassar Nazar	v New Zealand, Hyderabad, 1984-85
Mudassar Nazar	v New Zealand, Karachi, 1984-85
Mudassar Nazar	v New Zealand, Wellington, 1984-85
Mudassar Nazar	v England, Lahore, 1987-88
Mudassar Nazar	v England, Faisalabad, 1987-88
Mudassar Nazar	v Australia, Karachi, 1988-89
Mudassar Nazar	v Australia, Faisalabad, 1988-89
Mudassar Nazar	v Australia, Lahore, 1988-89

Sri Lanka

B. Warnapura	v England, Colombo, 1981-82
J.R. Ratnayeke	v India, Nagpur, 1986-87
J.R. Ratnayeke	v India, Calcutta, 1986-87

The 'Prince' of batsmen, Ranjitsinjhi, playing at Manchester in 1896. He scored 154 not out for England in this match against Australia.

Australian cricket stars of the 19th century: George Giffen, Harry Boyle, Billy Murdoch and Hugh Trumble.

SOME NOTABLE 'FIRSTS' AND 'LASTS'

1 L. Hone was the first player to represent England in a Test without playing for a county. (England v Australia, Melbourne, 1878-79.)

2 D.C.H. Townsend was the last player to represent England in a Test match without having played for a first-class county. (England v West Indies, at Port-of-Spain, Georgetown, and Kingston, 1934-35.)

3 Rt Rev. D.S. Sheppard (later Bishop of Liverpool) was the first ordained minister to play Test cricket. Although he played his first Test in 1950, he played his first Test as an ordained minister in 1956.

4 A. Sandham (England) was the first batsman to score 300 in a Test innings. He scored 325 in the match against the West Indies at Kingston in 1929-30.

5 W. Bardsley (Australia) was the first batsman to score a century in each innings of a Test match. He scored 136 and 130 in the match against England at The Oval in 1909.

6 A.K. Davison (Australia) was the first player to complete the match double of 100 runs and 10 wickets in a Test. Playing against the West Indies at Brisbane in 1960-61, he scored 44 and 80 runs, and his bowling figures were 30-2-135-5 and 24.6-4-87-6.

7 S. Morris (Australia) was the first black man to play in a Test match (Australia v England at Melbourne, 1884-85). Morris was born in Hobart of West Indian parents. When the 11 players from the first Test at Adelaide demanded 50 per cent of the gate money for the second Test and were refused by officials, Morris got his chance when a new team was formed as a result. He scored 4 and 10* and 2 for 73 in his only Test.

8 Gloucestershire-born W.E. Midwinter is the only cricketer to have played for and against Australia in Test matches. Midwinter played eight times for Australia against England — 1876-77 (2), 1882-83 (1), 1884 (3), 1886-87 (2). He played four times for England against Australia in 1881-82.

9 In the second Test at Melbourne in 1882-83, W. Bates achieved the first hat-trick for England when he dismissed P.S. McDonnell, G. Giffen and G.J. Bonnor in Australia's first innings. He became the first player to score a fifty and take 10 or more wickets in the same Test. He scored 55 runs, and his bowling figures were 26.2-14-28-7 and 33-14-74-7. This was the first Test to be won by an innings.

10 The first double-century in Test cricket was scored by the Australian captain W.L. Murdoch (211) against England at The Oval in 1884.

11 P.S. McDonnell (Australia) was the first batsman to score two centuries in successive Test innings. He scored 103 at The Oval against England in 1884, and 124 at Adelaide, also against England, in 1884-85.

12 A. Shrewsbury (England) became the first batsman to score 1000 runs in Test cricket. He scored his 1000th run in a match against Australia played at Lord's in 1893.

13 J. Briggs (England) became the first player to take 100 Test wickets, during the fourth Test against Australia played at Sydney in 1894-95. In the same match, C.T.B. Turner became the first Australian bowler to capture 100 Test wickets.

14 G.A. Lohmann (England) was the first bowler to take 9 wickets in a Test innings. This occurred during a match against South Africa played at Johannesburg in 1895-96. His figures were 14.2-6-28-9.

15 J. Darling (Australia) was the first left-hander to score a century in a Test match with 101 against England at Sydney in 1897-98. During the season, Darling became the first batsman to score three centuries in the same series, and the first to aggregate 500 in the same series.

A FEW MORE FIRSTS

1 *First time a country won a Test series after losing the first two matches:* In the 1936-37 series played in Australia, Australia won the last three matches in the five-match series to defeat England 3-2.

2 *First drawn match in Australia since 1881-82:* The third Test between Australia and England at Melbourne in 1946-47.

3 *First time an extra day was added to a Test:* This occurred during the match between New Zealand and England at Christchurch in 1946-47. The third day had been washed-out, but rain prevented play on the extra day as well.

4 *First time Test cricket was played on Christmas Day:* This occurred during the third Test between Australia and the West Indies at Adelaide in 1951-52.

5 *First ball bowled in Test cricket:* A. Shaw (England) bowled from the eastern end of the MCG. (Australia v England, Melbourne, 1876-77.)

6 *First run in Test cricket:* C. Bannerman (Australia), scored the first run off the second ball of A. Shaw's first over. (Australia v England, Melbourne, 1876-77.)

7 *First wicket taken in Test cricket:* A. Hill (England) clean-bowled N. Thompson (Australia) in the fourth over bowled in Test cricket. (Australia v England, Melbourne, 1876-77.)

8 *First 5-wickets-in-an-innings haul:* W.E. Midwinter (Australia), 5 for 78. (Australia v England, Melbourne, 1876-77.)

9 *First 10-wickets-in-a-match haul:* F.R. Spofforth (Australia), 6 for 48 and 7 for 62. (Australia v England, Melbourne, 1878-79.)

10 *First catch taken in Test cricket:* A. Hill (England) caught the Australian batsman T.P. Horan at third man. (Australia v England, Melbourne, 1876-77.).

11 *First stumping completed in Test cricket:* J.M. Blackham stumped England's A. Shaw for 2 in the second innings of the first Test match. (Australia v England, Melbourne, 1876-77.)

12 *First boundary hit:* T.P. Horan (Australia) hit the first boundary with a snick through slips. (Australia v England, Melbourne, 1876-77.)

13 *First 100 partnership:* W.G. Grace (152) and A.P. Lucas (55) put on 120 for England's second wicket against Australia. (England v Australia, The Oval, 1880.)

14 *First century:* C. Bannerman (Australia), 165 retired hurt. (Australia v England, Melbourne, 1876-77.)

15 *First to score 50 in each innings:* G. Ulyett (England), 52 and 63*. (England v Australia, Melbourne, 1876-77.)

* Ulyett also became the first cricketer to score a century and 50 in the same Test. This occurred in the match against Australia played in Melbourne in 1881-82.

16 *First hat-trick in Test cricket:* F.R. Spofforth (Australia) dismissed the England batsmen V.P.F.A. Royle (bowled), F.A. McKinnon (bowled) and T. Emmett (caught by T.P. Horan) for a hat-trick. (Australia v England, Melbourne, 1878-79.)

17 *First declaration in Test cricket:* A.E. Stoddart (England) declared at 8 for 234 during a match that was eventually drawn. (England v Australia, Lord's, 1893.)

18 *First six (without overthrows) in a Test:* J. Darling (Australia) hit the first six. To be a six in those early days, the ball had to be hit out of the ground, and not merely over the boundary. (Australia v England, Adelaide, 1897-98.)

19 *First bowler to be 'no-balled' for throwing:* E. Jones (Australia) was given the first no ball by umpire J. Phillips. (Australia v England, Melbourne, 1897-98.)

20 *First century before lunch:* K.S. Ranjitsinhji (England) finished not out on 154 in his first Test. 'Ranji' was also the first Indian to play Test cricket. (England v Australia, Manchester, 1896.)

21 *First batsman to carry his bat through a completed innings:* A.B. Tancred (South Africa) carried his bat with 26* from a team total of 47. (South Africa v England, Cape Town, 1888-89.)

22 *First Sunday Test match play:* India v England, Bombay, 1933-34 (first Test).

23 *First Test match streaker:* Michael Angelow streaked on the fourth day of the second Test between England and Australia at Lord's in August 1975. He did it to win a bet, but lost the proceeds to the magistrate in court on the next day.

24 *First US President to watch a Test match:* Dwight D. Eisenhower. (Pakistan v Australia, Karachi, 1959-60.)

25 *First batsman to wear a protective helmet in a Test:* D.L. Amiss. (England v West Indies, The Oval, 1976.)

ATTENDANCE RECORDS

Single day:

On 11 February 1961, 90 800 spectators watched the second day of the fifth Test between Australia and the West Indies at the MCG.

Match:

The third Test at Melbourne between Australia and England in 1936-37 attracted 350 534 spectators, the record for any cricket match. The Test was played on 1, 2, 4, 5, 6, 7 January 1937.

Series:

The five matches in the 1936-37 series between Australia and England attracted 943 000 spectators, the biggest attendance for any Test rubber.

GAMES ABANDONED WITHOUT A BALL BEING BOWLED

1 England v Australia, Manchester, 1890. Rain washed out play on each day.

2 England v Australia, Manchester, 1938. Rain washed out play on each day.

3 Australia v England, Melbourne, 1970-71. This game, originally scheduled as the third Test of the series, was abandoned after solid rain on the first three days. A replacement Test, becoming an historic seventh Test of the series, was arranged to replace the washed-out game.

4 West Indies v England, Georgetown, 1980-81. Two days before this match was due to start, England bowler Robin Jackman (who had been flown to Georgetown to replace the injured Bob Willis) had his visitor's permit revoked by the Guyanese government and was ordered to leave the country. This was because he had spent several English winters in South Africa (as, incidentally, had several other members of the England team). The Tour Manager Alan Smith issued a statement saying that England would not play this second Test of the series 'as it is no longer possible for the Test team to be chosen without restrictions being imposed'. The game was then abandoned.

5 New Zealand v Pakistan, Dunedin, 1988-89. Heavy, sweeping rain caused the match to be called off on the third day.

6 West Indies v England, Georgetown, 1989-90. Torrential rain, falling nightly for five days, left the ground under water, and a contentiously-early decision to abandon the match was made on the rest day.

FAVOURITE GROUNDS

1 W.R. Hammond (England) scored 808 runs at Sydney: 251 (1928-29); 112; 101 and 75* (1932-33); 231* (1936-37); 1 and 37 (1946-47). Average: 161.60.

2 L. Hutton (England) scored 1521 runs at The Oval: 12 (1937), 73 and 165* (1939), 25 (1946); 83 and 36 (1947); 30 and 64 (1948); 206 (1949); 20* and 2 (1950); 28 and 27 (1951); 86 (1952); 82 and 17 (1953); 14 and 5 (1954). Average: 89.47.

3 D.C.S. Compton (England) scored 955 runs at Nottingham: 102 (1938); 65 and 163 (1947); 19 and 184 (1948); 112 and 5 (1951); 0 (1953); 278 (1954); 27 (1955). Average: 95.50.

4 D.G. Bradman (Australia) scored 963 runs at Leeds: 334 (1930); 304 (1934); 103 and 16 (1938); 33 and 173* (1948). Average: 192.60.

5 D.G. Bradman (Australia) scored 1681 runs at Melbourne: 79 and 112; 123 and 37* (1928-29); 152 (1930-31); 0 and 103* (1932-33); 13 and 270; 169 (1936-37); 79 and 49 (1946-47); 132 and 127*; 57 retired hurt (1947-48). Average: 129.30.

6 S.M. Gavaskar (India) scored 793 runs at Port-of-Spain: 64 and 67*; 124 and 220 (1970-71); 156; 26 and 10 (1975-76); 1 and 32 (1982-83). Average 113.28.

7 H. Sutcliffe (England) scored 724 runs at Melbourne: 176 and 127; 143 (1924-25); 58 and 135 (1928-29); 52 and 53 (1932-33). Average: 103.50.

BATTING CURIOSITIES

1 A.C. Bannerman scored off only five of 208 balls bowled to him by W. Attewell. Attewell bowled 46 overs (6-ball), 24 of which were maidens, for figures of 1 for 43. Bannerman batted for 421 minutes for his 91 (Australia v England, Sydney, 1891-92).

2 C.F. Root (England) played in three Test matches during his career — and failed to get a hit in any of them (all against Australia in 1926).

3 C.S. Nayudu (India) played only four scoring strokes in a stay of 145 minutes during the match against England at Calcutta in 1933-34. He hit a six, 2 fours and a single.

4 W.J. Edrich (England) played two innings before lunch on the third day of the Test against South Africa at Nottingham in 1947. Edrich had been not out at the start of play, and came in at No. 3 when England followed-on.

5 A.R. Morris (Australia) batted at one end and D.G. Bradman and I.W. Johnson at the other for 100 minutes during the match against England at The Oval in 1948. The first single was eventually scored and the batsmen changed ends.

6 Three batsmen in the Australian team playing against England at Nottingham in 1953 scored 237 out of 244 runs from the bat in Australia's first innings of 249. A.R. Morris hit 67, A.L. Hassett 115, and K.R. Miller 55. Morris and Hassett shared a stand of 122 for the second wicket, and Hassett and Miller shared one of 109 for the fourth. Next highest score was 4.

7 Each batsman to go to the crease in the India v New Zealand Test at Delhi in 1955-56 reached double figures. The highest score of the fifteen who batted was 230* (B. Sutcliffe, New Zealand) and the lowest 10* (J.W. Guy, also playing for New Zealand).

8 There have been eight instances of all 11 batsmen reaching double figures in an innings of a Test match. On each occasion, a team score of over 350 has been recorded. The most recent instance was for India during its match against New Zealand at Kanpur in 1976-77.

9 Only once has an innings been completed without a single batsman reaching double figures. This occurred when South Africa was all out for 30 against England at Birmingham in 1924. The highest score was 7 (H.W. Taylor, England) and there were 11 extras.

10 In 1932, the Nawab of Pataudi Sr scored a century in his first Test against Australia. Thirty-two years later, his son, the Nawab of Pataudi Jnr, achieved the same distinction during the match against Australia played at Madras in 1964-65.

11 W.J. Edrich (England), who batted on 63 occasions for his country at an average of 40.00, had an incredible run of failures during 1938 and 1939. In consecutive innings, he scored 5, 0, 10, 12, 28, 12, 4, 10, 0, 6 and 1. In his next innings, he notched up 219.

12 In the second Test between South Africa and New Zealand in 1953-54, two New Zealand batsmen retired hurt before scoring. Both had been hit by balls from N.A.T. Adcock — B. Sutcliffe on the head, and L.S.M. Miller on the chest. Both returned later — Sutcliffe scoring 80*, including 7 sixes, and Miller 14.

13 In the first Test of the 1957-58 series between the West Indies and Pakistan at Bridgetown, Pakistan scored 106 in its first innings and 8d-

657 in its second — a difference of 551 between the two innings.

14 R.E. Foster's score of 287 at Sydney in the first Test of the 1903-04 series is the highest score by any player in his first Test. He was the first player to share in three century partnerships in the same innings.

15 In the first Test of the Triangular Tournament at Manchester in 1912, T.A. Ward (South Africa) bagged a 'king pair'. He was the third victim of T.J. Matthews's two hat-tricks and was dismissed twice on the one day (28 May).

16 In the fourth Test between Australia and England at Melbourne in 1920-21, J.W.H. Makepeace (England) became the oldest player to score a maiden Test century. He was aged 38 years and 173 days.

17 At Lord's in 1926, W. Bardsley, aged 42 years and 201 days, carried his bat in scoring 193*. His record as the oldest player to score a century for Australia against England still stands.

18 With scores of 176, 114, 112, and 223, G.A. Headley (West Indies) is the only batsman to have scored four Test centuries before turning 21.

19 With scores of 53* and 71*, G.C. Grant (West Indies) was the first batsman to score a not-out fifty in each innings of a Test in the match against Australia at Adelaide in 1930-31.

20 A.G. Ganteaume (West Indies) scored 112 in his only Test innings at Port-of-Spain against England in 1947-48.

21 At Durban in 1964-65, K.F. Barrington (England) became the first batsman to score a Test century in all seven Test-playing countries. (Since Barrington's retirement, Sri Lanka has been granted Test match status — in 1981 — and played its first Test in 1982. Zimbabwe was granted Test match status in 1992.)

22 Playing against the West Indies at Bridgetown in 1964-65, Australia's W.M. Lawry, 210, and R.B. Simpson, 201, became the first opening pair to score double-centuries in the same Test innings.

23 I.M. Chappell (Australia), 165, scored the 1000th Test century in the match against the West Indies played at Melbourne in 1968-69. This was the 643rd Test match.

24 G.M. Turner (New Zealand) became the youngest player to carry his bat through a completed Test innings. Turner was 22 years and 63 days when he scored 43* in this match against England played at Lord's in 1969.

25 In South Africa's last official Test series against Australia before its 22-year isolation, B.A. Richards became the only batsman to score 500 runs in his first series for South Africa (508 runs, average 72.57).

26 The record aggregate for a batsman playing in his first series is 774 (average 154.80), scored by S.M. Gavaskar (India) against the West Indies in 1970-71.

27 The highest aggregate by a batsman in his debut calendar year is 1219 (average 64.15), by M.A. Taylor (Australia) in 1989.

28 The first time brothers scored centuries in the same innings of a Test was at The Oval in 1972. I.M. Chappell scored 118 and his brother, G.S. Chappell, 113 for Australia in this match against England.

29 The first time brothers scored centuries in each innings of the same Test was at Wellington in 1973-74. I.M. Chappell (145 and 121) and G.S. Chappell (247* and 133) scored four centuries between them for Australia in this match against New Zealand.

30 R.E. Redmond (New Zealand) scored 107 and 56 in his only Test match, at Auckland against Pakistan in 1972-73.

31 M.E. Waugh and S.R. Waugh (Australia) provided the first instance in Test cricket of twins playing in the same Test when playing against the West Indies at Port-of-Spain in 1990-91.

32 G.S. Chappell (Australia) became the first player to score centuries in each innings of his first

Test as Captain with 123 and 109* against the West Indies at Brisbane in 1975-76.

33 When S. Amarnath (India) scored 124 against New Zealand at Auckland in 1975-76, he became the first player to emulate his father by scoring a century in his first Test. ('Lala' Amarnath scored 118 against England in 1933-34.)

34 The record number of runs scored in Tests in a calendar year was achieved by I.V.A. Richards (West Indies) with 1710 runs in 1976 (average: 90.00).

35 India scored 524 in the second Test against New Zealand at Kanpur in 1976-77. This is the highest total in Test cricket in which no batsman scored a century.

36 At Leeds in 1977, G. Boycott (England) became the first batsman to score his 100th first-class century in a Test match when he scored 191 against Australia.

37 C. Hill (Australia) became the only batsman to be dismissed for three consecutive 90s. This occurred in the series against England in 1901-02. He scored 99 in the second innings of the second Test, and 98 and 97 in the third Test. He also became the first player to score 500 runs in a series without making a century. His scores were 46 and 0, 15 and 99, 98 and 97, 21 and 30, and 28 and 87.

The only other batsman to score 500 runs in a series without making a century is C.C. Hunte (West Indies), against Australia in 1964-65. His scores were 41 and 81, 89 and 53, 31 and 38, 75 and 31, and 1 and 60*.

In his career, Hill made the following 'nervous '90s' scores: 96, 99, 98, 97, 91*, 98.

38 In the West Indies's first innings of the fourth Test against England at Leeds in 1957, F.C.M. Alexander, who went in at the fall of the seventh wicket, was not called upon to face a single ball. F.S. Trueman took a wicket with the last ball of the over, and in the next P.J. Loader took a hat-trick to dismiss the last three batsmen and end the innings. Four wickets fell in consecutive balls.

39 M.C. Cowdrey (England) became the first cricketer to play 100 Tests when he played against Australia at Birmingham in 1968. He duly celebrated this feat by scoring 104.

SIXES TO WIN TEST MATCHES

1 In the fifth Test between Australia and England played in Sydney in 1932-33, W.R. Hammond (England) won the match by hitting a six.

2 In the first Test between the West Indies and England played at Bridgetown in 1934-35, W.R. Hammond (England) won the match by hitting a six. (This is the last Test that the West Indies has lost at Bridgetown.)

3 In the fifth Test between South Africa and Australia played at Port Elizabeth, H.R. Lance (South Africa) won the match by hitting a six.

4 In the fourth Test between Australia and England played at Brisbane in 1932-33,. E. Paynter won the match, and the Ashes, for England by hitting a six.

FAMOUS BATSMEN WHO BAGGED A TEST MATCH 'PAIR'

Australia	Career Runs	Career Average	HS	100s
A.C.Bannerman	1108	23.08	94	-
R.Benaud	2201	24.45	122	3
J.Darling	1657	28.56	178	3
R.Edwards	1171	40.37	170*	2
J.H.W.Fingleton	1189	42.46	136	5
S.E.Gregory	2282	24.53	201	4
R.N.Harvey	6149	48.41	205	21
D.W.Hookes	1306	34.36	143*	1
K.J.Hughes	4415	37.41	213	9
D.M.Jones	3631	46.55	216	11
P.S.McDonnell	950	28.78	147	3
R.W.Marsh	3633	26.51	132	3
M.A.Noble	1997	30.25	133	1
V.Y.Richardson	706	23.53	138	1
K.R.Stackpole	2807	37.42	207	7
V.T.Trumper (3 'ducks' in a row)	3163	39.04	214*	8
G.M.Wood	3374	31.83	172	9

England	Career Runs	Career Average	HS	100s
D.L.Amiss (twice)	3612	46.30	262*	11
T.E.Bailey	2290	29.74	134*	1
I.T.Botham	5200	33.54	208	14
G.A.Gooch	7571	43.76	333	17
A.P.E.Knott	4389	32.75	135	5
B.W.Luckhurst	1298	36.05	131	4
G.Pullar	1974	43.86	175	4
M.J.K.Smith	2278	31.61	121	3
R.A.Woolmer	1059	33.09	149	3

West Indies	Career Runs	Career Average	HS	100s
F.C.M.Alexander	961	30.03	108	1
P.J.L.Dujon	3322	31.94	139	5
C.G.Greenidge	7558	44.72	226	19
A.I.Kallicharran (twice)	4399	44.43	187	12
A.L.Logie	2470	35.79	130	2
D.L.Murray	1993	22.90	91	-
C.A.Roach (twice)	952	30.70	209	2
O.G.Smith	1331	31.69	168	4
J.S.Solomon	1326	34.00	100*	1
E.D.Weekes	4455	58.61	207	15
F.M.M.Worrell	3860	49.48	261	9

India	Career Runs	Career Average	HS	100s
M.Amarnath (twice in a run of 0 + 0, 1 + 0, 0 + 0)	4378	42.50	138	11
F.M.Engineer	2611	31.08	121	2
V.S.Hazare	2192	47.65	164*	7
M.L.Jaisimha	2056	30.68	129	3
Pankaj Roy	2442	32.56	173	5
G.S.Ramchand	1180	24.58	109	2
D.N.Sardesai	2001	39.23	212	5
D.B.Vengsarkar	6868	42.13	166	17
Yashpal Sharma	1606	33.45	140	2

Pakistan	Career Runs	Career Average	HS	100s
Imtiaz Ahmed	2079	29.28	209	3
Javed Burki	1341	30.47	140	3
Majid J.Khan	3930	38.91	167	8
Mudassar Nazar	4114	38.09	231	10
Wazir Mohammad	801	27.62	189	2

New Zealand	Career Runs	Career Average	HS	100s
J.V.Coney	2668	37.57	174*	3
T.W.Jarvis	625	29.76	182	1
I.D.S.Smith	1815	25.56	173	2
J.G.Wright	4964	37.61	185	12

South Africa	Career Runs	Career Average	HS	100s
W.R.Endean	1630	33.95	162*	3
D.J.McGlew	2440	42.06	255*	7

Sri Lanka	Career Runs	Career Average	HS	100s
A.Ranatunga	1830	33.88	135*	2

BATSMEN WHO SCORED THEIR ONE AND ONLY TEST CENTURY IN THEIR DEBUT MATCH

C. Bannerman	Australia	165*	v England	1876-77
P.F. Warner	England	132*	v South Africa	1898-9
R.E. Foster	England	287	v Australia	1903-04
R.J. Hartigan	Australia	116	v England	1907-08
A. Jackson	Australia	164	v England	1928-29
J.E. Mills	New Zealand	117	v England	1929-30
Nawab of Pataudi Sr	England	102	v Australia	1932-33
N.B. Amarnath	India	118	v England	1933-34
S.C. Griffith	England	140	v West Indies	1947-48
A.G. Ganteaume	West Indies	112	v England	1947-48
R.H. Shodhan	India	110	v Pakistan	1952-53
B.H. Pairaudeau	West Indies	115	v India	1952-53
A.G. Kripal Singh	India	100*	v New Zealand	1955-56
C.A. Milton	England	104*	v New Zealand	1958
A.A. Baig	India	112	v England	1959
Hanumant Singh	India	105	v England	1963-64
Khalid Ibadulla	Pakistan	166	v Australia	1964-65
J.H. Hampshire	England	107	v West Indies	1969
R.E. Redmond	New Zealand	107	v Pakistan	1973
F.C. Hayes	England	106*	v West Indies	1973
L. Baichan	West Indies	105*	v Pakistan	1974-75
S. Amarnath	India	124	v New Zealand	1975-76
D.M. Wellham	Australia	103	v England	1981
D.S.B.P. Kuruppu §	Sri Lanka	201*	v New Zealand	1986-87
A.C. Hudson §	South Africa	163	v West Indies	1991-92
R.S. Kaluwitharana	Sri Lanka	132*	v Australia	1992-93

§ to date

FAMOUS BATSMEN WHO SCORED A 'DUCK' IN THEIR FIRST TEST INNINGS

It's been said of some cricketers, 'he batted so badly he was lucky to make a "duck"', and, on occasions, this applies as much to batsmen of proven ability as it does to their less-accomplished colleagues.

One occasion which seems to have overawed a number of otherwise reliable batsmen is their first Test innings. Below is a list of some who failed this, their first big test. The results of their second appearance is shown in brackets.

Hon.I.F.W. Bligh §	England	v Australia	Melbourne	1882-83	(3)
S.E. Gregory	Australia	v England	Lord's	1890	(9)
J. Darling	Australia	v England	Sydney	1894-95	(53)
V.T. Trumper	Australia	v England	Nottingham	1899	(11)
G.E. Tyldesley	England	v Australia	Nottingham	1921	(7)
R.E.S. Wyatt	England	v South Africa	Johannesburg	1927-28	(2)†
M. Leyland	England	v West Indies	The Oval	1928	(137)†
L. Hutton	England	v New Zealand	Lord's	1937	(1)
G.E. Gomez	West Indies	v England	Manchester	1939	(11)
D.B. Close	England	v New Zealand	Manchester	1949	(0)†
J.G. Leggatt	New Zealand	v West Indies	Auckland	1951-52	(6*)
K.F. Barrington	England	v South Africa	Nottingham	1955	(34)†
M.J.K. Smith	England	v New Zealand	Birmingham	1958	(7)
C. Milburn	England	v West Indies	Manchester	1966	(94)
A.P.E. Knott	England	v Pakistan	Nottingham	1967	(28)†
K.W.R. Fletcher	England	v Australia	Leeds	1968	(23*)
G.M. Turner	New Zealand	v West Indies	Auckland	1968-69	(40)
G.R. Viswanath	India	v Australia	Kanpur	1969-70	(137)†
A.R. Lewis §	England	v India	Delhi	1972-73	(70*)
G.A. Gooch	England	v Australia	Birmingham	1975	(0)
J.M. Brearley	England	v West Indies	Nottingham	1976	(17)

§ Captained England on first Test appearance
† Not in the same match

MOST RUNS OFF ONE BALL

1 8: E.H. Hendren (169), England v Australia, Brisbane, 1928-29 (four boundary overthrows).

2 8: J.G. Wright (44), New Zealand v Australia, Melbourne, 1980-81 (four boundary overthrows).

3 7: A. Sandham (325), England v West Indies, Kingston, 1929-30 (four boundary overthrows).

4 7: A.P.E. Knott (116), England v West Indies, Leeds, 1976 (one, plus two overthrows, plus four boundary overthrows).

PARTNERSHIP FEATS

1 H. Sutcliffe (England), playing against Australia at Sydney in 1932-33, shared in century stands for the first three wickets.

2 J.B. Hobbs and H. Sutcliffe (England) shared four century opening stands against Australia in 1924-25. Three of these were recorded in the first three innings in which they partnered each other.

3 L. Hutton and C. Washbrook (England) shared three consecutive opening stands of over 100 against Australia in 1946-47.

4 R.S. Modi and V.S. Hazare (India) shared three consecutive century stands for the third wicket against the West Indies in 1948-49.

5 C.G. Greenidge partnered D.L. Haynes in 16 century opening stands for the West Indies.

6 J.B. Hobbs (England) shared in 24 century opening stands (15 with H. Sutcliffe, 8 with W. Rhodes, and one with C.B. Fry). S.M. Gavaskar (India) and C.G. Greenidge (West Indies) in 22; H. Sutcliffe (England) 21; G. Boycott (England) 20.

7 G. Boycott, B.W. Luckhurst and J.H. Edrich (England) figure in four successive opening stands of more than 100 against Australia in 1970-71. In eight successive innings, these pairs registered six century opening stands.

8 I.M. Chappell (Australia) and S.M. Gavaskar (India) figured in 18 century partnerships for the second wicket.

9 Batsmen who have featured in the most century partnerships are: S.M. Gavaskar (India) with 58; A.R. Border (Australia) 51; Javed Miandad (Pakistan) 48; G. Boycott (England) 47; C.G. Greenidge (West Indies) 46; G.S. Chappell (Australia) and I.V.A. Richards (West Indies) 44; M.C. Cowdrey (England) 42; L. Hutton (England) and C.H. Lloyd (West Indies) 41.

CENTURIES BY TAIL-ENDERS*

*Lower than No. 8 in the order

1 W.W. Read (England). Read batted at No. 10 in the match against Australia at The Oval in 1884, and in the second innings came in with England facing defeat at 8 for 181. It was said that Read was in a towering rage at his captain's decision to place him so low in the order, and he made his point with a brilliant 117 in two hours, during which time he added 151 with W.H. Scotton (90 in five and three-quarter hours).

2 R.A. Duff (Australia). Duff batted at No. 6 in the first innings of the second Test against England at Melbourne in 1901-02, but was held back to No. 10 in the second innings. Duff scored 104 and shared in a 10th-wicket partnership of 120 with fellow debutant W.W. Armstrong.

3 R.J. Hartigan (Australia). Hartigan, batting at No. 9 in his Test debut against England at Adelaide in 1907-08, came in when Australia, in its second innings, led by only 102 with 7 wickets down. He joined C. Hill (who was suffering a bout of influenza); the two defied the English bowling and the 42°C heat to put on 243 for the eighth wicket, of which Hartigan's share was 116. Their record stand enabled Australia to win the match.

4 J.M. Gregory (Australia). After taking 7 for 69 earlier in the match against England at Melbourne in 1920-21, Gregory, batting at No. 9, joined C.E. Pellew with Australia 7 for 282 in their second innings. Together, they put on 173; Gregory's share was exactly 100.

5 G.O.B. Allen (England). Batting at No. 9, Allen joined the wicketkeeper, L.E.G. Ames, with England 7 for 190 in its first innings against New Zealand at Lord's in 1931. The two added 246 runs, with Allen making 122.

6 R.R. Lindwall (Australia). Batting at No. 9 in Australia's second innings against England at Melbourne in 1946-47, Lindwall joined wicketkeeper D. Tallon with Australia 7 for 341. These two then shared a blistering partnership, adding 154 in 88 minutes of brilliant hitting. Lindwall made 100 (1 six and 13 fours) in 109 minutes.

GOOD EFFORTS BY 'NIGHT-WATCHMEN'

1 H. Larwood (England), playing against Australia at Sydney in 1932-33, went in to bat late on the second evening when England was 2 for 153. The Australian bowlers did not see his back until the score had reached 310, of which Larwood's share in 135 minutes was a grand 98. His innings was ended by a catch to Bert Ironmonger, who was not noted as a safe catcher (he held only 3 in 14 Test matches).

2 A.V. Bedser (England) came in late on the first day in the match against Australia at Leeds in 1948. England was 2 for 268. The following morning, Bedser defied the Australian attack of R.R. Lindwall, K.R. Miller, W.A. Johnston, E.R.H. Toshack and I.W. Johnson to make his highest Test score — 79 — and to help add 155 for the third wicket with W.J. Edrich.

3 Nasim-ul-Ghani (Pakistan) played against England at Lord's in 1962. Normally batting at No. 8, he was promoted two places and sent in as a night-watchman when Pakistan was 4 for 77 in its second innings. Nasim stayed to score 101, and shared in a Pakistan record 5th-wicket partnership of 197 with Javed Burki — a record which still stands. Nasim's century was his first in first-class cricket, and the first by a Pakistan batsman in England.

4 A.L. Mann (Australia), playing against India at Perth in 1977-78, came in with the score of 1 for 13 late on the fourth day, having batted at No. 8 in the first innings. The following day, he proceeded to score 105 out of a total of 8 for 342, sharing a partnership of 139 for the third wicket with P.M. Toohey. Mann's other seven Test innings in a four-Test career netted a mere 84 runs.

5 Wasim Bari (Pakistan) was sent in as a night-watchman in the match against India at Lahore in 1978-79. The score was 1 for 19. He achieved a Test-career highest score of 85, sharing in a 2nd-wicket partnership stand of 115 with Majid J. Khan, and was dismissed when the score was 3 for 161.

6 R.R. Jumadeen (West Indies) came in late on the third day in the match against India at Kanpur in 1978-79. The score was 2 for 134, but Jumadeen stayed long enough to score his only Test fifty (56), and shared a 3rd-wicket stand of 129 with S.F.A.F. Bacchus.

7 S.M.H. Kirmani (India), when playing against Australia at Bombay in 1979-80, came in late on the first day as a night-watchman when India was 3 for 231. Scoring 0* overnight, Kirmani (in his side as wicketkeeper) batted for the remainder of the innings until India declared at 8 for 458. He scored 101* in five hours, adding 127 with K.D. Ghavri for the eighth wicket.

8 E.E. Hemmings (England) came in late on the fourth day of the match against Australia at Sydney in 1982-83. England was 1 for 3 in the second innings, but Hemmings batted for 226 minutes to record his highest Test score of 95.

9 W.W. Davis (West Indies) played against England at Manchester of 1984. He came in late on the first day when the score was 5 for 267, and scored 77, sharing in a 6th-wicket stand of 170 with C.G. Greenidge.

HIGHEST SCORES BY A NO. 11

1 68*: R.O. Collinge (New Zealand), New Zealand v Pakistan, Auckland, 1972-73. He added 151 for the tenth wicket with B.F. Hastings (110) — a record for Test cricket.

2 62*: A.E.E. Vogler (South Africa), South Africa v England, Cape Town, 1905-06.

3 60*: Wasim Bari (Pakistan), Pakistan v West Indies, Bridgetown, 1976-77.

4 59*: J.A. Snow (England), England v West Indies, The Oval, 1966.

5 50*: W.W. Hall (West Indies), West Indies v India, Port-of-Spain, 1961-62.

6 50: F.R. Spofforth (Australia), Australia v England, Melbourne, 1884-85.

7 50: Ghulam Ahmed (India), India v Pakistan, Delhi, 1952-53.

SLOW SCORING MEMORABILIA

1 Fourteen consecutive (4-ball) maiden overs were bowled to A.C. Bannerman and W.L. Murdoch (Australia) during their 2nd-wicket partnership against England at Melbourne in 1882-83.

2 A.C. Bannerman (Australia) scored 19 runs in 200 minutes during the match against England at Sydney in 1886-87. Bannerman made 15* in two hours in the first innings, and 4 in 80 minutes in the second.

3 Australia's total of 175 in 325 minutes in the match against England at Manchester in 1921 included 58 maiden overs.

4 B. Mitchell, on debut for South Africa against England at Birminghan in 1929, made a combined total of 149 in 575 minutes — 88 in 420 minutes, and 61* in 155 minutes.

5 England scored only 37 runs in the pre-lunch session against Australia at Adelaide in 1932-33.

6 I.D. Craig (Australia) scored 38 in four and a half hours, spread over four days, in the match against England at Manchester in 1956.

7 P.G. van der Bijl (South Africa) scored 125 against England at Durban in 1938-39, but did not hit his first boundary until he had been at the wicket for three hours. The first four of the South African innings came after 130 minutes.

8 England took 972 minutes and 1723 balls to score 442 runs against Australia at Leeds in 1953 — 167 in 386 minutes (658 balls), and 275 in 586 minutes (1065 balls).

9 England scored only 27 (39 overs) before lunch on the third day against the West Indies at Bridgetown in 1953-54. The new ball (at that time taken after 65 overs) arrived with the score at 77.

10 Hanif Mohammad scored 59 runs in 337 minutes for the match against England at Lord's in 1954 — 20 in 197 minutes, and 39 in 140 minutes.

11 New Zealand had scored only 24 at lunch (after 90 minutes) on the first day of the match against England at Dunedin in 1954-55. The total for the day was 125 in 292 minutes.

12 New Zealand scored only 69 off 90 6-ball overs (56 maidens) against Pakistan at Dacca in 1955-56.

13 New Zealand scored 6 for 32 and 3 for 37 in two pre-lunch sessions against England at Birmingham in 1958.

14 England scored only 19 runs before lunch (90 minutes) in the match against Australia at Brisbane in 1958-59, taking an overnight score of 2 for 92 to 4 for 114. T.E. Bailey scored 8 of the 19 runs in the session.

15 Pakistan scored 24 before lunch against Australia at Karachi in 1959-1960. The innings of 8 (dec.) for 194 lasted 8 hours.

16 M.L. Jaisimha (India), playing against Australia at Calcutta in 1959-60, batted through a whole day's play, taking his overnight score of 0* to 59*.

17 T.E. Bailey (England), in the first Test against Australia at Brisbane in 1958-59, scored 68 runs in 458 minutes — less than 9 runs an hour. He took 357 minutes to reach 50, and scored off only 40 of the 425 balls bowled to him.

COURAGEOUS PERFORMANCES

1 During the second Test of the 1970-71 series between Australia and England at Perth, England batsman B.W. Luckhurst damaged his thumb early in his innings but carried on to score 131 runs. In the fifth Test, played a little over a month later at Melbourne, Luckhurst's left little finger was fractured early in his innings, and on this occasion he scored 109 runs.

2 During the first Test at Dunedin of the 1967-68 series between New Zealand and India, R.B. Desai (India) had his jaw fractured by a rising ball from R.C. Motz, but went on to score 32* in a 10th-wicket partnership of 57 with B.S. Bedi.

3 A.R. Border (Australia), despite batting in considerable pain from a broken finger during the 1981 series against England, scored in succession 123*, 106*, and 84, batting in all for 15 hours and 2 minutes before losing his wicket.

4 E. Paynter (England) was hospitalised with acute tonsilitis during the fourth Test against Australia in 1932-33, but he insisted on taking his place at the crease where he stayed for four hours, scoring 83 runs. In the second innings, he struck a six which won the match and regained the Ashes for England.

5 A.D. Nourse (South Africa) batted for 550 minutes to score 208 in the first Test against

England at Nottingham in 1951 — with a broken thumb.

6 W.M. Lawry (Australia) had ten stitches inserted in a head wound caused by a fast rising ball from P.M. Pollock in the third Test against South Africa at Durban in 1966-67. He returned to the crease and top-scored with 44 out of the first innings total of 147.

7 R.B. McCosker (Australia) suffered a fractured jaw while batting in the first innings of the Centenary Test between Australia and England at Melbourne in March 1977. He returned to the crease, however, with his face swathed in bandages to help Australia to a second-innings total of 9 (dec.) for 419.

8 S.M. Patil (India), playing in the first Test against Australia at Sydney in 1980-81 was knocked unconscious by a 'bouncer' from L.S. Pascoe. Three weeks later in the second Test at Adelaide, he scored 174 in 301 minutes.

SHORTEST TEAM TEST MATCH INNINGS

1 50 minutes: South Africa was all out for 30 in 12.3 overs (6-ball) in the first innings against England at Birmingham in 1924.

2 80 minutes: England was all out for 45 in 35.3 overs (4-ball) in the first innings against Australia at Sydney in 1886-87.

3 90 minutes: Australia was all out for 36 in 23 overs (6-ball) in the first innings against England at Birmingham in 1902.

4 225 minutes: India was all out twice in one day for 58 in 21.4 overs (6-ball) and 82 in 37.3 overs when playing against England at Manchester in 1952.

UNUSUAL DISMISSALS

1 S.J. Snooke (South Africa) was stumped for 53 by N.C. Tufnell in the match against England at Durban in 1909-10. Tufnell was keeping wicket as a substitute for H. Strudwick (injured).

2 A.Ducat (England) had scored 3 against Australia at Leeds in 1921 when the shoulder of his bat was broken by an express delivery from E.A. McDonald. The broken piece knocked off a bail and the ball was caught by J.M. Gregory. The umpire's decision was 'out caught'.

3 W.H. Brann (South Africa) was given 'not out' for a catch at the wicket during the Test against South Africa in Cape Town in 1922-23. The bowler, G.G. Macauley, appealed for lbw and the appeal was granted.

4 Musthaq Ali (India), playing in the match against England at Manchester in 1936, was run out when a ball hit by his partner, V.M. Merchant, hit the back of Mushthaq Ali's bat and deflected to mid-off; there A.E. Fagg fielded and threw down the non-striker's wicket, with Mushtaq Ali out of his ground.

5 D.G. Bradman (Australia) was batting against India at Brisbane in 1947-48 when he played back so far to N.B. 'Lala' Amarnath that the downward swing of his bat broke the wicket from behind. Bradman was out 'hit wicket' to Amarnath for 185.

6 W.A. Brown (Australia) was run out by the bowler, M.H. 'Vinoon' Mankad, when batting for Australia against India at Sydney in 1947-48. Brown had been backing up too far and Mankad removed the bails as he ran in to bowl. Mankad did not deliver a warning as he had been involved in a similar incident with Brown only four weeks before the Test in a match between an Australian XI and the touring Indian team.

7 L. Hutton (England) was dismissed for 'obstructing the field' when playing against South Africa at The Oval in 1951. A delivery hit Hutton's bat handle or hand and lobbed into the air, and wicketkeeper W.R. Endean prepared to take the catch. Hutton, however, hit the ball away as it fell (with the intention of preventing it hitting his wicket), and upon appeal was given out.

8 Ironically, W. R. Endean (South Africa) was given out 'handled the ball' against England at Cape Town in 1956-57; a ball from J.C. Laker rose sharply and Endean palmed it away with his hand in hockey-goalkeeper style.

9 Pervez Sajjad (Pakistan) was stumped by B.E. Congdon (New Zealand) at Lahore in 1964-65. Congdon was substituting as wicketkeeper for A.E. Dick, who had been injured.

10 I.R. Redpath (Australia) was run out by bowler C.C. Griffith (West Indies) when backing-up too far at Adelaide in 1968-69. (Interestingly, I.M. Chappell was caught out of his ground in the same way by bowler D.A.J. Holford only minutes later, but in this instance the bowler refrained from removing the bails.)

11 D.W. Randall (England) was run out by the bowler E.J. Chatfield (New Zealand) in the Test at Christchurch in 1977-78.

12 Sikander Bakht (Pakistan) was similarly dismissed by bowler A.G. Hurst (Australia) at Perth in 1978-79.

13 A.M.J. Hilditch (Australia), when batting against Pakistan at Perth in 1978-79, took pity on the perspiring fast bowler Sarfraz Nawaz. He bent down and collected the ball by his feet at the bowler's end and handed it to Sarfraz. Instead of thanking Hilditch, the bowler appealed for 'handled the ball' and the umpire had no option but to uphold the appeal.

14 R.M. Hogg (Australia), when batting against Pakistan at Melbourne in 1978-79, ran a single, then, between deliveries, walked up the pitch to prod down some loose turf. The ball, however, was still in the possession of a fielder, Javed Miandad, who put down the stumps with Hogg yards down the wicket to run the batsman out for 9.

15 West Indies batsman J.S. Solomon was adjudged out 'hit wicket' when his cap fell off, dislodging the bails during the second Test of the 1960-61 series against Australia at Melbourne.

16 J.W. Zulch (South Africa), playing against Australia in the second Test at Johannesburg in 1921-22, was given out 'hit wicket' when a splinter of wood from his bat, dislodged by a ball from E.A. McDonald, removed the bails.

17 B.L. D'Oliveira (England) batted with J.M. Parks in the first innings of the second Test against the West Indies at Lord's in 1966. Parks, facing W.W. Hall, drove a ball back down the pitch which rebounded off D'Oliveira's boot onto the stumps while he was out of his crease. Thinking he was run out, D'Oliveira 'walked', whereupon Hall picked up the ball and removed a stump with the hand holding the ball, thus correctly completing the dismissal. Had the batsman stood his ground, he would not have been out, as no fielder had touched the ball when the wicket was first broken.

18 S.P. Jones (Australia), playing against England in the 1882 'Ashes' Test at The Oval, was run out by W.G. Grace when, after completing a run, he left his crease to pat the pitch down. This was said to so infuriate F.R. Spofforth that he bowled like a man possessed; taking 7 for 44 in England's second innings, Spofforth was instrumental in gaining Australia's first-ever win in a Test on English soil.

19 D.M. Jones (Australia), when playing against the West Indies at Georgetown in 1990-91, was bowled by a no-ball from C.A. Walsh. Because of his helmet and the noise from the crowd, he did not hear the umpire's call, and started to walk off the field. C.L. Hooper grabbed the ball and snatched up a stump with the hand holding the ball. The umpire then, incorrectly, gave the batsman out. The laws of cricket had been changed in 1980 so that the umpire can call back a batsman leaving the ground under a misapprehension that he had been dismissed.

Note: In 1973-74 at Port-of-Spain, A.W. Greig (England) ran out I.A. Kallicharran when B.D. Julien played the last ball on the second day down the pitch. Greig picked up the ball and, seeing Kallicharran out of his ground, threw down the non-striker's wicket and appealed. Umpire D. Sang Hue ruled Kallicharran 'run out'. That evening, lengthy off-field discussions between the captains, officials and umpires led to the appeal being withdrawn in the interests of cricket.

A FEW SURPRISE SELECTIONS

1 E.J.K. Burn (Australia) was selected for the 1890 Australian team going to England as the second wicketkeeper. It was only when the

team was assembled in Adelaide that it became known that he had never kept wicket in his life.

2 S.F. Barnes (England) was selected to tour Australia in 1901-02, mainly at the instigation of A.C. McLaren. Barnes, then a professional with Burnley in the Lancashire League, had taken only 9 wickets in first-class cricket — but then proceeded to take 19 wickets in his first two Tests on the way to becoming recognised as one of the greatest bowlers the world has every seen.

3 A.L. Valentine (West Indies) was taken to England in 1950 after only two first-class matches in which he took 2 wickets for 190 runs.

4 S. Ramadhin (West Indies) was pulled out of Trinidad club cricket to tour England in 1950. While on tour, he and A.L. Valentine mystified the best batsmen in England, and both were on their way to becoming Test 'greats'. Ramadhin, like Valentine, had played only two games of first-class cricket — both on matting.

5 G.S. Sobers (West Indies) was called into the West Indies Test side to play against England at Kingston in 1953-54. Previously, Sobers (who replaced the injured A.L. Valentine) had played only two first-class matches.

6 J.E.F. Beck (New Zealand) had played only club cricket and had never appeared in a first-class match when he was chosen to tour South Africa in 1953-54. He was run out for 99 at Cape Town in his second Test match.

7 J.R. Watkins (Australia) was chosen to play against Pakistan in Sydney in 1972-73 after A.A. Mallett announced he was unavailable for the forthcoming tour of the West Indies. Although Watkins's first-class record for New South Wales was not particularly distinguished, he made a fine 36 in the second innings, and shared in a stand of 83 with R.A.L. Massie after Australia had collapsed to 8 for 101; and, with the ball, he delivered probably the six most inaccurate overs ever bowled in Sydney.

8 The English selectors pulled off three of the most amazing selections in history for the 1956 series against Australia.

For the third Test at Leeds, they included 41-year-old C. Washbrook, who had not played Test cricket for five years. Coming in to bat with the score at 3 for 17, Washbrook made 98 and shared in a stand of 177 with P.B.H. May.

For the next Test at Manchester, the Rev. David Sheppard was included. Because of clerical duties, he had played only four innings that year for Sussex — but promptly made 113 to help England win the Test.

For the Oval Test, the selectors brought in Denis Compton — 18 years after he had played his first Test and not long after he had undergone an operation for the removal of a knee-cap. Compton completed the 'hat-trick' for the selectors with scores of 94 and 35.

9 Australian selectors had a 'double' selection bonanza in 1907-08 when they brought J.D.A. O'Connor and R.J. Hartigan into the side for the Adelaide Test against England. Hartigan scored 48 and 116 (sharing in a record stand of 243 with C. Hill after Australia had been 7 for 180), and O'Connor bowled Australia to victory with 5 for 40 in the vital fourth innings of the match.

10 W. Rhodes (England) was brought back into the England team for the vital fifth Test of the 1926 series against Australia. He was aged 48! With England needing to win to regain the Ashes, Rhodes bowled the team to victory with 2 for 35 and 4 for 44.

11 M.R. Whitney (Australia) was in England to play League cricket, and to appear occasionally for Gloucestershire, when he was brought into the Australian Test team in 1981 (injuries to G.F. Lawson and R.M. Hogg had left the team short of players). Previously, Whitney had made only four appearances for NSW.

12 P.L. Taylor (Australia) was selected for the fifth Test against England at Sydney in 1986-87 after only six first-class matches, and only one of them during the season. There was speculation in the media whether the selectors had chosen the wrong Taylor, for M.A. Taylor, an opening batsman for NSW, had experienced a successful debut in first-class cricket the previous season. P.L. Taylor, bowling off-spin, took a career-best 6 for 78 and 2 for 76, as well as scoring a crucial 42 runs in Australia's

second innings; Australia won its first Test against England since June 1985.

UNUSUAL INCIDENTS

1 In the series between Australia and England played in Australia in 1936-37, Middlesex captain R.W.V. Robins played under the leadership of his county vice-captain, G.O.B. Allen. A similar situation occurred in the 1980 England v West Indies series played in England when the Somerset captain B.C. Rose played under the leadership of Somerset vice-captain I.T. Botham.

2 The West Indies, playing against England at St John's in 1980-81, opened the Test by scoring 45 from the first seven overs — made up of 11 fours and a single.

3 The start of the Pakistan v West Indies Test at Multan in 1980-81 was delayed because of the late arrival of one of the umpires.

4 When given out lbw in the match against Australia at Melbourne in 1980-81, the Indian captain, S.M. Gavaskar, indicated that the ball had hit his bat, and was so angry at the decision that he ordered his batting partner, C.P.S. Chauhan, to accompany him from the field and forfeit the match. Both players were only metres inside the boundary when India's manager, Wing-Commander Durani, intervened and ordered Chauhan back to the crease. The following day, Kapil Dev and D.R. Doshi bowled India to victory as Australia was dismissed for 83 (while chasing a target of 143).

5 In the match between the West Indies and Pakistan at Multan in 1980-81, bowler S.T. Clarke (West Indies) was bombarded by a shower of oranges and a brick, thrown from the crowd as he fielded on the fine-leg fence. Enraged, Clarke picked up the brick and threw it back into the crowd, injuring a young student. Play was immediately held up, and only the West Indies vice-captain A.I. Kallicharran's calming plea restored order in the angry crowd. Clarke was later suspended for three matches by the West Indies Cricket Board of Control.

6 During the Test between India and Australia at Bangalore in 1979-80, the Australian pace-bowler R.M. Hogg became upset with the feather-bed pitch and with his own spate of no-balls (7 in five overs) — so he kicked down the stumps at the bowler's end! His captain, K.J. Hughes, tendered an immediate apology to the umpire, an action which Hogg duplicated at the end of play.

7 M.A. Holding, in the Test between the West Indies and New Zealand at Dunedin in 1979-80, duplicated the behaviour of R.M. Hogg (see above) by kicking down the stumps at the batsman's end after having an appeal disallowed.

8 In the New Zealand v West Indies Test at Christchurch in 1979-80, the West Indies fast-bowler C.E.H. Croft took bad sportsmanship to the brink. After being no-balled and showing his displeasure several times, Croft ran in very close to the umpire (F.R. Goodall) — so close that the batsman could not see him — and shouldered Goodall heavily. Croft was later suspended for his actions, but the West Indians were so upset about Goodall's umpiring that they refused to take the field after tea on the third day unless he was replaced. They were finally persuaded to resume, twelve minutes late.

9 In the seventh Test between Australia and England at Sydney in 1970-71, England nearly became the first team to forfeit a Test. English paceman J.A. Snow felled Australian tail-ender T.J. Jenner with a 'bouncer', and became involved in a war of words with the umpire L.P. Rowan when warned for 'intimidatory' bowling. R. Illingworth, England's captain, joined in, and the crowd began to boo and hiss. Cans came flying onto the field and, when Snow was sent to field right on the fine-leg boundary, a drunken spectator leaned over the fence and grabbed his arm. Illingworth immediately motioned his team from the ground, and it was only the umpire's advice that if they did not return they would forfeit the match that persuaded Illingworth to resume.

10 In the Test between Australia and England at Perth in 1979-80, Australian batsman D.K. Lillee, not out overnight, continued his innings the next morning using an aluminium bat (which he had used once previously). After two balls had been played (rather noisily), England captain J.M. Brearley complained to the umpires that the aluminium bat was damaging the ball! The umpires asked Lillee to change his bat, but Lillee, quite within his rights, refused and argued heatedly with Brearley. Finally, the umpires ordered him off for a replacement, but after stalking from the ground, Lillee re-appeared — still carrying his aluminium bat. Still more argument ensued, and eventually Lillee threw the bat away in disgust, accepted a willow replacement, and play was allowed to resume.

11 G.J. Bonnor (Australia), in making 87 against England at Sydney in 1882-83, was dropped eight (yes, eight!) times. A.G. Steel dropped four of the chances when Bonnor was 2, 17, 24, and 80. When England batted, Steel himself was dropped four times — but went on to make 135*.

CAPTAINCY CURIOSITIES

1 H.M. Taberer captained South Africa in his one and only Test match appearance when he led his country against England at Johannesburg in the first Test of 1902-03. For the second Test, less than a week later, J.H. Anderson led South Africa in his only Test appearance.

2 N. Betancourt captained the West Indies in his only Test match, which was against England in 1929-30.

3 In the fourth Test between the West Indies and England at Kingston in 1934-35, both captains were forced off the field through injury. England's R.E.S. Wyatt suffered a broken jaw, and the West Indies's C.G. Grant retired with an ankle injury.

4 C.A. Smith (England) captained his country at his only appearance in a Test match, which was against South Africa in 1888-89. Smith, later knighted, was afterwards famous as a Hollywood film actor.

5 P.W. Sherwell (South Africa) captained his country in his first Test appearance, which was against England at Johannesburg in 1905-06.

6 During his period as captain of England (12 matches from June 1980 to July 1981), I.T. Botham scored 276 runs at an average of 13.80, and took 35 wickets at 32.00 average. Compare these figures to his overall career-to-date statistics of 33.93 runs per innings and 28.24 for each wicket.

ODDMENTS

1 In the second Test match between Australia and England in 1877, played at the Melbourne Cricket Ground, Australian batsman T.J.D. Kelly hit 8 consecutive fours in the second innings, and C. Bannerman scored 30 in 15 minutes. Despite these spirited efforts, Australia lost by four wickets.

2 In the first Test of the 1881-82 season between Australia and England, played at Melbourne, E.W. Midwinter made his debut for England, after having played for Australia in the first two Tests between the two countries. (In the same match, T.P. Horan and G. Giffen scored Australia's first-ever century partnership: 107 for the fifth wicket.)

3 W.L. Murdoch of Australia scored the first double-century in Test cricket when he knocked up 211 against England at The Oval during the third Test in 1884. In the same match, all 11 English players were called upon to bowl while Australia scored 55 runs. The match was drawn.

4 The only other instance of 11 players bowling in an innings occurred at Faisalabad in 1979-80 during the second Test between Pakistan and Australia. The entire Australian team, including wicketkeeper R.W. Marsh, had a spell at the bowling crease during Pakistan's only innings. The match was drawn. Australia made 617 and Pakistan 2 for 382.

5 In the fifth Test between Australia and England at Melbourne during the 1884-85 season, umpire J. Hodges refused to take the field after tea on the third day because of complaints

made by some English players about his decisions. The Australian player T.W. Garrett deputised for Hodges during the last session, and the English manager, J. Lillywhite, took over on the last day. There is nothing in the records to indicate how Garrett performed in this unusual role.

6 The appearance of a mouse on the field held up play for several minutes during the Test between England and Pakistan at Birmingham in 1962.

7 Four players with the same surname played in the Test between South Africa and England at Cape Town in 1891-92: A., G.E., and J.T. Hearne for England; F. Hearne for South Africa.

8 In his debut Test match, G.G. Macaulay (playing for England against South Africa at Cape Town in 1922-23) took a wicket with his first ball, and made the winning hit when England won the match by 1 wicket.

9 In the Test between Pakistan and England at Lahore in 1977-78, England off-spinner G.A. Cope dismissed Abdul Qadir lbw, and then bowled Sarfraz Nawaz with the first ball. Iqbal Qasim then snicked the next delivery to J.M. Brearley, the England captain, at slip, and the umpire confirmed the catch and Copes's hat-trick. However, Brearley indicated that the 'catch' had been taken on the bounce, and Qasim was allowed to bat on. It would be difficult to get much closer to a Test hat-trick than Cope did on that day.

10 M.H. Mankad (India), in 72 innings, and W. Rhodes (England), in 98 innings, are the only two batsmen in the history of Test cricket to bat in every position from 1 to 11 in their Test match careers.

11 The only occasion when one country simultaneously played official Test matches in two different countries was in 1929-30 when England played New Zealand at Christchurch on 10, 11, and 13 January, and played the West Indies at Bridgetown on 11, 13, 14, 15 and 16 January.

12 In 1880, an Australian team advertised for opponents. This unique event occurred during the Australian's vist to England; apparently, it was not certain until the late spring of that year that the Australians would be touring, and consequently the county programmes had already been drawn up. The Australians therefore found the large part of their tour consisted of fixtures with local clubs in the North and Midlands, usually against the odds. It was during this period that the team took out newspaper advertisements for opponents.

Finally, at the end of August, and mainly through the efforts of one man, C.W. Alcock, a match against a representative England team was organised. This became the first Test match on English soil.

13 The most expensive miss occurred when B.A. Barnett, while keeping wicket for Australia, missed stumping L. Hutton off L.O. Fleetwood-Smith in the match against England at The Oval in 1938. Hutton was on 40, and went on to make 364.

14 In the first Test against India at Madras in 1979-80, Australia's first seven batsmen in the batting order each opened their score with a boundary. The batsmen were A.M.J. Hilditch, G.M. Wood, A.R. Border, K.J. Hughes, G.N. Yallop, D.F. Whatmore and K.J. Wright.

BOWLERS NO-BALLED FOR THROWING IN TEST MATCHES

The following bowlers have been no-balled for throwing:

1 E. Jones (Australia), once by umpire J. Phillips in the second Test against England at Melbourne in 1897-98.

2 G.A.R. Lock (England), in the first Test against the West Indies at Kingston in 1953-54.

3 G.M. Griffin (South Africa), 11 times by umpire F.S. Lee in the second Test against England at Lord's in 1960. In England's only innings, Griffin claimed the only Test hat-trick achieved for South Africa when he took the wickets of M.J.K. Smith, P.M. Walker and F.S. Trueman.

4 Haseeb Ahsan (Pakistan), in the first Test against India at Bombay in 1960-61.

5 I. Meckiff (Australia), four times by umpire C.J. Egar in his only over in the first Test against South Africa at Brisbane in 1963-64.

6 S. Abid Ali, India, once by umpire F.R. Goodall in the second Test against New Zealand at Christchurch in 1967-68. He deliberately threw the ball in protest at the action of G.A. Bartlett who had not been 'called' for throwing.

HAT-TRICKS TO END A TEST

1 In the second Test between Australia and England at Melbourne in 1901-02, H. Trumble completed Australia's win by taking a hat-trick. He dismissed A.O. Jones, J.R. Gunn and S.F. Barnes. Australian won by 229 runs.

2 In the second Test between South Africa and Australia at Cape Town in 1957-58, L.F. Kline completed Australia's win when he did the hat-trick. He dismissed E.R.H. Fuller, H.J. Tayfield and N.A.T. Addock. Australia won by an innings and 141 runs.

Note: In the third Test between England and Pakistan at Leeds in 1971, P. Lever completed England's win by taking 3 wickets in four balls. He dismissed Wasim Bari, Asif Masood and Pervez Sajjad. England won by 25 runs.

BOWLING CURIOSITIES

1 J. Briggs (England), playing against South Africa at Cape Town in 1888-89, took all of his wickets unaided. He bowled 14 and trapped one lbw. His figures were 7 for 17 and 8 for 11.

2 W.W. Armstrong (Australia), playing against England at Nottingham in 1905, bowled off-breaks wide outside leg stump in an attempt to slow the scoring. From 204 consecutive balls, the England batsmen scored from only 25. Of the remaining 179 balls, only 19 were played by the batsmen, the other 160 being allowed to go through to the wicketkeeper.

3 T.J. Matthews (Australia) took a hat-trick in each innings of the match between Australia and South Africa at Manchester in 1912. This is the only instance of this kind in all Test cricket history. These 6 wickets were the only ones taken by Matthews in the match, and constituted over one-third of his Test career 'bag'.

4 W.W. Armstrong (Australia) became the first man in Test history to bowl two consecutive overs when he did so against England at Manchester in 1921. England closed its innings on the second day but, as the first day had been washed out, it was discovered that Australia was not left with sufficient batting time under the laws of cricket (as they stood). After some confusion, the England innings was resumed, and Armstrong, who had bowled the last over before the break, bowled the first one after it.

5 G.O.B. Allen (England) opened the bowling against Australia at Manchester in 1934 with a 13-ball over — three wides and four no-balls.

6 England's score of 7 (dec.) for 469 against South Africa at Durban in 1938-39 did not include a single maiden over (8-ball overs).

7 N.B.F. Mann (South Africa), making his debut against England at Nottingham in 1947, bowled eight consecutive maiden overs before giving up his first run in Test cricket.

8 A.M. Moir (New Zealand) equalled the record of W.W. Armstrong by sending down two consecutive overs. In the Test against England at Wellington in 1950-51, Moir bowled the last over before tea and then the first over after tea.

9 H.J. Tayfield (South Africa), while playing against New Zealand at Johannesburg in 1953-54, bowled 14 8-ball overs, 7 of which were maidens, for figures of 6 for 13. There were only nine scoring shots made from 112 balls.

10 H.J. Tayfield (South Africa), playing against England at Durban in 1956-57, bowled 16 consecutive (8-ball) maiden overs. He delivered 137 successive balls all told from which no runs were scored.

11 K.R. Miller (Australia) bowled unchanged before lunch on the first day of the match against England at Melbourne in 1954-55, for figures of 9-8-5-3. All 5 runs scored off Miller came in his fourth over.

12 S. Ramadhin (West Indies), playing against England at Lord's in 1950, bowled 10 consecutive maidens in the first innings, and 11 in the second.

13 In the Test between England and Australia at The Oval in 1882, the England bowlers E. Peate and R.G. Barlow delivered 14 consecutive maidens in Australia's first innings of 63. Peate's return for the innings was 24 maidens in 38 overs, while Barlow's 31 overs included 22 maidens.

14 In the third Test between the West Indies and England played at Bridgetown in the 1973-74 season, a total of 79 no-balls were bowled. With 20 runs scored off them, the bowlers had given away almost a century.

15 In the six-match Test series between Australia and England played in Australia in 1970-71, not one lbw appeal was upheld against an Australian batsman.

16 In the second innings of the Test between the West Indies and India at Bridgetown in 1961-62, L.R. Gibbs (West Indies) achieved figures of 53.3 overs, 37 maidens, 38 runs and 8 wickets. These included figures of 15.3-14-6-8 in the final session of the match.

17 In the Test between India and England played at Madras in 1963-64, R.G. Nadkarni bowled 21 consecutive maiden overs in the first innings, but didn't take a wicket. His first innings figures were 32-27-5-0. In the second innings, he took 2 for 6 off 6 overs (with 4 maidens).

18 H. Verity (England) bowled a Chinaman when he dismissed E.E. Achong (West Indies) in the second Test at Manchester in 1933.

19 Because of an umpiring error, J.T. Sparling (New Zealand) bowled an 11-ball over (excluding no-balls and wides) in the first Test against England at Auckland in 1962-63.

20 At Lord's in 1972, R.A.L. Massie (Australia) returned match figures of 16 for 137, 32.5-7-84-8 and 27.2-9-53-8. At Madras in 1987-88, N.D. Hirwani equalled this feat by taking 16 for 136, 18.3-3-61-8 and 15.2-3-75-8. This is the record for any bowler in his first Test. A.E. Trott and A.L. Valentine are the only other bowlers to have taken 8 wickets in an innings in their first Test.

MOST CONSECUTIVE MAIDENS

6-ball overs

1 21: R.G. Nadkarni, India v England, Madras, 1963-64. (He bowled 131 consecutive balls from which no runs were scored.)

2 15: M.C. Carew, West Indies v England, Port-of-Spain, 1967-68. (He bowled 90 consecutive balls from which no runs were scored.)

3 13: J.H. Wardle, England v South Africa, Nottingham, 1955.

4 11: J.A. Young, England v Australia, Nottingham, 1948.

5 11: S. Ramadhin, West Indies v England, Lord's, 1950 (second innings).

6 10: S. Ramadhin, West Indies v England, Lord's 1950 (first innings).

8-ball overs

1 16: H.J. Tayfield, South Africa v England, Durban 1956-57. (He bowled 137 consecutive balls from which no runs were scored.)

2 9: H.J. Tayfield, South Africa v Australia, Melbourne 1952-53.

LONG BOWLING SPELLS

1 The Australian bowlers G.E. Palmer (53-36-68-7) and E. Evans (57-32-64-3) bowled unchanged for the entire English innings of 133, scored in 190 minutes during the match between England and Australia played at Sydney in 1881-82.

2 T. Richardson, playing for England against Australia at Manchester in 1896, bowled unchanged for three hours in the second innings to try to stave off an England defeat. Richardson, a pace bowler, delivered 42.3 overs with 16 maidens, and took 6 for 76.

3 A.M.B. Brown (South Africa) bowled unchanged for 46 6-ball overs against England at Leeds in 1947, for figures of 46-12-89-1.

4 Ghulam Ahmed, playing for India against Pakistan at Dacca in 1954-55, bowled 40 overs unchanged on the first day, his figures being 40-8-84-4.

5 T.L. Goddard (South Africa) bowled 46 overs unchanged on the last day of the match against England at Leeds in 1955. His spell resulted in figures of 46-27-45-4.

6 H.J. Tayfield (South Africa) had an unchanged spell of 53.4-29-60-5 during England's second innings in the match played at The Oval in 1955.

7 T.R. Veivers (Australia) bowled 55 consecutive overs in the Test against England at Manchester in 1964. Veivers bowled 75 of the last 80 overs sent down from the city end.

GOOD BOWLING SPELLS

1 7 wickets for 1 run in 26 balls: Sarfraz Nawaz, Pakistan v Australia, Australia, 1978-79.

2 7 wickets for 8 runs in 22 balls: J.C. Laker, England v Australia, Manchester, 1956.

3 6 wickets for 6 runs in 45 balls: S. Haigh, England v South Africa, Cape Town, 1898-99.

4 7 wickets for 17 runs in 46 balls: M.A. Noble, Australia v England, Melbourne, 1901-02.

5 8 wickets for 7 runs in 49 balls: G.A. Lohmann, England v South Africa, Johannesburg, 1895-96.

6 6 wickets for 7 runs in 29 balls: S.J. Pegler, South Africa v England, Lord's, 1912.

7 5 wickets for 1 run in 17 balls: G.R. Hazlitt, Australia v England, The Oval, 1912.

8 5 wickets for 7 runs in 31 balls: E.P. Nupen, South Africa v England, Durban, 1927-28.

9 6 wickets for 11 runs in 24 balls: E.P. Nupen, South Africa v England, Johannesburg, 1930-31.

10 6 wickets for 8 runs in 36 balls: H. Ironmonger, Australia v South Africa, Adelaide, 1931-32.

11 6 wickets for 9 runs in 56 balls: C.V.Grimmett, Australia v South Africa, Adelaide, 1931-32.

12 5 wickets for 1 run in 28 balls: I.T. Botham, England v Australia, Birmingham, 1981.

13 5 wickets for 2 runs in 19 balls: E.R.H. Toshack, Australia v India, Brisbane, 1947-48.

MOST WIDES BY ONE BOWLER

1 8: B.J.T. Bosanquet, England v Australia, Leeds, 1905.

2 6: M.A. Noble, Australia v England, Leeds, 1905. 3 6: J.R. Watkins, Australia v Pakistan, Sydney, 1972-73.

INEXPENSIVE ANALYSES

1 25-19-18-0: Fazal Mahmood, Pakistan v India, Dacca, 1954-55.

2 28-17-21-2: A.H. Kardar, Pakistan v New Zealand, Dacca, 1955-56.

3 30-19-20-2: Khan Mohammad, Pakistan v New Zealand, Dacca, 1955-56.

4 32-27-5-0: R.G. Nadkarni, India v England, Madras 1963-64.

5 32-23-24 4: J.H. Wardle, England v South Africa, Nottingham, 1955.

6 36-23-27-3: J.C. Laker, England v New Zealand, Leeds, 1958.

7 45-28-48-4: A.L. Valentine, West Indies v England, Lord's 1950.

8 45-26-42-6: K.D. Mackay, Australia v Pakistan, Dacca, 1959-60.

9 46-24-43-1: W. Attewell, England v Australia, Sydney, 1891-92.

10 46.1-20-42-1: G.E. Gomez, West Indies v India, Port-of-Spain, 1952-53.

11 46.3-24-42-6: Zulfiqar Ahmed, Pakistan v New Zealand, Karachi, 1955-56.

12 47-29-42-5: H. Ironmonger, Australia v South Africa, Brisbane 1931-32.

13 47-28-39-3: C.V. Grimmett, Australia v England, Nottingham, 1934.

14 53-30-50-4: S. Ramadhin, West Indies v England, Bridgetown, 1953-54.

15 53.3-37-38-8: L.R. Gibbs, West Indies v India, Bridgetown, 1961-62.

16 54-38-43-4: B.W. Yuile, New Zealand v Pakistan, Auckland, 1964-65.

17 57-30-64-1: J.C. White, England v Australia, Melbourne, 1928-29.

18 61-34-71-1: M.H. Mankand, India v Pakistan, Peshawar, 1954-55.

19 61-32-51-3: W. Attewell, England v Australia, Melbourne, 1891-92.

20 62-37-69-4: T.L. Goddard, South Africa v England, Leeds, 1955.

21 62-35-61-1: D.S. Atkinson, West Indies v Pakistan, Bridgetown, 1957-58.

22 69-34-79-2: D.R. Doshi, India v New Zealand, Auckland, 1980-81.

23 71-47-79-3: A.L. Valentine, West Indies v England, Lord's, 1950.

24 72-43-86-6: S. Ramadhin, West Indies v England, Lord's, 1950.

25 76-47-58-4: M.H. Mankad, India v England, Delhi, 1951-52.

26 81-36-105-5: G. Geary, England v Australia, Melbourne, 1928-29.

All the above instances concerned 6-ball overs.

EXPENSIVE ANALYSES

1 87-11-298-1: L.O. Fleetwood-Smith, Australia v England, The Oval, 1938.

2 80.2-13-266-5: O.C. Smith, West Indies v England, Kingston, 1929-30.

3 54-5-259-0: Khan Mohammad Pakistan v West Indies, Kingston, 1957-58.

4 85.2-20-247-2: Fazal Mahmood, Pakistan v West Indies, Kingston, 1957-58.

5 70-10-229-1: S.L. Boock, New Zealand v Pakistan, Auckland, 1988-89.

6 82-17-228-5: M.H. Mankad, India v West Indies, Kingston, 1952-53.

7 64.2-8-226-6: B.S. Bedi, India v England, Lord's, 1974.

8 38.4-3-220-7: Kapil Dev, India v Pakistan, Faisalabad, 1982-83.

9 54-7-217-3: I.T. Botham, England v Pakistan, The Oval, 1987.

10 71-8-204-6: I.A.R. Peebles, England v Australia, The Oval, 1930.

11 75-16-202-3: M.H. Mankad, India v West Indies, Bombay, 1948-49.

12 84-19-202-6: Haseeb Ahsan, Pakistan v India, Madras, 1960-61.

WICKETKEEPING CURIOSITIES

1 In the first-ever Test between England and South Africa, played at Port Elizabeth in March 1889, both wicketkeepers were at one stage off the field.

South Africa's W.H. Milton deputised for the regular keeper F.W. Smith in England's second innings, while M.P. Bowden filled in for H. Wood when he was unavailable.

Ironically, deputy Milton was caught behind by deputy Bowden.

2 In the first Test between England and New Zealand at Lord's in 1986, four different players shared the wicketkeeping duties for England in the New Zealand first innings. The selected keeper, B.N. French, was injured while batting. C.W.J. Athey kept wickets for the first two overs before handing over the gloves to R.W.

Taylor (substitute). After a further 74 overs, R.J. Parks (substitute) took over the gloves until the end of the 140th over of the innings. B.N. French then returned and kept wicket for the remainder of the innings — namely, one ball!

WICKETKEEPERS WHO HAVE OPENED THE BOWLING IN A TEST MATCH

1 C.L. Walcott (West Indies) opened the bowling in England's second innings at Manchester in 1950, replacing the injured H.H.H. Johnson. R.J. Christiani deputised behind the stumps, while Walcott bowled four overs without success.

BOUNDARY CURIOSITIES

1 E.H. Hendren (England), playing against Australia at Brisbane in 1928-29, scored an eight (including four overthrows) from the bowling of P.M. Hornibrook.

2 G.S. Sobers (West Indies) hit 10 fours in an innings of 43 in the Test against Australia at Bridgetown in 1954-55. His other scoring shots consisted of 3 singles.

3 J.H. Edrich (England) scored 238 in boundary hits (5 sixes and 52 fours) in the match against New Zealand at Leeds in 1965. His final score was 310*. Edrich is the only batsman to accumulate more than 200 runs through boundaries in a Test innings.

4 K.H. Weekes (West Indies), playing against England at The Oval in 1939, scored 4 successive fours from the bowling of R.T.D. Perks.

5 D.T. Lindsay (South Africa) scored 5 successive fours from the bowling of J.W. Gleeson in the match against Australia at Port Elizabeth in 1969-70.

6 R.E. Redmond (New Zealand) scored 5 successive fours from the bowling of Majid J. Khan in the match against Pakistan at Auckland in 1972-73.

7 D.W. Hookes (Australia) scored 5 successive fours from the bowling of A.W. Greig in the match against England at Melbourne in 1976-77.

8 S.M. Patil (India) scored 6 successive fours from the bowling of R.G.D. Willis in the match against England at Manchester in 1982.

9 B. Sutcliffe (New Zealand) hit 4 sixes (3 in four balls) off one 8-ball over bowled by H.J. Tayfield in the match against South Africa at Johannesburg in 1953-54.

10 F.S. Trueman (England) hit 3 sixes from one 6-ball over bowled by S. Ramadhin in the match against the West Indies at Lord's in 1957.

11 W.R. Hammond (England) hit 3 successive sixes from the bowling of J. Newman in the match against New Zealand at Auckland in 1932-33.

12 W. Voce (England) hit 3 sixes from four balls bowled by A.E. Hall in the match against South Africa at Johannesburg in 1930-31.

13 R.C. Motz (New Zealand) hit 3 sixes from five balls bowled by D.A. Allen in the match against England at Dunedin in 1965-66.

14 A.M.E. Roberts (West Indies) hit 3 sixes and a four from five balls bowled by I.T. Botham in the match against England at Port-of-Spain in 1980-81.

15 S.T. Clarke (West Indies) hit 3 sixes from three successive balls bowled by Mohammad Nazir in the match against Pakistan played at Faisalabad in 1980-81.

16 I.V.A. Richards (West Indies), in making 145 against England at Lord's in 1980, hit 106 runs in boundaries — 25 fours and 1 six.

17 B.L. Cairns (New Zealand) hit 3 sixes in one over off the bowling of D.R. Parry in the match against the West Indies at Dunedin in 1979-80.

18 Intikhab Alam (Pakistan) hit 11 fours in his score of 48 against Australia at Melbourne in 1972-73.

19 Kapil Dev (India) scored 70 runs from boundaries in an innings of 89 during the match against England at Lord's in 1982. He hit 13 fours and 3 sixes.

20 Kapil Dev (India) hit 4 successive sixes off the last four balls of an over from E.E. Hemmings to avoid the follow-on in the match against England at Lord's in 1990.

ALPHABETICAL TEAMS

After studying the information in this book, one cannot help wondering what great teams could be assembled if different cricketers from different countries and times were available for selection. And so, just for fun — and as an exercise in team selection — we have compiled 'Alphabetical Teams', based on the players' surnames. In doing so, we have produced some very interesting combinations!

We soon found that selecting a Test team was much more difficult than first expected. How can one compare the career performances of John Briggs and Bishen Bedi, or the batting deeds of J.T. Tyldesley and the latest prodigy, Sachin Tendulkar? There were some hard decisions to make, but in all cases we strived to select the best-balanced team to play in all types of conditions.

Which of these teams would you back? Do you agree with our selections? Should Alexander or Ames be the wicketkeeper for the 'A' team, and why did we leave Bardsley, Butcher, Blyth and Briggs out of the 'Bs'? Which players would you choose? Let's have a quick look at the line-ups:

The 'A's: One of the strongest teams. The bowling has hostility and variety. The batting has depth with all players through to Ames, the wicketkeeper, at No. 7, having scored Test centuries.

The 'B's: A difficult team to beat. The batting has a perfect mix of stroke-players and defenders. The attack has variety and penetration, with Barlow and Border a bonus.

The 'C's: Another of the strong teams, with the batting going to No. 8. Once again, the attack has a hostile new-ball battery, with plenty of variety to back it up.

The 'D's: Another powerful batting line-up that goes down to No. 9; however, this combination may struggle to bowl some of the better teams out.

The 'E's: This side would struggle against some of the more powerful opposition, although the batting looks stronger than the bowling, and there is no problem with the wicketkeeping or fielding.

The 'F's: Not in the silk department, but a more than useful outfit, just the same. Runs would be scored quickly, while the bowlers would be hard to keep out.

The 'G's: One of the favourites. An outstanding all-round team with a superbly balanced attack, top-quality batting and excellent wicketkeeping and fielding.

The 'H's: This outfit is almost unbeatable. Hanif will keep and bat at No. 7, and that thought would be enough to break any bowler's heart. The all pace attack would be capable of breaking through the strongest batting line-up.

The 'I's: This is not likely to be one of the stronger teams. The spin attack could pose some problems while Imran would be required to carry the pace department.

The 'J's: Batting is the strength of this outfit with the Jacksons leading the way. The attack does have variety, but Jones is the only bowler with real pace.

The 'K's: Other teams look classier than this one. It does, however, bat right down the order, with Knott at No. 9 and Knight at No. 10 being century-makers. Kapil Dev would be required to carry the attack.

The 'L's: This is a team to contend with, with its solid opening batsmen, dashing stroke-players and a lethal attack. There would not be many batsmen lining-up to open the innings against the likes of Larwood, Lillee and Lindwall.

The 'Mc's: The Australian influence is to the fore in this team. The batting has a balance of soundness and flair while the pace attack is aggressive.

The 'M's: Another one of the favourites. The batting is all class and should score heavily. The bowling doesn't have the same quality as the batting, but it is still strong enough to bowl out the opposition.

The 'N's: A team not likely to trouble the toughest teams; however, any side that is led by 'Monty' Noble should not be taken lightly.

The 'O's: This team would be down the table, but 'Tiger' O'Reilly would make sure the opposition earned each and every run.

The 'P's and 'Q's: One of the surprise packets. Not too many 'Q's have played Test cricket, but Qasim Omar deserves his place at No. 3 in this powerful line-up.

The 'R's: The strength of this team is the batting. Runs would be scored quickly and with elegance. Reid (who did his share of bowling) would be required to wicketkeep here. Rhodes and Richardson were two of the finest bowlers ever to play for England.

The 'S's: Another of the strong teams, comprised of a superb batting line-up supported by a pace quartet of the highest standard that could capture wickets under any conditions.

The 'T's: The batting may be a little thin, but the bowling is the opposite. Some of these champions would have to wait patiently to get a turn at the crease. Close-to-the-wicket catching would be another strength.

The 'U's and 'V's: A team that would struggle, but it should not be discounted entirely. What about the array of left-armers: Underwood, Valentine, and Verity would be hard to get away.

The 'W's: Another of the strong combinations. Walcott could bat anywhere from 1 to 7, but in this team he would have to be satisfied with the latter and taking the gloves. Wasim Akram and Wardle provide variety to a more than useful attack.

The 'X,Y,Z's: Not a particularly competitive team, but there weren't many players to select from.

The 'Left-Overs': Several quality 'left-over' sides could have been selected, but this one is a more than useful line-up.

And now for the teams:

A

1	D.L. Amiss	England
2	R. Abel	England
3	M. Amarnath	India
4	M. Azharuddin	India
5	Asif Iqbal	Pakistan
6	W.W. Armstrong	Australia (Capt.)
7	L.E.G.Ames	England (WK)
8	Abdul Qadir	Pakistan
9.	C.E.L. Ambrose	West Indies
10	N.A.T. Adcock	South Africa
11	T.M. Alderman	Australia

B

1	G. Boycott	England
2	E.J. Barlow	South Africa
3	D.G. Bradman	Australia (Capt.)
4	K.F. Barrington	England
5	A.R. Border	Australia
6	I.T. Botham	England
7	R. Benaud	Australia
8	A.V. Bedser	England
9	J.McC. Blackham	Australia (WK)
10	B.S. Bedi	India
11	S.F. Barnes	England

C

1	M.C. Cowdrey	England
2	H.L. Collins	Australia
3	I.M. Chappell	Australia (Capt.)
4	G.S. Chappell	Australia
5	D.C.S. Compton	England
6	M.D. Crowe	New Zealand
7	H.B. Cameron	South Africa (WK)
8	L.N. Constantine	West Indies
9	C.E.H. Croft	West Indies
10	A. Cotter	Australia
11	B.S.Chandrasekhar	India

D

1	R.A.Duff	Australia
2	C.S.Dempster	New Zealand
3	E.R. Dexter	England
4	J. Darling	Australia (Capt.)
5	M.P Donnelly	New Zealand
6	K.S. Duleepsinhji	England
7	P.J.L. Dujon	West Indies (WK)
8	B.L. D'Oliveira	England
9	A.K. Davidson	Australia
10	G.R. Dilley	England
11	D.R. Doshi	India

E

1 B.A. Edgar New Zealand
2 F.M. Engineer India
3 J.H. Edrich England (Capt.)
4 W.J. Edrich England
5 W.R. Endean South Africa
6 R. Edwards Australia
7 T.G. Evans England (WK)
8 J.E. Emburey England
9 P.H. Edmonds England
10 R.M. Ellison England
11 Ehtesham-ud-din Pakistan

F

1 R.C. Fredericks West Indies
2 J.H.W. Fingleton Australia
3 C.B. Fry England (Capt.)
4 R.E. Foster England
5 K.W.R. Fletcher England
6 A.G. Fairfax Australia
7 G.A. Faulkner South Africa
8 G.M. Fullerton South Africa (WK)
9 Fazal Mahmood Pakistan
10 J.J. Ferris England/Australia
11 A.P. Freeman England

G

1 S.M. Gavaskar India
2 C.G. Greenidge West Indies
3 W.G. Grace England (Capt.)
4 D.I. Gower England
5 T.L. Goddard South Africa
6 J.M. Gregory Australia
7 G. Giffen Australia
8 A.W.T. Grout Australia (WK)
9 J. Garner West Indies
10 L.R. Gibbs West Indies
11 C.V. Grimmett Australia

H

1 J.B. Hobbs England
2 L. Hutton England (Capt.)
3 R.N. Harvey Australia
4 W.R. Hammond England
5 G.A. Headley West Indies
6 C. Hill Australia
7 Hanif Mohammad Pakistan (WK)
8 R.J. Hadlee New Zealand
9 M.A. Holding West Indies
10 G.L. Hirst England
11 W.W. Hall WestIndies

I

1 F.A. Iredale Australia
2 Imtiaz Ahmed Pakistan (WK)
3 B.L. Irvine South Africa
4 Ijaz Ahmed Pakistan
5 D.J. Insole England
6 Imran Khan Pakistan
7 R. Illingworth England (Capt.)
8 Intikhab Alam Pakistan
9 Iqbal Qasim Pakistan
10 J.B. Iverson Australia
11 H. Ironmonger Australia

J

1 A. Jackson Australia
2 T.W. Jarvis New Zealand
3 D.R. Jardine England (Capt.)
4 Javed Miandad Pakistan
5 D.M. Jones Australia
6 Hon. F.S. Jackson England
7 G.L. Jessop England
8 I.W. Johnson Australia
9 B.N. Jarman Australia (WK)
10 E. Jones Australia
11 W.A. Johnston Australia

K

1 D.S.B.P Kuruppu Sri Lanka
2 B.K. Kunderan India
3 R.B. Kanhai West Indies
4 A.I. Kallicharran West Indies
5 A.F. Kippax Australia
6 A.G. Kripal Singh India
7 Kapil Dev India (Capt.)
8 C. Kelleway Australia
9 A.P.E. Knott England (WK)
10 B.R. Knight England
11 L.F. Kline Australia

L

1 W.M. Lawry Australia
2 B.W. Luckhurst England
3 M. Leyland England
4 C.H. Lloyd West Indies (Capt.)
5 A.J. Lamb England
6 D.T. Lindsay South Africa (WK)
7 R.R. Lindwall Australia

8	H. Larwood	England
9	D.K. Lillee	Australia
10	G.A. Lohmann	England
11	J.C. Laker	England

Mc, Mac

1	C.C. McDonald	Australia
2	D.J. McGlew	South Africa
3	C.G. Macartney	Australia
4	S.J. McCabe	Australia
5	A.C. MacLaren	England (Capt.)
6	K.D. Mackay	Australia
7	C.L. McCool	Australia
8	J.A. Maclean	Australia (WK)
9	C.J. McDermott	Australia
10	G.D. McKenzie	Australia
11	E.A. McDonald	Australia

M

1	A.R. Morris	Australia
2	W.L. Murdoch	Australia
3	B. Mitchell	South Africa
4	P.B.H. May	England (Capt.)
5	C.P. Mead	England
6	Mushtaq Mohammad	Pakistan
7	K.R. Miller	Australia
8	M.H. Mankad	India
9	R.W. Marsh	Australia (WK)
10	M.D. Marshall	West Indies
11	A.A. Mailey	Australia

N

1	Nazar Mohammad	Pakistan
2	A.W. Nourse	South Africa
3	A.D. Nourse	South Africa
4	S.M. Nurse	West Indies
5	M.A. Noble	Australia (Capt.)
6	R.G. Nadkarni	India
7	Nasim-Ul-Ghani	Pakistan
8	M.S. Nichols	England
9	R.K. Nunes	West Indies (WK)
10	E.P. Nupen	South Africa
11	J.M. Noreiga	West Indies

O

1	L.P.J. O'Brien	Australia
2	H.G. Owen-Smith	South Africa (Capt.)
3	N.C. O'Neill	Australia
4	N. Oldfield	England
5	S. O'Linn	South Africa
6	J. O'Connor	England
7	C.M. Old	England
8	K.J. O'Keeffe	Australia
9	W.A.S.Oldfield	Australia (WK)
10	J.D.A. O'Connor	Australia
11	W.J. O'Reilly	Australia

P & Q

1	W.H. Ponsford	Australia
2	G. Pullar	England
3	Qasim Omar	Pakistan
4	R.G. Pollock	South Africa
5	Pataudi, Nawab of Jnr.	India (Capt.)
6	E. Paynter	England
7	J.M. Parks	England (WK)
8	M.J. Procter	South Africa
9	P.M. Pollock	South Africa
10	R. Peel	England
11	E.A.S. Prasanna	India

R

1	B.A. Richards	South Africa
2	I.R. Redpath	Australia
3	R.B. Richardson	West Indies
4	I.V.A. Richards	West Indies (Capt.)
5	K.S. Ranjitsinhji	England
6	C.A.G. Russell	England
7	J.R. Reid	New Zealand (WK)
8	W. Rhodes	England
9	A.M.E. Roberts	West Indies
10	T. Richardson	England
11	S. Ramadhin	West Indies

S

1	H. Sutcliffe	England
2	R.B. Simpson	Australia
3	B. Sutcliffe	New Zealand
4	A. Shrewsbury	England (Capt.)
5	G.S. Sobers	Indies
7	P.W. Sherwell	South Africa (WK)
8	J.A. Snow	England
9	Sarfraz Nawaz	Pakistan
10	J.B. Statham	England
11	F.R. Spofforth	Australia

T

1	G.M. Turner	New Zealand
2	M.A. Taylor	Australia
3	V.T. Trumper	Australia
4	H.W. Taylor	South Africa (Capt.)

5 S.R. Tendulkar India
6 M.W. Tate England
7 D. Tallon Australia (WK)
8 H. Trumble Australia
9 H.J. Tayfield South Africa
10 F.S. Trueman England
11 C.T.B. Turner Australia

U & V

1 P.G.V. Van Der Bijl South Africa
2 H.G. Vivian New Zealand
3 D.B. Vengsarkar India
4 G.R. Vishwanath India
5 K.G. Viljoen South Africa (WK)
6 P.R. Umrigar India (Capt.)
7 G. Ulyett England
8 W. Voce England
9 H. Verity England
10 D.L. Underwood England
11 A.L. Valentine West Indies

W

1 W.M. Woodfull Australia
2 C. Washbrook England
3 E.D. Weekes West Indies
4 F.M.M. Worrell West Indies (Capt.)
5 F.E. Woolley England
6 K.D. Walters Australia
7 C.L. Walcott West Indies (WK)
8 Wasim Akram Pakistan
9 M.H.N. Walker Australia
10 J.H. Wardle England
11 R.G.D. Willis England

X,Y & Z

1 J.W. Zulch South Africa
2 Yashpal Sharma India
3 Zaheer Abbas Pakistan
4 G.N. Yallop Australia
5 Younis Ahmed Pakistan
6 N.W.D. Yardley England (Capt.)
7 T.J. Zoehrer Australia (WK)
8 B. Yardley Australia
9 N.S. Yadav India
10 Zulfiqar Ahmed Pakistan
11 H.I. Young England

The LEFT-OVERS

1 G.A. Gooch England
2 C.C. Hunte West Indies
3 W. Bardsley Australia
4 V.S. Hazare India
5 E.H. Hendren England
6 A.L. Hassett Australia (Capt.)
7 A.W. Greig England
8 Wasim Bari Pakistan (WK)
9 J.R. Thomson Australia
10 F.H. Tyson England
11 G.A.R. Lock England

A TEAM OF PLAYERS WHO APPEARED IN ONLY ONE TEST

* Figures represent each player's Test match figures)

		BATTING		BOWLING	
		1st	2nd	1st	2nd
1	A.G. Ganteaume (WI)	112	-	-	-
2	R.E. Redmond (NZ)	107	-	-	-
3	V.H. Stollmeyer (WI)	96	-	-	-
4	N. Oldfield (E)	80	19	-	-
5	Patiala, Yuvaraj (I) Capt.	24	60	-	-
6	Azmat Rana (P)	49	-	-	-
7	G.B. Street (E)	4	7*	1 STUMPING	
8	M.F. Malone (A)	46	-	5-63	1-14
9	L.J. Johnson (A)	25*	-	3-66	3-8
10	G.A. Chevalier (SA)	0	0*	3-68	2-32
11	C.S. Marriott (E)	0	-	5-37	6-59

A TEAM OF PLAYERS WHO APPEARED IN ONLY TWO TESTS

*Figures represent each player's Test career figures

		RUNS	H.S.	BATTING AVE.	WKTS	BOWLING AVE.
1	S.K. Coen (SA)	101	41*	50.50	-	-
2	R.J. Hartigaan (A)	170	116	42.50	-	-
3	K.H. Weekes (WI)	173	137	57.66	-	-
4	R.G. Gregory (A) Capt.	153	80	51.00	-	-
5.	C. Ramaswami (I)	10	60	56.66	-	-
6	R.E. Grieveson (SA)	114	75	57.00	-	-
7	I.L. Mendonca (WI) WK	81	78	40.50	8 Catches, 2 stumpings	
8	H.I Young (E)	43	43	21.50	12	21.83
9	H.J. Butler (E)	15	15*	15.00	12	17.91
10	T.K. Kendall (A)	39	17*	13.00	14	15.35
11	F. Martin (E)	14	13	7.00	14	10.07

PART 3
TEST MATCH RESULTS & RECORDS

Summary of Tests

SUMMARY OF ALL TEST MATCHES 1876-77 TO 1992

			won by									
	Opponent	Tests	A	E	SA	WI	NZ	I	P	SL	Tied	Drawn
Australia	v England	274	104	88	-	-	-	-	-	-	-	82
	v South Africa	53	29	-	11	-	-	-	-	-	-	13
	v West Indies	72	29	-	-	24	-	-	-	-	1	18
	v New Zealand	26	10	-	-	-	6	-	-	-	-	10
	v India	50	23	-	-	-	-	8	-	-	1	18
	v Pakistan	34	12	-	-	-	-	-	9	-	-	13
	v Sri Lanka	7	4	-	-	-	-	-	-	0	-	3
England	v South Africa	102	-	46	18	-	-	-	-	-	-	38
	v West Indies	104	-	24	-	43	-	-	-	-	-	37
	v New Zealand	72	-	33	-	-	4	-	-	-	-	35
	v India	78	-	31	-	-	-	11	-	-	-	36
	v Pakistan	52	-	14	-	-	-	-	7	-	-	31
	v Sri Lanka	4	-	3	-	-	-	-	-	0	-	1
South Africa	v New Zealand	17	-	-	9	-	2	-	-	-	-	6
	v West Indies	1	-	-	0	1	-	-	-	-	-	0
West Indies	v New Zealand	24	-	-	-	8	4	-	-	-	-	12
	v India	62	-	-	-	26	-	6	-	-	-	30
	v Pakistan	28	-	-	-	10	-	-	7	-	-	11
New Zealand	v India	31	-	-	-	-	6	12	-	-	-	13
	v Pakistan	32	-	-	-	-	3	-	13	-	-	16
	v Sri Lanka	9	-	-	-	-	4	-	-	0	-	5
India	v Pakistan	44	-	-	-	-	-	4	7	-	-	33
	v Sri Lanka	8	-	-	-	-	-	3	-	1	-	4
Pakistan	v Sri Lanka	12	-	-	-	-	-	-	6	1	-	5
		1196	211	238	38	112	29	44	49	2	2	470

	Tests	Won	Lost	Drawn	Tied	Toss Won
Australia	516	211	146	157	2	259
England	686	239	187	260	-	339
South Africa	173	38	78	57	-	81
West Indies	291	112	70	108	1	152
New Zealand	211	29	85	97	-	105
India	273	44	94	134	1	135
Pakistan	202	49	44	109	-	104
Sri Lanka	40	2	20	18	-	21
	1196	724	724	940	4	1196

The Grounds

TEST MATCH GROUNDS

The Tests played at the Khettamara Stadium, Colombo and the Tyrone Fernando Stadium, Moratura have lifted the number of Test match grounds to 67. Colombo has now used four grounds, Johannesburg and Bombay three apiece, whilst Brisbane, Durban, Madras and Lahore have each played Test matches on two different grounds. For these seven cities the exact ground is denoted by a superscript numeral (e.g. Brisbane[1]) except for Colombo, where the ground is shown in brackets. This key to this numeral is given in the tables below. The tables show the full title, date of the first day's play and number of Tests staged for each ground.

Test Match Centres	Grounds	First Test Match Day	No.of Tests
AUSTRALIA			(268)
Adelaide	Adelaide Oval	12 Dec 1884	50
Brisbane	[1]Exhibition Ground (1928-29 to 1930-31)	30 Nov 1928	2
	[2]Woolloongabba	27 Nov 1931	34
Hobart	Bellerive Oval	16 Dec 1989	1
Melbourne	Melbourne Cricket Ground	15 Mar 1877	84
Perth	Western Australia Cricket Association (WACA) Ground	11 Dec 1970	19
Sydney	Sydney Cricket Ground (No.1)	17 Feb 1882	78
ENGLAND			(347)
Birmingham	Edgbaston	29 May 1902	29
Leeds	Headingley	29 Jun 1899	54
Lord's, London	Lord's Cricket Ground	21 Jul 1884	89
Manchester	Old Trafford	†10 Jul 1884	59
Nottingham	Trent Bridge	1 Jun 1899	40
The Oval, London	Kennington Oval	6 Sep 1880	75
Sheffield	Bramall Lane	3 Jul 1902	1
SOUTH AFRICA			(98)
Cape Town	Newlands	25 Mar 1889	24
Durban	[1]Lord's (1909-10 to 1921-22)	21 Jan 1910	4
	[2]Kingsmead	18 Jan 1923	19
Johannesburg	[1]Old Wanderers (1895-96 to 1938-39)	2 Mar 1896	22
	[2]Ellis Park (1948-49 to 1953-54)	27 Dec 1948	6
	[3]Wanderers Stadium	24 Dec 1956	11
Port Elizabeth	St George's Park	12 Mar 1889	12
WEST INDIES			(126)
Bridgetown, Barbados	Kensington Oval	11 Jan 1930	28
Georgetown, Guyana	Bourda	21 Feb 1930	22
Kingston, Jamaica	Sabina Park	3 Apr 1930	29
Port-of-Spain, Trinidad	Queen's Park Oval	1 Feb 1930	41
St John's, Antigua	Recreation Ground	27 Mar 1981	6
NEW ZEALAND			(102)
Auckland	Eden Park	#14 Feb 1930	34
Christchurch	Lancaster Park	10 Jan 1930	30
Dunedin	Carisbrook	11 Mar 1955	8
Hamilton	Trust Bank Park	22 Feb 1991	1
Napier	McLean Park	16 Feb 1979	2
Wellington	Basin Reserve	24 Jan 1930	27

INDIA			(146)
Ahmedabad	Gujarat Stadium	12 Nov 1983	2
Bangalore	Karnataka State Cricket Association Stadium (Chinnaswamy Stadium)	22 Nov 1974	9
Bombay	[1]Gymkhana (1933-34 Only)	15 Dec 1933	1
	[2]Brabourne Stadium (1948-49 to 1972-73)	9 Dec 1948	17
	[3]Wankhede Stadium	23 Jan 1975	13
Calcutta	Eden Gardens	5 Jan 1934	26
Chandigarh	Sector 16 Stadium	23 Nov 1990	1
Cuttack	Barabati Stadium	4 Jan 1987	1
Delhi	Feroz Shah Kotla	10 Nov 1948	22
Hyderabad (Deccan)	Fateh Maidan (Lal Bahadur Stadium)	19 Nov 1955	3
Jaipur	Sawai Mansingh Stadium	21 Feb 1987	1
Jullundur	Burlton Park	24 Sep 1983	1
Kanpur	Green Park (Modi Stadium)	12 Jan 1952	16
Lucknow	University Ground	23 Oct 1952	1
Madras	[1]Chepauk (Chidambaram Stadium)	10 Feb 1934	20
	[2]Corporation (Nehru) Stadium (1955-56 to 1964-65)	6 Jan 1956	9
Nagpur	Vidarbha Cricket Association Ground	3 Oct 1969	3
PAKISTAN			(94)
Bahawalpur	Dring Stadium	15 Jan 1955	1
Dacca	Dacca Stadium	1 Jan 1955	7
Faisalabad	Iqbal Stadium	16 Oct 1978	16
Gujranwala	Municipal Stadium	20 Dec 1991	1
Hyderabad (Sind)	Niaz Stadium	16 Mar 1973	5
Karachi	National Stadium	26 Feb 1955	30
Lahore	[1]Lawrence Gardens (Bagh-i-Jinnah) (1954-55 to 1958-59)	29 Jan 1955	3
	[2]Lahore (Gaddafi) Stadium	21 Nov 1959	25
Multan	Ibn-e-Qasim Bagh Stadium	30 Dec 1980	1
Peshawar	Services Club Ground	13 Feb 1955	1
Rawalpindi	Pindi Club Ground	27 Mar 1965	1
Sialkot	Jinnah Stadium	27 Oct 1985	3
SRI LANKA			(15)
Colombo	P.Saravanamuttu Stadium (PSS)	17 Feb 1982	3
	Sinhalese Sports Club Ground (SSC)	16 Mar 1984	4
	Colombo Cricket Club Ground (CCC)	24 Mar 1984	2
	Khettamara Stadium (KS)	28 Aug 1992	1
Kandy	Asgiriya Stadium	22 Apr 1983	4
Moratuwa	Tyrone Fernando Stadium	8 Sep 1992	1

† Rain prevented play until 11 July 1884. # Rain prevented play until 17 February 1930.
The 1890 and 1938 Tests at Manchester, the 1970-71 Third Test at Melbourne, the 1988-89 Test at Dunedin and the 1989-90 Test at Georgetown, all abandoned without a ball being bowled, plus the cancelled 1980-81 Second Test at Georgetown are excluded from these figures.

RECORD TOTALS FOR EACH TEST MATCH GROUND

Centre	**Highest Total**			**Lowest Total**		
Adelaide	674	Australia v India	1947-48	82	Australia v West Indies	1951-52
Brisbane[1]	558	Australia v West Indies	1930-31	66	Australia v England	1928-29
Brisbane[2]	645	Australia v England	1946-47	58	Australia v England	1936-37
				58	India v Australia	1947-48
Hobart	513-5d	Australia v Sri Lanka	1989-90	216	Sri Lanka v Australia	1989-90
Melbourne	604	Australia v England	1936-37	36	South Africa v Australia	1931-32
Perth	592-8d	England v Australia	1986-87	62	Pakistan v Australia	1981-82
Sydney	659-8d	Australia v England	1946-47	42	Australia v England	1887-88

Centre		Highest Total			Lowest Total	
Birmingham	633-5d	England v India	1979	30	South Africa v England	1924
Leeds	601-7d	Australia v England	1989	67	New Zealand v England	1958
Lord's	729-6d	Australia v England	1930	42	India v England	1974
Manchester	656-8d	Australia v England	1964	58	India v England	1952
Nottingham	658-8d	England v Australia	1938	88	South Africa v England	1960
The Oval	903-7d	England v Australia	1938	44	Australia v England	1896
Sheffield	289	Australia v England	1902	145	England v Australia	1902
Cape Town	559-9d	England v South Africa	1938-39	35	South Africa v England	1898-99
Durban[1]	450	England v South Africa	1913-14	111	South Africa v England	1913-14
Durban[2]	654-5	England v South Africa	1938-39	75	Australia v South Africa	1949-50
Johannesburg[1]	482	England v South Africa	1895-96	85	South Africa v Australia	1902-03
Johannesburg[2]	608	England v South Africa	1948-49	79	New Zealand v South Africa	1953-54
Johannesburg[3]	620	South Africa v Australia	1966-67	72	South Africa v England	1956-57
Port Elizabeth	549-7d	Australia v South Africa	1949-50	30	South Africa v England	1895-96
Bridgetown	668	Australia v West Indies	1954-55	94	New Zealand v West Indies	1984-85
Georgetown	569	West Indies v Australia	1990-91	109	West Indies v Australia	1972-73
Kingston	849	England v West Indies	1929-30	97†	India v West Indies	1975-76
Port-of-Spain	681-8d	West Indies v England	1953-54	90	Australia v West Indies	1977-78
St John's	550	West Indies v India	1982-83	154	England v West Indies	1989-90
Auckland	616-5d	Pakistan v New Zealand	1988-89	26	New Zealand v England	1954-55
Christchurch	560-8d	England v New Zealand	1932-33	65	New Zealand v England	1970-71
Dunedin	507-6d	Pakistan v New Zealand	1972-73	74	New Zealand v West Indies	1955-56
Hamilton	374-6d	New Zealand v Sri Lanka	1990-91	253	Sri Lanka v New Zealand	1990-91
Napier	402	New Zealand v Pakistan	1978-79	360	Pakistan v New Zealand	1978-79
Wellington	671-4	New Zealand v Sri Lanka	1990-91	42	New Zealand v Australia	1945-46
Ahmedabad	395	Pakistan v India	1986-87	103	India v West Indies	1983-84
Bangalore	457-5d	India v Australia	1979-80	116	Pakistan v India	1986-87
Bombay[1]	438	England v India	1933-34	219	India v England	1933-34
Bombay[2]	629-6d	West Indies v India	1948-49	88	India v New Zealand	1964-65
Bombay[3]	604-6d	West Indies v India	1974-75	102	England v India	1981-82
Calcutta	614-5d	West Indies v India	1958-59	90	India v West Indies	1983-84
Chandigarh	288	India v Sri Lanka	1990-91	82	Sri Lanka v India	1990-91
Cuttack	400	India v Sri Lanka	1986-87	142	Sri Lanka v India	1986-87
Delhi	644-8d	West Indies v India	1958-59	75	India v West Indies	1987-88
Hyderabad	498-4d	India v New Zealand	1955-56	89	India v New Zealand	1969-70
Jaipur	465-8d	India v Pakistan	1986-87	341	Pakistan v India	1986-87
Jullundur	374	India v Pakistan	1983-84	337	Pakistan v India	1983-84
Kanpur	676-7	India v Sri Lanka	1986-87	105	Australia v India	1959-60
Lucknow	331	Pakistan v India	1952-53	106	India v Pakistan	1952-53
Madras[1]	652-7d	England v India	1984-85	83	India v England	1976-77
Madras[2]	539-9d	India v Pakistan	1960-61	138	India v Australia	1959-60
Nagpur	451-6d	India v Sri Lanka	1986-87	109	India v New Zealand	1969-70
Bahawalpur	312-9d	Pakistan v India	1954-55	235	India v Pakistan	1954-55
Dacca	439	England v Pakistan	1961-62	70	New Zealand v Pakistan	1955-56
Faisalabad	674-6	Pakistan v India	1984-85	53	West Indies v Pakistan	1986-87
Gujranwala	109-2	Pakistan v Sri Lanka	1991-92		no instance	
Hyderabad	581-3d	Pakistan v India	1982-83	189	India v Pakistan	1982-83
				189	New Zealand v Pakistan	1984-85
Karachi	565-9d	Pakistan v New Zealand	1976-77	80	Australia v Pakistan	1956-57
Lahore[1]	561	Pakistan v New Zealand	1955-56	104	Pakistan v West Indies	1958-59
Lahore[2]	699-5	Pakistan v India	1989-90	77	Pakistan v West Indies	1986-87
Multan	249	West Indies v Pakistan	1980-81	166	Pakistan v West Indies	1980-81
Peshawar	245	India v Pakistan	1954-55	182	Pakistan v India	1954-55

Centre		Highest Total			Lowest Total	
Rawalpindi	318	Pakistan v New Zealand	1964-65	79	New Zealand v Pakistan	1964-65
Sialkot	423-5d	Pakistan v Sri Lanka	1991-92	157	Sri Lanka v Pakistan	1985-86
Colombo (PSS)	385	Sri Lanka v India	1985-86	175	Sri Lanka v England	1981-82
Colombo (SSC)	547-8d	Sri Lanka v Australia	1992-93	164	Sri Lanka v Australia	1992-93
Colombo (CCC)	459	New Zealand v Sri Lanka	1983-84	132	Pakistan v Sri Lanka	1985-86
Colombo (KS)	296-6d	Australia v Sri Lanka	1992-93	247	Australia v Sri Lanka	1992-93
Kandy	514-4d	Australia v Sri Lanka	1982-83	97	Sri Lanka v New Zealand	1983-84
Moratuwa	337	Australia v Sri Lanka	1992-93	337	Australia v Sri Lanka	1992-93

†Five men were absent hurt. The second lowest total at Kingston is 103 by England in 1934-35.

HIGHEST INDIVIDUAL SCORE FOR EACH TEST MATCH GROUND

Adelaide	299*	D.G.Bradman	Australia v South Africa	1931-32
Brisbane[1]	223	D.G.Bradman	Australia v West Indies	1930-31
Brisbane[2]	226	D.G.Bradman	Australia v South Africa	1931-32
Hobart	134*	S.R.Waugh	Australia v Sri Lanka	1989-90
Melbourne	307	R.M.Cowper	Australia v England	1965-66
Perth	200	D.C.Boon	Australia v New Zealand	1989-90
Sydney	287	R.E.Foster	England v Australia	1903-04
Birmingham	285*	P.B.H.May	England v West Indies	1957
Leeds	334	D.G.Bradman	Australia v England	1930
Lord's	333	G.A.Gooch	England v India	1990
Manchester	311	R.B.Simpson	Australia v England	1964
Nottingham	278	D.C.S.Compton	England v Pakistan	1954
The Oval	364	L.Hutton	England v Australia	1938
Sheffield	119	C.Hill	Australia v England	1902
Cape Town	209	R.G.Pollock	South Africa v Australia	1966-67
Durban[1]	119	J.W.H.T.Douglas	England v South Africa	1913-14
Durban[2]	274	R.G.Pollock	South Africa v Australia	1969-70
Johannesburg[1]	231	A.D.Nourse	South Africa v Australia	1935-36
Johannesburg[2]	195	C.Washbrook	England v South Africa	1948-49
Johannesburg[3]	185	D.T.Lindsay	South Africa v Australia	1966-67
Port Elizabeth	167	A.L.Hassett	Australia v South Africa	1949-50
Bridgetown	337	Hanif Mohammad	Pakistan v West Indies	1957-58
Georgetown	259	G.M.Turner	New Zealand v West Indies	1971-72
Kingston	365*	G.S.Sobers	West Indies v Pakistan	1957-58
Port-of-Spain	220	S.M.Gavaskar	India v West Indies	1970-71
St John's	178	I.V.A.Richards	West Indies v Australia	1983-84
Auckland	336*	W.R.Hammond	England v New Zealand	1932-33
Christchurch	258	S.M.Nurse	West Indies v New Zealand	1968-69
Dunedin	201	Mushtaq Mohammad	Pakistan v New Zealand	1972-73
Hamilton	122	A.H.Jones	New Zealand v Sri Lanka	1990-91
Napier	119*	Majid Khan	Pakistan v New Zealand	1978-79
Wellington	299	M.D.Crowe	New Zealand v Sri Lanka	1990-91
Ahmedabad	109	D.B.Vengsarkar	India v Pakistan	1986-87
Bangalore	172	S.M.Gavaskar	India v England	1981-82
Bombay[1]	136	B.H.Valentine	England v India	1933-34
Bombay[2]	223	M.H.Mankad	India v New Zealand	1955-56
Bombay[3]	242*	C.H.Lloyd	West Indies v India	1974-75
Calcutta	256	R.B.Kanhai	West Indies v India	1958-59
Chandigarh	88	R.J.Shastri	India v Sri Lanka	1990-91
Cuttack	166	D.B.Vengsarkar	India v Sri Lanka	1986-87
Delhi	230*	B.Sutcliffe	New Zealand v India	1955-56

Hyderabad	223	P.R.Umrigar	India v New Zealand	1955-56
Jaipur	125	R.J.Shastri	India v Pakistan	1986-87
Jullundur	201	A.D.Gaekwad	India v Pakistan	1983-84
Kanpur	250	S.F.A.F.Bacchus	West Indies v India	1978-79
Lucknow	124*	Nazar Mohammad	Pakistan v India	1952-53
Madras[1]	236*	S.M.Gavaskar	India v West Indies	1983-84
Madras[2]	231	M.H.Mankad	India v New Zealand	1955-56
Nagpur	153	D.B.Vengsarkar	India v Sri Lanka	1986-87
Bahawalpur	142	Hanif Mohammad	Pakistan v India	1954-55
Dacca	165	G.Pullar	England v Pakistan	1961-62
Faisalabad	235	G.S.Chappell	Australia v Pakistan	1979-80
Gujranwala	51*	Rameez Raja	Pakistan v Sri Lanka	1991-92
Hyderabad	280*	Javed Miandad	Pakistan v India	1982-83
Karachi	211	Javed Miandad	West Indies v Pakistan	1958-59
Lahore[1]	217	R.B.Kanhai	Pakistan v India	1978-79
Lahore[2]	235*	Zaheer Abbas	Pakistan v India	1978-79
Multan	120*	I.V.A.Richards	West Indies v Pakistan	1980-81
Peshawar	108	P.R.Umrigar	India v Pakistan	1954-55
Rawalpindi	76	B.R.Taylor	New Zealand v Pakistan	1964-65
Sialkot	101	Saleem Malik	Pakistan v Sri Lanka	1991-92
Colombo (PSS)	135*	A.Ranatunga	Sri Lanka v Pakistan	1985-86
Colombo (SSC)	137	A.P.Gurusinha	Sri Lanka v Australia	1992-93
Colombo (CCC)	201*	D.S.B.P.Kuruppu	Sri Lanka v New Zealand	1986-87
Colombo (KS)	100*	D.M.Jones	Australia v Sri Lanka	1992-93
Kandy	143*	D.W.Hookes	Australia v Sri Lanka	1982-83
Moratuwa	106	A.R.Border	Australia v Sri Lanka	1992-93

HIGHEST WICKET PARTNERSHIPS FOR EACH TEST GROUND

	Runs	Wkt			
Adelaide	341	3rd	E.J.Barlow, R.G.Pollock	South Africa v Australia	1963-64
Brisbane[1]	229	2nd	W.H.Ponsford, D.G.Bradman	Australia v West Indies	1930-31
Brisbane[2]	276	3rd	D.G.Bradman, A.L.Hassett	Australia v England	1946-47
Hobart	260*	6th	D.M.Jones, S.R.Waugh	Australia v Sri Lanka	1989-90
Melbourne	346	6th	J.H.W.Fingleton, D.G.Bradman	Australia v England	1936-37
Perth	259	2nd	W.B.Phillips, G.N.Yallop	Australia v Pakistan	1983-84
Sydney	405	5th	S.G.Barnes, D.G.Bradman	Australia v England	1946-47
Birmingham	411	4th	P.B.H.May, M.C.Cowdrey	England v West Indies	1957
Leeds	388	4th	W.H.Ponsford, D.G.Bradman	Australia v England	1934
Lord's	370	3rd	W.J.Edrich, D.C.S.Compton	England v South Africa	1947
Manchester	246	3rd	E.R.Dexter, K.F.Barrington	England v Australia	1964
Nottingham	329	1st	G.R.Marsh, M.A.Taylor	Australia v England	1989
The Oval	451	2nd	W.H.Ponsford, D.G.Bradman	Australia v England	1934
Sheffield	107	4th	C.Hill, S.E.Gregory	Australia v England	1902
Cape Town	260	1st	B.Mitchell, I.J.Siedle	South Africa v England	1930-31
Durban[1]	143	4th	G.C.White, A.W.Nourse	South Africa v England	1909-10
Durban[2]	280	2nd	P.A.Gibb, W.J.Edrich	England v South Africa	1938-39
Johannesburg[1]	230	2nd	H.Sutcliffe, G.E.Tyldesley	England v South Africa	1927-28
Johannesburg[2]	359	1st	L.Hutton, C.Washbrook	England v South Africa	1948-49
Johannesburg[3]	221	7th	D.T.Lindsay, P.L.van der Merwe	South Africa v Australia	1966-67
Port Elizabeth	187	3rd	A.R.Morris, R.N.Harvey	Australia v South Africa	1949-50
Bridgetown	399	4th	G.S.Sobers.F.M.M.Worrell	West Indies v England	1959-60
Georgetown	387	1st	G.M.Turner, T.W.Jarvis	New Zealand v West Indies	1971-72
Kingston	446	2nd	C.C.Hunte, G.S.Sobers	West Indies v Pakistan	1957-58
Port-of-Spain	338	3rd	E.D.Weekes, F.M.M.Worrell	West Indies v England	1953-54
St John's	308	3rd	R.B.Richardson, I.V.A.Richards	West Indies v Australia	1983-84

Auckland	266	4th	M.H.Denness, K.W.R.Fletcher	England v New Zealand	1974-75
Christchurch	242	5th	W.R.Hammond, L.E.G.Ames	England v New Zealand	1932-33
Dunedin	350	4th	Mushtaq Mohammad, Asif Iqbal	Pakistan v New Zealand	1972-73
Hamilton	161	1st	T.J.Franklin, J.G.Wright	New Zealand v Sri Lanka	1990-91
Napier	195	2nd	J.G.Wright, G.P.Howarth	New Zealand v Pakistan	1978-79
Wellington	467	3rd	M.D.Crowe, A.H.Jones	New Zealand v Sri Lanka	1990-91
Ahmedabad	154	7th	Imran Khan, Ijaz Faqih	Pakistan v India	1986-87
Bangalore	207	4th	C.G.Greenidge, C.H.Lloyd	West Indies v India	1974-75
Bombay[1]	186	3rd	N.B.Amarnath, C.K.Nayudu	India v England	1933-34
Bombay[2]	254	5th	K.W.R.Fletcher, A.W.Greig	England v India	1972-73
Bombay[3]	298*	6th	D.B.Vengsarkar, R.J.Shastri	India v Australia	1986-87
Calcutta	344*	2nd	S.M.Gavaskar, D.B.Vengsarkar	India v West Indies	1978-79
Chandigarh	76	2nd	R.J.Shastri, S.V.Manjrekar	India v Sri Lanka	1990-91
Cuttack	111	6th	D.B.Vengsarkar, Kapil Dev	India v Sri Lanka	1986-87
Delhi	267	4th	C.L.Walcott, G.E.Gomez	West Indies v India	1948-49
Hyderabad	238	3rd	P.R.Umrigar, V.L.Manjrekar	India v New Zealand	1955-56
Jaipur	130	5th	M.Azharuddin, R.J.Shastri	India v Pakistan	1986-87
Jullundur	121	6th	A.D.Gaekwad, R.M.H.Binny	India v Pakistan	1983-84
Kanpur	272	6th	M.Azharuddin, Kapil Dev	India v Sri Lanka	1986-87
Lucknow	63	8th	Nazar Mohammad, Zulfiqar Ahmed	Pakistan v India	1952-53
Madras[1]	316	3rd	G.R.Viswanath, Yashpal Sharma	India v England	1981-82
Madras[2]	413	1st	M.H.Mankad, P.Roy	India v New Zealand	1955-56
Nagpur	173	3rd	M.Amarnath, D.B.Vengsarkar	India v Sri Lanka	1986-87
Bahawalpur	127	1st	Hanif Mohammad, Alimuddin	Pakistan v India	1954-55
Dacca	198	1st	G.Pullar, R.W.Barber	England v Pakistan	1961-62
Faisalabad	397	3rd	Qasim Omar, Javed Miandad	Pakistan v Sri Lanka	1985-86
Gujranwala	59	2nd	Rameez Raja, Zahid Fazal	Pakistan v Sri Lanka	1991-92
Hyderabad	451	3rd	Mudassar Nazar, Javed Miandad	Pakistan v India	1982-83
Karachi	252	4th	Javed Miandad, Mushtaq Mohammad	Pakistan v New Zealand	1976-77
Lahore[1]	308	7th	Waqar Hassan, Imtiaz Ahmed	Pakistan v New Zealand	1955-56
Lahore[2]	281	5th	Javed Miandad, Asif Iqbal	Pakistan v New Zealand	1976-77
Multan	100	3rd	Majid Khan, Javed Miandad	Pakistan v West Indies	1980-81
Peshawar	91	3rd	P.R.Umrigar, V.L.Manjrekar	India v Pakistan	1954-55
Rawalpindi	114	2nd	Mohammad Ilyas, Saeed Ahmed	Pakistan v New Zealand	1964-65
Sialkot	128	3rd	S.V.Manjrekar, M.Azharuddin	India v Pakistan	1985-86
Colombo (PSS)	240*	4th	A.P.Gurusinha, A.Ranatunga	Sri Lanka v Pakistan	1985-86
Colombo (SSC)	230	4th	A.P.Gurusinha, A.Ranatunga	Sri Lanka v Australia	1992-93
Colombo (CCC)	246*	6th	J.J.Crowe, R.J.Hadlee	New Zealand v Sri Lanka	1986-87
Colombo (KS)	131	6th	D.M.Jones, G.R.J.Matthews	Australia v Sri Lanka	1992-93
Kandy	216	4th	R.L.Dias, L.R.D.Mendis	Sri Lanka v India	1985-86
Moratuwa	129	7th	G.R.J.Matthews, I.A.Healy	Australia v Sri Lanka	1992-93

BEST INNINGS BOWLING ANALYSIS FOR EACH TEST GROUND

Adelaide	8-43	A.E.Trott	Australia v England	1894-95
Brisbane[1]	6-32	H.Larwood	England v Australia	1928-29
Brisbane[2]	9-52	R.J.Hadlee	New Zealand v Australia	1985-86
Hobart	6-66	R.J.Ratnayake	Sri Lanka v Australia	1989-90
Melbourne	9-86	Sarfraz Nawaz	Pakistan v Australia	1978-79
Perth	8-87	M.G.Hughes	Australia v West Indies	1988-89
Sydney	8-35	G.A.Lohmann	England v Australia	1886-87
Birmingham	7-17	W.Rhodes	England v Australia	1902
Leeds	8-43	R.G.D.Willis	England v Australia	1981
Lord's	8-34	I.T.Botham	England v Pakistan	1978
Manchester	10-53	J.C.Laker	England v Australia	1956
Nottingham	8-107	B.J.T.Bosanquet	England v Australia	1905

The Oval	8-29	S.F.Barnes	England v South Africa	1912
Sheffield	6-49	S.F.Barnes	England v Australia	1902
Cape Town	8-11	J.Briggs	England v South Africa	1888-89
Durban[1]	7-56	S.F.Barnes	England v South Africa	1913-14
Durban[2]	8-69	H.J Tayfield	South Africa v England	1956-57
Johannesburg[1]	9-28	G.A.Lohmann	England v South Africa	1895-96
Johannesburg[2]	6-13	H.J.Tayfield	South Africa v New Zealand	1953-54
Johannesburg[3]	9-113	H.J.Tayfield	South Africa v England	1956-57
Port Elizabeth	8-7	G.A.Lohmann	England v South Africa	1895-96
Bridgetown	8-38	L.R.Gibbs	West Indies v India	1961-62
Georgetown	7-44	I.W.Johnson	Australia v West Indies	1954-55
Kingston	7-34	T.E.Bailey	England v West Indies	1953-54
Port-of-Spain	9-95	J.M.Noreiga	West Indies v India	1970-71
St John's	6-74	C.E.H.Croft	West Indies v England	1980-81
Auckland	8-76	E.A.S.Prasanna	India v New Zealand	1975-76
Christchurch	7-75	F.S.Trueman	England v New Zealand	1962-63
Dunedin	7-52	Intikhab Alam	Pakistan v New Zealand	1972-73
Hamilton	5-77	R.J.Ratnayake	Sri Lanka v New Zealand	1990-91
Napier	5-98	D.K.Morrison	New Zealand v India	1989-90
Wellington	7-23	R.J.Hadlee	New Zealand v India	1975-76
Ahmedabad	9-83	Kapil Dev	India v West Indies	1983-84
Bangalore	7-27	Maninder Singh	India v Pakistan	1986-87
Bombay[1]	5-55	M.S.Nichols	England v India	1933-34
Bombay[2]	7-157	B.S.Chandrasekhar	India v West Indies	1966-67
Bombay[3]	7-48	I.T.Botham	England v India	1979-80
Calcutta	7-49	Ghulam Ahmed	India v Australia	1956-57
Chandigarh	6-12	S.L.Venkatapathy Raju	India v Sri Lanka	1990-91
Cuttack	5-85	J.R.Ratnayeke	Sri Lanka v India	1986-87
Delhi	8-52	M.H.Mankad	India v Pakistan	1952-53
Hyderabad	7-128	S.P.Gupte	India v New Zealand	1955-56
Jaipur	4-88	G.Sharma	India v Pakistan	1986-87
Jullundur	4-50	Wasim Raja	Pakistan v India	1983-84
Kanpur	9-69	J.M.Patel	India v Australia	1959-60
Lucknow	7-42	Fazal Mahmood	Pakistan v India	1952-53
Madras[1]	8-55	M.H.Mankad	India v England	1951-52
Madras[2]	7-43	R.R.Lindwall	Australia v India	1956-57
Nagpur	7-51	Maninder Singh	India v Sri Lanka	1986-87
Bahawalpur	6-74	P.R.Umrigar	India v Pakistan	1954-55
Dacca	6-21	Khan Mohammad	Pakistan v New Zealand	1955-56
Faisalabad	7-52	C.Pringle	New Zealand v Pakistan	1990-91
Gujranwala	1-27	G.P.Wickramasinghe	Sri Lanka v Pakistan	1991-92
Hyderabad	7-87	S.L.Boock	New Zealand v Pakistan	1984-85
Karachi	8-60	Imran Khan	Pakistan v India	1982-83
Lahore[1]	5-87	W.W.Hall	West Indies v Pakistan	1958-59
Lahore[2]	9-56	Abdul Qadir	Pakistan v England	1987-88
Multan	5-62	Imran Khan	Pakistan v West Indies	1980-81
Peshawar	5-63	S.P.Gupte	India v Pakistan	1954-55
Rawalpindi	4-5	Pervez Sajjad	Pakistan v New Zealand	1964-65
Sialkot	8-83	J.R.Ratnayeke	Sri Lanka v Pakistan	1985-86
Colombo (PSS)	6-33	J.E.Emburey	England v Sri Lanka	1981-82
Colombo (SSC)	6-85	R.J.Ratnayake	Sri Lanka v India	1985-86
Colombo (CCC)	5-29	R.I.Hadlee	New Zealand v Sri Lanka	1983-84
Colombo (KS)	4-53	C.J.McDermott	Australia v Sri Lanka	1992-93
Kandy	6-45	Tauseef Ahmed	Pakistan v Sri Lanka	1985-86
Moratuwa	5-82	C.P.H.Ramanayake	Sri Lanka v Australia	1992-93

BEST MATCH BOWLING ANALYSIS FOR EACH TEST GROUND

Adelaide	14-199	C.V.Grimmett	Australia v South Africa	1931-32
Brisbane[1]	9-144	C.V.Grimmett	Australia v West Indies	1930-31
Brisbane[2]	15-123	R.J.Hadlee	New Zealand v Australia	1985-86
Hobart	8-156	M.G.Hughes	Australia v Sri Lanka	1989-90
Melbourne	15-124	W.Rhodes	England v Australia	1903-04
Perth	13-217	M.G.Hughes	Australia v West Indies	1988-89
Sydney	12-87	C.T.B.Turner	Australia v England	1887-88
Birmingham	12-119	F.S.Trueman	England v West Indies	1963
Leeds	15-99	C.Blythe	England v South Africa	1907
Lord's	16-137	R.A.L.Massie	Australia v England	1972
Manchester	19-90	J.C.Laker	England v Australia	1956
Nottingham	14-99	A.V.Bedser	England v Australia	1953
The Oval	14-90	F.R.Spofforth	Australia v England	1882
Sheffield	11-103	M.A.Noble	Australia v England	1902
Cape Town	15-28	J.Briggs	England v South Africa	1888-89
Durban[1]	14-144	S.F.Barnes	England v South Africa	1913-14
Durban[2]	13-173	C.V.Grimmett	Australia v South Africa	1935-36
Johannesburg[1]	17-159	S.F.Barnes	England v South Africa	1913-14
Johannesburg[2]	8-61	H.J.Tayfield	South Africa v New Zealand	1953-54
Johannesburg[3]	13-192	H.J.Tayfield	South Africa v England	1956-57
Port Elizabeth	15-45	G.A.Lohmann	England v South Africa	1895-96
Bridgetown	11-120	M.D.Marshall	West Indies v New Zealand	1984-85
Georgetown	11-121	Imran Khan	Pakistan v West Indies	1987-88
Kingston	10-96	H.H.H.Johnson	West Indies v England	1947-48
Port-of-Spain	13-156	A.W.Greig	England v West Indies	1973-74
St John's	8-113	C.E.H.Croft	West Indies v England	1980-81
Auckland	11-123	D.K.Lillee	Australia v New Zealand	1976-77
Christchurch	12-97	D.L.Underwood	England v New Zealand	1970-71
Dunedin	11-102	R.J.Hadlee	New Zealand v West Indies	1979-80
Hamilton	6-147	R.J.Ratnayake	Sri Lanka v New Zealand	1990-91
Napier	5-98	D.K.Morrison	New Zealand v India	1989-90
Wellington	11-58	R.J.Hadlee	New Zealand v India	1975-76
Ahmedabad	10-135	Kapil Dev	India v West Indies	1983-84
Bangalore	10-126	Maninder Singh	India v Pakistan	1986-87
Bombay[1]	8-108	M.S.Nichols	England v India	1933-34
Bombay[2]	11-235	B.S.Chandrasekhar	India v West Indies	1966-67
Bombay[3]	13-106	I.T.Botham	England v India	1979-80
Calcutta	11-105	R.Benaud	Australia v India	1956-57
Chandigarh	8-37	S.L.Venkatapathy Raju	India v Sri Lanka	1990-91
Cuttack	6-83	Maninder Singh	India v Sri Lanka	1986-87
Delhi	13-131	M.H.Mankad	India v Pakistan	1952-53
Hyderabad	8-109	E.A.S.Prasanna	India v New Zealand	1969-70
Jaipur	4-88	G.Sharma	India v Pakistan	1986-87
Jullundur	4-50	Wasim Raja	Pakistan v India	1983-84
Kanpur	14-124	J.M.Patel	India v Australia	1959-60
Lucknow	12-94	Fazal Mahmood	Pakistan v India	1952-53
Madras[1]	16-136	N.D.Hirwani	India v West Indies	1987-88
Madras[2]	11-122	R.G.Nadkarni	India v Australia	1964-65
Nagpur	10-107	Maninder Singh	India v Sri Lanka	1986-87
Bahawalpur	7-124	Khan Mohammad	Pakistan v India	1954-55
Dacca	12-100	Fazal Mahmood	Pakistan v West Indies	1958-59
Faisalabad	12-130	Waqar Younis	Pakistan v New Zealand	1990-91

Gujranwala	1-27	G.P.Wickramasinghe	Sri Lanka v Pakistan	1991-92
Hyderabad	8-80	Imran Khan	Pakistan v India	1982-83
Karachi	13-114	Fazal Mahmood	Pakistan v Australia	1956-57
Lahore[1]	7-167	S.P.Gupte	India v Pakistan	1954-55
Lahore[2]	14-116	Imran Khan	Pakistan v Sri Lanka	1981-82
Multan	5-89	Imran Khan	Pakistan v West Indies	1980-81
Peshawar	6-115	S.P.Gupte	India v Pakistan	1954-55
Rawalpindi	8-47	Pervez Sajjad	Pakistan v New Zealand	1964-65
Sialkot	9-95	Imran Khan	Pakistan v Sri Lanka	1985-86
Colombo (PSS)	9-125	R.J.Ratnayake	Sri Lanka v India	1985-86
Colombo (SSC)	8-149	R.J.Ratnayake	Sri Lanka v India	1985-86
Colombo (CCC)	10-102	R.J.Hadlee	New Zealand v Sri Lanka	1983-84
Colombo (KS)	6-85	C.J.McDermott	Australia v Sri Lanka	1992-93
Kandy	9-77	Tauseef Ahmed	Pakistan v Sri Lanka	1985-86
Moratuwa	8-157	C.P.H.Ramanayake	Sri Lanka v Australia	1992-93

Series by Series Records

AUSTRALIA v ENGLAND

** denotes batted first (where a captain's name appears only once he was captain throughout the entire series.)*

Venue and Result	Australia 1st	Australia 2nd	England 1st	England 2nd	Captains Australia	Captains England
1876-77 in AUSTRALIA						
Melbourne-Australia 45 runs	*245	104	196	108	D.W.Gregory	J.Lillywhite
Melbourne-England 4 wkts	*122	259	261	6-122		
1878-79 in AUSTRALIA						
Melbourne-Australia 10 wkts	256	0-19	*113	160	D.W.Gregory	Lord Harris
1880 in ENGLAND						
The Oval-England 5 wkts	149	327	*420	5-57	W.L.Murdoch	Lord Harris
1881-82 in AUSTRALIA						
Melbourne-Drawn	320	3-127	*294	308	W.L.Murdoch	A.Shaw
Sydney-Australia 5 wkts	197	5-169	*133	232		
Sydney-Australia 6 wkts	260	4-66	*188	134		
Melbourne-Drawn	300	-	*309	2-234		
1882 in ENGLAND						
The Oval-Australia 7 runs	*63	122	101	77	W.L.Murdoch	A.N.Hornby
1882-83 in AUSTRALIA						
Melbourne-Australia 9 wkts	*291	1-58	177	169	W.L.Murdoch	Hon.I.F.W.Bligh
Melbourne-England inns & 27 runs	114	153	*294	-		
Sydney-England 69 runs	218	83	*247	123		
Sydney-Australia 4 wkts	262	6-199	*263	197		
1884 in ENGLAND						
Manchester-Drawn	182	-	*95	9-180	W.L.Murdoch	A.N.Hornby
Lord's-England inns & 5 runs	*229	145	379	-		Lord Harris
The Oval-Drawn	*551	-	346	2-85		Lord Harris
1884-85 in AUSTRALIA						
Adelaide-England 8 wkts	*243	191	369	2-67	W.L.Murdoch	A.Shrewsbury
Melbourne-England 10 wkts	279	126	*401	0-7	T.P.Horan	
Sydney-Australia 6 runs	*181	165	133	207	H.H.Massie	
Sydney-Australia 8 wkts	309	2-40	*269	77	J.M.Blackham	
Melbourne-England inns & 98 runs	*163	125	386	-	T.P.Horan	
1886 in ENGLAND						
Manchester-England 4 wkts	*205	123	223	6-107	H.J.H.Scott	A.G.Steel
Lord's-England inns & 106 runs	121	126	*353	-		
The Oval-England inns & 217 runs	68	149	*434	-		
1886-87 in AUSTRALIA						
Sydney-England 13 runs	119	97	*45	184	P.S.McDonnell	A.Shrewsbury
Sydney-England 71 runs	84	150	*151	154		
1887-88 in AUSTRALIA						
Sydney-England 126 runs	42	82	*113	137	P.S.McDonnell	W.W.Read

AUSTRALIA v ENGLAND (cont.)	Australia		England		Captains	
Venue and Result	1st	2nd	1st	2nd	Australia	England
1888 in ENGLAND						
Lord's-Australia 61 runs	*116	60	53	62	P.S.McDonnell	A.G.Steel
The Oval-England inns & 137 runs	*80	100	317	-		W.G.Grace
Manchester-England inns & 21 runs	81	70	*172	-		W.G.Grace
1890 in ENGLAND						
Lord's-England 7 wkts	*132	176	173	3-137	W.L.Murdoch	W.G.Grace
The Oval-England 2 wkts	*92	102	100	8-95		
Manchester-Abandoned	-	-	-	-		
1891-92 in AUSTRALIA						
Melbourne-Australia 54 runs	*240	236	264	158	J.M.Blackham	W.G.Grace
Sydney-Australia 72 runs	*145	391	307	157		
Adelaide-England inns & 230 runs	100	169	*499			
1893 in ENGLAND						
Lord's-Drawn	269	-	*334	8d-234	J.M.Blackham	A.E.Stoddart
The Oval-England inns & 43 runs	91	349	*483	-		W.G.Grace
Manchester-Drawn	*240	236	243	4-118		W.G.Grace
1894-95 in AUSTRALIA						
Sydney-England 10 runs	*586	166	325	437	J.M.Blackham	A.E.Stoddart
Melbourne-England 94 runs	123	333	*75	475	G.Giffen	
Adelaide-Australia 382 runs	*238	411	124	143	G.Giffen	
Sydney-Australia inns & 147 runs	*284	-	65	72	G.Giffen	
Melbourne-England 6 wkts	*414	267	385	4-298	G.Giffen	
1896 in ENGLAND						
Lord's-England 6 wkts	*53	347	292	4-111	G.H.S.Trott	W.G.Grace
Manchester-Australia 3 wkts	*412	7-125	231	305		
The Oval-England 66 runs	119	44	*145	84		
1897-98 in AUSTRALIA						
Sydney-England 9 wkts	237	408	*551	1-96	G.H.S.Trott	A.C.MacLaren
Melbourne-Australia inns & 55 runs	*520	-	315	150		A.C.MacLaren
Adelaide-Australia inns & 13 runs	*573	-	278	282		A.E.Stoddart
Melbourne-Australia 8 wkts	*323	2-115	174	263		A.E.Stoddart
Sydney-Australia 6 wkts	239	4-276	*335	178		A.C.MacLaren
1899 in ENGLAND						
Nottingham-Drawn	*252	8d-230	193	7-155	J.Darling	W.G.Grace
Lord's-Australia 10 wkts	421	0-28	*206	240		A.C.MacLaren
Leeds-Drawn	*172	224	220	0-19		A.C.MacLaren
Manchester-Drawn	196	7d-346	*372	3-94		A.C.MacLaren
The Oval-Drawn	352	5-254	*576	-		A.C.MacLaren
1901-02 in AUSTRALIA						
Sydney-England inns & 124 runs	168	172	*464	-	J.Darling	A.C.MacLaren
Melbourne-Australia 229 runs	*112	353	61	175	J.Darling	
Adelaide-Australia 4 wkts	321	6-315	*388	247	J.Darling	
Sydney-Australia 7 wkts	299	3-121	*317	99	H.Trumble	
Melbourne-Australia 32 runs	*144	255	189	178	H.Trumble	

AUSTRALIA v ENGLAND (cont.) Venue and Result	Australia 1st	Australia 2nd	England 1st	England 2nd	Captains Australia	Captains England
1902 in ENGLAND						
Birmingham-Drawn	36	2-46	*9d-376	-	J.Darling	A.C.MacLaren
Lord's-Drawn	-	-	*2-102	-		
Sheffield-Australia 143 runs	*194	289	145	195		
Manchester-Australia 3 runs	*299	86	262	120		
The Oval-England 1 wkt	*324	121	183	9-263		
1903-04 in AUSTRALIA						
Sydney-England 5 wkts	*285	485	577	5-194	M.A.Noble	P.F.Warner
Melbourne-England 185 runs	122	111	*315	103		
Adelaide-Australia 216 runs	*388	351	245	278		
Sydney-England 157 runs	131	171	*249	210		
Melbourne-Australia 218 runs	*247	133	61	101		
1905 in ENGLAND						
Nottingham-England 213 runs	221	188	*196	5d-426	J.Darling	Hon.F.S.Jackson
Lord's-Drawn	181	-	*282	5-151		
Leeds-Drawn	195	7-224	*301	5d-295		
Manchester-England inns & 80 runs	197	169	*446	-		
The Oval-Drawn	363	4-124	*430	6d-261		
1907-08 in AUSTRALIA						
Sydney-Australia 2 wkts	300	8-275	*273	300	M.A.Noble	F.L.Fane
Melbourne-England 1 wkt	*266	397	382	9-282		F.L.Fane
Adelaide-Australia 245 runs	*285	506	363	183		F.L.Fane
Melbourne-Australia 308 runs	*214	385	105	186		A.O.Jones
Sydney-Australia 49 runs	*137	422	281	229		A.O.Jones
1909 in ENGLAND						
Birmingham-England 10 wkts	*74	151	121	0-105	M.A.Noble	A.C.MacLaren
Lord's-Australia 9 wkts	350	1-41	*269	121		
Leeds-Australia 126 runs	*188	207	182	87		
Manchester-Drawn	*147	9d-279	119	3-108		
The Oval-Drawn	*325	5d-339	352	3-104		
1911-12 in AUSTRALIA						
Sydney-Australia 146 runs	*447	308	318	291	C.Hill	J.W.H.T.Douglas
Melbourne-England 8 wkts	*184	299	265	2-219		
Adelaide-England 7 wkts	*133	476	501	3-112		
Melbourne-England inns & 225 runs	*191	173	589	-		
Sydney-England 70 runs	176	292	*324	214		
1912 in ENGLAND						
Lord's-Drawn	7-282	-	*7d-310	-	S.E.Gregory	C.B.Fry
Manchester-Drawn	0-14	-	*203	-		
The Oval-England 244 runs	111	65	*245	175		
1920-21 in AUSTRALIA						
Sydney-Australia 377 runs	*267	581	190	281	W.W.Armstrong	J.W.H.T.Douglas
Melbourne-Australia inns & 91 runs	*499	-	251	157		
Adelaide-Australia 119 runs	*354	582	447	370		
Melbourne-Australia 8 wkts	389	2-211	*284	315		
Sydney-Australia 9 wkts	392	1-93	*204	280		

AUSTRALIA v ENGLAND (cont.) Venue and Result	Australia 1st	Australia 2nd	England 1st	England 2nd	Captains Australia	Captains England
1921 in ENGLAND						
Nottingham-Australia 10 wkts	232	0-30	*112	147	W.W.Armstrong	J.W.H.T.Douglas
Lord's-Australia 8 wkts	342	2-131	*187	283		J.W.H.T Douglas
Leeds-Australia 219 runs	*407	7d-273	259	202		Hon.L.H.Tennyson
Manchester-Drawn	175	-	*4d-362	1-44		Hon.L.H.Tennyson
The Oval-Drawn	389	-	*8d-403	2-244		Hon.L.H.Tennyson
1924-25 in AUSTRALIA						
Sydney-Australia 193 runs	*450	452	298	411	H.L.Collins	A.E.R.Gilligan
Melbourne-Australia 81 runs	*600	250	479	290		
Adelaide-Australia 11 runs	*489	250	365	363		
Melbourne-England inns & 29 runs	269	250	*548	-		
Sydney-Australia 307 runs	*295	325	167	146		
1926 in ENGLAND						
Nottingham-Drawn	-	-	*0-32	-	H.L.Collins	A.W.Carr
Lord's-Drawn	*383	5-194	3d-475	-	H.L.Collins	A.W.Carr
Leeds-Drawn	*494	-	294	3-254	W.Bardsley	A.W.Carr
Manchester-Drawn	*335	-	5-305	-	W.Bardsley	A.W.Carr
The Oval-England 289 runs	302	125	*280	436	H.L.Collins	A.P.F.Chapman
1928-29 in AUSTRALIA						
Brisbane[1]-England 675 runs	122	66	*521	8d-342	J.Ryder	A.P.F.Chapman
Sydney-England 8 wkts	*253	397	636	2-16		A.P.F.Chapman
Melbourne-England 3 wkts	*397	351	417	7-332		A.P.F.Chapman
Adelaide-England 12 runs	369	336	*334	383		A.P.F.Chapman
Melbourne-Australia 5 wkts	491	5-287	*519	257		J.C.White
1930 in ENGLAND						
Nottingham-England 93 runs	144	335	*270	302	W.M.Woodfull	A.P.F.Chapman
Lord's-Australia 7 wkts	6d-729	3-72	*425	375		A.P.F.Chapman
Leeds-Drawn	*566	-	391	3-95		A.P.F.Chapman
Manchester-Drawn	*345	-	8-251	-		A.P.F.Chapman
The Oval-Australia inns & 39 runs	695	-	*405	251		R.E.S.Wyatt
1932-33 in AUSTRALIA						
Sydney-England 10 wkts	*360	164	524	0-1	W.M.Woodfull	D.R.Jardine
Melbourne-Australia 111 runs	*228	191	169	139		
Adelaide-England 338 runs	222	193	*341	412		
Brisbane[2]-England 6 wkts	*340	175	356	4-162		
Sydney-England 8 wkts	*435	182	454	2-168		
1934 in ENGLAND						
Nottingham-Australia 238 runs	*374	8d-273	268	141	W.M.Woodfull	C.F.Walters
Lord's-England inns & 38 runs	284	118	*440	-		R.E.S.Wyatt
Manchester-Drawn	491	1-66	*9d-627	0d-123		R.E.S.Wyatt
Leeds-Drawn	584	-	*200	6-229		R.E.S.Wyatt
The Oval-Australia 562 runs	*701	327	321	145		R.E.S.Wyatt
1936-37 in AUSTRALIA						
Brisbane[2]-England 322 runs	234	58	*358	256	D.G.Bradman	G.O.B.Allen
Sydney-England inns & 22 runs	80	324	*6d-426	-		
Melbourne-Australia 365 runs	*9d-200	564	9d-76	323		
Adelaide-Australia 148 runs	*288	433	330	243		
Melbourne-Australia inns & 200 runs	*604	-	239	165		

AUSTRALIA v ENGLAND (cont.) Venue and Result	Australia 1st	Australia 2nd	England 1st	England 2nd	Captains Australia	Captains England
1938 in ENGLAND						
Nottingham-Drawn	411	6-427	*8d-658	-	D.G.Bradman	W.R.Hammond
Lord's-Drawn	422	6-204	*494	8d-242		
Manchester-Abandoned	-	-	-	-		
Leeds-Australia 5 wkts	242	5-107	*223	123		
The Oval-England inns & 579 runs	201	123	*7d-903	-		
1946-47 in AUSTRALIA						
Brisbane²-Australia inns & 332 runs	*645	-	141	172	D.G.Bradman	W.R.Hammond
Sydney-Australia inns & 33 runs	8d-659	-	*255	371		W.R.Hammond
Melbourne-Drawn	*365	536	351	7-310		W.R.Hammond
Adelaide-Drawn	487	1-215	*460	8d-340		W.R.Hammond
Sydney-Australia 5 wkts	253	5-214	*280	186		N.W.D.Yardley
1948 in ENGLAND						
Nottingham-Australia 8 wkts	509	2-98	*165	441	D.G.Bradman	N.W.D.Yardley
Lord's-Australia 409 runs	*350	7d-460	215	186		
Manchester-Drawn	221	1-92	*363	3d-174		
Leeds-Australia 7 wkts	458	3-404	*496	8d-365		
The Oval-Australia inns & 149 runs	389	-	*52	188		
1950-51 in AUSTRALIA						
Brisbane²-Australia 70 runs	*228	7d-32	7d-68	122	A.L.Hassett	F.R.Brown
Melbourne-Australia 28 runs	*194	181	197	150		
Sydney-Australia inns &13 runs	426	-	*290	123		
Adelaide-Australia 274 runs	*371	8d-403	272	228		
Melbourne-England 8 wkts	*217	197	320	2-95		
1953 in ENGLAND						
Nottingham-Drawn	*249	123	144	1-120	A.L.Hassett	L.Hutton
Lord's-Drawn	*346	368	372	7-282		
Manchester-Drawn	*318	8-35	276	-		
Leeds-Drawn	266	4-147	*167	275		
The Oval-England 8 wkts	*275	162	306	2-132		
1954-55 in AUSTRALIA						
Brisbane²-Australia inns & 154 runs	*8d-601	-	190	257	I.W.Johnson	L.Hutton
Sydney-England 38 runs	228	184	*154	296	A.R.Morris	
Melbourne-England 128 runs	231	111	*191	279	I.W.Johnson	
Adelaide-England 5 wkts	*323	111	341	5-97	I.W.Johnson	
Sydney-Drawn	221	6-118	*7d-371	-	I.W.Johnson	
1956 In ENGLAND						
Nottingham-Drawn	148	3-120	*8d-217	3d-188	I.W.Johnson	P.B.H.May
Lord's-Australia 185 runs	*285	257	171	186		
Leeds-England inns & 42 runs	143	140	*325	-		
Manchester-England inns & 170 runs	84	205	*459	-		
The Oval-Drawn	202	5-27	*247	3d-182		
1958-59 In AUSTRALIA						
Brisbane²-Australia 8 wkts	186	2-147	*134	198	R.Benaud	P.B.H.May
Melbourne-Australia 8 wkts	308	2-42	*259	87		
Sydney-Drawn	357	2-54	*219	7d-287		
Adelaide-Australia 10 wkts	*476	0-36	240	270		
Melbourne-Australia 9 wkts	351	1-69	*205	214		

AUSTRALIA v ENGLAND (cont.)	Australia		England		Captains	
Venue and Result	1st	2nd	1st	2nd	Australia	England
1961 In ENGLAND						
Birmingham-Drawn	9d-516	-	*195	4-401	R.Benaud	M.C.Cowdrey
Lord's-Australia 5 wkts	340	5-71	*206	202	R.N.Harvey	M.C.Cowdrey
Leeds-England 8 wkts	*237	120	299	2-62	R.Benaud	P.B.H.May
Manchester-Australia 54 runs	*190	432	367	201	R.Benaud	P.B.H.May
The Oval-Drawn	494	-	*256	8-370	R.Benaud	P.B.H.May
1962-63 in AUSTRALIA						
Brisbane²-Drawn	*404	4d-362	389	6-278	R.Benaud	E.R.Dexter
Melbourne-England 7 wkts	*316	248	331	3-237		
Sydney-Australia 8 wkts	319	2-67	*279	104		
Adelaide-Drawn	*393	293	331	4-223		
Sydney-Drawn	349	4-152	*321	8d-268		
1964 in ENGLAND						
Nottingham-Drawn	168	2-40	*8d-216	9d-193	R.B.Simpson	E.R.Dexter
Lord's-Drawn	*176	4-168	246	-		
Leeds-Australia 7 wkts	389	3-111	*268	229		
Manchester-Drawn	*8d-656	0-4	611	-		
The Oval-Drawn	379	-	*182	4-381		
1965-66 in AUSTRALIA						
Brisbane²-Drawn	*6d-443	-	280	3-186	B.C.Booth	M.J K.Smith
Melbourne-Drawn	*358	426	558	0-5	R.B.Simpson	
Sydney-England inns & 93 runs	221	174	*488	-	B.C.Booth	
Adelaide-Australia inns & 9 runs	516	-	*241	266	R.B.Simpson	
Melbourne-Drawn	8d-543	-	*9d-485	3-69	R.B Simpson	
1968 in ENGLAND						
Manchester-Australia 159 runs	*357	220	165	253	W.M.Lawry	M.C.Cowdrey
Lord's-Drawn	78	4-127	*7d-351	-	W.M.Lawry	M.C.Cowdrey
Birmingham-Drawn	222	1-68	*409	3d-142	W.M.Lawry	M.C.Cowdrey
Leeds-Drawn	*315	312	302	4-230	B.N.Jarman	T.W.Graveney
The Oval-England 226 runs	324	125	*494	181	W.M.Lawry	M.C.Cowdrey
1970-71 in AUSTRALIA						
Brisbane²-Drawn	*433	214	464	1-39	W.M.Lawry	R.Illingworth
Perth-Drawn	440	3-100	*397	6d-287	W.M.Lawry	
Melbourne-Abandoned	-	-	-	-	W.M.Lawry	
Sydney-England 299 runs	236	116	*332	5d-319	W.M.Lawry	
Melbourne-Drawn	*9d-493	4d-169	392	0-161	W.M.Lawry	
Adelaide-Drawn	235	3-328	*470	4d-233	W.M.Lawry	
Sydney-England 62 runs	264	160	*184	302	I.M.Chappell	
1972 in ENGLAND						
Manchester-England 89 runs	142	252	*249	234	I.M.Chappell	R.Illingworth
Lord's-Australia 8 wkts	308	2-81	*272	116		
Nottingham-Drawn	*315	4d-324	189	4-290		
Leeds-England 9 wkts	*146	136	263	1-21		
The Oval-Australia 5 wkts	399	5-242	*284	356		

AUSTRALIA v ENGLAND (cont.) Venue and Result	Australia 1st	Australia 2nd	England 1st	England 2nd	Captains Australia	Captains England
1974-75 in AUSTRALIA						
Brisbane²-Australia 166 runs	*309	5d-288	265	166	I.M.Chappell	M.H.Denness
Perth-Australia 9 wkts	481	1-23	*208	293		M.H.Denness
Melbourne-Drawn	241	8-238	*242	244		M.H.Denness
Sydney-Australia 171 runs	*405	4d-289	295	228		J.H.Edrich
Adelaide-Australia 163 runs	304	5d-272	172	241		M.H.Denness
Melbourne-England inns & 4 runs	*152	373	529	-		M.H.Denness
1975 in ENGLAND						
Birmingham-Australia inns & 85 runs	*359	-	101	173	I.M.Chappell	M.H.Denness
Lord's-Drawn	268	3-329	*315	7d-436		A.W.Greig
Leeds-Drawn	135	3-220	*288	291		A.W.Greig
The Oval-Drawn	*9d-532	2-40	191	538		A.W.Greig
1976-77 in AUSTRALIA (CENTENARY TEST)						
Melbourne-Australia 45 runs	*138	9d-419	95	417	G.S.Chappell	A.W.Greig
1977 in ENGLAND						
Lord's-Drawn	296	6-114	*216	305	G.S.Chappell	J.M.Brearley
Manchester-England 9 wkts	*297	218	437	1-82		
Nottingham-England 7 wkts	*243	309	364	3-189		
Leeds-England inns & 85 runs	103	248	*436	-		
The Oval-Drawn	385	-	*214	2-57		
1978-79 in AUSTRALIA						
Brisbane²-England 7 wkts	*116	339	286	3-170	G.N.Yallop	J.M.Brearley
Perth-England 166 runs	190	161	*309	208		
Melbourne-Australia 103 runs	*258	167	143	179		
Sydney-England 93 runs	294	111	*152	346		
Adelaide-England 205 runs	164	160	*169	360		
Sydney-England 9 wkts	198	143	308	1-35		
1979-80 in AUSTRALIA						
Perth-Australia 138 runs	*244	337	228	215	G.S.Chappell	J.M.Brearley
Sydney-Australia 6 wkts	145	4-219	*123	237		
Melbourne-Australia 8 wkts	477	2-103	*306	273		
1980 in ENGLAND (CENTENARY TEST)						
Lord's-Drawn	*5d-385	4d-189	205	3-244	G.S.Chappell	I.T.Botham
1981 in ENGLAND						
Nottingham-Australia 4 wkts	179	6-132	*185	125	K.J.Hughes	I.T.Botham
Lord's-Drawn	345	4-90	*311	8-265		I.T.Botham
Leeds-England 18 runs	*9-401	111	174	356		J.M.Brearley
Birmingham-England 29 runs	258	121	*189	219		J.M.Brearley
Manchester-England 103 runs	130	402	*231	404		J.M.Brearley
The Oval-Drawn	*352	9d-344	314	7-261		J.M.Brearley
1982-83 in AUSTRALIA						
Perth-Drawn	9d-424	2-73	*411	358	K.J.Hughes	R.G.D.Willis
Brisbane²-Australia 7 wkts	341	3-190	*219	309		
Adelaide-Australia 8 wkts	*438	2-83	216	304		
Melbourne-England 3 runs	287	288	*284	294		
Sydney-Drawn	*314	382	237	7-314		

AUSTRALIA v ENGLAND (cont.) Venue and Result	Australia 1st	Australia 2nd	England 1st	England 2nd	Captains Australia	Captains England
1985 in ENGLAND						
Leeds-England 5 wkts	*331	324	533	5-123	A.R.Border	D.I.Gower
Lord's-Australia 4 wkts	425	6-127	*290	261		
Nottingham-Drawn	539	-	*456	2-196		
Manchester-Drawn	*257	5-340	9d-482	-		
Birmingham-England inns & 118 runs	*335	142	5d-595	-		
The Oval-England inns & 94 runs	241	129	*464	-		
1986-87 in AUSTRALIA						
Brisbane²-England 7 wkts	248	282	*456	3-77	A.R.Border	M.W.Gatting
Perth-Drawn	401	4-197	*8d-592	8d-199		
Adelaide-Drawn	*5d-514	3d-201	455	2-39		
Melbourne-England inns & 14 runs	*141	194	349	-		
Sydney-Australia 55 runs	*343	251	275	264		
1987-88 in AUSTRALIA (BICENTENNIAL TEST)						
Sydney-Drawn	214	2-328	*425	-	A.R.Border	M.W.Gatting
1989 in ENGLAND						
Leeds-Australia 210 runs	*7d-601	3d-230	430	191	A.R.Border	D.I.Gower
Lord's-Australia 6 wkts	528	4-119	*286	359		
Birmingham-Drawn	*189	219	258	121		
Manchester-Australia 9 wkts	*231	404	130	402		
Nottingham-Australia inns & 180 runs	*6d-602	-	255	167		
The Oval-Drawn	*468	4d-219	285	5-143		
1990-91 in AUSTRALIA						
Brisbane²-Australia 10 wkts	152	0-157	*194	114	A.R.Border	A.J.Lamb
Melbourne-Australia 8 wkts	306	2-197	*352	150		G.A.Gooch
Sydney-Drawn	*518	205	8d-469	4-113		G.A.Gooch
Adelaide-Drawn	*386	6d-314	229	5-335		G.A.Gooch
Perth-Australia 9 wkts	307	1-120	*244	182		G.A.Gooch

Test Match Results Summary

AUSTRALIA v ENGLAND — IN AUSTRALIA

		Result			Melbourne			Sydney			Adelaide			Brisbane			Perth		
	Tests	A	E	D	A	E	D	A	E	D	A	E	D	A	E	D	A	E	D
1876-77	2	1	1	-	1	1	-	-	-	-	-	-	-	-	-	-	-	-	-
1878-79	1	1	-	-	1	-	-	-	-	-	-	-	-	-	-	-	-	-	-
1881-82	4	2	-	2	-	-	2	2	-	-	-	-	-	-	-	-	-	-	-
1882-83	4	2	2	-	1	1	-	1	1	-	-	-	-	-	-	-	-	-	-
1884-85	5	2	3	-	-	2	-	2	-	-	-	1	-	-	-	-	-	-	-
1886-87	2	-	2	-	-	-	-	-	2	-	-	-	-	-	-	-	-	-	-
1887-88	1	-	1	-	-	-	-	-	1	-	-	-	-	-	-	-	-	-	-
1891-92	3	2	1	-	1	-	-	1	-	-	-	1	-	-	-	-	-	-	-
1894-95	5	2	3	-	-	2	-	1	1	-	1	-	-	-	-	-	-	-	-
1897-98	5	4	1	-	2	-	-	1	1	-	1	-	-	-	-	-	-	-	-
1901-02	5	4	1	-	2	-	-	1	1	-	1	-	-	-	-	-	-	-	-
1903-04	5	2	3	-	1	1	-	-	2	-	1	-	-	-	-	-	-	-	-
1907-08	5	4	1	-	1	1	-	2	-	-	1	-	-	-	-	-	-	-	-
1911-12	5	1	4	-	-	2	-	1	1	-	-	1	-	-	-	-	-	-	-
1920-21	5	5	-	-	2	-	-	2	-	-	1	-	-	-	-	-	-	-	-
1924-25	5	4	1	-	1	1	-	2	-	-	1	-	-	-	-	-	-	-	-
1928-29	5	1	4	-	1	1	-	-	1	-	-	1	-	-	1	-	-	-	-
1932-33	5	1	4	-	1	-	-	-	2	-	-	1	-	-	1	-	-	-	-
1936-37	5	3	2	-	2	-	-	-	1	-	1	-	-	-	1	-	-	-	-
1946-47	5	3	-	2	-	-	1	2	-	-	-	-	1	1	-	-	-	-	-
1950-51	5	4	1	-	1	1	-	1	-	-	1	-	-	1	-	-	-	-	-
1954-55	5	1	3	1	-	1	-	-	1	1	-	1	-	1	-	-	-	-	-
1958-59	5	4	-	1	2	-	-	-	-	1	1	-	-	1	-	-	-	-	-
1962-63	5	1	1	3	-	1	-	1	-	1	-	-	1	-	-	1	-	-	-
1965-66	5	1	1	3	-	-	2	-	1	-	1	-	-	-	-	1	-	-	-
1970-71	6	-	2	4	-	-	1	-	2	-	-	-	1	-	-	1	-	-	1
1974-75	6	4	1	1	-	1	1	1	-	-	1	-	-	1	-	-	1	-	-
1976-77	1	1	-	-	1	-	-	-	-	-	-	-	-	-	-	-	-	-	-
1978-79	6	1	5	-	1	-	-	-	2	-	-	1	-	-	1	-	-	1	-
1979-80	3	3	-	-	-	1	-	-	1	-	-	-	-	-	-	-	1	-	-
1982-83	5	2	1	2	-	1	-	-	-	1	1	-	-	1	-	-	-	-	1
1986-87	5	1	2	2	-	1	-	1	-	-	-	-	1	-	1	-	-	-	1
1987-88	1	-	-	1	-	-	-	-	-	1	-	-	-	-	-	-	-	-	-
1990-91	5	3	-	2	1	-	-	-	-	1	-	-	1	1	-	-	1	-	-
	145	70	51	24	24	18	7	23	20	6	13	7	5	7	5	3	3	1	3

AUSTRALIA v ENGLAND — IN ENGLAND

	Tests	Result A	Result E	Result D	The Oval A	The Oval E	The Oval D	Manch. A	Manch. E	Manch. D	Lord's A	Lord's E	Lord's D	Notting. A	Notting. E	Notting. D	Leeds A	Leeds E	Leeds D	Birming. A	Birming. E	Birming. D	Sheffield A	Sheffield E	Sheffield D
1880	1	-	1	-	-	1	-	-	-	-	-	-	-	-	-	-	-	-	-	-	-	-	-	-	-
1882	1	1	-	-	1	-	-	-	-	-	-	-	-	-	-	-	-	-	-	-	-	-	-	-	-
1884	3	-	1	2	-	-	1	-	-	1	-	1	-	-	-	-	-	-	-	-	-	-	-	-	-
1886	3	-	3	-	-	1	-	-	1	-	-	1	-	-	-	-	-	-	-	-	-	-	-	-	-
1888	3	1	2	-	-	1	-	-	1	-	1	-	-	-	-	-	-	-	-	-	-	-	-	-	-
1890	2	-	2	-	-	1	-	-	-	-	-	1	-	-	-	-	-	-	-	-	-	-	-	-	-
1893	3	-	1	2	-	1	-	-	-	1	-	-	1	-	-	-	-	-	-	-	-	-	-	-	-
1896	3	1	2	-	-	1	-	1	-	-	-	1	-	-	-	-	-	-	-	-	-	-	-	-	-
1899	5	1	-	4	-	-	1	-	-	1	1	-	-	-	-	1	-	-	1	-	-	-	-	-	-
1902	5	2	1	2	-	1	-	1	-	-	-	-	1	-	-	-	-	-	-	-	-	1	1	-	-
1905	5	-	2	3	-	-	1	-	1	-	-	-	1	-	1	-	-	-	1	-	-	-	-	-	-
1909	5	2	1	2	-	-	1	-	-	1	1	-	-	-	-	-	1	-	-	-	1	-	-	-	-
1912	3	-	1	2	-	1	-	-	-	1	-	-	1	-	-	-	-	-	-	-	-	-	-	-	-
1921	5	3	-	2	-	-	1	-	-	1	1	-	-	1	-	-	1	-	-	-	-	-	-	-	-
1926	5	-	1	4	-	1	-	-	-	1	-	-	1	-	-	1	-	-	1	-	-	-	-	-	-
1930	5	2	1	2	1	-	-	-	-	1	1	-	-	-	1	-	-	-	1	-	-	-	-	-	-
1934	5	2	1	2	1	-	-	-	-	1	-	1	-	1	-	-	-	-	1	-	-	-	-	-	-
1938	4	1	1	2	-	1	-	-	-	-	-	-	1	-	-	1	1	-	-	-	-	-	-	-	-
1948	5	4	-	1	1	-	-	-	-	1	1	-	-	1	-	-	1	-	-	-	-	-	-	-	-
1953	5	-	1	4	-	1	-	-	-	1	-	-	1	-	-	1	-	-	1	-	-	-	-	-	-
1956	5	1	2	2	-	-	1	-	1	-	1	-	-	-	-	1	-	1	-	-	-	-	-	-	-
1961	5	2	1	2	-	-	1	1	-	-	1	-	-	-	-	-	-	1	-	-	-	1	-	-	-
1964	5	1	-	4	-	-	1	-	-	1	-	-	1	-	-	1	1	-	-	-	-	-	-	-	-
1968	5	1	1	3	-	1	-	1	-	-	-	-	1	-	-	-	-	-	1	-	-	1	-	-	-
1972	5	2	2	1	1	-	-	-	1	-	1	-	-	-	-	1	-	1	-	-	-	-	-	-	-
1975	4	1	-	3	-	-	1	-	-	-	-	-	1	-	-	-	-	-	1	1	-	-	-	-	-
1977	5	-	3	2	-	-	1	-	1	-	-	-	1	-	1	-	-	1	-	-	-	-	-	-	-
1980	1	-	-	1	-	-	-	-	-	-	-	-	1	-	-	-	-	-	-	-	-	-	-	-	-
1981	6	1	3	2	-	-	1	-	1	-	-	-	1	1	-	-	-	1	-	-	1	-	-	-	-
1985	6	1	3	2	-	1	-	-	-	1	1	-	-	-	-	1	-	1	-	-	1	-	-	-	-
1989	6	4	-	2	-	-	1	1	-	-	1	-	-	1	-	-	1	-	-	-	-	1	-	-	-
	129	34	37	58	5	13	12	5	7	13	11	5	13	5	3	8	6	6	8	1	3	4	1	-	-
Totals	246	82	93	71																					

Key to ground abbreviations: Manch. - Manchester; Notting. - Nottingham; Birming. - Birmingham.
The matches abandoned without a ball being bowled at Manchester in 1890 and 1938 and at Melbourne in 1970-71 are excluded from these tables.

HIGHEST INNINGS TOTALS

Australia in England	6d-729	Lord's	1930
Australia in Australia	8d-659	Sydney	1946-47
England in England	7d-903	The Oval	1938
England in Australia	636	Sydney	1928-29

LOWEST INNINGS TOTALS

Australia in England	36	Birmingham	1902
Australia in Australia	42	Sydney	1887-88
England in England	52	The Oval	1948
England in Australia	45	Sydney	1886-87

HIGHEST MATCH AGGREGATE	1753 for 40 wickets	Adelaide	1920-21
LOWEST MATCH AGGREGATE	291 for 40 wickets	Lord's	1888

HIGHEST INDIVIDUAL INNINGS

Australia in England	334	D.G.Bradman	Leeds	1930
Australia in Australia	307	R.M.Cowper	Melbourne	1965-66
England in England	364	L.Hutton	The Oval	1938
England in Australia	287	R.E.Foster	Sydney	1903-04

HIGHEST AGGREGATE OF RUNS IN A SERIES

Australia in England	974 (av 139.14)	D.G.Bradman	1930
Australia in Australia	810 (av 90.00)	D.G.Bradman	1936-37
England in England	732 (av 81.33)	D.I.Gower	1985
England in Australia	905 (av 113.12)	W.R.Hammond	1928-29

RECORD WICKET PARTNERSHIPS-AUSTRALIA

1st	329	G.R.Marsh (138), M.A.Taylor(219)	Nottingham	1989
2nd	451	W.H.Ponsford (266), D.G.Bradman (244)	The Oval	1934
3rd	276	D.G.Bradman (187), A.L.Hassett (128)	Brisbane2	1946-47
4th	388	W H.Ponsford (181), D.G.Bradman (304)	Leeds	1934
5th	405	S.G.Barnes (234), D.G.Bradman (234)	Sydney	1946-47
6th	346	J.H.W Fingleton (136), D.G Bradman (270)	Melbourne	1936-37
7th	165	C.Hill (188), H.Trumble (46)	Melbourne	1897-98
8th	243	R.J.Hartigan (113), C.Hill (160)	Adelaide	1907-08
9th	154	S.E.Gregory (201), J.M.Blackham (74)	Sydney	1894-95
10th	127	J.M.Taylor (108), A.A.Mailey (46*)	Sydney	1924-25

RECORD WICKET PARTNERSHIPS-ENGLAND

1st	323	J.B.Hobbs (178), W.Rhodes (179)	Melbourne	1911-12
2nd	382	L.Hutton (364), M.Leyland (187)	The Oval	1938
3rd	262	W.R.Hammond (177), D.R.Jardine (98)	Adelaide	1928-29
4th	222	W.R.Hammond (240), E.Paynter (99)	Lord's	1938
5th	206	E.Paynter (216*), D.C.S.Compton (102)	Nottingham	1938
6th	215	L.Hutton (364), J.Hardstaff, jr (169 *)	The Oval	1938
	215	G.Boycott (107), A.P.E.Knott (135)	Nottingham	1977
7th	143	F.E.Woolley (133 *), J.Vine (36)	Sydney	1911-12
8th	124	E.H.Hendren (169), H.Larwood (70)	Brisbane[1]	1928-29
9th	151	W.H.Scotton (90), W.W.Read (117)	The Oval	1884
10th	130	R.E.Foster (287), W.Rhodes (40 *)	Sydney	1903-04

BEST INNINGS BOWLING ANALYSIS

Australia in England	8-31	F.J.Laver	Manchester	1909
Australia in Australia	9-121	A.A.Mailey	Melbourne	1920-21
England in England	10-53	J.C.Laker	Manchester	1956
England in Australia	8-35	G.A.Lohmann	Sydney	1886-87

BEST MATCH BOWLING ANALYSIS

Australia in England	16-137	R.A.L.Massie	Lord's	1972
Australia in Australia	13-77	M.A.Noble	Melbourne	1901-02
England in England	19-90	J.C.Laker	Manchester	1956
England in Australia	15-124	W.Rhodes	Melbourne	1903-04

HIGHEST AGGREGATE OF WICKETS IN A SERIES

Australia in England	42 (av 21.26)	T.M.Alderman	1981
Australia in Australia	41 (av 12.85)	R.M.Hogg	1978-79
England in England	46 (av 9.60)	J.C.Laker	1956
England in Australia	38 (av 23.18)	M.W.Tate	1924-25

AUSTRALIA v SOUTH AFRICA

Venue and Result	Australia 1st	Australia 2nd	South Africa 1st	South Africa 2nd	Captains Australia	Captains South Africa
1902-03 in SOUTH AFRICA						
Johannesburg[1]-Drawn	296	7d-372	*454	4-101	J.Darling	H.M.Taberer
Johannesburg[1]-Australia 159 runs	*175	309	240	85		J.H.Anderson
Cape Town-Australia 10 wkts	*252	0-59	85	225		E.A.Halliwell
1910-11 in AUSTRALIA						
Sydney-Australia inns &114 runs	*528	-	174	240	C.Hill	P.W.Sherwell
Melbourne-Australia 89 runs	*348	327	506	80		
Adelaide-South Africa 38 runs	465	339	*482	360		
Melbourne-Australia 530 runs	*328	578	205	171		
Sydney-Australia 7 wkts	*364	3-198	160	401		
1912 in ENGLAND						
Manchester-Australia inns & 88 runs	*448	-	265	95	S.E.Gregory	F.Mitchell
Lord's-Australia 10 wkts	390	0-48	*263	173		F.Mitchell
Nottingham-Drawn	219	-	*329	-		L.J.Tancred
1921-22 in SOUTH AFRICA						
Durban[1]-Drawn	*299	7d-324	232	7-184	H.L.Collins	H.W.Taylor
Johannesburg[1]-Drawn	*450	0-7	243	8d-472		
Cape Town-Australia 10 wkts	396	0-1	*180	216		
1931-32 in AUSTRALIA						
Brisbane[2]-Australia inns & 163 runs	*450	-	170	117	W.M.Woodfull	H.B.Cameron
Sydney-Australia inns & 155 runs	469	-	*153	161		
Melbourne-Australia 169 runs	*198	554	358	225		
Adelaide-Australia 10 wkts	513	0-73	*308	274		
Melbourne-Australia inns & 72 runs	153	-	*36	45		
1935-36 in SOUTH AFRICA						
Durban[2]-Australia 9 wkts	429	1-102	*248	282	V.Y.Richardson	H.F.Wade
Johannesburg[1]-Drawn	250	2-274	*157	491		
Cape Town-Australia inns & 78 runs	*8d-362	-	102	182		
Johannesburg[1]-Australia inns & 184 runs	439	-	*157	98		
Durban[2]-Australia inns & 6 runs	455	-	*222	227		
1949-50 in SOUTH AFRICA						
Johannesburg[2]-Australia inns & 85 runs	*413	-	137	191	A.L.Hassett	A.D.Nourse
Cape Town-Australia 8 wkts	*7d-526	2-87	278	333		
Durban[2]-Australia 5 wkts	75	5-336	*311	99		
Johannesburg[2]-Drawn	*8d-465	2-259	352	-		
Port Elizabeth-Australia inns & 259 runs	*7d-549	-	158	132		
1952-53 in AUSTRALIA						
Brisbane[2]-Australia 96 runs	*280	277	221	240	A.L.Hassett	J.E.Cheetham
Melbourne-South Africa 82 runs	243	290	*227	388		
Sydney-Australia inns & 38 runs	443	-	*173	232		
Adelaide-Drawn	*530	3d-233	387	6-177		
Melbourne-South Africa 6 wkts	*520	209	435	4-297		

AUSTRALIA v SOUTH AFRICA (cont.) Venue and Result	Australia 1st	Australia 2nd	South Africa 1st	South Africa 2nd	Captains Australia	Captains South Africa
1957-58 in SOUTH AFRICA						
Johannesburg[3]-Drawn	368	3-162	*9d-470	201	I.D.Craig	D.J.McGlew
Cape Town-Australia inns & 141 runs	*449	-	209	99		C.B.van Ryneveld
Durban[2]-Drawn	*163	7-292	384	-		C.B.van Ryneveld
Johannesburg[3]-Australia 10 wkts	*401	0-1	203	198		C.B.van Ryneveld
Port Elizabeth-Australia 8 wkts	291	2-68	*214	144		C.B.van Ryneveld
1963-64 in AUSTRALIA						
Brisbane[2]-Drawn	*435	1d-144	346	1-13	R.Benaud	T.L.Goddard
Melbourne-Australia 8 wkts	447	2-136	*274	306	R.B.Simpson	
Sydney-Drawn	*260	9d-450	302	5-326	R.B.Simpson	
Adelaide-South Africa 10 wkts	*345	331	595	0-82	R.B.Simpson	
Sydney-Drawn	*311	270	411	0-76	R.B.Simpson	
1966-67 in SOUTH AFRICA						
Johannesburg[3]-South Africa 233 runs	325	261	*199	620	R.B.Simpson	P.L.van der Merwe
Cape Town-Australia 6 wkts	*542	4-180	353	367		
Durban[2]-South Africa 8 wkts	147	334	*300	2-185		
Johannesburg[3]-Drawn	*143	8-148	9d-332	-		
Port Elizabeth-South Africa 7 wkts	*173	278	276	3-179		
1969-70 in SOUTH AFRICA						
Cape Town-South Africa 170 runs	164	280	*382	232	W.M.Lawry	A.Bacher
Durban[2]-South Africa inns &129 runs	157	336	*9d-622	-		
Johannesburg[3]-South Africa 307 runs	202	178	*279	408		
Port Elizabeth-South Africa 323 runs	212	246	*311	8d-470		

Test Match Results Summary

AUSTRALIA v SOUTH AFRICA — IN AUSTRALIA

	Tests	Result			Sydney			Melbourne			Adelaide			Brisbane		
		A	SA	D	A	SA	D	A	SA	D	A	SA	D	A	SA	D
1910-11	5	4	1	-	2	-	-	2	-	-	-	1	-	-	-	-
1931-32	5	5	-	-	1	-	-	2	-	-	1	-	-	1	-	-
1952-53	5	2	2	1	1	-	-	-	2	-	-	-	1	1	-	-
1963-64	5	1	1	3	-	-	2	1	-	-	-	1	-	-	-	1
	20	12	4	4	4	-	2	5	2	-	1	2	1	2	-	1

AUSTRALIA v SOUTH AFRICA — IN SOUTH AFRICA

	Tests	Result			Johannesburg			Cape Town			Durban			P.Elizabeth		
		A	SA	D	A	SA	D	A	SA	D	A	SA	D	A	SA	D
1902-03	3	2	-	1	1	-	1	1	-	-	-	-	-	-	-	-
1921-22	3	1	-	2	-	-	1	1	-	-	-	-	1	-	-	-
1935-36	5	4	-	1	1	-	1	1	-	-	2	-	-	-	-	-
1949-50	5	4	-	1	1	-	1	1	-	-	1	-	-	1	-	-
1957-58	5	3	-	2	1	-	1	1	-	-	-	-	1	1	-	-
1966-67	5	1	3	1	-	1	1	1	-	-	-	1	-	-	1	-
1969-70	4	-	4	-	-	1	-	-	1	-	-	1	-	-	1	-
	30	15	7	8	4	2	6	6	1	-	3	2	2	2	2	-

AUSTRALIA v SOUTH AFRICA—IN ENGLAND

	Tests	Result A	Result SA	Result D	Manchester A	Manchester SA	Manchester D	Lord's A	Lord's SA	Lord's D	Nottingham A	Nottingham SA	Nottingham D
1912	3	2	-	1	1	-	-	1	-	-	-	-	1
Totals	53	29	11	13									

HIGHEST INNINGS TOTALS

Australia in Australia	578	Melbourne	1910-11
Australia in South Africa	7d-549	Port Elizabeth	1949-50
South Africa in Australia	595	Adelaide	1963-64
South Africa in South Africa	9d-622	Durban[2]	1969-70

LOWEST INNINGS TOTALS

Australia in Australia	153	Melbourne	1931-32
Australia in South Africa	75	Durban[2]	1949-50
South Africa in Australia	36	Melbourne	1931-32
South Africa in South Africa	85	Johannesburg[1]	1902-03
	85	Cape Town	1902-03

HIGHEST MATCH AGGREGATE	1646 for 40 wickets	Adelaide	1910-11
LOWEST MATCH AGGREGATE	234 for 29 wickets	Melbourne	1931-32

HIGHEST INDIVIDUAL INNINGS

Australia in Australia	299*	D.G.Bradman	Adelaide	1931-32
Australia in South Africa	203	H.L.Collins	Johannesburg[1]	1921-22
South Africa in Australia	204	G.A.Faulkner	Melbourne	1910-11
South Africa in South Africa	274	R.G.Pollock	Durban[2]	1969-70

HIGHEST AGGREGATE OF RUNS IN A SERIES

Australia in Australia	834 (av 92.66)	R.N.Harvey	1952-53
Australia in South Africa	660 (av 132.00)	R.N.Harvey	1949-50
South Africa in Australia	732 (av 73.20)	G.A.Faulkner	1910-11
South Africa in South Africa	606 (av 86.57)	D.T.Lindsay	1966-67

RECORD WICKET PARTNERSHIPS—AUSTRALIA

1st	233	J.H.W.Fingleton (112), W.A.Brown (121)	Cape Town	1935-36
2nd	275	C.C.McDonald (154), A.L.Hassett (163)	Adelaide	1952-53
3rd	242	C.Kelleway (102), W.Bardsley (164)	Lord's	1912
4th	168	R.N.Harvey (190), K.R.Miller (55)	Sydney	1952-53
5th	143	W.W.Armstrong (132), V.T.Trumper (87)	Melbourne	1910-11
6th	107	C.Kelleway (59), V.S.Ransford (75)	Melbourne	1910-11
7th	160	R.Benaud (90), G.D.McKenzie (76)	Sydney	1963-64
8th	83	A.G.Chipperfield (109), C.V.Grimmett (15)	Durban[2]	1935-36
9th	78	D.G.Bradman (299*), W.J.O'Reilly (23)	Adelaide	1931-32
	78	K.D.Mackay (83*), I.Meckiff (26)	Johannesburg[3]	1957-58
10th	82	V.S.Ransford (95), W.J.Whitty (39*)	Melbourne	1910-11

RECORD WICKET PARTNERSHIPS—SOUTH AFRICA

1st	176	D.J.McGlew (108), T.L.Goddard (90)	Johannesburg[3]	1957-58
2nd	173	L.J.Tancred (97), C.B.Llewellyn (90)	Johannesburg[1]	1902-03
3rd	341	E.J.Barlow (201), R.G.Pollock (175)	Adelaide	1963-64
4th	206	C.N.Frank (152), A.W.Nourse (111)	Johannesburg[1]	1921-22
5th	129	J.H.B.Waite (59), W.R.Endean (77)	Johannesburg[3]	1957-58
6th	200	R.G.Pollock (274), H.R.Lance (61)	Durban[2]	1969-70
7th	221	D.T.Lindsay (182), P.L.van der Merwe (76)	Johannesburg[3]	1966-67
8th	124	A.W.Nourse (72), E.A.Halliwell (57)	Johannesburg[1]	1902-03
9th	85	R.G.Pollock (209), P.M.Pollock (41)	Cape Town	1966-67
10th	53	L.A.Stricker (48), S.J.Pegler (24*)	Adelaide	1910-11

BEST INNINGS BOWLING ANALYSIS

Australia in Australia	7-83	C.V.Grimmett	Adelaide	1931-32
Australia in South Africa	7-34	J.V.Saunders	Johannesburg[1]	1902-03
South Africa in Australia	7-81	H.J.Tayfield	Melbourne	1952-53
South Africa in South Africa	7-23	H.J.Tayfield	Durban[2]	1949-50

BEST MATCH BOWLING ANALYSIS

Australia in Australia	14-199	C.V.Grimmett	Adelaide	1931-32
Australia in South Africa	13-173	C.V.Grimmett	Durban[2]	1935-36
South Africa in Australia	13-165	H.J.Tayfield	Melbourne	1952-53
South Africa in South Africa	10-116	C.B.Llewellyn	Johannesburg[1]	1902-03

HIGHEST AGGREGATE OF WICKETS IN A SERIES

Australia in Australia	37 (av 17.08)	W.J.Whitty	1910-11
Australia in South Africa	44 (av 14.59)	C.V.Grimmett	1935-36
South Africa in Australia	30 (av 28.10)	H.J.Tayfield	1952-53
South Africa in South Africa	26 (av 16.23)	T.L.Goddard	1966-67
	26 (av 13.57)	M.J.Procter	1969-70

AUSTRALIA v WEST INDIES

Venue and Result	Australia 1st	Australia 2nd	West Indies 1st	West Indies 2nd	Captains: Australia	Captains: West Indies
1930-31 in AUSTRALIA						
Adelaide-Australia 10 wkts	376	0-172	*296	249	W.M.Woodfull	G.C.Grant
Sydney-Australia inns & 172 runs	*369	-	107	90		
Brisbane[1]-Australia inns & 217 runs	*558	-	193	148		
Melbourne-Australia inns & 122 runs	8d-328	-	*99	107		
Sydney-West Indies 30 runs	224	220	*6d-350	5d-124		
1951-52 in AUSTRALIA						
Brisbane[2]-Australia 3 wkts	226	7-236	*216	245	A.L.Hassett	J.D.C.Goddard
Sydney-Australia 7 wkts	517	3-137	*362	290	A.L.Hassett	J.D.C.Goddard
Adelaide-West Indies 6 wkts	*82	255	105	4-233	A.R.Morris	J.D.C.Goddard
Melbourne-Australia 1 wkt	216	9-260	*272	203	A.L.Hassett	J.D.C.Goddard
Sydney-Australia 202 runs	*116	377	78	213	A.L.Hassett	J.B.Stollmeyer
1954-55 in WEST INDIES						
Kingston-Australia 9 wkts	*9d-515	1-20	259	275	I.W.Johnson	D.S.Atkinson
Port-of-Spain-Drawn	9d-600	-	*382	4-273		J.B.Stollmeyer
Georgetown-Australia 8 wkts	257	2-133	*182	207		J.B.Stollmeyer
Bridgetown-Drawn	*668	249	510	6-234		D.S.Atkinson
Kingston-Australia inns & 82 runs	8d-758	-	*357	319		D.S.Atkinson

AUSTRALIA v WEST INDIES (cont.)	Australia		West Indies		Captains	
Venue and Result	1st	2nd	1st	2nd	Australia	West Indies
1960-61 in AUSTRALIA						
Brisbane²-Tied	505	232	*453	284	R.Benaud	F.M.M.Worrell
Melbourne-Australia 7 wkts	*348	3-70	181	233		
Sydney-West Indies 222 runs	202	241	*339	326		
Adelaide-Drawn	366	9-273	*393	6d-432		
Melbourne-Australia 2 wkts	356	8-258	*292	321		
1964-65 in WEST INDIES						
Kingston-West Indies 179 runs	217	216	*239	373	R.B.Simpson	G.S.Sobers
Port-of-Spain-Drawn	516	-	*429	386		
Georgetown-West Indies 212 runs	179	144	*355	180		
Bridgetown-Drawn	*6d-650	4d-175	573	5-242		
Port-of-Spain-Australia 10 wkts	294	0-63	*224	131		
1968-69 in AUSTRALIA						
Brisbane ²-West Indies 125 runs	284	240	*296	353	W.M.Lawry	G.S.Sobers
Melbourne-Australia inns & 30 runs	510	-	*200	280		
Sydney-Australia 10 wkts	547	0-42	*264	324		
Adelaide-Drawn	533	9-339	*276	616		
Sydney-Australia 382 runs	*619	8d-394	279	352		
1972-73 in WEST INDIES						
Kingston-Drawn	*7d-428	2d-260	428	3-67	I.M.Chappell	R.B.Kanhai
Bridgetown-Drawn	*324	2d-300	391	0-36		
Port-of-Spain-Australia 44 runs	*332	281	280	289		
Georgetown-Australia 10 wkts	341	0-135	*366	109		
Port-of-Spain-Drawn	*8d-419	7d-218	319	5-135		
1975-76 in AUSTRALIA						
Brisbane²-Australia 8 wkts	366	2-219	*214	370	G.S.Chappell	C.H.Lloyd
Perth-West Indies inns & 87 runs	*329	169	585	-		
Melbourne-Australia 8 wkts	485	2-55	*224	312		
Sydney-Australia 7 wkts	405	3-82	*355	128		
Adelaide-Australia 190 runs	*418	7d-345	274	299		
Melbourne-Australia 165 runs	*351	3d-300	160	326		
1977-78 in WEST INDIES						
Port-of-Spain-West Indies inns & 106 runs	*90	209	405	-	R.B.Simpson	C.H.Lloyd
Bridgetown-West Indies 9 wkts	*250	178	288	1-141		C.H.Lloyd
Georgetown-Australia 3 wkts	286	7-362	*205	439		A.I.Kallicharran
Port-of-Spain-West Indies 198 runs	290	94	*292	290		A.I.Kallicharran
Kingston-Drawn	*343	3d-305	280	9-258		A.I.Kallicharran
1979-80 in AUSTRALIA						
Brisbane²-Drawn	*268	6d-448	441	3-40	G.S.Chappell	D L.Murray
Melbourne-West Indies 10 wkts	*156	259	397	0-22		C.H.Lloyd
Adelaide-West Indies 408 runs	203	165	*328	448		C.H.Lloyd
1981-82 in AUSTRALIA						
Melbourne-Australia 58 runs	*198	222	201	161	G.S.Chappell	C H.Lloyd
Sydney-Drawn	267	4-200	*384	255		
Adelaide-West Indies 5 wkts	*238	386	389	5-239		

AUSTRALIA v WEST INDIES (cont.) Venue and Result	Australia 1st	Australia 2nd	West Indies 1st	West Indies 2nd	Captains Australia	Captains West Indies
1983-84 in WEST INDIES						
Georgetown-Drawn	*279	9d-273	230	0-250	K.J.Hughes	C.H.Lloyd
Port-of-Spain-Drawn	*255	9d-299	8d-468	-		I.V.A.Richards
Bridgetown-West Indies 10 wkts	*429	97	509	0-21		C.H.Lloyd
St John's-West Indies inns & 36 runs	*262	200	498	-		C.H.Lloyd
Kingston-West Indies 10 wkts	*199	160	305	0-55		C.H.Lloyd
1984-85 in AUSTRALIA						
Perth-West Indies inns & 112 runs	76	228	*416	-	K.J.Hughes	C.H.Lloyd
Brisbane²-West Indies 8 wkts	*175	271	424	2-26	K.J.Hughes	
Adelaide-West Indies 191 runs	284	173	*356	7d-292	A.R.Border	
Melbourne-Drawn	298	8-198	*479	5d-186	A.R.Border	
Sydney-Australia inns & 55 runs	*9d-471	-	163	253	A.R.Border	
1988-89 in AUSTRALIA						
Brisbane²-West Indies 8 wkts	*167	289	394	2-63	A.R.Border	I.V.A.Richards
Perth-West Indies 169 runs	8d-395	234	*449	9d-349		
Melbourne-West Indies 285 runs	242	114	*280	9d-361		
Sydney-Australia 7 wkts	401	3-82	*224	256		
Adelaide-Drawn	*515	4d-224	369	4-233		
1990-91 in WEST INDIES						
Kingston-Drawn	371	-	*264	3-334	A.R.Border	I.V.A.Richards
Georgetown-West Indies 10 wkts	*348	248	569	0-31		
Port-of-Spain-Drawn	*294	3-123	227	-		
Bridgetown-West Indies 343 runs	134	208	*149	9d-536		
St John's-Australia 157 runs	*403	265	214	297		

Test Match Results Summary

AUSTRALIA v WEST INDIES—IN AUSTRALIA

		Result				Adelaide				Sydney				Brisbane				Melbourne				Perth			
	Tests	A	WI	D	T	A	WI	D	T	A	WI	D	T	A	WI	D	T	A	WI	D	T	A	WI	D	T
1930-31	5	4	1	-	-	1	-	-	-	-	1	-	-	1	-	-	-	1	-	-	-	-	-	-	-
1951-52	5	4	1	-	-	-	1	-	-	2	-	-	-	1	-	-	-	1	-	-	-	-	-	-	-
1960-61	5	2	1	1	1	-	-	1	-	-	1	-	-	-	-	-	1	2	-	-	-	-	-	-	-
1968-69	5	3	1	1	-	-	-	1	2	-	-	-	-	-	-	-	-	-	-	-	-	-	-	-	-
1975-76	6	5	1	-	-	1	-	-	-	1	-	-	-	1	-	-	-	2	-	-	-	-	1	-	-
1979-80	3	-	2	1	-	-	1	-	-	-	-	-	-	-	-	1	-	-	1	-	-	-	-	-	-
1981-82	3	1	1	1	-	-	1	-	-	-	-	1	-	-	-	-	-	1	-	-	-	-	-	-	-
1984-85	5	1	3	1	-	-	1	-	-	1	-	-	-	-	1	-	-	-	-	1	-	-	1	-	-
1988-89	5	1	3	1	-	-	-	1	-	1	-	-	-	-	1	-	-	-	1	-	-	-	1	-	-
	42	21	14	6	1	2	4	3	-	8	2	1	-	3	3	1	1	8	2	1	-	-	3	-	-

AUSTRALIA v WEST INDIES—IN WEST INDIES

		Result				Kingston				Port-of-Spain				Georgetown				Bridgetown				St John's			
	Tests	A	WI	D	T	A	WI	D	T	A	WI	D	T	A	WI	D	T	A	WI	D	T	A	WI	D	T
1954-55	5	3	-	2	-	2	-	-	-	-	-	1	-	1	-	-	-	-	-	1	-	-	-	-	-
1964-65	5	1	2	2	-	-	1	-	-	1	-	1	-	-	1	-	-	-	-	1	-	-	-	-	-
1972-73	5	2	-	3	-	-	-	1	-	1	-	1	-	1	-	-	-	-	-	1	-	-	-	-	-
1977-78	5	1	3	1	-	-	-	1	-	-	2	-	-	1	-	-	-	-	1	-	-	-	-	-	-
1983-84	5	-	3	2	-	-	1	-	-	-	-	1	-	-	-	1	-	-	1	-	-	-	1	-	-
1990-91	5	1	2	2	-	-	-	1	-	-	-	1	-	-	1	-	-	-	1	-	-	1	-	-	-
	30	8	10	12	-	2	2	3	-	2	2	5	-	3	2	1	-	-	3	3	-	1	1	-	-
Totals	72	29	24	18	1																				

HIGHEST INNINGS TOTALS

Australia in Australia	619	Sydney	1968-69
Australia in West Indies	8d-758	Kingston	1954-55
West Indies in Australia	616	Adelaide	1968-69
West Indies in West Indies	573	Bridgetown	1964-65

LOWEST INNINGS TOTALS

Australia in Australia	76	Perth	1984-85
Australia in West Indies	90	Port-of-Spain	1977-78
West Indies in Australia	78	Sydney	1951-52
West Indies in West Indies	109	Georgetown	1972-73

HIGHEST MATCH AGGREGATE	1764 for 39 wickets	Adelaide	1968-69
LOWEST MATCH AGGREGATE	534 for 28 wickets	Melbourne	1930-31

HIGHEST INDIVIDUAL INNINGS

Australia in Australia	242	K.D.Walters	Sydney	1968-69
Australia in West Indies	210	W.M.Lawry	Bridgetown	1964-65
West Indies in Australia	208	I.V.A.Richards	Melbourne	1988-89
West Indies in West Indies	226	C.G.Greenidge	Bridgetown	1990-91

HIGHEST AGGREGATE OF RUNS IN A SERIES

Australia in Australia	702 (av 117.00)	G.S.Chappell	1975-76
Australia in West Indies	650 (av 108.33)	R.N.Harvey	1954-55
West Indies in Australia	537 (av 59.66)	D.L.Haynes	1988-89
West Indies in West Indies	827 (av 82.70)	C.L.Walcott	1954-55

RECORD WICKET PARTNERSHIPS—AUSTRALIA

1st	382	W.M.Lawry (210), R.B.Simpson (201)	Bridgetown	1964-65
2nd	298	W.M.Lawry (205), I.M.Chappell (165)	Melbourne	1968-69
3rd	295	C.C.McDonald (127), R.N.Harvey (204)	Kingston	1954-55
4th	336	W.M.Lawry (151), K.D.Walters (242)	Sydney	1968-69
5th	220	K.R.Miller (109), R.G.Archer (128)	Kingston	1954-55
6th	206	K.R.Miller (137), R.G.Archer (98)	Bridgetown	1954-55
7th	134	R.Benaud (52), A.K.Davidson (80)	Brisbane[2]	1960-61
8th	137	R.Benaud (128), I.W.Johnson (27*)	Kingston	1954-55
9th	114	D.M.Jones (216), M.G. Hughes (72*)	Adelaide	1988-89
10th	97	T.G.Hogan (42*), R.M.Hogg (52)	Georgetown	1983-84

RECORD WICKET PARTNERSHIPS—WEST INDIES

1st	250*	C.G.Greenidge (120*), D.L.Haynes (103*)	Georgetown	1983-84
2nd	297	D.L.Haynes (111), R.B.Richardson (182)	Georgetown	1990-91
3rd	308	R.B.Richardson (154), I.V.A.Richards (178)	Antigua	1983-84
4th	198	L.G.Rowe (107), A.I.Kallicharran (101)	Brisbane²	1975-76
5th	210	R.B.Kanhai (84), M.L.C.Foster (125)	Kingston	1972-73
6th	165	R.B.Kanhai (105), D.L.Murray (90)	Bridgetown	1972-73
7th	347	D.S.Atkinson (219), C.C.Depeiza (122)	Bridgetown	1954-55
8th	87	P.J.L.Dujon (70), C.E.L.Ambrose (53)	Port-of-Spain	1990-91
9th	122	D.A.J.Holford (80), J.L.Hendriks (37*)	Adelaide	1968-69
10th	56	J.Garner (60), C.E.H.Croft (2*)	Brisbane²	1979-80

BEST INNINGS BOWLING ANALYSIS

Australia in Australia	8-71	G.D.McKenzie	Melbourne	1968-69
Australia in West Indies	7-44	I.W.Johnson	Georgetown	1954-55
West Indies in Australia	7-54	A.M.E.Roberts	Perth	1975-76
West Indies in West Indies	6-29	L R.Gibbs	Georgetown	1964-65

BEST MATCH BOWLING ANALYSIS

Australia in Australia	13-217	M.G.Hughes	Perth	1988-89
Australia in West Indies	10-115	N.J.N.Hawke	Georgetown	1964-65
West Indies in Australia	11-107	M.A.Holding	Melbourne	1981-82
West Indies in West Indies	9-80	L.R.Gibbs	Georgetown	1964-65

HIGHEST AGGREGATE OF WICKETS IN A SERIES

Australia in Australia	33 (av 17 96)	C.V.Grimmett	1930-31
	33 (av 18 54)	A.K.Davidson	1960-61
Australia in West Indies	26 (av 20.73)	M.H.N.Walker	1972-73
West Indies in Australia	28 (av 19.78)	M.D.Marshall	1984-85
West Indies in West Indies	31 (av 16.87)	J.Garner	1983-84

AUSTRALIA v NEW ZEALAND

Venue and Result	Australia 1st	Australia 2nd	New Zealand 1st	New Zealand 2nd	Captains Australia	Captains New Zealand
1945-46 in NEW ZEALAND						
Wellington-Australia inns & 103 runs	8d-199	-	*42	54	W.A.Brown	W.A.Hadlee
1973-74 in AUSTRALIA						
Melbourne-Australia inns & 25 runs	*8d-462	-	237	200	I.M.Chappell	B.E.Congdon
Sydney-Drawn	162	2-30	*312	9d-305		
Adelaide-Australia inns & 57 runs	*477	-	218	202		
1973-74 in NEW ZEALAND						
Wellington-Drawn	*6d-511	8-460	484	-	I.M.Chappell	B.E.Congdon
Christchurch-New Zealand 5 wkts	*223	259	255	5-230		
Auckland-Australia 297 runs	*221	346	112	158		
1976-77 in NEW ZEALAND						
Christchurch-Drawn	*552	4d-154	357	8-293	G.S.Chappell	G.M.Turner
Auckland-Australia 10 wkts	377	0-28	*229	175		
1980-81 in AUSTRALIA						
Brisbane²-Australia 10 wkts	305	0-63	*225	142	G.S.Chappell	G.P.Howarth
Perth-Australia 8 wkts	265	2-55	*196	121		M.G.Burgess
Melbourne-Drawn	*321	188	317	6-128		G.P.Howarth

AUSTRALIA v NEW ZEALAND (cont)	Australia		New Zealand		Captains	
Venue and Result	1st	2nd	1st	2nd	Australia	New Zealand
1981-82 in NEW ZEALAND						
Wellington-Drawn	1-85	-	*7d-266	-	G.S.Chappell	G.P.Howarth
Auckland-New Zealand 5 wkts	*210	280	387	5-109		
Christchurch-Australia 8 wkts	*353	2-69	149	272		
1985-86 in AUSTRALIA						
Brisbane²-New Zealand inns & 41 runs	*179	333	7d-553	-	A.R.Border	J.V.Coney
Sydney-Australia 4 wkts	227	6-260	*293	193		
Perth-New Zealand 6 wkts	*203	259	299	4-164		
1985-86 in NEW ZEALAND						
Wellington-Drawn	*435	-	6-379	-	A.R.Border	J.V.Coney
Auckland-Drawn	*364	7d-219	339	1-16		
Christchurch-New Zealand 8 wkts	*314	103	258	2-160		
1987-88 in AUSTRALIA						
Brisbane²-Australia 9 wkts	305	1-97	*186	212	A.R.Border	J.J.Crowe
Adelaide-Drawn	496	-	*9d-485	7-182		
Melbourne-Drawn	357	9-230	*317	286		
1989-90 in AUSTRALIA						
Perth-Drawn	*9d-521	-	231	7-322	A.R.Border	J.G.Wright
1989-90 in NEW ZEALAND						
Wellington-New Zealand 9 wkts	*110	269	202	1-181	A.R.Border	J.G.Wright

Test Match Results Summary

AUSTRALIA v NEW ZEALAND—IN AUSTRALIA

		Result			Melbourne			Sydney			Adelaide			Brisbane			Perth		
	Tests	A	NZ	D	A	NZ	D	A	NZ	D	A	NZ	D	A	NZ	D	A	NZ	D
1973-74	3	2	-	1	1	-	-	-	-	1	1	-	-	-	-	-	-	-	-
1980-81	3	2	-	1	-	-	1	-	-	-	-	-	-	1	-	-	1	-	-
1985-86	3	1	2	-	-	-	-	1	-	-	-	-	-	-	1	-	-	1	-
1987-88	3	1	-	2	-	-	1	-	-	-	-	-	1	1	-	-	-	-	-
1989-90	1	-	-	1	-	-	-	-	-	-	-	-	-	-	-	-	-	-	1
	13	6	2	5	1	-	2	1	-	1	1	-	1	2	1	-	1	1	1

AUSTRALIA v NEW ZEALAND—IN NEW ZEALAND

		Result			Wellington			Christchurch			Auckland		
	Tests	A	NZ	D	A	NZ	D	A	NZ	D	A	NZ	D
1945-46	1	1	-	-	1	-	-	-	-	-	-	-	-
1973-74	3	1	1	1	-	-	1	-	1	-	1	-	-
1976-77	2	1	-	1	-	-	-	-	-	1	1	-	-
1981-82	3	1	1	1	-	-	1	1	-	-	-	1	-
1985-86	3	-	1	2	-	-	1	-	-	1	-	1	-
1989-90	1	-	1	-	-	1	-	-	-	-	-	-	-
	13	4	4	5	1	1	3	1	1	2	2	2	-
Totals	26	10	6	10									

HIGHEST INNINGS TOTALS

Australia in Australia	9d-521	Perth	1989-90
Australia in New Zealand	552	Christchurch	1976-77
New Zealand in Australia	7d-553	Brisbane^2	1985-86
New Zealand in New Zealand	484	Wellington	1973-74

LOWEST INNINGS TOTALS

Australia in Australia	162	Sydney	1973-74
Australia in New Zealand	103	Auckland	1985-86
New Zealand in Australia	121	Perth	1980-81
New Zealand in New Zealand	42	Wellington	1945-46

HIGHEST MATCH AGGREGATE	1455 for 24 wickets	Wellington	1973-74
LOWEST MATCH AGGREGATE	295 for 28 wickets	Wellington	1945-46

HIGHEST INDIVIDUAL INNINGS

Australia in Australia	205	A.R.Border	Adelaide	1987-88
Australia in New Zealand	250	K.D.Walters	Christchurch	1976-77
New Zealand in Australia	188	M.D.Crowe	Sydney	1985-86
New Zealand in New Zealand	161	B.A.Edgar	Auckland	1981-82

HIGHEST AGGREGATE OF RUNS IN A SERIES

Australia in Australia	288 (av 72.00)	A.R.Border	1987-88
Australia in New Zealand	449 (av 89.80)	G.S.Chappell	1973-74
New Zealand in Australia	396 (av 66.00)	M.D.Crowe	1987-88
New Zealand in New Zealand	403 (av 100.75)	G.M.Turner	1973-74

RECORD WICKET PARTNERSHIPS—AUSTRALIA

1st	106	B.M.Laird (39), G.M.Wood (100)	Auckland	1981-82
2nd	168	G.R.Marsh (118), W.B.Phillips (62)	Auckland	1985-86
3rd	264	I.M.Chappell (145), G.S.Chappell (247*)	Wellington	1973-74
4th	116	A.R.Border (205), S.R.Waugh (61)	Adelaide	1987-88
5th	213	G.M.Ritchie (92), G.R.J.Matthews (130)	Wellington	1985-86
6th	197	A.R.Border (152*), G.R.J.Matthews (115)	Brisbane^2	1985-86
7th	217	K.D.Walters (250), G.J.Gilmour (101)	Christchurch	1976-77
8th	93	G.J.Gilmour (64), K.J.O'Keeffe (32)	Auckland	1976-77
9th	61	A.I.C.Dodemaide (50), C.J.McDermott (33)	Melbourne	1987-88
10th	60	K.D.Walters (107), J.D.Higgs (6*)	Melbourne	1980-81

RECORD WICKET PARTNERSHIPS—NEW ZEALAND

1st	107	G.M.Turner (72), J.M.Parker (34)	Auckland	1973-74
2nd	128	J.G.Wright (45), A.H.Jones (150)	Adelaide	1987-88
	128*	J.G.Wright (117*), A.H.Jones (33*)	Wellington	1989-90
3rd	224	J.F.Reid (108), M.D.Crowe (188)	Brisbane^2	1985-86
4th	229	B.E.Congdon (132), B.F.Hastings (101)	Wellington	1973-74
5th	88	J.V.Coney (71), M.G.Burgess (43)	Perth	1980-81
6th	109	K.R.Rutherford (65), J.V.Coney (101*)	Wellington	1985-86
7th	132*	J.V.Coney (101*), R.J.Hadlee (81*)	Wellington	1985-86
8th	88*	M.J.Greatbatch (146*), M.C.Snedden (33*)	Perth	1989-90
9th	73	H.J.Howarth (60), D.R.Hadlee (37)	Christchurch	1976-77
10th	124	J.G.Bracewell (83*), S.L.Boock (37)	Sydney	1985-86

BEST INNINGS BOWLING ANALYSIS

Australia in Australia	6-53	D.K.Lillee	Brisbane^2	1980-81
Australia in New Zealand	6-72	D.K.Lillee	Auckland	1976-77
New Zealand in Australia	9-52	R.J.Hadlee	Melbourne	1985-86
New Zealand in New Zealand	7-116	R.J.Hadlee	Christchurch	1985-86

BEST MATCH BOWLING ANALYSIS

Australia in Australia	10-174	R.G.Holland	Sydney	1985-86
Australia in New Zealand	11-123	D.K.Lillee	Auckland	1976-77
New Zealand in Australia	15-123	R.J.Hadlee	Brisbane^2	1985-86
New Zealand in New Zealand	10-146	J.G.Bracewell	Auckland	1985-86

HIGHEST AGGREGATE OF WICKETS IN A SERIES

Australia in Australia	17 (av 25.05)	C.J.McDermott	1985-86
Australia in New Zealand	15 (av 20.80)	D.K.Lillee	1976-77
New Zealand in Australia	33 (av 12.15)	R.J.Hadlee	1985-86
New Zealand in New Zealand	17 (av 25.64)	R.O.Collinge	1973-74

AUSTRALIA v INDIA

Venue and Result	Australia 1st	Australia 2nd	India 1st	India 2nd	Captains Australia	Captains India
1947-48 in AUSTRALIA						
Brisbane²-Australia inns & 226 runs	*8d-382	-	58	98	D.G.Bradman	N.B.Amarnath
Sydney-Drawn	107	-	*188	7-61		
Melbourne-Australia 233 runs	*394	4d-255	9d-291	125		
Adelaide-Australia inns & 16 runs	*674	-	381	277		
Melbourne-Australia inns & 177 runs	*8d-575	-	331	67		
1956-57 in INDIA						
Madras²-Australia inns & 5 runs	319	-	*161	153	I.W.Johnson	P.R.Umrigar
Bombay²-Drawn	7d-523	-	*251	5-250	R.R.Lindwall	
Calcutta-Australia 94 runs	*177	9d-189	136	136	I.W.Johnson	
1959-60 in INDIA						
Delhi-Australia inns & 127 runs	468	-	*135	206	R.Benaud	G.S.Ramchand
Kanpur-India 119 runs	219	105	*152	291		
Bombay²-Drawn	8d-387	1-34	*289	5d-226		
Madras²-Australia inns & 55 runs	*342	-	149	138		
Calcutta-Drawn	331	2-121	*194	339		
1964-65 in INDIA						
Madras²-Australia 139 runs	*211	397	276	193	R.B.Simpson	Nawab of Pataudi, jr
Bombay²-India 2 wkts	*320	274	341	8-256		
Calcutta-Drawn	*174	1-143	235	-		
1967-68 in AUSTRALIA						
Adelaide-Australia 146 runs	*335	369	307	251	R.B.Simpson	C.G Borde
Melbourne-Australia inns & 4 runs	529	-	*173	352	R.B.Simpson	Nawab of Pataudi, jr
Brisbane²-Australia 39 runs	*379	294	279	355	W M.Lawry	Nawab of Pataudi, jr
Sydney-Australia 144 runs	*317	292	268	197	W.M.Lawry	Nawab of Pataudi, jr
1969-70 in INDIA						
Bombay²-Australia 8 wkts	345	2-67	*271	137	W.M.Lawry	Nawab of Pataudi, jr
Kanpur-Drawn	348	0-95	*320	7d-312		
Delhi-India 7 wkts	*296	107	223	3-181		
Calcutta-Australia 10 wkts	335	0-42	*212	161		
Madras¹-Australia 77 runs	*258	153	163	171		
1977-78 in AUSTRALIA						
Brisbane²-Australia 16 runs	*166	327	153	324	R.B.Simpson	B.S.Bedi
Perth-Australia 2 wkts	394	8-342	*402	9d-330		
Melbourne-India 222 runs	213	164	*256	343		
Sydney-India inns & 2 runs	*131	263	8d-396	-		
Adelaide-Australia 47 runs	*505	256	269	445		

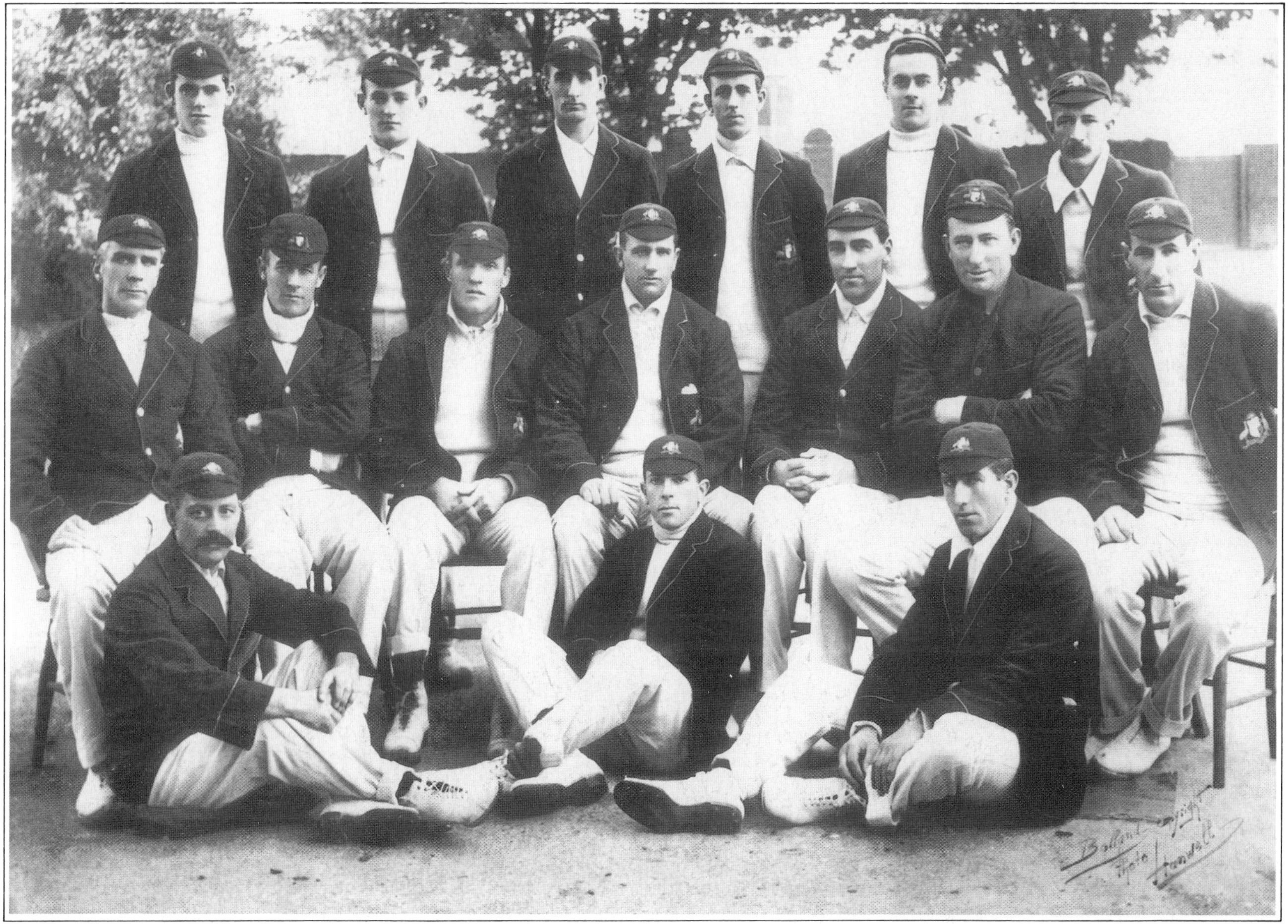

The Australian team, captained by Monty Noble, which toured England in 1909 and successfully retained the Ashes.

'The Big Ship' and captain of the Australian team, Warwick Armstrong, scoring a fine 158 against England at Sydney during the 1920-21 series.

AUSTRALIA v INDIA (cont.) Venue and Result	Australia 1st	Australia 2nd	India 1st	India 2nd	Captains Australia	Captains India
1979-80 in INDIA						
Madras[1]-Drawn	*390	7-212	425	-	K.J.Hughes	S.M.Gavaskar
Bangalore-Drawn	*333	3-77	5d-457	-		
Kanpur-India 153 runs	304	125	*271	311		
Delhi-Drawn	298	413	*7d-510	-		
Calcutta-Drawn	*442	6d-151	347	4-200		
Bombay[3]-India inns & 100 runs	160	198	*8d-458	-		
1980-81 In AUSTRALIA						
Sydney-Australia inns & 4 runs	406	-	*201	201	G.S.Chappell	S.M.Gavaskar
Adelaide-Drawn	*528	7d-221	419	8-135		
Melbourne-India 59 runs	419	83	*237	324		
1985-86 In AUSTRALIA						
Adelaide-Drawn	*381	0-17	520	-	A.R.Border	Kapil Dev
Melbourne-Drawn	*262	308	445	2-59		
Sydney-Drawn	396	6-119	*4d-600	-		
1986-87 in INDIA						
Madras[1]-Tied	*7d-574	5d-170	397	347	A.R.Border	Kapil Dev
Delhi-Drawn	*3d-207	-	3-107	-		
Bombay[3]-Drawn	*345	2-216	5d-517	-		
1991-92 in AUSTRALIA						
Brisbane[2]-Australia 10 wkts	340	0-58	*239	156	A.R.Border	M.Azharuddin
Melbourne-Australia 8 wkts	349	2-128	*263	213		
Sydney-Drawn	*313	8-173	483	-		
Adelaide-Australia 38 runs	*145	451	225	333		
Perth-Australia 300 runs	*346	6d-367	272	141		

Test Match Results Summary

AUSTRALIA v INDIA—IN AUSTRALIA

		Result				Brisbane				Sydney				Melbourne				Adelaide				Perth			
	Tests	A	I	D	T	A	I	D	T	A	I	D	T	A	I	D	T	A	I	D	T	A	I	D	T
1947-48	5	4	-	1	-	1	-	-	-	-	-	1	-	2	-	-	-	1	-	-	-	-	-	-	-
1967-68	4	4	-	-	-	1	-	-	-	1	-	-	-	1	-	-	-	1	-	-	-	-	-	-	-
1977-78	5	3	2	-	-	1	-	-	-	-	1	-	-	-	1	-	-	1	-	-	-	1	-	-	-
1980-81	3	1	1	1	-	-	-	-	-	1	-	-	-	-	1	-	-	-	-	1	-	-	-	-	-
1985-86	3	-	-	3	-	-	-	-	-	-	-	1	-	-	-	1	-	-	-	1	-	-	-	-	-
1991-92	5	4	-	1	-	1	-	-	-	-	-	1	-	1	-	-	-	1	-	-	-	1	-	-	-
	25	16	3	6	-	4	-	-	-	2	1	3	-	4	2	1	-	4	-	2	-	2	-	-	-

AUSTRALIA v INDIA—IN INDIA

		Result				Madras				Bombay				Calcutta				Delhi				Kanpur				Bangalore			
	Tests	A	I	D	T	A	I	D	T	A	I	D	T	A	I	D	T	A	I	D	T	A	I	D	T	A	I	D	T
1956-57	3	2	-	1	-	1	-	-	-	-	-	1	-	1	-	-	-	-	-	-	-	-	-	-	-	-	-	-	-
1959-60	5	2	1	2	-	1	-	-	-	-	-	1	-	-	-	1	-	1	-	-	-	-	1	-	-	-	-	-	-
1964-65	3	1	1	1	-	1	-	-	-	-	1	-	-	-	-	1	-	-	-	-	-	-	-	-	-	-	-	-	-
1969-70	5	3	1	1	-	1	-	-	-	1	-	-	-	1	-	-	-	-	1	-	-	-	-	1	-	-	-	-	-
1979-80	6	-	2	4	-	-	-	1	-	-	1	-	-	-	-	1	-	-	-	1	-	-	1	-	-	-	-	1	-
1986-87	3	-	-	2	1	-	-	-	1	-	-	1	-	-	-	-	-	-	-	1	-	-	-	-	-	-	-	-	-
	25	8	5	11	1	4	-	1	1	1	2	3	-	2	-	3	-	1	1	2	-	-	2	1	-	-	-	1	-
Totals	50	24	8	17	1																								

HIGHEST INNINGS TOTALS

Australia in Australia	674	Adelaide	1947-48
Australia in India	7d-574	Madras[1]	1986-87
India in Australia	4d-600	Sydney	1985-86
India in India	5d-517	Bombay[3]	1986-87

LOWEST INNINGS TOTALS

Australia in Australia	83	Melbourne	1980-81
Australia in India	105	Kanpur	1959-60
India in Australia	58	Brisbane[2]	1947-48
India in India	135	Delhi	1959-60

HIGHEST MATCH AGGREGATE	1488 for 32 wickets	Madras[1]	1986-87
LOWEST MATCH AGGREGATE	538 for 28 wickets	Brisbane[2]	1947-48

HIGHEST INDIVIDUAL INNINGS

Australia in Australia	213	K.J.Hughes	Adelaide	1980-81
Australia in India	210	D.M.Jones	Madras[1]	1986-87
India in Australia	206	R.J.Shastri	Sydney	1991-92
India in India	164*	D.B.Vengsarkar	Bombay[3]	1986-87

HIGHEST AGGREGATE OR RUNS IN A SERIES

Australia in Australia	715 (av 178.75)	D.G.Bradman	1947-48
Australia in India	594 (av 59.40)	K.J.Hughes	1979-80
India in Australia	473 (av 52.55)	G.R.Viswanath	1977-78
India in India	518 (av 74.00)	G.R.Viswanath	1979-80

RECORD WICKET PARTNERSHIPS—AUSTRALIA

1st	217	D.C.Boon (172), G.R.Marsh (116)	Sydney	1985-86
2nd	236	S.G.Barnes (112), D.G.Bradman (201)	Adelaide	1947-48
3rd	222	A.R.Border (162), K.J.Hughes (100)	Madras[1]	1979-80
4th	178	D.M.Jones (210), A.R.Border (106)	Madras[1]	1986-87
5th	223*	A.R.Morris (100*), D.G.Bradman (127*)	Melbourne	1947-48
6th	151	T.R.Veivers (67), B.N.Jarman (78)	Bombay[2]	1964-65
7th	66	G.R.J.Matthews (100), R.J.Bright (28)	Melbourne	1985-86
8th	73	T.R.Veivers (74), G.D.McKenzie (27)	Madras[2]	1964-65
9th	87	I.W.Johnson (73), W.P.A.Crawford (34)	Madras[2]	1956-57
10th	77	A.R.Border (163), D.R.Gilbert (10*)	Melbourne	1985-86

RECORD WICKET PARTNERSHIPS—INDIA

1st	192	S.M.Gavaskar (123), C.P.S.Chauhan (73)	Bombay[3]	1979-80
2nd	224	S.M.Gavaskar (172), M.Amarnath (138)	Sydney	1985-86
3rd	159	S.M.Gavaskar (115), G.R.Viswanath (131)	Delhi	1979-80
4th	159	D.B.Vengsarkar (112), G.R.Viswanath (161*)	Bangalore	1979-80
5th	196	R.J.Shastri (206), S.R.Tendulkar (148*)	Sydney	1991-92
6th	298*	D.B.Vengsarkar (164*), R.J.Shastri (121*)	Bombay[3]	1986-87
7th	132	V.S.Hazare (145), H.R.Adhikari (51)	Adelaide	1947-48
8th	127	S.M.H.Kirmani (101*), K.D.Ghavri (86)	Bombay[3]	1979-80
9th	81	S.R.Tendulkar (114), K.S.More (67*)	Perth	1991-92
10th	94	S.M.Gavaskar (166*), N.S.Yadav (41)	Adelaide	1985-86

BEST INNINGS BOWLING ANALYSIS

Australia in Australia	7-27	M.R.Whitney	Perth	1991-92
Australia in India	7-43	R.R.Lindwall	Madras[2]	1956-57
India in Australia	6-52	B.S.Chandrasekhar	Melbourne	1977-78
India in India	9-69	J.M.Patel	Kanpur	1959-60

BEST MATCH BOWLING ANALYSIS

Australia in Australia	11-31	E.R.H.Toshack	Brisbane[2]	1947-48
Australia in India	12-124	A.K.Davidson	Kanpur	1959-60
India in Australia	12-104	B.S.Chandrasekhar	Melbourne	1977-78
India in India	14-124	J.M.Patel	Kanpur	1959-60

HIGHEST AGGREGATE OF WICKETS IN A SERIES

Australia in Australia	31 (av 21.61)	C.J.McDermott	1991-92
Australia in India	29 (av 14 86)	A.K.Davidson	1959-60
	29 (av 19.58)	R.Benaud	1959-60
India in Australia	31 (av 23.87)	B.S.Bedi	1977-78
India in India	28 (av 22.32)	Kapil Dev	1979-80

AUSTRALIA v PAKISTAN

Venue and Result	Australia 1st	Australia 2nd	Pakistan 1st	Pakistan 2nd	Captains Australia	Captains Pakistan
1956-57 In PAKISTAN						
Karachi-Pakistan 9 wkts	*80	187	199	1-69	I.W.Johnson	A.H.Kardar
1959-60 In PAKISTAN						
Dacca-Australia 8 wkts	225	2-112	*200	134	R.Benaud	Fazal Mahmood
Lahore[2]-Australia 7 wkts	9d-391	3-123	*146	366		Imtiaz Ahmed
Karachi-Drawn	257	2-83	*287	8d-194		Fazal Mahmood
1964-65 in PAKISTAN						
Karachi-Drawn	352	2-227	*414	8d-279	R.B.Simpson	Hanif Mohammad
1964-65 in AUSTRALIA						
Melbourne-Drawn	448	2-88	*287	326	R.B.Simpson	Hanif Mohammad
1972-73 in AUSTRALIA						
Adelaide-Australia inns & 114 runs	585	-	*257	214	I.M.Chappell	Intikhab Alam
Melbourne-Australia 92 runs	*5d-441	425	8d-574	200		
Sydney-Australia 52 runs	*334	184	360	106		
1976-77 in AUSTRALIA						
Adelaide-Drawn	454	6-261	*272	466	G.S.Chappell	Mushtaq Mohammad
Melbourne-Australia 348 runs	*8d-517	8d-315	333	151		
Sydney-Pakistan 8 wkts	*211	180	360	232		

AUSTRALIA v PAKISTAN (cont.) Venue and Result	Australia 1st	Australia 2nd	Pakistan 1st	Pakistan 2nd	Captains Australia	Captains Pakistan
1978-79 in AUSTRALIA						
Melbourne-Pakistan 71 runs	168	310	*196	9d-353	G.N.Yallop	Mushtaq Mohammad
Perth-Australia 7 wkts	327	3-236	*277	285	K.J.Hughes	
1979-80 in PAKISTAN						
Karachi-Pakistan 7 wkts	*225	140	292	3-76	G.S.Chappell	Javed Miandad
Faisalabad-Drawn	*617	-	2-382	-		
Lahore[2]-Drawn	*7d-407	8-391	9d-420	-		
1981-82 in AUSTRALIA						
Perth-Australia 286 runs	*180	8d-424	62	256	G.S.Chappell	Javed Miandad
Brisbane[2]-Australia 10 wkts	9d-512	0-3	*291	223		
Melbourne-Pakistan inns & 82 runs	293	125	*8d-500	-		
1982-83 in PAKISTAN						
Karachi-Pakistan 9 wkts	*284	179	9d-419	1-47	K.J.Hughes	Javed Miandad
Faisalabad-Pakistan inns & 3 runs	168	330	*6d-501	-		
Lahore[2]-Pakistan 9 wkts	*316	214	7d-467	1-64		
1983-84 in AUSTRALIA						
Perth-Australia inns & 9 runs	*9d-436	-	129	298	K.J.Hughes	Zaheer Abbas
Brisbane[2]-Drawn	7d-506	-	*156	3-82		Zaheer Abbas
Adelaide-Drawn	*465	7-310	624	-		Zaheer Abbas
Melbourne-Drawn	555	-	*470	7-238		Imran Khan
Sydney-Australia 10 wkts	6d-454	0-35	*278	210		Imran Khan
1988-89 in PAKISTAN						
Karachi-Pakistan inns & 188 runs	185	116	*9d-469	-	A.R.Border	Javed Miandad
Faisalabad-Drawn	321	3-67	*316	9d-378		
Lahore[2]-Drawn	*340	3d-161	233	8-153		
1989-90 in AUSTRALIA						
Melbourne-Australia 92 runs	*223	8d-312	107	336	A.R.Border	Imran Khan
Adelaide-Drawn	341	6-233	*257	9d-387		
Sydney-Drawn	2-176	-	*199	-		

Test Match Results Summary

AUSTRALIA v PAKISTAN—IN AUSTRALIA

		Result			Melbourne			Adelaide			Sydney			Perth			Brisbane		
	Test	A	P	D	A	P	D	A	P	D	A	P	D	A	P	D	A	P	D
1964-65	1	-	-	1	-	-	1	-	-	-	-	-	-	-	-	-	-	-	-
1972-73	3	3	-	-	1	-	-	1	-	-	1	-	-	-	-	-	-	-	-
1976-77	3	1	1	1	1	-	-	-	-	1	-	1	-	-	-	-	-	-	-
1978-79	2	1	1	-	-	1	-	-	-	-	-	-	-	1	-	-	-	-	-
1981-82	3	2	1	-	-	1	-	-	-	-	-	-	-	1	-	-	1	-	-
1983-84	5	2	-	3	-	-	1	-	-	1	1	-	-	1	-	-	-	-	1
1989-90	3	1	-	2	1	-	-	-	-	1	-	-	1	-	-	-	-	-	-
	20	10	3	7	3	2	2	1	-	3	2	1	1	3	-	-	1	-	1

AUSTRALIA v PAKISTAN—IN PAKISTAN

	Tests	Result			Karachi			Dacca			Lahore			Faisalabad		
		A	P	D	A	P	D	A	P	D	A	P	D	A	P	D
1956-57	1	-	1	-	-	1	-	-	-	-	-	-	-	-	-	-
1959-60	3	2	-	1	-	-	1	1	-	-	1	-	-	-	-	-
1964-65	1	-	-	1	-	-	1	-	-	-	-	-	-	-	-	-
1979-80	3	-	1	2	-	1	-	-	-	-	-	-	1	-	-	1
1982-83	3	-	3	-	-	1	-	-	-	-	-	1	-	-	1	-
1988-89	3	-	1	2	-	1	-	-	-	-	-	-	1	-	-	1
	14	2	6	6	-	4	2	1	-	-	1	1	2	-	1	2
Totals	34	12	9	13												

HIGHEST INNINGS TOTALS

Australia in Australia	585	Adelaide	1972-73
Australia in Pakistan	617	Faisalabad	1979-80
Pakistan in Australia	624	Adelaide	1983-84
Pakistan in Pakistan	6d-501	Faisalabad	1982-83

LOWEST INNINGS TOTALS

Australia in Australia	125	Melbourne	1981-82
Australia in Pakistan	80	Karachi	1956-57
Pakistan in Australia	62	Perth	1981-82
Pakistan in Pakistan	134	Dacca	1959-60

HIGHEST MATCH AGGREGATE	1640 for 33 wickets	Melbourne	1972-73
LOWEST MATCH AGGREGATE	535 for 31 wickets	Karachi	1956-57

HIGHEST INDIVIDUAL INNINGS

Australia in Australia	268	G.N.Yallop	Melbourne	1983-84
Australia in Pakistan	235	G.S.Chappell	Faisalabad	1979-80
Pakistan in Australia	158	Majid Khan	Melbourne	1972-73
Pakistan in Pakistan	211	Javed Miandad	Karachi	1988-89

HIGHEST AGGREGATE ON RUNS IN A SERIES

Australia in Australia	554 (av 92.33)	G.N.Yallop	1983-84
Australia in Pakistan	395 (av 131.66)	A.R.Border	1979-80
Pakistan in Australia	390 (av 43.33)	Mohsin Khan	1983-84
Pakistan in Pakistan	412 (av 72.40)	Javed Miandad	1988-89

RECORD WICKET PARTNERSHIPS—AUSTRALIA

1st	134	I.C.Davis (56), A.Turner (82)	Melbourne	1976-77
2nd	259	W.B.Phillips (159), G.N.Yallop (141)	Perth	1983-84
3rd	203	G.N.Yallop (268), K.J.Hughes (94)	Melbourne	1983-84
4th	217	G.S.Chappell (235), G.N.Yallop (172)	Faisalabad	1979-80
5th	171	G.S.Chappell (121), G.J.Cosier (168)	Melbourne	1976-77
5th	171	A.R.Border (118), G.S.Chappell (150*)	Brisbane[2]	1983-84
6th	139	R.M.Cowper (83), T.R.Veivers (88)	Melbourne	1964-65
7th	185	G.N.Yallop (268), G.R.J.Matthews (75)	Melbourne	1983-84
8th	117	G.J.Cosier (168), K.J.O'Keeffe (28*)	Melbourne	1976-77
9th	83	J.R.Watkins (36), R.A.L.Massie (42)	Sydney	1972-73
10th	52	D.K.Lillee (14), M.H.N.Walker (34*)	Sydney	1976-77
10th	52	G.F.Lawson (57*), T.M.Alderman (7)	Lahore[2]	1982-83

RECORD WICKET PARTNERSHIPS—PAKISTAN

1st	249	Khalid Ibadulla (166), Abdul Kadir (95)	Karachi	1964-65
2nd	233	Mohsin Khan (149), Qasim Omar (113)	Adelaide	1983-84
3rd	223*	Taslim Arif (210*), Javed Miandad (106*)	Faisalabad	1979-80
4th	155	Mansoor Akhtar (111), Zaheer Abbas (126)	Faisalabad	1982-83
5th	186	Javed Miandad (131), Saleem Malik (77)	Adelaide	1983-84
6th	191	Imran Khan (136), Wasim Akram (123)	Adelaide	1976-77
7th	104	Intikhab Alam (64), Wasim Bari (72)	Adelaide	1972-73
8th	111	Majid Khan (110*), Imran Khan (56)	Lahore²	1979-80
9th	56	Intikhab Alam (61), Afaq Hussain (13*)	Melbourne	1964-65
10th	87	Asif Iqbal (152*), Iqbal Qasim (4)	Adelaide	1976-77

BEST INNINGS BOWLING ANALYSIS

Australia in Australia	8-59	A.A.Mallett	Adelaide	1972-73
Australia in Pakistan	7-75	L.F.Kline	Lahore²	1959-60
Pakistan in Australia	9-86	Sarfraz Nawaz	Melbourne	1978-79
Pakistan in Pakistan	7-49	Iqbal Qasim	Karachi	1979-80

BEST MATCH BOWLING ANALYSIS

Australia in Australia	11-118	C.G.Rackemann	Perth	1983-84
Australia in Pakistan	10-111	R.J.Bright	Karachi	1979-80
Pakistan in Australia	12-165	Imran Khan	Sydney	1976-77
Pakistan in Pakistan	13-114	Fazal Mahmood	Karachi	1956-57

HIGHEST AGGREGATE OF WICKETS IN A SERIES

Australia in Australia	24 (av 24.16)	G.F.Lawson	1983-84
Australia in Pakistan	18 (av 21.05)	R.Benaud	1959-60
Pakistan in Australia	19 (av 38.52)	Azeem Hafeez	1983-84
Pakistan in Pakistan	22 (av 25.54)	Abdul Qadir	1982-83

AUSTRALIA v SRI LANKA

Venue and Result	Australia 1st	Australia 2nd	Sri Lanka 1st	Sri Lanka 2nd	Captains Australia	Captains Sri Lanka
1982-83 in SRI LANKA						
Kandy-Australia inns & 38 runs	*4d-514	-	271	205	G.S.Chappell	L.R.D.Mendis
1987-88 in AUSTRALIA						
Perth-Australia inns & 108 runs	*455	-	194	153	A.R.Border	R.S.Madugalle
1989-90 in AUSTRALIA						
Brisbane²-Drawn	*367	6-375	418	-	A.R.Border	A.Ranatunga
Hobart-Australia 173 runs	*224	5d-513	216	348		
1992-93 in SRI LANKA						
Colombo (SSC)-Australia 16 runs	*256	471	8d-547	164	A.R.Border	A.Ranatunga
Colombo (KS)-Drawn	*247	6d-296	258	2-136		
Moratuwa-Drawn	*337	8-271	9d-274	-		

Test Match Results Summary

AUSTRALIA v SRI LANKA—IN AUSTRALIA

	Tests	Result A	Result SL	Result D	Perth A	Perth SL	Perth D	Brisbane A	Brisbane SL	Brisbane D	Hobart A	Hobart SL	Hobart D
1987-88	1	1	-	-	1	-	-	-	-	-	-	-	-
1989-90	2	1	-	1	-	-	-	-	-	1	1	-	-
	3	2	-	1	1	-	-	-	-	1	1	-	-

AUSTRALIA v SRI LANKA—IN SRI LANKA

		Result			Kandy			Colombo (SSC)			Colombo (KS)			Moratuwa		
	Tests	A	SL	D	A	SL	D	A	SL	D	A	SL	D	A	SL	D
1982-83	1	1	-	-	1	-	-	-	-	-	-	-	-	-	-	-
1992-93	3	1	-	2	-	-	-	1	-	-	-	-	1	-	-	1
	4	2	-	2	1	-	-	1	-	-	-	-	1	-	-	1
Totals	7	4	-	3												

HIGHEST INNINGS TOTALS

Australia in Australia	5d-513	Hobart	1989-90
Australia in Sri Lanka	4d-514	Kandy	1982-83
Sri Lanka in Australia	418	Brisbane[2]	1989-90
Sri Lanka in Sri Lanka	8d-547	Colombo (SSC)	1992-93

LOWEST INNINGS TOTALS

Australia in Australia	224	Hobart	1989-90
Australia in Sri Lanka	247	Colombo (KS)	1992-93
Sri Lanka in Australia	153	Perth	1987-88
Sri Lanka in Sri Lanka	164	Colombo (SSC)	1992-93

HIGHEST MATCH AGGREGATE	1438 for 39 wickets	Colombo (SSC)	1992-93
LOWEST MATCH AGGREGATE	802 for 30 wickets	Perth	1987-88

HIGHEST INDIVIDUAL INNINGS

Australia in Australia	164	M.A.Taylor	Brisbane[2]	1989-90
Australia in Sri Lanka	143*	D.W.Hookes	Kandy	1982-83
Sri Lanka in Australia	167	P.A.de Silva	Brisbane[2]	1989-90
Sri Lanka in Sri Lanka	137	A.P.Gurusinha	Colombo (SSC)	1992-93

HIGHEST AGGREGATE ON RUNS IN A SERIES

Australia in Australia	304 (av 76.00)	M.A.Taylor	1989-90
Australia in Sri Lanka	329 (av 54.83)	G.R.J.Matthews	1992-93
Sri Lanka in Australia	314 (av 104.66)	P.A.de Silva	1989-90
Sri Lanka in Sri Lanka	250 (av 50.00)	R.S.Mahanama	1992-93

RECORD WICKET PARTNERSHIPS—AUSTRALIA

1st	120	G.R.Marsh (53), D.C.Boon (64)	Perth	1987-88
2nd	170	K.C.Wessels (141), G.N.Yallop (98)	Kandy	1982-83
3rd	158	T.M.Moody (106), A.R.Border (56)	Brisbane[2]	1989-90
4th	163	M.A.Taylor (108), A.R.Border (85)	Hobart	1989-90
5th	155*	D.W.Hookes (143*), A.R.Border (47*)	Kandy	1982-83
6th	260*	D.M.Jones (118*), S.R.Waugh (134*)	Hobart	1989-90
7th	129	G.R.J.Matthews (96), I.A.Healy (49)	Moratuwa	1992-93
8th	56	G.R.J.Matthews (64), C.J.McDermott (40)	Colombo (SSC)	1992-93
9th	45	I.A.Healy (66*), S.K.Warne(24)	Colombo (SSC)	1992-93
10th	49	I.A.Healy (66*), M.R.Whitney (13)	Colombo (SSC)	1992-93

RECORD WICKET PARTNERSHIPS—SRI LANKA

1st	110	R.S.Mahanama (69), U.C.Hathurusingha (49)	Colombo (KS)	1992-93
2nd	92	R.S.Mahanama (78), A.P.Gurusinha (137)	Colombo (SSC)	1992-93
3rd	107	U.C.Hathurusingha (67), P.A.de Silva (85)	Colombo (KS)	1992-93
	107	R.S.Mahanama (50), P.A.de Silva (58)	Moratuwa	1992-93
4th	230	A.P.Gurusinha (137), A.Ranatunga (127)	Colombo (SSC)	1992-93
5th	116	H.P.Tillakaratne (82), A.Ranatunga (48)	Moratuwa	1992-93
6th	96	A.P.Gurusinha (137), R.S.Kaluwitharana (132*)	Colombo (SSC)	1992-93
7th	144	P.A.de Silva (167), J.R.Ratnayeke (56)	Brisbane[2]	1989-90
8th	33	A.Ranatunga (55), C.P.H.Ramanayake (9)	Perth	1987-88
9th	44*	R.S.Kaluwitharana (132*), M.A.W.R.Madurasinghe (5*)	Colombo (SSC)	1992-93
10th	27	P.A.de Silva (167), C.P.H.Ramanayake (10*)	Brisbane[2]	1989-90

BEST INNINGS BOWLING ANALYSIS

Australia in Australia	5-67	M.G.Hughes	Perth	1987-88
Australia in Sri Lanka	5-66	T.G.Hogan	Kandy	1982-83
Sri Lanka in Australia	6-66	R.J.Ratnayake	Hobart	1989-90
Sri Lanka in Sri Lanka	5-82	C.P.H.Ramanayake	Moratuwa	1992-93

BEST MATCH BOWLING ANALYSIS

Australia in Australia	8-156	M.G.Hughes	Hobart	1989-90
Australia in Sri Lanka	7-166	B.Yardley	Kandy	1982-83
Sri Lanka in Australia	8-189	R.J.Ratnayake	Hobart	1989-90
Sri Lanka in Sri Lanka	8-157	C.P.H.Ramanayake	Moratuwa	1992-93

HIGHEST AGGREGATE OF WICKETS IN A SERIES

Australia in Australia	11 (av 25.36)	M.G.Hughes	1989-90
Australia in Sri Lanka	14 (av 24.42)	C.J.McDermott	1992-93
Sri Lanka in Australia	8 (av 23.62)	R.J.Ratnayake	1989-90
Sri Lanka in Sri Lanka	17 (av 25.52)	C.P.H.Ramanayake	1992-93

ENGLAND v SOUTH AFRICA

	England		South Africa		Captains	
Venue and Result	1st	2nd	1st	2nd	England	South Africa
1888-89 in SOUTH AFRICA						
Port Elizabeth-England 8 wkts	148	2-67	*84	129	C.A.Smith	O.R.Dunell
Cape Town-England inns & 202 runs	*292	-	47	43	M.P.Bowden	W.H.Milton
1891-92 in SOUTH AFRICA						
Cape Town-England inns & 189 runs	369	-	*97	83	W.W.Read	W.H.Milton
1895-96 in SOUTH AFRICA						
Port Elizabeth-England 288 runs	*185	226	93	30	Sir T.C.O'Brien	E.A.Halliwell
Johannesburg[1]-England inns & 197 runs	*482	-	151	134	Lord Hawke	E.A.Halliwell
Cape Town-England inns & 33 runs	265	-	*115	117	Lord Hawke	A.R.Richards
1898-99 in SOUTH AFRICA						
Johannesburg[1]-England 32 runs	*145	237	251	99	Lord Hawke	M.Bisset
Cape Town-England 210 runs	*92	330	177	35		
1905-06 in SOUTH AFRICA						
Johannesburg[1]-South Africa 1 wkt	*184	190	91	9-287	P.F.Warner	P.W.Sherwell
Johannesburg[1]-South Africa 9 wkts	*148	160	277	1-33		
Johannesburg[1]-South Africa 243 runs	295	196	*385	5d-349		
Cape Town-England 4 wkts	198	6-160	*218	138		
Cape Town-South Africa inns & 16 runs	*187	130	333	-		
1907 in ENGLAND						
Lord's-Drawn	*428	-	140	3-185	R.E.Foster	P.W.Sherwell
Leeds-England 53 runs	*76	162	110	75		
The Oval-Drawn	*295	138	178	5-159		
1909-10 in SOUTH AFRICA						
Johannesburg[1]-South Africa 19 runs	310	224	*208	345	H.D.G.Leveson Gower	S.J.Snooke
Durban[1]-South Africa 95 runs	199	252	*199	347	H.D.G.Leveson Gower	
Johannesburg[1]-England 3 wkts	322	7-221	*305	237	H.D.G.Leveson Gower	
Cape Town-South Africa 4 wkts	*203	178	207	6-175	F.L.Fane	
Cape Town-England 9 wkts	*417	1-16	103	327	F.L.Fane	

ENGLAND v SOUTH AFRICA (cont.)	England		South Africa		Captains	
Venue and Result	1st	2nd	1st	2nd	England	South Africa
1912 in ENGLAND						
Lord's-England inns & 62 runs	337	-	*58	217	C.B.Fry	F.Mitchell
Leeds-England 174 runs	*242	238	147	159		L.J.Tancred
The Oval-England 10 wkts	176	0-14	*95	93		L.J.Tancred
1913-14 in SOUTH AFRICA						
Durban[1]-England inns & 157 runs	450	-	*182	111	J.W.H.T.Douglas	H.W.Taylor
Johannesburg[1]-England inns & 12 runs	403	-	*160	231		
Johannesburg[1]-England 91 runs	*238	308	151	304		
Durban[1]-Drawn	163	5-154	*170	9d-305		
Port Elizabeth-England 10 wkts	411	0-11	*193	228		
1922-23 in SOUTH AFRICA						
Johannesburg[1]-South Africa 168 runs	182	218	*148	420	F.T.Mann	H.W.Taylor
Cape Town-England 1 wkt	183	9-173	*113	242		
Durban[2]-Drawn	*428	1-11	368	-		
Johannesburg[1]-Drawn	*244	6d-376	295	4-247		
Durban[2]-England 109 runs	*281	241	179	234		
1924 in ENGLAND						
Birmingham-England inns & 18 runs	*438	-	30	390	A.E.R.Gilligan	H.W.Taylor
Lord's-England inns & 18 runs	2d-531	-	*273	240	A.E.R.Gilligan	
Leeds-England 9 wkts	*396	1-60	132	323	A.E.R.Gilligan	
Manchester-Drawn	-	-	*4-116	-	J.W.H.T.Douglas	
The Oval-Drawn	8-421	-	*342	-	A.E.R.Gilligan	
1927-28 in SOUTH AFRICA						
Johannesburg[1]-England 10 wkts	313	0-57	*196	170	R.T.Stanyforth	H.G.Deane
Cape Town-England 87 runs	*133	428	250	224	R.T.Stanyforth	
Durban[2]-Drawn	430	2-132	*246	8d-464	R.T.Stanyforth	
Johannesburg[1]-South Africa 4 wkts	*265	215	328	6-156	R.T.Stanyforth	
Durban[2]-South Africa 8 wkts	*282	118	7d-332	2-69	G.T.S.Stevens	
1929 in ENGLAND						
Birmingham-Drawn	*245	4d-308	250	1-171	J C.White	H.G.Deane
Lord's-Drawn	*302	8d-312	322	5-90	J C.White	
Leeds-England 5 wkts	328	5-186	*236	275	J C.White	
Manchester-England inns & 32 runs	*7d-427	-	130	265	A.W.Carr	
The Oval-Drawn	*258	1-264	8d-492	-	A.W.Carr	
1930-31 in SOUTH AFRICA						
Johannesburg[1]-South Africa 28 runs	193	211	*126	306	A.P.F.Chapman	E.P.Nupen
Cape Town-Drawn	350	252	*8d-513	-		H.G.Deane
Durban[2]-Drawn	1d-223	-	*177	8-145		H.G.Deane
Johannesburg[1]-Drawn	*442	9d-169	295	7-280		H.B.Cameron
Durban[2]-Drawn	230	4-72	*252	7d-219		H.B.Cameron
1935 in ENGLAND						
Nottingham-Drawn	*7d-384	-	220	1-17	R.E.S.Wyatt	H.F.Wade
Lord's-South Africa 157 runs	198	151	*228	7d-278		
Leeds-Drawn	*216	7d-294	171	5-194		
Manchester-Drawn	*357	6d-231	318	2-169		
The Oval-Drawn	6d-534	-	*476	6-287		

ENGLAND v SOUTH AFRICA (cont.) Venue and Result	England 1st	England 2nd	South Africa 1st	South Africa 2nd	Captains England	Captains South Africa
1938-39 in SOUTH AFRICA						
Johannesburg[1]-Drawn	*422	4d-291	390	1-108	W.R.Hammond	A.Melville
Cape Town-Drawn	*9d-559	-	286	2-201		
Durban[2]-England inns & 13 runs	*4d-469	-	103	353		
Johannesburg[1]-Drawn	*215	4-203	8d-349	-		
Durban[2]-Drawn	316	6-654	*530	481		
1947 in ENGLAND						
Nottingham-Drawn	208	551	*533	1-166	N.W.D.Yardley	A.Melville
Lord's-England 10 wkts	*8d-554	0-26	327	252		
Manchester-England 7 wkts	478	3-130	*339	267		
Leeds-England 10 wkts	7d-317	0-47	*175	184		
The Oval-Drawn	*427	6d-325	302	7-423		
1948-49 in SOUTH AFRICA						
Durban[2]-England 2 wkts	253	8-128	*161	219	F.G.Mann	A.D.Nourse
Johannesburg[2]-Drawn	*608	-	315	2-270		
Cape Town-Drawn	*308	3d-276	356	4-142		
Johannesburg[2]-Drawn	*379	7d-253	9d-257	4-194		
Port Elizabeth-England 3 wkts	395	7-174	*379	3d-187		
1951 in ENGLAND						
Nottingham-South Africa 71 runs	9d-419	114	*9d-483	121	F.R.Brown	A.D.Nourse
Lord s-England 10 wkts	*311	0-16	115	211		
Manchester-England 9 wkts	211	1-142	*158	191		
Leeds-Drawn	505	-	*538	0-87		
The Oval-England 4 wkts	194	6-164	*202	154		
1955 in ENGLAND						
Nottingham-England inns & 5 runs	*334	-	181	148	P.B.H.May	J.E.Cheetham
Lord's-England 71 runs	*133	353	304	111		J.E.Cheetham
Manchester-South Africa 3 wkts	*284	381	8d-521	7-145		D.J.McGlew
Leeds-South Africa 224 runs	191	256	*171	500		D.J.McGlew
The Oval-England 92 runs	*151	204	112	151		J.E.Cheetham
1956-57 in SOUTH AFRICA						
Johannesburg[3]-England 131 runs	*268	150	215	72	P.B.H.May	C.B.van Ryneveld
Cape Town-England 312 runs	*369	6d-220	205	72		D.J.McGlew
Durban[2]-Drawn	*218	254	283	6-142		C.B.van Ryneveld
Johannesburg[3]-South Africa 17 runs	251	214	*340	142		C.B.van Ryneveld
Port Elizabeth-South Africa 58 runs	110	130	*164	134		C.B.van Ryneveld
1960 in ENGLAND						
Birmingham-England 100 runs	*292	203	186	209	M.C.Cowdrey	D.J.McGlew
Lord's-England inns & 73 runs	*8d-362	-	152	137		
Nottingham-England 8 wkts	*287	2-49	88	247		
Manchester-Drawn	*260	7d-153	229	0-46		
The Oval-Drawn	*155	9d-479	419	4-97		
1964-65 in SOUTH AFRICA						
Durban[2]-England inns & 104 runs	*5d-485	-	155	226	M J K.Smith	T L.Goddard
Johannesburg[3]-Drawn	*531	-	317	6-336		
Cape Town-Drawn	442	0 15	*7d-501	346		
Johannesburg[3]-Drawn	384	6-153	*6d-390	3d-307		
Port Elizabeth-Drawn	435	1-29	*502	4d-178		

ENGLAND v SOUTH AFRICA (cont.) Venue and Result	England 1st	England 2nd	South Africa 1st	South Africa 2nd	Captains England	Captains South Africa
1965 in ENGLAND						
Lord's-Drawn	338	7-145	*280	248	M.J.K.Smith	P L.van der Merwe
Nottingham-South Africa 94 runs	240	224	*269	289		
The Oval-Drawn	202	4-308	*208	392		

Test Match Results Summary

ENGLAND v SOUTH AFRICA—IN ENGLAND

		Result			Lord's			Leeds			The Oval			Birmingham			Manchester			Nottingham		
	Tests	E	SA	D	E	SA	D	E	SA	D	E	SA	D	E	SA	D	E	SA	D	E	SA	D
1907	3	1	-	2	-	-	1	1	-	-	-	-	1	-	-	-	-	-	-	-	-	-
1912	3	3	-	-	1	-	-	1	-	-	1	-	-	-	-	-	-	-	-	-	-	-
1924	5	3	-	2	1	-	-	1	-	-	-	-	1	1	-	-	-	-	1	-	-	-
1929	5	2	-	3	-	-	1	1	-	-	-	-	1	-	-	-	1	-	-	-	-	-
1935	5	-	1	4	-	1	-	-	-	1	-	-	1	-	-	-	-	-	1	-	-	1
1947	5	3	-	2	1	-	-	1	-	-	-	-	1	-	-	-	1	-	-	-	-	1
1951	5	3	1	1	1	-	-	-	-	1	1	-	-	-	-	-	1	-	-	-	1	-
1955	5	3	2	-	1	-	-	-	1	-	1	-	-	-	-	-	-	1	-	1	-	-
1960	5	3	-	2	1	-	-	-	-	-	-	-	1	1	-	-	-	-	1	1	-	-
1965	3	-	1	2	-	-	1	-	-	-	-	-	1	-	-	-	-	-	-	-	1	-
	44	21	5	18	6	1	3	5	1	2	3	-	7	2	-	1	3	1	3	2	2	2

ENGLAND v SOUTH AFRICA—IN SOUTH AFRICA

		Result			P.Elizabeth			Cape Town			Johannesburg			Durban		
	Tests	E	SA	D	E	SA	D	E	SA	D	E	SA	D	E	SA	D
1888-89	2	2	-	-	1	-	-	1	-	-	-	-	-	-	-	-
1891-92	1	1	-	-	-	-	-	1	-	-	-	-	-	-	-	-
1895-96	3	3	-	-	1	-	-	1	-	-	1	-	-	-	-	-
1898-99	2	2	-	-	-	-	-	1	-	-	1	-	-	-	-	-
1905-06	5	1	4	-	-	-	-	1	1	-	-	3	-	-	-	-
1909-10	5	2	3	-	-	-	-	1	1	-	1	1	-	-	1	-
1913-14	5	4	-	1	1	-	-	-	-	-	2	-	-	1	-	1
1922-23	5	2	1	2	-	-	-	1	-	-	-	1	1	1	-	1
1927-28	5	2	2	1	-	-	-	1	-	-	1	1	-	-	1	1
1930-31	5	-	1	4	-	-	-	-	-	1	-	1	1	-	-	2
1938-39	5	1	-	4	-	-	-	-	-	1	-	-	2	1	-	1
1948-49	5	2	-	3	1	-	-	-	-	1	-	-	2	1	-	-
1956-57	5	2	2	1	-	1	-	1	-	-	1	1	-	-	-	1
1964-65	5	1	-	4	-	-	1	-	-	1	-	-	2	1	-	-
	58	25	13	20	4	1	1	9	2	4	7	8	8	5	2	7
Totals	102	46	18	38												

HIGHEST INNINGS TOTALS

England in England	8d-554	Lord's	1947
England in South Africa	5-654	Durban[2]	1938-39
South Africa in England	538	Leeds	1951
South Africa in South Africa	530	Durban[2]	1938-39

LOWEST INNINGS TOTALS

England in England	76	Leeds	1907
England in South Africa	92	Cape Town	1898-99
South Africa in England	30	Birmingham	1924
South Africa in South Africa	30	Port Elizabeth	1895-96

HIGHEST MATCH AGGREGATE	1981 for 35 wickets	Durban[2]	1938-39
LOWEST MATCH AGGREGATE	378 for 30 wickets	The Oval	1912

HIGHEST INDIVIDUAL INNINGS

England in England	211	J.B.Hobbs	Lord's	1924
England in South Africa	243	E.Paynter	Durban[2]	1938-39
South Africa in England	236	E.A.B.Rowan	Leeds	1951
South Africa in South Africa	176	H.W.Taylor	Johannesburg[1]	1922-23

HIGHEST AGGREGATE OF RUNS IN A SERIES

England in England	753 (av 94.12)	D.C.S.Compton	1947
England in South Africa	653 (av 81.62)	E.Paynter	1938-39
South Africa in England	621 (av 69.00)	A.D.Nourse	1947
South Africa in South Africa	582 (av 64.66)	H.W.Taylor	1922-23

RECORD WICKET PARTNERSHIPS—ENGLAND

1st	359	L.Hutton (158), C.Washbrook (195)	Johannesburg[2]	1948-49
2nd	280	P.A.Gibb (120), W.J.Edrich (219)	Durban[2]	1938-39
3rd	370	W.J.Edrich (189), D.C.S.Compton (208)	Lord's	1947
4th	197	W.R.Hammond (181), L.E.G.Ames (115)	Cape Town	1938-39
5th	237	D.C.S.Compton (163), N.W.D.Yardley (99)	Nottingham	1947
6th	206*	K.F.Barrington (148*), J.M.Parks (108*)	Durban[2]	1964-65
7th	115	J.W.H.T.Douglas (119), M.C.Bird (61)	Durban[1]	1913-14
8th	154	C.W.Wright (71), H.R Bromley-Davenport (84)	Johannesburg[1]	1895-96
9th	71	H.Wood (134), J.T.Hearne (40)	Cape Town	1891-92
10th	92	C.A.G.Russell (111), A.E.R.Gilligan (39*)	Durban[2]	1922-23

RECORD WICKET PARTNERSHIPS—SOUTH AFRICA

1st	260	B.Mitchell (123), I.J.Siedle (141)	Cape Town	1930-31
2nd	198	E.A.B.Rowan (236).C.B.van Ryneveld (83)	Leeds	1951
3rd	319	A.Melville (189), A.D.Nourse (149)	Nottingham	1947
4th	214	H.W.Taylor (121), H.G.Deane (93)	The Oval	1929
5th	157	A.J.Pithey (95), J.H.B.Waite (64)	Johannesburg[3]	1964-65
6th	171	J.H.B.Waite (113), P.L.Winslow (108)	Manchester	1955
7th	123	H.G.Deane (73), E.P.Nupen (69)	Durban[2]	1927-28
8th	109*	B.Mitchell (189*), L.Tuckett (40*)	The Oval	1947
9th	137	E.L.Dalton (117), A.B.C.Langton (73*)	The Oval	1935
10th	103	H.G.Owen-Smith (129), A.J.Bell (26*)	Leeds	1929

BEST INNINGS BOWLING ANALYSIS

England in England	8-29	S.F.Barnes	The Oval	1912
England in South Africa	9-28	G.A.Lohmann	Johannesburg[1]	1895-96
South Africa in England	7-65	S.J.Pegler	Lord's	1912
South Africa in South Africa	9-113	H.J.Tayfield	Johannesburg[3]	1956-57

BEST MATCH BOWLING ANALYSIS

England in England	15-99	C.Blythe	Leeds	1907
England in South Africa	17-159	S.F.Barnes	Johannesburg[1]	1913-14
South Africa in England	10-87	P.M.Pollock	Nottingham	1965
South Africa in South Africa	13-192	H.J.Tayfield	Johannesburg[3]	1956-57

HIGHEST AGGREGATE OF WICKETS IN A SERIES

England in England	34 (av 8.29)	S F Barnes	1912
England in South Africa	49 (av 10.93)	S.F.Barnes	1913-14
South Africa in England	26 (av 21.84)	H.J.Tayfield	1955
	26 (av 22.57)	N.A T.Adcock	1960
South Africa in South Africa	37 (av 17.18)	H.J.Tayfield	1956-57

ENGLAND v WEST INDIES

Venue and Result	England 1st	England 2nd	West Indies 1st	West Indies 2nd	Captains England	Captains West Indies
1928 in ENGLAND						
Lord's-England inns & 58 runs	*401	-	177	166	A.P.F.Chapman	R.K.Nunes
Manchester-England inns & 30 runs	351	-	*206	115		
The Oval-England inns & 71 runs	438	-	*238	129		
1929-30 in WEST INDIES						
Bridgetown-Drawn	467	3-167	*369	384	Hon F.S.G.Calthorpe	E.L.G.Hoad
Port-of-Spain-England 167 runs	*208	8d-425	254	212		N.Betancourt
Georgetown-West Indies 289 runs	145	327	*471	290		M.P.Fernandes
Kingston-Drawn	*849	9d-272	286	5-408		R.K.Nunes
1933 in ENGLAND						
Lord's-England inns & 27 runs	*296	-	97	172	D.R.Jardine	G.C.Grant
Manchester-Drawn	374	-	*375	225	D.R.Jardine	
The Oval-England inns & 17 runs	*312	-	100	195	R.E.S.Wyatt	
1934-35 in WEST INDIES						
Bridgetown-England 4 wkts	7d-81	6-75	*102	6d-51	R.E.S.Wyatt	G.C.Grant
Port-of-Spain-West Indies 217 runs	258	107	*302	6d-280		
Georgetown-Drawn	*226	6d-160	184	5-104		
Kingston-West Indies inns & 161 runs	271	103	*7d-535	-		
1939 in ENGLAND						
Lord's-England 8 wkts	5d-404	2-100	*277	225	W.R.Hammond	R.S.Grant
Manchester-Drawn	*7d-164	6d-128	133	4-43		
The Oval-Drawn	*352	3d-366	498	-		
1947-48 in WEST INDIES						
Bridgetown-Drawn	253	4-86	*296	9d-351	K.Cranston	G.A.Headley
Port-of-Spain-Drawn	*362	275	497	3-72	G.O.B.Allen	G.E.Gomez
Georgetown-West Indies 7 wkts	111	263	*8d-297	3-78	G.O.B.Allen	J.D.C.Goddard
Kingston-West Indies 10 wkts	*227	336	490	0-76	G.O.B.Allen	J.D.C.Goddard
1950 in ENGLAND						
Manchester-England 202 runs	*312	288	215	183	N.W.D.Yardley	J.D.C.Goddard
Lord's-West Indies 326 runs	151	274	*326	6d-425	N.W.D Yardley	
Nottingham-West Indies 10 wkts	*223	436	558	0-103	N.W.D.Yardley	
The Oval-West Indies inns & 56 runs	344	103	*503	-	F.R.Brown	
1953-54 in WEST INDIES						
Kingston-West Indies 140 runs	170	316	*417	6d-209	L.Hutton	J.B.Stollmeyer
Bridgetown-West Indies 181 runs	181	313	*383	2d-292		
Georgetown-England 9 wkts	*435	1-75	251	256		
Port-of-Spain-Drawn	537	3-98	*8d-681	4d-212		
Kingston-England 9 wkts	414	1-72	*139	346		
1957 in ENGLAND						
Birmingham-Drawn	*186	4d-583	474	7-72	P.B.H.May	J.D.C.Goddard
Lord s-England inns & 36 runs	424	-	*127	261		
Nottingham-Drawn	*6d-619	1-64	372	367		
Leeds-England inns & 5 runs	279	-	*142	132		
The Oval-England inns & 237 runs	*412	-	89	86		

ENGLAND v WEST INDIES (cont.)	England		West Indies		Captains	
Venue and Result	1st	2nd	1st	2nd	England	West Indies
1959-60 in WEST INDIES						
Bridgetown-Drawn	*482	0-71	8d-563	-	P.B.H.May	F.C.M.Alexander
Port-of-Spain-England 256 runs	*382	9d-230	112	244	P.B.H.May	
Kingston-Drawn	*277	305	353	6-175	P.B.H.May	
Georgetown-Drawn	*295	8-334	8d-402	-	M.C.Cowdrey	
Port-of-Spain-Drawn	*393	7d-350	8d-338	5-209	M.C.Cowdrey	
1963 in ENGLAND						
Manchester-West Indies 10 wkts	205	296	*6d-501	0-1	E.R.Dexter	F.M.M.Worrell
Lord's-Drawn	297	9-228	*301	229		
Birmingham-England 217 runs	*216	9d-278	186	91		
Leeds-West Indies 221 runs	174	231	*397	229		
The Oval-West Indies 8 wkts	*275	223	246	2-255		
1966 in ENGLAND						
Manchester-West Indies inns & 40 runs	167	277	*484	-	M.J.K.Smith	G.S.Sobers
Lord's-Drawn	355	4-197	*269	5d-369	M.C.Cowdrey	
Nottingham-West Indies 139 runs	325	253	*235	5d-482	M.C.Cowdrey	
Leeds-West Indies inns & 55 runs	240	205	*9d-500	-	M.C.Cowdrey	
The Oval-England inns & 34 runs	527	-	*268	225	D.B.Close	
1967-68 in WEST INDIES						
Port-of-Spain-Drawn	*568	-	363	8-243	M.C.Cowdrey	G.S.Sobers
Kingston-Drawn	*376	8-68	143	9d-391		
Bridgetown-Drawn	449	-	*349	6-284		
Port-of-Spain-England 7 wkts	404	3-215	*7d-526	2d-92		
Georgetown-Drawn	371	9-206	*414	264		
1969 in ENGLAND						
Manchester-England 10 wkts	*413	0-12	147	275	R.Illingworth	G.S.Sobers
Lord's-Drawn	344	7-295	*380	9d-295		
Leeds-England 30 runs	*223	240	161	272		
1973 in ENGLAND						
The Oval-West Indies 158 runs	257	255	*415	255	R.Illingworth	R.B.Kanhai
Birmingham-Drawn	305	2-182	*327	302		
Lord's-West Indies inns & 226 runs	233	193	*8d-652	-		
1973-74 in WEST INDIES						
Port-of-Spain-West Indies 7 wkts	*131	392	392	3-132	M.H.Denness	R.B.Kanhai
Kingston-Drawn	*353	9-432	9d-583	-		
Bridgetown-Drawn	*395	7-277	8d-596	-		
Georgetown-Drawn	*448	-	4-198	-		
Port-of-Spain-England 26 runs	*267	263	305	199		
1976 in ENGLAND						
Nottingham-Drawn	332	2-156	*494	5d-176	A.W.Greig	C.H.Lloyd
Lord's-Drawn	*250	254	182	6-241		
Manchester-West Indies 425 runs	71	126	*211	5d-411		
Leeds-West Indies 55 runs	387	204	*450	196		
The Oval-West Indies 231 runs	435	203	*8d-687	0d-182		

ENGLAND v WEST INDIES (cont.) Venue and Result	England 1st	England 2nd	West Indies 1st	West Indies 2nd	Captains England	Captains West Indies
1980 in ENGLAND						
Nottingham-West Indies 2 wkts	*263	252	308	8-209	I.T.Botham	C.H.Lloyd
Lord's-Drawn	*269	2-133	518	-		C.H.Lloyd
Manchester-Drawn	*150	7-391	260	-		C.H.Lloyd
The Oval-Drawn	*370	9d-209	265	-		C.H.Lloyd
Leeds-Drawn	*143	6d-227	245	-		I.V.A.Richards
1980-81 in WEST INDIES						
Port-of-Spain-West Indies inns & 79 runs	178	169	*9-426	-	I.T.Botham	C.H.Lloyd
Georgetown-match cancelled	-	-	-	-		
Bridgetown-West Indies 298 runs	122	224	*265	7d-379		
St John's-Drawn	*271	3-234	9d-468	-		
Kingston-Drawn	*285	6d-302	442	-		
1984 in ENGLAND						
Birmingham-West Indies inns & 180 runs	*191	235	606	-	D.I.Gower	C.H.Lloyd
Lord's-West Indies 9 wkts	*286	9d-300	245	1-344		
Manchester-West Indies 8 wkts	*270	159	302	2-131		
Leeds-West Indies inns & 64 runs	280	156	*500	-		
The Oval-West Indies 172 runs	190	346	162	202		
1985-86 in WEST INDIES						
Kingston-West Indies 10 wkts	*159	152	307	0-5	D.I.Gower	I.V.A.Richards
Port-of-Spain-West Indies 7 wkts	*176	315	399	3-95		
Bridgetown-West Indies inns & 30 runs	189	199	*418	-		
Port-of-Spain-West Indies 10 wkts	*200	150	312	0-39		
St John's-West Indies 240 runs	310	170	*474	2d-246		
1988 in ENGLAND						
Nottingham-Drawn	*245	3-301	9d-448	-	M.W.Gatting	I.V.A.Richards
Lord's-West Indies 134 runs	165	307	*209	397	J.E.Emburey	
Manchester-West Indies inns & 156 runs	*135	93	7d-384	-	J.E.Emburey	
Leeds-West Indies 10 wkts	*201	138	275	0-67	C.S.Cowdrey	
The Oval-West Indies 8 wkts	*205	202	183	2-226	G.A.Gooch	
1989-90 in WEST INDIES						
Kingston-England 9 wkts	364	1-21	*164	240	G.A.Gooch	I.V.A.Richards
Georgetown-match abandoned	-	-	-	-	G.A.Gooch	I.V.A.Richards
Port-of-Spain-Drawn	288	5-120	*199	239	G.A.Gooch	D.L.Haynes
Bridgetown-West Indies 164 runs	358	191	*446	8d-267	A.J.Lamb	I.V.A.Richards
St John's-West Indies inns & 32 runs	*260	154	446	-	A.J.Lamb	I.V.A.Richards
1991 in ENGLAND						
Leeds-England 115 runs	*198	252	173	162	G.A.Gooch	I.V.A.Richards
Lord's-Drawn	354	-	*419	2-12		
Nottingham-West Indies 9 wkts	*300	211	397	1-115		
Birmingham-West Indies 7 wkts	*188	255	292	3-157		
The Oval-England 5 wkts	*419	5-146	176	385		

Test Match Results Summary

ENGLAND v WEST INDIES—IN ENGLAND

		Result			Lord's			Manchester			The Oval			Nottingham			Birmingham			Leeds		
	Tests	E	WI	D	E	WI	D	E	WI	D	E	WI	D	E	WI	D	E	WI	D	E	WI	D
1928	3	3	-	-	1	-	-	1	-	-	1	-	-	-	-	-	-	-	-	-	-	-
1933	3	2	-	1	1	-	-	-	-	1	1	-	-	-	-	-	-	-	-	-	-	-
1939	3	1	-	2	1	-	-	-	-	1	-	-	1	-	-	-	-	-	-	-	-	-
1950	4	1	3	-	-	1	-	1	-	-	-	1	-	-	1	-	-	-	-	-	-	-
1957	5	3	-	2	1	-	-	-	-	-	1	-	-	-	-	1	-	-	1	1	-	-
1963	5	1	3	1	-	-	1	-	1	-	-	1	-	-	-	-	1	-	-	-	1	-
1966	5	1	3	1	-	-	1	-	1	-	-	1	-	-	-	-	1	-	-	-	1	-
1969	3	2	-	1	-	-	1	1	-	-	-	-	-	-	-	-	-	-	-	1	-	-
1973	3	-	2	1	-	1	-	-	-	-	-	1	-	-	-	-	-	-	1	-	-	-
1976	5	-	3	2	-	-	1	-	1	-	-	1	-	-	-	1	-	-	-	-	1	-
1980	5	-	1	4	-	-	1	-	-	1	-	-	1	-	1	-	-	-	-	-	1	-
1984	5	-	5	-	-	1	-	-	1	-	-	1	-	-	-	-	-	1	-	-	1	-
1988	5	-	4	1	-	1	-	-	1	-	-	1	-	-	-	-	-	1	-	-	-	1
1991	5	2	2	-	-	-	1	1	-	-	1	-	-	-	-	1	-	-	-	-	-	1
	59	16	26	17	4	4	6	4	5	3	5	6	2	-	3	4	1	1	2	2	5	2

ENGLAND v WEST INDIES—IN WEST INDIES

		Result			Bridgetown			Port-of-Spain			Georgetown			Kingston			St John's		
	Tests	E	WI	D	E	WI	D	E	WI	D	E	WI	D	E	WI	D	E	WI	D
1929-30	4	1	1	2	-	-	1	1	-	-	-	1	-	-	-	1	-	-	-
1934-35	4	1	2	1	1	-	-	-	1	-	-	-	1	-	1	-	-	-	-
1947-48	4	-	2	2	-	-	1	-	-	1	-	1	-	-	1	-	-	-	-
1953-54	5	2	2	1	-	1	-	-	-	1	1	-	-	1	1	-	-	-	-
1959-60	5	1	-	4	-	-	1	1	-	1	-	-	1	-	-	1	-	-	-
1967-68	5	1	-	4	-	-	1	1	-	1	-	-	1	-	-	1	-	-	-
1973-74	5	1	1	3	-	-	1	1	1	-	-	-	1	-	-	1	-	-	-
1980-81	4	-	2	2	-	1	-	-	1	-	-	-	-	-	-	1	-	-	1
1985-86	5	-	5	-	-	1	-	-	2	-	-	-	-	-	1	-	-	1	-
1989-90	4	1	2	1	-	1	-	-	-	1	-	-	-	1	-	-	-	1	-
	45	8	17	20	1	4	5	4	5	5	1	2	4	2	4	5	-	2	1
Totals	104	24	43	37															

HIGHEST INNINGS TOTALS

England in England	6d-619	Nottingham	1957
England in West Indies	849	Kingston	1929-30
West Indies in England	8d-687	The Oval	1976
West Indies in West Indies	8d-681	Port-of-Spain	1953-54

LOWEST INNINGS TOTALS

England in England	71	Manchester	1976
England in West Indies	103	Kingston	1934-35
West Indies in England	86	The Oval	1957
West Indies in West Indies	102	Bridgetown	1934-35

HIGHEST MATCH AGGREGATE	1815 for 34 wickets	Kingston	1929-30
LOWEST MATCH AGGREGATE	309 for 29 wickets	Bridgetown	1934-35

HIGHEST INDIVIDUAL INNINGS

England in England	285*	P.B.H.May	Birmingham	1957
England in West Indies	325	A.Sandham	Kingston	1929-30
West Indies in England	291	I.V.A.Richards	The Oval	1976
West Indies in West Indies	302	L.G.Rowe	Bridgetown	1973-74

HIGHEST AGGREGATE OF RUNS IN A SERIES

England in England	489 (av 97.80)	P.B.H.May	1957
England in West Indies	693 (av 115.50)	E.H.Hendren	1929-30
West Indies in England	829 (av 118.42)	I.V.A.Richards	1976
West Indies in West Indies	709 (av 101.28)	G.S.Sobers	1959-60

RECORD WICKET PARTNERSHIPS—ENGLAND

1st	212	C.Washbrook (102), R.T.Simpson (94)	Nottingham	1950
2nd	266	P.E.Richardson (126), T.W.Graveney (258)	Nottingham	1957
3rd	264	L.Hutton (165*), W.R.Hammond (138)	The Oval	1939
4th	411	P.B.H.May (285*), M.C.Cowdrey (154)	Birmingham	1957
5th	130*	C.Milburn (126*), T.W.Graveney (30*)	Lord's	1966
6th	163	A.W.Greig (148), A.P.E.Knott (87)	Bridgetown	1973-74
7th	197	M.J.K.Smith (96), J.M.Parks (101*)	Port-of-Spain	1959-60
8th	217	T.W.Graveney (165), J.T.Murray (112)	The Oval	1966
9th	109	G.A.R.Lock (89), P.I.Pocock (13)	Georgetown	1967-68
10th	128	K.Higgs (63), J.A.Snow (59*)	The Oval	1966

RECORD WICKET PARTNERSHIPS— WEST INDIES

1st	298	C.G.Greenidge (149), D.L.Haynes (167)	St John's	1989-90
2nd	287*	C.G.Greenidge (214*), H.A.Gomes (92*)	Lord's	1984
3rd	338	E.D.Weekes (206), F.M.M.Worrell (167)	Port-of-Spain	1953-54
4th	399	G.S.Sobers (226), F.M.M.Worrell (197*)	Bridgetown	1959-60
5th	265	S.M.Nurse (137), G.S.Sobers (174)	Leeds	1966
6th	274*	G.S.Sobers (163*), D.A.J.Holford (105*)	Lord's	1966
7th	155*†	G.S.Sobers (150*), B.D.Julien (121)	Lord's	1973
8th	99	C.A.McWatt (54), J.K.Holt (48*)	Georgetown	1953-54
9th	150	E.A.E.Baptiste (87*), M.A.Holding (69)	Birmingham	1984
10th	67*	M.A.Holding (58*), C.E.H.Croft (17*)	St John's	1980-81

† 231 runs were added for this wicket, G.S.Sobers retired ill and was replaced by K.D.Boyce after 155 had been scored.

BEST INNINGS BOWLING ANALYSIS

England in England	8-103	I.T.Botham	Lord's	1984
England in West Indies	8-86	A.W.Greig	Port-of-Spain	1973-74
West Indies in England	8-92	M.A.Holding	The Oval	1976
West Indies in West Indies	8-45	C.E.L.Ambrose	Bridgetown	1989-90

BEST MATCH BOWLING ANALYSIS

England in England	12-119	F.S.Trueman	Birmingham	1963
England in West Indies	13-156	A.W.Greig	Port-of-Spain	1973-74
West Indies in England	14-149	M.A.Holding	The Oval	1976
West Indies in West Indies	11-229	W.Ferguson	Port-of-Spain	1947-48

HIGHEST AGGREGATE OF WICKETS IN A SERIES

England in England	34 (av 17.47)	F.S.Trueman	1963
England in West Indies	27 (av 18.66)	J.A.Snow	1967-68
West Indies in England	35 (av 12.65)	M.D.Marshall	1950
West Indies in West Indies	27 (av 16.14)	J.Garner	1985-86
	27 (av 17.65)	M.D.Marshall	1985-86

ENGLAND v NEW ZEALAND

Venue and Result	England 1st	England 2nd	New Zealand 1st	New Zealand 2nd	Captains England	Captains New Zealand
1929-30 in NEW ZEALAND						
Christchurch-England 8 wkts	181	2-66	*112	131	A.H.H.Gilligan	T.C.Lowry
Wellington-Drawn	320	4-107	*440	4d-164		
Auckland-Drawn	*4d-330	-	1-96	-		
Auckland-Drawn	*540	3-22	387	-		
1931 in ENGLAND						
Lord's-Drawn	454	5-146	*224	9d-469	D.R.Jardine	T.C.Lowry
The Oval-England inns & 26 runs	*4d-416	-	193	197		
Manchester-Drawn	*3-224	-	-	-		
1932-33 in NEW ZEALAND						
Christchurch-Drawn	*8d-560	-	223	0-35	D.R.Jardine	M.L.Page
Auckland-Drawn	7d-548	-	*158	0-16	R.E.S.Wyatt	
1937 in ENGLAND						
Lord's-Drawn	*424	4d-226	295	8-175	R.W.V.Robins	M.L.Page
Manchester-England 130 runs	*9d-358	187	281	134		
The Oval-Drawn	7d-254	1-31	*249	187		
1946-47 in NEW ZEALAND						
Christchurch-Drawn	7d-265	-	*9d-345	-	W.R.Hammond	W.A.Hadlee
1949 in ENGLAND						
Leeds-Drawn	*372	4d-267	341	2-195	F.G.Mann	W.A.Hadlee
Lord's-Drawn	*9d-313	5-306	484	-	F.G.Mann	
Manchester-Drawn	9d-440	-	*293	7-348	F.R.Brown	
The Oval-Drawn	482	-	*345	9d-308	F.R.Brown	
1950-51 in NEW ZEALAND						
Christchurch-Drawn	550	-	*8d-417	3-46	F.R.Brown	W.A.Hadlee
Wellington-England 6 wkts	227	4-91	*125	189		
1954-55 in NEW ZEALAND						
Dunedin-England 8 wkts	8d-209	2-49	*125	132	L.Hutton	G.O.Rabone
Auckland-England inns & 20 runs	246	-	*200	26		
1958 in ENGLAND						
Birmingham-England 205 runs	*221	6d-215	94	137	P.B.H.May	J.R.Reid
Lord's-England inns & 148 runs	*269	-	47	74		
Leeds-England inns & 71 runs	2d-267	-	*67	129		
Manchester-England inns & 13 runs	9d-365	-	*267	85		
The Oval-Drawn	9d-219	-	*161	3-91		
1958-59 in NEW ZEALAND						
Christchurch-England inns & 99 runs	*374	-	142	133	P.B.H.May	J.R.Reid
Auckland-Drawn	7-311	-	*181	-		
1962-63 in NEW ZEALAND						
Auckland-England inns & 215 runs	*7d-562	-	258	89	E.R.Dexter	J.R.Reid
Wellington-England inns & 47 runs	8d-428	-	*194	187		
Christchurch-England 7 wkts	253	3-173	*266	159		

ENGLAND v NEW ZEALAND (cont.) Venue and Result	England 1st	England 2nd	New Zealand 1st	New Zealand 2nd	Captains England	Captains New Zealand
1965 in ENGLAND						
Birmingham-England 9 wkts	*435	1-96	116	413	M.J.K.Smith	J.R.Reid
Lord's-England 7 wkts	307	3-218	*175	347		
Leeds-England inns & 187 runs	*4d-546	-	193	166		
1965-66 in NEW ZEALAND						
Christchurch-Drawn	*342	5d-201	347	8-48	M.J.K.Smith	M.E.Chapple
Dunedin-Drawn	8d-254	-	*192	9-147		B.W.Sinclair
Auckland-Drawn	222	4-159	*296	129		B.W.Sinclair
1969 in ENGLAND						
Lord's-England 230 runs	*190	340	169	131	R.Illingworth	G.T.Dowling
Nottingham-Drawn	8d-451	-	*294	1-66		
The Oval-England 8 wkts	242	2-138	*150	229		
1970-71 in NEW ZEALAND						
Christchurch-England 8 wkts	231	2-89	*65	254	R.Illingworth	G.T.Dowling
Auckland-Drawn	*321	237	7d-313	0-40		
1973 in ENGLAND						
Nottingham-England 38 runs	*250	8d-325	97	440	R.Illingworth	B.E.Congdon
Lord's-Drawn	*253	9-463	9d-551	-		
Leeds-England inns &1 run	419	-	*276	142		
1974-75 in NEW ZEALAND						
Auckland-England inns & 83 runs	*6d-593	-	326	184	M.H.Denness	B.E.Congdon
Christchurch-Drawn	2-272	-	*342	-		
1977-78 in NEW ZEALAND						
Wellington-New Zealand 72 runs	215	64	*228	123	G.Boycott	M.G.Burgess
Christchurch-England 174 runs	*418	4d-96	235	105		
Auckland-Drawn	429	-	*315	8-382		
1978 in ENGLAND						
The Oval-England 7 wkts	279	3-138	*234	182	J.M.Brearley	M.G.Burgess
Nottingham-England inns &119 runs	*429	-	120	190		
Lord's-England 7 wkts	289	3-118	*339	67		
1983 in ENGLAND						
The Oval-England 189 runs	*209	6d-446	196	270	R.G.D.Willis	G.P.Howarth
Leeds-New Zealand 5 wkts	*225	252	377	5-103		
Lord's-England 127 runs	*326	211	191	219		
Nottingham-England 165 runs	*420	297	207	345		
1983-84 in NEW ZEALAND						
Wellington-Drawn	463	0-69	*219	537	R.G.D.Willis	G.P.Howarth
Christchurch-New Zealand inns & 132 runs	82	93	*307	-		
Auckland-Drawn	439	-	*9d-496	0-16		
1986 in ENGLAND						
Lord's-Drawn	*317	6d-295	342	2-41	M.W.Gatting	J.V.Coney
Nottingham-New Zealand 8 wkts	*256	230	413	2-77		
The Oval-Drawn	5d-388	-	*287	0-7		

ENGLAND v NEW ZEALAND (cont.)	England		New Zealand		Captains	
Venue and Result	1st	2nd	1st	2nd	England	New Zealand
1987-88 in NEW ZEALAND						
Christchurch-Drawn	*319	152	168	4-130	M.W.Gatting	J.J.Crowe
Auckland-Drawn	323	-	*301	7-350		J.J.Crowe
Wellington-Drawn	2-183	-	*6d-512	-		J.G.Wright
1990 in ENGLAND						
Nottingham-Drawn	9d-345	-	*208	2-36	G.A.Gooch	J.G.Wright
Lord's-Drawn	*334	4d-272	9d-462	-		
Birmingham-England 114 runs	*435	158	249	230		
1991-92 in NEW ZEALAND						
Christchurch-England inns & 4 runs	*9d-580	-	312	264	G.A.Gooch	M.D.Crowe
Auckland-England 168 runs	*203	321	142	214		
Wellington-Drawn	*305	7d-359	9d-432	3-43		

Test Match Results Summary

ENGLAND v NEW ZEALAND—IN ENGLAND

		Result			Lord's			The Oval			Manchester			Leeds			Birmingham			Nottingham		
	Tests	E	NZ	D	E	NZ	D	E	NZ	D	E	NZ	D	E	NZ	D	E	NZ	D	E	NZ	D
1931	3	1	-	2	-	-	1	1	-	-	-	-	1	-	-	-	-	-	-	-	-	-
1937	3	1	-	2	-	-	-	-	-	1	1	-	-	-	-	-	-	-	-	-	-	-
1949	4	-	-	4	-	-	1	-	-	1	-	-	1	-	-	1	-	-	-	-	-	-
1958	5	4	-	1	1	-	-	-	-	1	1	-	-	1	-	-	1	-	-	-	-	-
1965	3	3	-	-	1	-	-	-	-	-	-	-	-	1	-	-	1	-	-	-	-	-
1969	3	2	-	1	1	-	-	1	-	-	-	-	-	-	-	-	-	-	-	-	-	1
1973	3	2	-	1	-	-	1	-	-	-	-	-	-	1	-	-	-	-	-	1	-	-
1978	3	3	-	-	1	-	-	1	-	-	-	-	-	-	-	-	-	-	-	1	-	-
1983	4	3	1	-	1	-	-	1	-	-	-	-	-	-	1	-	-	-	-	1	-	-
1986	3	-	1	2	-	-	1	-	-	1	-	-	-	-	-	-	-	-	-	-	-	1
1990	3	1	-	2	-	-	1	-	-	-	-	-	-	-	-	-	1	-	-	-	-	1
	37	20	2	15	5	-	6	4	-	4	2	-	2	3	1	1	3	-	-	3	1	2

ENGLAND v NEW ZEALAND—IN NEW ZEALAND

		Result			Christchurch			Wellington			Auckland			Dunedin		
	Tests	E	NZ	D	E	NZ	D	E	NZ	D	E	NZ	D	E	NZ	D
1929-30	4	1	-	3	1	-	-	-	-	1	-	-	2	-	-	-
1932-33	2	-	-	2	-	-	1	-	-	-	-	-	1	-	-	-
1946-47	1	-	-	1	-	-	1	-	-	-	-	-	-	-	-	-
1950-51	2	1	-	1	-	-	1	1	-	-	-	-	-	-	-	-
1954-55	2	2	-	-	-	-	-	-	-	-	1	-	-	1	-	-
1958-59	2	1	-	1	1	-	-	-	-	-	-	-	1	-	-	-
1962-63	3	3	-	-	1	-	-	1	-	-	1	-	-	-	-	-
1965-66	3	-	-	3	-	-	1	-	-	-	-	-	1	-	-	1
1970-71	2	1	-	1	1	-	-	-	-	-	-	-	1	-	-	-
1974-75	2	1	-	1	-	-	1	-	-	-	1	-	-	-	-	-
1977-78	3	1	1	1	1	-	-	-	1	-	-	-	1	-	-	-
1983-84	3	-	1	2	-	1	-	-	-	1	-	-	1	-	-	-
1987-88	3	-	-	3	-	-	1	-	-	1	-	-	1	-	-	-
1991-92	3	2	-	1	1	-	-	-	-	1	1	-	-	-	-	-
	35	13	2	20	6	1	6	2	1	4	4	-	9	1	-	1
Totals	72	33	4	35												

HIGHEST INNINGS TOTALS

England In England	4d-546	Leeds	1965
England in New Zealand	6d-593	Auckland	1974-75
New Zealand in England	9d-551	Lord's	1973
New Zealand in New Zealand	537	Wellington	1983-84

LOWEST INNINGS TOTALS

England in England	158	Birmingham	1990
England in New Zealand	64	Wellington	1977-78
New Zealand in England	47	Lord's	1958
New Zealand in New Zealand	26	Auckland	1954-55

HIGHEST MATCH AGGREGATE	1293 for 34 wickets	Lord's	1931
LOWEST MATCH AGGREGATE	390 for 30 wickets	Lord's	1958

HIGHEST INDIVIDUAL INNINGS

England in England	310*	J.H.Edrich	Leeds	1965
England in New Zealand	336*	W.R.Hammond	Auckland	1932-33
New Zealand in England	206	M.P.Donnelly	Lord's	1949
New Zealand in New Zealand	174*	J.V.Coney	Wellington	1983-84

HIGHEST AGGREGATE OF RUNS IN A SERIES

England in England	469 (av 78.16)	L.Hutton	1949
England in New Zealand	563 (av 563.00)	W.R.Hammond	1932-33
New Zealand in England	462 (av 77.00)	M.P.Donnelly	1949
New Zealand in New Zealand	341 (av 85.25)	C.S.Dempster	1929-30

RECORD WICKET PARTNERSHIPS—ENGLAND

1st	223	G.Fowler (105), C.J.Tavare (109)	The Oval	1983
2nd	369	J.H.Edrich (310*), K.F.Barrington (163)	Leeds	1965
3rd	245	J.Hardstaff, jr (114), W.R.Hammond (140)	Lord's	1937
4th	266	M H.Denness (188), K.W.R.Fletcher (216)	Auckland	1974-75
5th	242	W.R.Hammond (227), L.E.G.Ames (103)	Christchurch	1932-33
6th	240	P.H.Parfitt (131*), 8.R.Knight (125)	Auckland	1962-63
7th	149	A.P.E.Knott (104), P.Lever (64)	Auckland	1970-71
8th	246	L.E.G.Ames (137), G.O.B.Allen (122)	Lord's	1931
9th	163*	M.C.Cowdrey (128*), A.C.Smith (69*)	Wellington	1962-63
10th	59	A.P.E.Knott (49), N.Gifford (25*)	Nottingham	1973

RECORD WICKET PARTNERSHIPS—NEW ZEALAND

1st	276	C.S.Dempster (136), J.E.Mills (117)	Wellington	1929-30
2nd	241	J.G.Wright (116), A.H.Jones (143)	Wellington	1991-92
3rd	210	B.A.Edgar (83), M.D.Crowe (106)	Lord's	1986
4th	155	M.D.Crowe (143), M.J.Greatbatch (68)	Wellington	1987-88
5th	177	B.E.Congdon (176), V.Pollard (116)	Nottingham	1973
6th	134	K.R.Rutherford (107*), J.G.Bracewell (54)	Wellington	1987-88
7th	117	D.N.Patel (99), C.L.Cairns (61)	Christchurch	1991-92
8th	104	D.A.R.Moloney (64), A.W.Roberts (66*)	Lord's	1937
9th	118	J.V.Coney (174*), B.L.Cairns (64)	Wellington	1983-84
10th	57	F.L.H.Mooney (46), J.Cowie (26*)	Leeds	1949

BEST INNINGS BOWLING ANALYSIS

England in England	7-32	D.L.Underwood	Lord's	1969
England in New Zealand	7-47	P.C.R.Tufnell	Christchurch	1991-92
New Zealand in England	7-74	B.L.Cairns	Leeds	1983
New Zealand in New Zealand	7-143	B.L.Cairns	Wellington	1983-84

BEST MATCH BOWLING ANALYSIS

England in England	12-101	D.L.Underwood	The Oval	1969
England in New Zealand	12-97	D.L.Underwood	Christchurch	1970-71
New Zealand in England	10-140	J.Cowie	Manchester	1937
	10-140	R.J.Hadlee	Nottingham	1986
New Zealand in New Zealand	10-100	R.J.Hadlee	Wellington	1977-78

HIGHEST AGGREGATE OF WICKETS IN A SERIES

England in England	34 (av 7.47)	G.A.R.Lock	1958
England in New Zealand	17 (av 9.34)	K.Higgs	1965-66
	17 (av 12.05)	D.L.Underwood	1970-71
	17 (av 18.29)	I.T.Botham	1977-78
New Zealand in England	21 (av 26.61)	R.J.Hadlee	1983
New Zealand in New Zealand	15 (av 19.53)	R.O.Collinge	1977-78
	15 (av 24.73)	R.J.Hadlee	1977-78

ENGLAND v INDIA

Venue and Result	England 1st	England 2nd	India 1st	India 2nd	Captains England	Captains India
1932 in ENGLAND						
Lord's-England 158 runs	*259	8d-275	189	187	D.R.Jardine	C.K.Nayudu
1933-34 in INDIA						
Bombay[1]-England 9 wkts	438	1-40	*219	258	D.R.Jardine	C.K.Nayudu
Calcutta-Drawn	*403	2-7	247	237		
Madras[1]-England 202 runs	*335	7d-261	145	249		
1936 in ENGLAND						
Lord's-England 9 wkts	134	1-108	*147	93	G.O.B.Allen	Maharaj Vizianagram
Manchester-Drawn	8d-571	-	*203	5-390		
The Oval-England 9 wkts	*8d-471	1-64	222	312		
1946 in ENGLAND						
Lord's-England 10 wkts	428	0-48	*200	275	W.R.Hammond	Nawab of Pataudi, sr
Manchester-Drawn	*294	5d-153	170	9-152		
The Oval-Drawn	3-95	-	*331	-		
1951-52 in INDIA						
Delhi-Drawn	*203	6-368	6d-418	-	N.D.Howard	V.S.Hazare
Bombay[2]-Drawn	456	2-55	*9d-485	208	N.D.Howard	
Calcutta-Drawn	*342	5d-252	344	0-103	N.D.Howard	
Kanpur-England 8 wkts	203	2-76	*121	157	N.D.Howard	
Madras[1]-India inns & 8 runs	*266	183	9d-457	-	D.B.Carr	
1952 in ENGLAND						
Leeds-England 7 wkts	334	3-128	*293	165	L.Hutton	V.S.Hazare
Lord's-England 8 wkts	537	2-79	*235	378		
Manchester-England inns & 207 runs	*9d-347	-	58	82		
The Oval-Drawn	*6d-326	-	98	-		
1959 in ENGLAND						
Nottingham-England inns & 59 runs	*422	-	206	157	P.B.H.May	D.K.Gaekwad
Lord's-England 8 wkts	226	2-108	*168	165	P.B.H.May	P.Roy
Leeds-England inns & 173 runs	8d-483	-	*161	149	P.B.H.May	D.K.Gaekwad
Manchester-England 171 runs	*490	8d-265	208	376	M C Cowdrey	D.K.Gaekwad
The Oval-England inns & 27 runs	361	-	*140	194	M C Cowdrey	D.K.Gaekwad
1961-62 in INDIA						
Bombay[2]-Drawn	*8d-500	5d-184	390	5-180	E.R.Dexter	N.J.Contractor
Kanpur-Drawn	244	5-497	*8d-467	-		
Delhi-Drawn	3-256	-	*466	-		
Calcutta-India 187 runs	212	233	*380	252		
Madras[2]-India 128 runs	281	209	*428	190		

ENGLAND v INDIA (cont.) Venue and Result	England 1st	England 2nd	India 1st	India 2nd	Captains England	Captains India
1963-64 in INDIA						
Madras^2-Drawn	317	5-241	*7d-457	9d-152	M.J.K.Smith	Nawab of Pataudi, jr
Bombay^2-Drawn	233	3-206	*300	8d-249		
Calcutta-Drawn	267	2-145	*241	7d-300		
Delhi-Drawn	451	-	*344	4 463		
Kanpur-Drawn	*8d-559	-	266	3-347		
1967 in ENGLAND						
Leeds-England 6 wkts	*4d-550	4-126	164	510	D.B.Close	Nawab of Pataudi, jr
Lord's-England inns & 124 runs	386	-	*152	110		
Birmingham-England 132 runs	*298	203	92	277		
1971 in ENGLAND						
Lord's-Drawn	*304	191	313	8-145	R.Illingworth	A.L.Wadekar
Manchester-Drawn	*386	3d-245	212	3-65		
The Oval-India 4 wkts	*355	101	284	6-174		
1972-73 In INDIA						
Delhi-England 6 wkts	200	4-208	*173	233	A.R.Lewis	A.L.Wadekar
Calcutta-India 28 runs	174	163	*210	155		
Madras^1-India 4 wkts	*242	159	316	6-86		
Kanpur-Drawn	397	-	*357	6-186		
Bombay^2-Drawn	480	2-67	*448	5d-244		
1974 in ENGLAND						
Lord's-England 113 runs	*9d-328	3d-213	246	182	M.H.Denness	A.L.Wadekar
Lord's-England inns & 285 runs	*629	-	302	42		
Birmingham-England inns & 78 runs	2d-459	-	*165	216		
1976-77 in INDIA						
Delhi-England inns & 25 runs	*381	-	122	234	A.W.Greig	B.S.Bedi
Calcutta-England 10 wkts	321	0-16	*155	181		
Madras^1-England 200 runs	*262	9d-185	164	83		
Bangalore-India 140 runs	195	177	*253	9d-259		
Bombay^3-Drawn	317	7-152	*338	192		
1979 in ENGLAND						
Birmingham-England inns & 83 runs	*5d-633	-	297	253	J.M.Brearley	S.Venkataraghavan
Lord's-Drawn	9d-419	-	*96	4-318		
Leeds-Drawn	*270	-	6-223	-		
The Oval-Drawn	*305	8d-334	202	8-429		
1979-80 in INDIA						
Bombay^3-England 10 wkts	296	0-98	*242	149	J.M.Brearley	G.R.Viswanath
1981-82 in INDIA						
Bombay^3-India 138 runs	166	102	*179	227	K.W.R.Fletcher	S.M.Gavaskar
Bangalore-Drawn	*400	3-174	428	-		
Delhi-Drawn	*9d-476	0-68	487	-		
Calcutta-Drawn	*248	5d-265	208	3-170		
Madras^1-Drawn	328	-	*4d-481	3-160		
Kanpur-Drawn	*9d-378	-	7-377	-		

ENGLAND v INDIA (cont.) Venue and Result	England 1st	England 2nd	India 1st	India 2nd	Captains England	Captains India
1982 in ENGLAND						
Lord's-England 7 wkts	*433	3-67	128	369	R.G.D.Willis	S.M.Gavaskar
Manchester-Drawn	*425	-	8-379	-		
The Oval-Drawn	*594	3d-191	410	3-111		
1984-85 in INDIA						
Bombay³-India 8 wkts	*195	317	8d-465	2-51	D.I.Gower	S.M.Gavaskar
Delhi-England 8 wkts	418	2-127	*307	235		
Calcutta-Drawn	276	-	*7d-437	1-29		
Madras¹-England 9 wkts	7d-652	1-35	*272	412		
Kanpur-Drawn	417	0-91	*8d-553	1d-97		
1986 in ENGLAND						
Lord's-India 5 wkts	*294	180	341	5-136	D.I.Gower	Kapil Dev
Manchester-India 279 runs	102	128	*272	237	M.W.Gatting	
The Oval-Drawn	*390	235	390	5-174	M.W.Gatting	
1990 in ENGLAND						
Lord's-England 247 runs	*4d-653	4d-272	454	224	G.A.Gooch	M.Azharuddin
Manchester-Drawn	*519	4d-320	432	6-343		
The Oval-Drawn	340	4d-477	*9d-606	-		

Test Match Results Summary

ENGLAND v INDIA — IN ENGLAND

	Tests	Result			Lord's			Manchester			The Oval			Leeds			Nottingham			Birmingham		
		E	I	D	E	I	D	E	I	D	E	I	D	E	I	D	E	I	D	E	I	D
1932	1	1	-	-	1	-	-	-	-	-	-	-	-	-	-	-	-	-	-	-	-	-
1936	3	2	-	1	1	-	-	-	-	1	1	-	-	-	-	-	-	-	-	-	-	-
1946	3	1	-	2	1	-	-	-	-	1	-	-	1	-	-	-	-	-	-	-	-	-
1952	4	3	-	1	1	-	-	1	-	-	-	-	1	1	-	-	-	-	-	-	-	-
1959	5	5	-	-	1	-	-	1	-	-	1	-	-	1	-	-	-	-	-	-	-	-
1967	3	3	-	-	1	-	-	-	-	-	-	-	-	-	-	-	1	-	-	1	-	-
1971	3	-	1	2	-	-	1	-	-	1	-	1	-	-	-	-	-	-	-	-	-	-
1974	3	3	-	-	1	-	-	1	-	-	-	-	-	-	-	-	-	-	-	1	-	-
1979	4	1	-	3	-	-	1	-	-	-	-	-	1	-	-	1	-	-	-	1	-	-
1982	3	1	-	2	1	-	-	-	-	1	-	-	1	-	-	-	-	-	-	-	-	-
1986	3	-	2	1	-	1	-	-	-	-	-	-	-	-	1	-	-	-	-	-	-	1
1990	3	1	-	2	1	-	-	-	-	1	-	-	1	-	-	-	-	-	-	-	-	-
	38	21	3	14	9	1	2	3	-	5	2	1	5	3	1	1	1	-	-	3	-	1

ENGLAND v INDIA—IN INDIA

	Tests	Result			Bombay			Calcutta			Madras			Delhi			Kanpur			Bangalore		
		E	I	D	E	I	D	E	I	D	E	I	D	E	I	D	E	I	D	E	I	D
1933-34	3	2	-	1	1	-	-	-	-	1	1	-	-	-	-	-	-	-	-	-	-	-
1951-52	5	1	1	3	-	-	1	-	-	1	-	1	-	-	-	1	1	-	-	-	-	-
1961-62	5	-	2	3	-	-	1	-	1	-	-	1	-	-	-	1	-	-	1	-	-	-
1963-64	5	-	-	5	-	-	1	-	-	1	-	-	1	-	-	1	-	-	1	-	-	-
1972-73	5	1	2	2	-	-	1	-	1	-	-	1	-	1	-	-	-	-	1	-	-	-
1976-77	5	3	1	1	-	-	1	1	-	-	1	-	-	1	-	-	-	-	-	-	-	1
1979-80	1	1	-	-	1	-	-	-	-	-	-	-	-	-	-	-	-	-	-	-	-	-
1981-82	6	-	1	5	-	1	-	-	-	1	-	-	1	-	-	1	-	-	1	-	-	1
1984-85	5	2	1	2	-	1	-	-	-	1	1	-	-	1	-	-	-	-	1	-	-	-
	40	10	8	22	2	2	5	1	2	5	3	3	2	3	-	4	1	-	5	-	1	1
Totals	67	28	8	31																		

HIGHEST INNINGS TOTALS

England in England	4d-653	Lord's	1990
England in India	7d-652	Madras[1]	1984-85
India in England	9d-606	The Oval	1990
India in India	8d-553	Kanpur	1984-85

LOWEST INNINGS TOTALS

England in England	101	The Oval	1971
England in India	102	Bombay[3]	1981-82
India in England	42	Lord's	1974
India in India	83	Madras[1]	1976-77

HIGHEST MATCH AGGREGATE	1614 for 30 wickets	Manchester	1990
LOWEST MATCH AGGREGATE	482 for 31 wickets	Lord's	1936

HIGHEST INDIVIDUAL INNINGS

England in England	333	G.A.Gooch	Lord's	1990
England in India	207	M.W.Gatting	Madras[1]	1984-85
India In England	221	S.M.Gavaskar	The Oval	1979
India in India	222	G.R.Viswanath	Madras[1]	1981-82

HIGHEST AGGREGATE OF RUNS IN A SERIES

England in England	752 (av 125.33)	G.A.Gooch	1990
England in India	594 (av 99.00)	K.F.Barrington	1961-62
India in England	542 (av 77.42)	S.M.Gavaskar	1979
India in India	586 (av 83.71)	V.L.Manjrekar	1961-62

RECORD WICKET PARTNERSHIPS—ENGLAND

1st	225	G.A.Gooch(116), M.A.Atherton(131)	Manchester	1990
2nd	241	G.Fowler (201), M.W.Gatting (207)	Madras[1]	1984-85
3rd	308	G.A.Gooch(333), A.J.Lamb(139)	Lord's	1990
4th	266	W.R.Hammond (217), T.S.Worthington (128)	Oval	1936
5th	254	K.W.R.Fletcher (113), A.W.Greig (148)	Bombay[2]	1972-73
6th	171	I.T.Botham (114), R.W.Taylor (43)	Bombay[3]	1979-80
7th	125	D.W.Randall (126), P.H.Edmonds (64)	Lord's	1982
8th	168	R.Illingworth (107), P.Lever (88*)	Manchester	1971
9th	83	K.W.R.Fletcher (97*), N.Gifford (19)	Madras[1]	1972-73
10th	70	P.J.W.Allott (41*), R.G.D.Willis (28)	Lord's	1982

RECORD WICKET PARTNERSHIPS—INDIA

1st	213	S.M.Gavaskar (221), C.P.S.Chauhan (80)	The Oval	1979
2nd	192	F.M.Engineer (121), A.L.Wadekar (87)	Bombay[2]	1972-73
3rd	316†	G.R.Viswanath (222), Yashpal Sharma (140)	Madras[1]	1981-82
4th	222	V.S.Hazare (89), V.L.Manjrekar (133)	Leeds	1952
5th	214	M.Azharuddin (110), R.J.Shastri (111)	Calcutta	1984-85
6th	130	S.M.H.Kirmani (43), Kapil Dev (97)	The Oval	1982
7th	235	R.J.Shastri (142), S.M.H.Kirmani (102)	Bombay[3]	1984-85
8th	128	R.J.Shastri (93), S.M.H.Kirmani (67)	Delhi	1981-82
9th	104	R.J.Shastri (93), S.Madan Lal (44)	Delhi	1981-82
10th	51	R.G.Nadkarni (43'), B.S.Chandrasekhar (16)	Calcutta	1963-64
	51	S.M.H.Kirmani (75), C.Sharma (17*)	Madras[1]	1984-85

† 415 runs were added for this wicket. D.B.Vengsarkar retired hurt after he had added 99 with Viswanath.

BEST INNINGS BOWLING ANALYSIS

England in England	8-31	F.S.Trueman	Manchester	1952
England in India	7-46	J.K.Lever	Delhi	1976-77
India in England	6-35	L.Amar Singh	Lord's	1936
India in India	8-55	M.H.Mankad	Madras[1]	1951-52

BEST MATCH BOWLING ANALYSIS

England in England	11-93	A.V.Bedser	Manchester	1946
England in India	13-106	I.T.Botham	Bombay[3]	1979-80
India in England	10-188	C.Sharma	Birmingham	1986
India in India	12-108	M.H.Mankad	Madras[1]	1951-52

HIGHEST AGGREGATE OF WICKETS IN A SERIES

England in England	29 (av 13.31)	F.S.Trueman	1952
England in India	29 (av 17.55)	D.L.Underwood	1976-77
India in England	17 (av 34.64)	S.P.Gupte	1959
India in India	35 (av 18.91)	B.S.Chandrasekhar	1972-73

ENGLAND v PAKISTAN

Venue and Result	England 1st	England 2nd	Pakistan 1st	Pakistan 2nd	Captains England	Captains Pakistan
1954 in ENGLAND						
Lord's-Drawn	9d-117	-	*87	3-121	L.Hutton	A.H.Kardar
Nottingham-England inns &129 runs	6d-558	-	*157	272	D.S.Sheppard	
Manchester-Drawn	*8d-359	-	90	4-25	D.S.Sheppard	
The Oval-Pakistan 24 runs	130	143	*133	164	L.Hutton	
1961-62 in PAKISTAN						
Lahore[2]-England 5 wkts	380	5-209	*9d-387	200	E.R.Dexter	Imtiaz Ahmed
Dacca-Drawn	439	0-38	*7d-393	216		
Karachi-Drawn	507	-	*253	8-404		
1962 in ENGLAND						
Birmingham-England inns & 24 runs	*5d-544	-	246	274	E.R.Dexter	Javed Burki
Lord's-England 9 wkts	370	1-86	*100	355	E.R.Dexter	
Leeds-England inns & 117 runs	*428	-	131	180	M.C.Cowdrey	
Nottingham-Drawn	*5d-428	-	219	6-216	E.R.Dexter	
The Oval-England 10 wkts	*5d-480	0-27	183	323	E.R.Dexter	
1967 in ENGLAND						
Lord's-Drawn	*369	9d-241	354	3-88	D.B.Close	Hanif Mohammad
Nottingham-England 10 wkts	8d-252	0-3	*140	114		
The Oval-England 8 wkts	440	2-34	*216	255		

ENGLAND v PAKISTAN (cont.) Venue and Result	England 1st	England 2nd	Pakistan 1st	Pakistan 2nd	Captains England	Captains Pakistan
1968-69 In PAKISTAN						
Lahore²-Drawn	*306	9d-225	209	5-203	M.C.Cowdrey	Saeed Ahmed
Dacca-Drawn	274	0-33	*246	6d-195		
Karachi-Drawn	*7-502	-	-	-		
1971 in ENGLAND						
Birmingham-Drawn	353	5-229	*7d-608	-	R.Illingworth	Intikhab Alam
Lord's-Drawn	*2d-241	0-117	148	-		
Leeds-England 25 runs	*316	264	350	205		
1972-73 in PAKISTAN						
Lahore²-Drawn	*355	7d-306	422	3-124	A.R.Lewis	Majid Khan
Hyderabad-Drawn	*487	6-218	9d-569	-		
Karachi-Drawn	386	1-30	*6d-445	199		
1974 in ENGLAND						
Leeds-Drawn	183	6-238	*285	179	M.H.Denness	Intikhab Alam
Lord's-Drawn	270	0-27	*9d-130	226		
The Oval-Drawn	545	-	*7d-600	4-94		
1977-78 in PAKISTAN						
Lahore²-Drawn	288	-	*9d-407	3-106	J.M.Brearley	Wasim Bari
Hyderabad-Drawn	191	1-186	*275	4d-259	J.M.Brearley	
Karachi-Drawn	*266	5-222	281	-	G.Boycott	
1978 in ENGLAND						
Birmingham-England inns & 57 runs	8d-452	-	*164	231	J.M.Brearley	Wasim Bari
Lord's-England inns &120 runs	*364	-	105	139		
Leeds-Drawn	7-119	-	*201	-		
1982 in ENGLAND						
Birmingham-England 113 runs	*272	291	251	199	R.G.D.Willis	Imran Khan
Lord's-Pakistan 10 wkts	227	276	*8d-428	0-77	D.I.Gower	
Leeds-England 3 wkts	256	7-219	*275	199	R.G.D.Willis	
1983-84 in PAKISTAN						
Karachi-Pakistan 3 wkts	*182	159	277	7-66	R.G.D.Willis	Zaheer Abbas
Faisalabad-Drawn	8d-546	-	*8d-449	4-137	D.I.Gower	
Lahore²-Drawn	*241	9d-344	343	6-217	D.I.Gower	
1987 in ENGLAND						
Manchester-Drawn	*447	-	5-140	-	M.W.Gatting	Imran Khan
Lord's-Drawn	*368	-	-	-		
Leeds-Pakistan inns & 18 runs	*136	199	353	-		
Birmingham-Drawn	521	7-109	*439	205		
The Oval-Drawn	232	4-315	*708	-		
1987-88 in PAKISTAN						
Lahore²-Pakistan inns & 87 runs	*175	130	392	-	M.W.Gatting	Javed Miandad
Faisalabad-Drawn	*292	6d-137	191	1-51		
Karachi-Drawn	*294	9-258	353	-		

ENGLAND v PAKISTAN (cont.) Venue and Result	England 1st	England 2nd	Pakistan 1st	Pakistan 2nd	Captains England	Captains Pakistan
1992 in ENGLAND						
Leeds-Drawn	7-459	-	*4d-448	-	G.A.Gooch	Javed Miandad
Lord's-Pakistan 2 wkts	*255	175	293	8-141		
Manchester-Drawn	390	-	*505	5d-239		
Leeds-England 6 wkts	320	4-99	*197	221		
The Oval-Pakistan 10 wkts	*207	174	380	0-5		

Test Match Results Summary

ENGLAND v PAKISTAN—IN ENGLAND

		Result			Lords			Nottingham			Manchester			The Oval			Birmingham			Leeds		
	Tests	E	P	D	E	P	D	E	P	D	E	P	D	E	P	D	E	P	D	E	P	D
1954	4	1	1	2	-	-	1	1	-	-	-	-	1	-	1	-	-	-	-	-	-	-
1962	5	4	-	1	1	-	-	-	-	1	-	-	-	1	-	-	1	-	-	1	-	-
1967	3	2	-	1	-	-	1	1	-	-	-	-	-	1	-	-	-	-	-	-	-	-
1971	3	1	-	2	-	-	1	-	-	-	-	-	-	-	-	-	-	-	1	1	-	-
1974	3	-	-	3	-	-	1	-	-	-	-	-	-	-	-	1	-	-	-	-	-	1
1978	3	2	-	1	1	-	-	-	-	-	-	-	-	-	-	-	1	-	-	-	-	1
1982	3	2	1	-	-	1	-	-	-	-	-	-	-	-	-	-	1	-	-	1	-	-
1987	5	-	1	4	-	-	1	-	-	-	-	-	1	-	-	1	-	-	1	-	1	-
1992	5	1	2	2	-	1	-	-	-	-	-	-	1	-	1	-	-	-	1	1	-	-
	34	13	5	16	2	2	5	2	-	1	-	-	3	2	2	2	3	-	3	4	1	2

ENGLAND v PAKISTAN—IN PAKISTAN

		Result			Lahore			Dacca			Karachi			Hyderabad			Faisalabad		
	Tests	E	P	D	E	P	D	E	P	D	E	P	D	E	P	D	E	P	D
1961-62	3	1	-	2	1	-	-	-	-	1	-	-	1	-	-	-	-	-	-
1968-69	3	-	-	3	-	-	1	-	-	-	-	-	1	-	-	1	-	-	-
1972-73	3	-	-	3	-	-	1	-	-	-	-	-	1	-	-	1	-	-	-
1977-78	3	-	-	3	-	-	1	-	-	1	-	-	1	-	-	-	-	-	-
1983-84	3	-	1	2	-	-	1	-	-	-	-	1	-	-	-	-	-	-	1
1987-88	3	-	1	2	-	1	-	-	-	-	-	-	1	-	-	-	-	-	1
	18	1	2	15	1	1	4	-	-	2	-	1	5	-	-	2	-	-	2
Totals	52	14	7	31															

HIGHEST INNINGS TOTALS

England in England	6d-558	Nottingham	1954
England in Pakistan	8d-546	Faisalabad	1983-84
Pakistan in England	708	The Oval	1987
Pakistan in Pakistan	9d-569	Hyderabad	1972-73

LOWEST INNINGS TOTALS

England in England	130	The Oval	1954
England in Pakistan	130	Lahore[2]	1987-88
Pakistan in England	87	Lord's	1954
Pakistan in Pakistan	191	Faisalabad	1987-88

HIGHEST MATCH AGGREGATE	1274 for 25 wickets	Hyderabad	1972-73
LOWEST MATCH AGGREGATE	509 for 28 wickets	Nottingham	1967

HIGHEST INDIVIDUAL INNINGS

England in England	278	D.C.S.Compton	Nottingham	1954
England in Pakistan	205	E.R.Dexter	Karachi	1961-62
Pakistan in England	274	Zaheer Abbas	Birmingham	1971
Pakistan in Pakistan	157	Mushtaq Mohammad	Hyderabad	1972-73

HIGHEST AGGREGATE OF RUNS IN A SERIES

England in England	453 (av 90.60)	D.C.S.Compton	1954
England in Pakistan	449 (av 112.25)	D.I.Gower	1983-84
Pakistan in England	488 (av 81.33)	Saleem Malik	1992
Pakistan in Pakistan	407 (av 67.83)	Hanif Mohammad	1961-62

RECORD WICKET PARTNERSHIPS—ENGLAND

1st	198	G.Pullar (165), R.W.Barber (86)	Dacca	1961-62
2nd	248	M.C.Cowdrey (182), E.R.Dexter (172)	The Oval	1962
3rd	247	A.J.Stewart (190), R.A.Smith (127)	Birmingham	1992
4th	188	E.R.Dexter (205), P.H.Parfitt (111)	Karachi	1961-62
5th	192	D.C.S.Compton (278), T.E.Bailey (36*)	Nottingham	1954
6th	153*	P.H.Parfitt (101*), D.A.Allen (79*)	Birmingham	1962
7th	167	D.I.Gower (152), V.J.Marks (83)	Faisalabad	1983-84
8th	99	P.H.Parfitt (119), D.A.Allen (62)	Leeds	1962
9th	76	T.W.Graveney (153), F.S.Trueman (29)	Lord's	1962
10th	79	R.W.Taylor (54), R.G.D.Willis (28*)	Birmingham	1982

RECORD WICKET PARTNERSHIPS—PAKISTAN

1st	173	Mohsin Khan (104), Shoaib Mohammad (80)	Lahore[2]	1983-84
2nd	291	Zaheer Abbas (274), Mushtaq Mohammad (100)	Birmingham	1971
3rd	180	Mudassar Nazar (114), Haroon Rashid (122)	Lahore[2]	1977-78
4th	332	Javed Miandad (153*), Saleem Malik (165)	Birmingham	1992
5th	197	Javed Burki (101), Nasim-ul-Ghani (101)	Lord's	1962
6th	145	Mushtaq Mohammad (157), Intikhab Alam (138)	Hyderabad	1972-73
7th	89	Ijaz Ahmed (69), Saleem Yousuf (42)	The Oval	1987
8th	130	Hanif Mohammad (187*), Asif Iqbal (76)	Lord's	1967
9th	190	Asif Iqbal (146), Intikhab Alam (51)	The Oval	1967
10th	62	Sarfraz Nawaz (53), Asif Masood (4*)	Leeds	1974

BEST INNINGS BOWLING ANALYSIS

England in England	8-34	I.T.Botham	Lord's	1978
England in Pakistan	7-66	P.H.Edmonds	Karachi	1977-78
Pakistan in England	7-40	Imran Khan	Leeds	1987
Pakistan in Pakistan	9-56	Abdul Qadir	Lahore[2]	1987-88

BEST MATCH BOWLING ANALYSIS

England in England	13-71	D.L.Underwood	Lord's	1974
England in Pakistan	11-83	N.G.B.Cook	Karachi	1983-84
Pakistan in England	12-99	Fazal Mahmood	The Oval	1954
Pakistan in Pakistan	13-101	Abdul Qadir	Lahore[2]	1987-88

HIGHEST AGGREGATE OF WICKETS IN A SERIES

England in England	22 (av 19.95)	F.S.Trueman	1962
England in Pakistan	14 (av 31.71)	N.G.B.Cook	1983-84
Pakistan in England	22 (av 25.31)	Waqar Younis	1992
Pakistan in Pakistan	30 (av 14.56)	Abdul Qadir	1987-88

ENGLAND v SRI LANKA

Venue and Result	England 1st	England 2nd	Sri Lanka 1st	Sri Lanka 2nd	Captains England	Captains Sri Lanka
1981-82 in SRI LANKA						
Colombo-England 7 wkts	223	3-171	*218	175	K.W.R.Fletcher	B.Warnapura
1984 in ENGLAND						
Lord's-Drawn	370	-	*7d-491	7d-294	D.I.Gower	L.R.D.Mendis
1988 in ENGLAND						
Lord's-England 7 wkts	429	3-100	*194	331	G.A.Gooch	R.S.Madugalle
1991 in ENGLAND						
Lord's-England 137 runs	*282	3d-364	224	285	G.A.Gooch	P.A.de Silva

Test Match Results Summary

ENGLAND v SRI LANKA—IN ENGLAND

	Tests	Result E	Result SL	Result D	Lord's E	Lord's SL	Lord's D
1984	1	-	-	1	-	-	1
1988	1	1	-	-	1	-	-
1991	1	1	-	-	1	-	-
	3	2	-	1	2	-	1

ENGLAND v SRI LANKA—IN SRI LANKA

	Tests	Result E	Result SL	Result D	Colombo (PSS) E	Colombo (PSS) SL	Colombo (PSS) D
1981-82	1	1	-	-	1	-	-
Totals	4	3	-	1			

HIGHEST INNINGS TOTALS

England in England	429	Lord's	1988
England in Sri Lanka	223	Colombo (PSS)	1981-82
Sri Lanka in England	7d-491	Lord's	1984
Sri Lanka in Sri Lanka	218	Colombo (PSS)	1981-82

LOWEST INNINGS TOTALS

England in England	282	Lord's	1991
England in Sri Lanka	223	Colombo (PSS)	1981-82
Sri Lanka in England	194	Lord's	1988
Sri Lanka in Sri Lanka	195	Colombo (PSS)	1981-82

HIGHEST MATCH AGGREGATE	1155 for 24 wickets	Lord's	1984
	1155 for 33 wickets	Lord's	1991
LOWEST MATCH AGGREGATE	787 for 33 wickets	Colombo (PSS)	1981-82

HIGHEST INDIVIDUAL INNINGS

England in England	174	G.A.Gooch	Lord's	1991
England in Sri Lanka	89	D.I.Gower	Colombo (PSS)	1981-82
Sri Lanka in England	190	S.Wettimuny	Lord's	1984
Sri Lanka in Sri Lanka	77	R.L.Dias	Colombo (PSS)	1981-82

HIGHEST AGGREGATE OF RUNS IN A SERIES

England in England	212 (av 90.60)	G.A.Gooch	1991
England in Sri Lanka	131 (av 112.25)	D.I.Gower	1981-82
Sri Lanka in England	205 (av 44.55)	L.R.D.Mendis	1984
Sri Lanka in Sri Lanka	77 (av 67.83)	R.L.Dias	1981-82

RECORD WICKET PARTNERSHIPS—ENGLAND

1st	78	G.A.Gooch (174), H.Morris (23)	Lord's	1991
2nd	139	G.A.Gooch (174), A.J.Stewart (43)	Lord's	1991
3rd	105	G.A.Gooch (174), R.A.Smith (63*)	Lord's	1991
4th	87	K.J.Barnett (86), D.I.Gower (55)	Lord's	1988
5th	40	A.J.Stewart (113*), I.T.Botham (22)	Lord's	1991
6th	87	A.J.Lamb (107), R.M.Ellison (41)	Lord's	1984
7th	63	A.J.Stewart (113*), R.C.Russell (17)	Lord's	1991
8th	12	A.J.Stewart (113*), P.A.J.DeFreitas (1)	Lord's	1991
9th	37	P.J.Newport (26), N.A.Foster (14*)	Lord's	1988
10th	9	N.A.Foster (14*), D.V.Lawrence (4)	Lord's	1988

RECORD WICKET PARTNERSHIPS—SRI LANKA

1st	50	D.S.B.P.Kuruppu (21), U.C.Hathurusingha (25)	Lord's	1991
2nd	83	B.Warnaweera (38), R.L.Dias (77)	Colombo (PSS)	1981-82
3rd	101	S.Wettimuny (190), R.L.Dias (32)	Lord's	1984
4th	148	S.Wettimuny (190), A.Ranatunga (84)	Lord's	1984
5th	150	S.Wettimuny (190), L.R.D.Mendis(111)	Lord's	1984
6th	138	S.A.R.Silva (102*), L.R.D.Mendis (94)	Lord's	1984
7th	74	U.C.Hathurusingha (66), R.J.Ratnayake (52)	Lord's	1991
8th	28	R.J.Ratnayake (17), C.P.H.Ramanayake (34*)	Lord's	1991
9th	12	J.R.Ratnayeke (32), G.F.Labrooy (9*)	Lord's	1988
	12	C.P.H.Ramanayake (34*), K.I.W.Wijegunawardene (4)	Lord's	1991
10th	64	J.R.Ratnayeke (59*), G.F.Labrooy (42)	Lord's	1988

BEST INNINGS BOWLING ANALYSIS

England in England	7-70	P.A.J.DeFreitas	Lord's	1991
England in Sri Lanka	6-33	J.E.Emburey	Colombo (PSS)	1981-82
Sri Lanka in England	5-69	R.J.Ratnayake	Lord's	1991
Sri Lanka in Sri Lanka	4-70	A.L.F.de Mel	Colombo (PSS)	1981-82

BEST MATCH BOWLING ANALYSIS

England in England	8-115	P.A.J.DeFreitas	Lord's	1991
England in Sri Lanka	8-95	D.L.Underwood	Colombo (PSS)	1981-82
Sri Lanka in England	5-160	R.J.Ratnayake	Lord's	1991
Sri Lanka in Sri Lanka	5-103	A.L.F.de Mel	Colombo (PSS)	1981-82

HIGHEST AGGREGATE OF WICKETS IN A SERIES

England in England	8 (av 14.37)	P.A.J.DeFreitas	1991
England in Sri Lanka	8 (av 11.87)	D.L.Underwood	1981-82
Sri Lanka in England	5 (av 32.00)	R.J.Ratnayake	1991
	5 (av 36.00)	S.D.Anurasiri	1991
Sri Lanka in Sri Lanka	5 (av 28.53)	A.L.F.de Mel	1981-82

SOUTH AFRICA v NEW ZEALAND

Venue and Result	South Africa 1st	South Africa 2nd	New Zealand 1st	New Zealand 2nd	Captains South Africa	Captains New Zealand
1931-32 In NEW ZEALAND						
Christchurch-South Africa inns & 12 runs	451	-	*293	146	H.B.Cameron	M.L.Page
Wellington-South Africa 8 wkts	410	2-150	*364	193		

SOUTH AFRICA v NEW ZEALAND (cont.) Venue and Result	SA 1st	SA 2nd	New Zealand 1st	New Zealand 2nd	Captains South Africa	Captains New Zealand
1952-53 In NEW ZEALAND						
Wellington-South Africa inns & 180 runs	*8d-524	-	172	172	J.E.Cheetham	W.M.Wallace
Auckland-Drawn	*377	5d-200	245	2-31		
1953-54 In SOUTH AFRICA						
Durban[2]-South Africa inns & 58 runs	*9d-437	-	230	149	J.E.Cheetham	G.O.Rabone
Johannesburg[2]-South Africa 132 runs	*271	148	187	100		G.O.Rabone
Cape Town-Drawn	326	3-159	*505	-		G.O.Rabone
Johannesburg[2]-South Africa 9 wkts	*243	1-25	79	188		B.Sutcliffe
Port Elizabeth-South Africa 5 wkts	237	5-215	*226	222		B.Sutcliffe
1961-62 In SOUTH AFRICA						
Durban[2]-South Africa 30 runs	*292	149	245	166	D.J.McGlew	J.R.Reid
Johannesburg[3]-Drawn	*322	6d-178	223	4-165		
Cape Town-New Zealand 72 runs	190	335	*385	9d-212		
Johannesburg[3]-South Africa inns & 51 runs	464	-	*164	249		
Port Elizabeth-New Zealand 40 runs	190	273	*275	228		
1963-64 in NEW ZEALAND						
Wellington-Drawn	*302	2d-218	253	6-138	T.L.Goddard	J.R.Reid
Dunedin-Drawn	223	3-42	*149	138		
Auckland-Drawn	*371	5d-200	263	8-191		

Test Match Results Summary

SOUTH AFRICA v NEW ZEALAND-IN SOUTH AFRICA

		Result			Durban			Johannesburg			Cape Town			P.Elizabeth		
	Tests	SA	NZ	D	SA	NZ	D	SA	NZ	D	SA	NZ	D	SA	NZ	D
1953-54	5	4	-	1	1	-	-	2	-	-	-	-	1	1	-	-
1961-62	5	2	2	1	1	-	-	1	-	1	-	1	-	-	1	-
	10	6	2	2	2	-	-	3	-	1	-	1	1	1	1	-

SOUTH AFRICA v NEW ZEALAND — IN NEW ZEALAND

		Result			Christchurch			Wellington			Auckland			Dunedin		
	Tests	SA	NZ	D	SA	NZ	D	SA	NZ	D	SA	NZ	D	SA	NZ	D
1931-32	2	2	-	-	1	-	-	1	-	-	-	-	-	-	-	-
1952-53	2	1	-	1	-	-	-	1	-	-	-	-	1	-	-	-
1963-64	3	-	-	3	-	-	-	-	-	1	-	-	1	-	-	1
	7	3	-	4	1	-	-	2	-	1	-	-	2	-	-	1
Totals	17	9	2	6												

HIGHEST INNINGS TOTALS

South Africa in South Africa	464	Johannesburg[3]	1961-62
South Africa in New Zealand	8d-524	Wellington	1952-53
New Zealand in South Africa	505	Cape Town	1953-54
New Zealand in New Zealand	364	Wellington	1931-32

Drama during the Bodyline series of 1932-33 when Australia's wicketkeeper Bertie Oldfield was struck by a ball bowled by England speedster Harold Larwood. This incident provoked ugly crowd scenes at the Adelaide Oval.

One of Australia's finest batsmen, Bill Ponsford, playing at The Oval in 1934 on his way to his highest Test innings score of 266.

The greatest batsman of all time, Don Bradman.

LOWEST INNINGS TOTALS

South Africa in South Africa	148	Johannesburg[2]	1953-54
South Africa in New Zealand	223	Dunedin	1963-64
New Zealand in South Africa	79	Johannesburg[2]	1953-54
New Zealand in New Zealand	138	Dunedin	1963-64

HIGHEST MATCH AGGREGATE	1122 for 39 wickets	Cape Town	1961-62
LOWEST MATCH AGGREGATE	535 for 31 wickets	Johannesburg[2]	1953-54

HIGHEST INDIVIDUAL INNINGS

South Africa in South Africa	127*	D.J.McGlew	Durban[2]	1961-62
South Africa in New Zealand	255*	D.J.McGlew	Wellington	1952-53
New Zealand in South Africa	142	J.R.Reid	Johannesburg[3]	1961-62
New Zealand in New Zealand	138	B.W.Sinclair	Auckland	1963-64

HIGHEST AGGREGATE OF RUNS IN A SERIES

South Africa in South Africa	426 (av 60.85)	D.J.McGlew	1961-62
South Africa in New Zealand	323 (av 161.50)	D.J.McGlew	1952-53
New Zealand in South Africa	546 (av 60.66)	J.R.Reid	1961-62
New Zealand in New Zealand	264 (av 44.00)	B.W.Sinclair	1963-64

RECORD WICKET PARTNERSHIPS — SOUTH AFRICA

1st	196	J.A.J.Christy (103), B.Mitchell (113)	Christchurch	1931-32
2nd	76	J.A.J.Christy (62), H.B.Cameron (44)	Wellington	1931-32
3rd	112	D.J.McGlew (120), R.A.McLean (78)	Johannesburg[3]	1961-62
4th	135	K.J.Funston (39), R.A McLean (101)	Durban[2]	1953-54
5th	130	W.R.Endean (116), J.E.Cheetham (54)	Auckland	1952-53
6th	83	K.C.Bland (83), D.T.Lindsay (37)	Auckland	1963-64
7th	246	D.J.McGlew (255*), A.R.A.Murray (109)	Wellington	1952-53
8th	95	J.E.Cheetham (89), H.J.Tayfield (34)	Cape Town	1953-54
9th	60	P.M.Pollock (54), N.A.T.Adcock (24)	Port Elizabeth	1961-62
10th	47	D.J.McGlew (28*), H.D.Bromfield (21)	Port Elizabeth	1961-62

RECORD WICKET PARTNERSHIPS — NEW ZEALAND

1st	126	G.O.Rabone (56), M.E.Chapple (76)	Cape Town	1953-54
2nd	51	W.P.Bradburn (32), B.W Sinclair (52)	Dunedin	1963-64
3rd	94	M.B.Poore (44), B.Sutcliffe (66)	Cape Town	1953-54
4th	171	B.W.Sinclair (138), S.N.McGregor (62)	Auckland	1963-64
5th	174	J.R.Reid (135), J.E.F.Beck (99)	Cape Town	1953-54
6th	100	H.G.Vivian (100), F.T Badcock (53)	Wellington	1931-32
7th	84	J.R.Reid (142), G.A.Bartlett (33)	Johannesburg[3]	1961-62
8th	73	P.G.Z.Harris (74), G.A.Bartlett (40)	Durban[2]	1961-62
9th	69	C.F.W.Allcott (26), I.B.Cromb (51*)	Wellington	1931-32
10th	49*	A.E.Dick (50*), F.J.Cameron (10*)	Cape Town	1961-62

BEST INNINGS BOWLING ANALYSIS

South Africa in South Africa	8-53	G.B.Lawrence	Johannesburg[3]	1961-62
South Africa in New Zealand	6-47	P.M.Pollock	Wellington	1963-64
New Zealand in South Africa	6-68	G.O.Rabone	Cape Town	1953-54
New Zealand in New Zealand	6-60	J.R.Reid	Dunedin	1963-64

BEST MATCH BOWLING ANALYSIS

South Africa in South Africa	11-196	S.F.Burke	Cape Town	1961-62
South Africa in New Zealand	9-127	Q.McMillan	Christchurch	1931-32
New Zealand in South Africa	8-180	J.C.Alabaster	Cape Town	1961-62
New Zealand in New Zealand	7-142	R.W.Blair	Auckland	1963-64

HIGHEST AGGREGATE OF WICKETS IN A SERIES

South Africa in South Africa	28 (av 18.28)	G.B.Lawrence	1961-62
South Africa in New Zealand	16 (av 20.18)	Q.McMillan	1931-32
New Zealand in South Africa	22 (av 20.63)	A.R.MacGibbon	1953-54
	22 (av 28.04)	J.C.Alabaster	1961-62
New Zealand in New Zealand	12 (av 23.16)	J.R.Reid	1963-64
	12 (av 27.16)	R.W.Blair	1963-64

SOUTH AFRICA v WEST INDIES

Venue and Result	South Africa 1st	South Africa 2nd	West Indies 1st	West Indies 2nd	Captains South Africa	Captains West Indies
1991-92 In WEST INDIES						
Bridgetown-West Indies 52 runs	345	148	*262	283	K.C.Wessels	R.B.Richardson

Test Match Results Summary

SOUTH AFRICA v WEST INDIES—IN WEST INDIES

	Tests	Result SA	Result W	Result D	Bridgetown SA	Bridgetown W	Bridgetown D
1991-92	1	-	1	-	-	1	-

HIGHEST INNINGS TOTALS

South Africa in West Indies	345	Bridgetown	1991-92
West Indies in West Indies	283	Bridgetown	1991-92

LOWEST INNINGS TOTALS

South Africa in West Indies	148	Bridgetown	1991-92
West Indies in West Indies	262	Bridgetown	1991-92

HIGHEST MATCH AGGREGATE 1038 for 40 wickets Bridgetown 1991-92

HIGHEST INDIVIDUAL INNINGS

South Africa in West Indies	163	A.C.Hudson	Bridgetown	1991-92
West Indies in West Indies	79*	J.C.Adams	Bridgetown	1991-92

HIGHEST AGGREGATE OF RUNS IN A SERIES

South Africa in West Indies	163 (av 81.50)	A.C.Hudson	1991-92
West Indies in West Indies	90 (av 90.00)	J.C.Adams	1991-92

HIGHEST WICKET PARTNERSHIP—SOUTH AFRICA

2nd	125	A.C.Hudson (163), K.C.Wessels (59)	Bridgetown	1991-92

HIGHEST WICKET PARTNERSHIP—WEST INDIES

1st	99	D.L.Haynes (58), P.V.Simmons (35)	Bridgetown	1991-92

BEST INNINGS BOWLING ANALYSIS

South Africa in West Indies	4-74	R.P.Snell	Bridgetown	1991-92
West Indies in West Indies	6-34	C.E.L.Ambrose	Bridgetown	1991-92

BEST MATCH BOWLING ANALYSIS

South Africa in West Indies	8-157	R.P.Snell	Bridgetown	1991-92
West Indies in West Indies	8-81	C.E.L.Ambrose	Bridgetown	1991-92

HIGHEST AGGREGATE OF WICKETS IN A SERIES

South Africa in West Indies	8 (av 19.62)	R.P.Snell	1991-92
West Indies in West Indies	8 (av 10.12)	C.E.L.Ambrose	1991-92

WEST INDIES v NEW ZEALAND

Venue and Result	West Indies 1st	West Indies 2nd	New Zealand 1st	New Zealand 2nd	Captains West Indies	Captains New Zealand
1951-52 in NEW ZEALAND						
Christchurch-West Indies 5 wkts	287	5-142	*236	189	J.D.C.Goddard	B.Sutcliffe
Auckland-Drawn	*6d-546	-	160	1-17		
1955-56 In NEW ZEALAND						
Dunedin-West Indies inns & 71 runs	353	-	*74	208	D.S.Atkinson	H.B.Cave
Christchurch-West Indies inns & 64 runs	*386	-	158	164		J.R.Reid
Wellington-West Indies 9 wkts	*404	1-13	208	208		J.R.Reid
Auckland-New Zealand 190 runs	145	77	*255	9d-157		J.R.Reid
1968-69 in NEW ZEALAND						
Auckland-West Indies 5 wkts	276	5-348	*323	8d-297	G.S.Sobers	G.T.Dowling
Wellington-New Zealand 6 wkts	*297	148	282	4-166		
Christchurch-Drawn	*417	-	217	6-367		
1971-72 in WEST INDIES						
Kingston-Drawn	*4d-508	3d-218	386	6-236	G.S.Sobers	G.T.Dowling
Port-of-Spain-Drawn	341	5-121	*348	3d-288		G.T.Dowling
Bridgetown-Drawn	*133	8-564	422	-		B.E.Congdon
Georgetown-Drawn	*7d-365	0-86	3d-543	-		B.E.Congdon
Port-of-Spain-Drawn	*368	194	162	7-253		B.E.Congdon
1979-80 in NEW ZEALAND						
Dunedin-New Zealand 1 wkt	*140	212	249	9-104	C.H.Lloyd	G.P.Howarth
Christchurch-Drawn	*228	5d-447	460	-		
Auckland-Drawn	*220	9d-264	305	4-73		
1984-85 in WEST INDIES						
Port-of-Spain-Drawn	*307	8d-261	262	6-187	I.V.A.Richards	G.P.Howarth
Georgetown-Drawn	*6d-511	6d-268	440	-		
Bridgetown-West Indies 10 wkts	336	0-10	*94	248		
Kingston-West Indies 10 wkts	*363	0-59	138	283		
1986-87 in NEW ZEALAND						
Wellington-Drawn	345	2-50	*228	5d-386	I.V.A.Richards	J.V.Coney
Auckland-West Indies 10 wkts	*9d-419	0-16	157	273		
Christchurch-New Zealand 5 wkts	*100	264	9d-332	5-33		

Test Match Results Summary

WEST INDIES v NEW ZEALAND—IN WEST INDIES

	Tests	Result			Kingston			Port-of-Spain			Bridgetown			Georgetown		
		WI	NZ	D	WI	NZ	D	WI	NZ	D	WI	NZ	D	WI	NZ	D
1971-72	5	-	-	5	-	-	1	-	-	2	-	-	1	-	-	1
1984-85	4	2	-	2	1	-	-	-	-	1	1	-	-	-	-	1
	9	2	-	7	1	-	1	-	-	3	1	-	1	-	-	2

WEST INDIES v NEW ZEALAND—IN NEW ZEALAND

		Result			Christchurch			Auckland			Dunedin			Wellington		
	Tests	WI	NZ	D	WI	NZ	D	WI	NZ	D	WI	NZ	D	WI	NZ	D
1951-52	2	1	-	1	1	-	-	-	-	1	-	-	-	-	-	-
1955-56	4	3	1	-	1	-	-	-	1	-	1	-	-	1	-	-
1968-69	3	1	1	1	-	-	1	1	-	-	-	-	-	-	1	-
1979-80	3	-	1	2	-	-	1	-	-	1	-	1	-	-	-	-
1986-87	3	1	1	1	-	1	-	1	-	-	-	-	-	-	-	1
	15	6	4	5	2	1	2	2	1	2	1	1	-	1	1	1
Totals	24	8	4	12												

HIGHEST INNINGS TOTALS

West Indies in West Indies	8-564	Bridgetown	1971-72
West Indies in New Zealand	6d-546	Auckland	1951-52
New Zealand in West Indies	3d-543	Georgetown	1971-72
New Zealand in New Zealand	460	Christchurch	1979-80

LOWEST INNINGS TOTALS

West Indies in West Indies	133	Bridgetown	1971-72
West Indies in New Zealand	77	Auckland	1955-56
New Zealand in West Indies	94	Bridgetown	1984-85
New Zealand in New Zealand	74	Dunedin	1955-56

HIGHEST MATCH AGGREGATE	1348 for 23 wickets	Kingston	1971-72
LOWEST MATCH AGGREGATE	634 for 39 wickets	Auckland	1955-56

HIGHEST INDIVIDUAL INNINGS

West Indies in West Indies	214	L.G.Rowe	Kingston	1971-72
West Indies in New Zealand	258	S.M.Nurse	Christchurch	1968-69
New Zealand in West Indies	259	G.M.Turner	Georgetown	1971-72
New Zealand in New Zealand	147	G.P.Howarth	Christchurch	1979-80

HIGHEST AGGREGATE OF RUNS IN A SERIES

West Indies in West Indies	487 (av 54.11)	R.C.Fredericks	1971-72
New Zealand in New Zealand	558 (av 111.60)	S.M.Nurse	1968-69
New Zealand in West Indies	672 (av 98.00)	G.M.Turner	1971-72
New Zealand in New Zealand	328 (av 65.60)	M.D.Crowe	1986-87

RECORD WICKET PARTNERSHIPS—WEST INDIES

1st	225	C.G.Greenidge (97), D.L.Haynes (122)	Christchurch	1979-80
2nd	269	R.C.Fredericks (163), L.G.Rowe (214)	Kingston	1971-72
3rd	185	C.G.Greenidge (100), R.B.Richardson (78)	Port-of-Spain	1984-85
4th	162	E.D.Weekes (123), O.G.Smith (64)	Dunedin	1955-56
	162	C.G.Greenidge (91), A.I.Kallicharran (75)	Christchurch	1979-80
5th	189	F.M.M.Worrell (100), C.L.Walcott (115)	Auckland	1951-52
6th	254	C.A.Davis (183), G.S.Sobers (142)	Bridgetown	1971-72
7th	143	D.S Atkinson (85), J.D.C.Goddard (83*)	Christchurch	1955-56
8th	83	I.V.A.Richards (105), M.D.Marshall (63)	Bridgetown	1984-85
9th	70	M.D.Marshall (63), J.Garner (37*)	Bridgetown	1984-85
10th	31	T.M.Findlay (44*), G.C.Shillingford (15)	Bridgetown	1971-72

RECORD WICKET PARTNERSHIPS — NEW ZEALAND

1st	387	G.M.Turner (259), T.W.Jarvis (182)	Georgetown	1971-72
2nd	210	G.P.Howarth (84), J.J.Crowe (112)	Kingston	1984-85
3rd	241	J.G.Wright (138), M.D.Crowe (119)	Wellington	1986-87
4th	175	B.E.Congdon (126), B.F.Hastings (105)	Bridgetown	1971-72
5th	142	M.D.Crowe (188), J.V.Coney (73)	Georgetown	1984-85
6th	220	G.M.Turner (223*), K.J.Wadsworth (78)	Kingston	1971-72
7th	143	M.D.Crowe (188), I.D.S.Smith (53)	Georgetown	1984-85
8th	136	B.E.Congdon (166*), R.S.Cunis (51)	Port-of-Spain	1971-72
9th	62*	V.Pollard (51*), R.S.Cunis (20*)	Auckland	1968-69
10th	41	B.E.Congdon (166*), J.C.Alabaster (18)	Port-of-Spain	1971-72

BEST INNINGS BOWLING ANALYSIS

West Indies in West Indies	7-80	M.D.Marshall	Bridgetown	1984-85
West Indies in New Zealand	7-53	D.S.Atkinson	Auckland	1955-56
New Zealand in West Indies	7 74	B.R.Taylor	Bridgetown	1971-72
New Zealand in New Zealand	6-50	R.J.Hadlee	Christchurch	1986-87

BEST MATCH BOWLING ANALYSIS

West Indies in West Indies	11-120	M.D.Marshall	Bridgetown	1984-85
West Indies in New Zealand	9-81	S.Ramadhin	Dunedin	1955-56
New Zealand in West Indies	10-124	E.J.Chatfield	Port-of-Spain	1984-85
New Zealand in New Zealand	11-102	R.J Hadlee	Dunedin	1979-80

HIGHEST AGGREGATE OF WICKETS IN A SERIES

West Indies in West Indies	27 (av 18.00)	M.D.Marshall	1984-85
West Indies In New Zealand	20 (av 15.80)	S.Ramadhin	1955-56
New Zealand in West Indies	27 (av 17.70)	B.R.Taylor	1971-72
New Zealand In New Zealand	19 (av 19.00)	R.J Hadlee	1979-80

WEST INDIES v INDIA

Venue and Result	West Indies 1st	West Indies 2nd	India 1st	India 2nd	Captains West Indies	Captains India
1948-49 in INDIA						
Delhi-Drawn	*631	-	454	6-220	J.D.C.Goddard	N.B.Amarnath
Bombay²-Drawn	*6d-629	-	273	3-333		
Calcutta-Drawn	*366	9d-336	272	3-325		
Madras¹-West Indies inns & 193 runs	*582	-	245	144		
Bombay²-Drawn	*286	267	193	8-355		
1952-53 in WEST INDIES						
Port-of-Spain-Drawn	438	0-142	*417	294	J.B.Stollmeyer	V.S.Hazare
Bridgetown-West Indies 142 runs	*296	228	253	129		
Port-of-Spain-Drawn	315	2-192	*279	7d-362		
Georgetown-Drawn	364	-	*262	5-190		
Kingston-Drawn	576	4-92	*312	444		
1958-59 in INDIA						
Bombay²-Drawn	*227	4d-323	152	5-289	F.C.M.Alexander	P.R.Umrigar
Kanpur-West Indies 203 runs	*222	7d-443	222	240		Ghulam Ahmed
Calcutta-West Indies inns & 336 runs	*5d-614	-	124	154		Ghulam Ahmed
Madras²-West Indies 295 runs	*500	5d-168	222	151		M.H.Mankad
Delhi-Drawn	8d-644	-	*415	275		H.R.Adhikari

WEST INDIES v INDIA (cont.) Venue and Result	West Indies 1st	West Indies 2nd	India 1st	India 2nd	Captains West Indies	Captains India
1961-62 in WEST INDIES						
Port-of-Spain-West Indies 10 wkts	289	0-15	*203	98	F.M.M.Worrell	N.J.Contractor
Kingston-West Indies inns & 18 runs	8d-631	-	*395	218		N.J.Contractor
Bridgetown-West Indies inns & 30 runs	475	-	*258	187	-	Nawab of Pataudi, jr
Port-of-Spain-West Indies 7 wkts	*9d-444	3-176	197	422		Nawab of Pataudi, jr
Kingston-West Indies 123 runs	*253	283	178	235		Nawab of Pataudi, jr
1966-67 in INDIA						
Bombay[2]-West Indies 6 wkts	421	4-192	*296	316	G.S.Sobers	Nawab of Pataudi, jr
Calcutta-West Indies inns & 45 runs	*390	-	167	178		
Madras[1]-Drawn	406	7-270	*404	323		
1970-71 in WEST INDIES						
Kingston-Drawn	217	5-385	*387	-	G.S.Sobers	A.L.Wadekar
Port-of-Spain-India 7 wkts	*214	261	352	3-125		
Georgetown-Drawn	*363	3d-307	376	0-123		
Bridgetown-Drawn	*5d-501	6d-180	347	5-221		
Port-of-Spain-Drawn	526	8-165	*360	427		
1974-75 in INDIA						
Bangalore-West Indies 267 runs	*289	6d-356	260	118	C.H.Lloyd	Nawab of Pataudi, jr
Delhi-West Indies inns & 17 runs	493	-	*220	256		S.Venkataraghavan
Calcutta-India 85 runs	240	224	*233	316		Nawab of Pataudi, jr
Madras[1]-India 100 runs	192	154	*190	256		Nawab of Pataudi, jr
Bombay[3]-West Indies 201 runs	*6d-604	3d-205	406	202		Nawab of Pataudi, jr
1975-76 in WEST INDIES						
Bridgetown-West Indies inns & 97 runs	9d-488	-	*177	214	C.H.Lloyd	B.S.Bedi
Port-of-Spain-Drawn	*241	8-215	5d-402	-		
Port-of-Spain-India 6 wkts	*359	6d-271	228	4-406		
Kingston-West Indies 10 wkts	391	0-13	*6d-306	97		
1978-79 in INDIA						
Bombay[3]-Drawn	493	-	*424	2-224	A.I.Kallicharran	S.M.Gavaskar
Bangalore-Drawn	*437	8-200	371	-		
Calcutta-Drawn	327	9-197	*300	1d-361		
Madras[1]-India 3 wkts	*228	151	255	7-125		
Delhi-Drawn	172	3-179	*8d-566	-		
Kanpur-Drawn	8-452	-	*7d-644	-		
1982-83 in WEST INDIES						
Kingston-West Indies 4 wkts	254	6-173	*251	174	C.H.Lloyd	Kapil Dev
Port-of-Spain-Drawn	394	-	*175	7-469		
Georgetown-Drawn	*470	-	3-284	-		
Bridgetown-West Indies 10 wkts	486	0-1	*209	277		
St John's-Drawn	550	-	*457	5d-247		
1983-84 in INDIA						
Kanpur-West Indies inns & 83 runs	*454	-	207	164	C.H.Lloyd	Kapil Dev
Delhi-Drawn	384	2-120	*464	233		
Ahmedabad-West Indies 138 runs	*281	201	241	103		
Bombay[3]-Drawn	393	4-104	*463	5d-173		
Calcutta-West Indies inns & 46 runs	377	-	*241	90		
Madras[1]-Drawn	*313	1-64	8d-451	-		

WEST INDIES v INDIA (cont.)	West Indies		India		Captains	
Venue and Result	1st	2nd	1st	2nd	West Indies	India
1987-88 in INDIA						
Delhi-West Indies 5 wkts	127	5-276	*75	327	I.V.A.Richards	D.B.Vengsarkar
Bombay[3]-Drawn	337	1-4	*281	173		D.B.Vengsarkar
Calcutta-Drawn	*5d-530	2-157	565	-		D.B.Vengsarkar
Madras[1]-India 255 runs	184	160	*382	8d-217		R.J.Shastri
1988-89 in WEST INDIES						
Georgetown-Drawn	*437	-	1-86	-	I.V.A.Richards	D.B.Vengsarkar
Bridgetown-West Indies 8 wkts	377	2-196	*321	251		
Port-of-Spain-West Indies 217 runs	*314	266	150	213		
Kingston-West Indies 7 wkts	384	3-60	*289	152		

Test Match Results Summary

WEST INDIES v INDIA — IN WEST INDIES

		Result			Port-of-Spain			Bridgetown			Georgetown			Kingston			St John's		
	Tests	WI	I	D	WI	I	D	WI	I	D	WI	I	D	WI	I	D	WI	I	D
1952-53	5	1	-	4	-	-	2	1	-	-	-	-	1	-	-	1	-	-	-
1961-62	5	5	-	-	2	-	-	1	-	-	-	-	-	2	-	-	-	-	-
1970-71	5	-	1	4	-	1	1	-	-	1	-	-	1	-	-	1	-	-	-
1975-76	4	2	1	1	-	1	1	1	-	-	-	-	-	1	-	-	-	-	-
1982-83	5	2	-	3	-	-	1	1	-	-	-	-	1	1	-	-	-	-	1
1988-89	4	3	-	1	1	-	-	1	-	-	-	-	1	1	-	-	-	-	-
	28	13	2	13	3	2	5	5	-	1	-	-	4	5	-	2	-	-	1

WEST INDIES v INDIA — IN INDIA

		Result			Delhi			Bombay			Calcutta			Madras			Kanpur			Bangalore			Ahmedabad		
	Tests	WI	I	D	WI	I	D	WI	I	D	WI	I	D	WI	I	D	WI	I	D	WI	I	D	WI	I	D
1948-49	5	1	-	4	-	-	1	-	-	2	-	-	1	1	-	-	-	-	-	-	-	-	-	-	-
1958-59	5	3	-	2	-	-	1	-	-	1	1	-	-	1	-	-	1	-	-	-	-	-	-	-	-
1966-67	3	2	-	1	-	-	-	1	-	-	1	-	-	-	-	1	-	-	-	-	-	-	-	-	-
1974-75	5	3	2	-	1	-	-	1	-	-	-	1	-	-	1	-	-	-	-	1	-	-	-	-	-
1978-79	6	-	1	5	-	-	1	-	-	1	-	-	1	-	1	-	-	-	1	-	-	1	-	-	-
1983-84	6	3	-	3	-	-	1	-	-	1	1	-	-	-	-	1	1	-	-	-	-	-	1	-	-
1987-88	4	1	1	2	1	-	-	-	-	1	-	-	1	-	1	-	-	-	-	-	-	-	-	-	-
	34	13	4	17	2	-	4	2	-	6	3	1	3	2	3	2	2	-	1	1	-	1	1	-	
Totals	62	26	6	30																					

HIGHEST INNINGS TOTALS

West Indies in West Indies	8d-631	Kingston	1961-62
West Indies in India	8d-644	Delhi	1958-59
India in West Indies	7-469	Port-of-Spain	1982-83
India in India	7d-644	Kanpur	1978-79

LOWEST INNINGS TOTALS

West Indies in West Indies	214	Port-of-Spain	1970-71
West Indies in India	127	Delhi	1987-88
India in West Indies	97	Kingston	1975-76
India in India	75	Delhi	1987-88

HIGHEST MATCH AGGREGATE	1478 for 38 wickets	Port-of-Spain	1970-71
LOWEST MATCH AGGREGATE	605 for 30 wickets	Port-of-Spain	1961-62

HIGHEST INDIVIDUAL INNINGS

West Indies in West Indies	237	F.M.M.Worrell	Kingston	1952-53
West Indies in India	256	R.B.Kanhai	Calcutta	1958-59
India in West Indies	220	S.M.Gavaskar	Port-of-Spain	1970-71
India in India	236*	S.M.Gavaskar	Madras[1]	1983-84

HIGHEST AGGREGATE OF RUNS IN A SERIES

West Indies in West Indies	716 (av 102.28)	E.D.Weekes	1952-53
West Indies in India	779 (av 111.28)	E.D.Weekes	1948-49
India in West Indies	774 (av 154.80)	S.M.Gavaskar	1970-71
India in India	732 (av 91.50)	S.M.Gavaskar	1978-79

RECORD WICKET PARTNERSHIPS — WEST INDIES

1st	296	C.G.Greenidge (154*), D.L.Haynes (136)	St John's	1982-83
2nd	255	E.D A.S.McMorris (125), R.B.Kanhai (158)	Kingston	1961-62
3rd	220	I V.A Richards (142), A.I.Kallicharran (93)	Bridgetown	1975-76
4th	267	C.L.Walcott (152) ,G.E.Gomez (101)	Delhi	1948-49
5th	219	E.D.Weekes (207) ,B.H.Pairaudeau (115)	Port-of-Spain	1952-53
6th	250	C.H.Lloyd (242), D.L.Murray (91)	Bombay[3]	1974-75
7th	130	C.G.Greenidge (194), M.D.Marshall (92)	Kanpur	1983-84
8th	124	I.V.A Richards (192), K.D.Boyce (68)	Delhi	1974-75
9th	161	C.H.Lloyd (161*), A.M.E.Roberts (68)	Calcutta	1983-84
10th	98*	F.M.M.Worrell (73*), W.W.Hall (50*)	Port-of-Spain	1961-62

RECORD WICKET PARTNERSHIPS — INDIA

1st	153	S.M.Gavaskar (73), C.P.S.Chauhan (84)	Bombay[3]	1978-79
2nd	344*	S.M.Gavaskar (182), D.B.Vengsarkar (157)	Calcutta	1978-79
3rd	159	M.Amarnath (85), G.R.Viswanath (112)	Port-of-Spain	1975-76
4th	172	G.R.Viswanath (179), A.D.Gaekwad (102)	Kanpur	1978-79
5th	204	S.M.Gavaskar (156), B.P.Patel (115)	Port-of-Spain	1975-76
6th	170	S.M.Gavaskar (236*), R.J.Shastri (72)	Madras[1]	1983-84
7th	186	D.N.Sardesai (150), E.D.Solkar (65)	Bridgetown	1970-71
8th	107	Yashpal Sharma (63), B.S.Sandhu (68)	Kingston	1982-83
9th	143*	S.M.Gavaskar (236*), S.M.H.Kirmani (63*)	Madras[1]	1983-84
10th	62	D.N.Sardesai (150), B.S.Bedi (20*)	Bridgetown	1970-71

BEST INNINGS BOWLING ANALYSIS

West Indies in West Indies	9-95	J.M.Noreiga	Port-of-Spain	1970-71
West Indies in India	7-64	A.M.E.Roberts	Madras[1]	1974-75
India in West Indies	7-162	S.P.Gupte	Port-of-Spain	1952-53
India in India	9-83	Kapil Dev	Ahmedabad	1983-84

BEST MATCH BOWLING ANALYSIS

West Indies in West Indies	11-89	M.D.Marshall	Port-of-Spain	1988-89
West Indies in India	12-121	A.M.E.Roberts	Madras[1]	1974-75
India in West Indies	8-118	Kapil Dev	Kingston	1982-83
India in India	16-136	N.D.Hirwani	Madras[1]	1987-88

HIGHEST AGGREGATE OF WICKETS IN A SERIES

West Indies in West Indies	28 (av 29.57)	A.L.Valentine	1952-53
West Indies in India	33 (av 18.81)	M.D.Marshall	1983-84
India in West Indies	27 (av 29.22)	S.P.Gupte	1952-53
India in India	29 (av 18.51)	Kapil Dev	1983-84

WEST INDIES v PAKISTAN

Venue and Result	West Indies 1st	West Indies 2nd	Pakistan 1st	Pakistan 2nd	Captains West Indies	Captains Pakistan
1957-58 In WEST INDIES						
Bridgetown-Drawn	*9d-579	0-28	106	8d-657	F.C.M.Alexander	A.H.Kardar
Port-of-Spain-West Indies 120 runs	*325	312	282	235		
Kingston-West Indies inns & 174 runs	3d-790	-	*328	288		
Georgetown-West Indies 8 wkts	410	2-317	*408	318		
Port-of-Spain-Pakistan inns & 1 run	*268	227	496	-		
1958-59 In PAKISTAN						
Karachi-Pakistan 10 wkts	*146	245	304	0-88	F.C.M.Alexander	Fazal Mahmood
Dacca-Pakistan 41 runs	76	172	*145	144		
Lahore[1]-West Indies & 156 runs	*469	-	209	104		
1974-75 in PAKISTAN						
Lahore[2]-Drawn	214	4-258	*199	7d-373	C.H.Lloyd	Intikhab Alam
Karachi-Drawn	493	0-1	*8d-406	256		
1976-77 in WEST INDIES						
Bridgetown-Drawn	421	9-251	*435	291	C.H.Lloyd	Mushtaq Mohammad
Port-of-Spain-West Indies 6 wkts	316	4-206	*180	340		
Georgetown-Drawn	448	1-154	*194	540		
Port-of-Spain-Pakistan 266 runs	154	222	*341	9d-301		
Kingston-West Indies 140 runs	*280	359	198	301		
1980-81 in PAKISTAN						
Lahore[2]-Drawn	297	-	*369	7-156	C.H.Lloyd	Javed Miandad
Faisalabad-West Indies 156 runs	*235	242	176	145		
Karachi-Drawn	169	-	*128	9-204		
Multan-Drawn	*249	5-116	166	-		
1986-87 in PAKISTAN						
Faisalabad-Pakistan 186 runs	248	53	*159	328	I.V.A.Richards	Imran Khan
Lahore[2]-West Indies inns & 10 runs	218	-	*131	77		
Karachi-Drawn	*240	211	239	7-125		
1987-88 in WEST INDIES						
Georgetown-Pakistan 9 wkts	*292	172	435	1-32	C.G.Greenidge	Imran Khan
Port-of-Spain-Drawn	*174	391	194	341	I.V.A.Richards	
Bridgetown-West Indies 2 wkts	306	8-268	*309	262	I.V.A.Richards	
1990-91 in PAKISTAN						
Karachi-Pakistan 8 wkts	*216	181	345	2-98	D.L.Haynes	Imran Khan
Faisalabad-West Indies 7 wkts	195	3-130	*170	154		
Lahore[2]-Drawn	*294	173	122	6-242		

Test Match Results Summary

WEST INDIES v PAKISTAN — IN WEST INDIES

		Result			Bridgetown			Port-of-Spain			Kingston			Georgetown		
	Tests	WI	P	D	WI	P	D	WI	P	D	WI	P	D	WI	P	D
1957-58	5	3	1	1	-	-	1	1	1	-	1	-	-	1	-	-
1976-77	5	2	1	2	-	-	1	1	1	-	1	-	-	-	-	1
1987-88	3	1	1	1	1	-	-	-	-	1	-	-	-	-	1	-
	13	6	3	4	1	-	2	2	2	1	2	-	-	1	1	1

WEST INDIES v PAKISTAN — IN PAKISTAN

		Result			Karachi			Dacca			Lahore			Faisalabad			Multan		
	Tests	WI	P	D	WI	P	D	WI	P	D	WI	P	D	WI	P	D	WI	P	D
1958-59	3	1	2	-	-	1	-	-	1	-	1	-	-	-	-	-	-	-	-
1974-75	2	-	-	2	-	-	1	-	-	-	-	-	1	-	-	-	-	-	-
1980-81	4	1	-	3	-	-	1	-	-	-	-	-	1	1	-	-	-	-	1
1986-87	3	1	1	1	-	-	1	-	-	-	1	-	-	-	1	-	-	-	-
1990-91	3	1	1	1	-	1	-	-	-	-	-	-	1	1	-	-	-	-	-
	15	4	4	7	-	2	3	-	1	-	2	-	3	2	1	-	-	-	1
Totals	28	10	7	11															

HIGHEST INNINGS TOTALS

West Indies in West Indies	3d-790	Kingston	1957-58
West Indies in Pakistan	493	Karachi	1974-75
Pakistan in West Indies	8d-657	Bridgetown	1957-58
Pakistan in Pakistan	8d-406	Karachi	1974-75

LOWEST INNINGS TOTALS

West Indies in West Indies	154	Port-of-Spain	1976-77
West Indies in Pakistan	53	Faisalabad	1986-84
Pakistan in West Indies	106	Bridgetown	1957-58
Pakistan in Pakistan	77	Lahore[2]	1986-84

HIGHEST MATCH AGGREGATE	1453 for 32 wickets	Georgetown	1957-58
LOWEST MATCH AGGREGATE	426 for 30 wickets	Lahore[2]	1986-84

HIGHEST INDIVIDUAL INNINGS

West Indies in West Indies	365	G.S.Sobers	Kingston	1957-58
West Indies in Pakistan	217	R.B.Kanhai	Lahore[1]	1958-59
Pakistan in West Indies	337	Hanif Mohammad	Bridgetown	1957-58
Pakistan in Pakistan	123	Mushtaq Mohammad	Lahore[2]	1974-75
	123	Imran Khan	Lahore[2]	1980-81

HIGHEST AGGREGATE OF RUNS IN A SERIES

West Indies in West Indies	824 (av 137.33)	G.S.Sobers	1957-58
West Indies in Pakistan	364 (av 72.80)	I.V.A.Richards	1980-81
Pakistan in West Indies	628 (av 69.77)	Hanif Mohammad	1957-58
Pakistan in Pakistan	285 (av 57.00)	Saleem Malik	1990-91

RECORD WICKET PARTNERSHIPS — WEST INDIES

1st	182	R.C.Fredericks (83), C.G.Greenidge (82)	Kingston	1976-77
2nd	446	C.C.Hunte (260), G.S.Sobers (365*)	Kingston	1957-58
3rd	162	R.B Kanhai (217), G S.Sobers (72)	Lahore[1]	1958-59
4th	188*	G.S Sobers (365*), C.L.Walcott (88*)	Kingston	1957-58
5th	185	E.D.Weekes (197), O.G Smith (78)	Bridgetown	1957-58
6th	151	C.H.Lloyd (157), D.L.Murray (52)	Bridgetown	1976-77
7th	70	C.H.Lloyd (157), J.Garner (43)	Bridgetown	1976-77
8th	50	B.D.Julien (101) V.A.Holder (29)	Karachi	1974-75
9th	61*	P.J.L.Dujon (29*), W.K.M.Benjamin (40*)	Bridgetown	1987-88
10th	44	R.Nanan (8), S.T.Clarke (35)	Faisalabad	1980-81

RECORD WICKET PARTNERSHIPS — PAKISTAN

1st	159†	Majid Khan (167), Zaheer Abbas (80)	Georgetown	1976-77
2nd	178	Hanif Mohammad (103), Saeed Ahmed (78)	Karachi	1958-59
3rd	169	Saeed Ahmed (97), Wazir Mohammad (189)	Port-of-Spain	1957-58
4th	174	Shoaib Mohammad (86), Saleem Malik (102)	Karachi	1990-91
5th	87	Mushtaq Mohammad (17), Asif Iqbal (135)	Kingston	1976-77
6th	166	Wazir Mohammad (106), A.H.Kardar (57)	Kingston	1957-58
7th	128	Wasim Raja (107*), Wasim Bari (58)	Karachi	1974-75
8th	94	Saleem Malik (66), Saleem Yousuf (39)	Port-of-Spain	1987-88
9th	73	Wasim Raja (117*), Sarfraz Nawaz (38)	Bridgetown	1976-77
10th	133	Wasim Raja (71), Wasim Bari (60*)	Bridgetown	1976-77

† 219 runs were added for this wicket, Sadiq Mohammad retired hurt and was replaced by Zaheer Abbas after 60 had been scored.

BEST INNINGS BOWLING ANALYSIS

West Indies in West Indies	8-29	C.E.H.Croft	Port-of-Spain	1976-77
West Indies in Pakistan	5-33	M.D.Marshall	Lahore[2]	1986-87
Pakistan in West Indies	7-80	Imran Khan	Georgetown	1987-88
Pakistan in Pakistan	6-16	Abdul Qadir	Faisalabad	1986-87

BEST MATCH BOWLING ANALYSIS

West Indies in West Indies	9-95	C.E.H.Croft	Port-of-Spain	1976-77
West Indies in Pakistan	9-187	A.M.E.Roberts	Lahore[2]	1974-75
Pakistan in West Indies	11-121	Imran Khan	Georgetown	1987-88
Pakistan in Pakistan	12-100	Fazal Mahmood	Dacca	1959-60

HIGHEST AGGREGATE OF WICKETS IN A SERIES

West Indies in West Indies	33 (av 20.48)	C E.H.Croft	1976-77
West Indies in Pakistan	17 (av 17.76)	C.E.H.Croft	1980-81
Pakistan in West Indies	25 (av 31.60)	Imran Khan	1976-77
Pakistan in Pakistan	21 (av 15.85)	Fazal Mahmood	1958-59
	21 (av 14.19)	Wasim Akram	1990-91

NEW ZEALAND v INDIA

Venue and Result	New Zealand 1st	New Zealand 2nd	India 1st	India 2nd	Captains New Zealand	Captains India
1955-56 in INDIA						
Hyderabad-Drawn	326	2-212	*4d-498	-	H.B.Cave	Ghulam Ahmed
Bombay[2]-India inns & 27 runs	258	136	*8d-421	-		P.R.Umrigar
Delhi-Drawn	*2d-450	1-112	7d-531	-		P.R.Umrigar
Calcutta-Drawn	336	6-75	*132	7d-438		P.R.Umrigar
Madras[1]-India inns & 109 runs	209	219	*3d-537	-		P.R.Umrigar

NEW ZEALAND v INDIA (cont.) Venue and Result	New Zealand 1st	New Zealand 2nd	India 1st	India 2nd	Captains New Zealand	Captains India
1964-65 in INDIA						
Madras[2]-Drawn	315	0-62	*397	2d-199	J.R.Reid	Nawab of Pataudi, jr
Calcutta-Drawn	*9d-462	9d-191	380	3-92		
Bombay[2]-Drawn	*297	8-80	88	5d-463		
Delhi-India 7 wkts	*262	272	8d-465	3-73		
1967-68 in NEW ZEALAND						
Dunedin-India 5 wkts	*350	208	359	5-200	B.W.Sinclair	Nawab of Pataudi, jr
Christchurch-New Zealand 6 wkts	*502	4-88	288	301	G.T.Dowling	
Wellington-India 8 wkts	*186	199	327	2-59	G.T.Dowling	
Auckland-India 272 runs	140	101	*252	5d-261	G.T.Dowling	
1969-70 in INDIA						
Bombay[2]-India 60 runs	229	127	*156	260	G.T.Dowling	Nawab of Pataudi, jr
Nagpur-New Zealand 167 runs	*319	214	257	109		
Hyderabad-Drawn	*181	8d-175	89	7-67		
1975-76 in NEW ZEALAND						
Auckland-India 8 wkts	*266	215	414	2-71	G.M.Turner	S.M.Gavaskar
Christchurch-Drawn	403	-	*270	6-255		B.S.Bedi
Wellington-New Zealand inns & 33 runs	334	-	*220	81		B.S.Bedi
1976-77 in INDIA						
Bombay[3]-India 162 runs	298	141	*399	4d-202	G.M.Turner	B.S.Bedi
Kanpur-Drawn	350	7-193	*9d-524	2d-208		
Madras[1]-India 216 runs	140	143	*298	5d-201		
1980-81 in NEW ZEALAND						
Wellington-New Zealand 62 runs	*375	100	223	190	G.P.Howarth	S.M.Gavaskar
Christchurch-Drawn	5-286	-	*255	-		
Auckland-Drawn	366	5-95	*238	284		
1988-89 in INDIA						
Bangalore-India 172 runs	189	164	*9d-384	1d-141	J.G.Wright	D.B.Vengsarkar
Bombay[3]-New Zealand 136 runs	*236	279	234	145		
Hyderabad-India 10 wkts	*254	124	358	0-22		
1989-90 in NEW ZEALAND						
Christchurch-New Zealand 10 wkts	*459	0-2	164	296	J.G.Wright	M.Azharuddin
Napier-Drawn	1-178	-	*358	-		
Auckland-Drawn	*391	5d-483	482	0-149		

Test Match Results Summary

NEW ZEALAND v INDIA — IN NEW ZEALAND

		Result			Dunedin			Christchurch			Wellington			Auckland			Napier		
	Tests	NZ	I	D	NZ	I	D	NZ	I	D	NZ	I	D	NZ	I	D	NZ	I	D
1967-68	4	1	3	-	-	1	-	1	-	-	-	1	-	-	1	-	-	-	-
1975-76	3	1	1	1	-	-	-	-	-	1	1	-	-	-	1	-	-	-	-
1980-81	3	1	-	2	-	-	-	-	-	1	1	-	-	-	-	1	-	-	-
1989-90	3	1	-	2	-	-	-	1	-	-	-	-	-	-	-	1	-	-	1
	13	4	4	5	-	1	-	2	-	2	2	1	-	-	2	2	-	-	1

NEW ZEALAND v INDIA — IN INDIA

		Result			Hyder.			Bombay			Delhi			Calcutta			Madras			Nagpur			Kanpur			Bangalore		
	Tests	NZ	I	D	NZ	I	D	NZ	I	D	NZ	I	D	NZ	I	D	NZ	I	D	NZ	I	D	NZ	I	D	NZ	I	D
1955-56	5	-	2	3	-	-	1	-	1	-	-	-	1	-	-	1	-	1	-	-	-	-	-	-	-	-	-	-
1964-65	4	-	1	3	-	-	-	-	-	1	-	1	-	-	-	1	-	-	1	-	-	-	-	-	-	-	-	-
1969-70	3	1	1	1	-	-	1	-	1	-	-	-	-	-	-	-	-	-	-	1	-	-	-	-	-	-	-	-
1976-77	3	-	2	1	-	-	-	-	1	-	-	-	-	-	-	-	-	1	-	-	-	-	-	-	1	-	-	-
1988-89	3	1	2	-	-	1	-	1	-	-	-	-	-	-	-	-	-	-	-	-	-	-	-	-	-	-	1	-
	18	2	8	8	-	1	2	1	3	1	-	1	1	-	-	2	-	2	1	1	-	-	-	-	1	-	1	-
Totals	31	5	12	11																								

Key to ground abbreviation: Hyder. - Hyderabad.

HIGHEST INNINGS TOTALS

New Zealand in New Zealand	502	Christchurch	1967-68
New Zealand in India	9d-462	Calcutta	1964-65
India in New Zealand	482	Auckland	1989-90
India in India	3d-537	Madras[2]	1955-56

LOWEST INNINGS TOTALS

New Zealand in New Zealand	100	Wellington	1980-81
New Zealand in India	124	Hyderabad	1988-89
India in New Zealand	81	Wellington	1975-76
India in India	88	Bombay[2]	1964-65

HIGHEST MATCH AGGREGATE	1505 for 25 wickets	Auckland	1989-90
LOWEST MATCH AGGREGATE	635 for 29 wickets	Wellington	1975-76

HIGHEST INDIVIDUAL INNINGS

New Zealand in New Zealand	239	G.T.Dowling	Christchurch	1967-68
New Zealand in India	230*	B.Sutcliffe	Delhi	1955-56
India in New Zealand	192	M.Azharuddin	Auckland	1989-90
India in India	231	M.H.Mankad	Madras[2]	1955-56

HIGHEST AGGREGATE OF RUNS IN A SERIES

New Zealand in New Zealand	471 (av 58.87)	G.T.Dowling	1967-68
New Zealand in India	611 (av 87.28)	B.Sutcliffe	1955-56
India in New Zealand	330 (av 47.14)	A.L.Wadekar	1967-68
India in India	526 (av 105.20)	M.H.Mankad	1955-56

RECORD WICKET PARTNERSHIPS — NEW ZEALAND

1st	126	T.J.Franklin (50), J.G.Wright (113*)	Napier	1989-90
2nd	155	G.T.Dowling (143), B.E.Congdon (58)	Dunedin	1967-68
3rd	222*	B.Sutcliffe (230*), J.R Reid (119*)	Delhi	1955-56
4th	125	J.G.Wright (185), M.J.Greatbatch (46)	Christchurch	1989-90
5th	119	G.T.Dowling (239), K Thomson (69)	Christchurch	1967-68
6th	87	J.W.Guy (102), A.R MacGibbon (59)	Hyderabad	1955-56
7th	163	B.Sutcliffe (151*), B.R Taylor (105)	Calcutta	1964-65
8th	103	R.J.Hadlee (87), I.D.S.Smith (173)	Auckland	1989-90
9th	136	I.D.S.Smith (173), M.C.Snedden (22)	Auckland	1989-90
10th	61	J.T.Ward (35*), R.O.Collinge (34)	Madras[2]	1964-65

RECORD WICKET PARTNERSHIPS — INDIA

1st	413	M.H.Mankad (231), P.Roy (173)	Madras[2]	1955-56
2nd	204	S.M Gavaskar (116), S Amarnath (124)	Auckland	1975-76
3rd	238	P.R Umrigar (223), V.L.Manjrekar (118)	Hyderabad	1955-56
4th	171	P R Umrigar (223), A.G Kripal Singh (100*)	Hyderabad	1955-56
5th	127	V.L.Manjrekar (177), G.S Ramchand (72)	Delhi	1955-56
6th	193*	D.N Sardesai (200), Hanumant Singh (75*)	Bombay[3]	1964-65
7th	128	S.R.Tendulkar (88), K.S.More (73)	Napier	1989-90
8th	143	R.G.Nadkarni (75), F.M.Engineer (90)	Madras[2]	1964-65
9th	105	S.M.H.Kirmani (88), B.S.Bedi (36)	Bombay[3]	1976-77
	105	S.M.H.Kirmani (78), N.S.Yadav (43)	Auckland	1980-81
10th	57	R.B.Desai (32*), B.S.Bedi (22)	Dunedin	1967-68

BEST INNINGS BOWLING ANALYSIS

New Zealand in New Zealand	7-23	R.J.Hadlee	Wellington	1975-76
New Zealand in India	6-49	R.J.Hadlee	Bombay[3]	1964-65
India in New Zealand	8-76	E.A.S.Prasanna	Auckland	1975-76
India in India	8-72	S.Venkataraghavan	Delhi	1964-65

BEST MATCH BOWLING ANALYSIS

New Zealand in New Zealand	11-58	R.J.Hadlee	Wellington	1975-76
New Zealand in India	10-88	R.J.Hadlee	Bombay[3]	1969-70
India in New Zealand	11-140	E.A.S.Prasanna	Auckland	1975-76
India in India	12-152	S.Venkataraghavan	Delhi	1964-65

HIGHEST AGGREGATE OF WICKETS IN A SERIES

New Zealand in New Zealand	16 (av 27.87)	D.K.Morrison	1989-90
New Zealand in India	18 (av 14.00)	R.J.Hadlee	1988-89
India in New Zealand	24 (av 18.79)	E.A.S.Prasanna	1967-68
India in India	34 (av 19.17)	S.P.Gupte	1955-55

NEW ZEALAND v PAKISTAN

	New Zealand		Pakistan		Captains	
Venue and Result	1st	2nd	1st	2nd	New Zealand	Pakistan
1955-56 in PAKISTAN						
Karachi-Pakistan inns & 1 run	*164	124	289	-	H.B.Cave	A.H.Kardar
Lahore[1]-Pakistan 4 wkts	*348	328	561	6-117		
Dacca-Drawn	*70	6-69	6d-195	-		
1964-65 in NEW ZEALAND						
Wellington-Drawn	*266	7d-179	187	7-140	J.R.Reid	Hanif Mohammad
Auckland-Drawn	214	7-166	*226	207		
Christchurch-Drawn	202	5-223	*206	8d-309		
1964-65 in PAKISTAN						
Rawalpindi-Pakistan inns & 64 runs	*175	79	318	-	J.R.Reid	Hanif Mohammad
Lahore[2]-Drawn	6d-482	-	*7d-385	8d-194		
Karachi-Pakistan 8 wkts	*285	223	8d-307	2-202		
1969-70 in PAKISTAN						
Karachi-Drawn	274	5-112	*220	8d-283	G.T.Dowling	Intikhab Alam
Lahore[2]-New Zealand 5 wkts	241	5-82	*114	208		
Dacca-Drawn	*273	200	7d-290	4-51		

NEW ZEALAND v PAKISTAN Venue and Result	New Zealand 1st	New Zealand 2nd	Pakistan 1st	Pakistan 2nd	Captains New Zealand	Captains Pakistan
1972-73 in NEW ZEALAND						
Wellington-Drawn	325	3-78	*357	6d-290	B.E.Congdon	Intikhab Alam
Dunedin-Pakistan inns & 166 runs	156	185	*6d-507	-		
Auckland-Drawn	402	3-92	*402	271		
1976-77 in PAKISTAN						
Lahore²-Pakistan 6 wkts	157	360	*417	4-105	G.M.Turner	Mushtaq Mohammad
Hyderabad-Pakistan 10 wkts	219	254	*8d-473	0-4	G.M.Turner	
Karachi-Drawn	468	7-262	*9d-565	5d-290	J.M.Parker	
1978-79 in NEW ZEALAND						
Christchurch-Pakistan 128 runs	290	176	*271	6d-323	M.G.Burgess	Mushtaq Mohammad
Napier-Drawn	402	-	*360	3d-234		
Auckland-Drawn	*254	8d-281	359	0-8		
1984-85 in PAKISTAN						
Lahore²-Pakistan 6 wkts	*157	241	221	4-181	J.V.Coney	Zaheer Abbas
Hyderabad-Pakistan 7 wkts	*267	189	230	3-230		
Karachi-Drawn	426	-	328	5-308		
1984-85 in NEW ZEALAND						
Wellington-Drawn	*492	4-103	322	-	G.P.Howarth	Javed Miandad
Christchurch-New Zealand inns & 99 runs	9d-451	-	169	183		
Dunedin-New Zealand 2 wkts	220	8-278	*274	223		
1988-89 in NEW ZEALAND						
Dunedin-Abandoned	-	-	-	-	J.G.Wright	Imran Khan
Wellington-Drawn	*447	8-186	7d-438	-		
Auckland-Drawn	403	3-99	5d-616	-		
1990-91 in PAKISTAN						
Karachi-Pakistan inns & 43 runs	*196	194	6d-433	-	M.D.Crowe	Javed Miandad
Lahore²-Pakistan 9 wkts	*160	287	9d-373	1-77		
Faisalabad-Pakistan 65 runs	217	177	*102	357		

Test Match Results Summary

NEW ZEALAND v PAKISTAN — IN NEW ZEALAND

	Tests	Result			Wellington			Auckland			Christchurch			Dunedin			Napier		
		NZ	P	D	NZ	P	D	NZ	P	D	NZ	P	D	NZ	P	D	NZ	P	D
1964-65	3	-	-	3	-	-	1	-	-	1	-	-	1	-	-	-	-	-	-
1972-73	3	-	1	2	-	-	1	-	-	1	-	-	-	-	1	-	-	-	-
1978-79	3	-	1	2	-	-	-	-	-	1	-	1	-	-	-	-	-	-	1
1984-85	3	2	-	1	-	-	1	1	-	-	-	-	-	1	-	-	-	-	-
1988-89	2	-	-	2	-	-	1	-	-	1	-	-	-	-	-	-	-	-	-
	14	2	2	10	-	-	4	1	-	4	-	1	1	1	1	-	-	-	1

NEW ZEALAND v PAKISTAN — IN PAKISTAN

		Result			Karachi			Lahore			Dacca			Rawalpindi			Hyderabad			Faisalabad		
	Tests	NZ	P	D	NZ	P	D	NZ	P	D	NZ	P	D	NZ	P	D	NZ	P	D	NZ	P	D
1955-56	3	-	2	1	-	1	-	-	1	-	-	-	1	-	-	-	-	-	-	-	-	-
1964-65	3	-	2	1	-	1	-	-	-	1	-	-	-	-	1	-	-	-	-	-	-	-
1969-70	3	1	-	2	-	-	1	1	-	-	-	-	1	-	-	-	-	-	-	-	-	-
1976-77	3	-	2	1	-	-	1	-	1	-	-	-	-	-	-	-	-	1	-	-	-	-
1984-85	3	-	2	1	-	-	1	-	1	-	-	-	-	-	-	-	-	1	-	-	-	-
1990-91	3	-	3	-	-	1	-	-	1	-	-	-	-	-	-	-	-	-	-	-	1	-
	18	1	11	6	-	3	3	1	4	1	-	-	2	-	1	-	-	2	-	-	1	-
Totals	32	3	13	16																		

HIGHEST INNINGS TOTALS

New Zealand in New Zealand	492	Wellington	1984-85
New Zealand in Pakistan	6d-482	Lahore²	1964-65
Pakistan in New Zealand	5d-616	Auckland	1988-89
Pakistan in Pakistan	9d-565	Karachi	1976-77

LOWEST INNINGS TOTALS

New Zealand in New Zealand	156	Dunedin	1972-73
New Zealand in Pakistan	70	Dacca	1955-56
Pakistan in New Zealand	169	Auckland	1984-85
Pakistan in Pakistan	102	Faisalabad	1990-91

HIGHEST MATCH AGGREGATE	1585 for 31 wickets	Karachi	1976-77
LOWEST MATCH AGGREGATE	572 for 30 wickets	Rawalpindi	1964-65

HIGHEST INDIVIDUAL INNINGS

New Zealand in New Zealand	174	M.D.Crowe	Wellington	1988-89
New Zealand in Pakistan	152	W.K.Lees	Karachi	1976-77
Pakistan in New Zealand	201	Javed Miandad	Auckland	1988-89
Pakistan in Pakistan	209	Imtiaz Ahmed	Lahore¹	1955-56

HIGHEST AGGREGATE OF RUNS IN A SERIES

New Zealand in New Zealand	333 (av 83.25)	J.F.Reid	1984-85
New Zealand in Pakistan	296 (av 59.20)	J.R.Reid	1964-65
Pakistan in New Zealand	389 (av 194.50)	Javed Miandad	1988-89
Pakistan in Pakistan	507 (av 169.00)	Shoaib Mohammad	1990-91

RECORD WICKET PARTNERSHIPS — NEW ZEALAND

1st	159	R.E.Redmond (107), G.M.Turner (58)	Auckland	1972-73
2nd	195	J.G.Wright (88), G.P.Howarth (114)	Napier	1978-79
3rd	178	B.W.Sinclair (130), J.R.Reid (88)	Lahore²	1964-65
4th	128	B.F.Hastings (72), M.G.Burgess (79)	Wellington	1972-73
5th	183	M.G.Burgess (111), R.W.Anderson (92)	Lahore²	1976-77
6th	145	J.F.Reid (148), R.J.Hadlee (87)	Wellington	1984-85
7th	186	W.K.Lees (152), R.J.Hadlee (87)	Karachi	1976-77
8th	100	B.W.Yuile (47*), D.R.Hadlee (56)	Karachi	1969-70
9th	96	M.G.Burgess (119*), R.S.Cunis (23)	Dacca	1969-70
10th	151	B.F.Hastings (110), R.O.Collinge (68*)	Auckland	1972-73

RECORD WICKET PARTNERSHIPS—PAKISTAN

1st	172	Rameez Raja (78), Shoaib Mohammad (203*)	Karachi	1990-91
2nd	114	Mohammad Ilyas (56), Saeed Ahmed (68)	Rawalpindi	1964-65
3rd	248	Shoaib Mohammad (112), Javed Miandad (271)	Auckland	1988-89
4th	350	Mushtaq Mohammad (201), Asif Iqbal (175)	Dunedin	1972-73
5th	281	Javed Miandad (163), Asif Iqbal (166)	Lahore[2]	1976-77
6th	217	Hanif Mohammad (203*), Majid Khan (80)	Lahore[2]	1964-65
7th	308	Waqar Hassan (189), Imtiaz Ahmed (209)	Lahore[1]	1955-56
8th	89	Anil Dalpat (52), Iqbal Qasim (45*)	Karachi	1984-85
9th	52	Intikhab Alam (45), Arif Butt (20)	Auckland	1964-65
10th	65	Salahuddin (34*), Mohammad Farooq (47)	Rawalpindi	1964-65

BEST INNINGS BOWLING ANALYSIS

New Zealand in New Zealand	6-51	R.J.Hadlee	Dunedin	1984-85
New Zealand in Pakistan	7-52	C.Pringle	Faisalabad	1990-91
Pakistan in New Zealand	7-52	Intikhab Alam	Dunedin	1972-73
Pakistan in Pakistan	7-52	Waqar Younis	Faisalabad	1990-91

BEST MATCH BOWLING ANALYSIS

New Zealand in New Zealand	9-70	F.J.Cameron	Auckland	1964-65
New Zealand in Pakistan	11-152	C.Pringle	Faisalabad	1990-91
Pakistan in New Zealand	11-130	Intikhab Alam	Dunedin	1972-73
Pakistan in Pakistan	12-130	Waqar Younis	Faisalabad	1990-91

HIGHEST AGGREGATE OF WICKETS IN A SERIES

New Zealand in New Zealand	18 (av 23.00)	R.J.Hadlee	1978-79
New Zealand in Pakistan	16 (av 20.18)	H.J.Howarth	1969-70
Pakistan in New Zealand	18 (av 13 94)	Intikhab Alam	1972-73
Pakistan in Pakistan	29 (av 10.86)	Waqar Younis	1990-91

NEW ZEALAND v SRI LANKA

Venue and Result	New Zealand 1st	New Zealand 2nd	Sri Lanka 1st	Sri Lanka 2nd	Captains New Zealand	Captains Sri Lanka
1982-83 in NEW ZEALAND						
Christchurch-New Zealand inns & 25 runs	*344	-	144	175	G.P.Howarth	D.S.de Silva
Wellington-New Zealand 6 wkts	201	4-134	*240	93		
1983-84 in SRI LANKA						
Kandy-New Zealand 165 runs	*276	8d-201	215	97	G.P.Howarth	L.R.D.Mendis
Colombo (SSC)-Drawn	198	4-123	*174	9d-289		
Colombo (CCC)-New Zealand inns & 61 runs	459	-	*256	142		
1986-87 in SRI LANKA						
Colombo (SSC)-Drawn	5-406	-	*9d-397	-	J.J.Crowe	L.R.D.Mendis
1990-91 in NEW ZEALAND						
Wellington-Drawn	*174	4-671	497	-	M.D.Crowe	A.Ranatunga
Hamilton-Drawn	*296	6d-374	253	6-344	M.D.Crowe	
Auckland-Drawn	317	5-261	*380	319	I.D.S.Smith	

Test Match Results Summary

NEW ZEALAND v SRI LANKA — IN NEW ZEALAND

		Result			Christchurch			Wellington			Hamilton			Auckland		
	Tests	NZ	SL	D	NZ	SL	D	NZ	SL	D	NZ	SL	D	NZ	SL	D
1982-83	2	2	-	-	1	-	-	1	-	-	-	-	-	-	-	-
1990-91	3	-	-	3	-	-	-	-	-	1	-	-	1	-	-	1
	5	2	-	3	1	-	-	1	-	1	-	-	1	-	-	1

NEW ZEALAND v SRI LANKA — IN SRI LANKA

		Result			Kandy			Colombo (SSC)			Colombo (CCC)		
	Tests	NZ	SL	D	NZ	SL	D	NZ	SL	D	NZ	SL	D
1983-84	3	2	-	1	1	-	-	-	-	1	1	-	-
1986-87	1	-	-	1	-	-	-	-	-	-	-	-	1
	4	2	-	2	1	-	-	-	-	1	1	-	1
Totals	9	4	-	5									

HIGHEST INNINGS TOTALS

New Zealand in New Zealand	4-671	Wellington	1990-91
New Zealand in Sri Lanka	459	Colombo (CCC)	1983-84
Sri Lanka in New Zealand	497	Wellington	1990-91
Sri Lanka in Sri Lanka	9d-397	Colombo (CCC)	1986-87

LOWEST INNINGS TOTALS

New Zealand in New Zealand	174	Wellington	1990-91
New Zealand in Sri Lanka	198	Colombo (SSC)	1983-84
Sri Lanka in New Zealand	93	Wellington	1987-88
Sri Lanka in Sri Lanka	97	Kandy	1983-84

HIGHEST MATCH AGGREGATE	1342 for 23 wickets	Wellington	1990-91
LOWEST MATCH AGGREGATE	663 for 30 wickets	Christchurch	1982-83

HIGHEST INDIVIDUAL INNINGS

New Zealand in New Zealand	299	M.D.Crowe	Wellington	1990-91
New Zealand in Sri Lanka	180	J.F.Reid	Colombo (CCC)	1983-84
Sri Lanka in New Zealand	267	P.A.de Silva	Wellington	1990-91
Sri Lanka in Sri Lanka	201*	D.S.B.P.Kuruppu	Colombo (CCC)	1986-87

HIGHEST AGGREGATE ON RUNS IN A SERIES

New Zealand in New Zealand	513 (av 102.60)	A.H.Jones	1990-91
New Zealand in Sri Lanka	243 (av 48.60)	J.F.Reid	1983-84
Sri Lanka in New Zealand	493 (av 98.60)	P.A.de Silva	1990-91
Sri Lanka in Sri Lanka	242 (av 60.50)	R.S.Madugalle	1983-84

RECORD WICKET PARTNERSHIPS — NEW ZEALAND

1st	161	T.J.Franklin (69), J.G.Wright (101)	Hamilton	1990-91
2nd	76	J.G.Wright (84), A.H.Jones (27)	Auckland	1990-91
3rd	467	A.H.Jones (188), M.D.Crowe (299)	Wellington	1990-91
4th	82	J.F.Reid (180), S.L.Boock (35)	Colombo (CCC)	1983-84
5th	113	A.H.Jones (100*), S.A.Thomson (55)	Hamilton	1990-91
6th	246*	J.J.Crowe (120*), R.J.Hadlee (151*)	Colombo (CCC)	1986-87
7th	30	R.J.Hadlee (29), I.D.S.Smith (30)	Kandy	1983-84
	30	R.J.Hadlee (27), J.J.Crowe (9)	Kandy	1983-84
8th	79	J.V.Coney (84), W.K.Lees (89)	Christchurch	1982-83
9th	42	W.K.Lees (89), M.C.Snedden (22)	Christchurch	1982-83
10th	52	W.K.Lees (89), E.J.Chatfield (10*)	Christchurch	1982-83

RECORD WICKET PARTNERSHIPS—SRI LANKA

1st	95	C.P.Senanayake (64), U.C.Hathurusingha (81)	Hamilton	1990-91
2nd	57	S.M.S.Kaluperuma (18), R.S.Madugalle (38)	Colombo (CCC)	1983-84
3rd	159*	S.Wettimuny (65), R.L.Dias (108)	Colombo (SSC)	1983-84
4th	178	P.A.de Silva (267), A.Ranatunga (55)	Wellington	1990-91
5th	130	R.S.Madugalle (79), D.S.de Silva (61)	Wellington	1982-83
6th	109	R.S.Madugalle (89*), A.Ranatunga (37)	Colombo (CCC)	1983-84
	109	D.S.B.P.Kuruppu (201*), R.S.Madugalle (60)	Colombo (CCC)	1986-87
7th	55	A.P.Gurusinha (119), A.Ranatunga (21)	Hamilton	1990-91
8th	52	H.P.Tillakaratne (31), G.F.Labrooy (70*)	Auckland	1990-91
9th	31	G.F.Labrooy (70*), R.J.Ratnayake (18)	Auckland	1990-91
	31	S.T.Jayasuriya (12*), R.J.Ratnayake (20)	Auckland	1990-91
10th	60	V.B.John (27*), A.M.J.G.Amerasinghe (34)	Kandy	1983-84

† 163 runs were added for this wicket, S.Wettimuny retired hurt and was replaced by L.R.D.Mendis after 159 had been scored.

§ 119 runs were added for this wicket, R.S.Madugalle retired hurt and was replaced by D.S.de Silva after 109 had been scored.

BEST INNINGS BOWLING ANALYSIS

New Zealand in New Zealand	5-75	C.L.Cairns	Auckland	1990-91
New Zealand in Sri Lanka	5-28	S.L.Boock	Kandy	1983-84
Sri Lanka in New Zealand	5-77	R.J.Ratnayake	Hamilton	1990-91
Sri Lanka in Sri Lanka	5-42	J.R.Ratnayeke	Colombo (SSC)	1983-84

BEST MATCH BOWLING ANALYSIS

New Zealand in New Zealand	9-211	C.L.Cairns	Auckland	1990-91
New Zealand in Sri Lanka	10-102	R.J.Hadlee	Colombo (CCC)	1983-84
Sri Lanka in New Zealand	7-90	G.F.Labrooy	Auckland	1990-91
Sri Lanka in Sri Lanka	8-159	V.B.John	Kandy	1983-84

HIGHEST AGGREGATE OF WICKETS IN A SERIES

New Zealand in New Zealand	13 (av 36.61)	D.K.Morrison	1990-91
New Zealand in Sri Lanka	23 (av 10.00)	R.J.Hadlee	1983-84
Sri Lanka in New Zealand	13 (av 27.46)	G.F.Labrooy	1990-91
	13 (av 32.30)	R.J.Ratnayake	1990-91
Sri Lanka in Sri Lanka	16 (av 23.31)	V.B.John	1983-84

INDIA v PAKISTAN

Venue and Result	India 1st	India 2nd	Pakistan 1st	Pakistan 2nd	Captains India	Captains Pakistan
1952-53 In INDIA						
Delhi-India inns & 70 runs	*372	-	150	152	N.B.Amarnath	A.H.Kardar
Lucknow-Pakistan inns & 43 runs	*106	182	331	-		
Bombay²-India 10 wkts	4d-387	0-45	*186	242		
Madras¹-Drawn	6-175	-	*344	-		
Calcutta-Drawn	397	0-28	*257	7d-236		
1954-55 In PAKISTAN						
Dacca-Drawn	148	2-147	*257	158	M.H.Mankad	A.H.Kardar
Bahawalpur-Drawn	*235	5-209	9d-312	-		
Lahore¹-Drawn	251	2-74	*328	5d-136		
Peshawar-Drawn	245	1-23	*188	182		
Karachi-Drawn	145	2-69	*162	5d-241		

INDIA v PAKISTAN (cont.) Venue and Result	India 1st	India 2nd	Pakistan 1st	Pakistan 2nd	Captains India	Captains Pakistan
1978-79 In PAKISTAN						
Faisalabad-Drawn	9d-462	0-43	*8d-503	4d-264	B.S.Bedi	Mushtaq Mohammad
Lahore²-Pakistan 8 wkts	*199	465	6d-539	2-182		
Karachi-Pakistan 8 wkts	*344	300	9d-481	2-164		
1960-61 in INDIA						
Bombay²-Drawn	9d-449	-	*350	4-166	N.J.Contractor	Fazal Mahmood
Kanpur-Drawn	404	-	*335	3-140		
Calcutta-Drawn	180	4-127	*301	3d-146		
Madras²-Drawn	9d-539	-	*8d-448	0-59		
Delhi-Drawn	*463	0-16	286	250		
1979-80 IN INDIA						
Bangalore-Drawn	416	-	*9d-431	2-108	S.M.Gavaskar	Asif Iqbal
Delhi-Drawn	126	6-364	*273	242	S.M.Gavaskar	
Bombay³-India 131 runs	*334	160	173	190	S.M.Gavaskar	
Kanpur-Drawn	*162	2-193	249	-	S.M.Gavaskar	
Madras¹-India 10 wkts	430	0-78	*272	233	S.M.Gavaskar	
Calcutta-Drawn	*331	205	4d-272	6-179	G.R.Viswanath	
1982-83 In PAKISTAN						
Lahore²-Drawn	379	-	*485	1-135	S.M.Gavaskar	Imran Khan
Karachi-Pakistan inns & 86 runs	*169	197	452	-		
Faisalabad-Pakistan 10 wkts	*372	286	652	0-10		
Hyderabad-Pakistan inns & 119 runs	189	273	*3d-581	-		
Lahore²-Drawn	3-235	-	*323	-		
Karachi-Drawn	*8d-393	2-224	6d-420	-		
1983-84 IN INDIA						
Bangalore-Drawn	*275	0-176	288	-	Kapil Dev	Zaheer Abbas
Jullundur-Drawn	374	-	*337	0-16		
Nagpur-Drawn	*245	8d-262	322	1-42		
1984-85 In PAKISTAN						
Lahore²-Drawn	156	6-371	*9d-428	-	S.M.Gavaskar	Zaheer Abbas
Faisalabad-Drawn	*500	-	6-674	-		
1986-87 IN INDIA						
Madras¹-Drawn	9d-527	-	*9d-487	3-182	Kapil Dev	Imran Khan
Calcutta-Drawn	*403	3d-181	229	5-179		
Jaipur-Drawn	*8d-465	2-114	341	-		
Ahmedabad-Drawn	323	-	*395	2-135		
Bangalore-Pakistan 16 runs	145	204	*116	249		
1989-90 In PAKISTAN						
Karachi-Drawn	262	3-303	*409	5d-305	K.Srikkanth	Imran Khan
Faisalabad-Drawn	*288	7-398	9d-423	-		
Lahore²-Drawn	*509	-	5-699	-		
Sialkot-Drawn	*324	7-234	250	-		

Test Match Results Summary

INDIA v PAKISTAN — IN INDIA

	T	Result I P D	Delhi I P D	Luck. I P D	Bomb. I P D	Madras I P D	Calc. I P D	Kanpur I P D	Bang. I P D	Jull. I P D	Nagpur I P D	Jaipur I P D	Ahmed. I P D
1952-53	5	2 1 2	1 - -	- 1 -	1 - -	- - 1	- - 1	- - -	- - -	- - -	- - -	- - -	- - -
1960-61	5	- - 5	- - 1	- - -	- - 1	- - 1	- - 1	- - 1	- - -	- - -	- - -	- - -	- - -
1979-80	6	2 - 4	- - 1	- - -	1 - -	1 - -	- - 1	- - 1	- - 1	- - -	- - -	- - -	- - -
1983-84	3	- - 3	- - -	- - -	- - -	- - -	- - -	- - -	- - 1	- - 1	- - 1	- - -	- - -
1986-87	5	- 1 4	- - -	- - -	- - -	- - 1	- - 1	- - -	- 1 -	- - -	- - -	- - 1	- - 1
	24	4 2 18	1 - 2	- 1 -	2 - 1	1 - 3	- - 4	- - 2	- 1 2	- - 1	- - 1	- - 1	- - 1

INDIA v PAKISTAN — IN PAKISTAN

	Tests	Result I	Result P	Result D	Dacca I P D	Bah. I P D	Lahore I P D	Pesh. I P D	Karachi I P D	Fais. I P D	Hyd. I P D	Sialkot I P D
1954-55	5	-	-	5	- - 1	- - 1	- - 1	- - 1	- - 1	- - -	- - -	- - -
1978-79	3	-	2	1	- - -	- - -	- 1 -	- - -	- 1 -	- - 1	- - -	- - -
1982-83	6	-	3	3	- - -	- - -	- - 2	- - -	- 1 1	- 1 -	- 1 -	- - -
1984-85	2	-	-	2	- - -	- - -	- - 1	- - -	- - -	- - 1	- - -	- - -
1989-90	4	-	-	4	- - -	- - -	- - 1	- - -	- - 1	- - 1	- - -	- - 1
	20	-	5	15	- - 1	- - 1	- 1 5	- - 1	- 2 3	- 1 3	- 1 -	- - 1
Totals	44	4	7	33								

Key to ground abbreviations: Luck. - Lucknow; Bomb. - Bombay; Calc. - Calcutta; Bang. - Bangalore; Jull. - Jullundur; Ahmed. - Ahmedabad; Bah. - Bahawalpur; Pesh. - Peshawar; Fais. - Faisalabad; Hyd. - Hyderabad.

HIGHEST INNINGS TOTALS

India in India	9d-539	Madras[2]	1960-61
India in Pakistan	509	Lahore[2]	1989-90
Pakistan in India	9d-487	Madras[2]	1960-61
Pakistan in Pakistan	5-699	Lahore[2]	1989-90

LOWEST INNINGS TOTALS

India in India	106	Lucknow	1952-53
India in Pakistan	145	Karachi	1954-55
Pakistan in India	116	Delhi	1986-87
Pakistan in Pakistan	158	Dacca	1954-55

HIGHEST MATCH AGGREGATE	1331 for 28 wickets	Lahore[2]	1978-79
LOWEST MATCH AGGREGATE	619 for 30 wickets	Lucknow	1952-53

HIGHEST INDIVIDUAL INNINGS

India in India	201	A.D.Gaekwad	Jullundur	1983-84
India in Pakistan	218	S.V.Manjrekar	Lahore[2]	1989-90
Pakistan in India	160	Hanif Mohammad	Bombay[2]	1960-61
Pakistan in Pakistan	280*	Javed Miandad	Hyderabad	1982-83

HIGHEST AGGREGATE OF RUNS IN A SERIES

India in India	529 (av 52.90)	S.M.Gavaskar	1979-80
India in Pakistan	584 (av 73.00)	M.Amarnath	1982-83
Pakistan in India	460 (av 51.11)	Saeed Ahmed	1960-61
Pakistan in Pakistan	761 (av 126.83)	Mudassar Nazar	1982-83

RECORD WICKET PARTNERSHIPS—INDIA

1st	200	S.M.Gavaskar (91), K.Srikkanth (123)	Madras[1]	1986-87
2nd	135	N.S.Sidhu (85), S.V.Manjrekar (113)	Karachi	1989-90
3rd	190	M.Amarnath (120), Yashpal Sharma (63*)	Lahore[2]	1982-83
4th	186	S.V.Manjrekar (218), R.J.Shastri (61)	Lahore[2]	1989-90
5th	200	S.M.Patil (127), R.J.Shastri (139)	Faisalabad	1984-85
6th	143	M.Azharuddin (141), Kapil Dev (66)	Calcutta	1986-87
7th	155	R.M.H.Binny (83*), S.Madan Lal (74)	Bangalore	1983-84
8th	122	S.M.H.Kirmani (66), S.Madan Lal (54)	Faisalabad	1982-83
9th	149	P.G.Joshi (52*), R.B.Desai (85)	Bombay[2]	1960-61
10th	109	H.R.Adhikari (81*), Ghulam Ahmed (50)	Delhi	1952-53

RECORD WICKET PARTNERSHIPS-PAKISTAN

1st	162	Hanif Mohammad (62), Imtiaz Ahmed (135)	Madras[2]	1960-61
2nd	250	Mudassar Nazar (199), Qasim Omar (210)	Faisalabad	1984-85
3rd	451	Mudassar Nazar (230), Javed Miandad (280*)	Hyderabad	1982-83
4th	287	Javed Miandad (126), Zaheer Abbas (168)	Faisalabad	1982-83
5th	213	Zaheer Abbas (186), Mudassar Nazar (119)	Karachi	1982-83
6th	207	Saleem Malik (107), Imran Khan (117)	Faisalabad	1982-83
7th	154	Imran Khan (72), Ijaz Faqih (105)	Ahmedabad	1986-87
8th	112	Imran Khan (135*), Wasim Akram (62)	Madras[1]	1986-87
9th	60	Wasim Bari (49*), Iqbal Qasim (20)	Bangalore	1979-80
10th	104	Zulfiqar Ahmed (63*), Amir Elahi (47)	Madras[1]	1952-53

BEST INNINGS BOWLING ANALYSIS

India in India	8-52	M.H.Mankad	Delhi	1952-53
India in Pakistan	8-85	Kapil Dev	Lahore[2]	1982-83
Pakistan In India	8-69	Sikander Bakht	Delhi	1979-80
Pakistan in Pakistan	8-60	Imran Khan	Karachi	1982-83

BEST MATCH BOWLING ANALYSIS

India in India	13-131	M.H.Mankad	Delhi	1952-53
India in Pakistan	8-85	Kapil Dev	Lahore[2]	1982-83
Pakistan in India	12-94	Fazal Mahmood	Lucknow	1952-53
Pakistan in Pakistan	11-79	Imran Khan	Karachi	1982-83

HIGHEST AGGREGATE OF WICKETS IN A SERIES

India in India	32 (av 17.68)	Kapil Dev	1979-80
India in Pakistan	21 (av 22.61)	Kapil Dev	1982-83
Pakistan in India	24 (av 26.70)	Sikander Bakht	1979-80
Pakistan in Pakistan	22 (av 15.86)	Imran Khan	1982-83

INDIA v SRI LANKA

Venue and Result	India 1st	India 2nd	Sri Lanka 1st	Sri Lanka 2nd	Captains India	Captains Sri Lanka
1982-83 in INDIA						
Madras[1]-Drawn	6d-566	7-135	*346	394	S.M.Gavaskar	B.Warnaweera
1985-86 in SRI LANKA						
Colombo (SSC)-Drawn	*218	251	347	4-61	Kapil Dev	L.R.D.Mendis
Colombo (CCC)-Sri Lanka 149 runs	244	198	*385	3d-206		
Kandy-Drawn	*249	5d-325	198	7-307		
1986-87 in INDIA						
Kanpur-Drawn	7-676	-	*420	-	Kapil Dev	L.R.D.Mendis
Nagpur-India inns & 106 runs	6d-451	-	*204	141		
Cuttack-India inns & 67 runs	*400	-	191	142		
1990-91 in INDIA						
Chandigarh-India inns & 8 runs	*288	-	82	198	M.Azharuddin	A.Ranatunga

Test Match Results Summary

INDIA v SRI LANKA—IN INDIA

	Tests	Result			Madras			Kanpur			Nagpur			Cuttack			Chandigarh		
		I	SL	D	I	SL	D	I	SL	D	I	SL	D	I	SL	D	I	SL	D
1982-83	1	-	-	1	-	-	1	-	-	-	-	-	-	-	-	-	-	-	-
1986-87	3	2	-	1	-	-	-	1	-	-	-	-	1	1	-	-	-	-	-
1990-91	1	1	-	-	-	-	-	-	-	-	-	-	-	-	-	-	-	-	1
	5	3	-	2	-	-	1	1	-	-	-	-	1	1	-	-	-	-	1

INDIA v SRI LANKA—IN SRI LANKA

	Tests	Result			Colombo (SSC)			Colombo (PSS)			Kandy		
		I	SL	D	I	SL	D	I	SL	D	I	SL	D
1985-86	3	-	1	2	-	-	1	-	1	-	-	-	1
Totals	8	3	1	4									

HIGHEST INNINGS TOTALS

India in India	7-676	Kanpur	1986-87
India in Sri Lanka	5d-325	Kandy	1985-86
Sri Lanka in India	420	Kanpur	1986-87
Sri Lanka in Sri Lanka	385	Colombo (PSS)	1985-86

LOWEST INNINGS TOTALS

India in India	288	Chandigarh	1990-91
India in Sri Lanka	198	Colombo (PSS)	1985-86
Sri Lanka in India	82	Chandigarh	1990-91
Sri Lanka in Sri Lanka	198	Kandy	1985-86

HIGHEST MATCH AGGREGATE	1441 for 33 wickets	Madras[1]	1982-83
LOWEST MATCH AGGREGATE	568 for 30 wickets	Chandigarh	1990-91

HIGHEST INDIVIDUAL INNINGS

India in India	199	M.Azharuddin	Kanpur	1986-87
India in Sri Lanka	116*	M.Amarnath	Kandy	1985-86
Sri Lanka in India	105 (twice) 1982-83	L.R.D.Mendis	Madras[1]	
Sri Lanka in Sri Lanka	124	L.R.D.Mendis	Kandy	1985-86

HIGHEST AGGREGATE ON RUNS IN A SERIES

India in India	376 (av 125.33)	D.B.Vengsarkar	1986-87
India in Sri Lanka	216 (av 72.00)	M.Amarnath	1985-86
Sri Lanka in India	210 (av 105.00)	L.R.D.Mendis	1982-83
Sri Lanka in Sri Lanka	310 (av 62.00)	L.R.D.Mendis	1985-86

RECORD WICKET PARTNERSHIPS — INDIA

1st	156	S.M.Gavaskar (155), Arun Lal (63)	Madras[1]	1982-83
2nd	173	S.M.Gavaskar (155), D.B.Vengsarkar (90)	Madras[1]	1982-83
3rd	173	M.Amarnath (131), D.B.Vengsarkar (153)	Nagpur	1986-87
4th	163	S.M.Gavaskar (176), M.Azharuddin (199)	Kanpur	1986-87
5th	78	M.Amarnath (116*), M.Azharuddin (43)	Kandy	1985-86
6th	272	M.Azharuddin (199), Kapil Dev (163)	Kanpur	1986-87
7th	78*	S.M.Patil (114*), S.Madan Lal (37*)	Madras[1]	1982-83
8th	70	Kapil Dev (78), L.Sivaramakrishnan (21)	Colombo (PSS)	1985-86
9th	16	S.M.Gavaskar (51), G.Sharma (10*)	Colombo (SSC)	1985-86
10th	29	Kapil Dev (78), C.Sharma (0*)	Colombo (PSS)	1985-86

RECORD WICKET PARTNERSHIPS — SRI LANKA

1st	159	S.Wettimuny (79), J.R.Ratnayeke (93)	Kanpur	1986-87
2nd	95	S.A.R.Silva (111), R.S.Madugalle (54)	Colombo (PSS)	1985-86
3rd	153	R.L.Dias (60), L.R.D.Mendis (105)	Madras[1]	1982-83
4th	216	R.L.Dias (106), L.R.D.Mendis (124)	Kandy	1985-86
5th	144	R.S.Madugalle (103), A.Ranatunga (111)	Colombo (SSC)	1985-86
6th	89	L.R.D.Mendis (105), A.N.Ranasinghe (77)	Madras[1]	1982-83
7th	77	R.S.Madugalle (46), D.S.de Silva (49)	Madras[1]	1982-83
8th	40*	P.A.de Silva (29*), A.L.F.de Mel (9*)	Kandy	1985-86
9th	60	H.P.Tillakaratne (55), M.A.W.R.Madurasinghe (11)	Madras[1]	1982-83
10th	44	R.J.Ratnayake (32*), E.A.R.de Silva (16)	Nagpur	1986-87

BEST INNINGS BOWLING ANALYSIS

India in India	7-51	Maninder Singh	Nagpur	1986-87
India in Sri Lanka	5-118	C.Sharma	Colombo (PSS)	1985-86
Sri Lanka in India	5-68	A.L.F.de Mel	Madras[1]	1982-83
Sri Lanka in Sri Lanka	6-85	R.J.Ratnayake	Colombo (SSC)	1985-86

BEST MATCH BOWLING ANALYSIS

India in India	10-107	Maninder Singh	Nagpur	1986-87
India in Sri Lanka	6-173	C.Sharma	Colombo (PSS)	1985-86
Sri Lanka in India	7-201	A.L.F.de Mel	Madras[1]	1982-83
Sri Lanka in Sri Lanka	9-125	R.J.Ratnayake	Colombo (PSS)	1985-86

HIGHEST AGGREGATE OF WICKETS IN A SERIES

India in India	18 (av 15.50)	Maninder Singh	1986-87
India in Sri Lanka	14 (av 27.35)	C.Sharma	1985-86
Sri Lanka in India	9 (av 34.00)	J.R.Ratnayeke	1986-87
Sri Lanka in Sri Lanka	20 (av 22.95)	R.J.Ratnayake	1985-86

PAKISTAN v SRI LANKA

Venue and Result	Pakistan 1st	Pakistan 2nd	Sri Lanka 1st	Sri Lanka 2nd	Captains Pakistan	Captains Sri Lanka
1981-82 in PAKISTAN						
Karachi-Pakistan 204 runs	*396	4d-301	344	149	Javed Miandad	B Warnapura
Faisalabad-Drawn	270	7-186	*454	8d-154		L. R. D. Mendis
Lahore²-Pakistan inns & 102 runs	7d-500	-	*240	158		B. Warnapura
1985-86 in PAKISTAN						
Faisalabad-Drawn	3-555	-	*479	-	Javed Miandad	L. R. D. Mendis
Sialkot-Pakistan 8 wkts	259	2-100	*157	200		
Karachi-Pakistan 10 wkts	295	0-98	*162	230		
1985-86 in SRI LANKA						
Kandy-Pakistan inns & 20 runs	230	-	*109	101	Imran Khan	L. R. D. Mendis
Colombo (CCC)-Sri Lanka 149 runs	*132	172	273	2-32		
Colombo (PSS)-Drawn	318	-	*281	3-323		
1991-92 in PAKISTAN						
Sialkot-Drawn	5d-423	-	*270	5-137	Imran Khan	P.A.de Silva
Gujranwala-Drawn	*2-109	-	-	-		
Faisalabad-Pakistan 3 wkts	221	7-188	*240	165		

Test Match Results Summary

PAKISTAN v SRI LANKA—IN PAKISTAN

	Tests	Results			Karachi			Faisalabad			Lahore			Sialkot			Gujranwala		
		P	SL	D	P	SL	D	P	SL	D	P	SL	D	P	SL	D	P	SL	D
1981-82	3	2	-	1	1	-	-	-	-	1	1	-	-	-	-	-	-	-	-
1985-86	3	2	-	1	1	-	-	-	-	1	-	-	-	1	-	-	-	-	-
1991-92	3	1	-	2	-	-	1	1	-	-	-	-	-	-	-	1	-	-	1
	9	5	-	4	2	-	1	1	-	2	1	-	-	1	-	1	-	-	1

PAKISTAN v SRI LANKA—IN SRI LANKA

	Tests	Result			Kandy			Colombo (CCC)			Colombo (PSS)		
		P	SL	D	P	SL	D	P	SL	D	P	SL	D
1985-86	3	1	1	1	1	-	-	-	1	-	-	-	1
Totals	12	6	1	5									

HIGHEST INNINGS TOTALS

Pakistan in Pakistan	3-555	Faisalabad	1985-86
Pakistan in Sri Lanka	318	Colombo (PSS)	1985-86
Sri Lanka in Pakistan	479	Faisalabad	1985-86
Sri Lanka in Sri Lanka	3-323	Colombo (PSS)	1985-86

LOWEST INNINGS TOTALS

Pakistan in Pakistan	221	Faisalabad	1991-92
Pakistan in Sri Lanka	132	Colombo (CCC)	1985-86
Sri Lanka in Pakistan	149	Karachi	1981-82
Sri Lanka in Sri Lanka	101	Kandy	1985-86

HIGHEST MATCH AGGREGATE	1190 for 34 wickets	Karachi	1981-82
LOWEST MATCH AGGREGATE	440 for 30 wickets	Kandy	1985-86

HIGHEST INDIVIDUAL INNINGS

Pakistan in Pakistan	206	Qasim Omar	Faisalabad	1985-86
Pakistan in Sri Lanka	122	Rameez Raja	Colombo (PSS)	1985-86
Sri Lanka in Pakistan	157	S.Wettimuny	Faisalabad	1981-82
Sri Lanka in Sri Lanka	135*	A.Ranatunga	Colombo (PSS)	1985-86

HIGHEST AGGREGATE OF RUNS IN A SERIES

Pakistan in Pakistan	306 (av 153.00)	Javed Miandad	1985-86
Pakistan in Sri Lanka	178 (av 44.50)	Rameez Raja	1985-86
Sri Lanka in Pakistan	316 (av 52.66)	S.Wettimuny	1985-86
Sri Lanka in Sri Lanka	316 (av 79.00)	A.Ranatunga	1985-86

RECORD WICKET PARTNERSHIPS—PAKISTAN

1st	128	Rameez Raja (98), Shoaib Mohammad (43)	Sialkot	1991-92
2nd	151	Mohsin Khan (129), Majid Khan (63)	Lahore[2]	1981-82
3rd	397	Qasim Omar (206), Javed Miandad (203*)	Faisalabad	1985-86
4th	162	Saleem Malik (100*), Javed Miandad (92)	Karachi	1981-82
5th	132	Saleem Malik (101), Imran Khan (93*)	Sialkot	1991-92
6th	100	Zaheer Abbas (134), Imran Khan (39)	Lahore[2]	1981-82
7th	104	Haroon Rashid (153), Tahir Naqqash (57)	Karachi	1981-82
8th	29	Ashraf Ali (58), Iqbal Qasim (5)	Faisalabad	1981-82
	29	Saleem Yousuf (23), Abdul Qadir (10)	Sialkot	1985-86
	29	Saleem Yousuf (27), Abdul Qadir (19)	Karachi	1985-86
9th	127	Haroon Rashid (153), Rashid Khan (59)	Karachi	1981-82
10th	48	Rashid Khan (43*), Tauseef Ahmed (18)	Faisalabad	1981-82

RECORD WICKET PARTNERSHIPS—SRI LANKA

1st	81	R.S.Mahanama (58), U.C.Hathurusingha (49)	Faisalabad	1991-92
2nd	217	S.Wettimuny (157), R.L.Dias (98)	Faisalabad	1981-82
3rd	85	S.Wettimuny (157), R.L.Dias (48)	Faisalabad	1985-86
4th	240*	A.P.Gurusinha (116*), A.Ranatunga (135*)	Colombo (PSS)	1985-86
5th	58	R.L.Dias (109), L.R.D.Mendis (26)	Lahore[2]	1981-82
6th	121	A.Ranatunga (79), P.A.de Silva (122)	Faisalabad	1985-86
7th	66	P.A.de Silva (122), J.R.Ratnayeke (34)	Faisalabad	1985-86
8th	61	R.S.Madugalle (91*), D.S.de Silva (29*)	Faisalabad	1981-82
9th	52	P.A.de Silva (122), R.J.Ratnayake (56)	Faisalabad	1985-86
10th	36	R.J.Ratnayake (356), R.G.C.E.Wijesuriya (7*)	Faisalabad	1985-86

BEST INNINGS BOWLING ANALYSIS

Pakistan in Pakistan	8-58	Imran Khan	Lahore[2]	1981-82
Pakistan in Sri Lanka	6-45	Tauseef Ahmed	Kandy	1985-86
Sri Lanka in Pakistan	8-83	J.R.Ratnayeke	Faisalabad	1985-86
Sri Lanka in Sri Lanka	5-37	J.R.Ratnayeke	Colombo (CCC)	1985-86

BEST MATCH BOWLING ANALYSIS

Pakistan in Pakistan	14-116	Imran Khan	Lahore[2]	1981-82
Pakistan in Sri Lanka	9-77	Tauseef Ahmed	Kandy	1985-86
Sri Lanka in Pakistan	9-162	D.S.de Silva	Faisalabad	1981-82
Sri Lanka in Sri Lanka	7-66	J.R.Ratnayeke	Colombo (CCC)	1985-86

HIGHEST AGGREGATE OF WICKETS IN SERIES

Pakistan in Pakistan	17 (av 15.94)	Imran Khan	1985-86
Pakistan in Sri Lanka	15 (av 18.00)	Imran Khan	1985-86
Sri Lanka in Pakistan	17 (av 28.94)	D.S.de Silva	1981-82
Sri Lanka in Sri Lanka	11 (av 18.90)	J.R.Ratnayeke	1985-86

The Teams

HIGHEST INNINGS TOTALS

903-7d	England	v	Australia	The Oval	1938
849	England	v	West Indies	Kingston	1929-30
790-3d	West Indies	v	Pakistan	Kingston	1957-58
758-8d	Australia	v	West Indies	Kingston	1954-55
729-6d	Australia	v	England	Lord's	1930
708	Pakistan	v	England	The Oval	1987
701	Australia	v	England	The Oval	1934
699-5	Pakistan	v	India	Lahore[2]	1989-90
695	Australia	v	England	The Oval	1930
687-8d	West Indies	v	England	The Oval	1976
681-8d	West Indies	v	England	Port-of-Spain	1953-54
676-7	India	v	Sri Lanka	Kanpur	1986-87
674-6	Pakistan	v	India	Faisalabad	1984-85
674	Australia	v	India	Adelaide	1947-48
671-4	New Zealand	v	Sri Lanka	Wellington	1990-91
668	Australia	v	West Indies	Bridgetown	1954-55
659-8d	Australia	v	England	Sydney	1946-47
658-8d	England	v	Australia	Nottingham	1938
657-8d	Pakistan	v	West Indies	Bridgetown	1957-58
656-8d	Australia	v	England	Manchester	1964
654-5	England	v	South Africa	Durban[2]	1938-39
653-4d	England	v	India	Lord's	1990
652-7d	England	v	India	Madras[1]	1984-85
652-8d	West Indies	v	England	Lord's	1973
652	Pakistan	v	India	Faisalabad	1982-83
650-6d	Australia	v	West Indies	Bridgetown	1964-65
645	Australia	v	England	Brisbane[2]	1946-47
644-7d	India	v	West Indies	Kanpur	1978-79
644-8d	West Indies	v	India	Delhi	1958-59
636	England	v	Australia	Sydney	1928-29
633-5d	England	v	India	Birmingham	1979
631-8d	West Indies	v	India	Kingston	1961-62
631	West Indies	v	India	Delhi	1948-49
629-6d	West Indies	v	India	Bombay[2]	1948-49
629	England	v	India	Lord's	1974
627-9d	England	v	Australia	Manchester	1934
624	Pakistan	v	Australia	Adelaide	1983-84
622-9d	South Africa	v	Australia	Durban[2]	1969-70
620	South Africa	v	Australia	Johannesburg[3]	1966-67
619-6d	England	v	West Indies	Nottingham	1957
619	Australia	v	West Indies	Sydney	1968-69
617	Australia	v	Pakistan	Faisalabad	1979-80
616-5d	Pakistan	v	New Zealand	Auckland	1988-89
616	West Indies	v	Australia	Adelaide	1968-69
614-5d	West Indies	v	India	Calcutta	1958-59
611	England	v	Australia	Manchester	1964
608-7d	Pakistan	v	England	Birmingham	1971
608	England	v	South Africa	Johannesburg[2]	1948-49
606	West Indies	v	England	Birmingham	1984
606	India	v	England	The Oval	1990
604-6d	West Indies	v	India	Bombay[3]	1974-75
604	Australia	v	England	Melbourne	1936-37
602-6d	Australia	v	England	Nottingham	1989

601-7d	Australia	v	England	Leeds	1989
601-8d	Australia	v	England	Brisbane[2]	1954-55
600-4d	India	v	Australia	Sydney	1985-86
600-7d	Pakistan	v	England	The Oval	1974
600-9d	Australia	v	West Indies	Port-of-Spain	1954-55
600	Australia	v	England	Melbourne	1924-25

The highest total for Sri Lanka is:

547-8d	Sri Lanka	v	Australia	Colombo (SSC)	1992-93

BOTH TEAMS SCORING 600

Australia (8d-656)	v	England (611)	Manchester	1964

RECORD SECOND INNINGS TOTALS

First innings in brackets (§ After following on.)

671-4	(174)	New Zealand	v	Sri Lanka	Wellington	1990-91
657-8d §	(106)	Pakistan	v	West Indies	Bridgetown	1957-58
654-5	(316)	England	v	South Africa	Durban[2]	1938-39
620	(199)	South Africa	v	Australia	Johannesburg[3]	1966-67
616	(276)	West Indies	v	Australia	Adelaide	1968-69
583-4d	(186)	England	v	West Indies	Birmingham	1957
582	(354)	Australia	v	England	Adelaide	1920-21
581	(267)	Australia	v	England	Sydney	1920-21
578	(328)	Australia	v	South Africa	Melbourne	1910-11
564-8	(133)	West Indies	v	New Zealand	Bridgetown	1971-72
564	(200-9d)	Australia	v	England	Melbourne	1936-37
554	(198)	Australia	v	South Africa	Melbourne	1931-32
551 §	(208)	England	v	South Africa	Nottingham	1947

RECORD FOURTH INNINGS TOTALS

						Runs set in 4th innings
TO WIN						
406-4	India	v	West Indies	Port-of-Spain	1975-76	403
404-3	Australia	v	England	Leeds	1948	404
362-7	Australia	v	West Indies	Georgetown	1977-78	359
348-5	West Indies	v	New Zealand	Auckland	1968-69	345
344-1	West Indies	v	England	Lord's	1984	342
342-8	Australia	v	India	Perth	1977-78	339
332-5	Australia	v	South Africa	Durban[2]	1949-50	336
336-7	England	v	Australia	Melbourne	1928-29	332
317-5	West Indies	v	Pakistan	Georgetown	1957-58	317
315-6	Australia	v	England	Adelaide	1901-02	315
TO TIE						
347	India	v	Australia	Madras[1]	1986-87	

						Runs set in 4th innings
TO DRAW						
654-5	England	v	South Africa	Durban[2]	1938-39	696
429-8	India	v	England	The Oval	1979	438
423-7	South Africa	v	England	The Oval	1947	451
408-5	West Indies	v	England	Kingston	1929-30	836
364-6	India	v	Pakistan	Delhi	1979-80	390
355-8	India	v	West Indies	Bombay[2]	1948-49	361
344-6	Sri Lanka	v	New Zealand	Hamilton	1990-91	418
343-6	India	v	England	Manchester	1990	408
341-9	Pakistan	v	West Indies	Port-of-Spain	1987-88	372
339-9	Australia	v	West Indies	Adelaide	1968-69	360
335-5	England	v	Australia	Adelaide	1990-90	472
329-3	Australia	v	England	Lord's	1975	484
328-3	Australia	v	England	Adelaide	1970-71	469
326-5	South Africa	v	Australia	Sydney	1963-64	409
325-3	India	v	West Indies	Calcutta	1948-49	431
314-7	England	v	Australia	Sydney	1982-83	460

TO LOSE						Losing Margin
445	India	v	Australia	Adelaide	1977-78	47
440	New Zealand	v	England	Nottingham	1973	38
417	England	v	Australia	Melbourne	1976-77	45
411	England	v	Australia	Sydney	1924-25	193
402	Australia	v	England	Manchester	1981	103
376	India	v	England	Manchester	1959	171
370	England	v	Australia	Adelaide	1920-21	119
363	England	v	Australia	Adelaide	1924-25	11
355	India	v	Australia	Brisbane²	1967-68	39
352	West Indies	v	Australia	Sydney	1968-69	382
345	New Zealand	v	England	Nottingham	1983	165
348	Sri Lanka	v	Australia	Hobart	1989-90	173
339	Australia	v	South Africa	Adelaide	1910-11	38
336	Australia	v	England	Adelaide	1928-29	12
336	Pakistan	v	Australia	Melbourne	1989-90	92
335	Australia	v	England	Nottingham	1930	93
335	South Africa	v	New Zealand	Cape Town	1961-62	72
333	Australia	v	England	Melbourne	1894-95	94
333	India	v	Australia	Adelaide	1991-92	38
327	England	v	West Indies	Georgetown	1929-30	289
326	West Indies	v	Australia	Melbourne	1975-76	165
324	India	v	Australia	Brisbane²	1977-78	16
323	England	v	Australia	Melbourne	1936-37	365
316	England	v	West Indies	Kingston	1953-54	140
313	England	v	West Indies	Bridgetown	1953-54	181
310	Australia	v	Pakistan	Melbourne	1978-79	71

RECORD MATCH AGGREGATES - BOTH SIDES

Runs	Wkts						Days Played
1981	35	South Africa	v	England	Durban²	1938-39	§10
1815	34	West Indies	v	England	Kingston	1929-30	†9
1764	39	Australia	v	West Indies	Adelaide	1968-69	5
1753	40	Australia	v	England	Adelaide	1920-21	6
1723	31	England	v	Australia	Leeds	1948	5
1661	36	West Indies	v	Australia	Bridgetown	1954-55	6
1646	40	Australia	v	South Africa	Adelaide	1910-11	6
1644	38	Australia	v	West Indies	Sydney	1968-69	6
1640	24	West Indies	v	Australia	Bridgetown	1964-65	6
1640	33	Australia	v	Pakistan	Melbourne	1972-73	5
1619	20	Australia	v	England	Melbourne	1924-25	7
1614	30	England	v	India	Manchester	1990	5
1611	40	Australia	v	England	Sydney	1924-25	7
1603	28	England	v	India	Lord's	1990	5
1601	29	England	v	Australia	Lord's	1930	4
1585	31	Pakistan	v	New Zealand	Karachi	1976-77	5
1562	37	Australia	v	England	Melbourne	1946-47	6
1554	35	Australia	v	England	Melbourne	1928-29	8
1541	35	Australia	v	England	Sydney	1903-04	6
1528	24	West Indies	v	England	Port-of-Spain	1953-54	6
1514	40	Australia	v	England	Sydney	1894-95	6
1507	28	England	v	West Indies	The Oval	1976	5
1505	25	New Zealand	v	India	Auckland	1989-90	5
1502	29	Australia	v	England	Adelaide	1946-47	6

§ No play on one day. † No play on two days.

RECORD MATCH AGGREGATES - ONE SIDE

Runs	Wkts					
1121	19	England	v	West Indies	Kingston	1929-30
1028	20	Australia	v	England	The Oval	1934
1013	18	Australia	v	West Indies	Sydney	1968-69
1011	20	South Africa	v	England	Durban[2]	1938-39

LOWEST COMPLETED INNINGS TOTALS

26	New Zealand	v	England	Auckland	1954-55
30	South Africa	v	England	Port Elizabeth	1895-96
30	South Africa	v	England	Birmingham	1924
35	South Africa	v	England	Cape Town	1898-99
36	Australia	v	England	Birmingham	1902
36	South Africa	v	Australia	Melbourne	1931-32
42	Australia	v	England	Sydney	1887-88
42	New Zealand	v	Australia	Wellington	1945-46
42 §	India	v	England	Lord's	1974
43	South Africa	v	England	Cape Town	1888-89
44	Australia	v	England	The Oval	1896
45	England	v	Australia	Sydney	1886-87
45	South Africa	v	Australia	Melbourne	1931-32
47	South Africa	v	England	Cape Town	1888-89
47	New Zealand	v	England	Lord's	1958
52	England	v	Australia	The Oval	1948
53	England	v	Australia	Lord's	1888
53	Australia	v	England	Lord's	1896
53	West Indies	v	Pakistan	Faisalabad	1986-87
54	New Zealand	v	Australia	Wellington	1945-46
58	South Africa	v	England	Lord's	1912
58 §	Australia	v	England	Brisbane[2]	1936-37
58	India	v	Australia	Brisbane[2]	1947-48
58	India	v	England	Manchester	1952
60	Australia	v	England	Lord's	1888
61	Australia	v	England	Melbourne	1901-02
61	England	v	Australia	Melbourne	1903-04
62	England	v	Australia	Lord's	1888
62	Pakistan	v	Australia	Perth	1981-82
63	Australia	v	England	The Oval	1882
64	England	v	New Zealand	Wellington	1977-78
65	England	v	Australia	Sydney	1894-95
65	Australia	v	England	The Oval	1912
65	New Zealand	v	England	Christchurch	1970-71

§ One batsman absent hurt/ill.

The lowest completed innings total by Sri Lanka is :

82	Sri Lanka	v	India	Chandigarh	1990-91

The following innings closed at a low total:

32-7d	Australia	v	England	Brisbane[2]	1950-51
35-8	Australia	v	England	Manchester	1953
48-8	New Zealand	v	England	Christchurch	1965-66
51-6d	West Indies	v	England	Bridgetown	1934-35

DISMISSED FOR UNDER 100 IN BOTH INNINGS

42	82	Australia	v	England	Sydney	1887-88
53	62	England	v	Australia	Lord's	1888
81	70	Australia	v	England	Manchester	1888
47	43	South Africa	v	England	Cape Town	1888-89
97	83	South Africa	v	England	Cape Town	1891-92
65	72	England	v	Australia	Sydney	1894-95
93	30	South Africa	v	England	Port Elizabeth	1895-96
95	93	South Africa	v	England	The Oval	1912
36	45	South Africa	v	Australia	Melbourne	1931-32
42	54	New Zealand	v	Australia	Wellington	1945-46
58	98	India	v	Australia	Brisbane[2]	1947-48
58	82	India	v	England	Manchester	1952
89	86	West Indies	v	England	The Oval	1957
47	74	New Zealand	v	England	Lord's	1958
82	93	England	v	New Zealand	Christchurch	1983-84

RESULTS BY NARROW MARGINS - TIE

Australia	v	West Indies	Brisbane[2]	1960-61
India	v	Australia	Madras[1]	1986-87

RESULTS BY NARROW MARGINS - WON BY ONE WICKET

				10th Wicket Partnership	
England	v	Australia	The Oval	15*	1902
South Africa	v	England	Johannesburg[2]	48*	1905-06
England	v	Australia	Melbourne	39*	1907-08
England	v	South Africa	Cape Town	5*	1922-23
Australia	v	West Indies	Melbourne	38*	1951-52
New Zealand	v	West Indies	Dunedin	4*	1979-80

** (unbroken)*

RESULTS BY NARROW MARGINS - WON BY TWO WICKETS

England	v	Australia	The Oval	1890
Australia	v	England	Sydney	1907-08
§England	v	South Africa	Durban[2]	1948-49
Australia	v	West Indies	Melbourne	1960-61
India	v	Australia	Bombay[2]	1964-65
Australia	v	India	Perth	1977-78
West Indies	v	England	Nottingham	1980
New Zealand	v	Pakistan	Dunedin	1984-85
West Indies	v	Pakistan	Bridgetown	1987-88
Pakistan	v	England	Lord's	1992

§ England won by a leg bye off the last possible ball

RESULTS BY NARROW MARGINS - LESS THAN TWENTY RUNS

3	Australia	v	England	Manchester	1902
3	England	v	Australia	Melbourne	1982-83
6	Australia	v	England	Sydney	1884-85
7	Australia	v	England	The Oval	1882
10	England	v	Australia	Sydney	1894-95
11	Australia	v	England	Adelaide	1924-25
12	England	v	Australia	Adelaide	1928-29
13	England	v	Australia	Sydney	1886-87
16	Australia	v	India	Brisbane[2]	1977-78
16	Pakistan	v	India	Bangalore	1986-87
16	Australia	v	Sri Lanka	Colombo (SSC)	1992-93
17	South Africa	v	England	Johannesburg[3]	1956-57
18	England	v	Australia	Leeds	1981
19	South Africa	v	England	Johannesburg[1]	1909-10

At Port-of-Spain in 1934-35, West Indies took England's last second innings wicket with the fifth ball of the last possible over to win by 217 runs.

DRAWS

	Target	Total	Opponents		
India	361	355-8	West Indies	Bombay[2]	1948-49
England	234	228-9	West Indies	Lord's	1963
Australia	360	339-9	West Indies	Adelaide	1968-69
Australia	246	238-8	England	Melbourne	1974-75
India	438	429-8	England	The Oval	1979
Australia	247	230-9	New Zealand	Melbourne	1987-88
Pakistan	372	341-9	West Indies	Port-of-Spain	1987-88

LOWEST MATCH AGGREGATES

(Completed match)

Runs	Wkts						Days Played
234	29	Australia	v	South Africa	Melbourne	1931-32	§3
291	40	England	v	Australia	Lord's	1888	2
295	28	New Zealand	v	Australia	Wellington	1945-46	2
309	29	West Indies	v	England	Bridgetown	1934-35	3
323	30	England	v	Australia	Manchester	1888	2
363	40	England	v	Australia	The Oval	1882	2
374	40	Australia	v	England	Sydney	1887-88	†5
378	30	England	v	South Africa	The Oval	1912	2
382	30	South Africa	v	England	Cape Town	1888-89	2
389	38	England	v	Australia	The Oval	1890	2
390	30	England	v	New Zealand	Lord's	1958	3
392	40	England	v	Australia	The Oval	1896	3

§ No play on one day. † No play on two days.

GREATEST TEST VICTORIES

Inns and 579 runs	England	v	Australia	The Oval	1938
Inns and 336 runs	West Indies	v	India	Calcutta	1958-59
Inns and 332 runs	Australia	v	England	Brisbane[2]	1946-47
Inns and 285 runs	England	v	India	Lord's	1974
Inns and 259 runs	Australia	v	South Africa	Port Elizabeth	1949-50
Inns and 237 runs	England	v	West Indies	The Oval	1957
Inns and 230 runs	England	v	Australia	Adelaide	1891-92
Inns and 226 runs	Australia	v	India	Brisbane[2]	1947-48
Inns and 226 runs	West Indies	v	England	Lord's	1973
Inns and 225 runs	England	v	Australia	Melbourne	1911-12
Inns and 217 runs	England	v	Australia	The Oval	1886
Inns and 217 runs	Australia	v	West Indies	Brisbane[1]	1930-31
Inns and 215 runs	England	v	New Zealand	Auckland	1962-63
Inns and 207 runs	England	v	India	Manchester	1952
Inns and 202 runs	England	v	South Africa	Cape Town	1888-89
Inns and 200 runs	Australia	v	England	Melbourne	1936-37
675 runs	England	v	Australia	Brisbane[1]	1928-29
562 runs	Australia	v	England	The Oval	1934
530 runs	Australia	v	South Africa	Melbourne	1910-11
425 runs	West Indies	v	England	Manchester	1976
409 runs	Australia	v	England	Lord's	1948
408 runs	West Indies	v	Australia	Adelaide	1979-80
382 runs	Australia	v	England	Adelaide	1894-95
382 runs	Australia	v	West Indies	Sydney	1968-69
377 runs	Australia	v	England	Sydney	1920-21
365 runs	Australia	v	England	Melbourne	1936-37
348 runs	Australia	v	Pakistan	Melbourne	1976-77
343 runs	West Indies	v	Australia	Bridgetown	1990-91
338 runs	England	v	Australia	Adelaide	1932-33
326 runs	West Indies	v	England	Lord's	1950
323 runs	South Africa	v	Australia	Port Elizabeth	1969-70
322 runs	England	v	Australia	Brisbane[2]	1936-37
312 runs	England	v	South Africa	Cape Town	1956-57

England batsman John Lever is caught behind by Rodney Marsh from the bowling of Dennis Lillee during the Centenary Test played at Melbourne in March 1977. In attaining his 188th wicketkeeping dismissal, Marsh broke Wally Grout's long-standing record of 187.

(Courtesy the Melbourne Herald and Weekly Times.*)*

Pakistan's finest allrounder Imran Khan forcing through the off-side field during his innings of 33 against Australia at Melbourne in March 1979.

(Courtesy David Syme & Co. Limited.)

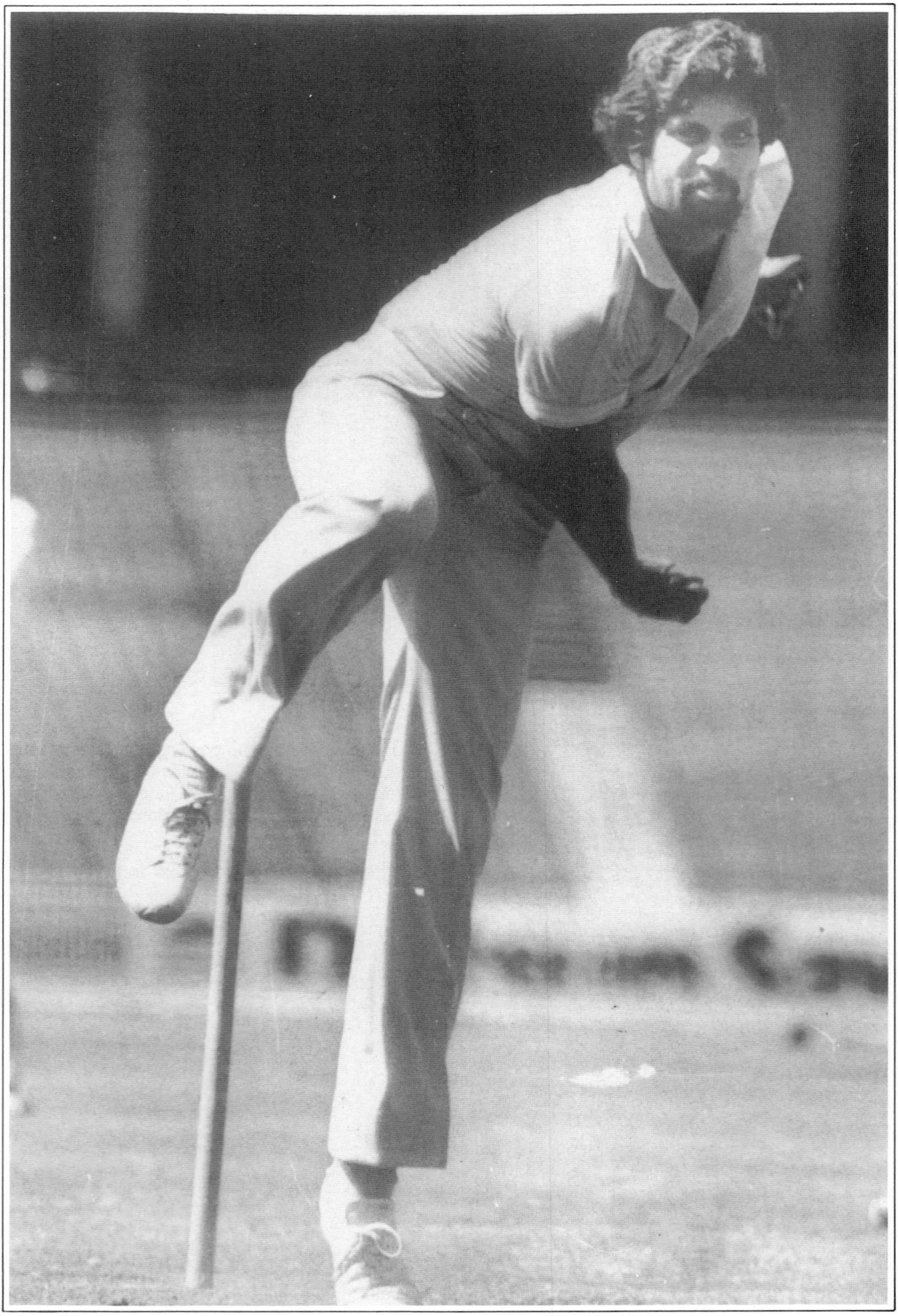

India's greatest fast bowler, Kapil Dev, in action at Melbourne during the 1980-81 tour of Australia. *(Courtesy the Melbourne* Herald and Weekly Times.*)*

VICTORY LOSING FEWEST WICKETS

TWO WICKETS

England (2d-531)	v	South Africa (273 + 240)	Lord's	1924
England (2d-267)	v	New Zealand (67 + 129)	Leeds	1958
England (2d-459)	v	India (165 + 216)	Birmingham	1974

VICTORY AFTER FOLLOWING-ON

England (325 + 437)	beat	Australia (586 +166) by 10 runs	Sydney	1894-95
England (174 + 356)	beat	Australia (9d-401 + 111) by 12 runs	Leeds	1981

LONGEST MATCHES

10 days	South Africa	v	England	Durban[2]	1938-39
9 days	West Indies	v	England	Kingston	1929-30
8 days	Australia	v	England	Melbourne	1928-29

MATCHES COMPLETED IN TWO DAYS

England	(101 + 77)	v	Australia	(63 + 122)	The Oval	1882
England	(53 + 62)	v	Australia	(116 + 60)	Lord's	1888
England	(317)	v	Australia	(80 + 100)	The Oval	1888
England	(172)	v	Australia	(81 + 70)	Manchester	1888
South Africa	(84 + 129)	v	England	(148 + 2-67)	Port Elizabeth	1888-89
South Africa	(47 + 43)	v	England	(292)	Cape Town	1888-89
England	(100 + 8-95)	v	Australia	(92 + 102)	The Oval	1890
South Africa	(93 + 30)	v	England	(185 + 226)	Port Elizabeth	1895-96
South Africa	(115 + 117)	v	England	(265)	Cape Town	1895-96
England	(176 + 0-14)	v	South Africa	(95 + 93)	The Oval	1912
Australia	(448)	v	South Africa	(265 + 95)	Manchester	1912
England	(112 + 147)	v	Australia	(232 + 0-30)	Nottingham	1921
Australia	(8d-328)	v	West Indies	(99 + 107)	Melbourne	1930-31
South Africa	(157 + 98)	v	Australia	(439)	Johannesburg[1]	1935-36
New Zealand	(42 + 54)	v	Australia	(8d-199)	Wellington	1945-46

COMPLETE SIDE DISMISSED TWICE IN A DAY

					Day	
India	(58 + 82)	v	England	Manchester	3rd	1952

BATSMEN'S PARADISE

(Over 60 runs per wicket)

Runs per Wkt	Runs-Wkts					
109.30	(1093-10)	India	v	New Zealand	Delhi	1955-56
99.40	(994-10)	West Indies	v	New Zealand	Georgetown	1971-72
86.87	(695-8)	New Zealand	v	England	Wellington	1987-88
83.25	(999-12)	Pakistan	v	Australia	Faisalabad	1979-80
82.27	(905-11)	England	v	Pakistan	Birmingham	1992
80.53	(1208-15)	Pakistan	v	India	Lahore[2]	1989-90
79.53	(1034-13)	Pakistan	v	Sri Lanka	Faisalabad	1985-86
78.25	(1252-16)	India	v	West Indies	Calcutta	1987-88
73.37	(1174-16)	Pakistan	v	India	Faisalabad	1984-85
73.06	(1096-15)	India	v	West Indies	Kanpur	1978-79
70.61	(1271-18)	England	v	Australia	Manchester	1964
68.33	(1640-24)	West Indies	v	Australia	Bridgetown	1964-65
66.95	(1406-21)	West Indies	v	Pakistan	Kingston	1957-58
65.35	(1307-20)	England	v	Australia	Manchester	1934
65.00	(1235-19)	India	v	West Indies	Bombay[2]	1948-49
64.81	(1037-16)	Pakistan	v	India	Karachi	1989-90
64.75	(1036-16)	India	v	New Zealand	Hyderabad	1955-56
64.47	(1096-17)	India	v	Sri Lanka	Kanpur	1986-87
63.66	(1528-24)	West Indies	v	England	Port-of-Spain	1953-54
63.41	(1078-17)	India	v	Australia	Bombay[3]	1986-87

62.33	(1496-24)	England	v	Australia	Nottingham	1938
62.11	(1118-18)	New Zealand	v	Pakistan	Auckland	1988-89
62.00	(1116-18)	West Indies	v	England	Bridgetown	1959-60
61.86	(1423-23)	England	v	India	The Oval	1990
61.52	(1042-17)	India	v	Pakistan	Madras[2]	1960-61
60.94	(1158-12)	India	v	England	Kanpur	1984-85
60.62	(1455-24)	New Zealand	v	Australia	Wellington	1973-74
60.57	(1272-21)	Pakistan	v	India	Faisalabad	1978-79
60.45	(1209-20)	Australia	v	England	Adelaide	1986-87
60.20	(1505-25)	New Zealand	v	India	Auckland	1989-90

HIGHEST SCORES FOR EACH BATTING POSITION

No							
1	364	L.Hutton	England	v	Australia	The Oval	1938
2	325	A.Sandham	England	v	West Indies	Kingston	1929-30
3	365*	G.S.Sobers	West Indies	v	Pakistan	Kingston	1957-58
4	307	R.M.Cowper	Australia	v	England	Melbourne	1965-66
5	304	D.G.Bradman	Australia	v	England	Leeds	1934
6	250	K.D.Walters	Australia	v	New Zealand	Christchurch	1976-77
7	270	D.G.Bradman	Australia	v	England	Melbourne	1936-37
8	209	Imtiaz Ahmed	Pakistan	v	New Zealand	Lahore[1]	1955-56
9	173	I.D.S.Smith	New Zealand	v	India	Auckland	1989-90
10	117	W.W.Read	England	v	Australia	The Oval	1884
11	68*	R.O.Collinge	New Zealand	v	Pakistan	Auckland	1972-73

HIGHEST SCORE AT THE FALL OF EACH WICKET

1st	413	India (3d-537)	v	New Zealand	Madras[2]	1955-56
2nd	533	West Indies (3d-790)	v	Pakistan	Kingston	1957-58
3rd	615	New Zealand (4-671)	v	Sri Lanka	Wellington	1990-91
4th	671	New Zealand (4-671)	v	Sri Lanka	Wellington	1990-91
5th	720	England (849)	v	West Indies	Kingston	1929-30
6th	770	England (7d-903)	v	Australia	The Oval	1938
7th	876	England (7d-903)	v	Australia	The Oval	1938
8th	813	England (849)	v	West Indies	Kingston	1929-30
9th	821	England (849)	v	West Indies	Kingston	1929-30
10th	849	England (849)	v	West Indies	Kingston	1929-30

LOWEST SCORE AT THE FALL OF EACH WICKET

1st	0	Numerous instances				
2nd	0	Numerous instances				
3rd	0	{Australia(7d-32)	v	England	Brisbane[2]	1950-51
		{India (165)	v	England	Leeds	1952
4th	0	India (165)	v	England	Leeds	1952
5th	6	India (98)	v	England	The Oval	1952
6th	7	Australia (70)	v	England	Manchester	1888
7th	14	Australia (44)	v	England	The Oval	1896
8th	19	Australia (44)	v	England	The Oval	1896
9th	25	Australia (44)	v	England	The Oval	1896
10th	26	New Zealand (26)	v	England	Auckland	1954-55

MOST CENTURIES IN AN INNINGS

5	Australia (8d-758)	v	West Indies	Kingston	1954-55
4	England (8d-658)	v	Australia	Nottingham	1938
4	West Indies (631)	v	India	Delhi	1948-49
4	Pakistan (652)	v	India	Faisalabad	1982-83
4	West Indies (550)	v	India	St John's	1982-83

The most fifties in a Test innings is seven by England (9d-627) v Australia at Manchester in 1934.

MOST CENTURIES IN A MATCH (BOTH TEAMS)

7	England (4)	v	Australia (3)	Nottingham	1938
7	West Indies (2)	v	Australia (5)	Kingston	1954-55

The most fifties in a Test match is 17 by Australia (10) and West Indies (7) at Adelaide in 1968-69.

MOST CENTURIES IN A SERIES (ONE TEAM)

				Venue		Tests
12	Australia	v	West Indies	West Indies	1954-55	5
12	Pakistan	v	India	Pakistan	1982-83	6
11	England	v	South Africa	South Africa	1938-39	5
11	West Indies	v	India	India	1948-49	5
11	Australia	v	South Africa	South Africa	1949-50	5
11	India	v	West Indies	India	1978-79	6

MOST CENTURIES IN A SERIES (BOTH TEAMS)

				Venue		Tests
21	West Indies (9)	v	Australia (12)	West Indies	1954-55	5
17	Australia (9)	v	England (8)	Australia	1928-29	5
17	South Africa (6)	v	England (11)	South Africa	1938-39	5
17	Pakistan (12)	v	India (5)	Pakistan	1982-83	6
16	India (5)	v	West Indies (11)	India	1948-49	5
16	Australia (10)	v	West Indies (6)	Australia	1968-69	5
16	Australia (10)	v	West Indies (6)	Australia	1975-76	6
15	Australia (10)	v	England (5)	Australia	1946-47	5

TEAM UNCHANGED THROUGHOUT A SERIES

			Venue		Tests
England	v	Australia	Australia	1884-85	5
South Africa	v	England	South Africa	1905-06	5
England	v	Australia	Australia	1881-82	4
Australia	v	England	England	1884	3
Australia	v	England	England	1893	3
Pakistan	v	New Zealand	Pakistan	1964-65	3
Australia	v	New Zealand	New Zealand	1981-82	3
West Indies	v	Australia	West Indies	1990-91	5

MOST PLAYERS ENGAGED BY ONE SIDE IN A SERIES

				Venue	
30 in 5 Tests	England	v	Australia	England	1921
29 in 6 Tests	England	v	Australia	England	1989
28 in 5 Tests	Australia	v	England	Australia	1884-85
27 in 4 Tests	West Indies	v	England	West Indies	1929-30
26 in 5 Tests	India	v	Pakistan	India	1952-53
25 in 4 Tests	England	v	West Indies	England	1950
25 in 5 Tests	England	v	Australia	England	1909
25 in 5 Tests	England	v	South Africa	England	1935
25 in 5 Tests	England	v	South Africa	England	1955

South Africa used 20 players in the 3-match rubber of 1895-96 against England in South Africa.

WINNING EVERY TEST IN A SERIES (Minimum: 4 matches)

			Venue		Tests
Australia	v	England	Australia	1920-21	5
Australia	v	South Africa	Australia	1931-32	5
England	v	India	England	1959	5
West Indies	v	India	West Indies	1961-62	5
Australia	v	India	Australia	1967-68	4
South Africa	v	Australia	South Africa	1969-70	4
West Indies	v	England	England	1984	5
West Indies	v	England	West Indies	1985-86	5

The following countries won 6-match series in Australia by 5 Tests to one: Australia (v West Indies 1975-76) England (v Australia 1978-79).

MOST CONSECUTIVE WINS

11	West Indies	Bridgetown	1983-84	to	Adelaide	1984-85
8	Australia	Sydney	1920-21	to	Leeds	1921
7	England	Melbourne	1884-85	to	Sydney	1887-88
7	England	Lord's	1928	to	Adelaide	1928-29
7	West Indies	Bridgetown	1984-85	to	St John's	1985-86
7	West Indies	Lord's	1988	to	Melbourne	1988-89
6	England	The Oval	1888	to	The Oval	1890
6	England	Leeds	1957	to	Manchester	1958
6	West Indies	Port-of-Spain	1961-62	to	Manchester	1963

MOST CONSECUTIVE MATCHES WITHOUT DEFEAT

27	West Indies	Sydney	1981-82	to	Melbourne	1984-85
26	England	Lord's	1968	to	Manchester	1971
25	Australia	Wellington	1945-46	to	Adelaide	1950-51
18	England	Christchurch	1958-59	to	Birmingham	1961
17	Australia	Madras[2]	1956-57	to	Delhi	1959-60
17	India	Kandy	1985-86	to	Ahmedabad	1986-87
16	Australia	Sydney	1920-21	to	Adelaide	1924-25
16	Pakistan	Karachi	1986-87	to	Port-of-Spain	1987-88
15	England	Melbourne	1911-12	to	Port Elizabeth	1913-14
15	Pakistan	Wellington	1972-73	to	Adelaide	1976-77
15	India	Lord's	1979	to	Calcutta	1979-80
15	West Indies	Christchurch	1979-80	to	Kingston	1980-81
14	Australia	Sydney	1988-89	to	Sydney	1989-90
13	India	Port-of-Spain	1952-53	to	Madras[2]	1955-56
13	Australia	The Oval	1972	to	Wellington	1973-74
12	England	The Oval	1938	to	The Oval	1946
12	Pakistan	Manchester	1954	to	Bridgetown	1957-58
12	England	The Oval	1966	to	Georgetown	1967-68
12	Pakistan	Karachi	1982-83	to	Nagpur	1983-84

MOST CONSECUTIVE DEFEATS

8 †	South Africa	Port Elizabeth	1888-89	to	Cape Town	1898-99
8	England	Sydney	1920-21	to	Leeds	1921
7	Australia	Melbourne	1884-85	to	Sydney	1887-88
7	England	Lord's	1950	to	Adelaide	1950-51
7	India	Leeds	1967	to	Sydney	1967-68
7	England	Kingston	1985-86	to	Leeds	1986
6	South Africa	Melbourne	1910-11	to	Lord's	1912
6	New Zealand	Johannesburg[2]	1953-54	to	Lahore[1]	1955-56
6	India	Nottingham	1959	to	Delhi	1959-60
6	Australia	Bridgetown	1983-84	to	Adelaide	1984-85

† South Africa's first 8 Tests

MOST CONSECUTIVE MATCHES WITHOUT VICTORY

44 †	New Zealand	Christchurch	1929-30	to	Wellington	1955-56
31	India	Bangalore	1981-82	to	Faisalabad	1984-85
28	South Africa	Leeds	1935	to	Port Elizabeth	1949-50
24	India	Lord's	1932	to	Kanpur	1951-52
23	New Zealand	Auckland	1962-63	to	Dunedin	1967-68
22	Pakistan	Lahore[1]	1958-59	to	Christchurch	1964-65
20	West Indies	Wellington	1968-69	to	Port-of-Spain	1972-73
20 §	Sri Lanka	Colombo (PSS)	1985-86	to	Moratuwa	1992-93
18	New Zealand	Dacca	1969-70	to	Wellington	1973-74
18	England	Sydney	1986-87	to	The Oval	1988
16	South Africa	Melbourne	1910-11	to	Cape Town	1921-22
16	Pakistan	Lord's	1967	to	Wellington	1972-73

14	India	Madras[2]	1956-57	to	Delhi	1959-60
14	Australia	Perth	1985-86	to	Melbourne	1928-29
14	India	Georgetown	1988-89	to	The Oval	1990
13	India	Madras[1]	1952-53	to	Hyderabad	1955-56
13	England	Wellington	1983-84	to	Bombay[3]	1984-85
13	Sri Lanka	Colombo (PSS)	1981-82	to	Colombo (SSC)	1985-86
12	South Africa	Cape Town	1922-23	to	Durban[2]	1927-28
12	England	Leeds	1963	to	The Oval	1964
12	England	Nottingham	1980	to	Lord's	1981

† New Zealand's first 44 Tests *§to date.*

MOST CONSECUTIVE DRAWS

10	West Indies	Georgetown	1970-71	to	Bridgetown	1972-73
9	India	Port-of-Spain	1952-53	to	Hyderabad	1955-56
9	India	Calcutta	1959-60	to	Delhi	1961-62

DRAWING EVERY TEST IN A FIVE-MATCH SERIES

Pakistan	v	India	1954-55
India	v	Pakistan	1960-61
India	v	England	1963-64
West Indies	v	New Zealand	1971-72

ELEVEN BATSMEN REACHING DOUBLE FIGURES IN AN INNINGS

				Venue	Lowest Score
1894-95	England (475)	v	Australia	Melbourne	11
1905-06	South Africa (385)	v	England	Johannesburg[2]	10
1928-29	England (636)	v	Australia	Sydney	11
1931-32	South Africa (358)	v	Australia	Melbourne	10*
1947-48	Australia (8d-575)	v	India	Melbourne	11
1952-53	India (397)	v	Pakistan	Calcutta	11
1967-68	India (359)	v	New Zealand	Dunedin	12
1976-77	India (9d-524)	v	New Zealand	Kanpur	10*
1992-93	Australia (471)	v	Sri Lanka	Colombo (SSC)	10*

NO BATSMAN REACHING DOUBLE FIGURES IN A COMPLETED INNINGS

South Africa (30 - highest score 7)	v	England	Birmingham	1924

ONLY FOUR BOWLERS IN AN INNINGS OF OVER 400 RUNS

Australia	v	England (8d-403)	The Oval	1921
South Africa	v	England (8-421)	The Oval	1924
New Zealand	v	England (482)	The Oval	1949
England	v	Australia (426)	Sydney	1950-51
India	v	England (9d-419)	Lord's	1979
India	v	Australia (528)	Adelaide	1980-81
Australia	v	England (404)	Manchester	1981
England	v	India (428)	Bangalore	1981-82
Sri Lanka	v	Pakistan (7d-500)	Lahore[2]	1981-82
Pakistan	v	Australia (6d-454)	Sydney	1983-84
Australia	v	West Indies (8d-468)	Port-of-Spain	1983-84
Australia	v	West Indies (498)	St John's	1983-84
Australia	v	West Indies (416)	Perth	1984-85
Australia	v	England (456)	Nottingham	1985
Pakistan	v	England (447)	Manchester	1987
New Zealand	v	India (482)	Auckland	1989-90
England	v	West Indies (446)	Bridgetown	1989-90
England	v	West Indies (446)	St John's	1989-90

ELEVEN BOWLERS IN AN INNINGS

England	v	Australia (551)	The Oval	1884
Australia	v	Pakistan (2-382)	Faisalabad	1979-80

TWENTY BOWLERS IN A MATCH

South Africa (7d-501 + 346)	v	England (442 + 0-15)	Cape Town	1964-65

MOST RUNS IN ONE DAY

By one team

						Day
503-2	England (0-28 to 2d-531)	v	South Africa	Lord's	1924	2nd
494-6	Australia (6-496)	v	South Africa	Sydney	1910-11	1st
475-2	Australia (2-475)	v	England	The Oval	1934	1st
471-8	England (8d-471)	v	India	The Oval	1936	1st
458-3	Australia (3-458)	v	England	Leeds	1930	1st
455-1	Australia (3-93 to 4-494)	v	England	Leeds	1934	2nd
451-10	South Africa (451 all out)	v	New Zealand	Christchurch	1931-32	2nd
450-10	Australia (450 all out)	v	South Africa	Johannesburg[1]	1921-22	1st

By both teams

						Day
588-6	England (2-173 to 8d-571)	v	India (0-190)	Manchester	1936	2nd
522-2	England (0-28 to 2d-531)	v	South Africa (0-19)	Lord's	1924	2nd
508-8	England (4-313- to 6d-534)	v	South Africa (6-287)	The Oval	1935	3rd
496-4	England (2-121 to 6d-558)	v	Pakistan (0-59)	Nottingham	1952	2nd
492-8	South Africa (6-297 to 476 all out)	v	England (4-313)	The Oval	1935	2nd
491-7	New Zealand (9-312 to 341 all out + 2-195)	v	England (4d-267)	Leeds	1949	3rd
473-4	South Africa (5-283 to 8d-492)	v	England (1-264)	The Oval	1929	3rd
471-9	Australia (3-162 to 389 all out)	v	England (2-244)	The Oval	1921	3rd
469-7	West Indies (6-395 to 498 all out)	v	England (3d-366)	The Oval	1939	3rd
464-11	Australia (448 all out)	v	South Africa (1-16)	Manchester	1912	1st
458-12	Australia (3-239 to 8d-394)	v	West Indies (7-303)	Sydney	1968-69	5th

FEWEST RUNS IN A FULL DAY'S PLAY

						Day
95-12	Australia (80 all out)	v	Pakistan (2-15)	Karachi	1956-57	1st
104-5	Pakistan (5-104)	v	Australia	Karachi	1959-60	4th
106-8	England (2-92 to 198 all out)	v	Australia	Brisbane[2]	1958-59	4th
112-5	Australia (6-138 to 187 all out)	v	Pakistan (1-63)	Karachi	1956-57	4th
115-10	Australia (5-117 to 165 all out + 5-66)	v	Pakistan	Karachi	1988-89	4th
117-5	India (5-117)	v	Australia	Madras[2]	1956-57	1st
117-1	New Zealand (0-6 to 1-123)	v	Sri Lanka	Colombo (SSC)	1983-84	5th

MOST WICKETS IN ONE DAY

						Day
27-157	England (3-18 to 53 all out + 62)	v	Australia (60)	Lord's	1888	2nd
25-221	Australia (112 + 5-48)	v	England (61)	Melbourne	1901-02	1st
24-255	England (1-69 to 145 all out + 5-60)	v	Australia (61)	The Oval	1896	2nd
22-197	Australia (92 + 2-5)	v	England (100)	The Oval	1890	1st
22-207	Australia (82 + 2-0)	v	West Indies (105)	Adelaide	1951-52	1st
22-195	England (7-292 to 9d-347)	v	India (58 + 82)	Manchester	1952	3rd
21-278	England (185 + 1-0)	v	South Africa (93)	Port Elizabeth	1895-96	1st

MOST WICKETS BEFORE LUNCH

						Day
18	Australia (2-32 to 81 out + 70)	v	England	Manchester	1888	2nd

NO WICKETS IN A FULL DAY'S PLAY

				Day	
England (0-283)	v	Australia	Melbourne	3rd	1924-25
West Indies (6-187 to 6-494)	v	Australia	Bridgetown	4th	1954-55
India (0-234)	v	New Zealand	Madras²	1st	1955-56
West Indies (1-147 to 1-504)	v	Pakistan	Kingston	3rd	1957-58
West Indies (3-279 to 3-486)	v	England §	Bridgetown	5th	1959-60
West Indies (2-81 to 2-291)	v	England	Kingston	3rd	1959-60
Australia (0-263)	v	West Indies	Bridgetown	1st	1964-65
West Indies (7-310 to 7d-365)	v	New Zealand (0-163)	Georgetown	3rd	1971-72
India (1-70 to 1d-361)	v	West Indies 0-15)	Calcutta	4th	1978-79
India (2-178 to 395-2)	v	England	Madras²	2nd	1981-82
Sri Lanka (3-83 to 3-323)	v	Pakistan	Colombo (PSS)	5th	1985-86
Australia (0-301)	v	England	Nottingham	1st	1989

§ G.S.Sobers (226) and F.M.M.Worrell (197) added 399 for the fourth wicket in the longest partnership in Test cricket (579 minutes) and remain the only pair of batsmen to bat throughout two consecutive days of Test cricket, although the final hour of the fourth day was lost to rain and a rest day intervened.*
The following pairs of batsmen have batted throughout one full day's play in the above matches: J.B.Hobbs and H.Sutcliffe (1924-25), D.S.Atkinson and C.C.Depeiza (1954-55), M.H.Mankad and Pankaj Roy (1955-56), C.C.Hunte and G.S.Sobers (1957-58) W.M.Lawry and R.B.Simpson (1964-65), G.R.Viswanath and Yashpal Sharma (1981-82), A.P.Gurusinha and A.Ranatunga (1985-86), and G.R.Marsh and M.A.Taylor (1989).

EXTRAS TOP SCORING IN A COMPLETED INNINGS

	Total	HS	Extras	Opponents		
South Africa	58	13	17	England	Lord's	1912
South Africa	30	7	11	England	Birmingham	1924
New Zealand	97	19	20	England	Nottingham	1973
England	126	24	25	West Indies	Manchester	1976
England	227	33	46	Pakistan	Lord's	1982
Australia	200	29	36	West Indies	St John's	1983-84
England	315	47	59	West Indies	Port-of-Spain	1985-86
New Zealand	160	33	38	Pakistan	Lahore²	1990-91
Australia	248	47	53	West Indies	Georgetown	1990-91

60 OR MORE EXTRAS IN AN INNINGS

71 (B 21, LB 8, NB 38, W 4)	Pakistan (435)	v	West Indies	Georgetown	1987-88
68 (B 29, LB 11, NB 28)	Pakistan (291)	v	West Indies	Bridgetown	1976-77
64 (B 12, LB 25, NB 27)	India (565)	v	West Indies	Calcutta	1987-88
61 (B 17, LB 17, NB 25, W 2)	Pakistan (9-341)	v	West Indies	Port-of-Spain	1987-88
61 (B 6, LB 23, NB 29, W 3)	Australia (6d-602)	v	England	Nottingham	1989
60 (B 4, LB 27, NB 18, W 11)	England (5d-633)	v	India	Birmingham	1979

25 OR MORE BYES IN AN INNINGS

37	Australia (327)	v	England	The Oval	1934
33	India (390)	v	England	Bombay²	1961-62
33	West Indies (9d-391)	v	England	Kingston	1967-68
31	New Zealand (387)	v	England	Auckland	1929-30
29	Pakistan (291)	v	West Indies	Bridgetown	1976-77
28	India (372)	v	Pakistan	Delhi	1952-53

25 OR MORE LEG BYES IN AN INNINGS

30	West Indies (5d-411)	v	England	Manchester	1976
27	England (5d-633)	v	India	Birmingham	1979
26	England (8d-452)	v	Pakistan	Birmingham	1978
25	West Indies (509)	v	Australia	Bridgetown	1983-84
25	India (565)	v	West Indies	Calcutta	1987-88

35 OR MORE NO BALLS IN AN INNINGS *(from which no runs were scored by batsmen)*

40	England (310)	v	West Indies	St John's	1985-86
40	Australia (515)	v	West Indies	Adelaide	1988-89
38	Pakistan (435)	v	West Indies	Georgetown	1987-88
37	Australia (234) (2nd innings)	v	West Indies	Perth	1988-89
35	West Indies (8d-596)	v	England	Bridgetown	1973-74
35	England (309)	v	Australia	Brisbane[2]	1982-83
35	Australia (8d-395) (1st innings)	v	West Indies	Perth	1988-89
35	New Zealand (4-671)	v	Sri Lanka	Wellington	1990-91
35	England (419)	v	West Indies	The Oval	1991
35	England (390)	v	Pakistan	Manchester	1992

10 OR MORE WIDES IN AN INNINGS

15	India (288)	v	Pakistan	Faisalabad	1989-90
15	England (260)	v	West Indies	St John's	1989-90
13	England (227)	v	Pakistan	Lord's	1982
12	India (6d-306)	v	West Indies	Kingston	1975-76
11	England (288)	v	Australia	Leeds	1975
11	England (5d-633)	v	India	Birmingham	1979
11	England (521)	v	Pakistan	Birmingham	1987
10	England (252)	v	West Indies	Nottingham	1980
10	England (370)	v	West Indies	The Oval	1980

MOST EXTRAS IN A MATCH

173 (B 37, LB 31, NB 103, W 2) West Indies	v	Pakistan	Bridgetown	1976-77
149 (B 25, LB 34, NB 90) Australia	v	West Indies	Perth	1988-89
140 (B 20, LB 48, NB 71, W 1) Australia	v	West Indies	Adelaide	1988-89
136 (B 28, LB 29, NB 75, W 4) West Indies	v	Australia	Georgetown	1990-91
127 (B 22, LB 38, NB 62, W 5) West Indies	v	England	Bridgetown	1989-90
124 (B 21, LB 36, NB 63, W 4) West Indies	v	England	Antigua	1985-86
122 (B 19, LB 33, NB 58, W 12) England	v	West Indies	Leeds	1976
122 (B 31, LB 39, NB 37, W 15) England	v	India	The Oval	1990

COMPLETED INNINGS WITHOUT EXTRAS

Total	Wicket-keeper					
328	N.S.Tamhane	India	v	Pakistan	Lahore[1]	1954-55
252	W.Farrimond	England	v	South Africa	Durban[2]	1930-31
247	J.M.Parks	England	v	South Africa	Nottingham	1960
236	G.MacGregor	England	v	Australia	Melbourne	1891-92
200	R.W.Marsh	Australia	v	Pakistan	Melbourne	1972-73
174	J.J.Kelly	Australia	v	England	Melbourne	1897-98
128	R.W.Marsh	Australia	v	West Indies	Sydney	1975-76
126	J.Hunter	England	v	Australia	Melbourne	1884-85
111	A.F.A.Lilley	England	v	Australia	Melbourne	1903-04
96	R.W.Taylor	England	v	India	Lord's	1979
94	T.G.Evans	England	v	New Zealand	Birmingham	1958
92	G.MacGregor	England	v	Australia	The Oval	1890
84	T.G.Evans	England	v	Australia	Manchester	1956
77	S.C.Guillen	New Zealand	v	West Indies	Auckland	1955-56
74	T.G.Evans	England	v	New Zealand	Lord's	1958
62	J.M.Blackham	Australia	v	England	Lord's	1888
42	A.P.E.Knott	England	v	India	Lord's	1974
30	H.R.Butt	England	v	South Africa	Port Elizabeth	1895-96
26	T.G.Evans	England	v	New Zealand	Auckland	1954-55

UNUSUAL DISMISSALS

Handled the ball

W.R.Endean (3)	South Africa	v	England	Cape Town	1956-57
A.M.J.Hilditch (29)	Australia	v	Pakistan	Perth	1978-79
Mohsin Khan (58)	Pakistan	v	Australia	Karachi	1982-83
D.L.Haynes (55)	West Indies	v	India	Bombay[3]	1983-84

Obstructed the field

L.Hutton (27)	England	v	South Africa	The Oval	1951

Run out by the bowler

(while backing up before the ball had been bowled)

W.A.Brown (18) by M.H.Mankad	Australia	v	India	Sydney	1947-48
I.R.Redpath (9) by C.C.Griffith	Australia	v	West Indies	Adelaide	1968-69
D.W Randall (13) by E.J.Chatfield	England	v	New Zealand	Christchurch	1977-78
Sikander Bakht (0) by A.G.Hurst	Pakistan	v	Australia	Perth	1978-79

Stumped by a substitute

S.J.Snooke by N.C.Tufnell (sub for H.Strudwick)	South Africa	v	England	Durban[1]	1909-10
Pervez Sajjad by B.E.Congdon (sub for A.E.Dick)	Pakistan	v	New Zealand	Lahore[1]	1964-65

TEN BATSMEN CAUGHT IN AN INNINGS

Australia	v	England	Melbourne	1903-04
South Africa	v	Australia	Melbourne	1931-32
England	v	South Africa	Durban[2]	1948-49
New Zealand	v	England	Leeds	1949
England	v	Pakistan	The Oval	1954
England	v	Australia	Melbourne	1958-59
West Indies	v	Australia	Sydney	1960-61
New Zealand	v	India	Wellington	1967-68
New Zealand	v	West Indies	Auckland	1968-69
New Zealand	v	India	Bombay[2]	1969-70
India	v	West Indies	Port-of-Spain	1970-71
India	v	England	Lord's	1971
Australia	v	England	Nottingham	1972
England	v	India	Madras[1]	1972-73
England	v	West Indies	Lord's	1973
Australia	v	New Zealand	Auckland	1973-74
New Zealand	v	Pakistan	Auckland	1978-79
§England	v	Australia	Brisbane[2]	1982-83
England	v	Australia	Melbourne	1982-83
India	v	West Indies	Bridgetown	1982-83
West Indies	v	India	Bridgetown	1982-83
Sri Lanka	v	Australia	Kandy	1982-83
England	v	New Zealand	Christchurch	1987-88
England	v	West Indies	The Oval	1988
India	v	New Zealand	Hyderabad	1988-89
Pakistan	v	India	Karachi	1989-90
West Indies	v	Australia	Bridgetown	1990-91
Australia	v	India	Perth	1991-92
India	v	Australia	Perth	1991-92

§Australia held nine catches in England's second innings to become the only side to hold 19 catches in a Test.

MOST BATSMEN CAUGHT IN A MATCH

33	Australia	v	India	Perth	1991-92

(of the 36 batsmen dismissed not one was bowled - a unique feat for a completed Test match)

MOST BATSMEN CAUGHT AND BOWLED IN AN INNINGS

4	Australia	v	England	Lord's	1890
4	Australia	v	New Zealand	Sydney	1985-86

MOST BATSMEN CAUGHT AND BOWLED IN A MATCH

6	Australia	v	England	Lord's	1890

MOST BATSMEN BOWLED IN AN INNINGS

9	South Africa	v	England	Cape Town	1888-89

MOST BATSMEN BOWLED IN A MATCH

23	South Africa	v	England	Port Elizabeth	1895-96

MOST BATSMEN LBW IN AN INNINGS

6	England	v	South Africa	Leeds	1955
6	England	v	West Indies	Kingston	1959-60
6	England	v	Pakistan	Karachi	1977-78
6	West Indies	v	England	Kingston	1985-86
6	Pakistan	v	Australia	Melbourne	1989-90
6	India	v	Sri Lanka	Chandigarh	1990-91
6	Pakistan	v	Sri Lanka	Faisalabad	1991-92

MOST BATSMEN LBW IN A MATCH

14	Pakistan	v	Sri Lanka	Faisalabad	1991-92
13	New Zealand	v	England	Auckland	1991-92

MOST BATSMEN RUN OUT IN AN INNINGS

4	India	v	Pakistan	Peshawar	1954-55
4	Australia	v	West Indies	Adelaide	1968-69

MOST BATSMEN RUN OUT IN A MATCH

7	Australia	v	Pakistan	Melbourne	1972-73

MOST BATSMEN STUMPED IN AN INNINGS

5	West Indies	v	India (K.S.More)	Madras[1]	1987-88

MOST BATSMEN STUMPED IN A MATCH

6	Australia	v	England	Sydney	1894-95
6	India	v	England	Madras[1]	1951-52
6	West Indies	v	India (all by K.S.More)	Madras[1]	1987-88

Batting

6000 RUNS IN TESTS

	M	I	Runs	Opponent: A	E	SA	WI	NZ	I	P	SL
S.M.Gavaskar (I)	125	215	**10122**	1550	2483	-	2749	651	-	2089	600
A.R.Border (A)	133	230	**9775**	-	3115	-	1754	1130	1567	1666	543
I.V.A.Richards (W)	121	182	**8540**	2266	2869	-	-	387	1927	1091	-
Javed Miandad (P)	117	178	**8465**	2092	1034	-	714	1815	2228	-	582
D.I.Gower (E)	117	204	**8231**	3269	-	-	1149	1051	1391	1185	186
G.Boycott (E)	108	193	**8114**	2945	-	373	2205	916	1084	591	-
G.S.Sobers (W)	93	160	**8032**	1510	3214	-	-	404	1920	984	-
M.C.Cowdrey (E)	114	188	**7624**	2433	-	1021	1751	1133	653	633	-
G.A.Gooch (E)	99	179	**7573**	1714	-	-	2197	925	1678	683	376
C.G.Greenidge (W)	108	185	**7558**	1819	2318	-	-	882	1678	861	-
C.H.Lloyd (W)	110	175	**7515**	2211	2120	-	-	234	2344	606	-
W.R.Hammond (E)	85	140	**7249**	2852	-	2188	639	1015	555	-	-
G.S.Chappell (A)	87	151	**7110**	-	2619	-	1400	1076	368	1581	66
D.G.Bradman (A)	52	80	**6996**	-	5028	806	447	-	715	-	-
L.Hutton (E)	79	138	**6971**	2428	-	1564	1661	777	522	19	-
D.B.Vengsarkar (E)	116	185	**6868**	1304	1589	-	1596	440	-	1284	655
K.F.Barrington (E)	82	131	**6806**	2111	-	989	1042	594	1355	715	-
D.L.Haynes (W)	102	178	**6644**	1893	2392	-	-	843	990	526	-
R.B.Kanhai (W)	79	137	**6227**	1694	2267	-	-	-	1693	573	-
R.N.Harvey (A)	79	137	**6149**	-	2416	1625	1054	-	775	279	-
G.R.Viswanath (I)	91	155	**6080**	1538	1880	-	1455	585	-	611	11

2000 RUNS IN TESTS

AUSTRALIA	Tests	I	NO	Runs	HS	Avge	100	50
A.R.Border	133	230	42	9775	205	51.99	24	56
G.S.Chappell	87	151	19	7110	247*	53.86	24	31
D.G.Bradman	52	80	10	6996	334	99.94	29	13
R.N.Harvey	79	137	10	6149	205	48.41	21	24
K.D.Walters	74	125	14	5357	250	48.26	15	33
I.M.Chappell	75	136	10	5345	196	42.42	14	26
W.M.Lawry	67	123	12	5234	210	47.15	13	27
R.B.Simpson	62	111	7	4869	311	46.81	10	27
I.R.Redpath	66	120	11	4737	171	43.45	8	31
D.C.Boon	66	121	12	4699	200	43.11	13	20
K.J.Hughes	70	124	6	4415	213	37.41	9	22
R.W.Marsh	96	150	13	3633	132	26.51	3	16
D.M.Jones	52	89	11	3631	216	46.55	11	14
A.R.Morris	46	79	3	3533	206	46.48	12	12
C.Hill	49	89	2	3412	191	39.21	7	19
G.M.Wood	59	112	6	3374	172	31.83	9	12
V.T.Trumper	48	89	8	3163	214*	39.04	8	13
C.C.McDonald	47	83	4	3107	170	39.32	5	17
A.L.Hassett	43	69	3	3073	198*	46.56	10	11
K.R.Miller	55	87	7	2958	147	36.97	7	13
W.W.Armstrong	50	84	10	2863	159*	38.68	6	8
G.R.Marsh	50	93	7	2854	138	33.18	4	15
M.A.Taylor	33	62	4	2842	219	49.00	8	17
K.R.Stackpole	43	80	5	2807	207	37.42	7	14
N.C.O'Neill	42	69	8	2779	181	45.55	6	15
G.N.Yallop	39	70	3	2756	268	41.13	8	9
S.J.McCabe	39	62	5	2748	232	48.21	6	13
W.Bardsley	41	66	5	2469	193*	40.47	6	14
W.M.Woodfull	35	54	4	2300	161	46.00	7	13

	Tests	I	NO	Runs	HS	Avge	100	50
P.J.P.Burge	42	68	8	2290	181	38.16	4	12
S.E.Gregory	58	100	7	2282	201	24.53	4	8
R.Benaud	63	97	7	2201	122	24.45	3	9
C.G.Macartney	35	55	4	2131	170	41.78	7	9
W.H.Ponsford	29	48	4	2122	266	48.22	7	6
S.R.Waugh	44	67	11	2097	177*	37.44	3	13
R.M.Cowper	27	46	2	2061	307	46.84	5	10

ENGLAND	Tests	I	NO	Runs	HS	Avge	100	50
D.I.Gower	117	204	18	8231	215	44.25	18	39
G.Boycott	108	193	23	8114	246*	47.72	22	42
M.C.Cowdrey	114	188	15	7624	182	44.06	22	38
G.A.Gooch	99	179	6	7573	333	43.77	17	41
W.R.Hammond	85	140	16	7249	336*	58.45	22	24
L.Hutton	79	138	15	6971	364	56.67	19	33
K.F.Barrington	82	131	15	6806	256	58.67	20	35
D.C.S.Compton	78	131	15	5807	278	50.06	17	28
J.B.Hobbs	61	102	7	5410	211	56.94	15	28
I.T.Botham	102	161	6	5200	208	33.54	14	22
J.H.Edrich	77	127	9	5138	310*	43.54	12	24
T.W.Graveney	79	123	13	4882	258	44.38	11	20
A.J.Lamb	80	139	10	4656	142	36.09	14	18
H.Sutcliffe	54	84	9	4555	194	60.73	16	23
P.B.H.May	66	106	9	4537	285*	46.77	13	22
E.R.Dexter	62	102	8	4502	205	47.89	9	27
A.P.E.Knott	95	149	15	4389	135	32.75	5	30
M.W.Gatting	68	117	14	3870	207	37.57	9	18
D.L.Amiss	50	88	10	3612	262*	46.30	11	11
A.W.Greig	58	93	4	3599	148	40.43	8	20
E.H.Hendren	51	83	9	3525	205*	47.63	7	21
F.E.Woolley	64	98	7	3283	154	36.07	5	23
K.W.R.Fletcher	59	96	14	3272	216	39.90	7	19
M.Leyland	41	65	5	2764	187	46.06	9	10
R.A.Smith	36	66	14	2645	148*	50.86	7	18
C.Washbrook	37	66	6	2569	195	42.81	6	12
B.L.D'Oliveira	44	70	8	2484	158	40.06	5	15
D.W.Randall	47	79	5	2470	174	33.37	7	12
W.J.Edrich	39	63	2	2440	219	40.00	6	13
T.G.Evans	91	133	14	2439	104	20.49	2	8
L.E.G.Ames	47	72	12	2434	149	40.56	8	7
W.Rhodes	58	98	21	2325	179	30.19	2	11
T.E.Bailey	61	91	14	2290	134*	29.74	1	10
M.J.K.Smith	50	78	6	2278	121	31.63	3	11
P.E.Richardson	34	56	1	2061	126	37.47	5	9

SOUTH AFRICA	Tests	I	NO	Runs	HS	Avge	100	50
B.Mitchell	42	80	9	3471	189*	48.88	8	21
A.D.Nourse	34	62	7	2960	231	53.81	9	14
H.W.Taylor	42	76	4	2936	176	40.77	7	17
E.J.Barlow	30	57	2	2516	201	45.74	6	15
T.L.Goddard	41	78	5	2516	112	34.46	1	18
D.J.McGlew	34	64	6	2440	255*	42.06	7	10
J.H.B.Waite	50	86	7	2405	134	30.44	4	16
R.G.Pollock	23	41	4	2256	274	60.97	7	11
A.W.Nourse	45	83	8	2234	111	29.78	1	15
R.A.McLean	40	73	3	2120	142	30.28	5	10

WEST INDIES	Tests	I	NO	Runs	HS	Avge	100	50
I.V.A.Richards	121	182	12	8540	291	50.23	24	45
G.S.Sobers	93	160	21	8032	365*	57.78	26	30
C.G.Greenidge	108	185	16	7558	226	44.72	19	34
C.H.Lloyd	110	175	14	7515	242*	46.67	19	39
D.L.Haynes	103	180	21	6725	184	42.29	16	37
R.B.Kanhai	79	137	6	6227	256	47.53	15	28
R.B.Richardson	63	109	10	4693	194	47.40	14	18
E.D.Weekes	48	81	5	4455	207	58.61	15	19
A.I.Kallicharran	66	109	10	4399	187	44.43	12	21
R.C.Fredericks	59	109	7	4334	169	42.49	8	26
F.M.M.Worrell	51	87	9	3860	261	49.48	9	22
C.L.Walcott	44	74	7	3798	220	56.68	15	14
P.J.L.Dujon	81	115	11	3322	139	31.94	5	16
C.C.Hunte	44	78	6	3245	260	45.06	8	13
H.A.Gomes	60	91	11	3171	143	39.63	9	13
B.F.Butcher	44	78	6	3104	209*	43.11	7	16
S.M.Nurse	29	54	1	2523	258	47.60	6	10
A.L.Logie	52	78	9	2470	130	35.79	2	16
G.A.Headley	22	40	4	2190	270*	60.83	10	5
J.B.Stollmeyer	32	56	5	2159	160	42.33	4	12
L.G.Rowe	30	49	2	2047	302	43.55	7	7

NEW ZEALAND	Tests	I	NO	Runs	HS	Avge	100	50
J.G.Wright	77	138	6	4964	185	37.60	12	21
M.D.Crowe	59	98	10	4205	299	47.78	13	14
B.E.Congdon	61	114	7	3448	176	32.22	7	19
J..R.Reid	58	108	5	3428	142	33.28	6	22
R.J.Hadlee	86	134	19	3124	151*	27.16	2	15
G.M.Turner	41	73	6	2991	259	44.64	7	14
B.Sutcliffe	42	76	8	2727	230*	40.10	5	15
M.G.Burgess	50	92	6	2684	119*	31.20	5	14
J.V.Coney	52	85	14	2668	174*	37.57	3	16
G.P.Howarth	47	83	5	2531	147	32.44	6	11
G.T.Dowling	39	77	3	2306	239	31.16	3	11

INDIA	Tests	I	NO	Runs	HS	Avge	100	50
S.M.Gavaskar	125	214	16	10122	236*	51.12	34	45
D.B.Vengsarkar	116	185	22	6868	166	42.13	17	35
G.R.Viswanath	91	155	10	6080	222	41.93	14	35
Kapil Dev	115	168	13	4690	163	30.25	7	24
M.Amarnath	69	113	10	4378	138	42.50	11	24
R.J.Shastri	76	115	14	3760	206	37.22	11	12
P.R.Umrigar	59	94	8	3631	223	42.22	12	14
V.L.Manjrekar	55	92	10	3208	189*	39.12	7	15
M.Azharuddin	46	70	3	3168	199	47.28	11	10
C.G.Borde	55	97	11	3061	177*	35.59	5	18
Nawab of Pataudi, jr	46	83	3	2793	203*	34.91	6	16
S.M.H.Kirmani	88	124	22	2759	102	27.04	2	12
F.M.Engineer	46	87	3	2611	121	31.08	2	16
Pankaj Roy	43	79	4	2442	173	32.56	5	9
V.S.Hazare	30	52	6	2192	164*	47.65	7	9
A.L.Wadekar	37	71	3	2113	143	31.07	1	14
M.H.Mankad	44	72	5	2109	231	31.47	5	6
C.P.S.Chauhan	40	68	2	2084	97	31.57	-	16
K.Srikkanth	43	72	3	2062	123	29.88	2	12
M.L.Jaisimha	39	71	4	2056	129	30.68	3	12
D.N.Sardesai	30	55	4	2001	212	39.23	5	9

PAKISTAN	Tests	I	NO	Runs	HS	Avge	100	50
Javed Miandad	117	178	21	8465	280*	53.91	23	41
Zaheer Abbas	78	124	11	5062	274	44.79	12	20
Mudassar Nazar	76	116	8	4114	231	38.09	10	17
Majid Khan	63	106	5	3930	167	38.91	8	19
Hanif Mohammad	55	97	8	3915	337	43.98	12	15
Imran Khan	88	126	25	3807	136	37.69	6	18
Saleem Malik	71	101	18	3743	165	45.09	10	21
Mushtaq Mohammad	57	100	7	3643	201	39.17	10	19
Asif Iqbal	58	99	7	3575	175	38.85	11	12
Saeed Ahmed	41	78	4	2991	172	40.41	5	16
Wasim Raja	57	92	14	2821	125	36.16	4	18
Mohsin Khan	48	79	6	2709	200	37.10	7	9
Sadiq Mohammad	41	74	2	2579	166	35.81	5	10
Shoaib Mohammad	39	58	6	2443	203*	46.98	7	10
Rameez Raja	44	71	5	2149	122	32.56	2	16
Imtiaz Ahmed	41	72	1	2079	209	29.28	3	11

SRI LANKA	Tests	I	NO	Runs	HS	Avge	100	50
A.Ranatunga	36	61	3	2023	135*	34.87	3	13

BATSMEN WITH 1000 RUNS IN THE CALENDAR YEAR

Player (Country)	Year	Tests	I	NO	Runs	HS	Avge	100	50
I.V.A.Richards (W)	1976	11	19	0	1710	291	90.00	7	5
S.M.Gavaskar (I)	1979	18	27	1	1555	221	59.80	5	8
G.R.Viswanath (I)	1979	17	26	3	1388	179	60.34	5	6
R.B.Simpson (A)	1964	14	26	3	1381	311	60.04	3	7
D.L.Amiss (E)	1974	13	22	2	1379	262*	68.95	5	3
S.M.Gavaskar (I)	1983	18	32	4	1310	236*	46.78	5	5
G.A.Gooch (E)	1990	9	17	1	1264	333	79.00	4	5
M.A.Taylor (A)	1989	11	20	1	1219	219	64.15	4	5 #
G.S.Sobers (W)	1958	7	12	3	1193	365*	132.55	5	3
D.B.Vengsarkar (I)	1979	18	27	4	1174	146*	51.04	5	6
K.J.Hughes (A)	1979	15	28	4	1163	130*	48.45	2	8
D.C.S.Compton (E)	1947	9	15	1	1159	208	82.78	6	3
C.G.Greenidge (W)	1984	14	22	4	1149	223	63.83	4	3
A.R.Border (A)	1985	11	20	3	1099	196	64.64	4	2
D.M.Jones (A)	1989	11	18	3	1099	216	73.26	4	4
I.T.Botham (E)	1982	14	22	0	1095	208	49.77	3	6
K.W.R.Fletcher (E)	1973	13	22	4	1090	178	60.55	2	9
M.Amarnath (I)	1983	14	24	1	1077	120	46.82	4	7
A.R.Border (A)	1979	14	27	3	1073	162	44.70	3	6
C.Hill (A)	1902	12	21	2	1061	142	55.78	2	7
D.I.Gower (E)	1982	14	25	2	1061	114	46.13	1	8
D.I.Gower (E)	1986	14	25	1	1059	136	44.12	2	6
W.M.Lawry (A)	1964	14	27	2	1056	157	42.24	2	6
S.M.Gavaskar (I)	1978	9	15	2	1044	205	80.30	4	4
G.A.Gooch (E)	1991	9	17	1	1040	174	65.00	3	5
K.F.Barrington (E)	1963	12	22	2	1039	132*	51.95	3	5
E.R.Dexter (E)	1962	11	15	1	1038	205	74.14	2	6
K.F.Barrington (E)	1961	10	17	4	1032	172	79.38	4	5
Mohsin Khan (P)	1982	10	17	3	1029	200	73.50	4	4
D.G.Bradman (A)	1948	8	13	4	1025	201	113.88	5	2
S.M.Gavaskar (I)	1976	11	20	1	1024	156	53.89	4	4
A.R.Border (A)	1986	11	19	3	1000	140	62.50	5	3

 # Taylor achieved the feat in his debut calendar year.

HIGHEST INDIVIDUAL INNINGS

365*	G.S.Sobers	West Indies	v	Pakistan	Kingston	1957-58
364	L.Hutton	England	v	Australia	The Oval	1938
337	Hanif Mohammad	Pakistan	v	West Indies	Bridgetown	1957-58
336*	W.R.Hammond	England	v	New Zealand	Auckland	1932-33
334	D.G.Bradman	Australia	v	England	Leeds	1930
333	G.A.Gooch	England	v	India	Lord's	1990
325	A.Sandham	England	v	West Indies	Kingston	1929-30
311	R.B.Simpson	Australia	v	England	Manchester	1964
310*	J.H.Edrich	England	v	New Zealand	Leeds	1965
307	R.M.Cowper	Australia	v	England	Melbourne	1965-66
304	D.G.Bradman	Australia	v	England	Leeds	1934
302	L.G.Rowe	West Indies	v	England	Bridgetown	1973-74
299*	D.G.Bradman	Australia	v	South Africa	Adelaide	1931-32
299	M.D.Crowe	New Zealand	v	Sri Lanka	Wellington	1990-91
291	I.V.A.Richards	West Indies	v	England	The Oval	1976
287	R.E.Foster	England	v	Australia	Sydney	1903-04
285*	P.B.H.May	England	v	West Indies	Birmingham	1958
280*	Javed Miandad	Pakistan	v	India	Hyderabad	1982-83
278	D.C.S.Compton	England	v	Pakistan	Nottingham	1954
274	R.G.Pollock	South Africa	v	Australia	Durban[2]	1969-70
274	Zaheer Abbas	Pakistan	v	England	Birmingham	1971
271	Javed Miandad	Pakistan	v	New Zealand	Auckland	1988-89
270*	G.A.Headley	West Indies	v	England	Kingston	1934-35
270	D.G.Bradman	Australia	v	England	Melbourne	1936-37
268	G.N.Yallop	Australia	v	Pakistan	Melbourne	1983-84
267	P.A.de Silva	Sri Lanka	v	New Zealand	Wellington	1990-91
266	W.H.Ponsford	Australia	v	England	The Oval	1934
262*	D.L.Amiss	England	v	West Indies	Kingston	1973-74
261	F.M.M.Worrell	West Indies	v	England	Nottingham	1950
260	C.C.Hunte	West Indies	v	Pakistan	Kingston	1957-58
260	Javed Miandad	Pakistan	v	England	The Oval	1987
259	G.M.Turner	New Zealand	v	West Indies	Georgetown	1971-72
258	T.W.Graveney	England	v	West Indies	Nottingham	1957
258	S.M.Nurse	West Indies	v	New Zealand	Christchurch	1968-69
256	R.B.Kanhai	West Indies	v	India	Calcutta	1958-59
256	K.F.Barrington	England	v	Australia	Manchester	1964
255*	D.J.McGlew	South Africa	v	New Zealand	Wellington	1952-53
254	D.G.Bradman	Australia	v	England	Lord's	1930
251	W.R.Hammond	England	v	Australia	Sydney	1928-29
250	K.D.Walters	Australia	v	New Zealand	Christchurch	1976-77
250	S.F.A.F.Bacchus	West Indies	v	India	Kanpur	1978-79
247*	G.S.Chappell	Australia	v	New Zealand	Wellington	1973-74
246*	G.Boycott	England	v	India	Leeds	1967
244	D.G.Bradman	Australia	v	England	The Oval	1934
243	E.Paynter	England	v	South Africa	Durban[2]	1938-39
242*	C.H.Lloyd	West Indies	v	India	Bombay[3]	1974-75
242	K.D.Walters	Australia	v	West Indies	Sydney	1968-69
240	W.R.Hammond	England	v	Australia	Lord's	1938
240	Zaheer Abbas	Pakistan	v	England	The Oval	1974
239	G.T.Dowling	New Zealand	v	India	Christchurch	1967-68
237	F.M.M.Worrell	West Indies	v	India	Kingston	1952-53
236*	S.M.Gavaskar	India	v	West Indies	Madras[1]	1983-84
236	E.A.B.Rowan	South Africa	v	England	Leeds	1951
235*	Zaheer Abbas	Pakistan	v	India	Lahore[2]	1978-79
235	G.S.Chappell	Australia	v	Pakistan	Faisalabad	1979-80
234	D.G.Bradman	Australia	v	England	Sydney	1946-47
234	S.G.Barnes	Australia	v	England	Sydney	1946-47

232	D.G.Bradman	Australia	v	England	The Oval	1930
232	S.J.McCabe	Australia	v	England	Nottingham	1938
232	I.V.A.Richards	West Indies	v	England	Nottingham	1976
231*	W.R.Hammond	England	v	Australia	Sydney	1936-37
231	A.D.Nourse	South Africa	v	Australia	Johannesburg[1]	1935-36
231	M.H.Mankad	India	v	New Zealand	Madras[2]	1955-56
231	Mudassar Nazar	Pakistan	v	India	Hyderabad	1982-83
230*	B.Sutcliffe	New Zealand	v	India	Delhi	1955-56
227	W.R.Hammond	England	v	New Zealand	Christchurch	1932-33
226	D.G.Bradman	Australia	v	South Africa	Brisbane[2]	1931-32
226	G.S.Sobers	West Indies	v	England	Bridgetown	1959-60
226	C.G.Greenidge	West Indies	v	Australia	Bridgetown	1990-91
225	R.B.Simpson	Australia	v	England	Adelaide	1965-66
223*	G.M.Turner	New Zealand	v	West Indies	Kingston	1971-72
223	G.A.Headley	West Indies	v	England	Kingston	1929-30
223	D.G.Bradman	Australia	v	West Indies	Brisbane[1]	1930-31
223	P.R.Umrigar	India	v	New Zealand	Hyderabad	1955-56
223	M.H.Mankad	India	v	New Zealand	Bombay[2]	1955-56
223	C.G.Greenidge	West Indies	v	England	Manchester	1984
222	G.R.Viswanath	India	v	England	Madras[1]	1981-82
221	S.M.Gavaskar	India	v	England	The Oval	1979
220	C.L.Walcott	West Indies	v	England	Bridgetown	1953-54
220	S.M.Gavaskar	India	v	West Indies	Port-of-Spain	1970-71
219	W.J.Edrich	England	v	South Africa	Durban[2]	1938-39
219	D.S.Atkinson	West Indies	v	Australia	Bridgetown	1954-55
219	M.A.Taylor	Australia	v	England	Nottingham	1989
218	S.V.Manjrekar	India	v	Pakistan	Lahore[2]	1989-90
217	W.R.Hammond	England	v	India	The Oval	1936
217	R.B.Kanhai	West Indies	v	Pakistan	Lahore[1]	1958-59
216*	E.Paynter	England	v	Australia	Nottingham	1938
216	K.W.R.Fletcher	England	v	New Zealand	Auckland	1974-75
216	D.M.Jones	Australia	v	West Indies	Adelaide	1988-89
215	Zaheer Abbas	Pakistan	v	India	Lahore[2]	1982-83
215	D.I.Gower	England	v	West Indies	Birmingham	1985
214*	V.T.Trumper	Australia	v	South Africa	Adelaide	1910-11
214*	D.Lloyd	England	v	India	Birmingham	1974
214*	C.G.Greenidge	West Indies	v	England	Lord's	1984
214	L.G.Rowe	West Indies	v	New Zealand	Kingston	1971-72
213	K.J.Hughes	Australia	v	India	Adelaide	1980-81
213	C.G.Greenidge	West Indies	v	New Zealand	Auckland	1986-87
212	D.G.Bradman	Australia	v	England	Adelaide	1936-37
212	D.N.Sardesai	India	v	West Indies	Kingston	1970-71
211	W.L.Murdoch	Australia	v	England	The Oval	1884
211	J.B.Hobbs	England	v	South Africa	Lord's	1924
211	Javed Miandad	Pakistan	v	Australia	Karachi	1988-89
210*	Taslim Arif	Pakistan	v	Australia	Faisalabad	1979-80
210	W.M.Lawry	Australia	v	West Indies	Bridgetown	1964-65
210	Qasim Omar	Pakistan	v	India	Faisalabad	1984-85
210	D.M.Jones	Australia	v	India	Madras[1]	1986-87
209*	B.F.Butcher	West Indies	v	England	Nottingham	1966
209	C.A.Roach	West Indies	v	England	Georgetown	1929-30
209	Imtiaz Ahmed	Pakistan	v	New Zealand	Lahore[1]	1955-56
209	R.G.Pollock	South Africa	v	Australia	Cape Town	1966-67
208	D.C.S.Compton	England	v	South Africa	Lord's	1947
208	A.D.Nourse	South Africa	v	England	Nottingham	1951
208	I.T.Botham	England	v	India	The Oval	1982
208	I.V.A.Richards	West Indies	v	Australia	Melbourne	1984-85
207	E.D.Weekes	West Indies	v	India	Port-of-Spain	1952-53
207	K.R.Stackpole	Australia	v	England	Brisbane[2]	1970-71

207	M.W.Gatting	England	v	India	Madras[1]	1984-85
206*	W.A.Brown	Australia	v	England	Lord's	1938
206	M.P.Donnelly	New Zealand	v	England	Lord's	1949
206	L.Hutton	England	v	New Zealand	The Oval	1949
206	A.R.Morris	Australia	v	England	Adelaide	1950-51
206	E.D.Weekes	West Indies	v	England	Port-of-Spain	1953-54
206	Javed Miandad	Pakistan	v	New Zealand	Karachi	1976-77
206	Qasim Omar	Pakistan	v	Sri Lanka	Faisalabad	1985-86
206	R.J.Shastri	India	v	Australia	Sydney	1991-92
205*	E.H.Hendren	England	v	West Indies	Port-of-Spain	1929-30
205*	J.Hardstaff, jr	England	v	India	Lord's	1946
205	R.N.Harvey	Australia	v	South Africa	Melbourne	1952-53
205	L.Hutton	England	v	West Indies	Kingston	1953-54
205	E.R.Dexter	England	v	Pakistan	Karachi	1961-62
205	W.M.Lawry	Australia	v	West Indies	Melbourne	1968-69
205	S.M.Gavaskar	India	v	West Indies	Bombay[3]	1978-79
205	A.R.Border	Australia	v	New Zealand	Adelaide	1987-88
205	Aamer Sohail	Pakistan	v	England	Manchester	1992
204	G.A.Faulkner	South Africa	v	Australia	Melbourne	1910-11
204	R.N.Harvey	Australia	v	West Indies	Kingston	1954-55
204	G.S.Chappell	Australia	v	India	Sydney	1980-81
203*	Nawab of Pataudi, jr	India	v	England	Delhi	1963-64
203*	Hanif Mohammad	Pakistan	v	New Zealand	Lahore[2]	1964-65
203*	Javed Miandad	Pakistan	v	Sri Lanka	Faisalabad	1985-86
203*	Shoaib Mohammad	Pakistan	v	India	Lahore[2]	1989-90
203*	Shoaib Mohammad	Pakistan	v	New Zealand	Karachi	1990-91
203	H.L.Collins	Australia	v	South Africa	Johannesburg[1]	1921-22
203	D.L.Amiss	England	v	West Indies	The Oval	1976
202*	L.Hutton	England	v	West Indies	The Oval	1950
201*	J.Ryder	Australia	v	England	Adelaide	1924-25
201*	D.S.B.P.Kuruppu	Sri Lanka	v	New Zealand	Colombo (CCC)	1986-87
201	S.E.Gregory	Australia	v	England	Sydney	1894-95
201	D.G.Bradman	Australia	v	India	Adelaide	1947-48
201	E.J.Barlow	South Africa	v	Australia	Adelaide	1963-64
201	R.B.Simpson	Australia	v	West Indies	Bridgetown	1964-65
201	S.M.Nurse	West Indies	v	Australia	Bridgetown	1964-65
201	Mushtaq Mohammad	Pakistan	v	New Zealand	Dunedin	1972-73
201	G.S.Chappell	Australia	v	Pakistan	Brisbane[2]	1981-82
201	A.D.Gaekwad	India	v	Pakistan	Jullundur	1983-84
201	G.Fowler	England	v	India	Madras[1]	1984-85
200*	D.N.Sardesai	India	v	New Zealand	Bombay[2]	1964-65
200*	D.I.Gower	England	v	India	Birmingham	1979
200	W.R.Hammond	England	v	Australia	Melbourne	1928-29
200	Mohsin Khan	Pakistan	v	England	Lord's	1982
200	D.C.Boon	Australia	v	New Zealand	Perth	1989-90

HIGHEST BATTING AVERAGES

(Qualification: 15 innings)

	Country	Tests	I	NO	Runs	HS	Avge	100	50
D.G.Bradman	Australia	52	80	10	6996	334	**99.94**	29	13
C.S.Dempster	New Zealand	10	15	4	723	136	**65.72**	2	5
S.G.Barnes	Australia	13	19	2	1072	234	**63.05**	3	5
R.G.Pollock	South Africa	23	41	4	2256	274	**60.97**	7	11
G.A.Headley	West Indies	22	40	4	2190	270*	**60.83**	10	5
H.Sutcliffe	England	54	84	9	4555	194	**60.73**	16	23
E.Paynter	England	20	31	5	1540	243	**59.23**	4	7
K.F.Barrington	England	82	131	15	6806	256	**58.67**	20	35
E.D.Weekes	West Indies	48	81	5	4455	207	**58.61**	15	19
K.S.Duleepsinhji	England	12	19	2	995	173	**58.52**	3	5

W.R.Hammond	England	85	140	16	7249	336*	**58.15**	22	24
G.S.Sobers	West Indies	93	160	21	8032	365*	**57.78**	26	30
J.B.Hobbs	England	61	102	7	5410	211	**56.94**	15	28
C.A.G.Russell	England	10	18	2	990	140	**56.87**	5	2
C.L.Walcott	West Indies	44	74	7	3798	220	**56.68**	15	14
L.Hutton	England	79	138	15	6971	364	**56.67**	19	33
G.E.Tyldesley	England	14	20	2	990	122	**55.00**	3	6
C.A.Davis	West Indies	15	29	5	1301	183	**54.20**	4	4
Javed Miandad	Pakistan	117	178	21	8465	280*	**53.91**	23	41
G.S.Chappell	Australia	87	151	19	7110	247*	**53.86**	24	31
A.D.Nourse	South Africa	34	62	7	2960	231	**53.81**	9	14
A.Melville	South Africa	11	19	2	894	189*	**52.58**	4	3
C.F.Walters	England	11	18	3	784	102	**52.26**	1	7
A.H.Jones	New Zealand	23	42	5	1929	186	**52.13**	6	6
A.R.Border	Australia	133	230	42	9775	205	**51.99**	24	56
J.Ryder	Australia	20	32	5	1394	201*	**51.62**	3	9
S.M.Gavaskar	India	125	214	12	10122	236*	**51.12**	34	45
R.A.Smith	England	36	66	14	2645	148*	**50.86**	7	18
I.V.A.Richards	West Indies	121	182	12	8540	291	**50.23**	24	45
D.C.S.Compton	England	78	131	15	5807	278	**50.06**	17	28

500 RUNS IN A TEST SERIES

(§ first Test series. # last Test series. † only Test Series)

AUSTRALIA	Opp	Season	Tests	I	NO	Runs	HS	Avge	100	50
D.G.Bradman	ENG	1930	5	7	0	974	334	139.14	4	-
M.A.Taylor	ENG	1989	6	11	1	839	219	83.90	2	5
R.N.Harvey	SA	1952-53	5	9	0	834	205	92.66	4	3
D.G.Bradman	ENG	1936-37	5	9	0	810	270	90.00	3	1
D.G.Bradman	SA	1931-32	5	5	1	806	299*	201.50	4	-
D.G.Bradman	ENG	1934	5	8	0	758	304	94.75	2	1
D.G.Bradman	IND	1947-48	5	6	2	715	201	178.75	4	1
G.S.Chappell	WI	1975-76	6	11	5	702	182*	117.00	3	3
K.D.Walters	WI	1968-69	4	6	0	699	242	116.50	4	2
A.R.Morris	ENG	1948	5	9	1	696	196	87.00	3	3
D.G.Bradman	ENG	1946-47	5	8	1	680	234	97.14	2	3
W.M.Lawry	WI	1968-69	5	8	0	667	205	83.38	3	2
V.T.Trumper	SA	1910-11	5	9	2	661	214*	94.42	2	2
R.N.Harvey	SA	1949-50	5	8	3	660	178	132.00	4	1
R.N.Harvey	WI	1954-55	5	7	1	650	204	108.33	3	1
K.R.Stackpole	ENG	1970-71	6	12	0	627	207	52.25	2	2
G.S.Chappell	ENG	1974-75	6	11	0	608	144	55.27	2	5
A.R.Border	ENG	1985	6	11	2	597	196	66.33	2	1
K.J.Hughes	IND	1979-80	6	12	2	594	100	59.40	1	5
W.M.Lawry	ENG	1965-66	5	7	0	592	166	84.57	3	2
I.R.Redpath	WI	1975-76	6	11	0	575	103	52.27	3	2
V.T.Trumper	ENG	1903-04	5	10	1	574	185*	63.77	2	3
W.Bardsley	SA	1910-11	5	9	0	573	132	63.66	1	5
W.H.Ponsford #	ENG	1934	4	7	1	569	266	94.83	2	1
D.M.Jones	ENG	1989	6	9	1	566	157	70.75	2	3
H.L.Collins §	ENG	1920-21	5	9	0	557	162	61.88	2	3
D.C.Boon	IND	1991-92	5	9	2	556	135	79.42	3	1
G.N.Yallop	PAK	1983-84	5	6	0	554	268	92.33	2	1
I.M.Chappell	WI	1968-69	5	8	0	548	165	68.50	2	3
I.M.Chappell	WI	1972-73	5	9	2	542	109	77.42	2	3
J.M.Taylor	ENG	1924-25	5	10	0	541	108	54.10	1	4
R.B.Simpson	IND	1977-78	5	10	0	539	176	53.90	2	2
J.Darling	ENG	1897-98	5	8	0	537	178	67.12	3	-
A.R.Border	ENG	1981	6	12	3	533	123*	59.22	2	3
B.C.Booth	SA	1963-64	4	7	1	531	169	88.50	2	3

D.C.Boon	ENG	1990-91	5	9	2	530	121	75.71	1	3
N.C.O'Neill	WI	1960-61	5	10	0	522	181	52.20	1	3
C.Hill	ENG	1901-02	5	10	0	521	99	52.10	-	4
A.R.Border	IND	1979-80	6	12	0	521	162	49.63	2	6
A.R.Border	WI	1983-84	5	10	3	521	100*	74.42	1	4
C.C.McDonald	ENG	1958-59	5	9	1	519	170	64.87	2	1
W.A.Brown	ENG	1938	4	8	1	512	206*	73.14	2	1
D.M.Jones	ENG	1986-87	5	10	1	511	184*	56.77	1	3
D.G.Bradman #	ENG	1948	5	9	2	508	173*	72.57	2	1
S.R.Waugh	ENG	1989	6	8	4	506	177	126.50	2	1
K.C.Wessels	WI	1984-85	5	9	0	505	173	56.11	1	4
A.R.Morris §	ENG	1946-47	5	8	1	503	155	71.85	3	1

ENGLAND	Opp	Season	Tests	I	NO	Runs	HS	Avge	100	50
W.R.Hammond	AUST	1928-29	5	9	1	905	251	113.12	4	-
D.C.S.Compton	SA	1947	5	8	0	753	208	94.12	4	2
G.A.Gooch	IND	1990	3	6	0	752	333	125.33	3	2
H.Sutcliffe	AUST	1924-25	5	9	0	734	176	81.56	4	2
D.I.Gower	AUST	1985	6	9	0	732	215	81.33	3	1
E.H.Hendren	WI	1929-30	4	8	2	693	205*	115.50	2	5
L.Hutton	WI	1953-54	5	8	1	667	205	96.71	2	3
D.L.Amiss	WI	1973-74	5	9	1	663	262*	82.87	3	-
J.B.Hobbs	AUST	1911-12	5	9	1	662	187	82.75	3	1
G.Boycott	AUST	1970-71	5	10	3	657	142*	93.85	2	5
E.Paynter #	SA	1938-39	5	8	0	653	243	81.62	3	2
J.H.Edrich	AUST	1970-71	6	11	2	648	130	72.00	2	4
W.R.Hammond	SA	1938-39	5	8	1	609	181	87.00	3	2
K.F.Barrington	IND	1961-62	5	9	3	594	172	99.00	3	1
A.Sandham #	WI	1929-30	4	8	0	592	325	74.00	2	2
K.F.Barrington	AUST	1962-63	5	10	2	582	132	72.75	2	3
P.B.H.May	SA	1955	5	9	1	582	117	72.75	2	3
L.Hutton	SA	1948-49	5	9	0	577	158	64.11	2	2
M.W.Gatting	IND	1984-85	5	9	3	575	207	95.83	2	1
J.B.Hobbs	AUST	1924-25	5	9	0	573	154	63.66	3	2
W.R.Hammond	NZ	1932-33	2	2	1	563	336*	64.49	2	-
D.C.S.Compton	AUST	1948	5	10	1	562	184	62.44	2	2
J.H.Edrich	AUST	1968	5	9	0	554	164	61.55	1	4
R.A.Smith	AUST	1989	5	10	1	553	143	61.44	2	3
W.J.Edrich	SA	1947	4	6	1	552	191	110.40	2	2
C.Washbrook	SA	1948-49	5	9	0	542	195	60.22	1	2
J.B.Hobbs	SA	1909-10	5	9	1	539	187	67.37	1	4
M.C.Cowdrey	WI	1967-68	5	8	0	534	148	66.75	2	4
L.Hutton	AUST	1950-51	5	10	4	533	156*	88.83	1	4
K.F.Barrington	AUST	1964	5	8	1	531	256	75.85	1	2
M.W.Gatting	AUST	1985	6	9	3	527	160	87.83	2	3
E.R.Dexter	WI	1959-60	5	9	1	526	136*	65.75	2	2
G.E.Tyldesley	SA	1927-28	5	9	1	520	122	65.00	2	3
W.R.Hammond	SA	1930-31	5	9	1	517	136*	64.62	1	4
H.Sutcliffe	AUST	1929	5	9	1	513	114	64.12	4	-
K.F.Barrington	SA	1964-65	5	7	2	508	148*	101.60	2	2
J.B.Hobbs	AUST	1920-21	5	10	0	505	123	50.50	2	1

SOUTH AFRICA	Opp	Season	Tests	I	NO	Runs	HS	Avge	100	50
G.A.Faulkner	AUST	1910-11	5	10	0	732	204	73.20	2	5
A.D.Nourse	ENG	1947	5	9	0	621	149	69.00	2	5
D.T.Lindsay	AUST	1966-67	5	7	0	606	182	86.57	3	1
E.J.Barlow	AUST	1963-64	5	10	2	603	201	75.37	3	1
B.Mitchell	ENG	1947	5	10	1	597	189*	66.33	2	3
H.W.Taylor	ENG	1922-23	5	9	0	582	176	64.66	3	2

K.C.Bland	ENG	1964-65	5	10	2	572	144*	71.50	1	4
A.Melville	ENG	1947	5	10	1	569	189	63.22	3	1
E.J.Barlow	ENG	1964-65	5	10	0	558	138	55.80	1	4
G.A.Faulkner	ENG	1909-10	5	10	1	545	123	60.55	1	3
R.G.Pollock	AUST	1966-67	5	9	2	537	209	76.71	2	2
A.D.Nourse	ENG	1948-49	5	10	3	536	129*	76.57	2	2
A.D.Nourse	AUST	1935-36	5	10	1	518	231	57.55	1	2
R.G.Pollock #	AUST	1969-70	4	7	0	517	274	73.85	1	3
E.A.B.Rowan #	ENG	1951	5	10	1	515	236	57.22	1	3
B.A.Richards †	AUST	1969-70	4	7	0	508	140	72.57	2	2
H.W.Taylor	ENG	1913-14	5	10	0	508	109	35.10	1	3

WEST INDIES	Opp	Season	Tests	I	NO	Runs	HS	Avge	100	50
I.V.A.Richards	ENG	1976	4	7	0	829	291	118.42	3	2
C.L.Walcott	AUST	1954-55	5	10	0	827	155	82.70	5	2
G.S.Sobers	PAK	1957-58	5	8	2	824	365*	137.33	3	3
E.D.Weekes	IND	1948-49	5	7	0	779	194	111.28	4	2
G.S.Sobers	ENG	1966	5	8	1	722	174	103.14	3	2
E.D.Weekes	IND	1952-53	5	8	1	716	207	102.28	3	2
G.S.Sobers	ENG	1959-60	5	8	1	709	226	101.28	3	1
G.A.Headley §	ENG	1929-30	4	8	0	703	223	87.87	4	-
C.L.Walcott	ENG	1953-54	5	10	2	698	220	87.25	3	3
C.H.Lloyd	IND	1974-75	5	9	1	636	242*	79.50	2	1
C.C.Hunte §	PAK	1957-58	5	9	1	622	260	79.75	3	-
R.B.Richardson	IND	1988-89	4	7	0	619	194	88.42	2	3
L.G.Rowe	ENG	1973-74	5	7	0	616	302	88.00	3	-
G.S.Sobers	IND	1970-71	5	10	2	597	178*	74.62	3	1
C.G.Greenidge	ENG	1976	5	10	1	592	134	65.66	3	2
C.G.Greenidge	ENG	1984	5	8	1	572	223	81.71	2	-
S.M.Nurse †	NZ	1968-69	3	5	0	558	258	111.60	2	1
G.S.Sobers	IND	1958-59	5	8	2	557	198	92.83	3	-
I.V.A.Richards	IND	1975-76	4	7	0	556	177	92.66	3	1
C.C.Hunte	AUST	1964-65	5	10	1	550	89	61.11	-	6
G.S.Sobers	ENG	1967-68	5	9	3	545	152	90.83	2	2
F.M.M.Worrell	ENG	1950	4	6	0	539	261	89.33	2	1
A.I.Kallicharran	IND	1978-79	6	10	1	538	187	59.77	1	3
R.B.Kanhai	IND	1958-59	5	8	0	538	256	67.25	1	2
C.G.Greenidge	PAK	1976-77	5	10	0	536	100	53.60	1	4
R.B.Kanhai	ENG	1967-68	5	10	1	535	153	59.44	2	1
C.A.Davis	IND	1970-71	4	8	4	529	125*	132.25	2	3
R.C.Fredericks	ENG	1976	5	10	1	517	138	57.44	2	3
R.B.Kanhai	AUST	1960-61	5	10	0	503	117	50.30	2	2
S.M.Nurse	ENG	1966	5	8	0	501	137	62.65	1	4

NEW ZEALAND	Opp	Season	Tests	I	NO	Runs	HS	Avge	100	50
G.M.Turner	WI	1971-72	5	8	1	672	259	96.00	2	2
B.Sutcliffe	IND	1955-56	5	9	2	611	230*	87.28	2	1
J.R.Reid	SA	1961-62	5	10	1	546	142	60.66	1	4
B.E.Congdon	WI	1971-72	5	8	2	531	166*	88.50	2	3
A.H.Jones	SL	1990-91	3	6	1	513	186	102.60	3	1

INDIA	Opp	Season	Tests	I	NO	Runs	HS	Avge	100	50
S.M.Gavaskar §	WI	1970-71	4	8	3	774	220	154.80	4	3
S.M.Gavaskar	WI	1978-79	6	9	1	732	205*	91.50	4	1
D.N.Sardesai	WI	1970-71	5	8	0	642	212	80.25	3	1
M.Amarnath	WI	1982-83	5	9	0	598	117	66.44	2	4
V.L.Manjrekar	ENG	1961-62	5	8	1	586	189*	83.71	1	4
M.Amarnath	PAK	1982-83	6	10	2	584	120	73.00	3	3
S.V.Manjrekar	PAK	1989-90	4	7	1	569	218	94.83	2	3

G.R.Viswanath	WI	1974-75	5	10	1	568	139	63.11	1	3
R.S.Modi	WI	1948-49	5	10	0	560	112	56.00	1	5
P.R.Umrigar	WI	1952-53	5	10	1	560	130	62.22	2	4
V.S.Hazare	WI	1948-49	5	10	2	543	134*	67.87	2	3
S.M.Gavaskar	ENG	1979	4	7	0	542	221	77.42	1	4
S.M.Gavaskar	PAK	1979-80	6	11	1	529	166	52.90	1	2
M.H.Mankad	NZ	1955-56	4	5	0	526	231	105.20	2	-
B.K.Kunderan	ENG	1963-64	5	10	0	525	192	52.50	2	1
G.R.Viswanath	A	1979-80	6	8	1	518	161*	74.00	2	2
S.M.Gavaskar	WI	1983-84	6	11	1	505	236*	50.50	2	1
S.M.Gavaskar	ENG	1981-82	6	9	1	500	172	62.50	1	3

PAKISTAN	Opp	Season	Tests	I	NO	Runs	HS	Avge	100	50
Mudassar Nazar	IND	1982-83	6	8	2	761	231	126.83	4	1
Zaheer Abbas	IND	1982-83	6	6	1	650	215	130.00	3	-
Hanif Mohammad	WI	1957-58	5	9	0	628	337	39.10	1	3
Javed Miandad	IND	1982-83	6	6	1	594	280*	118.88	2	1
Zaheer Abbas	IND	1978-79	3	5	2	583	235	174.33	2	1
Majid.J.Khan	WI	1976-77	5	10	0	530	167	53.00	1	3
Wasim Raja	WI	1976-77	5	10	1	517	117*	57.44	1	5
Saeed Ahmed §	WI	1957-58	5	9	0	508	150	56.44	1	4
Shoaib Mohammad	NZ	1990-91	3	5	2	507	203*	169.00	3	-
Javed Miandad §	NZ	1976-77	3	5	1	504	206	126.00	2	1

Best for Sri Lanka:

SRI LANKA	Opp	Season	Tests	I	NO	Runs	HS	Avge	100	50
P.A.de Silva	NZ	1990-91	3	5	0	493	267	98.60	2	1

MOST RUNS IN A MATCH

456	G.A.Gooch (333 + 123)	England	v	India	Lord's	1990
380	G.S.Chappell (247* + 133)	Australia	v	New Zealand	Wellington	1973-71
375	A.Sandham (325 + 50)	England	v	West Indies	Kingston	1929-30
365	G.S.Sobers (365*)	West Indies	v	Pakistan	Kingston	1957-58
364	L.Hutton (364)	England	v	Australia	The Oval	1938
354	Hanif Mohammad (17 + 337)	Pakistan	v	West Indies	Bridgetown	1957-58

The most for the other countries are as follows:

344	S.M.Gavaskar (124 + 220)	India	v	West Indies	Port-of-Spain	1970-71
329	M.D.Crowe (30 + 299)	New Zealand	v	Sri Lanka	Wellington	1990-91
309	B.Mitchell (120 + 189*)	South Africa	v	England	The Oval	1947
267	P.A.de Silva (267)	Sri Lanka	v	New Zealand	Wellington	1990-91

CARRYING BAT THROUGH A COMPLETED INNINGS

(§ on Test debut. ∫ one or more batsmen absent or retired hurt)

AUSTRALIA	Score	Total	Opponents		
J.E.Barrett §	67*	176	England	Lord's	1890
W.W.Armstrong	159*	309	South Africa	Johannesburg[1]	1902-03
W.Bardsley	193*	383	England	Lord's	1926
W.M.Woodfull	30*	66∫	England	Brisbane[1]	1928-29
W.M.Woodfull	73*	193∫	England	Adelaide	1932-33
W.A.Brown	206*	422	England	Lord's	1938
W.M.Lawry	49*	107	India	Delhi	1969-70
W.M.Lawry	60*	116∫	England	Sydney	1970-71
I.R.Redpath	159*	346	New Zealand	Auckland	1973-74
D.C.Boon	58*	103	New Zealand	Auckland	1985-86

ENGLAND	Score	Total	Opponents		
R.Abel	132*	307	Australia	Sydney	1891-92
P.F.Warner	132*	237	South Africa	Johannesburg[1]	1898-99
L.Hutton	202*	344	West Indies	The Oval	1950
L.Hutton	156*	272	Australia	Adelaide	1950-51
G.Boycott	99*	215	Australia	Perth	1979-80
G.A.Gooch	154*	252	West Indies	Leeds	1991
A.J.Stewart	69*	175	Pakistan	Lord's	1992

SOUTH AFRICA	Score	Total	Opponents		
A.B.Tancred	26*	47	England	Cape Town	1888-89
J.W.Zulch	43*	103	England	Cape Town	1909-10
T.L.Goddard	56*	99	Australia	Cape Town	1957-58
D.J.McGlew	127*	292	New Zealand	Durban[2]	1961-62

WEST INDIES	Score	Total	Opponents		
F.M.M.Worrell	191*	372	England	Nottingham	1957
C.C.Hunte	60*	131	Australia	Port-of-Spain	1964-65
D.L.Haynes	88*	211	Pakistan	Karachi	1986-87
D.L.Haynes	75*	176	England	The Oval	1991

NEW ZEALAND	Score	Total	Opponents		
G.M.Turner	43*	131	England	Lord's	1969
G.M.Turner	223*	386	West Indies	Kingston	1971-72

INDIA	Score	Total	Opponents		
S.M.Gavaskar	127*	286	Pakistan	Faisalabad	1982-83

PAKISTAN	Score	Total	Opponents		
Nazar Mohammad	124*	331	India	Lucknow	1952-53
Mudassar Nazar	152*	323	India	Lahore[2]	1982-83

SRI LANKA	Score	Total	Opponents		
S.Wettimuny	63*	144	New Zealand	Christchurch	1982-83

MOST CENTURIES

	Country	100	Inns	A	E	SA	WI	NZ	I	P	SL
S.M.Gavaskar	India	**34**	214	8	4	-	13	2	-	5	2
D.G.Bradman	Australia	**29**	80	-	19	4	2	-	4	-	-
G.S.Sobers	West Indies	**26**	160	4	10	-	-	1	8	3	-
A.R.Border	Australia	**24**	230	-	7	-	2	4	4	6	1
G.S.Chappell	Australia	**24**	151	-	9	-	5	3	1	6	-
I.V.A.Richards	West Indies	**24**	161	5	8	-	-	1	8	2	-
G.Boycott	England	**22**	193	7	-	1	5	2	4	3	-
M.C.Cowdrey	England	**22**	188	5	-	3	6	2	3	3	-
W.R.Hammond	England	**22**	140	9	-	6	1	4	2	-	-
Javed Miandad	Pakistan	**23**	178	6	2	-	2	7	5	-	1
R.N.Harvey	Australia	**21**	137	-	6	8	3	-	4	-	-
K.F.Barrington	England	**20**	131	5	-	2	3	3	3	4	-
C.G.Greenidge	West Indies	**19**	185	4	7	-	-	2	5	1	-
L.Hutton	England	**19**	138	5	-	4	5	3	2	-	-
C.H.Lloyd	West Indies	**19**	175	6	5	-	-	-	7	1	-
D.I.Gower	England	**18**	204	9	-	-	1	4	2	2	-
D.C.S.Compton	England	**17**	131	5	-	7	2	2	-	1	-
G.A.Gooch	England	**17**	179	2	-	-	5	3	5	2	1
D.B.Vengsarkar	India	**17**	168	2	5	-	6	-	-	2	2
D.L.Haynes	West Indies	**16**	180	5	5	-	-	3	2	1	-
H.Sutcliffe	England	**16**	84	8	-	6	-	2	-	-	-

J.B.Hobbs	England	**15**	102	12	-	2	1	-	-	-	-
R.B.Kanhai	West Indies	**15**	137	5	5	-	-	-	4	1	-
C.L.Walcott	West Indies	**15**	74	5	4	-	-	1	4	1	-
K.D.Walters	Australia	**15**	125	-	4	-	6	3	1	1	-
E.D.Weekes	West Indies	**15**	81	1	3	-	-	3	7	1	-
I.T.Botham	England	**14**	161	4	-	-	-	3	5	2	-
I.M.Chappell	Australia	**14**	136	-	4	-	5	2	2	1	-
A.J.Lamb	England	**14**	139	1	-	-	6	3	3	-	1
R.B.Richardson	West Indies	**14**	109	7	4	-	-	1	2	-	-
G.R.Viswanath	India	**14**	155	4	4	-	4	1	-	1	-
D.C.Boon	Australia	**13**	121	-	3	-	2	2	6	-	-
M.D.Crowe	New Zealand	**13**	98	3	3	-	3	1	2	1	-
W.M.Lawry	Australia	**13**	123	-	7	1	4	-	1	-	-
P.B.H.May	England	**13**	106	3	-	3	3	3	1	-	-
J.H.Edrich	England	**12**	127	7	-	-	1	3	1	-	-
Hanif Mohammad	Pakistan	**12**	97	2	3	-	2	3	2	-	-
A.I.Kallicharran	West Indies	**12**	109	4	2	-	-	2	3	1	-
A.R.Morris	Australia	**12**	79	-	8	2	1	-	1	-	-
P.R.Umrigar	India	**12**	94	-	3	-	3	1	-	5	-
J.G.Wright	New Zealand	**12**	138	2	4	-	1	-	3	1	1
Zaheer Abbas	Pakistan	**12**	124	2	2	-	-	1	6	-	1
M.Amarnath	India	**11**	113	2	-	-	3	-	-	4	2
M.Azharuddin	India	**11**	70	1	5	-	-	1	-	3	1
D.L.Amiss	England	**11**	88	-	-	-	4	2	2	3	-
Asif Iqbal	Pakistan	**11**	99	3	3	-	1	3	1	-	-
T.W.Graveney	England	**11**	123	1	-	-	5	-	2	3	-
D.M.Jones	Australia	**11**	89	-	3	-	1	-	2	2	3
R.J.Shastri	India	**11**	115	2	4	-	2	-	-	3	-
A.L.Hassett	Australia	**10**	69	-	4	3	2	-	1	-	-
G.A.Headley	West Indies	**10**	40	2	8	-	-	-	-	-	-
Mudassar Nazar	Pakistan	**10**	116	-	3	-	-	1	6	-	-
Mushtaq Mohammad	Pakistan	**10**	100	1	3	-	2	3	1	-	-
Saleem Malik	Pakistan	**10**	101	-	3	-	1	1	3	-	2
R.B.Simpson	Australia	**10**	111	-	2	1	1	-	4	2	-

The leading century-maker for South Africa is A.D.Nourse (9 in 62 innings) and for Sri Lanka P.A.de Silva (5 in 48 innings).

MOST CENTURIES IN A SERIES

FIVE				
C.L Walcott	West Indies	v	Australia	1954-55
FOUR				
D.G Bradman	Australia	v	England	1930
	Australia	v	South Africa	1931-32
	Australia	v	India	1947-48
D.C.S.Compton	England	v	South Africa	1947
S.M.Gavaskar	India	v	West Indies	1970-71
	India	v	West Indies	1978-79
W.R.Hammond	England	v	Australia	1928-29
R.N.Harvey	Australia	v	South Africa	1949-50
	Australia	v	South Africa	1952-53
G.A.Headley	West Indies	v	England	1929-30
Mudassar Nazar	Pakistan	v	India	1982-83
H.Sutcliffe	England	v	Australia	1924-25
	England	v	South Africa	1929
K.D.Walters	Australia	v	West Indies	1968-69
E.D.Weekes	West Indies	v	India	1948-49

MOST DOUBLE CENTURIES IN A SERIES

THREE				
D.G.Bradman	Australia	v	England	1930
TWO				
D.G.Bradman	Australia	v	South Africa	1931-32
	Australia	v	England	1934
	Australia	v	England	1936-37
C.G.Greenidge	West Indies	v	England	1984
W.R.Hammond	England	v	Australia	1928-29
	England	v	New Zealand	1932-33
M.H.Mankad	India	v	New Zealand	1955-56
I.V.A.Richards	West Indies	v	England	1976
G.M.Turner	New Zealand	v	West Indies	1971-72

CENTURIES IN MOST CONSECUTIVE INNINGS

FIVE			Opponents		
E.D.Weekes	West Indies	141	England	Kingston	1947-48
		128	India	Delhi	1947-48
		194	India	Bombay[2]	1947-48
		162)	India	Calcutta	1947-48
		101)			
Weekes was run out for 90 in his next innings (Madras[1] 1948-49).					
FOUR			Opponents		
J.H.W.Fingleton	Australia	112	South Africa	Cape Town	1935-36
		108	South Africa	Johannesburg[1]	1935-36
		118	South Africa	Durban[2]	1935-36
		100	England	Brisbane[2]	1936-37
A.Melville	South Africa	103	England	Durban[2]	1938-39
		189)	England	Nottingham	1947
		104*)			
		117	England	Lord's	1947
THREE			Opponents		
W.Bardsley	Australia	136)	England	The Oval	1909
		130)			
		132	South Africa	Sydney	1910-11
G.Boycott	England	119*	Australia	Adelaide	1970-71
		121*	Pakistan	Lord's	1971
		112	Pakistan	Leeds	1971
D G Bradman	Australia	132)	India	Melbourne	1947-48
		127*)			
		201	India	Adelaide	1947-48
D.C.S.Compton	England	163	South Africa	Nottingham	1947
		208	South Africa	Lord's	1947
		115	South Africa	Manchester	1947
S.M.Gavaskar	India	117*	West Indies	Bridgetown	1970-71
		124)	West Indies	Port-of-Spain	1970-71
		220)			
S.M.Gavaskar		111)	Pakistan	Karachi	1978-79
		137)			
		205	West Indies	Bombay[3]	1978-79
G.A.Gooch	England	333)	India	Lord's	1990
		123)			
		116	India	Manchester	1990

C G Greenidge	West Indies	134)	England	Manchester	1976
		101)			
		115	England	Leeds	1976
V.S.Hazare	India	122	West Indies	Bombay[2]	1948-49
		164*	England	Delhi	1951-52
		155	England	Bombay[2]	1951-52
G.A.Headley	West Indies	270*	England	Kingston	1934-35
		106)	England	Lord's	1939
		107)			
A.H.Jones	New Zealand	186	Sri Lanka	Wellington	1990-91
		122)	Sri Lanka	Hamilton	1990-91
		100*)			
C.G.Macartney	Australia	133*	England	Lord's	1926
		151	England	Leeds	1926
		109	England	Manchester	1926
A.R.Morris	Australia	155	England	Melbourne	1946-47
		122)	England	Adelaide	1946-47
		124*)			
Mudassar Nazar	Pakistan	231	India	Hyderabad	1982-83
		152*	India	Lahore[2]	1982-83
		152	India	Karachi	1982-83
G.S.Sobers	West Indies	365*	Pakistan	Kingston	1957-58
		125)	Pakistan	Georgetown	1957-58
		109*)			
H.Sutcliffe	England	115	Australia	Sydney	1924-25
		176)	Australia	Melbourne	1924-25
		127)			
P.R.Umrigar	India	117	Pakistan	Madras[2]	1960-61
		112	Pakistan	Delhi	1960-61
		147*	England	Kanpur	1961-62
E.D.Weekes	West Indies	123	New Zealand	Dunedin	1955-56
		103	New Zealand	Christchurch	1955-56
		156	New Zealand	Wellington	1955-56
Zaheer Abbas	Pakistan	215	India	Lahore[2]	1982-83
		186	India	Karachi	1982-83
		168	India	Faisalabad	1982-83

CENTURY IN EACH INNINGS OF A MATCH

AUSTRALIA			Opponents		
W.Bardsley	136	130	England	The Oval	1909
A.R.Morris	122	124*	England	Adelaide	1946-47
D.G.Bradman	132	127*	India	Melbourne	1947-48
J.Moroney	118	101*	South Africa	Johannesburg[2]	1949-50
R.B.Simpson	153	115	Pakistan	Karachi	1964-65
K.D.Walters	242	103	West Indies	Sydney	1968-69
I.M.Chappell	145	121	New Zealand	Wellington	1973-74
G.S.Chappell	247*	133	New Zealand	Wellington	1973-74
G.S.Chappell	123	109*	West Indies	Brisbane[2]	1975-76
A.R.Border	150*	153	Pakistan	Lahore[2]	1979-80
A.R.Border	140	114*	New Zealand	Christchurch	1985-86
D.M.Jones	116	121*	Pakistan	Adelaide	1989-90
ENGLAND			Opponents		
C.A.G.Russell	140	111	South Africa	Durban[2]	1922-23
H.Sutcliffe	176	127	Australia	Melbourne	1924-25
W.R.Hammond	119*	177	Australia	Adelaide	1928-29
H.Sutcliffe	104	109*	South Africa	The Oval	1929
E.Paynter	117	100	South Africa	Johannesburg[1]	1938-39
D.C.S.Compton	147	103*	Australia	Adelaide	1946-47
G.A.Gooch	333	123	India	Lord's	1990

SOUTH AFRICA			Opponents		
A.Melville	189	104*	England	Nottingham	1947
B.Mitchell	120	189*	England	The Oval	1947
WEST INDIES			Opponents		
G.A.Headley	114	112	England	Georgetown	1929-30
G.A.Headley	106	107	England	Lord's	1939
E.D.Weekes	162	101	India	Calcutta	1948-49
C.L.Walcott	126	110	Australia	Port-of-Spain	1954-55
C.L.Walcott	155	110	Australia	Kingston	1954-55
G.S.Sobers	125	109*	Pakistan	Georgetown	1957-58
R.B.Kanhai	117	115	Australia	Adelaide	1960-61
L.G.Rowe	214	100*	New Zealand	Kingston	1971-72
C.G.Greenidge	134	101	England	Manchester	1976
NEW ZEALAND			Opponents		
G.M.Turner	101	110*	Australia	Christchurch	1973-74
G.P.Howarth	122	102	England	Auckland	1977-78
A.H.Jones	122	100*	Sri Lanka	Hamilton	1990-91
INDIA			Opponents		
V.S.Hazare	116	145	Australia	Adelaide	1947-48
S.M.Gavaskar	124	220	West Indies	Port-of-Spain	1970-71
S.M.Gavaskar	111	137	Pakistan	Karachi	1978-79
S.M.Gavaskar	107	182*	West Indies	Calcutta	1978-79
PAKISTAN			Opponents		
Hanif Mohammad	111	104	England	Dacca	1961-62
Javed Miandad	104	103*	New Zealand	Hyderabad	1984-85
SRI LANKA			Opponents		
L.R.D.Mendis	105	105	India	Madras[1]	1982-83
A.P.Gurusinha	119	102	New Zealand	Hamilton	1990-91

CENTURY AND A NINETY IN A MATCH

(§ In first Test. † in last Test)

AUSTRALIA			Opponents		
R.M.Cowper	92	108	India	Adelaide	1967-68
P.M.Toohey	122	97	West Indies	Kingston	1977-78
A.R.Border	98*	100*	West Indies	Port-of-Spain	1983-84
ENGLAND			Opponents		
P.A.Gibb §	93	106	South Africa	Johannesburg[1]	1938-39
M.C.Cowdrey	114	97	West Indies	Kingston	1959-60
K.F.Barrington	101	94	Australia	Sydney	1962-63
A.P.E.Knott	101	96	New Zealand	Auckland	1970-71
G.Boycott	99	112	West Indies	Port-of-Spain	1973-74
SOUTH AFRICA			Opponents		
P.G.V.van der Bijl †	125	97	England	Durban[2]	1938-39
WEST INDIES			Opponents		
G.S.Sobers	152	92*	England	Georgetown	1967-68
S.M.Nurse	95	168	New Zealand	Auckland	1968-69
C.G.Greenidge §	93	107	India	Bangalore	1974-75
INDIA			Opponents		
C.G.Borde	109	96	West Indies	Delhi	1958-59
M.Amarnath	90	100	Australia	Perth	1977-78
PAKISTAN			Opponents		
Hanif Mohammad	104	93	Australia	Melbourne	1964-65
Zaheer Abbas	176	96	India	Faisalabad	1978-79
Mohsin Khan	94	101*	India	Lahore[2]	1982-83

SRI LANKA

			Opponents		
L.R.D.Mendis	111	94	England	Lord's	1984
P.A.de Silva	96	123	New Zealand	Auckland	1990-91

NINETY IN EACH INNINGS OF A MATCH

AUSTRALIA

			Opponents		
C.Hill	98	97	England	Adelaide	1901-02

ENGLAND

			Opponents		
F.E.Woolley	95	93	Australia	Lord's	1921

WEST INDIES

			Opponents		
C.G.Greenidge	91	96	Pakistan	Georgetown	1976-77
C.G.Greenidge	91	97	New Zealand	Christchurch	1979-80

CENTURIES IN MOST CONSECUTIVE MATCHES

SIX

D.G.Bradman	Australia	270, 212, 169, 144*, 102*, 103	1936-37 to 1938

Because of injury Bradman was unable to bat in his next Test but scored 187 and 234 in his following two matches in 1946-47.

CENTURY ON DEBUT

IN BOTH INNINGS

L.G.Rowe	214) 100*)	West Indies	v	New Zealand	Kingston	1971-72

IN FIRST INNINGS

C.Bannerman	165*	Australia	v	England	Melbourne	1876-77
W.G.Grace	152	England	v	Australia	The Oval	1880
H.Graham	107	Australia	v	England	Lord's	1890
R.E.Foster	287	England	v	Australia	Sydney	1903-04
G.Gunn	119	England	v	Australia	Sydney	1907-08
W.H.Ponsford †Ω	110	Australia	v	England	Sydney	1924-25
A.Jackson	164	Australia	v	England	Adelaide	1928-29
J.E.Mills	117	New Zealand	v	England	Wellington	1929-30
Nawab of Pataudi, sr	102	England	v	Australia	Sydney	1932-33
B.H.Valentine	136	England	v	India	Bombay[1]	1933-34
S.C.Griffith	140	England	v	West Indies	Port-of-Spain	1947-48
A.G.Ganteaume ∫	112	West Indies	v	England	Port-of-Spain	1947-48
P.B.H.May	138	England	v	South Africa	Leeds	1951
R.H.Shodhan	110	India	v	Pakistan	Calcutta	1952-53
B.H.Pairaudeau	115	West Indies	v	India	Port-of-Spain	1952-53
A.G.Kripal Singh	100*	India	v	New Zealand	Hyderabad	1955-56
C.C.Hunte	142	West Indies	v	Pakistan	Bridgetown	1957-58
C.A.Milton	104*	England	v	New Zealand	Leeds	1958
Hanumant Singh	105	India	v	England	Delhi	1963-64
Khalid Ibadulla	166	Pakistan	v	Australia	Karachi	1964-65
B.R.Taylor	105	New Zealand	v	India	Calcutta	1964-65
K.D.Walters Ω	155	Australia	v	England	Brisbane[2]	1965-66
J.H.Hampshire	107	England	v	West Indies	Lord's	1969
G.S.Chappell †	108	Australia	v	England	Perth	1970-71
A.I.Kallicharran Ω	100*	West Indies	v	New Zealand	Georgetown	1971-72
R.E.Redmond ∫	107	New Zealand	v	Pakistan	Auckland	1972-73
G.J.Cosier	109	Australia	v	West Indies	Melbourne	1975-76
S.Amarnath ¡	124	India	v	New Zealand	Auckland	1975-76
Javed Miandad	163	Pakistan	v	New Zealand	Lahore[2]	1976-77
K.C.Wessels	162	Australia	v	England	Brisbane[2]	1982-83
W.B.Phillips	159	Australia	v	Pakistan	Perth	1983-84
M.Azharuddin ¶	110	India	v	England	Calcutta	1984-85
D.S.B.P.Kuruppu	201*	Sri Lanka	v	New Zealand	Colombo (CCC)	1986-87
M.E.Waugh	138	Australia	v	England	Adelaide	1990-91
A.C.Hudson	163	South Africa	v	West Indies	Bridgetown	1991-92
R.S.Kaluwitharana	132*	Sri Lanka	v	Australia	Colombo (SSC)	1992-93

IN SECOND INNINGS

K.S.Ranjitsinhji	154*	England	v	Australia	Manchester	1896
P.F.Warner	132*	England	v	South Africa	Johannesburg[1]	1898-99
R.A.Duff †	104	Australia	v	England	Melbourne	1901-02
R.J.Hartigan	116	Australia	v	England	Adelaide	1907-08
H.L.Collins	104	Australia	v	England	Sydney	1920-21
G.A.Headley	176	West Indies	v	England	Bridgetown	1929-30
N.B.Amarnath ¡	118	India	v	England	Bombay[1]	1933-34
P.A.Gibb §	106	England	v	South Africa	Johannesburg[1]	1938-39
J.W.Burke	101*	Australia	v	England	Adelaide	1950-51
O.G.Smith	104	West Indies	v	Australia	Kingston	1954-55
A.A.Baig	112	India	v	England	Manchester	1959
G.R.Viswanath	137	India	v	Australia	Kanpur	1969-70
F.C.Hayes	106*	England	v	West Indies	The Oval	1973
C.G.Greenidge §	107	West Indies	v	India	Bangalore	1974-75
L.Baichan	105*	West Indies	v	Pakistan	Lahore[2]	1974-75
A.B.Williams	100	West Indies	v	Australia	Georgetown	1977-78
D.M.Wellham	103	Australia	v	England	The Oval	1981
Saleem Malik	100*	Pakistan	v	Sri Lanka	Karachi	1981-82
M.J.Greatbatch	107*	New Zealand	v	England	Auckland	1987-88

§ Gibb and Greenidge both scored 93 in the first innings. † Duff, Ponsford and Chappell also scored a century in their last Test (Chappell also scored a century in each innings of his first Test as captain). Ω Ponsford, Walters and Kallicharran also scored a century in their second Test. ∫ Only Test. ¶ Azharuddin scored a century in each of his first three Tests. ¡ N.B. and S.Amarnath provide the only instance of a father and son scoring a century on debut.

MOST RUNS IN FIRST TEST MATCH

314	L.G.Rowe	(211 + 100*)	West Indies	v	New Zealand	Kingston	1971-72
306	R.E.Foster	(287 + 19)	England	v	Australia	Sydney	1903-04

B.M.Laird (92 and 75) scored 167 runs for Australia v West Indies at Brisbane[2] in 1979-80 the highest aggregate without a century by a player in his first Test.

MAIDEN FIRST-CLASS CENTURY IN A TEST MATCH

C.Bannerman § †	165*	Australia	v	England	Melbourne	1876-77
W.L.Murdoch	153*	Australia	v	England	The Oval	1880
P.S.McDonnell	147	Australia	v	England	Sydney	1881-82
H.Wood †	134*	England	v	South Africa	Cape Town	1891-92
H.Graham §	107	Australia	v	England	Lord's	1893
A.J.L.Hill	124	England	v	South Africa	Cape Town	1895-96
J.H.Sinclair	106	South Africa	v	England	Cape Town	1898-99
P.W.Sherwell	115	South Africa	v	England	Lord's	1907
H.G.Owen-Smith	129	South Africa	v	England	Leeds	1929
C.A.Roach	122	West Indies	v	England	Bridgetown	1929-30
S.C.Griffith §	140	England	v	West Indies	Port-of-Spain	1947-48
V.L.Manjrekar	133	India	v	England	Leeds	1952
C.C.Depeiza †	122	West Indies	v	Australia	Bridgetown	1954-55
P.L.Winslow	108	South Africa	v	England	Manchester	1955
S.N.McGregor	111	New Zealand	v	Pakistan	Lahore[1]	1955-56
F.C.M.Alexander †	108	West Indies	v	Australia	Sydney	1960-61
Nasim-ul-Ghani	101	Pakistan	v	England	Lord's	1962
B.R.Taylor §	105	New Zealand	v	India	Calcutta	1964-65
B.D.Julien	121	West Indies	v	England	Lord's	1973

W.K.Lees	152	New Zealand	v	Pakistan	Karachi	1976-77
Kapil Dev	126*	India	v	West Indies	Delhi	1978-79
S.Wettimuny	157	Sri Lanka	v	Pakistan	Faisalabad	1981-82
S.A.R.Silva	102*	Sri Lanka	v	England	Lord's	1984
D.S.B.P.Kuruppu §	201*	Sri Lanka	v	New Zealand	Colombo (CCC)	1986-87
R.C.Russell	128*	England	v	Australia	Manchester	1989

§ On Test debut. † Only century in first-class cricket. H.Graham (105 v England at Sydney in 1894-95), C.A.Roach (209 v England at Georgetown in 1929-30) and B.R.Taylor (124 v West Indies at Auckland in 1968-69) also scored their second first-class century in a Test match.

YOUNGEST PLAYERS TO SCORE A CENTURY

Years	Days							
17	82	Mushtaq Mohammad	101	Pakistan	v	India	Delhi	1960-61
17	112	S.R.Tendulkar	119*	India	v	England	Manchester	1990
18	328	Saleem Malik	100*	Pakistan	v	Sri Lanka	Karachi	1981-82
19	26	Mohammad Ilyas	126	Pakistan	v	New Zealand	Karachi	1964-65
19	119	Javed Miandad	163	Pakistan	v	New Zealand	Lahore²	1976-77
19	121	H.G.Vivian	100	New Zealand	v	South Africa	Wellington	1931-32
19	121	R.N.Harvey	153	Australia	v	India	Melbourne	1947-48
19	152	A.Jackson	164	Australia	v	England	Adelaide	1928-29
19	192	A.P.Gurusinha	116*	Sri Lanka	v	Pakistan	Colombo (PSS)	1985-86
19	318	R.G.Pollock	122	South Africa	v	Australia	Sydney	1963-64
19	357	K.D.Walters	155	Australia	v	England	Brisbane²	1965-66
20	3	Ijaz Ahmed	122	Pakistan	v	Australia	Faisalabad	1988-89
20	19	D.C.S.Compton	203	England	v	Australia	Nottingham	1938
20	21	Kapil Dev	126*	India	v	West Indies	Delhi	1978-79
20	58	Hanif Mohammad	142	Pakistan	v	India	Bahawalpur	1954-55
20	129	D.G.Bradman	112	Australia	v	England	Melbourne	1928-29
20	131	A.A.Baig	112	India	v	England	Manchester	1959
20	148	H.G.Owen-Smith	129	South Africa	v	England	Leeds	1929
20	154	Saeed Ahmed	150	Pakistan	v	West Indies	Georgetown	1957-58
20	230	G.A.Headley	176	West Indies	v	England	Bridgetown	1929-30
20	240	J.W.Burke	101*	Australia	v	England	Adelaide	1950-51
20	249	R.J.Shastri	128	India	v	Pakistan	Karachi	1982-83
20	253	V.L.Manjrekar	133	India	v	England	Leeds	1952
20	281	G.R.Viswanath	137	India	v	Australia	Kanpur	1969-70
20	317	C.Hill	188	Australia	v	England	Melbourne	1897-98
20	324	J.W.Hearne	114	England	v	Australia	Melbourne	1911-12
20	330	O.G.Smith	104	West Indies	v	Australia	Kingston	1954-55

Only the first century for each player is given. S.R.Tendulkar scored three centuries before his 19th birthday, R.N.Harvey, R.G.Pollock, Javed Miandad and Saleem Malik each scored two before their 20th and G.A.Headley four before his 21st.

YOUNGEST PLAYERS TO SCORE A DOUBLE CENTURY

Years	Days							
19	141	Javed Miandad	206	Pakistan	v	New Zealand	Karachi	1976-77
20	315	G.A.Headley	223	West Indies	v	England	Kingston	1929-30

YOUNGEST PLAYERS TO SCORE A TRIPLE CENTURY

Years	Days							
21	216	G.S.Sobers	365*	West Indies	v	Pakistan	Kingston	1957-58
21	318	D.G.Bradman	334	Australia	v	England	Leeds	1930

OLDEST PLAYERS TO SCORE A CENTURY

Years	Days							
46	82	J.B.Hobbs	142	England	v	Australia	Melbourne	1928-29
45	240	J.B.Hobbs	159	England	v	West Indies	The Oval	1928
45	151	E.H.Hendren	132	England	v	Australia	Manchester	1934

DISTRIBUTION OF TEST MATCH CENTURIES

Conceded By	Scored For A	E	SA	WI	NZ	I	P	SL	Total Conceded
Australia	0	194	36	73	17	35	31	4	390
England	214	0	58	99	36	56	33	3	499
South Africa	55	87	0	0	7	0	0	0	149
West Indies	70	87	1	0	17	55	17	0	247
New Zealand	23	75	11	25	0	22	33	6	195
India	51	70	0	76	21	0	41	7	266
Pakistan	37	44	0	21	18	31	0	6	157
Sri Lanka	10	3	0	0	8	9	8	0	38
Total Scored	460	560	106	294	124	208	163	26	1941

CENTURIES IN TEST CRICKET

(§ Denotes century on first appearance against that country)

AUSTRALIA (460)			Opponents		
Archer,RG		128	West Indies	Kingston	1954-55
Armstrong,WW	(6)	159*	South Africa	Johannesburg[1]	1902-03
		133*	England	Melbourne	1907-08
		132	South Africa	Melbourne	1910-11
		158	England	Sydney	1920-21
		121	England	Adelaide	1920-21
		123*	England	Melbourne	1920-21
Badcock,CL		118	England	Melbourne	1936-37
Bannerman,C		165* §	England	Melbourne	1876-77
		(The first century in Test cricket)			
Bardsley,W	(6)	136)	England	The Oval	1909
		130)			
		132 §	South Africa	Sydney	1910-11
		121	South Africa	Manchester	1912
		164	South Africa	Lord's	1912
		193*	England	Lord's	1926
Barnes,SG	(3)	234	England	Sydney	1946-47
		112	India	Adelaide	1947-48
		141	England	Lord's	1948
Benaud,J		142	Pakistan	Melbourne	1972-73
Benaud,R	(3)	121	West Indies	Kingston	1954-55
		122	South Africa	Johannesburg[3]	1957-58
		100	South Africa	Johannesburg[3]	1957-58
Bonnor,GJ		128	England	Sydney	1884-85
Boon,DC	(13)	123 §	India	Adelaide	1985-86
		131	India	Sydney	1985-86
		122	India	Madras[1]	1986-87
		103	England	Adelaide	1986-87
		143	New Zealand	Brisbane[2]	1987-88
		184*	England	Sydney	1987-88
		149	West Indies	Sydney	1988-89
		200	New Zealand	Perth	1989-90
		121	England	Adelaide	1990-91
		109*	West Indies	Kingston	1990-91
		129*	India	Sydney	1991-92
		135	India	Adelaide	1991-92
		107	India	Perth	1991-92

Booth,BC	(5)	112	England	Brisbane[2]	1962-63
		103	England	Melbourne	1962-63
		169 §	South Africa	Brisbane[2]	1963-64
		102*	South Africa	Sydney	1963-64
		117	West Indies	Port-of-Spain	1964-65
Border,AR	(24)	105 §	Pakistan	Melbourne	1978-79
		162 §	India	Madras[1]	1979-80
		115	England	Perth	1979-80
		150*)	Pakistan	Lahore[2]	1979-80
		153)			
		124	India	Melbourne	1980-81
		123*	England	Manchester	1981
		106*	England	The Oval	1981
		126	West Indies	Adelaide	1981-82
		118	Pakistan	Brisbane[2]	1983-84
		117*	Pakistan	Adelaide	1983-84
		100*	West Indies	Port-of-Spain	1983-84
		196	England	Lord's	1985
		146*	England	Manchester	1985
		152*	New Zealand	Brisbane[2]	1985-86
		163	India	Melbourne	1985-86
		140)	New Zealand	Christchurch	1985-86
		114*)			
		106	India	Madras[1]	1986-87
		125	England	Perth	1986-87
		100*	England	Adelaide	1986-87
		205	New Zealand	Adelaide	1987-88
		113*	Pakistan	Faisalabad	1988-89
		106	Sri Lanka	Moratuwa	1992-93
Bradman,DG	(29)	112	England	Melbourne	1928-29
		123	England	Melbourne	1928-29
		131	England	Nottingham	1930
		254	England	Lord's	1930
		334	England	Leeds	1930
		232	England	The Oval	1930
		223	West Indies	Brisbane[1]	1930-31
		152	West Indies	Melbourne	1930-31
		226 §	South Africa	Brisbane[1]	1931-32
		112	South Africa	Sydney	1931-32
		167	South Africa	Melbourne	1931-32
		299*	South Africa	Adelaide	1931-32
		103*	England	Melbourne	1932-33
		304	England	Leeds	1934
		244	England	The Oval	1934
		270	England	Melbourne	1936-37
		212	England	Adelaide	1936-37
		169	England	Melbourne	1936-37
		144*	England	Nottingham	1938
		102*	England	Lord's	1938
		103	England	Leeds	1938
		187	England	Brisbane[2]	1946-47
		234	England	Sydney	1946-47
		185 §	India	Brisbane[2]	1947-48
		132)	India	Melbourne	1947-48
		127*)			
		201	India	Adelaide	1947-48
		138	England	Nottingham	1948
		173*	England	Leeds	1948

Brown,WA	(4)	105	England	Lord's	1934
		121	South Africa	Cape Town	1935-36
		133	England	Nottingham	1938
		206*	England	Lord's	1938
Burge,PJP	(4)	181	England	The Oval	1961
		103	England	Sydney	1962-63
		160	England	Leeds	1964
		120	England	Melbourne	1965-66
Burke,JW	(3)	101* §	England	Adelaide	1950-51
		161	India	Bombay[2]	1956-57
		189	South Africa	Cape Town	1957-58
Chappell,GS	(24)	108 §	England	Perth	1970-71
		131	England	Lord's	1972
		113	England	The Oval	1972
		116*	Pakistan	Melbourne	1972-73
		106	West Indies	Bridgetown	1972-73
		247*)	New Zealand	Wellington	1973-74
		133)			
		144	England	Sydney	1974-75
		102	England	Melbourne	1974-75
		123)	West Indies	Brisbane[2]	1975-76
		109*)			
		182*	West Indies	Sydney	1975-76
		121	Pakistan	Melbourne	1976-77
		112	England	Manchester	1977
		124	West Indies	Brisbane[2]	1979-80
		114	England	Melbourne	1979-80
		235	Pakistan	Faisalabad	1979-80
		204 §	India	Sydney	1980-81
		201	Pakistan	Brisbane[2]	1981-82
		176	New Zealand	Christchurch	1981-82
		117	England	Perth	1982-83
		115	England	Adelaide	1982-83
		150*	Pakistan	Brisbane[2]	1983-84
		182	Pakistan	Sydney	1983-84
Chappell,IM	(14)	151	India	Melbourne	1967-68
		117 §	West Indies	Brisbane[2]	1968-69
		165	West Indies	Melbourne	1968-69
		138	India	Delhi	1969-70
		111	England	Melbourne	1970-71
		104	England	Adelaide	1970-71
		118	England	The Oval	1972
		196	Pakistan	Adelaide	1972-73
		106*	West Indies	Bridgetown	1972-73
		109	West Indies	Georgetown	1972-73
		145)	New Zealand	Wellington	1973-74
		121)			
		192	England	The Oval	1975
		156	West Indies	Perth	1975-76
Chipperfield,AG		109 §	South Africa	Durban[2]	1935-36
Collins,HL	(4)	104 §	England	Sydney	1920-21
		162	England	Adelaide	1920-21
		203	South Africa	Johannesburg[1]	1921-22
		114	England	Sydney	1924-25
Cosier,GJ	(2)	109 §	West Indies	Melbourne	1975-76
		168	Pakistan	Melbourne	1976-77
Cowper,RM	(5)	143	West Indies	Port-of-Spain	1964-65
		102	West Indies	Bridgetown	1964-65
		307	England	Melbourne	1965-66

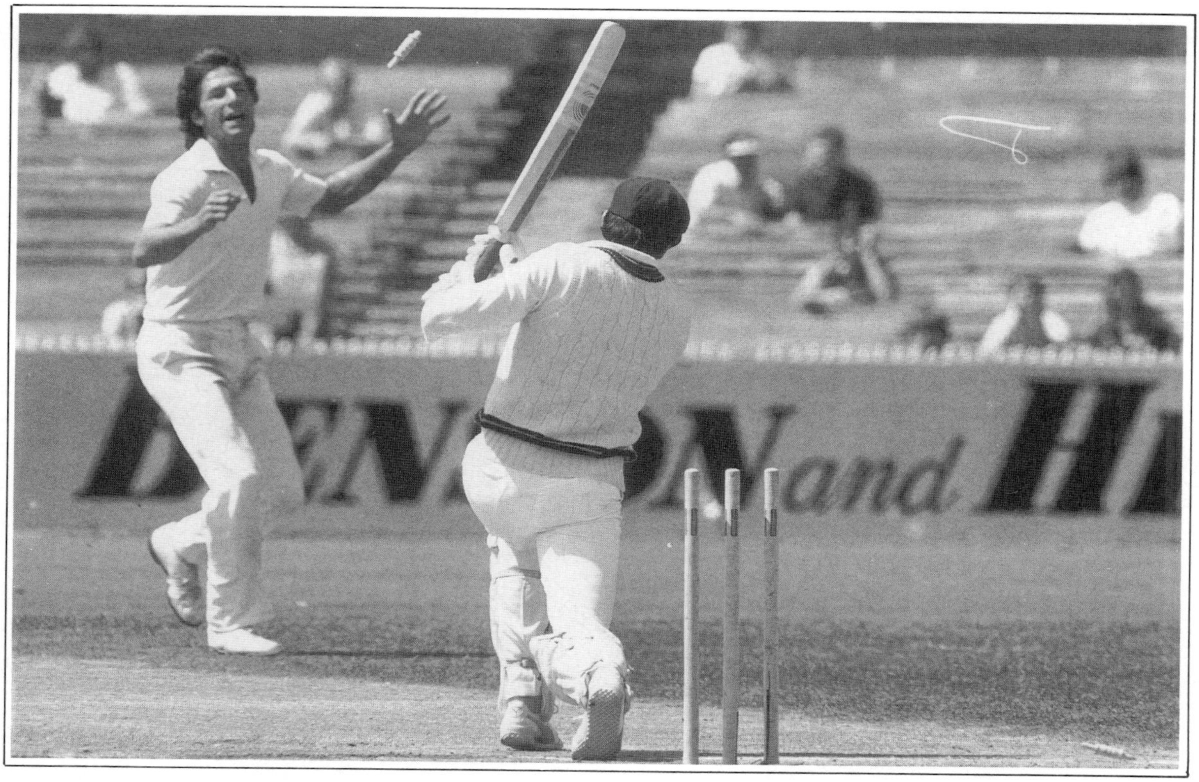

Pakistan's Imran Khan bowls Australia's Bruce Yardley for a duck in the third Test played at Melbourne in December 1981.
(Courtesy David Syme & Co. Limited.)

New Zealand's leading modern-day batsman, Martin Crowe, on his way to his maiden Test century against England at Wellington in January 1984.
(Courtesy the Wellington Dominion.*)*

Australian fast bowler Craig McDermott playing against the West Indies at Melbourne during the 1984-85 series. This was his first Test match.

(Courtesy the Melbourne Herald and Weekly Times.*)*

		108	India	Adelaide	1967-68
		165	India	Sydney	1967-68
Darling,J	(3)	101	England	Sydney	1897-98
		178	England	Adelaide	1897-98
		160	England	Sydney	1897-98
Davis,IC		105 §	Pakistan	Adelaide	1976-77
Duff,RA	(2)	104 §	England	Melbourne	1901-02
		146	England	The Oval	1905
Dyson,J	(2)	102	England	Leeds	1981
		127* §	West Indies	Sydney	1981-82
Edwards,R	(2)	170*	England	Nottingham	1972
		115	England	Perth	1974-75
Favell,LE		101	India	Madras[2]	1959-60
Fingleton,JHW	(5)	112	South Africa	Cape Town	1935-36
		108	South Africa	Johannesburg[1]	1935-36
		118	South Africa	Durban[2]	1935-36
		100	England	Brisbane[2]	1936-37
		136	England	Melbourne	1936-37
Giffen,G		161	England	Sydney	1894-95
Gilmour,GJ		101	New Zealand	Christchurch	1976-77
Graham,H	(2)	107 §	England	Lord's	1893
		105	England	Sydney	1894-95
Gregory,JM	(2)	100	England	Melbourne	1920-21
		119	South Africa	Johannesburg[1]	1921-22
		(Including the fastest Test century in 70 minutes)			
Gregory,SE	(4)	201	England	Sydney	1894-95
		103	England	Lord's	1896
		117	England	The Oval	1899
		112	England	Adelaide	1903-04
Hartigan,RJ		116 §	England	Adelaide	1907-08
Harvey,RN	(21)	153	India	Melbourne	1947-48
		112 §	England	Leeds	1948
		178	South Africa	Cape Town	1949-50
		151*	South Africa	Durban[2]	1949-50
		100	South Africa	Johannesburg[2]	1949-50
		116	South Africa	Port Elizabeth	1949-50
		109	South Africa	Brisbane[2]	1952-53
		190	South Africa	Sydney	1952-53
		116	South Africa	Adelaide	1952-53
		205	South Africa	Melbourne	1952-53
		122	England	Manchester	1953
		162	England	Brisbane[2]	1954-55
		133	West Indies	Kingston	1954-55
		133	West Indies	Port-of-Spain	1954-55
		204	West Indies	Kingston	1954-55
		140	India	Bombay[2]	1956-57
		167	England	Melbourne	1958-59
		114	India	Delhi	1959-60
		102	India	Bombay[2]	1959-60
		114	England	Birmingham	1961
		154	England	Adelaide	1962-63
Hassett,AL	(10)	128	England	Brisbane[2]	1946-47
		198*	India	Adelaide	1947-48
		137	England	Nottingham	1948
		112 §	South Africa	Johannesburg[1]	1949-50
		167	South Africa	Port Elizabeth	1949-50
		132	West Indies	Sydney	1951-52
		102	West Indies	Melbourne	1951-52
		163	South Africa	Adelaide	1952-53

		115	England	Nottingham	1953
		104	England	Lord's	1953
Hendry,HSTL		112	England	Sydney	1928-29
Hilditch,AMJ	(2)	113 §	West Indies	Melbourne	1984-85
		119	England	Leeds	1985
Hill,C	(7)	188	England	Melbourne	1897-98
		135	England	Lord's	1899
		119	England	Sheffield	1902
		142 §	South Africa	Johannesburg[1]	1902-03
		160	England	Adelaide	1907-08
		191	South Africa	Sydney	1910-11
		100	South Africa	Melbourne	1910-11
Hookes,DW		143* §	Sri Lanka	Kandy	1982-83
Horan,TP		124	England	Melbourne	1881-82
Hughes,KJ	(9)	129	England	Brisbane[2]	1978-79
		100	India	Madras[1]	1979-80
		130* §	West Indies	Brisbane[2]	1979-80
		117	England	Lord's	1980
		213	India	Adelaide	1980-81
		106	Pakistan	Perth	1981-82
		100*	West Indies	Melbourne	1981-82
		137	England	Sydney	1982-83
		106	Pakistan	Adelaide	1983-84
Iredale,FA	(2)	140	England	Adelaide	1894-95
		108	England	Manchester	1896
Jackson,AA		164 §	England	Adelaide	1928-29
Jones,DM	(11)	210 §	India	Madras[1]	1986-87
		184*	England	Sydney	1986-87
		102 §	Sri Lanka	Perth	1987-88
		216	West Indies	Adelaide	1988-89
		157	England	Birmingham	1989
		122	England	The Oval	1989
		118*	Sri Lanka	Hobart	1989-90
		116)	Pakistan	Adelaide	1989-90
		121*)			
		150*	India	Perth	1991-92
		100*	Sri Lanka	Colombo (KS)	1992-93
Kelleway,C	(3)	114	South Africa	Manchester	1912
		102	South Africa	Lord's	1912
		147	England	Adelaide	1920-21
Kippax,AF	(2)	100	England	Melbourne	1928-29
		146 §	West Indies	Adelaide	1930-31
Lawry,WM	(13)	130	England	Lord's	1961
		102	England	Manchester	1961
		157	South Africa	Melbourne	1963-64
		106	England	Manchester	1964
		210	West Indies	Bridgetown	1964-65
		166	England	Brisbane[2]	1965-66
		119	England	Adelaide	1965-66
		108	England	Melbourne	1965-66
		100	India	Melbourne	1967-68
		135	England	The Oval	1968
		105	West Indies	Brisbane[2]	1968-69
		205	West Indies	Melbourne	1968-69
		151	West Indies	Sydney	1968-69
Lindwall,RR	(2)	100	England	Melbourne	1946-47
		118	West Indies	Bridgetown	1954-55
Loxton,SJE		101 §	South Africa	Johannesburg[2]	1949-50
Lyons,JJ		134	England	Sydney	1891-92

Macartney,CG	(7)	137	South Africa	Sydney	1910-11
		170	England	Sydney	1920-21
		115	England	Leeds	1921
		116	South Africa	Durban[1]	1921-22
		133*	England	Lord's	1926
		151	England	Leeds	1926
		109	England	Manchester	1926
McCabe,SJ	(6)	187*	England	Sydney	1932-33
		137	England	Manchester	1934
		149	South Africa	Durban[2]	1935-36
		189*	South Africa	Johannesburg[1]	1935-36
		112	England	Melbourne	1936-37
		232	England	Nottingham	1938
McCool,CL		104*	England	Melbourne	1946-47
McCosker,RB	(4)	127	England	The Oval	1975
		109*	West Indies	Melbourne	1975-76
		105	Pakistan	Melbourne	1976-77
		107	England	Nottingham	1977
McDonald,CC	(5)	154	South Africa	Adelaide	1952-53
		110	West Indies	Port-of-Spain	1954-55
		127	West Indies	Kingston	1954-55
		170	England	Adelaide	1958-59
		133	England	Melbourne	1958-59
McDonnell,PS	(3)	147	England	Sydney	1881-82
		103	England	The Oval	1884
		124	England	Adelaide	1884-85
McLeod,CE		112	England	Melbourne	1897-98
Mann,AL		105	India	Perth	1977-78
Marsh,GR	(4)	118	New Zealand	Auckland	1985-86
		101	India	Bombay[3]	1986-87
		110 §	England	Brisbane[2]	1986-87
		138	England	Nottingham	1989
Marsh,RW	(3)	118 §	Pakistan	Adelaide	1972-73
		132	New Zealand	Adelaide	1973-74
		110*	England	Melbourne	1976-77
Matthews,GRJ	(4)	115 §	New Zealand	Brisbane[2]	1985-86
		100*	India	Melbourne	1985-86
		130	New Zealand	Wellington	1985-86
		128	England	Sydney	1990-91
Miller,KR	(7)	141*	England	Adelaide	1946-47
		145*	England	Sydney	1950-51
		129	West Indies	Sydney	1951-52
		109	England	Lord's	1953
		147	West Indies	Kingston	1954-55
		137	West Indies	Bridgetown	1954-55
		109	West Indies	Kingston	1954-55
Moody,TM	(2)	106 §	Sri Lanka	Brisbane[2]	1989-90
		101 §	India	Perth	1991-92
Moroney,J	(2)	118)	South Africa	Johannesburg[2]	1949-50
		101*)			
Morris,AR	(12)	155	England	Melbourne	1946-47
		122)	England	Adelaide	1946-47
		124*)			
		100*	India	Melbourne	1947-48
		105	England	Lord's	1948
		182	England	Leeds	1948
		196	England	The Oval	1948
		111	South Africa	Johannesburg[2]	1949-50
		157	South Africa	Port Elizabeth	1949-50

		206	England	Adelaide	1950-51
		153	England	Brisbane[2]	1954-55
		111	West Indies	Port-of-Spain	1954-55
Murdoch,WL	(2)	153*	England	The Oval	1880
		211	England	The Oval	1884
Noble,MA		133	England	Sydney	1903-04
O'Neill,NC	(6)	134	Pakistan	Lahore[2]	1959-60
		163	India	Bombay[2]	1959-60
		113	India	Calcutta	1959-60
		181 §	West Indies	Brisbane[2]	1960-61
		117	England	The Oval	1961
		100	England	Adelaide	1962-63
Pellew,CE	(2)	116	England	Melbourne	1920-21
		104	England	Adelaide	1920-21
Phillips,WB	(2)	159 §	Pakistan	Perth	1983-84
		120	West Indies	Bridgetown	1983-84
Ponsford,WH	(7)	110 §	England	Sydney	1924-25
		128	England	Melbourne	1924-25
		110	England	The Oval	1930
		183	West Indies	Sydney	1930-31
		109	West Indies	Brisbane[1]	1930-31
		181	England	Leeds	1934
		266	England	The Oval	1934
Ransford,VS		143*	England	Lord's	1909
Redpath,IR	(8)	132	West Indies	Sydney	1968-69
		171	England	Perth	1970-71
		135	Pakistan	Melbourne	1972-73
		159*	New Zealand	Auckland	1973-74
		105	England	Sydney	1974-75
		102	West Indies	Melbourne	1975-76
		103	West Indies	Adelaide	1975-76
		101	West Indies	Melbourne	1975-76
Richardson,AJ		100	England	Leeds	1926
Richardson,VY		138	England	Melbourne	1924-25
Rigg,KE		127 §	South Africa	Sydney	1931-32
Ritchie,GM	(3)	106*	Pakistan	Faisalabad	1982-83
		146	England	Nottingham	1985
		128 §	India	Adelaide	1985-86
Ryder,J	(3)	142	South Africa	Cape Town	1921-22
		201*	England	Adelaide	1924-25
		112	England	Melbourne	1928-29
Scott,HJH		102	England	The Oval	1884
Serjeant,CS		124	West Indies	Georgetown	1977-78
Sheahan,AP	(2)	114	India	Kanpur	1969-70
		127	Pakistan	Melbourne	1972-73
Simpson, RB	(10)	311	England	Manchester	1964
		153 §)	Pakistan	Karachi	1964-65
		115 §)			
		201	West Indies	Bridgetown	1964-65
		225	England	Adelaide	1965-66
		153	South Africa	Cape Town	1966-67
		103	India	Adelaide	1967-68
		109	India	Melbourne	1967-68
		176	India	Perth	1977-78
		100	India	Adelaide	1977-78
Stackpole,KR	(7)	134	South Africa	Cape Town	1966-67
		103 §	India	Bombay[2]	1969-70
		207	England	Brisbane[2]	1970-71
		136	England	Adelaide	1970-71

		114	England	Nottingham	1972
		142	West Indies	Kingston	1972-73
		122 §	New Zealand	Melbourne	1973-74
Taylor,JM		108	England	Sydney	1924-25
Taylor,MA	(8)	136 §	England	Leeds	1989
		219	England	Nottingham	1989
		164 §	Sri Lanka	Brisbane²	1989-90
		108	Sri Lanka	Hobart	1989-90
		101 §	Pakistan	Melbourne	1989-90
		101*	Pakistan	Sydney	1989-90
		144	West Indies	St John's	1990-91
		100	India	Adelaide	1991-92
Toohey,PM		122	West Indies	Kingston	1977-78
Trott,G HS		143	England	Lord's	1896
Trumper,VT	(8)	135*	England	Lord's	1899
		104	England	Manchester	1902
		185*	England	Sydney	1903-04
		113	England	Adelaide	1903-04
		166	England	Sydney	1907-08
		159	South Africa	Melbourne	1910-11
		214*	South Africa	Adelaide	1910-11
		113	England	Sydney	1911-12
Turner,A		136	West Indies	Adelaide	1975-76
Walters,KD	(15)	155 §	England	Brisbane²	1965-66
		115	England	Melbourne	1965-66
		118	West Indies	Sydney	1968-69
		110	West Indies	Adelaide	1968-68
		242)	West Indies	Sydney	1968-69
		103)			
		102	India	Madras¹	1969-70
		112	England	Brisbane²	1970-71
		102*	West Indies	Bridgetown	1972-73
		112	West Indies	Port-of-Spain	1972-73
		104*	New Zealand	Auckland	1973-74
		103	England	Perth	1974-75
		107	Pakistan	Adelaide	1976-77
		250	New Zealand	Christchurch	1976-77
		107	New Zealand	Melbourne	1980-81
Waugh,ME	(2)	138 §	England	Adelaide	1990-91
		139*	West Indies	St John's	1990-91
Waugh,SR	(3)	177*	England	Leeds	1989
		152*	England	Lord's	1989
		134*	Sri Lanka	Hobart	1989-90
Wellham,DM		103 §	England	The Oval	1981
Wessels,KC	(4)	162 §	England	Brisbane²	1982-83
		141 §	Sri Lanka	Kandy	1982-83
		179	Pakistan	Adelaide	1983-84
		173	West Indies	Sydney	1984-85
Wood,GM	(9)	126	West Indies	Georgetown	1977-78
		100	England	Melbourne	1978-79
		112	England	Lord's	1980
		111 §	New Zealand	Brisbane²	1980-81
		125	India	Adelaide	1980-81
		100	Pakistan	Melbourne	1981-82
		100	New Zealand	Auckland	1981-82
		172	England	Nottingham	1985
		111	West Indies	Perth	1988-89
Woodfull,WM	(7)	141	England	Leeds	1926
		117	England	Manchester	1926

		111	England	Sydney	1928-29
		107	England	Melbourne	1928-29
		102	England	Melbourne	1928-29
		155	England	Lord's	1930
		161	South Africa	Melbourne	1931-32
Yallop,GN	(8)	121 §	India	Adelaide	1977-78
		102 §	England	Brisbane²	1978-79
		121	England	Sydney	1978-79
		167	India	Calcutta	1979-80
		172	Pakistan	Faisalabad	1979-80
		114	England	Manchester	1981
		141	Pakistan	Perth	1983-84
		268	Pakistan	Melbourne	1983-84
ENGLAND (560)			Opponents		
Abel,R	(2)	120	South Africa	Cape Town	1888-89
		132*	Australia	Sydney	1891-92
Allen,GOB		122 §	New Zealand	Lord's	1931
Ames,LEG	(8)	105	West Indies	Port-of-Spain	1929-30
		149	West Indies	Kingston	1929-30
		137 §	New Zealand	Lord's	1931
		103	New Zealand	Christchurch	1932-33
		120	Australia	Lord's	1934
		126	West Indies	Kingston	1934-35
		148*	South Africa	The Oval	1935
		115	South Africa	Cape Town	1938-39
Amiss,DL	(11)	112	Pakistan	Lahore²	1972-73
		158	Pakistan	Hyderabad	1972-73
		138* §	New Zealand	Nottingham	1973
		174	West Indies	Port-of-Spain	1973-74
		262*	West Indies	Kingston	1973-74
		118	West Indies	Georgetown	1973-74
		188	India	Lord's	1974
		183	Pakistan	The Oval	1974
		164*	New Zealand	Christchurch	1974-75
		203	West Indies	The Oval	1976
		179	India	Delhi	1976-77
Atherton,MA	(3)	151	New Zealand	Nottingham	1990
		131	India	Manchester	1990
		105	Australia	Sydney	1990-91
Athey,CWJ		123	Pakistan	Lord's	1987
Bailey,TE		134*	New Zealand	Christchurch	1950-51
Bakewell,AH		107 §	West Indies	The Oval	1933
Barber,RW		185	Australia	Sydney	1965-66
Barnes,W		134	Australia	Adelaide	1884-85
Barnett,CJ	(2)	129	Australia	Adelaide	1936-37
		126	Australia	Nottingham	1938
Barrington,KF	(20)	128 §	West Indies	Bridgetown	1959-60
		121	West Indies	Port-of-Spain	1959-60
		139 §	Pakistan	Lahore²	1961-62
		151*	India	Bombay²	1961-62
		172	India	Kanpur	1961-62
		113*	India	Delhi	1961-62
		132*	Australia	Adelaide	1962-63
		101	Australia	Sydney	1962-63
		126 §	New Zealand	Auckland	1962-63
		256	Australia	Manchester	1964
		148*	South Africa	Durban²	1964-65
		121	South Africa	Johannesburg³	1964-65

		137	New Zealand	Birmingham	1965
		163	New Zealand	Leeds	1965
		102	Australia	Adelaide	1965-66
		115	Australia	Melbourne	1965-66
		148	Pakistan	Lord's	1967
		109*	Pakistan	Nottingham	1967
		142	Pakistan	The Oval	1967
		143	West Indies	Port-of-Spain	1967-68
Botham,IT	(14)	103	New Zealand	Christchurch	1977-78
		100 §	Pakistan	Birmingham	1978
		108	Pakistan	Lord's	1978
		137	India	Leeds	1979
		119*	Australia	Melbourne	1979-80
		114	India	Bombay[3]	1979-80
		149*	Australia	Leeds	1981
		118	Australia	Manchester	1981
		142	India	Kanpur	1981-82
		128	India	Manchester	1982
		208	India	The Oval	1982
		103	New Zealand	Nottingham	1983
		138	New Zealand	Wellington	1983-84
		138	Australia	Brisbane[2]	1986-87
Bowley,EH		109	New Zealand	Auckland	1929-30
Boycott,G	(22)	113	Australia	The Oval	1964
		117	South Africa	Port Elizabeth	1964-65
		246* §	India	Leeds	1967
		116	West Indies	Georgetown	1967-68
		128	West Indies	Manchester	1969
		106	West Indies	Lord's	1969
		142*	Australia	Sydney	1970-71
		119*	Australia	Adelaide	1970-71
		121*	Pakistan	Lord's	1971
		112	Pakistan	Leeds	1971
		115	New Zealand	Leeds	1973
		112	West Indies	Port-of-Spain	1973-74
		107	Australia	Nottingham	1977
		191	Australia	Leeds	1977
	(His 100th first-class century)				
		100*	Pakistan	Hyderabad	1977-78
		131	New Zealand	Nottingham	1978
		155	India	Birmingham	1979
		125	India	The Oval	1979
		128*	Australia	Lord's	1980
		104*	West Indies	St John's	1980-81
		137	Australia	The Oval	1981
		105	India	Delhi	1981-82
Braund,LC	(3)	103*	Australia	Adelaide	1901-02
		102	Australia	Sydney	1903-04
		104 §	South Africa	Lord's	1907
Briggs,J		121	Australia	Melbourne	1884-85
Broad,BC	(6)	162	Australia	Perth	1986-87
		116	Australia	Adelaide	1986-87
		112	Australia	Melbourne	1986-87
		116	Pakistan	Faisalabad	1987-88
		139	Australia	Sydney	1987-88
		114 §	New Zealand	Christchurch	1987-88
Brown,JT		140	Australia	Melbourne	1894-95
Chapman,APF		121	Australia	Lord's	1930

Compton,DCS	(17)	102 §	Australia	Nottingham	1938
		120 §	West Indies	Lord's	1939
		147)	Australia	Adelaide	1946-47
		103*)			
		163 §	South Africa	Nottingham	1947
		208	South Africa	Lord's	1947
		115	South Africa	Manchester	1947
		113	South Africa	The Oval	1947
		184	Australia	Nottingham	1948
		145*	Australia	Manchester	1948
		114	South Africa	Johannesburg[2]	1948-49
		114	New Zealand	Leeds	1949
		116	New Zealand	Lord's	1949
		112	South Africa	Nottingham	1951
		133	West Indies	Port-of-Spain	1953-54
		278	Pakistan	Nottingham	1954
		158	South Africa	Manchester	1955
Cowdrey,MC	(22)	102	Australia	Melbourne	1954-55
		101	South Africa	Cape Town	1956-57
		154 §	West Indies	Birmingham	1957
		152	West Indies	Lord's	1957
		100*	Australia	Sydney	1958-59
		160	India	Leeds	1959
		114	West Indies	Kingston	1959-60
		119	West Indies	Port-of-Spain	1959-60
		155	South Africa	The Oval	1960
		159 §	Pakistan	Birmingham	1962
		182	Pakistan	The Oval	1962
		113	Australia	Melbourne	1962-63
		128*	New Zealand	Wellington	1962-63
		107	India	Calcutta	1963-64
		151	India	Delhi	1963-64
		119	New Zealand	Lord's	1965
		105	South Africa	Nottingham	1965
		104	Australia	Melbourne	1965-66
		101	West Indies	Kingston	1967-68
		148	West Indies	Port-of-Spain	1967-68
		104	Australia	Birmingham	1968
		(In his 100th Test match)			
		100	Pakistan	Lahore[2]	1968-69
Denness,MH	(4)	118	India	Lord's	1974
		100	India	Birmingham	1974
		188	Australia	Melbourne	1974-75
		181	New Zealand	Auckland	1974-75
Denton, D		104	South Africa	Johannesburg[1]	1909-10
Dexter,ER	(9)	141	New Zealand	Christchurch	1958-59
		136* §	West Indies	Bridgetown	1959-60
		110	West Indies	Georgetown	1959-60
		180	Australia	Birmingham	1961
		126*	India	Kanpur	1961-62
		205	Pakistan	Karachi	1961-62
		172	Pakistan	The Oval	1962
		174	Australia	Manchester	1964
		172	South Africa	Johannesburg[3]	1964-65
D'Oliveira,BL	(5)	109 §	India	Leeds	1967
		158	Australia	The Oval	1968
		114*	Pakistan	Dacca	1968-69
		117	Australia	Melbourne	1970-71
		100	New Zealand	Christchurch	1970-71

Douglas,JWHT		119 §	South Africa	Durban[1]	1913-14
Duleepsinhji,KS	(3)	117	New Zealand	Auckland	1929-30
		173 §	Australia	Lord's	1930
		109	New Zealand	The Oval	1931
Edrich,JH	(12)	120 §	Australia	Lord's	1964
		310* §	New Zealand	Leeds	1965
		109	Australia	Melbourne	1965-66
		103	Australia	Sydney	1965-66
		146	West Indies	Bridgetown	1967-68
		164	Australia	The Oval	1968
		115	New Zealand	Lord's	1969
		115	New Zealand	Nottingham	1969
		115*	Australia	Perth	1970-71
		130	Australia	Adelaide	1970-71
		100*	India	Manchester	1974
		175	Australia	Lord's	1975
Edrich,WJ	(6)	219	South Africa	Durban[2]	1938-39
		119	Australia	Sydney	1946-47
		189	South Africa	Lord's	1947
		191	South Africa	Manchester	1947
		111	Australia	Leeds	1948
		100	New Zealand	The Oval	1949
Evans,TG	(2)	104	West Indies	Manchester	1950
		104	India	Lord's	1952
Fane,FL		143	South Africa	Johannesburg[1]	1905-06
Fletcher,KWR	(7)	113	India	Bombay[2]	1972-73
		178	New Zealand	Lord's	1973
		129*	West Indies	Bridgetown	1973-74
		123*	India	Manchester	1974
		122	Pakistan	The Oval	1974
		146	Australia	Melbourne	1974-75
		216	New Zealand	Auckland	1974-75
Foster,RE		287 §	Australia	Sydney	1903-04
Fowler,G	(3)	105 §	New Zealand	The Oval	1983
		106	West Indies	Lord's	1984
		201	India	Madras[1]	1984-85
Fry,CB	(2)	144	Australia	The Oval	1905
		129	South Africa	The Oval	1907
Gatting,MW	(9)	136	India	Bombay[3]	1984-85
		207	India	Madras[1]	1984-85
		100*	Australia	Birmingham	1985
		160	Australia	Manchester	1985
		183*	India	Birmingham	1986
		121	New Zealand	The Oval	1986
		100	Australia	Adelaide	1986-87
		124	Pakistan	Birmingham	1987
		150*	Pakistan	The Oval	1987
Gibb,PA	(2)	106 §	South Africa	Johannesburg[1]	1938-39
		120	South Africa	Durban[2]	1938-39
Gooch,GA	(17)	123	West Indies	Lord's	1980
		116	West Indies	Bridgetown	1980-81
		153	West Indies	Kingston	1980-81
		127	India	Madras[1]	1981-82
		196	Australia	The Oval	1985
		114	India	Lord's	1986
		183	New Zealand	Lord's	1986
		146	West Indies	Nottingham	1988
		154	New Zealand	Birmingham	1990

		333)	India	Lord's	1990
		123)			
		116	India	Manchester	1990
		117	Australia	Adelaide	1990-91
		154*	West Indies	Leeds	1991
		174	Sri Lanka	Lord's	1991
		114	New Zealand	Auckland	1991-92
		135	Pakistan	Leeds	1992
Gower,DI	(18)	111 §	New Zealand	The Oval	1978
		102	Australia	Perth	1978-79
		200* §	India	Birmingham	1979
		154*	West Indies	Kingston	1980-81
		114	Australia	Adelaide	1982-83
		112*	New Zealand	Leeds	1983
		108	New Zealand	Lord's	1983
		152	Pakistan	Faisalabad	1983-84
		173*	Pakistan	Lahore[2]	1983-84
		166	Australia	Nottingham	1985
		215	Australia	Birmingham	1985
		157	Australia	The Oval	1985
		131	New Zealand	The Oval	1986
		136	Australia	Perth	1986-87
		106	Australia	Lord's	1989
		157*	India	The Oval	1990
		100	Australia	Melbourne	1990-91
		123	Australia	Sydney	1990-91
Grace,WG	(2)	152 §	Australia	The Oval	1880
		170	Australia	The Oval	1886
Graveney,TW	(11)	175 §	India	Bombay[2]	1951-52
		111	Australia	Sydney	1954-55
		258	West Indies	Nottingham	1957
		164	West Indies	The Oval	1957
		153	Pakistan	Lord's	1962
		114	Pakistan	Nottingham	1962
		109	West Indies	Nottingham	1966
		165	West Indies	The Oval	1966
		151	India	Lord's	1967
		118	West Indies	Port-of-Spain	1967-68
		105	Pakistan	Karachi	1968-69
Greig,AW	(8)	148	India	Bombay[2]	1972-73
		139 §	New Zealand	Nottingham	1973
		148	West Indies	Bridgetown	1973-74
		121	West Indies	Georgetown	1973-74
		106	India	Lord's	1974
		110	Australia	Brisbane[2]	1974-75
		116	West Indies	Leeds	1976
		103	India	Calcutta	1976-77
Griffith,SC		140 §	West Indies	Port-of-Spain	1947-48
Gunn,G	(2)	119 §	Australia	Sydney	1907-08
		122*	Australia	Sydney	1907-08
Gunn,W		102*	Australia	Manchester	1893
Hammond,WR	(22)	251	Australia	Sydney	1928-29
		200	Australia	Melbourne	1928-29
		119*)	Australia	Adelaide	1928-29
		177)			
		138*	South Africa	Birmingham	1929
		101*	South Africa	The Oval	1929
		113	Australia	Leeds	1930
		136*	South Africa	Durban[2]	1930-31

		100*	New Zealand	The Oval	1931
		112	Australia	Sydney	1932-33
		101	Australia	Sydney	1932-33
		227	New Zealand	Christchurch	1932-33
		336*	New Zealand	Auckland	1932-33
		167	India	Manchester	1936
		217	India	The Oval	1936
		231*	Australia	Sydney	1936-37
		140	New Zealand	Lord's	1937
		240	Australia	Lord's	1938
		181	South Africa	Cape Town	1938-39
		120	South Africa	Durban[2]	1938-39
		140	South Africa	Durban[2]	1938-39
		138	West Indies	The Oval	1939
Hampshire,JH		107 §	West Indies	Lord's	1969
Hardstaff,J,jr	(4)	114 §	New Zealand	Lord's	1937
		103	New Zealand	The Oval	1937
		169*	Australia	The Oval	1938
		205*	India	Lord's	1946
Hayes,FC		106 §	West Indies	The Oval	1973
Hayward,TW	(3)	122	South Africa	Johannesburg[1]	1895-96
		130	Australia	Manchester	1899
		137	Australia	The Oval	1899
Hearne,JW		114	Australia	Melbourne	1911-12
Hendren,EH	(7)	132	South Africa	Leeds	1924
		142	South Africa	The Oval	1924
		127*	Australia	Lord's	1926
		169	Australia	Brisbane[1]	1928-29
		205*	West Indies	Port-of-Spain	1929-30
		123	West Indies	Georgetown	1929-30
		132	Australia	Manchester	1934
Hill,AJL		124	South Africa	Cape Town	1895-96
Hobbs,JB	(15)	187	South Africa	Cape Town	1909-10
		126*	Australia	Melbourne	1911-12
		187	Australia	Adelaide	1911-12
		178	Australia	Melbourne	1911-12
		107	Australia	Lord's	1912
		122	Australia	Melbourne	1920-21
		123	Australia	Adelaide	1920-21
		211	South Africa	Lord's	1924
		115	Australia	Sydney	1924-25
		154	Australia	Melbourne	1924-25
		119	Australia	Adelaide	1924-25
		119	Australia	Lord's	1926
		100	Australia	The Oval	1926
		159	West Indies	The Oval	1928
		142	Australia	Melbourne	1928-29
Hutchings,KL		126	Australia	Melbourne	1907-08
Hutton,L	(19)	100	New Zealand	Manchester	1937
		100 §	Australia	Nottingham	1938
		364	Australia	The Oval	1938
		196 §	West Indies	Lord's	1939
		165*	West Indies	The Oval	1939
		122*	Australia	Sydney	1946-47
		100	South Africa	Leeds	1947
		158	South Africa	Johannesburg[2]	1948-49
		123	South Africa	Johannesburg[2]	1948-49
		101	New Zealand	Leeds	1949
		206	New Zealand	The Oval	1949

		202*	West Indies	The Oval	1950
		156*	Australia	Adelaide	1950-51
		100	South Africa	Leeds	1951
		150	India	Lord's	1952
		104	India	Manchester	1952
		145	Australia	Lord's	1953
		169	West Indies	Georgetown	1953-54
		205	West Indies	Kingston	1953-54
Illingworth,R	(2)	113	West Indies	Lord's	1969
		107	India	Manchester	1971
Insole,DJ		110*	South Africa	Durban[2]	1956-57
Jackson,Hon.FS	(5)	103	Australia	The Oval	1893
		118	Australia	The Oval	1899
		128	Australia	Manchester	1902
		144*	Australia	Leeds	1905
		113	Australia	Manchester	1905
Jardine,DR		127	West Indies	Manchester	1933
Jessop,GL		104	Australia	The Oval	1902
Knight,B R	(2)	125 §	New Zealand	Auckland	1962-63
		127	India	Kanpur	1963-64
Knott,APE	(5)	101	New Zealand	Auckland	1970-71
		116	Pakistan	Birmingham	1971
		106*	Australia	Adelaide	1974-75
		116	West Indies	Leeds	1976
		135	Australia	Nottingham	1977
Lamb,AJ	(14)	107	India	The Oval	1982
		102* §	New Zealand	The Oval	1983
		137*	New Zealand	Nottingham	1983
		110	West Indies	Lord's	1984
		100	West Indies	Leeds	1984
		100*	West Indies	Manchester	1984
		107 §	Sri Lanka	Lord's	1984
		113	West Indies	Lord's	1988
		125	Australia	Leeds	1989
		132	West Indies	Kingston	1989-90
		119	West Indies	Bridgetown	1989-90
		139	India	Lord's	1990
		109	India	Manchester	1990
		142	New Zealand	Wellington	1991-92
Legge,GB		196	New Zealand	Auckland	1929-30
Lewis,AR		125	India	Kanpur	1972-73
Leyland,M	(9)	137 §	Australia	Melbourne	1928-29
		102	South Africa	Lord's	1929
		109	Australia	Lord's	1934
		153	Australia	Manchester	1934
		110	Australia	The Oval	1934
		161	South Africa	The Oval	1935
		126	Australia	Brisbane[2]	1936-37
		111*	Australia	Melbourne	1936-37
		187	Australia	The Oval	1938
Lloyd,D		214*	India	Birmingham	1974
Luckhurst,BW	(4)	131	Australia	Perth	1970-71
		109	Australia	Melbourne	1970-71
		108* §	Pakistan	Birmingham	1971
		101	India	Manchester	1971
MacLaren,AC	(5)	120	Australia	Melbourne	1894-95
		109	Australia	Sydney	1897-98
		124	Australia	Adelaide	1897-98
		116	Australia	Sydney	1901-02

		140	Australia	Nottingham	1905
Makepeace,JWH		117	Australia	Melbourne	1920-21
Mann,FG		136*	South Africa	Port Elizabeth	1948-49
May,PBH	(13)	138 §	South Africa	Leeds	1951
		135	West Indies	Port-of-Spain	1953-54
		104	Australia	Sydney	1954-55
		112	South Africa	Lord's	1955
		117	South Africa	Manchester	1955
		101	Australia	Leeds	1956
		285*	West Indies	Birmingham	1957
		104	West Indies	Nottingham	1957
		113*	New Zealand	Leeds	1958
		101	New Zealand	Manchester	1958
		113	Australia	Melbourne	1958-59
		124*	New Zealand	Auckland	1958-59
		106	India	Nottingham	1959
Mead,CP	(4)	102	South Africa	Johannesburg[1]	1913-14
		117	South Africa	Port Elizabeth	1913-14
		182*	Australia	The Oval	1921
		181	South Africa	Durban[2]	1922-23
Milburn,C	(2)	126*	West Indies	Lord's	1966
		139	Pakistan	Karachi	1968-69
Milton,CA		104* §	New Zealand	Leeds	1958
Murray,JT		112 §	West Indies	The Oval	1966
Parfitt,PH	(7)	111	Pakistan	Karachi	1961-62
		101*	Pakistan	Birmingham	1962
		119	Pakistan	Leeds	1962
		101*	Pakistan	Nottingham	1962
		131* §	New Zealand	Auckland	1962-63
		121	India	Kanpur	1963-64
		122*	South Africa	Johannesburg[3]	1964-65
Parks,JM	(2)	101* §	West Indies	Port-of-Spain	1959-60
		108*	South Africa	Durban[2]	1964-65
Pataudi,Nawab of,sr		102 §	Australia	Sydney	1932-33
Paynter,E	(4)	216*	Australia	Nottingham	1938
		117 §)	South Africa	Johannesburg[1]	1938-39
		100 §)			
		243	South Africa	Durban[2]	1938-39
Place,W		107	West Indies	Kingston	1947-48
Pullar,G	(4)	131	India	Manchester	1959
		175	South Africa	The Oval	1960
		119	India	Kanpur	1961-62
		165	Pakistan	Dacca	1961-62
Radley,CT	(2)	158	New Zealand	Auckland	1977-78
		106 §	Pakistan	Birmingham	1978
Randall,DW	(7)	174 §	Australia	Melbourne	1976-77
		150	Australia	Sydney	1978-79
		126	India	Lord's	1982
		105	Pakistan	Birmingham	1982
		115	Australia	Perth	1982-83
		164	New Zealand	Wellington	1983-84
		104	New Zealand	Auckland	1983-84
Ranjitsinhji,KS	(2)	154* §	Australia	Manchester	1896
		175	Australia	Sydney	1897-98
Read,WW		117	Australia	The Oval	1884
Rhodes,W	(2)	179	Australia	Melbourne	1911-12
		152	South Africa	Johannesburg[1]	1913-14
Richards,CJ		133	Australia	Perth	1986-87
Richardson,PE	(5)	104*	Australia	Manchester	1956

		117 §	South Africa	Johannesburg[3]	1956-57
		126	West Indies	Nottingham	1957
		107	West Indies	The Oval	1957
		100 §	New Zealand	Birmingham	1958
Robertson,JDB	(2)	133	West Indies	Port-of-Spain	1947-48
		121 §	New Zealand	Lord's	1949
Robins,RWV		108	South Africa	Manchester	1935
Robinson,RT	(4)	160	India	Delhi	1984-85
		175 §	Australia	Leeds	1985
		148	Australia	Birmingham	1985
		166 §	Pakistan	Manchester	1987
Russell,CAG	(5)	135*	Australia	Adelaide	1920-21
		101	Australia	Manchester	1921
		102*	Australia	The Oval	1921
		140)	South Africa	Durban[2]	1922-23
		111)			
Russell,RC	(1)	128*	Australia	Manchester	1989
Sandham,A	(2)	152 §	West Indies	Bridgetown	1929-30
		325	West Indies	Kingston	1929-30
Sharp,J		105	Australia	The Oval	1909
Sharpe,PJ		111	New Zealand	Nottingham	1969
Sheppard,Rev.DS	(3)	119	India	The Oval	1952
		113	Australia	Manchester	1956
		113	Australia	Melbourne	1962-63
Shrewsbury,A	(3)	105*	Australia	Melbourne	1884-85
		164	Australia	Lord's	1886
		106	Australia	Lord's	1893
Simpson,RT	(4)	103 §	New Zealand	Manchester	1949
		156*	Australia	Melbourne	1950-51
		137	South Africa	Nottingham	1951
		101	Pakistan	Nottingham	1954
Smith,MJK	(3)	100 §	India	Manchester	1959
		108	West Indies	Port-of-Spain	1959-60
		121	South Africa	Cape Town	1964-65
Smith,RA	(7)	143	Australia	Manchester	1989
		101	Australia	Nottingham	1989
		100* §	India	Lord's	1990
		121*	India	Manchester	1990
		148*	West Indies	Lord's	1991
		109	West Indies	The Oval	1991
		127 §	Pakistan	Birmingham	1992
Spooner,RH		119 §	South Africa	Lord's	1912
Steel,AG	(2)	135*	Australia	Sydney	1882-83
		148	Australia	Lord's	1884
Steele,DS		106 §	West Indies	Nottingham	1976
Stewart,AJ	(4)	113* §	Sri Lanka	Lord's	1991
		148	New Zealand	Christchurch	1991-92
		107	New Zealand	Wellington	1991-92
		190 §	Pakistan	Birmingham	1992
Stoddart,AE	(2)	134	Australia	Adelaide	1891-92
		173	Australia	Melbourne	1894-95
Sutcliffe,H	(16)	122	South Africa	Lord's	1924
		115 §	Australia	Sydney	1924-25
		176)	Australia	Melbourne	1924-25
		127)			
		143	Australia	Melbourne	1924-25
		161	Australia	The Oval	1926
		102	South Africa	Johannesburg[1]	1927-28
		135	Australia	Melbourne	1928-29

		114	South Africa	Birmingham	1929
		100	South Africa	Lord's	1929
		104)	South Africa	The Oval	1929
		109*)			
		161	Australia	The Oval	1930
		117 §	New Zealand	The Oval	1931
		109*	New Zealand	Manchester	1931
		194	Australia	Sydney	1932-33
Tate,MW		100*	South Africa	Lord's	1929
Tavare,CJ	(2)	149	India	Delhi	1981-82
		109 §	New Zealand	The Oval	1983
Tyldesley,GE	(3)	122	South Africa	Johannesburg[1]	1927-28
		100	South Africa	Durban[2]	1927-28
		122 §	West Indies	Birmingham	1928
Tyldesley,JT	(4)	112	South Africa	Cape Town	1898-99
		138	Australia	Birmingham	1902
		100	Australia	Leeds	1905
		112*	Australia	The Oval	1905
Ulyett,G		149	Australia	Melbourne	1881-82
Valentine,BH	(2)	136 §	India	Bombay[1]	1933-34
		112	South Africa	Cape Town	1938-39
Walters,CF		102	India	Madras[1]	1933-34
Ward,Albert		117	Australia	Sydney	1894-95
Warner,PF		132* §	South Africa	Johannesburg[1]	1898-99
Washbrook,C	(6)	112	Australia	Melbourne	1946-47
		143	Australia	Leeds	1948
		195	South Africa	Johannesburg[2]	1948-49
		103*	New Zealand	Leeds	1949
		114 §	West Indies	Lord's	1950
		102	West Indies	Nottingham	1950
Watkins,AJ	(2)	111	South Africa	Johannesburg[2]	1948-49
		137 §	India	Delhi	1951-52
Watson,W	(2)	109 §	Australia	Lord's	1953
		116 §	West Indies	Kingston	1953-54
Willey,P	(2)	100*	West Indies	The Oval	1980
		102*	West Indies	St John's	1980-81
Wood,H		134*	South Africa	Cape Town	1891-92
Woolley,FE	(5)	133*	Australia	Sydney	1911-12
		115*	South Africa	Johannesburg[1]	1922-23
		134*	South Africa	Lord's	1924
		123	Australia	Sydney	1924-25
		154	South Africa	Manchester	1929
Woolmer,RA	(3)	149	Australia	The Oval	1975
		120	Australia	Lord's	1977
		137	Australia	Manchester	1977
Worthington,TS		128	India	The Oval	1936
Wyatt,RES	(2)	113	South Africa	Manchester	1929
		149	South Africa	Nottingham	1935

SOUTH AFRICA (106)			Opponents		
Balaskas,XC		122*	New Zealand	Wellington	1931-32
Barlow,EJ	(6)	114 §	Australia	Brisbane[2]	1963-64
		109	Australia	Melbourne	1963-64
		201	Australia	Adelaide	1963-64
		138	England	Cape Town	1964-65
		127	Australia	Cape Town	1969-70
		110	Australia	Johannesburg[3]	1969-70
Bland,KC	(3)	126	Australia	Sydney	1963-64
		144*	England	Johannesburg[3]	1964-65

		127	England	The Oval	1965
Catterall,RH	(3)	120	England	Birmingham	1924
		120	England	Lord's	1924
		119	England	Durban[2]	1927-28
Christy,JAJ		103 §	New Zealand	Christchurch	1931-32
Dalton,EL	(2)	117	England	The Oval	1935
		102	England	Johannesburg[1]	1938-39
Endean,WR	(3)	162*	Australia	Melbourne	1952-53
		116	New Zealand	Auckland	1952-53
		116*	England	Leeds	1955
Faulkner,GA	(4)	123	England	Johannesburg[1]	1909-10
		204	Australia	Melbourne	1910-11
		115	Australia	Adelaide	1910-11
		122*	Australia	Manchester	1912
Frank,CN		152	Australia	Johannesburg[1]	1921-22
Goddard,TL		112	England	Johannesburg[3]	1964-65
Hathorn,CMH		102	England	Johannesburg[1]	1905-06
Hudson,AC		163 §	West Indies	Bridgetown	1991-92
Irvine,BL		102	Australia	Port Elizabeth	1969-70
Lindsay,DT	(3)	182	Australia	Johannesburg[3]	1966-67
		137	Australia	Durban[2]	1966-67
		131	Australia	Johannesburg[3]	1966-67
McGlew,DJ	(7)	255* §	New Zealand	Wellington	1952-53
		104*	England	Manchester	1955
		133	England	Leeds	1955
		108	Australia	Johannesburg[3]	1957-58
		105	Australia	Durban[2]	1957-58
		127*	New Zealand	Durban[2]	1961-62
		120	New Zealand	Johannesburg[3]	1961-62
McLean,RA	(5)	101	New Zealand	Durban[2]	1953-54
		142	England	Lord's	1955
		100	England	Durban[2]	1956-57
		109	England	Manchester	1960
		113	New Zealand	Cape Town	1961-62
Melville,A	(4)	103	England	Durban[2]	1938-39
		189)	England	Nottingham	1947
		104*)			
		117	England	Lord's	1947
Mitchell,B	(8)	123	England	Cape Town	1930-31
		113 §	New Zealand	Christchurch	1931-32
		164*	England	Lord's	1935
		128	England	The Oval	1935
		109	England	Durban[2]	1938-39
		120)	England	The Oval	1947
		189*)			
		120	England	Cape Town	1948-49
Murray,ARA		109 §	New Zealand	Wellington	1952-53
Nourse,AD	(9)	231	Australia	Johannesburg[1]	1935-36
		120	England	Cape Town	1938-39
		103	England	Durban[2]	1938-39
		149	England	Nottingham	1947
		115	England	Manchester	1947
		112	England	Cape Town	1948-49
		129*	England	Johannesburg[2]	1948-49
		114	Australia	Cape Town	1949-50
		208	England	Nottingham	1951
Nourse,AW		111	Australia	Johannesburg[1]	1921-22
Owen-Smith,HG		129	England	Leeds	1929
Pithey,AJ		154	England	Cape Town	1964-65

Pollock,RG	(7)	122	Australia	Sydney	1963-64
		175	Australia	Adelaide	1963-64
		137	England	Port Elizabeth	1964-65
		125	England	Nottingham	1965
		209	Australia	Cape Town	1966-67
		105	Australia	Port Elizabeth	1966-67
		274	Australia	Durban²	1969-70
Richards,BA	(2)	140	Australia	Durban²	1969-70
		126	Australia	Port Elizabeth	1969-70
Rowan,EAB	(3)	156*	England	Johannesburg²	1948-49
		143	Australia	Durban²	1949-50
		236	England	Leeds	1951
Sherwell,PW		115	England	Lord's	1907
Siedle,IJ		141	England	Cape Town	1930-31
Sinclair,JH	(3)	106	England	Cape Town	1898-99
		101	Australia	Johannesburg¹	1902-03
		104	Australia	Cape Town	1902-03
Snooke,SJ		103	Australia	Adelaide	1910-11
Taylor,HW	(7)	109	England	Durban¹	1913-14
		176	England	Johannesburg¹	1922-23
		101	England	Johannesburg¹	1922-23
		102	England	Durban²	1922-23
		101	England	Johannesburg¹	1927-28
		121	England	The Oval	1929
		117	England	Cape Town	1930-31
Van der Bijl,PGV		125	England	Durban²	1938-39
Viljoen,KG	(2)	111	Australia	Melbourne	1931-32
		124	England	Manchester	1935
Wade,WW		125	England	Port Elizabeth	1948-49
Waite,JHB	(4)	113	England	Manchester	1955
		115	Australia	Johannesburg³	1957-58
		134	Australia	Durban²	1957-58
		101	New Zealand	Johannesburg³	1961-62
White,GC	(2)	147	England	Johannesburg¹	1905-06
		118	England	Durban¹	1909-10
Winslow,PL		108	England	Manchester	1955
Zulch,JW	(2)	105	Australia	Adelaide	1910-11
		150	Australia	Sydney	1910-11

WEST INDIES (294)			Opponents		
Alexander,FCM		108	Australia	Sydney	1960-61
Atkinson,DS		219	Australia	Bridgetown	1954-55
Bacchus,SFAF		250	India	Kanpur	1978-79
Baichan,L		105* §	Pakistan	Lahore²	1974-75
Barrow,I		105	England	Manchester	1933
Best,CA		164	England	Bridgetown	1989-90
Butcher,BF	(7)	103	India	Calcutta	1958-59
		142	India	Madras²	1958-59
		133	England	Lord's	1963
		117	Australia	Port-of-Spain	1964-65
		209*	England	Nottingham	1966
		101	Australia	Sydney	1968-69
		118	Australia	Adelaide	1968-69
Carew,GM		107	England	Port-of-Spain	1947-48
Carew,MC		109 §	New Zealand	Auckland	1968-69
Christiani,RJ		107 §	India	Delhi	1948-49
Davis,CA	(4)	103	England	Lord's	1969
		125*	India	Georgetown	1970-71
		105	India	Port-of-Spain	1970-71

		183	New Zealand	Bridgetown	1971-72
Depeiza,CC		122	Australia	Bridgetown	1954-55
Dujon,PJL	(5)	110	India	St John's	1982-83
		130	Australia	Port-of-Spain	1983-84
		101	England	Manchester	1984
		139	Australia	Perth	1984-85
		106*	Pakistan	Port-of-Spain	1987-88
Foster,MLC		125 §	Australia	Kingston	1972-73
Fredericks,RC	(8)	163	New Zealand	Kingston	1971-72
		150	England	Birmingham	1973
		100	India	Calcutta	1974-75
		104	India	Bombay[3]	1974-75
		169	Australia	Perth	1975-76
		138	England	Lord's	1976
		109	England	Leeds	1976
		120	Pakistan	Port-of-Spain	1976-77
Ganteaume,AG		112 §	England	Port-of-Spain	1947-48
Gomes,HA	(9)	101 §	Australia	Georgetown	1977-78
		115	Australia	Kingston	1977-78
		126*	Australia	Sydney	1981-82
		124*	Australia	Adelaide	1981-82
		123	India	Port-of-Spain	1982-83
		143	England	Birmingham	1984
		104*	England	Leeds	1984
		127	Australia	Perth	1984-85
		120*	Australia	Adelaide	1984-85
Gomez,GE		101 §	India	Delhi	1948-49
Greenidge,CG	(19)	107 §	India	Bangalore	1974-75
		134)	England	Manchester	1976
		101)			
		115	England	Leeds	1976
		100	Pakistan	Kingston	1976-77
		154*	India	St John's	1982-83
		194	India	Kanpur	1983-84
		120*	Australia	Georgetown	1983-84
		127	Australia	Kingston	1983-84
		214*	England	Lord's	1984
		223	England	Manchester	1984
		100	New Zealand	Port-of-Spain	1984-85
		213	New Zealand	Auckland	1986-87
		141	India	Calcutta	1987-88
		103	England	Lord's	1988
		104	Australia	Adelaide	1988-89
		117	India	Bridgetown	1988-89
		149	England	St John's	1989-90
		(In his 100th Test match)			
		226	Australia	Bridgetown	1990-91
Haynes,DL	(16)	105 §	New Zealand	Dunedin	1979-80
		122	New Zealand	Christchurch	1979-80
		184	England	Lord's	1980
		136	India	St John's	1982-83
		103*	Australia	Georgetown	1983-84
		145	Australia	Bridgetown	1983-84
		125	England	The Oval	1984
		131	England	St John's	1985-86
		121	New Zealand	Wellington	1986-87
		100	Australia	Perth	1988-89
		143	Australia	Sydney	1988-89
		112*	India	Bridgetown	1988-89

		109	England	Bridgetown	1989-90
		167	England	St John's	1989-90
		117	Pakistan	Karachi	1990-91
		111	Australia	Georgetown	1990-91
Headley,GA	(10)	176 §	England	Bridgetown	1929-30
		114)	England	Georgetown	1929-30
		112)			
		223	England	Kingston	1929-30
		102*	Australia	Brisbane[1]	1930-31
		105	Australia	Sydney	1930-31
		169*	England	Manchester	1933
		270*	England	Kingston	1934-35
		106)	England	Lord's	1939
		107)			
Holford,DAJ		105*	England	Lord's	1966
Holt,JK	(2)	166	England	Bridgetown	1953-54
		123	India	Delhi	1958-59
Hooper,CL	(3)	100*	India	Calcutta	1987-88
		134	Pakistan	Lahore[2]	1990-91
		111	England	Lord's	1991
Hunte,CC	(8)	142 §	Pakistan	Bridgetown	1957-58
		260	Pakistan	Kingston	1957-58
		114	Pakistan	Georgetown	1957-58
		110	Australia	Melbourne	1960-61
		182	England	Manchester	1963
		108*	England	The Oval	1963
		135	England	Manchester	1966
		101	India	Bombay[2]	1966-67
Julien,BD	(2)	121	England	Lord's	1973
		101	Pakistan	Karachi	1974-75
Kallicharran,AI	(12)	100* §	New Zealand	Georgetown	1971-72
		101	New Zealand	Port-of-Spain	1971-72
		158	England	Port-of-Spain	1973-74
		119	England	Bridgetown	1973-74
		124 §	India	Bangalore	1974-75
		115	Pakistan	Karachi	1974-75
		101	Australia	Brisbane[2]	1975-76
		103*	India	Port-of-Spain	1975-76
		127	Australia	Port-of-Spain	1977-78
		126	Australia	Kingston	1977-78
		187	India	Bombay[3]	1978-79
		106	Australia	Adelaide	1979-80
Kanhai,RB	(15)	256	India	Calcutta	1958-59
		217	Pakistan	Lahore[1]	1958-59
		110	England	Port-of-Spain	1959-60
		117)	Australia	Adelaide	1960-61
		115)			
		138	India	Kingston	1961-62
		139	India	Port-of-Spain	1961-62
		129	Australia	Bridgetown	1964-65
		121	Australia	Port-of-Spain	1964-65
		104	England	The Oval	1966
		153	England	Port-of-Spain	1967-68
		150	England	Georgetown	1967-68
		158*	India	Kingston	1970-71
		105	Australia	Bridgetown	1972-73
		157	England	Lord's	1973
King,CL		100*	New Zealand	Christchurch	1979-80

Lloyd,CH	(19)	118 §	England	Port-of-Spain	1967-68
		113*	England	Bridgetown	1967-68
		129 §	Australia	Brisbane[2]	1968-69
		178	Australia	Georgetown	1972-73
		132	England	The Oval	1973
		163	India	Bangalore	1974-75
		242*	India	Bombay[3]	1974-75
		149	Australia	Perth	1975-76
		102	Australia	Melbourne	1975-76
		102	India	Bridgetown	1975-76
		157	Pakistan	Bridgetown	1976-77
		121	Australia	Adelaide	1979-80
		101	England	Manchester	1980
		100	England	Bridgetown	1980-81
		143	India	Port-of-Spain	1982-83
		106	India	St John's	1982-83
		103	India	Delhi	1983-84
		161*	India	Calcutta	1983-84
		114	Australia	Brisbane[2]	1984-85
Logie,AL	(2)	130	India	Bridgetown	1982-83
		101	India	Calcutta	1987-88
McMorris,EDAS		125 §	India	Kingston	1961-62
Martin,FR		123*	Australia	Sydney	1930-31
Nurse,SM	(6)	201	Australia	Bridgetown	1964-65
		137	England	Leeds	1966
		136	England	Port-of-Spain	1967-68
		137	Australia	Sydney	1968-69
		168 §	New Zealand	Auckland	1968-69
		258	New Zealand	Christchurch	1968-69
Pairaudeau,BH		115 §	India	Port-of-Spain	1952-53
Rae,AF	(4)	104	India	Bombay[2]	1948-49
		109	India	Madras[1]	1948-49
		106	England	Lord's	1950
		109	England	The Oval	1950
Richards,IVA	(24)	192*	India	Delhi	1974-75
		101	Australia	Adelaide	1975-76
		142	India	Bridgetown	1975-76
		130	India	Port-of-Spain	1975-76
		177	India	Port-of-Spain	1975-76
		232 §	England	Nottingham	1976
		135	England	Manchester	1976
		291	England	The Oval	1976
		140	Australia	Brisbane[2]	1979-80
		145	England	Lord's	1980
		120	Pakistan	Multan	1980-81
		182*	England	Bridgetown	1980-81
		114	England	St John's	1980-81
		109	India	Georgetown	1982-83
		120	India	Bombay[3]	1983-84
		178	Australia	St John's	1983-84
		117	England	Birmingham	1984
		208	Australia	Melbourne	1984-85
		105	New Zealand	Bridgetown	1984-85
		110*	England	St John's	1985-86
		109*	India	Delhi	1987-88
		123	Pakistan	Port-of-Spain	1987-88
		146	Australia	Perth	1988-89
		110	India	Kingston	1988-89

Richardson,RB	(14)	131*	Australia	Bridgetown	1983-84
		154	Australia	St John's	1983-84
		138	Australia	Brisbane²	1984-85
		185	New Zealand	Georgetown	1984-85
		102	England	Port-of-Spain	1985-86
		160	England	Bridgetown	1985-86
		122	Australia	Melbourne	1988-89
		106	Australia	Adelaide	1988-89
		194	India	Georgetown	1988-89
		156	India	Kingston	1988-89
		104*	Australia	Kingston	1990-91
		182	Australia	Georgetown	1990-91
		104	England	Birmingham	1991
		121	England	The Oval	1991
Roach,CA	(2)	122	England	Bridgetown	1929-30
		209	England	Georgetown	1929-30
Rowe,LG	(7)	214 §)	New Zealand	Kingston	1971-72
		100* §)			
		120	England	Kingston	1973-74
		302	England	Bridgetown	1973-74
		123	England	Port-of-Spain	1973-74
		107	Australia	Brisbane²	1975-76
		100	New Zealand	Christchurch	1979-80
Shillingford,IT		120	Pakistan	Georgetown	1976-77
Smith,OG	(4)	104 §	Australia	Kingston	1954-55
		161 §	England	Birmingham	1957
		168	England	Nottingham	1957
		100	India	Delhi	1958-59
Sobers,GS	(26)	365*	Pakistan	Kingston	1957-58
		125)	Pakistan	Georgetown	1957-58
		109*)			
		142* §	India	Bombay²	1958-59
		198	India	Kanpur	1958-59
		106*	India	Calcutta	1958-59
		226	England	Bridgetown	1959-60
		147	England	Kingston	1959-60
		145	England	Georgetown	1959-60
		132	Australia	Brisbane²	1960-61
		168	Australia	Sydney	1960-61
		153	India	Kingston	1961-62
		104	India	Kingston	1961-62
		102	England	Leeds	1963
		161	England	Manchester	1966
		163*	England	Lord's	1966
		174	England	Leeds	1966
		113*	England	Kingston	1967-68
		152	England	Georgetown	1967-68
		110	Australia	Adelaide	1968-69
		113	Australia	Sydney	1968-69
		108*	India	Georgetown	1970-71
		178	India	Bridgetown	1970-71
		132	India	Port-of-Spain	1970-71
		142	New Zealand	Bridgetown	1971-72
		150*	England	Lord's	1973
Solomon,JS		100*	India	Delhi	1958-59
Stollmeyer,JB	(4)	160	India	Madras¹	1948-49
		104	Australia	Sydney	1951-52
		152	New Zealand	Auckland	1951-52
		104*	India	Port-of-Spain	1952-53

Walcott,CL	(15)	152 §	India	Delhi	1948-49
		108	India	Calcutta	1948-49
		168*	England	Lord's	1950
		115	New Zealand	Auckland	1951-52
		125	India	Georgetown	1952-53
		118	India	Kingston	1952-53
		220	England	Bridgetown	1953-54
		124	England	Port-of-Spain	1953-54
		116	England	Kingston	1953-54
		108	Australia	Kingston	1954-55
		126)	Australia	Port-of-Spain	1954-55
		110)			
		155)	Australia	Kingston	1954-55
		110)			
		145	Pakistan	Georgetown	1957-58
Weekes,ED	(15)	141	England	Kingston	1947-48
		128 §	India	Delhi	1948-49
		194	India	Bombay[2]	1948-49
		162)	India	Calcutta	1948-49
		101)			
		129	England	Nottingham	1950
		207	India	Port-of-Spain	1952-53
		161	India	Port-of-Spain	1952-53
		109	India	Kingston	1952-53
		206	England	Port-of-Spain	1953-54
		139	Australia	Port-of-Spain	1954-55
		123	New Zealand	Dunedin	1955-56
		103	New Zealand	Christchurch	1955-56
		156	New Zealand	Wellington	1955-56
		197 §	Pakistan	Bridgetown	1957-58
Weekes,KH		137	England	The Oval	1939
Williams,AB	(2)	100 §	Australia	Georgetown	1977-78
		111	India	Calcutta	1978-79
Worrell,FMM	(9)	131*	England	Georgetown	1947-48
		261	England	Nottingham	1950
		138	England	The Oval	1950
		108	Australia	Melbourne	1951-52
		100	New Zealand	Auckland	1951-52
		237	India	Kingston	1952-53
		167	England	Port-of-Spain	1953-54
		191*	England	Nottingham	1957
		197*	England	Bridgetown	1959-60
NEW ZEALAND (124)			Opponents		
Barton,PT		109	South Africa	Port Elizabeth	1961-62
Bracewell,JG		110	England	Nottingham	1986
Burgess,MG	(5)	119*	Pakistan	Dacca	1969-70
		104	England	Auckland	1970-71
		101	West Indies	Kingston	1971-72
		105	England	Lord's	1973
		111	Pakistan	Lahore[2]	1976-77
Coney,JV	(3)	174*	England	Wellington	1983-84
		111*	Pakistan	Dunedin	1984-85
		101*	Australia	Wellington	1985-86
Congdon,BE	(7)	101	England	Christchurch	1965-66
		166*	West Indies	Port-of-Spain	1971-72
		126	West Indies	Bridgetown	1971-72
		176	England	Nottingham	1973
		175	England	Lord's	1973

		132	Australia	Wellington	1973-74
		107*	Australia	Christchurch	1976-77
Crowe,JJ	(3)	128	England	Auckland	1983-84
		112	West Indies	Kingston	1984-85
		120*	Sri Lanka	Colombo (CCC)	1986-87
Crowe,MD	(13)	100	England	Wellington	1983-84
		188	West Indies	Georgetown	1984-85
		188	Australia	Brisbane²	1985-86
		137	Australia	Christchurch	1985-86
		106	England	Lord's	1986
		119	West Indies	Wellington	1986-87
		104	West Indies	Auckland	1986-87
		137	Australia	Adelaide	1987-88
		143	England	Wellington	1987-88
		174	Pakistan	Wellington	1988-89
		113	India	Auckland	1989-90
		108*	Pakistan	Lahore²	1990-91
		299	Sri Lanka	Wellington	1990-91
Dempster,CS	(2)	136	England	Wellington	1929-30
		120	England	Lord's	1931
Donnelly,MP		206	England	Lord's	1949
Dowling,GT	(3)	129	India	Bombay²	1964-65
		143	India	Dunedin	1967-68
		239	India	Christchurch	1967-68
Edgar,BA	(3)	129 §	Pakistan	Christchurch	1978-79
		127	West Indies	Auckland	1979-80
		161	Australia	Auckland	1981-82
Franklin,TJ		101	England	Lord's	1990
Greatbatch,MJ	(2)	107* §	England	Auckland	1987-88
		146* §	Australia	Perth	1989-90
Guy,J W		102 §	India	Hyderabad	1955-56
Hadlee,RJ	(2)	103	West Indies	Christchurch	1979-80
		151*	Sri Lanka	Colombo (CCC)	1986-87
Hadlee,WA		116	England	Christchurch	1946-47
Harris,PGZ		101	South Africa	Cape Town	1961-62
Hastings,BF	(4)	117*	West Indies	Christchurch	1968-69
		105	West Indies	Bridgetown	1971-72
		110	Pakistan	Auckland	1972-73
		101	Australia	Wellington	1973-74
Howarth,GP	(6)	122)	England	Auckland	1977-78
		102)			
		123	England	Lord's	1978
		114	Pakistan	Napier	1978-79
		147	West Indies	Christchurch	1979-80
		137 §	India	Wellington	1980-81
Jarvis,TW		182	West Indies	Georgetown	1971-72
Jones,AH	(6)	150	Australia	Adelaide	1987-88
		170	India	Auckland	1989-90
		186	Sri Lanka	Wellington	1990-91
		122)	Sri Lanka	Hamilton	1990-91
		100*)			
		143	England	Wellington	1991-92
Lees,WK		152	Pakistan	Karachi	1976-77
McGregor,SN		111	Pakistan	Lahore¹	1955-56
Mills,JE		117 §	England	Wellington	1929-30
Morrison,JFM		117	Australia	Sydney	1973-74
Page,ML		104	England	Lord's	1931
Parker,JM	(3)	108	Australia	Sydney	1973-74
		121	England	Auckland	1974-75

		104	India	Bombay[3]	1976-77
Pollard,V	(2)	116	England	Nottingham	1973
		105*	England	Lord's	1973
Rabone,GO		107	South Africa	Durban[2]	1953-54
Redmond,RE		107 §	Pakistan	Auckland	1972-73
Reid,JF	(6)	123*	India	Christchurch	1980-81
		180	Sri Lanka	Colombo (CCC)	1983-84
		106	Pakistan	Hyderabad	1984-85
		148	Pakistan	Wellington	1984-85
		158*	Pakistan	Auckland	1984-85
		108 §	Australia	Brisbane[2]	1985-86
Reid,JR	(6)	135	South Africa	Cape Town	1953-54
		119*	India	Delhi	1955-56
		120	India	Calcutta	1955-56
		142	South Africa	Johannesburg[3]	1961-62
		100	England	Christchurch	1962-63
		128	Pakistan	Karachi	1964-65
Rutherford,KR		107*	England	Wellington	1987-88
Sinclair,BW	(3)	138	South Africa	Auckland	1963-64
		130	Pakistan	Lahore[2]	1964-65
		114	England	Auckland	1965-66
Smith,IDS	(2)	113*	England	Auckland	1983-84
		173	India	Auckland	1989-90
Sutcliffe,B	(5)	101	England	Manchester	1949
		116	England	Christchurch	1950-51
		137* §	India	Hyderabad	1955-56
		230*	India	Delhi	1955-56
		151*	India	Calcutta	1964-65
Taylor,BR	(2)	105 §	India	Calcutta	1964-65
		124 §	West Indies	Auckland	1968-69
Turner,GM	(7)	110 §	Pakistan	Dacca	1969-70
		223*	West Indies	Kingston	1971-72
		259	West Indies	Georgetown	1971-72
		101)	Australia	Christchurch	1973-74
		110*)			
		117	India	Christchurch	1975-76
		113	India	Kanpur	1976-77
Vivian,HG		100 §	South Africa	Wellington	1931-32
Wright,JG	(12)	110	India	Auckland	1980-81
		141	Australia	Christchurch	1981-82
		130	England	Auckland	1983-84
		107	Pakistan	Karachi	1984-85
		119	England	The Oval	1986
		138	West Indies	Wellington	1986-87
		103	England	Auckland	1987-88
		185	India	Christchurch	1989-90
		113*	India	Napier	1989-90
		117*	Australia	Wellington	1989-90
		101	Sri Lanka	Hamilton	1990-91
		116	England	Wellington	1991-92

INDIA (208)			Opponents		
Adhikari,HR		114* §	West Indies	Delhi	1948-49
Amarnath,M	(11)	100	Australia	Perth	1977-78
		101*	West Indies	Kanpur	1978-79
		109*	Pakistan	Lahore[2]	1982-83
		120	Pakistan	Lahore[2]	1982-83
		103*	Pakistan	Karachi	1982-83
		117	West Indies	Port-of-Spain	1982-83

		116	West Indies	St John's	1982-83
		101*	Pakistan	Lahore[2]	1984-85
		116*	Sri Lanka	Kandy	1985-86
		138	Australia	Sydney	1985-86
		131	Sri Lanka	Nagpur	1986-87
Amarnath,NB		118 §	England	Bombay[1]	1933-34
Amarnath,S		124 §	New Zealand	Auckland	1975-76
Apte,ML		163*	West Indies	Port-of-Spain	1952-53
Azharuddin,M	(11)	110 §	England	Calcutta	1984-85
		105	England	Madras[1]	1984-85
		122	England	Kanpur	1984-85
		199	Sri Lanka	Kanpur	1986-87
		141	Pakistan	Calcutta	1986-87
		110	Pakistan	Jaipur	1986-87
		109	Pakistan	Faisalabad	1989-90
		192	New Zealand	Auckland	1989-90
		121	England	Lord's	1990
		179	England	Manchester	1990
		106	Australia	Adelaide	1991-92
Baig,AA		112 §	England	Manchester	1959
Borde,CG	(5)	109	West Indies	Delhi	1958-59
		177*	Pakistan	Madras[2]	1960-61
		109	New Zealand	Bombay[2]	1964-65
		121	West Indies	Bombay[2]	1966-67
		125	West Indies	Madras[1]	1966-67
Contractor,NJ		108	Australia	Bombay[2]	1959-60
Durani,SA		104	West Indies	Port-of-Spain	1961-62
Engineer,FM	(2)	109	West Indies	Madras[1]	1966-67
		121	England	Bombay[2]	1972-73
Gaekwad,AD	(2)	102	West Indies	Kanpur	1978-79
		201	Pakistan	Jullundur	1983-84
Gavaskar,SM	(34)	116	West Indies	Georgetown	1970-71
		117*	West Indies	Bridgetown	1970-71
		124)	West Indies	Port-of-Spain	1970-71
		220)			
		101	England	Manchester	1974
		116 §	New Zealand	Auckland	1975-76
		156	West Indies	Port-of-Spain	1975-76
		102	West Indies	Port-of-Spain	1975-76
		119	New Zealand	Bombay[3]	1976-77
		108	England	Bombay[3]	1976-77
		113 §	Australia	Brisbane[2]	1977-78
		127	Australia	Perth	1977-78
		118	Australia	Melbourne	1977-78
		111)	Pakistan	Karachi	1978-79
		137)			
		205	West Indies	Bombay[3]	1978-79
		107)	West Indies	Calcutta	1978-79
		182*)			
		120	West Indies	Delhi	1978-79
		221	England	The Oval	1979
		115	Australia	Delhi	1979-80
		123	Australia	Bombay[3]	1979-80
		166	Pakistan	Madras[1]	1979-80
		172	England	Bangalore	1981-82
		155 §	Sri Lanka	Madras[1]	1982-83
		127*	Pakistan	Faisalabad	1982-83
		147*	West Indies	Georgetown	1982-83
		103*	Pakistan	Bangalore	1983-84

		121	West Indies	Delhi	1983-84
		236*	West Indies	Madras^1	1983-84
		166*	Australia	Adelaide	1985-86
		172	Australia	Sydney	1985-86
		103	Australia	Bombay^3	1986-87
		176	Sri Lanka	Kanpur	1986-87
Hanumant Singh		105 §	England	Delhi	1963-64
Hazare,VS	(7)	116)	Australia	Adelaide	1947-48
		145)			
		134*	West Indies	Bombay^2	1948-49
		122	West Indies	Bombay^2	1948-49
		164*	England	Delhi	1951-52
		155	England	Bombay^2	1951-52
		146*	Pakistan	Bombay^2	1952-53
Jaisimha,ML	(3)	127	England	Delhi	1961-62
		129	England	Calcutta	1963-64
		101	Australia	Brisbane^2	1967-68
Kapil Dev	(7)	126*	West Indies	Delhi	1978-79
		116	England	Kanpur	1981-82
		100*	West Indies	Port-of-Spain	1982-83
		119	Australia	Madras^1	1986-87
		163	Sri Lanka	Kanpur	1986-87
		109	West Indies	Madras^1	1987-88
		110	England	The Oval	1990
Kirmani,SMH	(2)	101*	Australia	Bombay^3	1979-80
		102	England	Bombay^3	1984-85
Kripal Singh,AG		100* §	New Zealand	Hyderabad	1955-56
Kunderan,BK	(2)	192	England	Madras^2	1963-64
		100	England	Delhi	1963-64
Manjrekar,SV	(3)	108	West Indies	Bridgetown	1988-89
		113*	Pakistan	Karachi	1989-90
		218	Pakistan	Lahore^2	1989-90
Manjrekar,VL	(7)	133	England	Leeds	1952
		118	West Indies	Kingston	1952-53
		118 §	New Zealand	Hyderabad	1955-56
		177	New Zealand	Delhi	1955-56
		189*	England	Delhi	1961-62
		108	England	Madras^2	1963-64
		102*	New Zealand	Madras^2	1964-65
Mankad,MH	(5)	116	Australia	Melbourne	1947-48
		111	Australia	Melbourne	1947-48
		184	England	Lord's	1952
		223	New Zealand	Bombay^2	1955-56
		231	New Zealand	Madras^2	1955-56
Merchant,VM	(3)	114	England	Manchester	1936
		128	England	The Oval	1946
		154	England	Delhi	1951-52
Modi,RS		112	West Indies	Bombay^2	1948-49
Mushtaq Ali	(2)	112	England	Manchester	1936
		106 §	West Indies	Calcutta	1948-49
Nadkarni,RG		122*	England	Kanpur	1963-64
Pataudi,Nawab of,jr	(6)	103	England	Madras^2	1961-62
		203*	England	Delhi	1963-64
		128* §	Australia	Madras^2	1964-65
		153	New Zealand	Calcutta	1964-65
		113	New Zealand	Delhi	1964-65
		148	England	Leeds	1967
Patel,BP		115*	West Indies	Port-of-Spain	1975-76

Patil,SM	(4)	174	Australia	Adelaide	1980-81
		129*	England	Manchester	1982
		114* §	Sri Lanka	Madras[1]	1982-83
		127	Pakistan	Faisalabad	1984-85
Phadkar,DG	(2)	123	Australia	Adelaide	1947-48
		115	England	Calcutta	1951-52
Ramchand,GS	(2)	106*	New Zealand	Calcutta	1955-56
		109	Australia	Bombay[2]	1956-57
Roy,Pankaj	(5)	140	England	Bombay[2]	1951-52
		111	England	Madras[1]	1951-52
		150	West Indies	Kingston	1952-53
		100	New Zealand	Calcutta	1955-56
		173	New Zealand	Madras[2]	1955-56
Sardesai,DN	(5)	200*	New Zealand	Bombay[2]	1964-65
		106	New Zealand	Delhi	1964-65
		212	West Indies	Kingston	1970-71
		112	West Indies	Port-of-Spain	1970-71
		150	West Indies	Bridgetown	1970-71
Shastri,RJ	(11)	128	Pakistan	Karachi	1982-83
		102	West Indies	St John's	1982-83
		139	Pakistan	Faisalabad	1984-85
		142	England	Bombay[3]	1984-85
		111	England	Calcutta	1984-85
		121*	Australia	Bombay[3]	1986-87
		125	Pakistan	Jaipur	1986-87
		107	West Indies	Bridgetown	1988-89
		100	England	Lord's	1990
		187	England	The Oval	1990
		206	Australia	Sydney	1991-92
Shodhan,RH		110 §	Pakistan	Calcutta	1952-53
Sidhu,NS	(2)	116 §	New Zealand	Bangalore	1988-89
		116	West Indies	Kingston	1988-89
Solkar,ED		102	West Indies	Bombay[3]	1974-75
Srikkanth,K	(2)	116	Australia	Sydney	1985-86
		123	Pakistan	Madras[1]	1986-87
Tendulkar,SR	(3)	119*	England	Manchester	1990
		148*	Australia	Sydney	1991-92
		114	Australia	Perth	1991-92
Umrigar,PR	(12)	130*	England	Madras[1]	1951-52
		102	Pakistan	Bombay[2]	1952-53
		130	West Indies	Port-of-Spain	1952-53
		117	West Indies	Kingston	1952-53
		108	Pakistan	Peshawar	1954-55
		223 §	New Zealand	Hyderabad	1955-56
		118	England	Manchester	1959
		115	Pakistan	Kanpur	1960-61
		117	Pakistan	Madras[2]	1960-61
		112	Pakistan	Delhi	1960-61
		147*	England	Kanpur	1961-62
		172*	West Indies	Port-of-Spain	1961-62
Vengsarkar,DB	(17)	157*	West Indies	Calcutta	1978-79
		109	West Indies	Delhi	1978-79
		103	England	Lord's	1979
		112	Australia	Bangalore	1979-80
		146*	Pakistan	Delhi	1979-80
		157	England	Lord's	1982
		159	West Indies	Delhi	1983-84
		100	West Indies	Bombay[3]	1983-84
		137	England	Kanpur	1984-85

		126*	England	Lord's	1986
		102*	England	Leeds	1986
		164*	Australia	Bombay[3]	1986-87
		153	Sri Lanka	Nagpur	1986-87
		166	Sri Lanka	Cuttack	1986-87
		109	Pakistan	Ahmedabad	1986-87
		102	West Indies	Delhi	1987-88
		102*	West Indies	Calcutta	1987-88
Viswanath,GR	(14)	137 §	Australia	Kanpur	1969-70
		113	England	Bombay[2]	1972-73
		139	West Indies	Calcutta	1974-75
		112	West Indies	Port-of-Spain	1975-76
		103*	New Zealand	Kanpur	1976-77
		145 §	Pakistan	Faisalabad	1978-79
		124	West Indies	Madras[1]	1978-79
		179	West Indies	Kanpur	1978-79
		113	England	Lord's	1979
		161*	Australia	Bangalore	1979-80
		131	Australia	Delhi	1979-80
		114	Australia	Melbourne	1980-81
		107	England	Delhi	1981-82
		222	England	Madras[1]	1981-82
Wadekar,AL		143	New Zealand	Wellington	1967-68
Yashpal Sharma	(2)	100*	Australia	Delhi	1979-80
		140	England	Madras[1]	1981-82
PAKISTAN (163)			Opponents		
Aamer Malik	(2)	117	India	Faisalabad	1989-90
		113	India	Lahore[2]	1989-90
Aamer Sohail		205	England	Manchester	1992
Alimuddin	(2)	103*	India	Karachi	1954-55
		109	England	Karachi	1961-62
Asif Iqbal	(11)	146	England	The Oval	1967
		104*	England	Birmingham	1971
		175	New Zealand	Dunedin	1972-73
		102	England	Lahore[2]	1972-73
		166	New Zealand	Lahore[2]	1976-77
		152*	Australia	Adelaide	1976-77
		120	Australia	Sydney	1976-77
		135	West Indies	Kingston	1976-77
		104 §	India	Faisalabad	1978-79
		104	New Zealand	Napier	1978-79
		134*	Australia	Perth	1978-79
Hanif Mohammad	(12)	142	India	Bahawalpur	1954-55
		103	New Zealand	Dacca	1955-56
		337 §	West Indies	Bridgetown	1957-58
		103	West Indies	Karachi	1958-59
		101*	Australia	Karachi	1959-60
		160	India	Bombay[2]	1960-61
		111)	England	Dacca	1961-62
		104)			
		104	Australia	Melbourne	1964-65
		100*	New Zealand	Christchurch	1964-65
		203*	New Zealand	Lahore[2]	1964-65
		187*	England	Lord's	1967
Haroon Rashid	(3)	122 §	England	Lahore[2]	1977-78
		108	England	Hyderabad	1977-78
		153 §	Sri Lanka	Karachi	1981-82

Ijaz Ahmed	(2)	122	Australia	Faisalabad	1988-89
		121	Australia	Melbourne	1989-90
Ijaz Faqih		105 §	India	Ahmedabad	1986-87
Imran Khan	(6)	123	West Indies	Lahore²	1980-81
		117	India	Faisalabad	1982-83
		135*	India	Madras¹	1986-87
		118	England	The Oval	1987
		109*	India	Karachi	1989-90
		136	Australia	Adelaide	1989-90
Imtiaz Ahmed	(3)	209	New Zealand	Lahore²	1955-56
		122	West Indies	Kingston	1957-58
		135	India	Madras²	1960-61
Intikhab Alam		138	England	Hyderabad	1972-73
Javed Burki		138 §	England	Lahore²	1961-62
		140	England	Dacca	1961-62
		101	England	Lord's	1962
Javed Miandad	(23)	163 §	New Zealand	Lahore²	1976-77
		206	New Zealand	Karachi	1976-77
		154* §	India	Faisalabad	1978-79
		100	India	Karachi	1978-79
		160*	New Zealand	Christchurch	1978-79
		129*	Australia	Perth	1978-79
		106*	Australia	Faisalabad	1979-80
		138	Australia	Lahore²	1982-83
		126	India	Faisalabad	1982-83
		280*	India	Hyderabad	1982-83
		131	Australia	Adelaide	1983-84
		104)	New Zealand	Hyderabad	1984-85
		103*)			
		203*	Sri Lanka	Faisalabad	1985-86
		260	England	The Oval	1987
		114	West Indies	Georgetown	1987-88
		102	West Indies	Port-of-Spain	1987-88
		211	Australia	Karachi	1988-89
		107	Australia	Faisalabad	1988-89
		118	New Zealand	Wellington	1988-89
		271	New Zealand	Auckland	1988-89
		145	India	Lahore²	1989-90
	(In his 100th Test match)				
		153*	England	Birmingham	1992
Khalid Ibadulla		166 §	Australia	Karachi	1964-65
Majid Khan	(8)	158	Australia	Melbourne	1972-73
		110	New Zealand	Auckland	1972-73
		100	West Indies	Karachi	1974-75
		112	New Zealand	Karachi	1976-77
		167	West Indies	Georgetown	1976-77
		119*	New Zealand	Napier	1978-79
		108	Australia	Melbourne	1978-79
		110*	Australia	Lahore²	1979-80
Mansoor Akhtar		111	Australia	Faisalabad	1982-83
Mohammad Ilyas		126	New Zealand	Karachi	1964-65
Mohsin Khan	(7)	129	Sri Lanka	Lahore²	1981-82
		200	England	Lord's	1982
		135	Australia	Lahore²	1982-83
		101* §	India	Lahore²	1982-83
		149	Australia	Adelaide	1983-84
		152	Australia	Melbourne	1983-84
		104	England	Lahore²	1983-84

Mudassar Nazar	(10)	114 §	England	Lahore[2]	1977-78
		126	India	Bangalore	1979-80
		119	India	Karachi	1982-83
		231	India	Hyderabad	1982-83
		152*	India	Lahore[2]	1982-83
		152	India	Karachi	1982-83
		199	India	Faisalabad	1984-85
		106	New Zealand	Hyderabad	1984-85
		124	England	Birmingham	1987
		120	England	Lahore[2]	1987-88
Mushtaq Mohammad	(10)	101	India	Delhi	1960-61
		100*	England	Nottingham	1962
		100	England	Birmingham	1971
		121	Australia	Sydney	1972-73
		201	New Zealand	Dunedin	1972-73
		157	England	Hyderabad	1972-73
		123	West Indies	Lahore[2]	1971-75
		101	New Zealand	Hyderabad	1976-77
		107	New Zealand	Karachi	1976-77
		121	West Indies	Port-of-Spain	1976-77
Nasim-ul-Ghani		101	England	Lord's	1962
Nazir Mohammad		124*	India	Lucknow	1952-53
Qasim Omar	(3)	113	Australia	Adelaide	1983-84
		210	India	Faisalabad	1984-85
		206 §	Sri Lanka	Faisalabad	1985-86
Rameez Raja	(2)	122	Sri Lanka	Colombo (PSS)	1985-86
		114	India	Jaipur	1986-87
Sadiq Mohammad	(5)	137	Australia	Melbourne	1972-73
		166	New Zealand	Wellington	1972-73
		119	England	Lahore[2]	1972-73
		103*	New Zealand	Hyderabad	1976-77
		105	Australia	Melbourne	1976-77
Saeed Ahmed	(5)	150	West Indies	Georgetown	1957-58
		166	Australia	Lahore[2]	1959-60
		121 §	India	Bombay[2]	1960-61
		103	India	Madras[2]	1960-61
		172	New Zealand	Karachi	1964-65
Saleem Malik	(10)	100* §	Sri Lanka	Karachi	1981-82
		107	India	Faisalabad	1982-83
		116	England	Faisalabad	1983-84
		102*	India	Faisalabad	1984-85
		119*	New Zealand	Karachi	1984-85
		102	England	The Oval	1987
		102*	India	Karachi	1989-90
		102	West Indies	Karachi	1990-91
		101	Sri Lanka	Sialkot	1991-92
		165	England	Birmingham	1992
Shoaib Mohammad	(7)	101	India	Madras[1]	1986-87
		163	New Zealand	Wellington	1988-89
		112	New Zealand	Auckland	1988-89
		203*	India	Lahore[2]	1989-90
		203*	New Zealand	Karachi	1990-91
		105	New Zealand	Lahore[2]	1990-91
		142	New Zealand	Faisalabad	1990-91
Taslim Arif		210*	Australia	Faisalabad	1979-80
Waqar Hassan		189	New Zealand	Lahore[1]	1955-56
Wasim Akram		123	Australia	Adelaide	1989-90
Wasim Raja	(4)	107*	West Indies	Karachi	1974-75
		117*	West Indies	Bridgetown	1976-77

		125	India	Jullundur	1983-84
		112	England	Faisalabad	1983-84
Wazir Mohammad	(2)	106	West Indies	Kingston	1957-58
		189	West Indies	Port-of-Spain	1957-58
Zaheer Abbas	(12)	274 §	England	Birmingham	1971
		240	England	The Oval	1974
		101	Australia	Adelaide	1976-77
		176 §	India	Faisalabad	1978-79
		235*	India	Lahore²	1978-79
		135	New Zealand	Auckland	1978-79
		134 §	Sri Lanka	Lahore²	1981-82
		126	Australia	Faisalabad	1982-83
		215	India	Lahore²	1982-83
	(His 100th first-class century)				
		186	India	Karachi	1982-83
		168	India	Faisalabad	1982-83
		168*	India	Lahore²	1984-85
SRI LANKA (26)			Opponents		
de Silva,PA	(5)	122 §	Pakistan	Faisalabad	1985-86
		105	Pakistan	Karachi	1985-86
		167	Australia	Brisbane²	1989-90
		267	New Zealand	Wellington	1990-91
		123	New Zealand	Auckland	1990-91
Dias,RL	(3)	109	Pakistan	Lahore²	1981-82
		108 §	New Zealand	Colombo (SSC)	1983-84
		106	India	Kandy	1985-86
Gurusinha,AP	(4)	116*	Pakistan	Colombo (PSS)	1985-86
		119)	New Zealand	Hamilton	1990-91
		102)			
		137	Australia	Colombo (SSC)	1992-93
Kaluwitharana,RS §		132*	Australia	Colombo (SSC)	1992-93
Kuruppu,DSBP		201* §	New Zealand	Colombo (CCC)	1986-87
Madugalle,RS		103	India	Colombo (SSC)	1985-86
Mendis,LRD	(4)	105 §)	India	Madras¹	1982-83
		105 §)			
		111	England	Lord's	1984
		124	India	Kandy	1985-86
Ranatunga,A	(3)	111	India	Colombo (SSC)	1985-86
		135*	Pakistan	Colombo (PSS)	1985-86
		127	Australia	Colombo (SSC)	1992-93
Silva,SAR	(2)	102* §	England	Lord's	1984
		111	India	Colombo (PSS)	1985-86
Wettimuny,S	(2)	157	Pakistan	Faisalabad	1981-82
		190	England	Lord's	1984

NOUGHT AND A CENTURY IN THE SAME MATCH

(§ in first Test. † in last Test)

AUSTRALIA	Scores		Opponents		
W.L.Murdoch	0	153*	England	The Oval	1880
G.H.S.Trott	0	143	England	Lord's	1896
C.Hill	188	0	England	Melbourne	1897-98
D.G.Bradman	0	103*	England	Melbourne	1932-33
J.H.W.Fingleton	100	0	England	Brisbane²	1936-37
D.G.Bradman	138	0	England	Nottingham	1948
S.G.Barnes	0	141	England	Lord's	1948
R.N.Harvey	122	0	England	Manchester	1953
I.R.Redpath	0	132	West Indies	Sydney	1968-69
I.M.Chappell	138	0	India	Delhi	1969-70
I.C.Davis	105	0	Pakistan	Adelaide	1976-77

R.B.McCosker	0	105	Pakistan	Melbourne	1976-77
C.S.Serjeant	0	124	West Indies	Georgetown	1977-78
G.N.Yallop	0	114	England	Manchester	1981
G.R.Marsh	118	0	New Zealand	Auckland	1985-86
D.C.Boon	103	0	England	Adelaide	1986-87
M.E.Waugh	139*	0	West Indies	St John's	1990-91

ENGLAND	Scores		Opponents		
L.C.Braund	102	0	Australia	Sydney	1903-04
J.T.Tyldesley	0	100	Australia	Leeds	1905
G.Gunn	122*	0	Australia	Sydney	1907-08
F.E.Woolley	0	123	Australia	Sydney	1924-25
G.B.Legge	196	0	New Zealand	Auckland	1929-30
D.C.S.Compton	145*	0	Australia	Manchester	1948
L.Hutton	101	0	New Zealand	Leeds	1949
P.B.H.May	0	112	South Africa	Lord's	1955
M.C.Cowdrey	119	0	West Indies	Port-of-Spain	1959-60
Rev.D.S.Sheppard	0	113	Australia	Melbourne	1962-63
M.C.Cowdrey	101	0	West Indies	Kingston	1967-68
D.L.Amiss	158	0	Pakistan	Hyderabad	1972-73
D.W.Randall	0	150	Australia	Sydney	1978-79
I.T.Botham	0	118	Australia	Manchester	1981
G.Boycott	137	0	Australia	The Oval	1981
M.W.Gatting	100	0	Australia	Adelaide	1986-87
D.I.Gower	100	0	Australia	Melbourne	1990-91

SOUTH AFRICA	Scores		Opponents		
J.H.Sinclair	0	104	Australia	Cape Town	1902-03
G.A.Faulkner	122*	0	Australia	Manchester	1912
R.H.Catterall	0	120	England	Birmingham	1924
A.D.Nourse	0	231	Australia	Johannesburg[1]	1935-36
E.J.Barlow	114	0	Australia	Brisbane[2]	1963-64
A.C.Hudson §	163	0	West Indies	Bridgetown	1991-92

WEST INDIES	Scores		Opponents		
I.Barrow	105	0	England	Manchester	1933
F.C.M.Alexander	0	108	Australia	Sydney	1960-61
S.M.Nurse	201	0	Australia	Bridgetown	1964-65
G.S.Sobers	0	113*	England	Kingston	1967-68
C.A.Davis	103	0	England	Lord's	1969
G.S.Sobers	132	0	India	Port-of-Spain	1970-71
A.I.Kallicharran	0	103*	India	Port-of-Spain	1975-76
R.C.Fredericks	0	138	England	Lord's	1976
D.L.Haynes	0	122	New Zealand	Christchurch	1979-80
C.L.King	0	100*	New Zealand	Christchurch	1979-80
I.V.A.Richards	0	182*	England	Bridgetown	1980-81
I.V.A.Richards	208	0	Australia	Melbourne	1984-85
D.L.Haynes	0	109	England	Bridgetown	1989-90
R.B.Richardson	104	0	England	Birmingham	1991

NEW ZEALAND	Scores		Opponents		
G.T.Dowling	129	0	India	Bombay[2]	1964-65
B.F.Hastings	0	117*	West Indies	Christchurch	1968-69
M.D.Crowe	174	0	Pakistan	Wellington	1988-89
J.G.Wright †	116	0	England	Wellington	1991-92

INDIA	Scores		Opponents		
M.H.Mankad	111	0	Australia	Melbourne	1947-48
Pankaj Roy	140	0	England	Bombay[2]	1951-52
V.L.Manjrekar	133	0	England	Leeds	1952

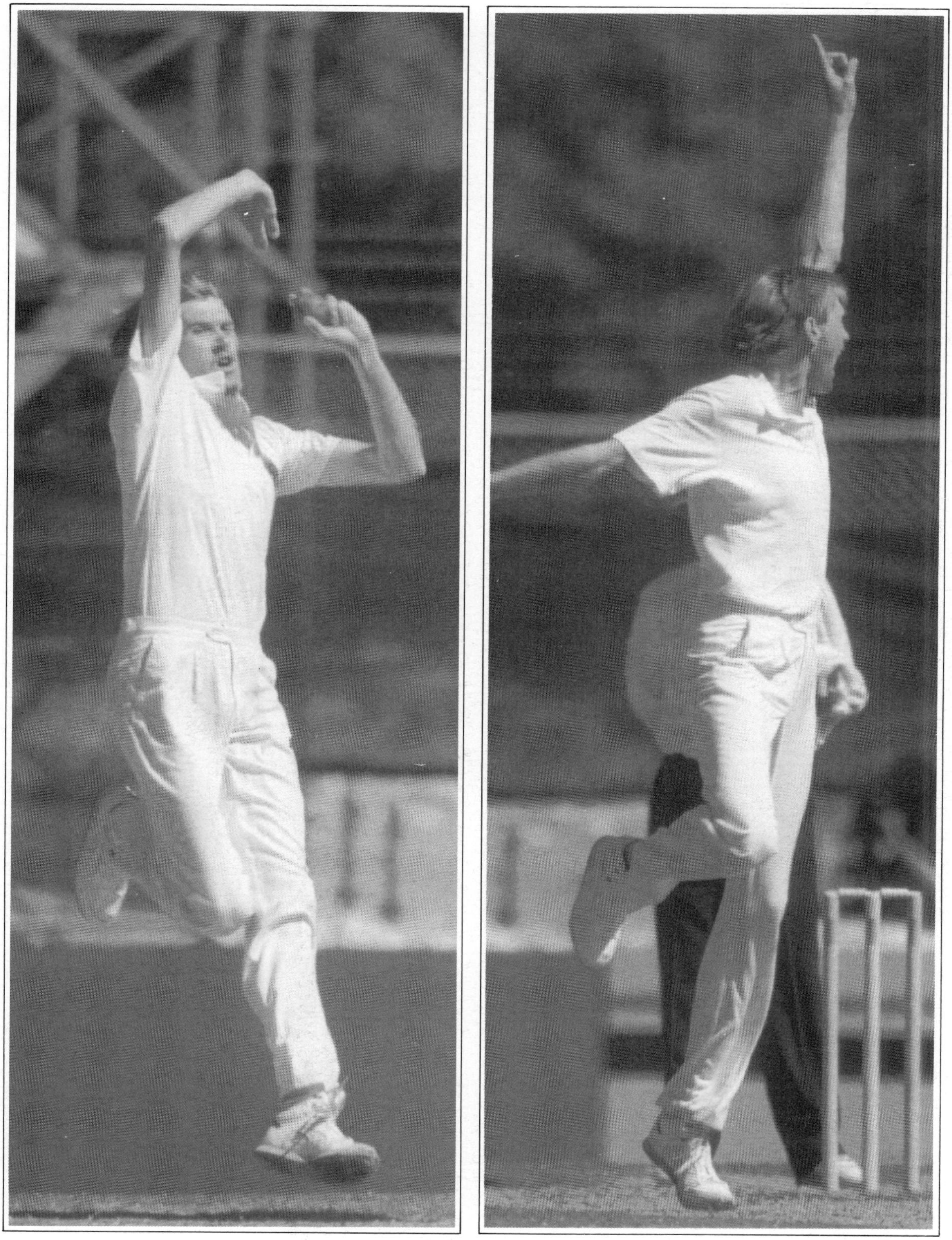

After a severe back injury interrupted his career, beanpole fast bowler Bruce Reid makes a successful return to the Australian team to rout England in the 1990-91 Ashes series. *(Courtesy PBL Marketing.)*

England batsman Alec Stewart fends off some fiery fast bowling from the Australian attack during the 1990-91 Ashes series.

(Courtesy PBL Marketing.)

M.L.Apte	0	163*	West Indies	Port-of-Spain	1952-53
V.L.Manjrekar	108	0	England	Madras[2]	1963-64
G.R.Viswanath §	0	137	Australia	Kanpur	1969-70
S.M.Gavaskar	0	118	Australia	Melbourne	1977-78
D.B.Vengsarkar	0	103	England	Lord's	1979
N.S.Sidhu	116	0	West Indies	Kingston	1988-89
M.Azharuddin	0	109	Pakistan	Faisalabad	1989-90

PAKISTAN	Scores		Opponents		
Imtiaz Ahmed	209	0	New Zealand	Lahore[1]	1955-56
Imtiaz Ahmed	122	0	West Indies	Kingston	1957-58
Hanif Mohammad	160	0	India	Bombay[2]	1960-61
Javed Burki	140	0	England	Dacca	1961-62
Asif Iqbal	0	152*	Australia	Adelaide	1976-77
Sadiq Mohammad	105	0	Australia	Melbourne	1976-77
Asif Iqbal	0	104	India	Faisalabad	1978-79
Ijaz Ahmed	122	0	Australia	Faisalabad	1988-89

SRI LANKA	Scores		Opponents		
A.Ranatunga	127	0	Australia	Colombo (SSC)	1992-93

NINETY-NINES IN TEST MATCHES

Over the years many batsmen have scored 99 runs in a Test innings. M.J.K.Smith, G.Boycott, R.B.Richardson and J.G.Wright are the only batsmen to score 99 twice in their careers. In the third Test between England and Pakistan at Karachi in 1972-73 three batsmen, Majid Khan, Mushtaq Mohammad and D.L.Amiss, were dismissed for 99.

AUSTRALIA *(§ on debut)*	How out	Opponent		
C.Hill	caught	England	Melbourne	1901-02
C.G.Macartney	caught	England	Lord's	1912
A.G.Chipperfield §	caught	England	Nottingham	1934
W.A.Brown	run out	India	Melbourne	1947-48
K.R.Miller	bowled	England	Adelaide	1950-51
A.R.Morris	run out	South Africa	Melbourne	1952-53
C.C.McDonald	caught	South Africa	Cape Town	1957-58
R.M.Cowper	caught	England	Melbourne	1965-66
I.M.Chappell	caught	India	Calcutta	1969-70
R.Edwards	lbw	England	Lord's	1975
K.J.Hughes	caught	England	Perth	1979-80
D.M.Jones	lbw	New Zealand	Perth	1989-90

ENGLAND	How out	Opponent		
H.Sutcliffe	bowled	South Africa	Cape Town	1927-28
E.Paynter	lbw	Australia	Lord's	1938
N.W.D.Yardley	caught	South Africa	Nottingham	1947
M.J.K.Smith	caught	South Africa	Lord's	1960
M.J.K.Smith	run out	Pakistan	Lahore[2]	1961-62
E.R.Dexter	bowled	Australia	Brisbane[2]	1962-63
D.L.Amiss	caught	Pakistan	Karachi	1972-73
G.Boycott	caught	West Indies	Port-of-Spain	1973-74
G.Boycott*	not out	Australia	Perth	1979-80
G.A.Gooch	run out	Australia	Melbourne	1979-80
M.D.Moxon	caught	New Zealand	Auckland	1987-88

** Boycott is the only player to register a not out 99.*

SOUTH AFRICA	How out	Opponent		
G.A.Faulkner	caught	England	Cape Town	1909-10
B.Mitchell	caught	England	Port Elizabeth	1948-49
T.L.Goddard	caught	England	The Oval	1960

WEST INDIES *(§ on debut)*	How out	Opponent		
R.J.Christiani §	lbw	England	Bridgetown	1947-48
A.F.Rae	bowled	New Zealand	Auckland	1951-52
R.B.Kanhai	run out	India	Madras[2]	1958-59
M.L.C.Foster	bowled	India	Port-of-Spain	1970-71
R.B.Richardson	bowled	India	Port-of-Spain	1988-89
R.B.Richardson	lbw	Australia	Bridgetown	1990-91

NEW ZEALAND	How out	Opponent		
J.E.F.Beck	run out	South Africa	Cape Town	1953-54
R.J.Hadlee	caught	England	Christchurch	1983-84
J.G.Wright	caught	Australia	Melbourne	1987-88
D.N.Patel	run out	England	Christchurch	1991-92
J.G.Wright	stumped	England	Christchurch	1991-92

INDIA	How out	Opponent		
Pankaj Roy	caught	Australia	Delhi	1959-60
M.L.Jaisimha	run out	Pakistan	Kanpur	1960-61
A.L.Wadekar	caught	Australia	Melbourne	1967-68
R.F.Surti	caught	New Zealand	Auckland	1967-68

PAKISTAN	How out	Opponent		
Maqsood Ahmed	stumped	India	Lahore[1]	1954-55
Majid Khan	caught	England	Karachi	1972-73
Mushtaq Mohammad	run out	England	Karachi	1972-73
Javed Miandad	caught	India	Bangalore	1983-84
Saleem Malik	caught	England	Leeds	1987

MOST FIFTIES *(All scores of 50 and over)*

Player	Country	50's	Inns	A	E	SA	WI	NZ	I	P	SL
A.R.Border	Australia	**80**	230	0	27	0	14	7	13	14	5
S.M.Gavaskar	India	**79**	214	20	12	0	20	5	0	17	5
I.V.A.Richards	West Indies	**69**	182	19	23	0	0	3	15	9	0
G.Boycott	England	**64**	193	0	21	3	20	8	6	6	0
Javed Miandad	Pakistan	**64**	178	13	11	0	6	12	19	0	3
M.C.Cowdrey	England	**60**	188	0	16	10	16	10	5	3	0
G.A.Gooch	England	**58**	179	13	0	0	18	6	13	6	2
C.H.Lloyd	West Indies	**58**	175	18	18	0	0	0	19	3	0
D.I.Gower	England	**57**	204	21	0	0	7	8	8	11	2
G.S.Sobers	West Indies	**56**	160	23	10	0	0	1	15	7	0
K.F.Barrington	England	**55**	131	0	18	8	7	4	12	6	0
G.S.Chappell	Australia	**55**	151	21	0	0	12	6	3	12	0
D.L.Haynes	West Indies	**54**	178	19	17	0	0	8	6	3	0
C.G.Greenidge	West Indies	**53**	185	15	12	1	0	7	13	6	0
L.Hutton	England	**52**	138	0	19	11	11	7	4	0	0
D.B.Vengsarkar	India	**52**	185	9	11	0	13	3	0	10	6

MOST CONSECUTIVE FIFTIES

SEVEN

E.D.Weekes	West Indies	141	128	194	162	101	90	56	1947-48 to 1948-49

SIX

J.Ryder	Australia	78*	58	56	142	201*	88	1921-22 to 1924-25
E.H.Hendren	England	77	205*	56	123	61	55	1929-30
G.A.Headley	West Indies	93	53	270*	106	107	51	1934-35 to 1939
A.Melville	South Africa	67	78	103	189	104*	117	1938-39 to 1947
G.S.Sobers	West Indies	52	52	80	365*	125	109*	1957-58

E.R.Dexter	England	85	172	70	99	93	52	1962 to 1962-63
K.F.Barrington	England	63	132*	101	94	126	76	1962-63
K.D.Walters	Australia	76	118	110	50	242	103	1968-69
G.S.Chappell	Australia	68	54*	52	70	121	67	1975-76 to 1976-77
G.R.Viswanath	India	59	54	79	89	73	145	1977-78 to 1978-79
A.R.Border	Australia	80	65*	76	51*	50	56	1989 to 1989-90
M.A.Taylor	Australia	108	52	101	77	59	101*	1989-90

G.Boycott (England) scored nine fifties in ten innings in 1970-71 and 1971: 70, 50, 77, 142,12, 76*, 58, 119*, 121*, 112.*

M.A.Noble (Australia) is the only player to score two separate fifties on the same day: 60 and 59* v England at Manchester in 1899 on the second day.*

OVER 60% OF A COMPLETED INNINGS TOTAL.

67.34	C.Bannerman	165*/245	Australia	v	England	Melbourne	1876-77
63.50	C.G.Greenidge	134/211	West Indies	v	England	Manchester	1976
63.41	A.P.Gurusinha	52*/82	Sri Lanka	v	India	Chandigarh	1990-91
62 89	J.R.Reid	100/159	New Zealand	v	England	Christchurch	1962-63
61 87	S.M.Nurse	258/417	West Indies	v	New Zealand	Christchurch	1968-69
61.85	M.Amarnath	60/97†	India	v	West Indies	Kingston	1975-76
61.11	G.N.Yallop	121/198	Australia	v	England	Sydney	1978-79
61.11	G.A.Gooch	154*/252	England	v	West Indies	Leeds	1991
60.65	V.T.Trumper	74/122	Australia	v	England	Melbourne	1903-04
60.26	H.A.Gomes	91/151	West Indies	v	India	Madras[1]	1978-79
60.19	J.T.Tyldesley	62/103	England	v	Australia	Melbourne	1903-04

† Five men were absent hurt.

D.L.Amiss (262) scored 60.64% of England 's total of 432 for 9 against West Indies at Kingston in 1973-74.*

THE NERVOUS NINETIES *(§ first Test, † last Test, ¶ only Test)*

AUSTRALIA		Opponents		
A.C.Bannerman	94	England	Sydney	1882-83
A.C.Bannerman	91	England	Sydney	1891-92
G.H.S.Trott	92	England	The Oval	1893
G.H.S.Trott	95	England	Melbourne	1894-95
C.Hill	96	England	Sydney	1897-98
C.Hill	99	England	Melbourne	1901-02
C.Hill	98) 97)	England	Adelaide	1901-02
C.Hill	91	South Africa	Cape Town	1902-03
V.S.Ransford	95	South Africa	Melbourne	1910-11
W.Bardsley	94	South Africa	Sydney	1910-11
R.B.Minnett §	90	England	Sydney	1911-12
W.W.Armstrong	90	England	Melbourne	1911-12
C.Hill	98*	England	Adelaide	1911-12
C.G.Macartney	99	England	Lord's	1912
J.M.Gregory	93	England	Sydney	1920-21
T.J.E.Andrews	92	England	Leeds	1921
T.J.E.Andrews	94	England	The Oval	1921
A.J.Richardson §	98	England	Sydney	1924-25
J.M.Taylor	90	England	Melbourne	1924-25
S.J.McCabe	90	West Indies	Adelaide	1930-31
W.H.Ponsford	92*	West Indies	Adelaide	1930-31
A.G.Chipperfield §	99	England	Nottingham	1934
S.J.McCabe	93	England	Sydney	1936-37
C.L.McCool	95	England	Brisbane[2]	1946-47
D.Tallon	92	England	Melbourne	1946-47
W.A.Brown	99	India	Melbourne	1947-48
S.J.E.Loxton	93	England	Leeds	1948

K.R.Miller	99	England	Adelaide	1950-51
A.L.Hassett	92	England	Melbourne	1950-51
A.R.Morris	99	South Africa	Melbourne	1952-53
R.N.Harvey	92*	England	Sydney	1954-55
R.G.Archer	98	West Indies	Bridgetown	1954-55
R.Benaud	97	England	Lord's	1956
C.C.McDonald	99	South Africa	Cape Town	1957-58
R.N.Harvey	96	Pakistan	Dacca	1959-60
C.C.McDonald	91	West Indies	Melbourne	1960-61
R.B.Simpson	92	West Indies	Brisbane[2]	1960-61
R.B.Simpson	92	West Indies	Melbourne	1960-61
W.M.Lawry	98	England	Brisbane[2]	1962-63
R.B.Simpson	91	England	Sydney	1962-63
I.R.Redpath §	97	South Africa	Melbourne	1963-64
B.K.Shepherd	96	South Africa	Melbourne	1963-64
R.Benaud	90	South Africa	Sydney	1963-64
P.J.P.Burge	91	South Africa	Adelaide	1963-64
B.C.Booth	98	England	Manchester	1964
W.M.Lawry	94	England	The Oval	1964
R.M.Cowper	99	England	Melbourne	1965-66
W.M.Lawry	98	South Africa	Johannesburg[3]	1966-67
R.B.Simpson	94	South Africa	Durban[2]	1966-67
R.M.Cowper	92	India	Adelaide	1967-68
K.D.Walters	93	India	Brisbane[2]	1967-68
K.D.Walters	94*	India	Sydney	1967-68
I.R.Redpath	92	England	Leeds	1968
I.M.Chappell	96	West Indies	Adelaide	1968-69
I.M.Chappell	99	India	Calcutta	1969-70
R.W.Marsh	92*	England	Melbourne	1970-71
R.W.Marsh	91	England	Manchester	1972
R.W.Marsh	97	West Indies	Kingston	1972-73
I.M.Chappell	97	West Indies	Port-of-Spain	1972-73
K.D.Walters	94	New Zealand	Adelaide	1973-74
I.R.Redpath	93	New Zealand	Wellington	1973-74
I.M.Chappell	90	England	Brisbane[2]	1974-75
R.Edwards	99	England	Lord's	1975
R.B.McCosker	95*	England	Leeds	1975
G.J.Gilmour	95	West Indies	Adelaide	1975-76
G.M.Wood	90	West Indies	Kingston	1977-78
P.M.Toohey	97	West Indies	Kingston	1977-78
W.M.Darling	91	England	Sydney	1978-79
K.J.Hughes	92	India	Calcutta	1979-80
B.M.Laird	93	West Indies	Brisbane[2]	1979-80
K.J.Hughes	99	England	Perth	1979-80
G.S.Chappell	98*	England	Sydney	1979-80
J.M.Wiener	93	Pakistan	Lahore[2]	1979-80
R.W.Marsh	91	New Zealand	Perth	1980-81
G.N.Yallop	98	Sri Lanka	Kandy	1982-83
K.J.Hughes	94	Pakistan	Melbourne	1983-84
A.R.Border	98*	West Indies	Port-of-Spain	1983-84
A.R.Border	98	West Indies	St John's	1983-84
K.C.Wessels	98	West Indies	Adelaide	1984-85
K.C.Wessels	90	West Indies	Melbourne	1984-85
W.B.Phillips	91	England	Leeds	1985
G.M.Ritchie	94	England	Lord's	1985
G.M.Ritchie	92	New Zealand	Wellington	1985-86
D.M.Jones	93	England	Adelaide	1986-87
P.R.Sleep	90	New Zealand	Melbourne	1987-88
S.R.Waugh	90	West Indies	Brisbane[2]	1988-89

S.R.Waugh	91	West Indies	Perth	1988-89
D.C.Boon	94	England	Lord's	1989
S.R.Waugh	92	England	Manchester	1989
D.M.Jones	99	New Zealand	Perth	1989-90
D.C.Boon	94*	England	Melbourne	1990-91
D.C.Boon	97	England	Sydney	1990-91
G.R.Marsh	94	West Indies	Georgetown	1990-91
M.A.Taylor	94	India	Brisbane²	1991-92
A.R.Border	91*	India	Adelaide	1991-92
G.R.J.Matthews	96	Sri Lanka	Moratuwa	1992-93
ENGLAND		Opponents		
W.H.Scotton	90	Australia	The Oval	1884
W.W.Read	94	Australia	The Oval	1886
F.S.Jackson §	91	Australia	Lord's	1893
A.Ward	93	Australia	Melbourne	1894-95
R.Abel	94	Australia	Lord's	1896
K.S.Ranjitsinhji	93*	Australia	Nottingham	1899
T.W.Hayward	90	Australia	Adelaide	1901-02
A.C.MacLaren	92	Australia	Sydney	1901-02
T.W.Hayward	91	Australia	Sydney	1903-04
J.T.Tyldesley	97	Australia	Melbourne	1903-04
G.L.Jessop	93	South Africa	Lord's	1907
J.B.Hobbs	93*	South Africa	Johannesburg¹	1909-10
W.Rhodes	92	Australia	Manchester	1912
J.B.Hobbs	92	South Africa	Johannesburg¹	1913-14
J.B.Hobbs	97	South Africa	Durban²	1913-14
F.E.Woolley	95) 93)	Australia	Lord's	1921
C.A.G.Russell	96	South Africa	Johannesburg¹	1922-23
E.H.Hendren	92	Australia	Adelaide	1924-25
H.Sutcliffe	94	Australia	Leeds	1926
H.Sutcliffe	99	South Africa	Cape Town	1927-28
R.E.S.Wyatt	91	South Africa	Cape Town	1927-28
W.R.Hammond	90	South Africa	Durban²	1927-28
D.R.Jardine	98	Australia	Adelaide	1928-29
E.H.Hendren	95	Australia	Melbourne	1928-29
F.E.Woolley	95*	South Africa	Leeds	1929
E.H.Hendren	93	South Africa	Cape Town	1930-31
M.Leyland	91	South Africa	Johannesburg¹	1930-31
H.Larwood	98	Australia	Sydney	1932-33
J.Hardstaff, jr	94	India	Manchester	1936
E.Paynter	99	Australia	Lord's	1938
P.A.Gibb §	93	South Africa	Johannesburg¹	1938-39
B.H.Valentine	97	South Africa	Johannesburg¹	1938-39
L.Hutton	92	South Africa	Johannesburg¹	1938-39
J.Hardstaff, jr	94	West Indies	The Oval	1939
L.Hutton	94	Australia	Adelaide	1946-47
N.W.D.Yardley	99	South Africa	Nottingham	1947
J.Hardstaff, jr	98	West Indies	Bridgetown	1947-48
C.Washbrook	97	South Africa	Johannesburg²	1948-49
T.E.Bailey	93	New Zealand	Lord's	1949
R.T.Simpson	94	West Indies	Nottingham	1950
L.Hutton	98*	South Africa	Manchester	1951
T.E.Bailey	95	South Africa	Leeds	1951
R.T.Spooner	92	India	Calcutta	1951-52
D.C.S.Compton	93	West Indies	Bridgetown	1953-54
T.W.Graveney	92	West Indies	Port-of-Spain	1953-54
D.C.S.Compton	93	Pakistan	Manchester	1954

P.B.H.May	91	Australia	Melbourne	1954-55
P.B.H.May	97	South Africa	Leeds	1955
C.Washbrook	98	Australia	Leeds	1956
D.C.S.Compton	94	Australia	The Oval	1956
P.B.H.May	92	Australia	Sydney	1958-59
R.Subba Row	94	India	The Oval	1959
M.J.K.Smith	98	India	The Oval	1959
M.C.Cowdrey	97	West Indies	Kingston	1959-60
M.J.K.Smith	96	West Indies	Port-of-Spain	1959-60
R.Subba Row	90	South Africa	Lord's	1960
M.J.K.Smith	99	South Africa	Lord's	1960
M.C.Cowdrey	93	Australia	Leeds	1961
P.B.H.May	95	Australia	Manchester	1961
M.J.K.Smith	99	Pakistan	Lahore[2]	1961-62
T.W.Graveney	97	Pakistan	Birmingham	1962
E.R.Dexter	99	Australia	Brisbane[2]	1962-63
E.R.Dexter	93	Australia	Melbourne	1962-63
K.F.Barrington	94	Australia	Sydney	1962-63
M.C.Cowdrey	93*	Australia	The Oval	1964
R.W.Barber	97	South Africa	Johannesburg[3]	1964-65
K.F.Barrington	93	South Africa	Johannesburg[3]	1964-65
K.F.Barrington	91	South Africa	Lord's	1965
C.Milburn §	94	West Indies	Manchester	1966
T.W.Graveney	96	West Indies	Lord's	1966
J.M.Parks	91	West Indies	Lord's	1966
M.C.Cowdrey	96	West Indies	Nottingham	1966
K.F.Barrington	93	India	Leeds	1967
K.F.Barrington	97	India	Lord's	1967
J.H.Edrich	96	West Indies	Kingston	1967-68
G.Boycott	90	West Indies	Bridgetown	1967-68
T.W.Graveney	96	Australia	Birmingham	1968
A.P.E.Knott	96*	Pakistan	Karachi	1968-69
A.P.E.Knott	96	New Zealand	Auckland	1970-71
A.P.E.Knott	90	India	The Oval	1971
B.W.Luckhurst	96	Australia	Nottingham	1972
A.P.E.Knott	92	Australia	The Oval	1972
B.Wood §	90	Australia	The Oval	1972
D.L.Amiss	99	Pakistan	Karachi	1972-73
G.Boycott	99	West Indies	Port-of-Spain	1973-74
G.Boycott	92	New Zealand	Lord's	1973
G.Boycott	97	West Indies	The Oval	1973
G.Boycott	93	West Indies	Port-of-Spain	1973-74
J.H.Edrich	96	India	Lord's	1974
D.L.Amiss	90	Australia	Melbourne	1974-75
A.W.Greig	96	Australia	Lord's	1975
D.S.Steele	92	Australia	Leeds	1975
J.H.Edrich	96	Australia	The Oval	1975
J.M.Brearley	91	India	Bombay[3]	1976-77
A.W.Greig	91	Australia	Lord's	1977
G.Miller	98*	Pakistan	Lahore[2]	1977-78
G.Boycott	99*	Australia	Perth	1979-80
G.A.Gooch	91*	New Zealand	The Oval	1978
R.W.Taylor	97	Australia	Adelaide	1978-79
D.I.Gower	98*	Australia	Sydney	1978-79
G.A.Gooch	99	Australia	Melbourne	1979-80
G.Miller	98	India	Manchester	1982
D.W.Randall	95	India	The Oval	1982
E.E.Hemmings	95	Australia	Sydney	1982-83
C.L.Smith	91	New Zealand	Auckland	1983-84

D.I.Gower	90	West Indies	St John's	1985-86
C.W.J.Athey	96	Australia	Perth	1986-87
M.W.Gatting	96	Australia	Sydney	1986-87
D.J.Capel	98	Pakistan	Karachi	1987-88
G.A.Gooch	93	Pakistan	Karachi	1987-88
M.D.Moxon	99	New Zealand	Auckland	1987-88
R.C.Russell §	94	Sri Lanka	Lord's	1988
R.A.Smith	96	Australia	Lord's	1989
A.J.Stewart	91	Australia	Sydney	1990-91
A.J.Lamb	91	Australia	Perth	1990-91
R.A.Smith	96	New Zealand	Christchurch	1991-92
A.J.Lamb	93	New Zealand	Christchurch	1991-92

SOUTH AFRICA		Opponents		
L.J.Tancred	97	Australia	Johannesburg[1]	1902-03
C.B.Llewellyn	90	Australia	Johannesburg[1]	1902-03
A.W.Nourse	93*	England	Johannesburg[1]	1902-03
G.A.Faulkner	99	England	Cape Town	1909-10
A.W.Nourse	92*	Australia	Melbourne	1910-11
G.A.Faulkner	92	Australia	Sydney	1910-11
H.W.Taylor	93	Australia	Lord's	1912
H.W.Taylor	93	England	Durban[1]	1913-14
H.W.Taylor	91	England	Durban[2]	1922-23
R.H.Catterall	95	England	The Oval	1924
R.H.Catterall	98	England	Birmingham	1929
H.G.Deane	93	England	The Oval	1929
B.Mitchell	95	Australia	Adelaide	1931-32
H.B.Cameron	90	England	Lord's	1935
A.D.Nourse	91	Australia	Durban[2]	1935-36
P.G.V.van der Bijl †	97	England	Durban[2]	1938-39
K.G.Viljoen	93	England	Manchester	1947
A.D.Nourse	97	England	The Oval	1947
B.Mitchell	99	England	Port Elizabeth	1948-49
P.N.F.Mansell §	90	England	Leeds	1951
K.J.Funston	92	Australia	Adelaide	1952-53
J.C.Watkins	92	Australia	Melbourne	1952-53
W.R.Endean	93	New Zealand	Johannesburg[2]	1953-54
R.A.McLean	93	England	Johannesburg[3]	1956-57
T.L.Goddard	90	Australia	Johannesburg[3]	1957-58
S.O'Linn	98	England	Nottingham	1960
T.L.Goddard	99	England	The Oval	1960
T.L.Goddard	93	Australia	Sydney	1963-64
E.J.Barlow	92	New Zealand	Wellington	1963-64
E.J.Barlow	96	England	Johannesburg[3]	1964-65
A.J.Pithey	95	England	Johannesburg[3]	1964-65
R.G.Pollock	90	Australia	Johannesburg[3]	1966-67

WEST INDIES		Opponents		
R.K.Nunes	92	England	Kingston	1929-30
J.E.D.Sealy	92	England	Port-of-Spain	1934-35
L.N.Constantine	90	England	Port-of-Spain	1934-35
G.A.Headley	93	England	Port-of-Spain	1934-35
J.E.D.Sealy	91	England	Kingston	1934-35
V.H.Stollmeyer ¶	96	England	The Oval	1939
R.J.Christiani §	99	England	Bridgetown	1947-48
F.M.M.Worrell §	97	England	Port-of-Spain	1947-48
E.D.Weekes	90	India	Madras[1]	1948-49
A.F.Rae	97	India	Bombay[2]	1948-49
A.F.Rae	99	New Zealand	Auckland	1951-52

C.L.Walcott	98	India	Bridgetown	1952-53
J.K.Holt §	94	England	Kingston	1953-54
E.D.Weekes	90*	England	Kingston	1953-54
E.D.Weekes	94	England	Georgetown	1953-54
C.L.Walcott	90	England	Birmingham	1957
E.D.Weekes	90	England	Lord's	1957
R.B.Kanhai	96	Pakistan	Port-of-Spain	1957-58
R.B.Kanhai	99	India	Madras[2]	1958-59
C.C.Hunte	92	India	Delhi	1958-59
G.S.Sobers	92	England	Port-of-Spain	1959-60
J.S.Solomon	96	India	Bridgetown	1961-62
F.M.M.Worrell	98*	India	Kingston	1961-62
R.B.Kanhai	90	England	Manchester	1963
R.B.Kanhai	92	England	Leeds	1963
S.M.Nurse	93	England	Nottingham	1966
G.S.Sobers	94	England	Nottingham	1966
R.B.Kanhai	90	India	Calcutta	1966-67
G.S.Sobers	95	India	Madras[1]	1966-67
G.S.Sobers	92*	England	Georgetown	1967-68
R.B.Kanhai	94	Australia	Brisbane[2]	1968-69
M.C.Carew	90	Australia	Adelaide	1968-69
M.C.Carew	91	New Zealand	Auckland	1968-69
S.M.Nurse	95	New Zealand	Auckland	1968-69
B.F.Butcher	91	England	Leeds	1969
G.S.Sobers	93	India	Kingston	1970-71
M.L.C.Foster	99	India	Port-of-Spain	1970-71
C.A.Davis	90	New Zealand	Port-of-Spain	1971-72
R.C.Fredericks	98	Australia	Bridgetown	1972-73
D.L.Murray	90	Australia	Bridgetown	1972-73
A.I.Kallicharran	91	Australia	Port-of-Spain	1972-73
C.H.Lloyd	94	England	Birmingham	1973
R.C.Fredericks	94	England	Kingston	1973-74
A.I.Kallicharran	93	England	Kingston	1973-74
R.C.Fredericks	98	England	Georgetown	1973-74
C.G.Greenidge §	93	India	Bangalore	1974-75
A.I.Kallicharran	98	India	Bombay[3]	1974-75
D.L.Murray	91	India	Bombay[3]	1974-75
A.I.Kallicharran	92*	Pakistan	Lahore[2]	1974-75
K.D.Boyce	95*	Australia	Adelaide	1975-76
I.V.A.Richards	98	Australia	Melbourne	1975-76
C.H.Lloyd	91*	Australia	Melbourne	1975-76
A.I.Kallicharran	93	India	Bridgetown	1975-76
A.I.Kallicharran	97	England	Nottingham	1976
I.V.A.Richards	92	Pakistan	Bridgetown	1976-77
C.G.Greenidge	91)	Pakistan	Georgetown	1976-77
	96)			
A.I.Kallicharran	92	Australia	Port-of-Spain	1977-78
S.F.A.F.Bacchus	98	India	Bangalore	1978-79
A.I.Kallicharran	98	India	Madras[1]	1978-79
H.A.Gomes	91	India	Madras[1]	1978-79
I.V.A.Richards	96	Australia	Melbourne	1979-80
C.G.Greenidge	91)	New Zealand	Christchurch	1979-80
	97)			
D.L.Haynes	96	England	Port-of-Spain	1980-81
C.H.Lloyd	95	England	Kingston	1980-81
H.A.Gomes	90*	England	Kingston	1980-81
D.L.Haynes	92	India	Bridgetown	1982-83
M.D.Marshall	92	India	Kanpur	1983-84
P.J.L.Dujon	98	India	Ahmedabad	1983-84

A.L.Logie	97	Australia	Port-of-Spain	1983-84
H.A.Gomes	92*	England	Lord's	1984
C.G.Greenidge	95	Australia	Adelaide	1984-85
D.L.Haynes	90	New Zealand	Georgetown	1984-85
A.L.Logie	93	Australia	Perth	1988-89
R.B.Richardson	93	India	Bridgetown	1988-89
R.B.Richardson	99	India	Port-of-Spain	1988-89
A.L.Logie	98	England	Port-of-Spain	1989-90
R.B.Richardson	99	Australia	Bridgetown	1990-91
NEW ZEALAND				
R.C.Blunt	96	England	Lord's	1931
W.A.Hadlee	93	England	Manchester	1937
F.B.Smith	96	England	Leeds	1949
J.R.Reid	93	England	The Oval	1949
J.E.F.Beck	99	South Africa	Cape Town	1953-54
N.S.Harford §	93	Pakistan	Lahore[1]	1955-56
J.W.Guy	91	India	Calcutta	1955-56
J.R.Reid	92	South Africa	Cape Town	1961-62
J.R.Reid	97	Pakistan	Wellington	1964-65
R.W.Morgan	97	Pakistan	Christchurch	1964-65
B.A.G.Murray	90	Pakistan	Lahore[2]	1969-70
G.M.Turner	95	West Indies	Port-of-Spain	1971-72
G.M.Turner	98	England	Christchurch	1974-75
M.G.Burgess	95	India	Wellington	1975-76
R.W.Anderson §	92	Pakistan	Lahore[2]	1976-77
G.P.Howarth	94	England	The Oval	1978
J.G.Wright	93	England	Leeds	1983
R.J.Hadlee	92*	England	Nottingham	1983
R.J.Hadlee	99	England	Christchurch	1983-84
J.V.Coney	92	Sri Lanka	Colombo (CCC)	1983-84
J.F.Reid	97	Pakistan	Karachi	1984-85
J.V.Coney	98	Australia	Christchurch	1985-86
J.V.Coney	93	Australia	Auckland	1985-86
J.G.Wright	99	Australia	Melbourne	1987-88
J.G.Wright	98	England	Lord's	1990
D.N.Patel	99	England	Christchurch	1991-92
J.G.Wright	99	England	Christchurch	1991-92
INDIA		Opponents		
M.H.Mankad	96	West Indies	Port-of-Spain	1952-53
V.L.Manjrekar	90	New Zealand	Calcutta	1955-56
Pankaj Roy	90	West Indies	Bombay[2]	1958-59
N.J.Contractor	92	West Indies	Delhi	1958-59
C.G.Borde	96	West Indies	Delhi	1958-59
Pankaj Roy	99	Australia	Delhi	1959-60
M.L.Jaisimha	99	Pakistan	Kanpur	1960-61
N.J.Contractor	92	Pakistan	Delhi	1960-61
V.L.Manjrekar	96	England	Kanpur	1961-62
C.G.Borde	93	West Indies	Kingston	1961-62
S.A.Durani	90	England	Bombay[2]	1963-64
Hanumant Singh	94	Australia	Madras[2]	1964-65
F.M.Engineer	90	New Zealand	Madras[2]	1964-65
A.L.Wadekar	91	England	Leeds	1967
A.L.Wadekar	99	Australia	Melbourne	1967-68
R.F.Surti	99	New Zealand	Auckland	1967-68
Nawab of Pataudi, jr	95	Australia	Bombay[2]	1969-70
A.V.Mankad	97	Australia	Delhi	1969-70
A.L.Wadekar	91*	Australia	Delhi	1969-70

A.L.Wadekar	90	England	Kanpur	1972-73
G.R.Viswanath	97*	West Indies	Madras[1]	1974-75
G.R.Viswanath	95	West Indies	Bombay[3]	1974-75
M.Amarnath	90	Australia	Perth	1977-78
C.P.S.Chauhan	93	Pakistan	Lahore[2]	1978-79
S.M.Gavaskar	97	Pakistan	Lahore[2]	1978-79
G.R.Viswanath	96	Australia	Calcutta	1979-80
C.P.S.Chauhan	97	Australia	Adelaide	1980-81
R.J.Shastri	93	England	Delhi	1981-82
Kapil Dev	97	England	The Oval	1982
D.B.Vengsarkar	90	Sri Lanka	Madras[1]	1982-83
M.Amarnath	91	West Indies	Bridgetown	1982-83
D.B.Vengsarkar	94	West Indies	St John's	1982-83
Kapil Dev	98	West Indies	St John's	1982-83
S.M.Gavaskar	90	West Indies	Ahmedabad	1983-84
M.Amarnath	95	England	Madras[1]	1984-85
D.B.Vengsarkar	98*	Sri Lanka	Colombo (SSC)	1985-86
S.M.Gavaskar	90	Australia	Madras[1]	1986-87
S.M.Gavaskar	91	Pakistan	Madras[1]	1986-87
D.B.Vengsarkar	96	Pakistan	Madras[1]	1986-87
S.M.Gavaskar	96	Pakistan	Bangalore	1986-87
Arun Lal	93	West Indies	Calcutta	1987-88
K.Srikkanth	94	New Zealand	Bombay[3]	1988-89
N.S.Sidhu	97	Pakistan	Sialkot	1989-90
W.V.Raman	96	New Zealand	Christchurch	1989-90
M.Prabhakar	95	New Zealand	Napier	1989-90
S.V.Manjrekar	93	England	Manchester	1990

PAKISTAN		Opponents		
Hanif Mohammad	96	India	Bombay[2]	1952-53
Waqar Hassan	97	India	Calcutta	1952-53
Maqsood Ahmed	99	India	Lahore[1]	1954-55
A.H.Kardar	93	India	Karachi	1954-55
Imtiaz Ahmed	91	West Indies	Bridgetown	1957-58
Wazir Mohammad	97*	West Indies	Georgetown	1957-58
Saeed Ahmed	97	West Indies	Port-of-Spain	1957-58
Saeed Ahmed	91	Australia	Karachi	1959-60
Imtiaz Ahmed	98	England	The Oval	1962
Abdul Kadir §	95	Australia	Karachi	1964-65
Hanif Mohammad	93	Australia	Melbourne	1964-65
Shafqat Rana	95	New Zealand	Lahore[2]	1969-70
Asif Iqbal	92	New Zealand	Dacca	1969-70
Sadiq Mohammad	91	England	Leeds	1971
Majid Khan	99	England	Karachi	1972-73
Mushtaq Mohammad	99	England	Karachi	1972-73
Majid Khan	98	England	The Oval	1974
Sadiq Mohammad	98*	Pakistan	Karachi	1974-75
Majid Khan	98	New Zealand	Hyderabad	1976-77
Zaheer Abbas	90	Australia	Melbourne	1976-77
Majid Khan	92	West Indies	Port-of-Spain	1976-77
Sadiq Mohammad	97	England	Leeds	1978
Zaheer Abbas	96	India	Faisalabad	1978-79
Wasim Raja	97	India	Delhi	1979-80
Wasim Raja	94*	India	Kanpur	1979-80
Taslim Arif §	90	India	Calcutta	1979-80
Zaheer Abbas	90	Australia	Melbourne	1981-82
Mudassar Nazar	95	Australia	Melbourne	1981-82
Javed Miandad	92	Sri Lanka	Karachi	1982-83
Zaheer Abbas	91	Australia	Faisalabad	1982-83

Mohsin Khan	94	India	Lahore²	1982-83
Mohsin Khan	91	India	Karachi	1982-83
Javed Miandad	99	India	Bangalore	1983-84
Sarfraz Nawaz	90	England	Lahore²	1983-84
Qasim Omar	96	New Zealand	Dunedin	1984-85
Javed Miandad	94	India	Madras¹	1986-87
Saleem Malik	99	England	Leeds	1987
Saleem Yousuf	91	England	Birmingham	1987
Aamer Malik	98*	England	Karachi	1987-88
Shoaib Mohammad	94	Australia	Karachi	1988-89
Shoaib Mohammad	95	India	Karachi	1989-90
Rameez Raja	98	Sri Lanka	Sialkot	1991-92
Imran Khan	93*	Sri Lanka	Sialkot	1991-92

SRI LANKA		Opponents		
R.L.Dias	98	Pakistan	Faisalabad	1981-82
R.S.Madugalle	91*	Pakistan	Faisalabad	1981-82
R.L.Dias	97	India	Madras¹	1982-83
A.Ranatunga	90	Australia	Kandy	1982-83
S.Wettimuny	91	Australia	Kandy	1982-83
L.R.D.Mendis	94	England	Lord's	1984
R.L.Dias	95	India	Colombo (PSS)	1985-86
J.R.Ratnayeke	93	India	Kanpur	1986-87
P.A.de Silva	96	New Zealand	Auckland	1990-91

There have been 449 scores in the nineties recorded in Test cricket (96 for Australia; 117 for England; 32 for South Africa; 79 for West Indies; 27 for New Zealand; 46 for India; 43 for Pakistan; and 9 for Sri Lanka). The following players scored these nineties:

8 A.I.Kallicharran(W)

6 G.Boycott(E), C.G.Greenidge(W), C.Hill(A), R.B.Kanhai(W)

5 K.F.Barrington(E), S.M.Gavaskar(I), G.S.Sobers(W)

4 I.M.Chappell(A), M.C.Cowdrey(E), T.W.Graveney(E), A.P.E.Knott(E), Majid Khan(P), R.W.Marsh(A), P.B.H.May(E), R.B.Simpson(A), M.J.K.Smith(E), D.B.Vengsarkar(I), A.L.Wadekar(I), E.D.Weekes(W), J.G.Wright(N), Zaheer Abbas(P)

3 M.Amarnath(I), D.C.Boon(A), A.R.Border(A), D.C.S.Compton(E), J.V.Coney(N), R.L.Dias(SL), J.H.Edrich(E), R.C.Fredericks(W), T.L.Goddard(SA), H.A.Gomes(W), G.A.Gooch(E), J.Hardstaff, jr(E), D.L.Haynes(W), E.H.Hendren(E), J.B.Hobbs(E), K.J.Hughes(A), L.Hutton(E), Javed Miandad(P), W.M.Lawry(A), C.H.Lloyd(W), A.L.Logie(W), I.R.Redpath(A), J.R.Reid(N), I.V.A.Richards(W), R.B.Richardson(W), Sadiq Mohammad(P), H.W.Taylor(SA), G.R.Viswanath, K.D.Walters(A), S.R.Waugh(A), F.E.Woolley(E)

2 D.L.Amiss(E), T.J.E.Andrews(A), T.E.Bailey(E), A.C.Bannerman(A), E.J.Barlow(SA), R.Benaud(A), C.G.Borde(I), M.C.Carew(W), R.H.Catterall(SA), C.P.S.Chauhan(I), N.J.Contractor(I), R.M.Cowper(A), E.R.Dexter(E), G.A.Faulkner(SA), D.I.Gower(E), A.W.Greig(E), R.J.Hadlee(N), Hanif Mohammad(P), R.N.Harvey(A), T.W.Hayward(E), Imtiaz Ahmed(P), D.M.Jones(A), Kapil Dev(I), A.J.Lamb(E), S.J.McCabe(A), C.C.McDonald(A), V.L.Manjrekar(I), G.Miller(E), B.Mitchell(SA), Mohsin Khan(P), D.L.Murray(W), A.D.Nourse(SA), A.W.Nourse(SA), S.M.Nurse(W), Pankaj Roy(I), A.F.Rae(W), G.M.Ritchie(A), Saeed Ahmed(P), J.E.D.Sealy(W), Shoaib Mohammad(P), R.A.Smith(E), R.Subba Row(E), H.Sutcliffe(E), G.H.S.Trott(A), G.M.Turner(N), C.L.Walcott(W), C.Washbrook(E), Wasim Raja(P), K.C.Wessels(A), F.M.M.Worrell(W)

1 Aamer Malik(P), Abdul Kadir(P), R.Abel(E), R.W.Anderson(N), R.G.Archer(A), W.W.Armstrong(A), Arun Lal(I), Asif Iqbal(P), C.W.J.Athey(E), S.F.A.F.Bacchus(A), R.W.Barber(E), W.Bardsley(A), J.E.F.Beck(N), R.C.Blunt(N), B.C.Booth(A), K.D.Boyce(W), J.M.Brearley(E), W.A.Brown(A), P.J.P.Burge(A), M.G.Burgess(N), B.F.Butcher(W), D.J.Capel(E), H.B.Cameron(SA), G.S.Chappell(A), A.G.Chipperfield(A), R.J.Christiani(W), L.N.Constantine(W), W.M.Darling(A), C.A.Davis(W), H.G.Deane(SA), P.A.de Silva(SL), P.J.L.Dujon(W), S.A.Durani(I), R.Edwards(A), W.R.Endean(SA), F.M.Engineer(I), M.L.C.Foster(W), K.J.Funston(SA), M.W.Gatting(E), P.A.Gibb(E), G.J.Gilmour(A), J.M.Gregory(A), J.W.Guy(N), W.A.Hadlee(N), W.R.Hammond(E), Hanumant Singh(I), N.S.Harford(N), A.L.Hassett(A), G.A.Headley(W), E.E.Hemmings(E), J.K.Holt(W), G.P.Howarth(N), C.C.Hunte(W), Imran Khan(P), F.S.Jackson(E), M.L.Jaisimha(I), D.R.Jardine(E), G.L.Jessop(E), A.H.Kardar(P),

B.M.Laird(A), H.Larwood(E), M.Leyland(E), C.B.Llewellyn(SA), S.J.E.Loxton(A), B.W.Luckhurst(E), C.G.Macartney(A), C.L.McCool(A), R.B.McCosker(A), A.C.MacLaren(E), R.A.McLean(SA), R.S.Madugalle(SL), S.V.Manjrekar(I), A.V.Mankad(I), M.H.Mankad(I), P.N.F.Mansell(SA), Maqsood Ahmed(P), G.R.Marsh(A), M.D.Marshall(W), G.R.J.Matthews(A), L.R.D.Mendis(SL), C.Milburn(E), K.R.Miller(A), R.B.Minnett(A), R.W.Morgan(N), A.R.Morris(A), M.D.Moxon(E), Mudassar Nazar(P), B.A.G.Murray(N), Mushtaq Mohammad(P), R.K.Nunes(W), S.O'Linn(SA), J.M.Parks(E), Nawab of Pataudi, jr(I), D.N.Patel(N), E.Paynter(E), W.B.Phillips(A), A.J.Pithey(SA), R.G.Pollock(SA), W.H.Ponsford(A), M.Prabhakar(I), Qasim Omar(P), W.V.Raman(I), Rameez Raja(P), A.Ranatunga(SL), D.W.Randall(E), K.S.Ranjitsinhji(E), V.S.Ransford(A), J.R.Ratnayeke(SL), W.W.Read(E), J.F.Reid(N), W.Rhodes(E), A.J.Richardson(A), C.A.G.Russell(E), R.C.Russell(E), Saleem Malik(P), Saleem Yousuf(P), Sarfraz Nawaz(P), W.H.Scotton(E), Shafqat Rana(P), R.J.Shastri(I), B.K.Shepherd(A), N.S.Sidhu(I), R.T.Simpson(E), P.R.Sleep(A), C.L.Smith(E), F.B.Smith(N), J.S.Solomon(W), R.T.Spooner(E), V.H.Stollmeyer(W), K.Srikkanth(I), D.S.Steele(E), A.J.Stewart(E), R.F.Surti(I), D.Tallon(A), L.J.Tancred(SA), Taslim Arif(P), J.M.Taylor(A), M.A.Taylor(A), R.W.Taylor(E), P.M.Toohey(A), J.T.Tyldesley(E), B.H.Valentine(E), P.G.V.van der Bijl(SA), K.G.Viljoen(SA), Waqar Hassan(P), A.Ward(E), J.C.Watkins(SA), Wazir Mohammad(P), S.Wettimuny(SL), J.M.Wiener(A), B.Wood(E), G.M.Wood(A), R.E.S.Wyatt(E), G.N.Yallop(A), N.W.D.Yardley(E)

LONGEST INNINGS FOR EACH COUNTRY

For	Min		Opponents		
Australia	762	R.B.Simpson (311)	England	Manchester	1964
England	797	L.Hutton (364)	Australia	Oval	1938
South Africa	575	D.J.McGlew (105)	Australia	Durban[2]	1957-58
West Indies	682	F.M.M.Worrell (197*)	England	Bridgetown	1959-60
New Zealand	704	G.M.Turner (259)	West Indies	Georgetown	1971-72
India	708	S.M.Gavaskar (172)	England	Bangalore	1981-82
Pakistan	970	Hanif Mohammad(337)	West Indies	Bridgetown	1957-58
Sri Lanka	777	D.S.B.P.Kuruppu (201*)	New Zealand	Colombo (CCC)	1986-87

BATTED ON EACH DAY OF A FIVE-DAY MATCH

	Scores						
M.L.Jaisimha	20*	74	India	v	Australia	Calcutta	1959-60
G.Boycott	107	80*	England	v	Australia	Nottingham	1977
K.J.Hughes	117	84	Australia	v	England	Lord's	1980
A.J.Lamb	23	110	England	v	West Indies	Lord's	1984
R.J.Shastri	111	7*	India	v	England	Calcutta	1984-85

MOST RUNS FROM STROKES WORTH FOUR OR MORE IN AN INNINGS

	6s	5s	4s							
238	5	-	52	J.H.Edrich	310*	England	v	New Zealand	Leeds	1965
196	10	-	34	W.R.Hammond	336*	England	v	New Zealand	Auckland	1932-33
190	3	-	43	G.A.Gooch	333	England	v	India	The Oval	1990
184	-	-	46	D.G.Bradman	334	Australia	v	England	Leeds	1930
184	2	-	43	D.G.Bradman	304	Australia	v	England	Leeds	1934
177	-	1	43	R.G.Pollock	274	South Africa	v	Australia	Durban[2]	1969-70
168	-	-	42	R.B.Kanhai	256	West Indies	v	India	Calcutta	1958-59
166	1	-	40	D.L.Amiss	262*	England	v	West Indies	Kingston	1973-74
160	-	-	40	P.A.de Silva	267	Sri Lanka	v	New Zealand	Wellington	1990-91
157	-	1	38	G.S.Sobers	365*	West Indies	v	Pakistan	Kingston	1957-58
152	2	-	35	F.M.M.Worrell	261	West Indies	v	England	Nottingham	1957
152	-	-	38	Zaheer Abbas	274	Pakistan	v	England	Birmingham	1971
152	-	-	38	I.V.A.Richards	291	West Indies	v	England	Oval	1976
150	1	-	36	L.G.Rowe	302	West Indies	v	England	Bridgetown	1973-74

MOST SIXES IN AN INNINGS

TEN	W.R.Hammond (336*)	England	v	New Zealand	Auckland	1932-33
SEVEN	B.Sutcliffe (80*)	New Zealand	v	South Africa	Johannesburg[2]	1953-54
	I.V.A.Richards (110*)	West Indies	v	England	St John's	1985-86
	C G.Greenidge (213)	West Indies	v	New Zealand	Auckland	1986-87
SIX	J.H.Sinclair (104)	South Africa	v	Australia	Cape Town	1902-03
	I.V.A.Richards (192*)	West Indies	v	India	Delhi	1974-75
	Haroon Rashid (108)	Pakistan	v	England	Hyderabad	1977-78
	I.T.Botham (118)	England	v	Australia	Manchester	1981
	R.J.Shastri (121*)	India	v	Australia	Bombay[3]	1986-87

MOST SIXES OFF CONSECUTIVE BALLS

FOUR	Kapil Dev (77*) off E.E.Hemmings	India	v	England	Lord's	1990
THREE	W.R.Hammond (336*) off J.Newman	England	v	New Zealand	Auckland	1932-33
	S.T.Clarke (35*) off Mohammad Nazir	West Indies	v	Pakistan	Faisalabad	1980-81

MOST FOURS OFF CONSECUTIVE BALLS

FIVE	D.T.Lindsay (60) off J.W.Gleeson	South Africa	v	Australia	Port Elizabeth	1969-70
	R.E.Redmond (107) off Majid Khan	New Zealand	v	Pakistan	Auckland	1972-73
	D.W.Hookes (56) off A.W.Greig	Australia	v	England	Melbourne	1976-77

MOST RUNS OFF ONE OVER

EIGHT-BALLS

25 (66061600)	B.Sutcliffe and R.W.Blair (off H.J.Tayfield)	New Zealand	v	South Africa	Johannesburg[2]	1953-54

SIX-BALLS

24 (462660§) (§ 1 leg-bye)	A.M.E.Roberts (off I.T.Botham)	West Indies	v	England	Port-Of-Spain	1980-81
24 (444#0444) (#no-ball)	S.M.Patil (off R.G.D.Willis)	India	v	England	Manchester	1982
24 (464604)	I.T.Botham (off D.A.Stirling)	England	v	New Zealand	The Oval	1986
24 (244266)	I.D.S.Smith (off A.S.Wassan)	New Zealand	v	India	Auckland	1989-90
24 (006666)	Kapil Dev (off E.E.Hemmings)	India	v	England	Lord's	1990

CENTURY BEFORE LUNCH

FIRST DAY

	Lunch score					
V.T.Trumper (101)	103*	Australia	v	England	Manchester	1902
C.G.Macartney (151)	112*	Australia	v	England	Leeds	1926
D.G.Bradman (334)	105*	Australia	v	England	Leeds	1930
Majid Khan (112)	108*	Pakistan	v	New Zealand	Karachi	1976-77

OTHER DAYS

	Overnight score	Lunch score						Day
K.S.Ranjitsinhji (154*)	41*	154*	England	v	Australia	Manchester	1896	3
C.Hill (142)	22*	138*	Australia	v	South Africa	Johannesburg[1]	1902-03	3
W.Bardsley (164)	32*	150*	Australia	v	South Africa	Lord's	1912	2
C.P.Mead (182*	19*	128*	England	v	Australia	The Oval	1921	2
J.B.Hobbs (211)	12*	114*	England	v	South Africa	Lord's	1924	2
H.G.Owen-Smith (129)	27*	129	South Africa	v	England	Leeds	1929	3
W.R.Hammond (336*)	41*	152*	England	v	New Zealand	Auckland	1932-33	2
L.E.G.Ames (148*)	25*	148*	England	v	South Africa	The Oval	1935	3
S.J.McCabe (189*)	59*	159*	Australia	v	South Africa	Johannesburg[1]	1935-36	4
G.S.Chappell (176)	76*	176	Australia	v	New Zealand	Christchurch	1981-82	2

FASTEST FIFTIES

Min						
22	V.T.Trumper (63)	Australia	v	South Africa	Johannesburg[1]	1902-03
28	J.T Brown (140)	England	v	Australia	Melbourne	1894-95
29	S.A.Durani (61*)	India	v	England	Kanpur	1963-64
30	E.A.V.Williams (72)	West Indies	v	England	Bridgetown	1947-48
30	B.R.Taylor (124)	New Zealand	v	West Indies	Auckland	1968-69
33	C.A.Roach (56)	West Indies	v	England	The Oval	1933
34	C.R.Browne (70*)	West Indies	v	England	Georgetown	1929-30
35	J.H.Sinclair (104)	South Africa	v	Australia	Cape Town	1902-03
35	C.G.Macartney (56)	Australia	v	South Africa	Sydney	1910-11
35	J.W.Hitch (51*)	England	v	Australia	The Oval	1921

FASTEST CENTURIES

Min						
70	J.M.Gregory (119)	Australia	v	South Africa	Johannesburg[1]	1921-22
75	G.L.Jessop (104)	England	v	Australia	The Oval	1902
78	R.Benaud (121)	Australia	v	West Indies	Kingston	1954-55
80	J.H.Sinclair (104)	South Africa	v	Australia	Cape Town	1902-03
81	I.V.A.Richards (110*)	West Indies	v	England	St John's	1985-86
86	B.R.Taylor (124)	New Zealand	v	West Indies	Auckland	1968-69
91	J.Darling (160)	Australia	v	England	Sydney	1897-98
91	S.J.McCabe (189*)	Australia	v	South Africa	Johannesburg[1]	1935-36
94	V.T.Trumper (185*)	Australia	v	England	Sydney	1903-04
95	J.T.Brown (140)	England	v	Australia	Melbourne	1894-95
95	P.W.Sherwell (115)	South Africa	v	England	Lord's	1907

FASTEST DOUBLE CENTURIES

Min						
214	D.G.Bradman (334)	Australia	v	England	Leeds	1930
223	S.J.McCabe (232)	Australia	v	England	Nottingham	1938
226	V.T.Trumper (214*)	Australia	v	South Africa	Adelaide	1910-11
234	D.G.Bradman (254)	Australia	v	England	Lord's	1930
240	W.R.Hammond (336*)	England	v	New Zealand	Auckland	1932-33
241	S.E.Gregory (201)	Australia	v	England	Sydney	1894-95
245	D.C S.Compton (278)	England	v	Pakistan	Nottingham	1954
251	D.G Bradman (223)	Australia	v	West Indies	Brisbane[1]	1930-31
253	D.G.Bradman (226)	Australia	v	South Africa	Brisbane[2]	1931-32

FASTEST TRIPLE CENTURIES

Min						
288	W.R.Hammond (336*)	England	v	New Zealand	Auckland	1932-33
336	D.G.Bradman (334)	Australia	v	England	Leeds	1930

W.R.Hammond's third hundred was scored in 48 minutes.
D.G.Bradman scored his three hundreds in 99, 115 and 122 minutes respectively and reached 309 at the end of the first day.*

MOST RUNS IN A DAY

309	(0-309*)	D.G.Bradman (334)	Australia	v	England	Leeds	1930
295	(41*-336*)	W.R.Hammond (336*)	England	v	New Zealand	Auckland	1932-33
273	(5*-278)	D.C.S.Compton (278)	England	v	Pakistan	Nottingham	1954
271	(0-271*)	D.G.Bradman (304)	Australia	v	England	Leeds	1934
244	(0-244)	D.G.Bradman (244)	Australia	v	England	The Oval	1934

239	(0-239*)	F.M.M.Worrell (261)	West Indies	v	England	Nottingham	1950
223	(0-223*)	W.R.Hammond (227)	England	v	New Zealand	Christchurch	1932-33
223	(0-223*)	D.G.Bradman (223)	Australia	v	West Indies	Brisbane[1]	1930-31
217	(0-217)	W.R.Hammond (217)	England	v	India	The Oval	1936
214	(73*-287)	R.E.Foster (287)	England	v	Australia	Sydney	1903-04
213	(19*-232)	S.J.McCabe (232)	Australia	v	England	Nottingham	1938
210	(0-210*)	W.R.Hammond (240)	England	v	Australia	Lord's	1938
209	(0-209)	C.A.Roach (209)	West Indies	v	England	Georgetown	1929-30
208	(20*-228*)	G.S.Sobers (365*)	West Indies	v	Pakistan	Kingston	1957-58
208	(0-208*)	V.T.Trumper (214*)	Australia	v	South Africa	Adelaide	1910-11
206	(0-206)	L.Hutton (206)	England	v	New Zealand	The Oval	1949
205	(0-205*)	W.H.Ponsford (266)	Australia	v	England	The Oval	1934
205	(0-205)	Aamer Sohail (205)	Pakistan	v	England	Manchester	1992
203	(0-203)	H.L.Collins (203)	Australia	v	South Africa	Johannesburg[1]	1921-22
203	(0-203*)	R B Kanhai (256)	West Indies	v	India	Calcutta	1958-59
203	(0*-203*)	P.A.de Silva (267)	Sri Lanka	v	New Zealand	Wellington	1990-91
201	(0-201)	D.G.Bradman (201)	Australia	v	India	Adelaide	1947-48
200	(0-200*)	D.G.Bradman (226)	Australia	v	South Africa	Brisbane[2]	1931-32
200	(0-200*)	I.V.A.Richards (291)	West Indies	v	England	The Oval	1976

FEWEST BOUNDARIES IN AN INNINGS

Runs	Fours						
84	0	W.M.Lawry	Australia	v	England	Brisbane[2]	1970-71
77	0	G.Boycott	England	v	Australia	Perth	1978-79
67	0	E.A.B.Rowan	South Africa	v	England	Durban	1938-39
120	2	P.A.Gibb	England	v	South Africa	Durban[2]	1938-39
94	2	K.F.Barrington	England	v	Australia	Sydney	1962-63
102	3	W.M.Woodfull	Australia	v	England	Melbourne	1928-29
161	5	W.M.Woodfull	Australia	v	South Africa	Melbourne	1931-32

G.Boycott's innings included one four but it was all-run and included two runs from an overthrow.

SLOWEST FIFTIES

Min						
357	T.E.Bailey (68)	England	v	Australia	Brisbane[2]	1958-59
350	C.J.Tavare (82)	England	v	Pakistan	Lord's	1982
326	S.M.Gavaskar (51)	India	v	Sri Lanka	Colombo (SSC)	1985-86
318	Rameez Raja (62)	Pakistan	v	West Indies	Karachi	1986-87
316	C.P.S.Chauhan (61)	India	v	Pakistan	Kanpur	1979-80
313	D.J.McGlew (70)	South Africa	v	Australia	Johannesburg[3]	1957-58
312	J.J.Crowe (120*)	New Zealand	v	Sri Lanka	Colombo (CCC)	1986-87
310	B.A.Edgar (55)	New Zealand	v	Australia	Wellington	1981-82
310	A.R.Border (75)	Australia	v	West Indies	Sydney	1988-89
306	C.J.Tavare (78)	England	v	Australia	Manchester	1981
302	D.N.Sardesai (60)	India	v	West Indies	Bridgetown	1961-62
300	G.S.Camacho (57)	West Indies	v	England	Bridgetown	1967-68
290	G.Boycott (63)	England	v	Pakistan	Lahore[2]	1977-78
290	K.R.Rutherford (50*)	New Zealand	v	Australia	Auckland	1985-86
289	C.J.Tavare (56)	England	v	India	Bombay[3]	1981-82
288	R.J.Shastri (109)	India	v	West Indies	Bridgetown	1988-89
285	P.R.Umrigar (78)	India	v	Australia	Bombay[2]	1956-57
285	G.A.Gooch (84)	England	v	West Indies	The Oval	1988
282	E.D.A.S.McMorris (73)	West Indies	v	England	Kingston	1959-60
280	P.E.Richardson (117)	England	v	South Africa	Johannesburg[3]	1956-57
278	G.Boycott (77)	England	v	Australia	Perth	1978-79

SLOWEST CENTURIES

Min						
557	Mudassar Nazar (111)	Pakistan	v	England	Lahore[2]	1977-78
545	D.J.McGlew (105)	South Africa	v	Australia	Durban[2]	1957-58
515	J.J.Crowe (120*)	New Zealand	v	Sri Lanka	Colombo (CCC)	1986-87
488	P.E.Richardson (117)	England	v	South Africa	Johannesburg[3]	1956-57
487	C.T.Radley (158)	England	v	New Zealand	Auckland	1977-78
468	Hanif Mohammad (142)	Pakistan	v	India	Bahawalpur	1954-55
462	M.J.Greatbatch (146*)	New Zealand	v	Australia	Perth	1989-90
461	M.D.Crowe (108*)	New Zealand	v	Pakistan	Lahore[2]	1990-91
460	Hanif Mohammad (111)	Pakistan	v	England	Dacca	1961-62
458	K.W.R.Fletcher (122)	England	v	Pakistan	The Oval	1974
457	S.A.R.Silva (111)	Sri Lanka	v	India	Colombo (SSC)	1985-86
455	G.P.Howarth (122)	New Zealand	v	England	Auckland	1977-78
440	A.J.Watkins (137*)	England	v	India	Delhi	1951-52
438	G.Boycott (105)	England	v	India	Delhi	1981-82
437	D.B.Vengsarkar (146*)	India	v	Pakistan	Delhi	1979-80
435	J.W.Guy (102)	New Zealand	v	India	Hyderabad	1955-56
434	M.C.Cowdrey (154)	England	v	West Indies	Birmingham	1957
434	T.J.Franklin (101)	New Zealand	v	England	Lord's	1990
428	S.M.Gavaskar (172)	India	v	England	Bangalore	1981-82
427	R.J.Shastri (109)	India	v	West Indies	Bridgetown	1988-89
424	R.J.Shastri (125)	India	v	Pakistan	Jaipur	1986-87
425	H.A.Gomes (127)	West Indies	v	Australia	Perth	1984-85
424	M.A.Atherton (105)	England	v	Australia	Sydney	1990-91
422	R.J.Shastri (111)	India	v	England	Calcutta	1984-85
420	M.D.Crowe (188)	New Zealand	v	West Indies	Georgetown	1984-85
414	J.H.B.Waite (134)	South Africa	v	Australia	Durban[2]	1957-58
414	A.W.Greig (103)	England	v	India	Calcutta	1976-77
414	J.G.Wright (110)	New Zealand	v	India	Auckland	1980-81
412	J.G.Wright (138)	New Zealand	v	West Indies	Wellington	1986-87
411	D.W.Randall (150)	England	v	Australia	Sydney	1978-79

SLOWEST DOUBLE CENTURIES

Min						
777	D.S.B.P.Kuruppu (201*)	Sri Lanka	v	New Zealand	Colombo (CCC)	1986-87
656	Shoaib Mohammad (203*)	Pakistan	v	New Zealand	Karachi	1990-91
652	A.D.Gaekwad (201)	India	v	Pakistan	Jullundur	1983-84
608	R.B.Simpson (311)	Australia	v	England	Manchester	1964
596	A.R.Border (205)	Australia	v	New Zealand	Adelaide	1987-88
591	Javed Miandad (211)	Pakistan	v	Australia	Karachi	1988-89
595	G.S.Sobers (226)	West Indies	v	England	Bridgetown	1959-60
584	Hanif Mohammad (337)	Pakistan	v	West Indies	Bridgetown	1957-58
570	S.G.Barnes (234)	Australia	v	England	Sydney	1946-47
568	G.R.Viswanath (222)	India	v	England	Madras[1]	1981-82

SLOWEST TRIPLE CENTURIES

Min						
858	Hanif Mohammad (337)	Pakistan	v	West Indies	Bridgetown	1957-58
753	R.B.Simpson (311)	Australia	v	England	Manchester	1964
693	R.M.Cowper (307)	Australia	v	England	Melbourne	1965-66
662	L.Hutton (364)	England	v	Australia	The Oval	1938

AN HOUR BEFORE SCORING FIRST RUN

Min						
97	T.G.Evans (10*)	England	v	Australia	Adelaide	1946-47
82	P.I.Pocock (13)	England	v	West Indies	Georgetown	1967-68
74	J.T.Murray (3*)	England	v	Australia	Sydney	1962-63
72	C.G.Rackemann (9)	Australia	v	England	Sydney	1990-91
70	W.L.Murdoch (17)	Australia	v	England	Sydney	1882-83
69	R.M.Hogg (7*)	Australia	v	West Indies	Adelaide	1984-85
67	C.J.Tavare (82)	England	v	Pakistan	Lord's	1982
66	J.G.Wright (38)	New Zealand	v	Australia	Wellington	1981-82
65	Shujauddin (45)	Pakistan	v	Australia	Lahore[2]	1959-60
63	C.J.Tavare (9)	England	v	Australia	Perth	1982-83

AN HOUR WITHOUT ADDING TO SCORE

Min						
91	M.C.Snedden (23)	New Zealand	v	Australia	Wellington	1989-90
91	J.J.Crowe (21)	New Zealand	v	West Indies	Bridgetown	1984-85
90	B.Mitchell (58)	South Africa	v	Australia	Brisbane[2]	1931-32
90	C.J.Tavare (89)	England	v	Australia	Perth	1982-83
79	T.E.Bailey (8)	England	v	South Africa	Leeds	1955
77	D.B.Close (20)	England	v	West Indies	Manchester	1976
75	A.Ranatunga (37)	Sri Lanka	v	New Zealand	Colombo (CCC)	1983-84
70	D.L.Haynes (9)	West Indies	v	New Zealand	Auckland	1979-80
69	G.A.Gooch (84)	England	v	West Indies	The Oval	1988
67	W.H.Scotton (34)	England	v	Australia	The Oval	1886
66	S.M.Gavaskar (52)	India	v	Sri Lanka	Colombo (PSS)	1985-86
65	Nawab of Pataudi, jr (5)	India	v	England	Bombay[2]	1972-73
64	Anil Dalpat (15)	Pakistan	v	New Zealand	Wellington	1984-85
64	M.A.Taylor (11)	Australia	v	England	Sydney	1990-91
63	D.R.Jardine (24)	England	v	Australia	Brisbane	1932-33
63	W.R.Endean (18)	South Africa	v	England	Johannesburg[3]	1956-57
63	W.R.Playle (18)	New Zealand	v	England	Leeds	1958
63	J.M.Brearley (48)	England	v	Australia	Birmingham	1981
62	K.F.Barrington (137)	England	v	New Zealand	Birmingham	1965
61	J.F.Reid (148)	New Zealand	v	Pakistan	Wellington	1984-85
60	B.Mitchell (73)	South Africa	v	England	Johannesburg[1]	1938-39
60	T.E.Bailey (80)	England	v	South Africa	Durban[2]	1956-57
60	C.J.Tavare (82)	England	v	Pakistan	Lord's	1982
60	A.R.Border (9)	Australia	v	Pakistan	Faisalabad	1982-83
60	S.M.Gavaskar (51)	India	v	Sri Lanka	Colombo (SSC)	1985-86

FEWEST RUNS IN A DAY

49	(5*-54*)	M.L.Jaisimha (99)	India	v	Pakistan	Kanpur	1960-61
52	(52*)	Mudassar Nazar(114)	Pakistan	v	England	Lahore[2]	1977-78
56	(1*-57*)	D.J.McGlew (70)	South Africa	v	Australia	Johannesburg[3]	1957-58
59	(0*-59*)	M.L.Jaisimha (74)	India	v	Australia	Calcutta	1959-60

PLAYER DISMISSED FROM THE FIRST BALL OF A TEST

Batsman	Bowler					
A.C.MacLaren	A.Coningham	England	v	Australia	Melbourne	1894-95
T.W.Hayward	A.E.E.Vogler	England	v	South Africa	The Oval	1907
W.Bardsley	M.W.Tate	Australia	v	England	Leeds	1926
H.Sutcliffe	F.T.Badcock	England	v	New Zealand	Christchurch	1932-33
T.S.Worthington	E.L.McCormick	England	v	Australia	Brisbane[2]	1936-37

C.C.Hunte	Fazal Mahmood	West Indies	v	Pakistan	Port-of-Spain	1957-58
E.J.Barlow	G.D.McKenzie	South Africa	v	Australia	Durban[2]	1966-67
R.C.Fredericks	S.Abid Ali	West Indies	v	India	Port-of-Spain	1970-71
K.R.Stackpole	R.J.Hadlee	Australia	v	New Zealand	Auckland	1973-74
S.M.Gavaskar	G.G.Arnold	India	v	England	Birmingham	1974
S.S.Naik	A.M.E.Roberts	India	v	West Indies	Calcutta	1974-75
J.F.M.Morrison	G.G.Arnold	New Zealand	v	England	Christchurch	1974-75
Mohsin Khan	Kapil Dev	Pakistan	v	India	Jullundur	1983-84
S.M.Gavaskar	M.D.Marshall	India	v	West Indies	Calcutta	1983-84
S.M.Gavaskar	Imran Khan	India	v	Pakistan	Jaipur	1986-87
W.V.Raman	R.J.Hadlee	India	v	New Zealand	Napier	1989-90

BATSMEN DISMISSED FOR A 'PAIR'

FOUR TIMES

B.S.Chandrasekhar (India): v NZ 1975-76; v E 1976-77; v A 1977-78 (twice).

THREE TIMES

R.Peel (England):v A 1894-95 (twice), 1896.
R.W.Blair (New Zealand): v WI 1955-56; v E 1962-63; v SA 1963-64.
DL.Underwood (England):v WI 1966; v A 1974-75; v WI 1976.
B.S.Bedi (India):v E 1974; v WI 1974-75; v E 1976-77.
A.G.Hurst (Australia):v E 1978-79 (twice); v P 1978-79.
C.E.L.Ambrose (West Indies):v E 1988; v P 1990-91; v E 1991.

TWICE

AUSTRALIA: K.D.Mackay v E 1956; v I 1959-60. G.D.McKenzie v SA 1963-64; v E 1968. J.W.Gleeson v SA 1969-70; v E 1970-71. W.M.Clark v WI 1977-78 (twice). R.M.Hogg v I 1979-80; v WI 1984-85. R.G.Holland v E 1985; v NZ 1985-86. M.E.Waugh v SL 1992-93.

ENGLAND: A.V.Bedser v A 1948; v WI 1950. D.L.Amiss v A 1968, 1974-75. P.I.Pocock v WI 1984 (twice). N.A.Foster v WI 1985-86; v P 1987-88. D.E.Malcolm v NZ 1990; v P 1992.

SOUTH AFRICA: L.J.Tancred v E 1907, 1912. Q.McMillan v A 1931-32 (twice). R.J.Crisp v A 1935-36 (twice).

WEST INDIES: C.A.Roach v E 1929-30, 1933. A.L.Valentine v E 1950, 1953-54. A.I.Kallicharran v E 1973-74; v NZ 1979-80.

NEW ZEALAND: D.K.Morrison v A 1987-88; v SL 1990-91.

INDIA: M.Amarnath v WI 1983-84 (twice). Maninder Singh v P 1982-83; v WI 1987-88.

PAKISTAN: Aaqib Javed v A 1989-90; v E 1992.

ONCE

AUSTRALIA: P.S.McDonnell v E 1882-83. T.W.Garrett v E 1882-83. E.Evans v E 1886. F.G.McShane v E 1887-88. A.C.Bannerman v E 1888. M.A.Noble v E 1899. S.E.Gregory v E 1899. C.E.McLeod v E 1901-02. J.Darling v E 1902. J.J.Kelly v E 1902. H.Trumble v E 1903-04. V.T.Trumper v E 1907-08. J.V.Saunders v E 1907-08. C.V.Grimmett v E 1930. W.A.S.Oldfield v SA 1931-32. J.H.W.Fingleton v E 1932-33. V.Y.Richardson v E 1932-33. C.L.Badcock v E 1938. I.W.Johnson v E 1946-47. J.Moroney v E 1950-51. J.B.Iverson v E 1950-51. L.V.Maddocks v E 1956. R.N.Harvey v E 1956. A.T.W.Grout v WI 1960-61. R.Benaud v E 1961. A.N.Connolly v WI 1968-69. R.Edwards v E 1972. K.R.Stackpole v NZ 1973-74. G.Dymock v E 1974-75. R.W.Marsh v E 1977. J.R.Thomson v E 1977. C.S.Serjeant v I 1977-78. A.L.Mann v I 1977-78. D.W.Hookes v P 1979-80. G.M.Wood v NZ 1980-81. M.R.Whitney v E 1981. B.Yardley v P 1982-83. R.J.Bright v P 1982-83. C.G.Rackemann v WI 1984-85. K.J.Hughes v WI 1984-85. M.G.Hughes v E 1986-87. D.M.Jones v P 1988-89. B.A.Reid v WI 1990-91.

ENGLAND: G.F.Grace v A 1880. W.Attewell v A 1891-92. G.A.Lohmann v SA 1895-96. E.G.Arnold v A 1903-04. A.E.Knight v A 1903-04. E.G.Hayes v SA 1905-06. M.C.Bird v SA 1909-10. H.Strudwick v A 1921. P.Holmes v SA 1927-28. C.I.J.Smith v WI 1934-35. J.T.Ikin v A 1946-47. J.J.Warr v A 1950-51. F.Ridgway v I 1951-52. R.T.Spooner v SA 1955. J.H.Wardle v A 1956. F.S.Trueman v A 1958-59. T.E.Bailey v A 1958-59. G.Pullar v P 1961-62. M.J.K.Smith v I 1961-62. J.T.Murray v P 1967. B.W.Luckhurst v P 1971. A.P.E.Knott v NZ 1973.

G.G.Arnold v A 1974-75. G.A.Gooch v A 1975. A.Ward v WI 1976. J.C.Balderstone v WI 1976. M.Hendrick v NZ 1977-78. R.A.Woolmer v A 1981. I.T.Botham v A 1981. E.E.Hemmings v A 1982-83. N.G.Cowans v I 1984-85. D.J.Capel v P 1987-88. W.Larkins v WI 1989-90. R.J.Bailey v WI 1989-90.

SOUTH AFRICA: C.S.Wimble v E 1891-92. J.T.Willoughby v E 1895-96. J.J.Kotze v A 1902-03. P.S.Twentyman-Jones v A 1902-03. A.E.E.Vogler v A 1910-11. T.A.Ward v A 1912. C.B.Llewellyn v E 1912. P.T.Lewis v E 1913-14. J.I.Cox v E 1913-14. C.D.Dixon v E 1913-14. G.A.L.Hearne v E 1922-23. A.E.Hall v E 1922-23. F.Nicholson v A 1935-36. X.C.Balaskas v A 1935-36. C.N.McCarthy v E 1948-49. D.J.McGlew v E 1955. W.R.Endean v E 1955. P.S.Heine v E 1956-57. C.Wesley v E 1960. M.A.Seymour v A 1969-70. A.A.Donald v WI 1991-92.

WEST INDIES: C.R.Browne v E 1929-30. H.C.Griffith v E 1933. E.E.Achong v E 1934-35. J.Trim v A 1951-52. A.P.Binns v A 1954-55. O.G.Smith v A 1954-55. S.Ramadhin v E 1957. E.D.Weekes v E 1957. F.C.M.Alexander v E 1957. L.R.Gibbs v P 1958-59. F.M.M.Worrell v A 1960-61. J.S.Solomon v I 1961-62. J.L.Hendriks v E 1966. W.W.Hall v E 1967-68. D.L.Murray v I 1974-75. C.G.Greenidge v A 1975-76. J.Garner v P 1976-77. D.A.Murray v P 1980-81. A.L.Logie v I 1983-84. M.A.Holding v A 1984-85. P.J.L.Dujon v P 1986-87. A.H.Gray v P 1986-87.

NEW ZEALAND: K.C.James v E 1929-30. F.T.Badcock v E 1929-30. J.Cowie v E 1937. C.G.Rowe v A 1945-46. L.A.Butterfield v A 1945-46. L.S.M.Miller v SA 1953-54. M.B.Poore v E 1954-55. I.A.Colquhoun v E 1954-55. J.A.Hayes v E 1954-55. A.R.MacGibbon v I 1955-56. H.B.Cave v WI 1955-56. N.S.Harford v E 1958. R.C.Motz v SA 1961-62. M.J.F.Shrimpton v SA 1963-64. A.E.Dick v P 1964-65. G.A.Bartlett v E 1965-66. T.W.Jarvis v P 1972-73. W.K.Lees v E 1977-78. B.P.Bracewell v E 1978. B.L.Cairns v A 1980-81. B.A.Edgar v A 1980-81. G.B.Troup v I 1980-81. J.V.Coney v A 1981-82. I.D.S.Smith v A 1981-82. J.G.Bracewell v P 1984-85. K.R.Rutherford v WI 1984-85. J.G.Wright v E 1986. C.M.Kuggeleijn v I 1988-89. M.C.Snedden v I 1988-89. B.R.Hartland v E 1991-92.

INDIA: V.S.Hazare v E 1951-52. G.S.Ramchand v E 1952. Pankaj Roy v E 1952. P.G.Joshi v WI 1952-53. C.V.Gadkari v WI 1952-53. N.S.Tamhane v WI 1958-59. Surendranath v E 1959. R.B.Desai v A 1959-60. D.N.Sardesai v WI 1961-62. M.L.Jaisimha v NZ 1969-70. E.A.S.Prasanna v WI 1974-75. F.M.Engineer v WI 1974-75. D.B.Vengsarkar v WI 1978-79. Yashpal Sharma v A 1979-80. R.M.H.Binny v P 1979-80. D.R.Doshi v P 1982-83. S.Venkataraghavan v WI 1982-83. R.G.Patel v NZ 1988-89.

PAKISTAN: M.E.Z.Ghazali v E 1954. Nasim-ul-Ghani v WI 1957-58. Wazir Mohammad v WI 1957-58. Imtiaz Ahmed v E 1961-62. Javed Burki v NZ 1964-65. Salim Altaf v A 1976-77. Iqbal Qasim v E 1978. Majid Khan v A 1978-79. Wasim Bari v A 1978-79. Sikander Bakht v A 1978-79. Mudassar Nazar v E 1982. Wasim Akram v SL 1985-86. Waqar Younis v NZ 1990-91. Saeed Anwar v WI 1990-91.

SRI LANKA: B.R.Jurangpathy v I 1986-87. R.G.de Alwis v I 1986-87. M.S.Ataputta v I 1990-91. R.J.Ratnayake v I 1990-91. G.F.Labrooy v I 1990-91. A.Ranatunga v P 1991-92. S.D.Anurasiri v P 1991-92.

FASTEST 'PAIRS'

Timed from the start of first innings to dismissal in the second innings

Minutes						
120	M.E.Z.Ghazali	Pakistan	v	England	Manchester	1954
124	R.N.Harvey	Australia	v	England	Manchester	1956
164	Pankaj Roy	India	v	England	Manchester	1952

DISMISSED FOR A 'PAIR' BY THE SAME FIELDING COMBINATION

R.Peel	st Jarvis b Turner	England	v	Australia	Sydney	1894-95
J.Darling	c Braund b Barnes	Australia	v	England	Sheffield	1902
P.T.Lewis	c Woolley b Barnes	South Africa	v	England	Durban[1]	1913-14
P.G.Joshi	c Worrell b Valentine	India	v	West Indies	Bridgetown	1952-53
K.D.Mackay	c Oakman b Laker	Australia	v	England	Manchester	1956
Maninder Singh	c Richardson b Walsh	India	v	West Indies	Bombay[3]	1987-88

THREE 'PAIRS' IN A MATCH BY THE SAME TEAM

M.B.Poore, I.A.Colquhoun, J A.Hayes	New Zealand	v	England	Auckland	1954-55
D L.Amiss, D L.Underwood, G G.Arnold	England	v	Australia	Adelaide	1974-75
Majid Khan, Wasim Bari, Sikander Bakht	Pakistan	v	Australia	Perth	1978-79
M.S.Ataputta, R.J.Ratnayake, G.F.Labrooy	Sri Lanka	v	India	Chandigarh	1990-91

MOST CONSECUTIVE 'DUCKS'

FIVE

R.G.Holland	(including two pairs in consecutive Tests)	Australia	v	England	1985
		Australia	v	New Zealand	1985-86

FOUR

R.Peel	(2 pairs in consecutive Tests)	England	v	Australia	1894-95
R.J.Crisp	(2 pairs in consecutive Tests)	South Africa	v	Australia	1935-36
Pankaj Roy	(including one pair)	India	v	England	1952
L.S.M.Miller	(including one pair)	New Zealand	v	South Africa	1953-54
W.M.Clark	(2 pairs in consecutive Tests)	Australia	v	West Indies	1977-78
P.I.Pocock	(2 pairs in consecutive Tests)	England	v	West Indies	1984
R.G.de Alwis	(including one pair)	Sri Lanka	v	India	1986-87
		Sri Lanka	v	Australia	1987-88
N.A.Foster	(including one pair)	England	v	Australia	1985
		England	v	West Indies	1985-86
M.E.Waugh	(2 pairs in consecutive Tests)	Australia	v	Sri Lanka	1992-93

R.J.Crisp was dismissed four times in five balls.

MOST 'DUCKS' IN A SERIES

					Innings	
SIX	A.G.Hurst	Australia	v	England	12	1978-79
FIVE	Pankaj Roy	India	v	England	7	1952
	R.C.Motz	New Zealand	v	South Africa	9	1961-62
	W.M.Clark	Australia	v	West Indies	7	1977-78
	M.Amarnath	India	v	West Indies	6	1983-84

FEWEST 'DUCKS' IN A CAREER

Ducks	Innings					
1	74	C.L.Walcott	West Indies	1947-48	to	1959-60
1	73	G.M.Turner	New Zealand	1968-69	to	1982-83
2	84	H.Sutcliffe	England	1924	to	1935
2	83	C.C.McDonald	Australia	1951-52	to	1961
4	175	C.H.Lloyd	West Indies	1966-67	to	1984-85
4	140	W.R.Hammond	England	1927-28	to	1946-47
5	131	K.F.Barrington	England	1955	to	1968

MOST INNINGS BEFORE FIRST 'DUCK'

58	C.H.Lloyd	West Indies	1966-67	to	1973-74
46	B.F.Butcher	West Indies	1958-59	to	1966-67
41	R.N.Harvey	Australia	1947-48	to	1953
40	W.H.Ponsford	Australia	1924-25	to	1932-33

MOST CONSECUTIVE INNINGS WITHOUT A 'DUCK'

119	D.I.Gower	England	1982	to	1990-91
89	A.R.Border	Australia	1982-83	to	1988-89
78	K.F.Barrington	England	1962	to	1967-68
74	C.H.Lloyd	West Indies	1976	to	1984
72	H.W.Taylor	South Africa	1912	to	1931-32
72	G.M.Turner	New Zealand	1968-69	to	1982-83
68	K.D.Walters	Australia	1969-70	to	1976-77
67	W.R.Hammond	England	1929	to	1936
67	G.Boycott	England	1969	to	1978-79

MOST 'DUCKS'

	Country	0's	Tests	A	E	SA	WI	NZ	I	P	SL
B.S.Chandrasekhar	India	**23**	58	6	8	-	4	3	-	2	-
B.S.Bedi	India	**20**	67	11	1	-	7	1	-	-	-
Wasim Bari	Pakistan	**19**	81	11	4	-	2	-	2	-	-
D.L.Underwood	England	**19**	86	8	-	-	7	-	2	1	1
J.Garner	West Indies	**18**	59	5	5	-	-	4	-	4	-
T.G.Evans	England	**17**	91	5	-	6	1	3	1	1	-
J.A.Snow	England	**16**	49	6	-	1	7	-	1	1	-
Kapil Dev	India	**16**	115	3	4	-	4	2	-	2	1
E.A.S.Prasanna	India	**15**	49	7	4	-	2	2	-	-	-
J.E.Emburey	England	**15**	60	5	-	-	6	-	2	1	1
M.A.Holding	West Indies	**15**	60	5	4	-	-	2	4	-	-
G.D.McKenzie	Australia	**15**	61	-	7	3	1	-	4	-	-
I.T.Botham	England	**15**	102	11	-	-	1	1	1	1	-
D.B.Vengsarkar	India	**15**	116	1	3	-	5	3	-	2	1
D.K.Morrison	New Zealand	**14**	25	4	4	-	-	-	1	3	2
D.R.Doshi	India	**14**	33	4	4	-	-	1	-	5	-
R.M.Hogg	Australia	**14**	38	-	7	-	2	1	3	1	-
S.Ramadhin	West Indies	**14**	43	7	6	-	-	1	-	-	-
Pankaj Roy	India	**14**	43	8	1	-	2	1	-	2	-
J.R.Thomson	Australia	**14**	43	-	5	-	6	-	2	1	-
D.W.Randall	England	**14**	47	6	-	-	1	2	3	2	-
L.R.Gibbs	West Indies	**14**	79	5	5	-	-	-	1	3	-
M.D.Marshall	West Indies	**14**	81	3	6	-	-	1	1	3	-
C.G.Borde	India	**13**	55	4	4	-	4	-	-	1	-
S.Venkataraghavan	India	**13**	57	5	2	-	5	1	-	-	-
F.E.Woolley	England	**13**	64	7	-	6	-	-	-	-	-
M.W.Gatting	England	**13**	68	3	-	-	2	2	3	3	-
J.B.Statham	England	**13**	70	5	-	5	2	-	-	1	-
G.S.Chappell	Australia	**13**	87	-	5	-	3	3	1	1	-
R.W.Marsh	Australia	**13**	96	-	6	-	1	2	1	3	-
R.W.Blair	New Zealand	**12**	19	-	6	4	2	-	-	-	-
K.R.Rutherford	New Zealand	**12**	30	3	2	-	3	-	1	2	1
R.C.Motz	New Zealand	**12**	32	-	2	6	-	-	1	3	-
A.L.Valentine	West Indies	**12**	36	5	4	-	-	1	2	-	-
R.A.McLean	South Africa	**12**	40	3	6	-	-	3	-	-	-
J.G.Bracewell	New Zealand	**12**	41	3	3	-	-	-	1	4	1
C.A.Walsh	West Indies	**12**	51	5	2	-	-	-	1	4	-
S.E.Gregory	Australia	**12**	58	-	11	1	-	-	-	-	-
M.Amarnath	India	**12**	69	3	3	-	5	-	-	1	-
R.J.Hadlee	New Zealand	**12**	86	3	5	-	1	-	3	2	-
R.G.D.Willis	England	**12**	90	5	-	-	3	1	2	-	1
G.S.Sobers	West Indies	**12**	93	6	1	-	-	2	2	1	-
S.M.Gavaskar	India	**12**	125	3	2	-	5	-	-	1	1
J.W.Gleeson	Australia	**11**	29	-	5	3	2	-	1	-	-
Maninder Singh	India	**11**	34	-	1	-	4	-	-	5	1
E.J.Chatfield	New Zealand	**11**	43	5	-	-	1	-	3	2	-
M.J.K.Smith	England	**11**	50	2	-	2	2	2	3	-	-
A.V.Bedser	England	**11**	51	5	-	2	3	1	-	-	-
D.M.Jones	Australia	**11**	52	-	3	-	1	2	2	3	-
A.T.W.Grout	Australia	**11**	51	-	4	2	3	-	1	1	-
F.M.M.Worrell	West Indies	**11**	51	8	2	-	-	-	1	-	-
V.L.Manjrekar	India	**11**	55	4	-	-	5	1	-	1	-
F.S.Trueman	England	**11**	67	6	-	2	1	1	1	-	-
G.A.Gooch	England	**11**	98	5	-	-	3	2	1	-	-
A.G.Hurst	Australia	**10**	12	-	6	-	-	-	2	2	-
P.I.Pocock	England	**10**	25	-	-	-	7	-	3	-	-
S.L.Boock	New Zealand	**10**	28	2	-	-	3	-	-	5	-

J.Briggs	England	**10**	33	9	-	1	-	-	-	-	-
C.E.L.Ambrose	West Indies	**10**	34	2	5	-	-	-	-	3	-
Fazal Mahmood	Pakistan	**10**	34	3	-	-	5	-	2	-	-
A.F.A.Lilley	England	**10**	35	9	-	1	-	-	-	-	-
A.A.Mallett	Australia	**10**	38	-	4	-	3	1	1	1	-
G.R.Dilley	England	**10**	39	2	-	-	5	1	1	1	-
Wasim Akram	Pakistan	**10**	44	-	1	-	4	1	2	-	2
I.W.Johnson	Australia	**10**	45	-	6	1	1	-	1	1	-
Intikhab Alam	Pakistan	**10**	47	4	1	-	1	3	1	-	-
Iqbal Qasim	Pakistan	**10**	47	5	-	-	2	-	3	-	-
W.W.Hall	West Indies	**10**	48	2	4	-	-	-	2	2	-
D.L.Amiss	England	**10**	50	7	-	-	-	-	2	1	-
R.W.Taylor	England	**10**	57	3	-	-	-	3	2	2	-
D.C.Boon	Australia	**10**	66	-	2	-	2	2	-	1	3
A.I.Kallicharran	West Indies	**10**	66	4	1	-	-	3	2	-	-
K.J.Hughes	Australia	**10**	70	-	3	-	4	1	1	1	-
I.M.Chappell	Australia	**10**	75	-	4	4	-	-	2	-	-
Zaheer Abbas	Pakistan	**10**	78	2	3	-	2	2	1	-	-
G.R.Viswanath	India	**10**	91	3	1	-	1	2	-	3	-
C.G.Greenidge	West Indies	**10**	96	3	5	-	-	-	2	-	-
D.L.Haynes	West Indies	**10**	103	1	2	-	-	3	1	3	-
G.Boycott	England	**10**	108	3	-	1	4	2	-	-	-

Most 'ducks' for Sri Lanka:

A.Ranatunga	Sri Lanka	**7**	36	1	1	-	-	-	1	4	-

Partnerships

HIGHEST PARTNERSHIP FOR EACH WICKET

1st	413	M.H.Mankad (231), Pankaj Roy (173)	IND	v	NZ	Madras[2]	1955-56
2nd	451	W.H.Ponsford (266), D.G.Bradman (244)	AUST	v	ENG	The Oval	1934
3rd	467	A.H.Jones (186), M.D.Crowe (299)	NZ	v	SL	Wellington	1990-91
4th	411	P.B.H.May (285*), M.C.Cowdrey (154)	ENG	v	WI	Birmingham	1957
5th	405	S.G.Barnes (234), D.G.Bradman (234)	AUST	v	ENG	Sydney	1946-47
6th	346	J.H.W.Fingleton (136), D.G.Bradman (270)	AUST	v	ENG	Melbourne	1936-37
7th	347	D.S.Atkinson (219), C.C.Depeiza (122)	WI	v	AUST	Bridgetown	1954-55
8th	246	L.E.G.Ames (137), G.O.B.Allen (122)	ENG	v	NZ	Lord's	1931
9th	190	Asif Iqbal (146), Intikhab Alam (51)	PAK	v	ENG	The Oval	1967
10th	151	B.F.Hastings (110), R.O.Collinge (68*)	NZ	v	PAK	Auckland	1972-73

PARTNERSHIPS OF 300 AND OVER

Runs	Wkt				
467	3rd	A.H.Jones (186), M.D.Crowe (299)	NZ v SL	Wellington	1990-91
451	2nd	W.H.Ponsford (266), D.G.Bradman (244)	AUST v ENG	The Oval	1938
451	3rd	Mudassar Nazar (231), Javed Miandad (280*)	PAK v IND	Hyderabad	1982-83
446	2nd	C.C.Hunte (260), G.S.Sobers (365*)	WI v PAK	Kingston	1957-58
413	1st	M.H.Mankad (231), Pankaj Roy (173)	IND v NZ	Madras[2]	1955-56
411	4th	P.B.H.May (285*), M.C.Cowdrey (154)	ENG v WI	Birmingham	1957
405	5th	S.G.Barnes (234), D.G.Bradman (234)	AUST v ENG	Sydney	1946-47
399	4th	G.S.Sobers (226), F.M.M.Worrell (197*)	WI v E	Bridgetown	1959-60
397	3rd	Qasim Omar (206), Javed Miandad (203*)	PAK v SL	Faisalabad	1985-86
388	4th	W.H.Ponsford (181), D.G.Bradman (304)	AUST v ENG	Leeds	1934
387	1st	G.M.Turner (259), T.W.Jarvis (182)	NZ v WI	Georgetown	1971-72
382	2nd	L.Hutton (364), M.Leyland (187)	ENG v AUST	The Oval	1938
382	1st	W.M.Lawry (210), R.B.Simpson (201)	AUST v WI	Bridgetown	1964-65
370	3rd	W.J.Edrich (189), D.C.S.Compton (208)	ENG v SA	Lord's	1947
369	2nd	J.H.Edrich (310*), K.F.Barrington (163)	ENG v NZ	Leeds	1965
359	1st	L.Hutton (158), C.Washbrook (195)	ENG v SA	Johannesburg[2]	1948-49
351	2nd	G.A.Gooch (196), D.I.Gower (157)	ENG v AUST	The Oval	1985
350	4th	Mushtaq Mohammad (201), Asif Iqbal (175)	PAK v NZ	Dunedin	1972-73
347	7th	D.S.Atkinson (219), C.C.Depeiza (122)	WI v AUST	Bridgetown	1954-55
346	6th	J.H.W.Fingleton (136), D.G.Bradman (270)	AUST v ENG	Melbourne	1936-37
344*	2nd	S.M.Gavaskar (182*), D.B.Vengsarkar (157*)	IND v WI	Calcutta	1978-79
341	3rd	E.J.Barlow (201), R.G.Pollock (175)	SA v AUST	Adelaide	1963-64
338	3rd	E.D.Weekes (206), F.M.M.Worrell (167)	WI v ENG	Port-of-Spain	1953-54
336	4th	W.M.Lawry (151), K.D.Walters (242)	AUST v WI	Sydney	1968-69
331	2nd	R.T.Robinson (148), D.I.Gower (215)	ENG v AUST	Birmingham	1985
329	1st	G.R.Marsh (138), M.A.Taylor (219)	AUST v ENG	Nottingham	1989
323	1st	J.B.Hobbs (178), W.Rhodes (179)	ENG v AUST	Melbourne	1911-12
322	4th	Javed Miandad (153*), Saleem Malik (165)	PAK v ENG	Birmingham	1992
319	3rd	A.Melville (189), A.D.Nourse (149)	SA v ENG	Nottingham	1947
316†	3rd	G.R.Viswanath (222), Yashpal Sharma (140)	IND v ENG	Madras[1]	1981-82
308	7th	Waqar Hassan (189), Imtiaz Ahmed (209)	PAK v IND	Lahore[1]	1955-56
308	3rd	R.B.Richardson (154), I.V.A.Richards (178)	WI v AUST	St John's	1983-84
308	3rd	G.A.Gooch (333), A.J.Lamb (139)	ENG v IND	Lord's	1990
303	3rd	I.V.A.Richards (232), A.I.Kallicharran (97)	WI v ENG	Nottingham	1976
301	2nd	A.R.Morris (182), D.G.Bradman (173*)	AUST v ENG	Leeds	1948

† 415 runs were scored for this wicket in two separate partnerships, D.B.Vengsarkar retiring hurt and being succeeded by Yashpal Sharma after 99 runs had been added.

MOST CENTURY PARTNERSHIPS IN AN INNINGS

FOUR		Opponents		
England	382 (2nd), 135 (3rd), 215 (6th), 106 (7th)	Australia	The Oval	1938
West Indies	267 (4th), 101 (6th), 118 (7th), 106 (9th)	India	Delhi	1948-49
Pakistan	152 (1st), 112 (2nd), 154 (3rd), 121 (4th)	West Indies	Bridgetown	1957-58
India	144 (3rd), 172 (4th), 109 (5th), 102 (6th)	West Indies	Kanpur	1978-79

SUMMARY OF CENTURY PARTNERSHIPS

	1st	2nd	3rd	4th	5th	6th	7th	8th	9th	10th	Total
Australia	62	104	93	94	62	35	21	12	7	2	492
England	131	124	110	102	66	67	32	11	7	3	653
South Africa	28	20	26	22	11	10	11	5	1	1	135
West Indies	43	54	58	56	41	44	15	1	4	-	316
New Zealand	20	22	26	18	22	12	8	4	2	2	136
India	33	43	45	40	28	23	15	6	7	1	241
Pakistan	21	26	38	31	23	18	6	4	3	2	172
Sri Lanka	2	2	9	6	4	5	2	-	-	-	30
Total	340	395	405	369	257	214	110	43	31	11	2175

BATSMEN SHARING IN MOST CENTURY PARTNERSHIPS

		Total	1st	2nd	3rd	4th	5th	6th	7th	8th	9th	10th
S.M.Gavaskar	India	**58**	22	18	8	6	2	1	-	-	1	-
A.R.Border	Australia	**52**	-	2	14	16	11	7	1	1	-	-
Javed Miandad	Pakistan	**50**	-	2	21	16	8	3	-	-	-	-
G.Boycott	England	**47**	20	8	9	8	-	2	-	-	-	-
C.G.Greenidge	West Indies	**46**	22	9	5	4	2	3	1	-	-	-
G.S.Chappell	Australia	**44**	-	2	15	13	11	2	1	-	-	-
I.V.A.Richards	West Indies	**44**	-	11	12	12	5	2	1	1	-	-
G.S.Sobers	West Indies	**43**	-	3	4	12	12	10	2	-	-	-
M.C.Cowdrey	England	**42**	5	9	6	13	4	3	1	-	1	-
L.Hutton	England	**41**	17	13	7	1	-	2	1	-	-	-
C.H.Lloyd	West Indies	**41**	-	-	6	14	9	10	1	-	1	-
G.A.Gooch	England	**38**	18	10	7	1	2	-	-	-	-	-
D.I.Gower	England	**38**	-	7	10	11	5	3	2	-	-	-
K.F.Barrington	England	**35**	-	6	10	14	4	1	-	-	-	-
D.G.Bradman	Australia	**35**	-	14	11	3	6	1	-	-	-	-
R.B.Kanhai	West Indies	**34**	2	9	11	7	3	2	-	-	-	-
W.R.Hammond	England	**33**	1	6	12	11	2	1	-	-	-	-
D.L.Haynes	West Indies	**34**	17	12	3	1	-	1	-	-	-	-
H.Sutcliffe	England	**33**	21	10	1	-	-	1	-	-	-	-
J.H.Edrich	England	**32**	9	11	6	5	1	-	-	-	-	-
R.N.Harvey	Australia	**32**	-	6	13	9	3	1	-	-	-	-
J.B.Hobbs	England	**32**	24	6	1	-	-	-	1	-	-	-
I.M.Chappell	Australia	**30**	-	18	8	1	1	2	-	-	-	-
D.C.S.Compton	England	**30**	-	-	14	7	7	1	-	1	-	-
D.B.Vengsarkar	India	**30**	-	9	9	9	1	2	-	-	-	-
The most for the other countries is:												
B.Mitchell	South Africa	**24**	9	3	8	2	-	-	1	1	-	-
J.G.Wright	New Zealand	**22**	6	11	3	1	1	-	-	-	-	-
P.A.de Silva	Sri Lanka	**9**	-	-	5	2	-	1	1	-	-	-

HIGHEST WICKET PARTNERSHIPS FOR EACH COUNTRY

AUSTRALIA

1st	382	W.M.Lawry (210), R.B.Simpson (201)	v	West Indies	Bridgetown	1964-65
2nd	451	W.H.Ponsford (266), D.G.Bradman (244)	v	England	The Oval	1934
3rd	295	C.C.McDonald (127), R.N.Harvey (204)	v	West Indies	Kingston	1954-55
4th	388	W.H.Ponsford (181), D.G.Bradman (304)	v	England	Leeds	1934
5th	405	S.G.Barnes (234), D.G.Bradman (234)	v	England	Sydney	1946-47
6th	346	J.H.W.Fingleton (136), D.G.Bradman (270)	v	England	Melbourne	1936-37
7th	217	K.D.Walters (250), G.J.Gilmour (101)	v	New Zealand	Christchurch	1976-77
8th	243	R.J.Hartigan (116), C.Hill (160)	v	England	Adelaide	1907-08
9th	154	S.E.Gregory (201), J.M.Blackham (74)	v	England	Sydney	1894-95
10th	127	J.M.Taylor (108), A.A.Mailey (46*)	v	England	Sydney	1924-25

ENGLAND

1st	359	L.Hutton (158), C.Washbrook (195)	v	South Africa	Johannesburg[2]	1948-49
2nd	382	L.Hutton (364), M.Leyland (187)	v	Australia	The Oval	1938
3rd	370	W.J.Edrich (189), D.C.S.Compton (208)	v	South Africa	Lord's	1947
4th	411	P.B.H.May (285*), M.C.Cowdrey (154)	v	West Indies	Birmingham	1957
5th	254	K.W.R.Fletcher (113), A.W.Greig (148)	v	India	Bombay[2]	1972-73
6th	240	P.H.Parfitt (131*), B.R.Knight (125)	v	New Zealand	Auckland	1962-62
7th	197	M.K.J.Smith (96), J.M.Parks (101*)	v	West Indies	Port-of-Spain	1959-60
8th	246	L.E.G.Ames (137), G.O.B.Allen (122)	v	New Zealand	Lord's	1931
9th	163*	M.C.Cowdrey (128*), A.C.Smith (69*)	v	New Zealand	Wellington	1962-62
10th	130	R.E.Foster (287), W.Rhodes (40*)	v	Australia	Sydney	1903-04

SOUTH AFRICA

1st	260	B.Mitchell (123), I.J.Siedle (141)	v	England	Cape Town	1930-31
2nd	198	E.A.B.Rowan (236), C.B.van Ryneveld (83)	v	England	Leeds	1951
3rd	341	E.J.Barlow (201), R.G.Pollock (175)	v	Australia	Adelaide	1963-64
4th	214	H.W.Taylor (121), H.G.Deane (93)	v	England	The Oval	1929
5th	157	A.J.Pithey (95), J.H.B.Waite (64)	v	England	Johannesburg[2]	1964-65
6th	200	R.G.Pollock (274), H.R.Lance (61)	v	Australia	Durban[2]	1969-70
7th	246	D.J.McGlew (255*), A.R.A.Murray (109)	v	New Zealand	Wellington	1952-53
8th	124	A.W.Nourse (72), E.A.Halliwell (57)	v	Australia	Johannesburg[1]	1902-03
9th	137	E.L.Dalton (117), A.B.C.Langton (73*)	v	England	The Oval	1935
10th	103	H.G.Owen-Smith (129), A.J.Bell (26*)	v	England	Leeds	1929

WEST INDIES

1st	298	C.G.Greenidge (149), D.L.Haynes (167)	v	England	St John's	1989-90
2nd	446	C.C.Hunte (260), G.S.Sobers (365*)	v	Pakistan	Kingston	1957-58
3rd	338	E.D.Weekes (206), F.M.M.Worrell (167)	v	England	Port-of-Spain	1953-54
4th	399	G.S.Sobers (226), F.M.M.Worrell (197*)	v	England	Bridgetown	1959-60
5th	265	S.M.Nurse (137), G.S.Sobers (174)	v	England	Leeds	1966
6th	274*	G.S.Sobers (163*), D.A.J.Holford (105*)	v	England	Lord's	1966
7th	347	D.S.Atkinson (219), C.C.Depeiza (122)	v	Australia	Bridgetown	1954-55
8th	124	I.V.A.Richards (192*), K.D.Boyce (68)	v	India	Delhi	1974-75
9th	161	C.H.Lloyd (161*), A.M.E.Roberts (68)	v	India	Calcutta	1983-84
10th	98*	F.M.M.Worrell (73*), W.W.Hall (50*)	v	India	Port-of-Spain	1961-62

NEW ZEALAND

1st	387	G.M.Turner (259), T.W.Jarvis (182)	v	West Indies	Georgetown	1971-72
2nd	241	J.G.Wright (116), A.H.Jones (143)	v	England	Wellington	1991-92
3rd	467	A.H.Jones (186), M.D.Crowe (299)	v	Sri Lanka	Wellington	1990-91
4th	229	B.E.Congdon (132), B.F.Hastings (101)	v	Australia	Wellington	1973-74
5th	183	M.G.Burgess (111), R.W.Anderson (92)	v	Pakistan	Lahore[2]	1976-77
6th	246*	J.J.Crowe (120*), R.J.Hadlee (151*)	v	Sri Lanka	Colombo (CCC)	1986-87
7th	186	W.K.Lees (152), R.J.Hadlee (87)	v	Pakistan	Karachi	1976-77
8th	136	B.E.Congdon (166*), R.S.Cunis (51)	v	West Indies	Port-of-Spain	1971-72
9th	136	I.D.S.Smith (173), M.C.Snedden (22)	v	India	Auckland	1989-90
10th	151	B.F.Hastings (110), R.O.Collinge (68*)	v	Pakistan	Auckland	1972-73

INDIA

1st	413	M.H.Mankad (231), Pankaj Roy (173)	v	New Zealand	Madras[2]	1955-56
2nd	344*	S.M.Gavaskar (182*), D.B.Vengsarkar (157*)	v	West Indies	Calcutta	1978-79
3rd	316	G.R.Viswanath (222), Yashpal Sharma (140)	v	England	Madras[1]	1981-82
4th	222	V.S.Hazare (89), V.L.Manjrekar (133)	v	England	Leeds	1952
5th	214	M.Azharuddin (110), R.J.Shastri (111)	v	England	Calcutta	1984-85
6th	298*	D.B.Vengsarkar (164*), R.J.Shastri (121*)	v	Australia	Bombay[3]	1986-87
7th	235	R.J.Shastri (142), S.M.H.Kirmani (102)	v	England	Bombay[2]	1984-85
8th	143	R.G.Nadkarni (75), F.M.Engineer (90)	v	New Zealand	Madras[2]	1964-65
9th	149	P.G.Joshi (52*), R.B.Desai (85)	v	Pakistan	Bombay[2]	1960-61
10th	109	H.R.Adhikari (81*), Ghulam Ahmed (50)	v	Pakistan	Delhi	1952-53

PAKISTAN

1st	249	Khalid Ibadulla (116), Abdul Kadir (95)	v	Australia	Karachi	1964-65
2nd	291	Zaheer Abbas (274), Mushtaq Mohammad (100)	v	England	Birmingham	1971
3rd	451	Mudassar Nazar (231), Javed Miandad (280*)	v	India	Hyderabad	1982-83
4th	350	Mushtaq Mohammad (201), Asif Iqbal (175)	v	New Zealand	Dunedin	1972-73
5th	281	Javed Miandad (163), Asif Iqbal (166)	v	New Zealand	Lahore[2]	1976-77
6th	217	Hanif Mohammad (203*), Majid Khan (80)	v	New Zealand	Lahore[2]	1964-65
7th	308	Waqar Hassan (189), Imtiaz Ahmed (209)	v	New Zealand	Lahore[1]	1955-56
8th	130	Hanif Mohammad (187*), Asif Iqbal (76)	v	England	Lord's	1967
9th	190	Asif Iqbal (146), Intikhab Alam (51)	v	England	The Oval	1967
10th	133	Wasim Raja (71), Wasim Bari (60*)	v	West Indies	Bridgetown	1976-77

SRI LANKA

1st	159	S.Wettimuny (79), J.R.Ratnayeke (93)	v	India	Kanpur	1986-87
2nd	217	S.Wettimuny (157), R.L.Dias (98)	v	Pakistan	Faisalabad	1981-82
3rd	159*	S.Wettimuny (65), R.L.Dias (108)	v	New Zealand	Colombo (SSC)	1983-84
4th	240*	A.P.Gurusinha (116*), A.Ranatunga (135*)	v	Pakistan	Colombo (PSS)	1985-86
5th	150	S.Wettimuny (190), L.R.D.Mendis (111)	v	England	Lord's	1984
6th	138	S.A.R.Silva (102*), L.R.D.Mendis (94)	v	England	Sialkot	1984
7th	144	P A de Silva (167), J R Ratnayeke (56)	v	Australia	Brisbane[2]	1989-90
8th	61	R.S.Madugalle (91*), D.S.de Silva (49)	v	Pakistan	Faisalabad	1981-82
9th	52	P.A.de Silva (122), R.J.Ratnayake (56)	v	Pakistan	Faisalabad	1985-86
10th	64	J.R.Ratnayeke (59*), G.F.Labrooy (42)	v	England	Lord's	1988

Bowling

200 TEST WICKETS

	Tests	Wkts	Avge	A	E	SA	WI	NZ	I	P	SL
							Opponents				
R.J.Hadlee (N)	86	**431**	22.29	130	97	-	51	-	65	51	37
Kapil Dev (I)	115	**401**	29.66	79	78	-	89	23	-	99	33
I.T.Botham (E)	102	**383**	28.40	148	-	-	61	64	59	40	11
M.D.Marshall (W)	81	**376**	20.94	87	127	-	-	36	76	50	-
Imran Khan (P)	88	**362**	22.81	64	47	-	80	31	94	-	46
D.K.Lillee (A)	70	**355**	23.92	-	167	-	55	38	21	71	3
R.G.D.Willis (E)	90	**325**	25.20	128	-	-	38	60	62	34	3
L.R.Gibbs (W)	79	**309**	29.09	103	100	-	-	11	63	32	-
F.S.Trueman (E)	67	**307**	21.57	79	-	27	86	40	53	22	-
D.L.Underwood (E)	86	**297**	25.83	105	-	-	38	48	62	36	8
B.S.Bedi (I)	67	**266**	28.71	56	85	-	62	57	-	6	-
J.Garner (W)	58	**259**	20.97	89	92	-	-	36	7	35	-
J.B.Statham (E)	70	**252**	24.84	69	-	69	42	20	25	27	-
M.A.Holding (W)	60	**249**	23.68	76	96	-	-	16	61	-	-
R.Benaud (A)	63	**248**	27.03	-	83	52	42	-	47	15	-
G.D.McKenzie (A)	61	**246**	29.78	-	96	41	47	-	47	15	-
B.S.Chandrasekhar (I)	58	**242**	29.74	38	95	-	65	36	-	8	-
A.V.Bedser (E)	51	**236**	24.89	104	-	54	11	13	44	10	-
Abdul Qadir (P)	67	**236**	32.80	45	82	-	42	26	27	-	14
G.S.Sobers (W)	93	**235**	34.03	51	102	-	-	19	59	4	-
R.R.Lindwall (A)	61	**228**	23.03	-	114	31	41	2	36	4	-
C.V.Grimmett (A)	37	**216**	24.21	-	106	77	33	-	-	-	-
J.A.Snow (E)	49	**202**	26.66	83	-	4	72	20	16	7	-
A.M.E.Roberts (W)	47	**202**	25.61	51	50	-	-	3	67	31	-
J.R.Thomson (A)	51	**200**	28.00	-	100	-	62	6	22	10	-

100 OR MORE TEST WICKETS

AUSTRALIA	Tests	Balls	Runs	Wkts	Avge	5wi	10wm	Best
D.K.Lillee	70	18467	8493	355	23.92	23	7	7/83
R.Benaud	63	19108	6704	248	27.03	16	1	7/72
G.D.McKenzie	61	17681	7328	246	29.78	16	3	8/71
R.R.Lindwall	61	13650	5251	228	23.03	12	-	7/38
C.V.Grimmett	37	14513	5231	216	24.21	21	7	7/40
J.R.Thomson	51	10535	5601	200	28.00	8	-	6/46
A.K.Davidson	44	11587	3819	186	20.53	14	2	7/93
G.F.Lawson	46	11118	5501	180	30.56	11	2	8/112
K.R.Miller	55	10461	3906	170	22.97	7	1	7/60
T.M.Alderman	41	10181	4616	170	27.15	14	1	6/47
C.J.McDermott	39	9100	4671	167	27.97	9	2	8/97
W.A.Johnston	40	11048	3826	160	23.91	7	-	6/44
W.J.O'Reilly	27	10024	3254	144	22.59	11	3	7/54
M.G.Hughes	37	8421	4154	144	28.84	5	1	8/87
H.Trumble	32	8099	3072	141	21.78	9	3	8/65
M.H.N.Walker	34	10094	3792	138	27.47	6	-	8/143
A.A.Mallett	39	9990	3940	132	29.84	6	1	8/59
B.Yardley	33	8909	3986	126	31.63	6	1	7/98
R.M.Hogg	38	7633	3503	123	28.47	6	2	6/74
M.A.Noble	42	7159	3025	121	25.00	9	2	7/17
I.W.Johnson	45	8780	3182	109	29.19	3	-	7/44
B.A.Reid	26	5926	2633	106	24.83	4	2	7/51
G.Giffen	31	6391	2791	103	27.09	7	1	7/117
A.N.Connolly	30	7818	2981	102	29.22	4	-	6/47
C.T.B.Turner	17	5179	1670	101	16.53	11	2	7/43

ENGLAND	Tests	Balls	Runs	Wkts	Avge	5wi	10wm	Best
I.T.Botham	102	21815	10878	383	28.40	27	4	8/34
R.G.D.Willis	90	17357	8190	325	25.20	16	-	8/43
F.S.Trueman	67	15178	6625	307	21.57	17	3	8/31
D.L.Underwood	86	21862	7674	297	25.83	17	6	8/51
J.B.Statham	70	16056	6261	252	24.84	9	1	7/39
A.V.Bedser	51	15918	5876	236	24.89	15	5	7/44
J.A.Snow	49	12021	5387	202	26.66	8	1	7/40
J.C.Laker	46	12027	4101	193	21.24	9	3	10/53
S.F.Barnes	27	7873	3106	189	16.43	24	7	9/103
G.A.R.Lock	49	13147	4451	174	25.58	9	3	7/35
M.W.Tate	39	12523	4055	155	26.16	7	1	6/42
F.J.Titmus	53	15118	4931	153	32.22	7	-	7/79
H.Verity	40	11173	3510	144	24.37	5	2	8/43
C.M.Old	46	8858	4020	143	28.11	4	-	7/50
A.W.Greig	58	9802	4541	141	32.20	6	2	8/86
G.R.Dilley	41	8192	4107	138	29.76	6	-	6/38
J.E.Emburey	60	14227	5105	138	36.99	6	-	7/78
T.E.Bailey	61	9712	3856	132	29.21	5	1	7/34
W.Rhodes	58	8231	3425	127	26.96	6	1	8/68
P.H.Edmonds	51	12028	4273	125	34.18	2	-	7/66
D.A.Allen	39	11297	3779	122	30.97	4	-	5/30
R.Illingworth	61	11934	3807	122	31.20	3	-	6/29
J.Briggs	33	5332	2094	118	17.74	9	4	8/11
G.G.Arnold	34	7650	3254	115	28.29	6	-	6/45
G.A.Lohmann	18	3821	1205	112	10.75	9	5	9/28
D.V.P.Wright	34	8135	4224	108	39.11	6	1	7/105
R.Peel	20	5216	1715	101	16.98	5	1	7/31
J.H.Wardle	28	6597	2080	102	20.39	5	1	7/36
C.Blythe	19	4546	1863	100	18.63	9	4	8/59

SOUTH AFRICA	Tests	Balls	Runs	Wkts	Avge	5wi	10wm	Best
H.J.Tayfield	37	13568	4405	170	25.91	14	2	9/113
T.L.Goddard	41	11736	3226	123	26.22	5	-	6/53
P.M.Pollock	28	6522	2806	116	24.18	9	1	6/38
N.A.T.Adcock	26	6391	2195	104	21.10	5	-	6/43

WEST INDIES	Tests	Balls	Runs	Wkts	Avge	5wi	10wm	Best
M.D.Marshall	81	17585	7876	376	20.94	22	4	7/22
L.R.Gibbs	79	27115	8989	309	29.09	18	2	8/38
J.Garner	58	13169	5433	259	20.97	7	-	6/56
M.A.Holding	60	12680	5898	249	23.68	13	2	8/92
G.S.Sobers	93	21599	7999	235	34.03	6	-	6/73
A.M.E.Roberts	47	111355	5174	202	25.61	11	2	7/54
W.W.Hall	48	10421	5066	192	26.38	9	1	7/69
C.A.Walsh	51	10114	4444	178	24.96	5	1	6/62
S.Ramadhin	43	13939	4579	158	28.98	10	1	7/49
C.E.L.Ambrose	34	8219	3320	148	22.43	6	1	8/45
A.L.Valentine	36	12953	4215	139	30.32	8	2	8/104
C.E.H.Croft	27	6165	2913	125	23.30	3	-	8/29
V.A.Holder	40	9095	3627	109	33.27	3	-	6/28

NEW ZEALAND	Tests	Balls	Runs	Wkts	Avge	5wi	10wm	Best
R.J.Hadlee	86	21918	9611	431	22.29	36	9	9/52
B.L.Cairns	43	10628	4279	130	32.91	6	1	7/74
E.J.Chatfield	43	10360	3958	123	32.17	3	1	6/73
R.O.Collinge	35	7689	3393	116	29.25	3	-	6/63
B.R.Taylor	30	6334	2953	111	26.60	4	-	7/74
J.G.Bracewell	41	8403	3653	102	35.81	4	1	6/32
R.C.Motz	32	7034	3148	100	31.48	5	-	6/63

INDIA	Tests	Balls	Runs	Wkts	Avge	5wi	10wm	Best
Kapil Dev	115	24967	11894	401	29.66	23	2	9/83
B.S.Bedi	67	21367	7637	266	28.71	14	1	7/98
B.S.Chandrasekhar	58	15963	7199	242	29.74	16	2	8/79
E.A.S.Prasanna	49	14353	5742	189	30.38	10	2	8/76
M.H.Mankad	44	14686	5236	162	32.32	8	2	8/52
S.Venkataraghavan	57	14877	5634	156	36.11	3	1	8/72
S.P.Gupte	36	11284	4403	149	29.55	12	1	9/102
R.J.Shastri	76	15391	6028	148	40.72	2	-	5/75
D.R.Doshi	33	9322	3502	114	30.71	6	-	6/102
K.D.Ghavri	39	7042	3656	109	33.54	4	-	5/33
N.S.Yadav	35	8349	3580	102	35.09	3	-	5/76

PAKISTAN	Tests	Balls	Runs	Wkts	Avge	5wi	10wm	Best
Imran Khan	88	19458	8258	362	22.81	23	6	8/58
Abdul Qadir	67	17126	7742	236	32.80	15	5	9/56
Sarfraz Nawaz	55	13926	5798	177	32.75	4	1	9/86
Iqbal Qasim	50	13019	4807	171	28.11	8	2	7/49
Wasim Akram	44	9643	4100	169	24.26	11	2	6/62
Fazal Mahmood	34	9834	3434	139	24.70	13	4	7/42
Intikhab Alam	47	10474	4494	125	35.92	5	2	7/52

Most wickets for Sri Lanka:

SRI LANKA	Tests	Balls	Runs	Wkts	Avge	5wi	10wm	Best
R.J.Ratnayake	23	4955	2563	73	35.11	5	-	6/66

BEST BOWLING AVERAGES

(Qualification: 25 wicket)		Tests	Balls	Runs	Wkts	Avge	5wi	10wm
G.A.Lohmann	England	18	3821	1205	112	**10.75**	9	5
J.J.Ferris	Australia/England	9	2302	775	61	**12.70**	6	1
A.E.Trott	Australia/England	5	948	390	26	**15.00**	2	-
M.J.Proctor	South Africa	7	1514	616	41	**15.02**	1	-
W.Barnes	England	21	2289	793	51	**14.54**	3	-
S.F.Barnes	England	27	7873	3106	189	**16.43**	24	7
C.T.B.Turner	Australia	17	5179	1670	101	**16.53**	11	2
R.Peel	England	20	5216	1715	101	**16.98**	5	1
J.Briggs	England	33	5332	2094	118	**17.74**	9	4
R.Appleyard	England	9	1596	534	31	**17.87**	1	-
W.S.Lees	England	5	1256	467	26	**17.96**	2	-
H.Ironmonger	Australia	14	4695	1330	74	**17.97**	4	2
G.B.Lawrence	South Africa	5	1334	512	28	**18.28**	2	-
F.R.Spofforth	Australia	18	4185	1731	94	**18.41**	7	4
F.H.Tyson	England	17	3452	1413	76	**18.56**	4	1
C.Blythe	England	19	4446	1863	100	**18.63**	9	4
G.F.Bissett	South Africa	4	989	469	25	**18.76**	2	-
A.S.Kennedy	England	5	1683	599	31	**19.32**	2	-

BEST STRIKE RATES

(Qualification: 25 wicket)		Balls/wkt	Tests	Balls	Runs	Wkts	Avge
G.A.Lohmann	England	**34.11**	18	3821	1205	112	10.75
A.E.Trott	Australia/England	**36.46**	5	948	390	26	15.00
M.J.Proctor	South Africa	**36.92**	7	1514	616	41	15.02
J.J.Ferris	Australia/England	**37.73**	9	2302	775	61	12.70
B.J.T.Bosanquet	England	**38.80**	7	970	604	25	24.16
G.F.Bissett	South Africa	**39.56**	4	989	469	25	18.76
Waqar Younis	Pakistan	**40.22**	19	1976	1908	93	20.51
S.F.Barnes	England	**41.65**	27	7873	3106	189	16.43

MOST ECONOMICAL CAREER BOWLING

(Qualification: 2000 balls)

		Runs/100 balls	Tests	Balls	Runs	Wkts	Avge
W.Attewell	England	**21.96**	10	2850	626	28	22.35
C.Gladwin	England	**26.82**	8	2129	571	15	38.06
T.L.Goddard	South Africa	**27.48**	41	11736	3226	123	26.22
R.G.Nadkarni	India	**27.92**	41	9165	2559	88	29.07
H.Ironmonger	Australia	**28.32**	14	4695	1330	74	17.97
J.C.Watkins	South Africa	**29.09**	15	2805	816	29	28.13
K.D.Mackay	Australia	**29.71**	37	5792	1721	50	34.42
A.R.A.Murray	South Africa	**29.90**	10	2374	710	18	39.44

25 OR MORE WICKETS IN A TEST SERIES

(§ in first series. # in last series. † in only series.)

AUSTRALIA	Opp	Season	Tests	Balls	Mdns	Runs	Wkts	Avge	5wi	10wm	Best
C.V.Grimmett #	SA	1935-36	5	2077	140	642	44	14.59	5	3	7/40
T.M.Alderman §	ENG	1981	6	1950	76	893	42	21.26	4	-	6/135
R.M.Hogg §	ENG	1978-79	6	1740	60	527	41	12.85	5	2	6/74
T.M.Alderman	ENG	1989	6	1622	68	712	41	17.36	6	1	6/128
D.K.Lillee	ENG	1981	6	1870	81	870	39	22.30	2	1	7/89
W.J.Whitty	SA	1910-11	5	1395	55	632	37	17.08	2	-	6/17
A.A.Mailey §	ENG	1920-21	5	1465	27	946	36	26.27	4	2	9/121
G.Giffen	ENG	1894-95	5	2060	111	820	34	24.11	3	-	6/155
G.F.Lawson	ENG	1982-83	5	1384	51	687	34	20.20	4	1	6/47
C.V.Grimmett	WI	1930-31	5	1433	60	593	33	17.96	2	1	7/87
C.V.Grimmett	SA	1931-32	5	1836	108	557	33	16.87	3	1	7/83
A.K.Davidson	WI	1960-61	4	1391	25	612	33	18.54	5	1	6/53
J.R.Thomson	ENG	1974-75	5	1401	34	592	33	17.93	2	-	6/46
M.A.Noble	ENG	1901-02	5	1380	68	608	32	19.00	4	1	7/17
H.V.Hordern #	ENG	1911-12	5	1665	43	780	32	24.37	4	2	7/90
J.V.Saunders #	ENG	1907-08	5	1603	52	716	31	23.09	3	-	5/28
H.Ironmonger	SA	1931-32	4	1331	112	296	31	9.54	3	1	6/18
R.Benaud	ENG	1958-59	5	1866	65	584	31	18.83	2	-	5/83
D.K.Lillee	ENG	1972	5	1499	83	548	31	17.67	3	1	6/66
C.J.McDermott	IND	1991-92	5	1586	75	670	31	21.61	3	1	5/54
R.Benaud	SA	1957-58	5	1937	56	658	30	21.93	4	-	5/49
G.D.McKenzie	WI	1968-69	5	1649	27	758	30	25.26	1	1	8/71
C.J.McDermott	ENG	1985	6	1406	21	901	30	30.03	2	-	8/141
C.V.Grimmett	ENG	1930	5	2098	78	925	29	31.89	4	1	6/167
A.K.Davidson	IND	1959-60	5	1469	85	431	29	14.86	2	1	7/93
R.Benaud	IND	1959-60	5	1934	146	568	29	19.58	2	-	5/43
G.D.McKenzie	ENG	1964	5	1536	61	654	29	22.55	2	-	7/153
J.R.Thomson	WI	1975-76	6	1205	15	831	29	28.65	2	-	6/50
G.F.Lawson	ENG	1989	6	1663	68	791	29	27.27	1	-	6/72
H.Trumble	ENG	1901-02	5	1604	93	561	28	20.03	2	-	6/74
W.J.O'Reilly	ENG	1934	5	2002	128	698	28	24.92	2	1	7/54
A.A.Mallett	IND	1969-70	5	1792	129	535	28	19.10	3	1	6/64
W.M.Clark §	IND	1977-78	5	1585	27	701	28	25.03	-	-	4/46
E.A.McDonald	ENG	1921	5	1235	32	668	27	24.74	2	-	5/32
W.J.O'Reilly	ENG	1932-33	5	2302	144	724	27	26.81	2	1	5/63
W.J.O'Reilly	SA	1935-36	5	1502	112	460	27	17.03	2	-	5/20
R.R.Lindwall	ENG	1948	5	1337	57	530	27	19.62	2	-	6/20
W.A.Johnston	ENG	1948	5	1856	91	630	27	23.33	1	-	5/36
D.K.Lillee	WI	1975-76	5	1035	7	712	27	26.37	1	-	5/63
B.A.Reid	ENG	1990-91	4	1039	47	432	27	16.00	2	1	7/51
E.Jones	ENG	1899	5	1276	73	657	26	25.26	2	1	7/88
H.Trumble	ENG	1902	3	1036	55	371	26	14.26	2	2	8/65
R.R.Lindwall	ENG	1953	5	1444	62	490	26	18.84	3	-	5/54
J.W.Gleeson	WI	1968-69	5	2006	57	844	26	32.46	2	-	5/61

M.H.N.Walker	WI	1972-73	5	1627	83	539	26	20.73	3	-	6/114
C.V.Grimmett	ENG	1934	5	2379	148	668	25	26.72	2	-	7/83
W.J.O'Reilly	ENG	1936-37	5	1982	89	555	25	22.20	2	-	5/51
A.K.Davidson	SA	1957-58	5	1613	47	425	25	17.00	2	-	6/34
D.K.Lillee	ENG	1974-75	6	1462	36	596	25	23.84	-	-	4/49
A.G.Hurst	ENG	1978-79	6	1634	44	577	25	23.08	1	-	5/28

ENGLAND	Opp	Season	Tests	Balls	Mdns	Runs	Wkts	Avge	5wi	10wm	Best
S.F.Barnes #	SA	1913-14	4	1356	56	536	49	10.93	7	3	9/103
J.C.Laker	AUST	1956	5	1703	127	442	46	9.60	4	2	10/53
A.V.Bedser	AUST	1953	5	1591	58	682	39	17.48	5	1	7/44
M.W.Tate	AUST	1924-25	5	2528	62	881	38	23.18	5	1	6/99
G.A.Lohmann	SA	1895-96	3	520	38	203	35	5.80	4	2	9/28
S.F.Barnes	AUST	1911-12	5	1782	64	778	34	22.88	3	-	5/44
S.F.Barnes	SA	1912	3	768	38	282	34	8.29	5	3	8/29
G.A.R.Lock	NZ	1958	5	1056	93	254	34	7.47	3	1	7/35
F.S.Trueman	WI	1963	5	1420	53	594	34	17.47	4	2	7/44
I.T.Botham	AUST	1981	6	1635	81	700	34	20.58	3	1	6/95
H.Larwood #	AUST	1932-33	5	1322	42	644	33	19.51	2	1	5/28
T.Richardson	AUST	1894-95	5	1747	63	849	32	26.53	4	-	6/104
F.R.Foster §	AUST	1911-12	5	1660	58	692	32	21.62	3	-	6/91
W.Rhodes	AUST	1903-04	5	1032	36	488	31	15.74	3	1	8/68
A.S.Kennedy †	SA	1922-23	5	1683	91	599	31	19.32	2	-	5/76
J.A.Snow	AUST	1970-71	6	1805	47	708	31	22.83	2	-	7/40
I.T.Botham	AUST	1985	6	1510	36	855	31	27.58	1	-	5/109
J.N.Crawford #	AUST	1907-08	5	1426	36	742	30	24.73	3	-	5/48
A.V.Bedser	AUST	1950-51	5	1560	34	482	30	16.06	2	1	5/46
A.V.Bedser	SA	1951	5	1655	84	517	30	17.23	3	1	7/58
F.S.Trueman §	IND	1952	4	718	25	386	29	13.31	2	-	8/31
D.L.Underwood	IND	1976-77	5	1517	95	509	29	17.55	1	-	5/84
R.G.D.Willis	AUST	1981	6	1516	56	666	29	22.96	1	-	8/43
F.H.Tyson	AUST	1954-55	5	1208	16	583	28	20.82	2	1	7/27
R.Peel	AUST	1894-95	5	1831	77	721	27	26.70	1	-	6/67
M.W.Tate §	SA	1924	5	1304	68	424	27	15.70	1	-	6/42
J.B.Statham	SA	1960	5	1218	54	491	27	18.18	2	1	6/63
F.J.Titmus	IND	1963-64	5	2393	156	747	27	27.66	2	-	6/73
J.A.Snow	WI	1967-68	4	990	29	504	27	18.66	3	1	7/49
R.G.D.Willis	AUST	1977	5	1000	36	534	27	19.77	3	-	7/78
W.S.Lees †	SA	1905-06	5	1256	69	467	26	17.96	2	-	6/78
C.Blythe	SA	1907	3	603	26	270	26	10.38	3	1	8/59
W.Voce	AUST	1936-37	5	1297	20	560	26	21.53	1	1	6/41
J.H.Wardle	SA	1956-57	4	1118	37	359	26	13.80	3	1	7/36
J.K.Lever §	IND	1976-77	5	898	29	380	26	14.61	2	1	7/46
A.Fielder #	AUST	1907-08	4	1299	31	627	25	25.08	1	-	6/82
J.C.White	AUST	1928-29	5	2440	134	760	25	30.40	3	1	8/126
F.S.Trueman	SA	1960	5	1083	31	508	25	20.32	1	-	5/27

SOUTH AFRICA	Opp	Season	Tests	Balls	Mdns	Runs	Wkts	Avge	5wi	10wm	Best
H.J.Tayfield	ENG	1956-57	5	2280	105	636	37	17.18	4	1	9/113
A.E.E.Vogler	ENG	1909-10	5	1349	33	783	36	21.75	4	1	7/94
H.J.Tayfield	AUST	1952-53	5	2228	58	843	30	28.10	2	1	7/81
G.A.Faulkner	ENG	1909-10	5	1255	45	635	29	21.89	2	-	6/87
G.B.Lawrence †	NZ	1961-62	5	1334	62	512	28	18.28	2	-	8/53
A.E.Hall §	ENG	1922-23	4	1505	82	501	27	18.55	2	1	7/63
H.J.Tayfield	ENG	1955	5	1881	124	568	26	21.84	3	-	5/60
N.A.T.Adcock	ENG	1960	5	1578	69	587	26	22.57	2	-	6/65
T.L.Goddard	AUST	1966-67	5	1533	101	422	26	16.23	1	-	6/53
M.J.Procter #	AUST	1969-70	4	858	50	353	26	13.57	1	-	6/73
C.B.Llewellyn	AUST	1902-03	3	796	23	448	25	17.92	4	1	6/92

R.O.Schwarz	AUST	1910-11	5	1006	19	651	25	26.04	2	-	6/47
J.M.Blanckenberg	ENG	1922-23	5	1510	60	613	25	24.52	2	-	6/76
G.F.Bissett †	ENG	1927-28	4	989	28	469	25	18.76	2	-	7/29
T.L.Goddard §	ENG	1955	5	1894	148	528	25	21.12	2	-	5/31
J.T.Partridge §	AUST	1963-64	5	1980	33	833	25	33.32	2	-	7/91
P.M.Pollock	AUST	1963-64	5	1275	11	710	25	28.40	2	-	6/95

WEST INDIES	Opp	Season	Tests	Balls	Mdns	Runs	Wkts	Avge	5wi	10wm	Best
M.D.Marshall	ENG	1988	5	1219	49	443	35	12.66	3	1	7/22
A.L.Valentine §	ENG	1950	4	2535	197	674	33	20.42	2	2	8/104
C.E.H.Croft §	PAK	1976-77	5	1307	45	676	33	20.48	1	-	8/29
M.D.Marshall	IND	1983-84	6	1326	59	621	33	18.81	2	-	6/37
C.C.Griffith	ENG	1963	5	1343	54	519	32	16.21	3	-	6/36
A.M.E.Roberts	IND	1974-75	5	1251	51	585	32	18.28	3	1	7/64
J.Garner	AUST	1983-84	5	1253	55	523	31	16.87	3	-	6/60
W.W.Hall	IND	1958-59	5	1330	65	530	30	17.66	2	1	6/50
M.A.Holding	IND	1983-84	6	1342	43	663	30	22.10	1	-	5/102
J.Garner	ENG	1984	5	1307	60	540	29	18.62	1	-	5/55
A.L.Valentine	IND	1952-53	5	2580	178	828	28	29.57	2	-	5/64
M.A.Holding	ENG	1976	4	957	54	356	28	12.71	3	1	8/92
A.M.E.Roberts	ENG	1976	5	1330	69	537	28	19.17	3	1	6/37
M.D.Marshall	AUST	1984-85	5	1277	47	554	28	19.78	4	1	5/38
C.E.L.Ambrose	ENG	1991	5	1494	63	560	28	20.00	2	-	6/52
W.W.Hall	IND	1961-62	5	1006	37	475	27	15.74	2	-	6/49
M.D.Marshall	NZ	1984-85	4	1021	30	486	27	18.00	1	1	7/80
J.Garner	ENG	1985-86	5	937	30	436	27	16.14	-	-	4/43
M.D.Marshall	ENG	1985-86	5	1017	36	482	27	17.85	-	-	4/38
S.Ramadhin §	ENG	1950	4	2267	170	604	26	23.23	3	1	6/86
R.Gilchrist #	IND	1958-59	4	1189	73	419	26	16.11	1	-	6/55
L.R.Gibbs	ENG	1963	5	1497	74	554	26	21.30	2	1	5/98
L.R.Gibbs	AUST	1972-73	5	1950	108	696	26	26.76	1	-	5/102
J.Garner	ENG	1980	5	1276	73	371	26	14.26	-	-	4/30
C.A.Walsh	IND	1987-88	4	823	24	437	26	16.80	2	-	5/54
C.E.L.Ambrose	AUST	1988-89	5	1227	38	558	26	21.46	1	-	5/72
J.Garner §	PAK	1976-77	5	1317	41	688	25	27.52	-	-	4/48

NEW ZEALAND	Opp	Season	Tests	Balls	Mdns	Runs	Wkts	Avge	5wi	10wm	Best
R.J.Hadlee	AUST	1985-86	3	1017	42	401	33	12.15	5	2	9/52
B.R.Taylor	WI	1971-72	4	1034	39	478	27	17.70	2	-	7/74

INDIA	Opp	Season	Tests	Balls	Mdns	Runs	Wkts	Avge	5wi	10wm	Best
B.S.Chandrasekhar	ENG	1972-73	5	1747	83	662	35	18.91	4	-	8/79
M.H.Mankad	ENG	1951-52	5	2224	151	571	34	16.79	1	1	8/55
S.P.Gupte	NZ	1955-56	5	2140	152	669	34	19.67	4	-	7/128
Kapil Dev	PAK	1979-80	6	1271	53	566	32	17.68	3	1	7/56
B.S.Bedi	AUST	1977-78	5	1759	39	740	31	23.87	3	1	5/55
Kapil Dev	WI	1983-84	6	1223	39	537	29	18.51	2	1	9/83
B.S.Chandrasekhar	AUST	1977-78	5	1579	24	704	28	25.14	3	1	6/52
Kapil Dev	AUST	1979-80	6	1339	53	625	28	22.32	2	-	5/74
S.P.Gupte	WI	1952-53	5	1977	87	789	27	29.22	3	-	7/162
K.D.Ghavri	WI	1978-79	6	1230	42	634	27	23.48	1	-	5/51
D.R.Doshi §	AUST	1979-80	6	1838	87	630	27	23.33	2	-	6/103
E.A.S.Prasanna	AUST	1969-70	5	1770	107	672	26	25.84	3	1	6/74
M.H.Mankad	PAK	1952-53	4	1592	100	514	25	20.56	3	1	8/52
E.A.S.Prasanna	AUST	1967-68	4	1581	34	686	25	27.44	2	-	6/104
B.S.Bedi	ENG	1972-73	5	2237	134	632	25	25.28	1	-	5/63
B.S.Bedi	ENG	1976-77	5	1788	106	574	25	22.96	2	-	6/71
Kapil Dev	AUST	1991-92	5	1704	76	645	25	25.80	2	-	5/97

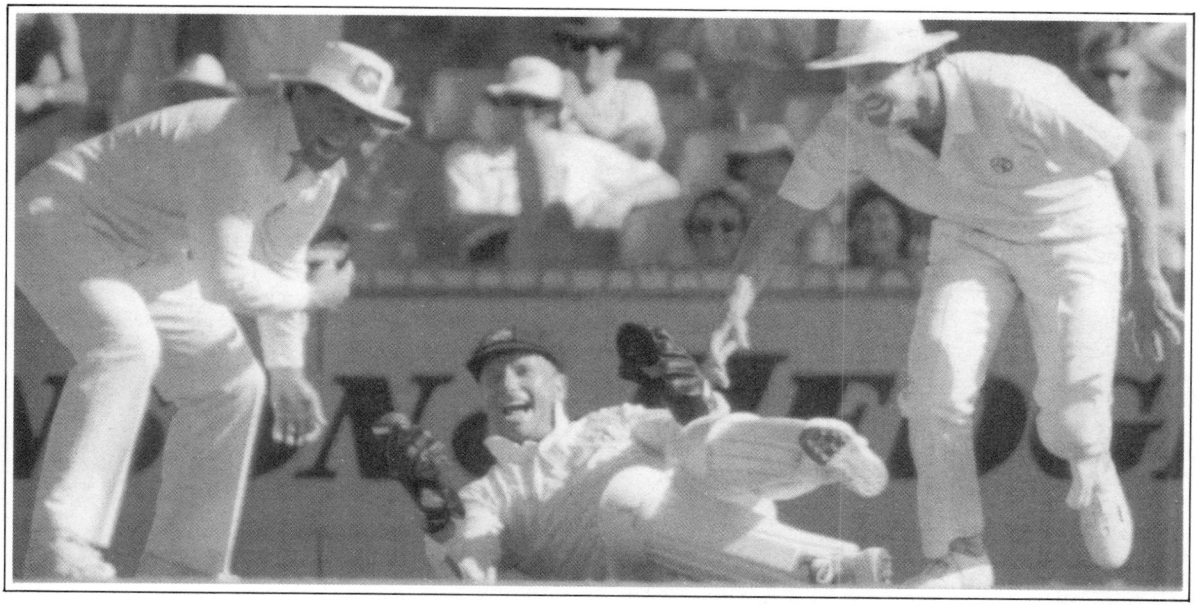

Australian wicketkeeper Ian Healy in action against England at the 'Gabba during the first Test of the 1990-91 series.
(Courtesy PBL Marketing.)

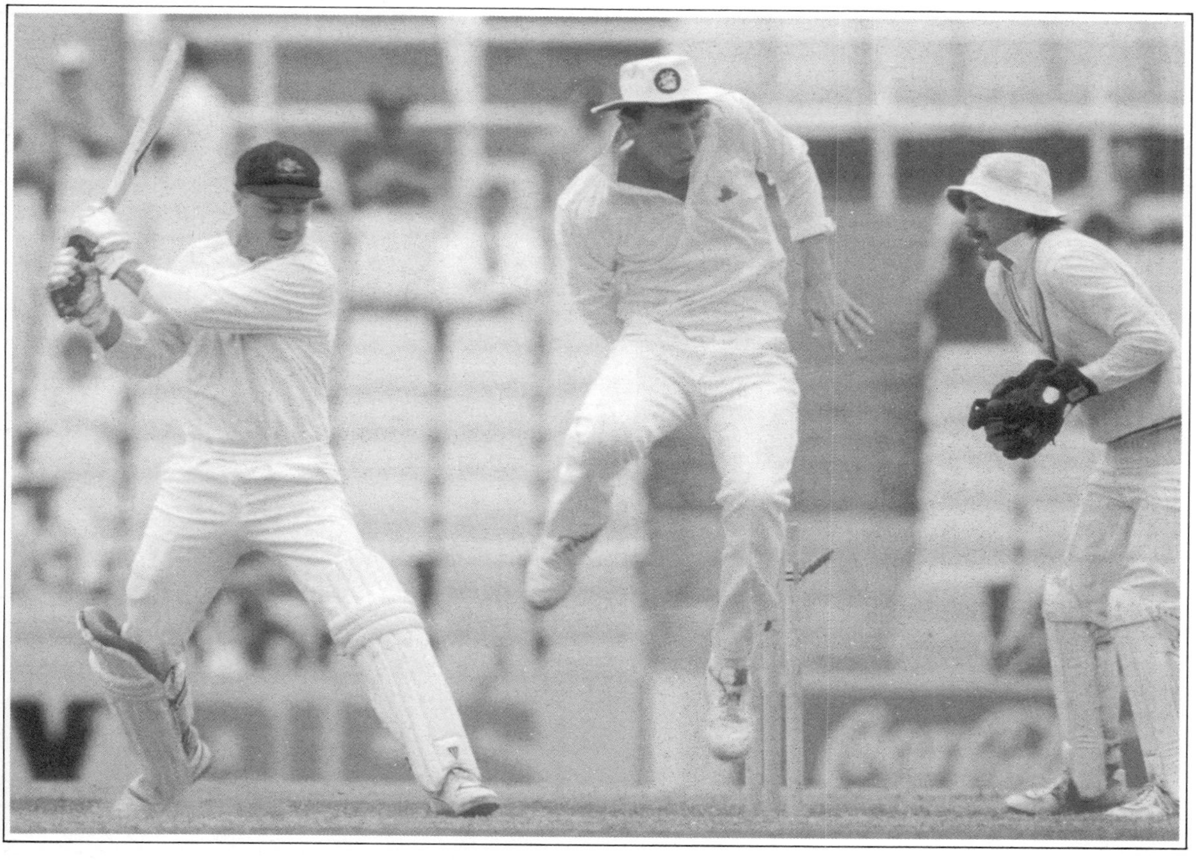

After scoring a century for Australia in the first innings, Greg Matthews is bowled by Eddie Hemmings for 19 in the second during the Test match against England played at Sydney in January 1991.
(Courtesy PBL Marketing.)

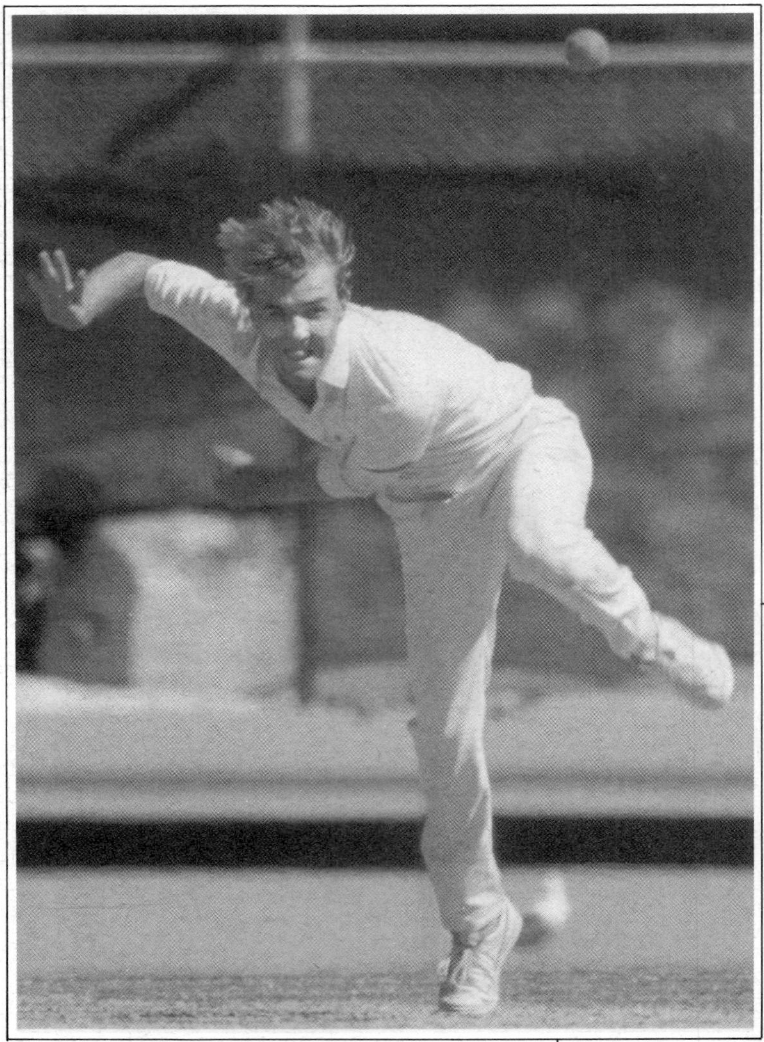

England left-arm spinner Phil Tufnell enjoyed the conditions at the Sydney Cricket Ground during the 1990-91 Ashes series. He captured five Australian wickets in the second innings.

(Courtesy PBL Marketing.)

England off-spinner Eddie Hemmings also enjoyed the pitch at Sydney during the 1990-91 series. He captured three Australian wickets in each innings.

(Courtesy PBL Marketing.)

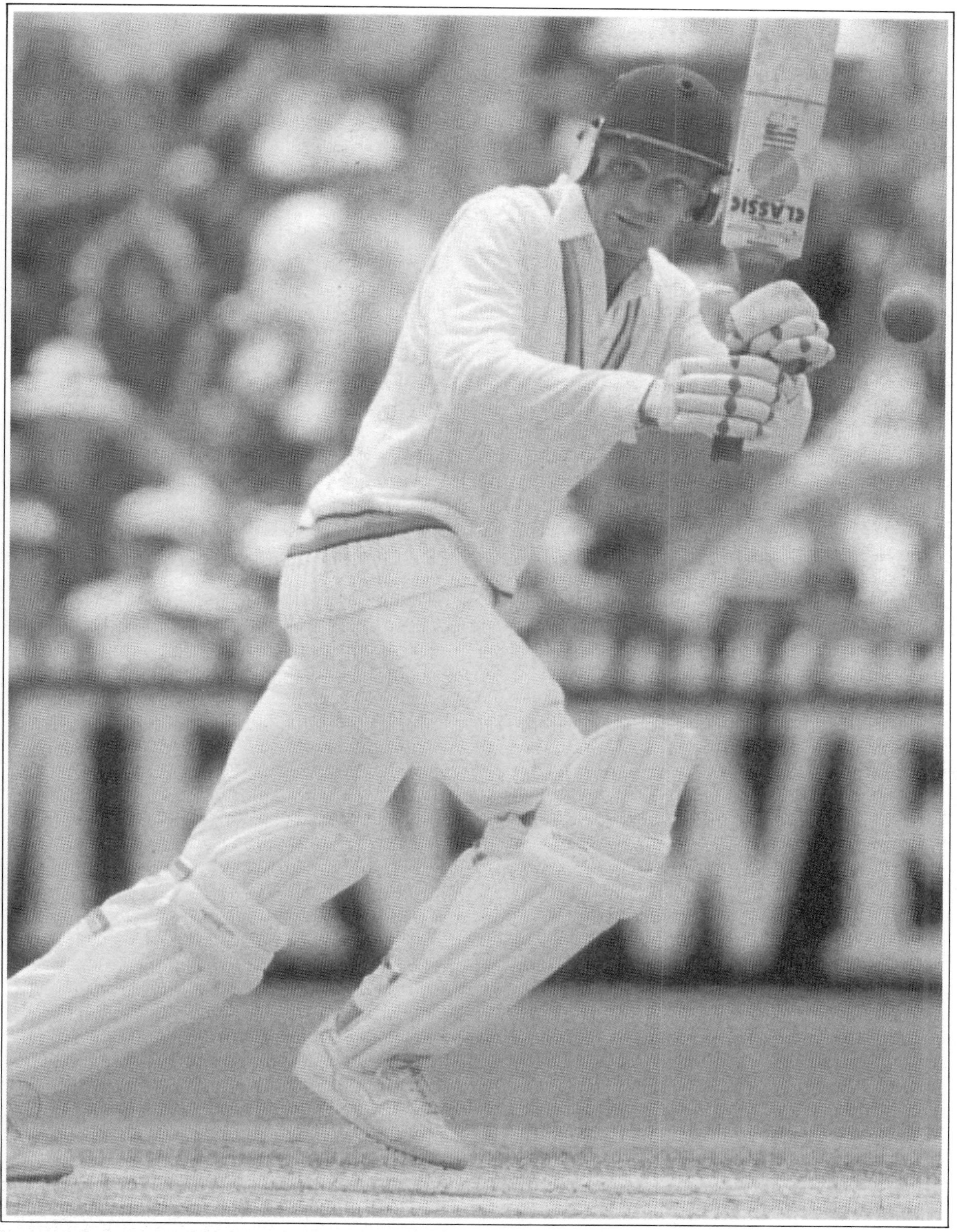

England's elegant left-handed batsman David Gower in full flight and on his way to another Test century. This time, he scored 123 in his first innings against Australia at Sydney during the 1990-91 series.
(Courtesy PBL Marketing.)

David Boon driving to the boundary on his way to a century for Australia against England at the Adelaide Oval in January 1991. *(Courtesy David Syme & Co. Limited/Bryan Charlton.)*

PAKISTAN	Opp	Season	Tests	Balls	Mdns	Runs	Wkts	Avge	5wi	10wm	Best
Imran Khan	IND	1982-83	6	1339	69	558	40	13.95	4	2	8/60
Abdul Qadir	ENG	1987-88	3	1408	69	437	30	14.56	3	2	9/56
Waqar Younis	NZ	1990-91	3	869	50	315	29	10.86	3	2	7/76
Imran Khan	WI	1976-77	5	1417	54	790	25	31.60	1	-	6/90

Most wickets in a series for Sri Lanka:

SRI LANKA	Opp	Season	Tests	Balls	Mdns	Runs	Wkts	Avge	5wi	10wm	Best
R.J.Ratnayake	IND	1985-86	3	977	35	459	20	22.95	2	-	6/85

TEN WICKETS IN A MATCH

(§ In first Test. # In last Test. † In only Test)

AUSTRALIA (70)		Opponents		
R.A.L.Massie §	16-137	England	Lord's	1972
F.R.Spofforth	14-90	England	The Oval	1882
C.V.Grimmett	14-199	South Africa	Adelaide	1931-32
M.A.Noble	13-77	England	Melbourne	1901-02
F.R.Spofforth	13-110	England	Melbourne	1878-79
B.A.Reid	13-148	England	Melbourne	1990-91
C.V.Grimmett #	13-173	South Africa	Durban[2]	1935-36
M.G.Hughes	13-217	West Indies	Perth	1988-89
A.A.Mailey	13-236	England	Melbourne	1920-21
C.T.B.Turner	12-87	England	Sydney	1887-88
H.Trumble	12-89	England	The Oval	1896
A.K.Davidson	12-124	India	Kanpur	1959-60
B.A.Reid	12-126	India	Melbourne	1991-92
G.Dymock	12-166	India	Kanpur	1979-80
H.Trumble	12-173	England	The Oval	1902
H.V.Hordern	12-175	England	Sydney	1911-12
H.Ironmonger	11-24	South Africa	Melbourne	1931-32
E.R.H.Toshack	11-31	India	Brisbane[2]	1947-48
H.Ironmonger	11-79	West Indies	Melbourne	1930-31
C.V.Grimmett §	11-82	England	Sydney	1924-25
C.G.Macartney	11-85	England	Leeds	1909
M.R.Whitney	11-95	India	Perth	1991-92
A.R.Border	11-96	West Indies	Sydney	1988-89
M.A.Noble	11-103	England	Sheffield	1902
R.Benaud	11-105	India	Calcutta	1956-57
F.R.Spofforth	11-117	England	Sydney	1882-83
C.G.Rackemann	11-118	Pakistan	Perth	1983-84
D.K.Lillee	11-123	New Zealand	Auckland	1976-77
W.J.O'Reilly	11-129	England	Nottingham	1934
G.F.Lawson	11-134	England	Brisbane[2]	1982-83
D.K.Lillee	11-138	England	Melbourne	1979-80
C.J.McDermott	11-157	England	Perth	1990-91
D.K.Lillee	11-159	England	The Oval	1981
G.E.Palmer	11-165	England	Sydney	1881-82
D.K.Lillee	11-165	England	Melbourne	1976-77
G.F.Lawson	11-181	West Indies	Adelaide	1984-85
C.V.Grimmett	11-183	West Indies	Adelaide	1930-31
A.K.Davidson	11-222	West Indies	Brisbane[2]	1960-61
C.T.B.Turner	10-63	England	Lord's	1888
R.M.Hogg	10-66	England	Melbourne	1978-79
C.V.Grimmett	10-88	South Africa	Cape Town	1935-36
G.D.McKenzie	10-91	India	Madras[2]	1964-65
C.V.Grimmett	10-110	South Africa	Johannesburg[1]	1935-36
R.J.Bright	10-111	Pakistan	Karachi	1979-80
N.J.N.Hawke	10-115	West Indies	Georgetown	1964-65
W.J.O'Reilly	10-122	England	Leeds	1938

R.M.Hogg	10-122	England	Perth	1978-79
G.E.Palmer	10-126	England	Melbourne	1882-83
D.K.Lillee	10-127	West Indies	Melbourne	1981-82
H.Trumble	10-128	England	Manchester	1902
W.J.O'Reilly	10-129	England	Melbourne	1932-33
D.K.Lillee	10-135	Pakistan	Melbourne	1976-77
F R.Spofforth	10-144	England	Sydney	1884-85
A.A.Mallett	10-144	India	Madras[1]	1969-70
R.G.Holland	10-144	West Indies	Sydney	1984-85
G.D.McKenzie	10-151	India	Melbourne	1967-68
T.M.Alderman	10-151	England	Leeds	1989
K.R.Miller	10-152	England	Lord's	1956
G.D.McKenzie	10-159	West Indies	Melbourne	1968-69
G.Giffen	10-160	England	Sydney	1891-92
H.V.Hordern #	10-161	England	Sydney	1911-12
E.Jones	10-164	England	Lord's	1899
C.J.McDermott	10-168	India	Adelaide	1991-92
R.G.Holland	10-174	New Zealand	Sydney	1985-86
D.K.Lillee	10-181	England	The Oval	1972
B.Yardley	10-185	West Indies	Sydney	1981-82
C.V.Grimmett	10-201	England	Nottingham	1930
L.O.Fleetwood-Smith	10-239	England	Adelaide	1936-37
G.R.J.Matthews	10-249	India	Madras[1]	1986-87
A.A.Mailey	10-302	England	Adelaide	1920-21

ENGLAND (88)		Opponents		
J.C.Laker	19-90	Australia	Manchester	1956
S.F.Barnes	17-159	South Africa	Johannesburg[1]	1913-14
J.Briggs	15-28	South Africa	Cape Town	1888-89
G.A Lohmann	15-45	South Africa	Port Elizabeth	1895-96
C.Blythe	15-99	South Africa	Leeds	1907
H.Verity	15-104	Australia	Lord's	1934
W.Rhodes	15-124	Australia	Melbourne	1903-04
A.V.Bedser	14-99	Australia	Nottingham	1953
W.Bates	14-102	Australia	Melbourne	1882-83
S.F.Barnes #	14-144	South Africa	Durban[1]	1913-14
S.F.Barnes	13-57	South Africa	The Oval	1912
D.L.Underwood	13-71	Pakistan	Lord's	1974
J.J.Ferris ¶	13-91	South Africa	Cape Town	1891-92
I.T.Botham	13-106	India	Bombay[3]	1979-88
A.W.Greig	13-156	West Indies	Port-of-Spain	1973-74
S.F.Barnes	13-162	Australia	Melbourne	1901-02
T.Richardson	13-244	Australia	Manchester	1896
J.C.White	13-256	Australia	Adelaide	1928-29
G.A.Lohmann	12-71	South Africa	Johannesburg[1]	1895-96
J.H.Wardle	12-89	South Africa	Cape Town	1956-57
D.L.Underwood	12-97	New Zealand	Christchurch	1970-71
R.Tattersall	12-101	South Africa	Lord's	1951
D.L.Underwood	12-101	New Zealand	The Oval	1969
F.Martin §	12-102	Australia	The Oval	1890
G.A.Lohmann	12-104	Australia	The Oval	1886
A.V.Bedser	12-112	South Africa	Manchester	1951
F.S.Trueman	12-119	West Indies	Birmingham	1963
G.Geary	12-130	South Africa	Johannesburg[1]	1927-28
J.Briggs	12-136	Australia	Adelaide	1891-92
A.P.Freeman	12-171	South Africa	Manchester	1929
G.A.R.Lock	11-48	West Indies	The Oval	1957
G.A.R.Lock	11-65	New Zealand	Leeds	1958
R.Peel	11-68	Australia	Manchester	1888

D.L.Underwood	11-70	New Zealand	Lord's	1969
J.Briggs	11-74	Australia	Lord's	1886
W.H.Lockwood	11-76	Australia	Manchester	1902
N.G.B.Cook	11-83	Pakistan	Karachi	1983-84
G.A.R.Lock	11-84	New Zealand	Christchurch	1958-59
F.S.Trueman	11-88	Australia	Leeds	1961
A.E.R.Gilligan	11-90	South Africa	Birmingham	1924
A.V.Bedser	11-93	India	Manchester	1946
C.S.Marriott †	11-96	West Indies	The Oval	1933
J.B.Statham	11-97	South Africa	Lord's	1960
T.E.Bailey	11-98	West Indies	Lord's	1957
C.Blythe	11-102	Australia	Birmingham	1909
S.F.Barnes	11-110	South Africa	Lord's	1912
J.C.Laker	11-113	Australia	Leeds	1956
C.Blythe	11-118	South Africa	Cape Town	1905-06
I.T.Botham	11-140	New Zealand	Lord's	1978
A.V.Bedser §	11-145	India	Lord's	1946
P.C.R.Tufnell	11-147	New Zealand	Christchurch	1991-92
W.Voce	11-149	West Indies	Port-of-Spain	1929-30
F.S.Trueman	11-152	West Indies	Lord's	1963
H.Verity	11-153	India	Madras[1]	1933-34
N.A.Foster	11-163	India	Madras[1]	1984-85
T.Richardson	11-173	Australia	Lord's	1896
I.T.Botham	11-176	Australia	Perth	1979-80
D.L.Underwood	11-215	Australia	Adelaide	1974-75
M.W.Tate	11-228	Australia	Sydney	1924-25
F.E.Woolley	10-49	Australia	The Oval	1912
W.Voce	10-57	Australia	Brisbane[2]	1936-37
R.Reel	10-58	Australia	Sydney	1887-88
J.T.Hearne	10-60	Australia	The Oval	1896
J.K.Lever §	10-70	India	Delhi	1976-77
G.O.B.Allen	10-78	India	Lord's	1936
D.L.Underwood	10-82	Australia	Leeds	1972
G.A.Lohmann	10-87	Australia	Sydney	1886-87
A.P.Freeman	10-93	West Indies	Manchester	1928
C.Blythe #	10-104	South Africa	Cape Town	1909-10
R.M.Ellison	10-104	Australia	Birmingham	1985
A.V.Bedser	10-105	Australia	Melbourne	1950-51
S.F.Barnes	10-105	South Africa	Durban[1]	1913-14
S.F.Barnes	10-115	South Africa	Leeds	1912
J.C.Laker	10-119	South Africa	The Oval	1951
H.Larwood	10-124	Australia	Sydney	1932-33
F.H.Tyson	10-130	Australia	Sydney	1954-55
D.E.Malcolm	10-137	West Indies	Port-of-Spain	1989-90
G.A Lohmann	10-142	Australia	Sydney	1891-92
J.A.Snow	10-142	West Indies	Georgetown	1967-68
J.Briggs	10-148	Australia	The Oval	1893
A.W.Greig	10-149	New Zealand	Auckland	1977
T.Richardson §	10-156	Australia	Manchester	1893
D.V.P.Wright	10-175	South Africa	Lord's	1947
K.Farnes §	10-179	Australia	Nottingham	1934
G.T.S.Stevens	10-195	West Indies	Bridgetown	1929-30
T.Richardson #	10-204	Australia	Sydney	1897-98
A.P.Freeman	10-207	South Africa	Leeds	1929
I.T.Botham	10-253	Australia	The Oval	1981

¶ Ferris's only Test for England.

SOUTH AFRICA (9)

		Opponents		
H.J.Tayfield	13-165	Australia	Melbourne	1952-53
H.J.Tayfield	13-192	England	Johannesburg[3]	1956-57
S.J.Snooke	12-127	England	Johannesburg[1]	1905-06
A.E.E.Vogler	12-181	England	Johannesburg[1]	1909-10
A.E.Hall §	11-112	England	Cape Town	1922-23
E.P.Nupen	11-150	England	Johannesburg[1]	1930-31
S.F.Burke §	11-196	New Zealand	Cape Town	1961-62
P.M.Pollock	10-87	England	Nottingham	1965
C.B.Llewellyn	10-116	Australia	Johannesburg[1]	1902-03

WEST INDIES (20)

		Opponents		
M.A.Holding	14-149	England	The Oval	1976
A.M.E.Roberts	12-121	India	Madras[1]	1974-75
M.D.Marshall	11-89	India	Port-of-Spain	1988-89
M.A.Holding	11-107	Australia	Melbourne	1981-82
M.D.Marshall	11-120	New Zealand	Bridgetown	1984-85
W.W.Hall	11-126	India	Kanpur	1958-59
K.D.Boyce	11-147	England	The Oval	1973
S.Ramadhin	11-152	England	Lord's	1950
L.R.Gibbs	11-157	England	Manchester	1963
A.L.Valentine §	11-204	England	Manchester	1950
W.Ferguson	11-229	England	Port-of-Spain	1947-48
M.D.Marshall	10-92	England	Lord's	1988
H.H.H.Johnson §	10-96	England	Kingston	1947-48
C A Walsh	10-101	India	Kingston	1988-89
L R Gibbs	10-106	England	Manchester	1966
M.D.Marshall	10-107	Australia	Adelaide	1984-85
G.E.Gomez	10-113	Australia	Sydney	1951-52
A.M.E.Roberts	10-123	England	Lord's	1976
C.E.L.Ambrose	10-127	England	Bridgetown	1989-90
A.L.Valentine	10-160	England	The Oval	1950

NEW ZEALAND (15)

		Opponents		
R.J.Hadlee	15-123	Australia	Brisbane[2]	1985-86
R.J.Hadlee	11-58	India	Wellington	1975-76
R.J.Hadlee	11-102	West Indies	Dunedin	1979-80
C.Pringle	11-152	Pakistan	Faisalabad	1990-91
R.J.Hadlee	11-155	Australia	Perth	1985-86
R.J.Hadlee	10-88	India	Bombay[3]	1988-89
R.J.Hadlee	10-100	England	Wellington	1977-78
R.J.Hadlee	10-102	Sri Lanka	Colombo (CCC)	1983-84
J.G.Bracewell	10-106	Australia	Auckland	1985-86
E.J.Chatfield	10-124	West Indies	Port-of-Spain	1984-85
J.Cowie	10-140	England	Manchester	1937
R.J.Hadlee	10-140	England	Nottingham	1986
B.L.Cairns	10-144	England	Leeds	1983
G.B.Troup	10-166	West Indies	Auckland	1979-80
R.J.Hadlee	10-176	Australia	Melbourne	1987-88

INDIA (20)

		Opponents		
N.D.Hirwani §	16-136	West Indies	Madras[1]	1987-88
J.M.Patel	14-124	Australia	Kanpur	1959-60
M.H.Mankad	13-131	Pakistan	Delhi	1952-53
B.S.Chandrasekhar	12-104	Australia	Melbourne	1977-78
M.H.Mankad	12-108	England	Madras[1]	1951-52
S.Venkataraghavan	12-152	New Zealand	Delhi	1964-65
L.Sivaramakrishnan	12-181	England	Bombay[3]	1984-85
R.G.Nadkarni	11-122	Australia	Madras[2]	1964-65

E.A.S.Prasanna	11-140	New Zealand	Auckland	1975-76
Kapil Dev	11-146	Pakistan	Madras[1]	1979-80
B.S.Chandrasekhar	11-235	West Indies	Bombay[2]	1966-67
Maninder Singh	10-107	Sri Lanka	Nagpur	1986-87
Maninder Singh	10-126	Pakistan	Bangalore	1986-87
Ghulam Ahmed	10-130	Australia	Calcutta	1956-57
Kapil Dev	10-135	West Indies	Ahmedabad	1983-84
E.A.S.Prasanna	10-174	Australia	Madras[1]	1969-70
S.A.Durani	10-177	England	Madras[2]	1961-62
C.Sharma	10-188	England	Birmingham	1986
B.S.Bedi	10-194	Australia	Perth	1977-78
S.P.Gupte	10-223		Kanpur	1958-59

PAKISTAN (26)		Opponents		
Imran Khan	14-116	Sri Lanka	Lahore[2]	1981-82
Abdul Qadir	13-101	England	Lahore[2]	1987-88
Fazal Mahmood	13-114	Australia	Karachi	1956-57
Fazal Mahmood	12-94	India	Lucknow	1952-53
Fazal Mahmood	12-99	England	The Oval	1954
Fazal Mahmood	12-100	West Indies	Dacca	1958-59
Waqar Younis	12-130	New Zealand	Faisalabad	1990-91
Imran Khan	12-165	Australia	Sydney	1976-77
Zulfiqar Ahmed	11-79	New Zealand	Karachi	1955-56
Imran Khan	11-79	India	Karachi	1982-83
Iqbal Qasim	11-118	Australia	Karachi	1979-80
Imran Khan	11-121	West Indies	Georgetown	1987-88
Sarfraz Nawaz	11-125	Australia	Melbourne	1978-79
Intikhab Alam	11-130	New Zealand	Dunedin	1972-73
Wasim Akram	11-160	Australia	Melbourne	1989-90
Imran Khan	11-180	India	Faisalabad	1982-83
Sikander Bakht	11-190	India	Delhi	1979-80
Abdul Qadir	11-218	Australia	Faisalabad	1982-83
Imran Khan	10-77	England	Leeds	1987
Waqar Younis	10-106	New Zealand	Lahore	1990-91
Wasim Akram	10-128	New Zealand	Dunedin	1984-85
Iqbal Qasim	10-175	India	Bombay[3]	1979-80
Intikhab Alam	10-182	New Zealand	Dacca	1969-70
Abdul Qadir	10-186	England	Karachi	1987-88
Abdul Qadir	10-194	England	Lahore[2]	1983-84
Abdul Qadir	10-211	England	The Oval	1987

Best for Sri Lanka:

SRI LANKA

R.J.Ratnayake	9-125	India	Colombo (PSS)	1985-86

SIX WICKETS IN AN INNINGS ON DEBUT

IN BOTH INNINGS

F.Martin	6/50) 6/52)	England	v	Australia	The Oval	1890
R.A.L.Massie	8/84) 8/52)	Australia	v	England	Lord's	1972
N.D.Hirwani	8/61) 8/75)	India	v	West Indies	Madras[1]	1987-88

IN FIRST INNINGS

W.H.Ashley	7/95	South Africa	v	England	Port Elizabeth	1888-89
W.H.Lockwood	6/101	England	v	Australia	Lord's	1893
G.H.T.Simpson-Hayward	6/43	England	v	South Africa	Johannesburg[1]	1909-10

G.M.Parker	6/152	South Africa	v	England	Birmingham	1924
A.J.Bell	6/99	South Africa	v	England	Lord's	1929
A.V.Bedser	7/49	England	v	India	Lord's	1946
J.C.Laker	7/103	England	v	West Indies	Bridgetown	1947-48
T.E.Bailey	6/118	England	v	New Zealand	Leeds	1949
G.F.Cresswell	6/168	New Zealand	v	England	The Oval	1949
A.L.Valentine	8/104	West Indies	v	England	Manchester	1950
A.M.Moir	6/155	New Zealand	v	England	Christchurch	1950-51
S.F.Burke	6/128	South Africa	v	New Zealand	Cape Town	1961-62
Arif Butt	6/89	Pakistan	v	Australia	Melbourne	1964-65
S.Abid Ali	6/55	India	v	Australia	Adelaide	1967-68
Mohammad Nazir	7/99	Pakistan	v	New Zealand	Karachi	1969-70
J.K.Lever	7/46	England	v	India	Delhi	1976-77
R.M.Hogg	6/74	Australia	v	England	Brisbane[2]	1978-79
D.R.Doshi	6/103	India	v	Australia	Madras[1]	1979-80
P.L.Taylor	6/78	Australia	v	England	Sydney	1986-87
IN SECOND INNINGS						
T.K.Kendall	7/55	Australia	v	England	Melbourne	1876-77
W.H.Cooper	6/120	Australia	v	England	Melbourne	1881-82
A.E.Trott	8/43	Australia	v	England	Adelaide	1894-95
M.A.Noble	6/49	Australia	v	England	Melbourne	1897-98
A.E.Hall	7/63	South Africa	v	England	Cape Town	1922-23
C.V.Grimmett	6/37	Australia	v	England	Sydney	1924-25
J.Langridge	7/56	England	v	West Indies	Manchester	1933
C.S.Marriott	6/59	England	v	West Indies	The Oval	1933
F.A.Ward	6/102	Australia	v	England	Brisbane[2]	1936-37
C.N.McCarthy	6/43	South Africa	v	England	Durban[2]	1948-49
P.S.Pollock	6/38	South Africa	v	New Zealand	Durban[2]	1961-62
L.J.Coldwell	6/85	England	v	Pakistan	Lord's	1962
A.I.C.Dodemaide	6/58	Australia	v	New Zealand	Melbourne	1987-88

TEN WICKETS IN A MATCH ON DEBUT

F.Martin	10/104	England	v	Australia	The Oval	1890
T.Richardson	10/156	England	v	Australia	Manchester	1893
A.E.Hall	11/112	South Africa	v	England	Cape Town	1922-23
C.V.Grimmett	11/82	Australia	v	England	Sydney	1924-25
C.S.Marriott	11/96	England	v	West Indies	The Oval	1933
K.Farnes	10/179	England	v	Australia	Nottingham	1934
A.V.Bedser	11/145	England	v	India	Lord's	1946
H.H.H.Johnson	10/96	West Indies	v	England	Kingston	1947-48
A.L.Valentine	11/204	West Indies	v	England	Manchester	1950
S.F.Burke	11/196	South Africa	v	New Zealand	Cape Town	1961-62
R.A.L.Massie	16/137	Australia	v	England	Lord's	1972
J.K.Lever	10/70	England	v	India	Delhi	1976-77
N.D.Hirwani	16/136	India	v	West Indies	Madras[1]	1987-88

EIGHT WICKETS IN AN INNINGS

(§ In first Test. # In last Test)

AUSTRALIA (13)		Opponents		
A.A.Mailey	9-121	England	Melbourne	1920-21
F.Laver	8-31	England	Manchester	1909
A.E.Trott §	8-43	England	Adelaide	1894-95
R.A.L.Massie §	8-53	England	Lord's	1972
A.A.Mallett	8-59	Pakistan	Adelaide	1972-73
H.Trumble	8-65	England	The Oval	1902
G.D.McKenzie	8-71	West Indies	Melbourne	1968-69
R.A.L.Massie §	8-84	England	Lord's	1972

M.G.Hughes	8-87	West Indies	Perth	1988-89
C.J.McDermott	8-97	England	Perth	1990-91
G.F.Lawson	8-112	West Indies	Adelaide	1984-85
C.J.McDermott	8-141	England	Manchester	1985
M.H.N.Walker	8-143	England	Melbourne	1974-75
ENGLAND (24)		Opponents		
J.C.Laker	10-53	Australia	Manchester	1956
G.A.Lohmann	9-28	South Africa	Johannesburg[1]	1895-96
J.C.Laker	9-37	Australia	Manchester	1956
S.F.Barnes	9-103	South Africa	Johannesburg[1]	1913-14
G.A.Lohmann	8-7	South Africa	Port Elizabeth	1895-96
J.Briggs	8-11	South Africa	Cape Town	1888-89
S.F.Barnes	8-29	South Africa	The Oval	1912
F.S.Trueman	8-31	India	Manchester	1952
I.T.Botham	8-34	Pakistan	Lord's	1978
G.A.Lohmann	8-35	Australia	Sydney	1886-87
H.Verity	8-43	Australia	Lord's	1934
R.G.D.Willis	8-43	Australia	Leeds	1981
D.L.Underwood	8-51	Pakistan	Lord's	1974
S.F.Barnes	8-56	South Africa	Johannesburg[1]	1913-14
G.A.Lohmann	8-58	Australia	Sydney	1891-92
C.Blythe	8-59	South Africa	Leeds	1907
W.Rhodes	8-68	Australia	Melbourne	1903-04
L.C.Braund	8-81	Australia	Melbourne	1903-04
A.W.Greig	8-86	West Indies	Port-of-Spain	1973-74
T.Richardson #	8-94	Australia	Sydney	1897-98
I.T.Botham	8-103	West Indies	Lord's	1984
B.J.T.Bosanquet	8-107	Australia	Nottingham	1905
N.A.Foster	8-107	Pakistan	Leeds	1987
J.C.White	8-126	Australia	Adelaide	1928-29
SOUTH AFRICA (4)		Opponents		
H.J.Tayfield	9-113	England	Johannesburg[3]	1956-57
G.B.Lawrence	8-53	New Zealand	Johannesburg[3]	1961-62
H.J.Tayfield	8-69	England	Durban[2]	1956-57
S.J.Snooke	8-70	England	Johannesburg[1]	1905-06
WEST INDIES (6)		Opponents		
J.M.Noreiga	9-95	India	Port-of-Spain	1970-71
C.E.H.Croft	8-29	Pakistan	Port-of-Spain	1976-77
L.R.Gibbs	8-38	India	Bridgetown	1961-62
C.E.L.Ambrose	8-45	England	Bridgetown	1989-90
M.A.Holding	8-92	England	The Oval	1976
A.L.Valentine §	8-104	England	Manchester	1950
NEW ZEALAND (1)		Opponents		
R.J.Hadlee	9-52	Australia	Brisbane[2]	1985-86
INDIA (12)		Opponents		
J.M.Patel	9-69	Australia	Kanpur	1959-60
Kapil Dev	9-83	West Indies	Ahmedabad	1983-84
S.P.Gupte	9-102	West Indies	Kanpur	1958-59
M.H.Mankad	8-52	Pakistan	Delhi	1952-53
M.H.Mankad	8-55	England	Madras[1]	1951-52
N.D.Hirwani §	8-61	West Indies	Madras[1]	1987-88
S.Venkataraghavan	8-72	New Zealand	Delhi	1964-65
N.D.Hirwani §	8-75	West Indies	Madras[1]	1987-88
E.A.S.Prasanna	8-76	New Zealand	Auckland	1975-76

B.S.Chandrasekhar	8-79	England	Delhi	1972-73
Kapil Dev	8-85	Pakistan	Lahore[2]	1982-83
Kapil Dev	8-106	Australia	Adelaide	1985-86

PAKISTAN (5)		Opponents		
Abdul Qadir	9-56	England	Lahore[2]	1887-88
Sarfraz Nawaz	9-86	Australia	Melbourne	1978-79
Imran Khan	8-58	Sri Lanka	Lahore[2]	1981-82
Imran Khan	8-60	India	Karachi	1982-83
Sikander Bakht	8-69	India	Delhi	1979-80

SRI LANKA (1)		Opponents		
J.R.Ratnayeke	8-83	Pakistan	Sialkot	1985-86

HAT-TRICKS IN TEST MATCHES

(§ In first Test. # On final Test appearance. ¶ Over both innings.)

F.R.Spofforth	Australia	v	England	Melbourne	1878-79
W.Bates	England	v	Australia	Melbourne	1882-83
J.Briggs	England	v	Australia	Sydney	1891-92
G.A.Lohmann	England	v	South Africa	Port Elizabeth	1895-96
J.T.Hearne	England	v	Australia	Leeds	1899
H.Trumble	Australia	v	England	Melbourne	1901-02
H.Trumble #	Australia	v	England	Melbourne	1903-04
T.J.Matthews (2)	Australia	v	South Africa	Manchester	1912
M.J.C.Allom §	England	v	New Zealand	Christchurch	1929-30
T.W.J.Goddard	England	v	South Africa	Johannesburg[1]	1938-39
P.J.Loader	England	v	West Indies	Leeds	1957
L.F.Kline	Australia	v	South Africa	Cape Town	1957-58
W.W.Hall	West Indies	v	Pakistan	Lahore[1]	1958-59
G.M.Griffin #	South Africa	v	England	Lord's	1960
L.R.Gibbs	West Indies	v	Australia	Adelaide	1960-61
P.J.Petherick §	New Zealand	v	Pakistan	Lahore[2]	1976-77
C.A.Walsh ¶	West Indies	v	Australia	Brisbane[2]	1988-89
M.G.Hughes ¶	Australia	v	West Indies	Perth	1988-89

Matthews did the hat-trick in each innings on the second afternoon of the match.

OUTSTANDING ANALYSES IN A TEST INNINGS

O	M	R	W						
51.2	23	53	10	J.C.Laker	England	v	Australia	Manchester	1956
14.2	6	28	9	G.A.Lohmann	England	v	South Africa	Johannesburg[1]	1895-96
16.4	4	37	9	J.C.Laker	England	v	Australia	Manchester	1956
9.4	5	7	8	G.A.Lohmann	England	v	South Africa	Port Elizabeth	1895-96
14.2	5	11	8	J.Briggs	England	v	South Africa	Cape Town	1888-89
19.1	11	17	7	J.Briggs	England	v	South Africa	Cape Town	1888-89
7.4	2	17	7	M.A.Noble	Australia	v	England	Melbourne	1901-02
11	3	17	7	W.Rhodes	England	v	Australia	Birmingham	1902
6.3	4	7	6	A.E.R.Gilligan	England	v	South Africa	Birmingham	1924
11.4	6	11	6	S.Haigh	England	v	South Africa	Cape Town	1898-99
11.6	7	12	6	D.L.Underwood	England	v	New Zealand	Christchurch	1970-71
17.5	13	12	6	S.L.Venkatapathy Raju	India	v	Sri Lanka	Chandigarh	1990-91
14	7	13	6	H.J.Tayfield	South Africa	v	New Zealand	Johannesburg[2]	1953-54
18	11	15	6	C.T.B.Turner	Australia	v	England	Sydney	1886-87
16	8	15	6	M.H.N.Walker	Australia	v	Pakistan	Sydney	1972-73
2.3	1	2	5	E.R.H.Toshack	Australia	v	India	Brisbane[2]	1947-48
7.2	5	6	5	H.Ironmonger	Australia	v	South Africa	Melbourne	1931-32
12	8	5	4	Pervez Sajjad	Pakistan	v	New Zealand	Rawalpindi	1964-65
9	7	5	4	K.Higgs	England	v	New Zealand	Christchurch	1965-66
8	6	6	4	P.H.Edmonds	England	v	Pakistan	Lord's	1978

6.3	2	7	4	J.C.White	England	v	Australia	Brisbane[1]	1928-29
5	2	7	4	J.H.Wardle	England	v	Australia	Manchester	1953
6	3	7	4	R.Appleyard	England	v	New Zealand	Auckland	1954-55
3.4	3	0	3	R.Benaud	Australia	v	India	Delhi	1959-60

FOUR WICKETS IN FIVE BALLS

M.J.C.Allom — England v New Zealand — Christchurch — 1929-30
In his first Test - in his eighth over (W0WWW).

C.M.Old — England v Pakistan — Birmingham — 1978
In the same over (WW0WW) his third ball was a no ball.

Wasim Akram — Pakistan v West Indies — Lahore[2] — 1990-91
In the same over (WW1WW) - a catch was dropped from the third ball.

THREE WICKETS IN FOUR BALLS

F.R.Spofforth	Australia	v	England	The Oval	1882
F.R.Spofforth	Australia	v	England	Sydney	1884-85
J.Briggs	England	v	South Africa	Cape Town	1888-89
W.P.Howell	Australia	v	South Africa	Cape Town	1902-03
J.M Gregory	Australia	v	England	Nottingham	1921
E.P.Nupen	South Africa	v	England	Johannesburg[1]	1930-31
W J.O'Reilly	Australia	v	England	Manchester	1934
B.Mitchell	South Africa	v	England	Johannesburg[1]	1935-36
W.Voce	England	v	Australia	Sydney	1936-37
R.R.Lindwall	Australia	v	England	Adelaide	1946-47
K.Cranston	England	v	South Africa	Leeds	1947
R.Appleyard	England	v	New Zealand	Auckland	1954-55
R.Benaud	Australia	v	West Indies	Georgetown	1954-55
Fazal Mahmood	Pakistan	v	Australia	Karachi	1956-57
J.W.Martin	Australia	v	West Indies	Melbourne	1960-61
L.R.Gibbs	West Indies	v	Australia	Sydney	1960-61
K.D.Mackay	Australia	v	England	Birmingham	1961
W.W.Hall	West Indies	v	India	Port-of-Spain	1961-62
D.Shackleton	England	v	West Indies	Lord's	1963
G.D.McKenzie	Australia	v	West Indies	Port-of-Spain	1964-65
F.J.Titmus	England	v	New Zealand	Leeds	1965
P.Lever	England	v	Pakistan	Leeds	1971
D.K.Lillee	Australia	v	England	Manchester	1972
D.K.Lillee	Australia	v	England	The Oval	1972
C.M.Old	England	v	Pakistan	Birmingham	1978
S.T.Clarke	West Indies	v	Pakistan	Karachi	1980-81
R..Hadlee	New Zealand	v	Australia	Melbourne	1980-81
R..Shastri	India	v	New Zealand	Wellington	1980-81
I.T.Botham	England	v	Australia	Leeds	1985
Kapil Dev	India	v	Australia	Adelaide	1985-86
C.G.Rackemann	Australia	v	Pakistan	Adelaide	1989-90
D.E.Malcolm	England	v	West Indies	Port-of-Spain	1989-90
Wasim Akram	Pakistan	v	West Indies	Lahore[2]	1990-91
A.R.Border	Australia	v	West Indies	Georgetown	1990-91
Wasim Akram	Pakistan	v	England	Lord's	1992
C.N. McCarthy	South Africa	v	England	Durban[2]	1948-49

K.Cranston, F.J.Titmus, C.M.Old and Wasim Akram each took four wickets in an over.

WICKET WITH FIRST BALL IN TEST CRICKET

	Batsman dismissed					
A.Coningham	A.C.MacLaren	Australia	v	England	Melbourne	1894-95
W.M.Bradley	F.J.Laver	England	v	Australia	Manchester	1899
E.G.Arnold	V.T.Trumper	England	v	Australia	Sydney	1903-04
G.G.Macaulay	G.A.L.Hearne	England	v	South Africa	Cape Town	1922-23

M.W.Tate	M.J.Susskind	England	v	South Africa	Birmingham	1924
M.Henderson	E.W.Dawson	New Zealand	v	England	Christchurch	1929-30
H.D.Smith	E.Paynter	New Zealand	v	England	Christchurch	1932-33
T.F.Johnson	W.W.Keeton	West Indies	v	England	The Oval	1939
R.Howorth	D.V.Dyer	England	v	South Africa	The Oval	1947
Intikhab Alam	C.C.McDonald	Pakistan	v	Australia	Karachi	1959-60
R.K.Illingworth	P.V.Simmons	England	v	West Indies	Nottingham	1991

MOST WICKETS BY A BOWLER IN ONE DAY

15	J.Briggs	15-28	England	v	South Africa	Cape Town	1888-89
14	H.Verity	14-80	England	v	Australia	Lord's	1934

500 BALLS IN AN INNINGS

		O	M	R	W					
588	S.Ramadhin	98	35	179	2	West Indies	v	England	Birmingham	1957
571	T.R.Veivers	95.1	36	155	3	Australia	v	England	Manchester	1964
552	A.L.Valentine	92	49	140	3	West Indies	v	England	Nottingham	1950
522	L.O.Fleetwood-Smith	87	11	298	1	Australia	v	England	The Oval	1938
512	Fazal Mahmood	85.2	20	247	2	Pakistan	v	West Indies	Kingston	1957-58
510	W.J.O'Reilly	85	26	178	3	Australia	v	England	The Oval	1938
504	Haseeb Ahsan	84	19	202	6	Pakistan	v	India	Madras[2]	1960-61

700 BALLS IN A MATCH

		O	M	R	W					
774	S.Ramadhin	129	51	228	9	West Indies	v	England	Birmingham	1957
766	H.Verity	95.6	23	184	4	England	v	South Africa	Durban[2]	1938-39
749	J.C.White	124.5	37	256	13	England	v	Australia	Adelaide	1928-29
738	N.Gordon	92.2	17	256	1	South Africa	v	England	Durban[2]	1938-39
728	A.B.C.Langton	91	24	203	4	South Africa	v	England	Durban[2]	1938-39
712	M.W.Tate	89	19	228	11	England	v	Australia	Sydney	1924-25
708	G.Giffen	118	42	239	8	Australia	v	England	Sydney	1894-95

DISMISSING ALL ELEVEN BATSMEN IN A MATCH

J.C.Laker	19-90	England	v	Australia	Manchester	1956
S.Venkataraghavan	12-152	India	v	New Zealand	Delhi	1964-65
G.Dymock	12-166	Australia	v	India	Kanpur	1979-80
Abdul Qadir	13-101	Pakistan	v	England	Lahore[2]	1987-88
Waqar Younis	12-130	Pakistan	v	New Zealand	Faisalabad	1990-91

OVER 200 RUNS CONCEDED IN AN INNINGS

O	M	R	W						
87	11	298	1	L.O.Fleetwood-Smith	Australia	v	England	The Oval	1938
80.2	13	266	5	O.C.Scott	West Indies	v	England	Kingston	1929-30
54	5	259	0	Khan Mohammad	Pakistan	v	West Indies	Kingston	1957-58
85.2	20	247	2	Fazal Mahmood	Pakistan	v	West Indies	Kingston	1957-58
70	10	229	1	S.L.Boock	New Zealand	v	Pakistan	Auckland	1988-89
82	17	228	5	M.H.Mankad	India	v	West Indies	Kingston	1952-53
64.2	8	226	6	B.S.Bedi	India	v	England	Lord's	1974
38.4	3	220	7	Kapil Dev	India	v	Pakistan	Faisalabad	1982-83
52	7	217	3	I.T.Botham	England	v	Pakistan	The Oval	1987
71	8	204	6	I.A.R.Peebles	England	v	Australia	The Oval	1930
75	16	202	3	M.H.Mankad	India	v	West Indies	Bombay[2]	1948-49
84	19	202	6	Haseeb Ahsan	Pakistan	v	India	Madras[2]	1960-61

OVER 300 RUNS CONCEDED IN A MATCH

O	M	R	W						
105.2	13	374	9	O.C.Scott	West Indies	v	England	Kingston	1929-30
63	3	308	7	A.A.Mailey	Australia	v	England	Sydney	1924-25
61.3	6	302	10	A.A.Mailey	Australia	v	England	Adelaide	1920-21

BOWLERS UNCHANGED IN A COMPLETED INNINGS

		Opponents		
AUSTRALIA				
G.E.Palmer (7-68)	E.Evans (3-64)	England (133)	Sydney	1881-82
F.R.Spofforth (5-30)	G.E.Palmer (4-32)	England (77)	Sydney	1884-85
C.T.B.Turner (6-15)	J.J.Ferris (4-27)	England (45)	Sydney	1886-87
C.T.B.Turner (5-36)	J.J.Ferris (5-26)	England (62)	Lord's	1888
G.Giffen (5-26)	C.T.B.Turner (4-33)	England (72)	Sydney	1894-95
H.Trumble (3-38)	M.A.Noble (7-17)	England (61)	Melbourne	1901-02
M.A.Noble (5-54)	J.V.Saunders (5-43)	England (99)	Sydney	1901-02
ENGLAND		Opponents		
F.Morley (2-34)	R.G.Barlow (7-40)	Australia (83)	Sydney	1882-83
G.A.Lohmann (7-36)	J.Briggs(3-28)	Australia (68)	The Oval	1886
G.A.Lohmann (5-17)	R.Peel (5-18)	Australia (42)	Sydney	1887-88
J.Briggs (8-11)	A.J.Fothergill (1-30)	South Africa (43)	Cape Town	1888-89
J.J.Ferris (7-37)	F.Martin (2-39)	South Africa (83)	Cape Town	1891-92
J.Briggs (6-49)	G.A.Lohmann (3-46)	Australia (100)	Adelaide	1891-92
T.Richardson (6-39)	G.A.Lohmann (3-13)	Australia (53)	Lord's	1896
S.Haigh (6-11)	A.E.Trott (4-19)	South Africa (35)	Cape Town	1898-99
S.F.Barnes (6-42)	C.Blythe (4-64)	Australia (112)	Melbourne	1901-02
G.H.Hirst (4-28)	C.Blythe (6-44)	Australia (74)	Birmingham	1909
F.R.Foster (5-16)	S.F.Barnes (5-25)	South Africa (58)	Lord's	1912
A.E.R.Gilligan (6-7)	M.W.Tate (4-12)	South Africa (30)	Birmingham	1924
G.O.B.Allen (5-36)	W.Voce (4-16)	Australia (58)	Brisbane[2]	1936-37
PAKISTAN		Opponents		
Fazal Mahmood (6-34)	Khan Mohammad (4-43)	Australia (80)	Karachi	1956-57

BOWLERS WITH 50 WICKETS IN THE CALENDAR YEAR

Player (Country)	Year	Tests	Balls	Mdns	Runs	Wkts	Avge	5w	10w	Best
D.K.Lillee (A)	1981	13	3710	162	1781	85	20.95	5	2	7/83
J.Garner (W)	1984	15	3620	149	1603	77	20.81	4	-	6/60
Kapil Dev (I)	1983	18	3469	112	1738	75	23.17	5	1	9/83
Kapil Dev (I)	1979	18	3651	147	1720	74	23.24	5	-	6/63
M.D.Marshall (W)	1984	13	3251	121	1471	73	20.15	9	1	7/53
G.D.McKenzie (A)	1964	14	4106	119	1737	71	24.46	4	1	7/153
S.F.Barnes (E)	1912	10	2394	106	959	64	14.98	8	3	8/29 #
R.J.Hadlee (N)	1985	10	2588	102	1116	64	17.43	6	2	9/52
I.T.Botham (E)	1978	12	2757	91	1160	63	18.41	6	1	8/34
F.S.Trueman (E)	1963	11	2563	90	1061	62	17.11	6	2	7/44
I.T.Botham (E)	1981	12	3338	136	1590	62	25.64	4	1	6/95
Imran Khan (P)	1982	9	2359	112	824	62	13.29	5	2	8/58
M.D.Marshall (W)	1988	10	2477	83	1072	60	17.86	4	1	7/22
R.G.D.Willis (E)	1978	14	2921	94	1056	57	18.52	4	-	5/32
C.J.McDermott (A)	1991	9	2416	84	1188	56	21.21	4	1	8/97
A.A.Mailey (A)	1921	10	2849	63	1567	55	28.49	4	2	9/121 #
R.Benaud (A)	1959	9	3248	177	1031	55	18.74	4	-	5/76
T.M.Alderman (A)	1981	9	2672	105	1222	54	22.62	4	-	6/135
M.D.Marshall (W)	1983	11	2371	99	1119	54	20.72	2	-	6/37
H.Trumble (A)	1902	8	2520	140	994	53	18.75	4	2	8/65
M.H.Mankad (I)	1952	10	3512	218	1170	53	22.07	5	2	8/52
M.A.Holding (W)	1976	11	2305	88	1080	53	20.37	4	1	8/92
B.S.Chandrasekhar (I)	1976	11	3139	108	1458	52	28.03	3	-	6/94
J.Garner (W)	1980	13	2758	139	897	52	17.25	1	-	6/56
R.G.D.Willis (E)	1982	13	2428	72	1236	52	23.76	2	-	6/101
M.A.Noble (A)	1902	12	2208	100	989	51	19.39	6	2	7/17
J.M.Gregory (A)	1921	12	2702	84	1292	51	25.33	3	-	7/69
R.G.D.Willis (E)	1977	11	2146	58	1108	50	22.16	5	-	7/78
T.M.Alderman (A)	1989	10	2414	106	1019	50	20.38	6	1	6/128

 # includes one match in which player did not bowl.

Wicketkeeping

MOST DISMISSALS IN TEST CAREER

		Tests	Dis	C	S	A	E	SA	WI	NZ	I	P	SL
						Opponents							
R.W.Marsh	A	96	**355**	343	12	-	148	-	65	58	16	68	-
P.J.L.Dujon	WI	81	**272**	267 ¶	5	86	84	-	-	20	60	22	-
A.P.E.Knott	E	95	**269**	250	19	105	-	-	43	26	54	41	-
Wasim Bari	P	81	**228**	201	27	66	54	-	21	32	55	-	-
T.G.Evans	E	91	**219**	173	46	76	-	59	37	28	12	7	-
S.M.H.Kirmani	I	88	**198**	160	38	41	42	-	36	28	-	50	1
D.L.Murray	WI	62	**189**	181	8	40	94	33	-	7	27	21	-
A.T.W.Grout	A	51	**187**	163	24	-	76	-	41	-	20	17	-
I.D.S.Smith	NZ	63	**176**	168	8	39	42	-	16	-	29	23	27
R.W.Taylor	E	57	**174**	167	7	57	-	-	-	45	40	29	3
J.H.B.Waite	SA	50	**141**	124	17	28	56	27	-	57	-	-	-
W.A.S.Oldfield	A	54	**130**	78	52	-	90	30	13	-	-	-	-
I.A.Healy	A	39	**117**	115	2	-	38	-	22	7	19	20	11
J.M.Parks	E	46	**114**	103 §	11	21	-	-	31	22	9	1	-
Saleem Yousuf	P	32	**104**	91	13	15	15	-	22	22	11	-	19
Best for Sri Lanka is:													
S.A.R.Silva	SL	9	**34**	33	1	-	6	-	-	2	22	4	-

§ Including 2 catches in 3 Tests when not keeping wicket. ¶ Including 2 catches in 2 Tests when not keeping wicket.

MOST DISMISSALS IN A MATCH

(§ In first Test)

AUSTRALIA				
9 (8c, 1s)	G.R.A.Langley	England	Lord's	1956
9 (9c)	R.W.Marsh	England	Brisbane[2]	1982-83
8 (8c)	J.J.Kelly	England	Sydney	1901-02
8 (8c)	G.R.A.Langley	West Indies	Kingston	1954-55
8 (6c, 2s)	A.T.W.Grout	Pakistan	Lahore[2]	1959-60
8 (8c)	A.T.W.Grout	England	Lord's	1961
8 (7c, 1s) §	H.B.Taber	South Africa	Johannesburg[3]	1966-67
8 (8c)	R.W.Marsh	West Indies	Melbourne	1975-76
8 (8c)	R.W.Marsh	New Zealand	Christchurch	1976-77
8 (7c, 1s)	R.W.Marsh	India	Sydney	1980-81
8 (8c)	R.W.Marsh	England	Adelaide	1982-83
ENGLAND				
10 (10c)	R.W.Taylor	India	Bombay[3]	1979-80
8 (6c, 2s)	L.E.G.Ames	West Indies	The Oval	1933
8 (8c)	J.M.Parks	New Zealand	Christchurch	1965-66
SOUTH AFRICA				
8 (8c)	D.T.Lindsay	Australia	Johannesburg[3]	1966-67
WEST INDIES				
9 (9c)	D.A.Murray	Australia	Melbourne	1981-82
NEW ZEALAND				
8 (8c)	W.K.Lees	Sri Lanka	Wellington	1982-83
8 (8c)	I.D.S.Smith	Sri Lanka	Hamilton	1990-91
INDIA				
7 (1c, 6s)	K.S.More	West Indies	Madras[1]	1987-88
PAKISTAN				
8 (8c)	Wasim Bari	England	Leeds	1971

SRI LANKA

9 (9c)	S.A.R.Silva	India	Colombo (SSC)	1985-86
9 (8c, 1s)	S.A.R.Silva	India	Colombo (PSS)	1985-86

MOST DISMISSALS IN A SERIES

(§ In first series. # In last series)

AUSTRALIA

Total	C	S	Tests	Player	Opponents	Season
28	28	-	5	R.W.Marsh	England	1982-83
26	26	-	6	R.W.Marsh	West Indies	1975-76
24	24	-	5	I.A.Healy	England	1990-91
23	20	3	5	A.T.W.Grout	West Indies	1960-61
23	21	2	5	R.W.Marsh	England	1972
23	23	-	6	R.W.Marsh	England	1981
22 §	22	-	5	S.J.Rixon	India	1977-78
21 #	13	8	5	R.A.Saggers	South Africa	1949-50
21 §	16	5	5	G.R.A.Langley	West Indies	1951-52
21	20	1	5	A.T.W.Grout	England	1961
21 #	21	-	5	R.W.Marsh	Pakistan	1983-84
20	16	4	5	D.Tallon	England	1946-47
20	16	4	4	G.R.A.Langley	West Indies	1954-55
20	17	3	5	A.T.W.Grout	England	1958-59
20 §	19	1	5	H.B.Taber	South Africa	1966-67

ENGLAND

Total	C	S	Tests	Player	Opponents	Season
24	21	3	6	A.P.E.Knott	Australia	1970-71
23	22	1	6	A.P.E.Knott	Australia	1974-75
21	21	-	5	H.Strudwick	South Africa	1913-14
20	20	-	-	T.G.Evans	South Africa	1956-57
20	18	2	6	R.W.Taylor	Australia	1978-79
20	19	1	6	P.R.Downton	Australia	1985

SOUTH AFRICA

Total	C	S	Tests	Player	Opponents	Season
26	23	3	5	J.H.B.Waite	New Zealand	1961-62
24	24	-	5	D.T.Lindsay	Australia	1966-67
23	16	7	5	J.H.B.Waite	New Zealand	1953-54

WEST INDIES

Total	C	S	Tests	Player	Opponents	Season
24 §	22	2	5	D.L.Murray	England	1963
23	22	1	5	F.C.M.Alexander	England	1959-60
23	23	-	5	P.J.L.Dujon	Australia	1990-91
20	19	1	5	P.J.L.Dujon	Australia	1983-84
20	20	-	5	P.J.L.Dujon	England	1988

NEW ZEALAND

Total	C	S	Tests	Player	Opponents	Season
23 §	21	2	5	A.E.Dick	South Africa	1961-62

INDIA

Total	C	S	Tests	Player	Opponents	Season
19 §	12	7	5	N.S.Tamhane	Pakistan	1954-55
19	17	2	6	S.M.H.Kirmani	Pakistan	1979-80

PAKISTAN

Total	C	S	Tests	Player	Opponents	Season
17	15	2	6	Wasim Bari	India	1982-83

SRI LANKA

Total	C	S	Tests	Player	Opponents	Season
22	21	1	3	S.A.R.Silva	India	1985-86

MOST DISMISSALS IN AN INNINGS

(§ In first Test. # in last Test)

AUSTRALIA				
6 (6c) §	A.T.W.Grout	South Africa	Johannesburg[3]	1957-58
6 (6c)	R.W.Marsh	England	Brisbane[2]	1982-83
5 (1c, 4s)	W.A.S.Oldfield	England	Melbourne	1924-25
5 (2c, 3s)	G.R.A.Langley	West Indies	Georgetown	1954-55
5 (5c)	G.R.A.Langley	West Indies	Kingston	1954-55
5 (5c)	G.R.A.Langley	England	Lord's	1956
5 (4c, 1s)	A.T.W.Grout	South Africa	Durban[2]	1957-58
5 (5c)	A.T.W.Grout	Pakistan	Lahore[2]	1959-60
5 (4c, 1s)	A.T.W.Grout	West Indies	Brisbane[2]	1960-61
5 (5c)	A.T.W.Grout	England	Lord's	1961
5 (5c)	A.T.W.Grout	England	Sydney	1965-66
5 (5c) §	H.B.Taber	South Africa	Johannesburg[3]	1966-67
5 (5c)	H.B.Taber	West Indies	Sydney	1968-69
5 (5c) #	H.B.Taber	South Africa	Port Elizabeth	1969-70
5 (5c)	R.W.Marsh	England	Manchester	1972
5 (5c)	R.W.Marsh	England	Nottingham	1972
5 (5c)	R.W.Marsh	New Zealand	Sydney	1973-74
5 (5c)	R.W.Marsh	New Zealand	Christchurch	1973-74
5 (5c)	R.W.Marsh	West Indies	Melbourne	1975-76
5 (5c)	R.W.Marsh	New Zealand	Christchurch	1976-77
5 (5c) §	J.A.Maclean	England	Brisbane[2]	1978-79
5 (5c)	K.J.Wright	Pakistan	Melbourne	1978-79
5 (5c)	R.W.Marsh	West Indies	Brisbane[2]	1979-80
5 (5c)	R.W.Marsh	India	Sydney	1980-81
5 (5c)	R.W.Marsh	Pakistan	Perth	1981-82
5 (5c)	R.W.Marsh	Pakistan	Perth	1983-84
5 (5c) #	R.W.Marsh	Pakistan	Sydney	1983-84
5 (5c)	W.B.Phillips	West Indies	Kingston	1983-84
5 (5c)	I.A.Healy	Pakistan	Adelaide	1989-90
5 (5c)	I.A.Healy	England	Melbourne	1990-91
5 (5c)	I.A.Healy	England	Adelaide	1990-91
ENGLAND				
7 (7c)	R.W.Taylor	India	Bombay[3]	1979-80
6 (6c)	J.T.Murray	India	Lord's	1967
6 (6c)	R.C.Russell	Australia	MCG	1990-91
5 (5c)	J.G.Binks	India	Calcutta	1963-64
5 (3c, 2s)	J.M.Parks	Australia	Sydney	1965-66
5 (5c)	J.M.Parks	New Zealand	Christchurch	1965-66
5 (4c, 1s)	A.P.E.Knott	India	Manchester	1974
5 (5c)	R.W.Taylor	New Zealand	Nottingham	1978
5 (5c)	R.W.Taylor	Australia	Brisbane[2]	1978-79
5 (5c)	C.J.Richards	Australia	Melbourne	1986-87
5 (5c)	R.C.Russell	West Indies	Bridgetown	1989-90
SOUTH AFRICA				
6 (6c)	D.T.Lindsay	Australia	Johannesburg[3]	1966-67
WEST INDIES				
5 (5c)	F.C.M.Alexander	England	Bridgetown	1959-60
5 (5c)	D.L.Murray	England	Leeds	1976
5 (5c)	D.L.Murray	Pakistan	Georgetown	1976-77
5 (5c)	D.A.Murray	India	Delhi	1978-79
5 (5c)	D.A.Murray	Australia	Melbourne	1981-82
5 (5c)	P.J.L.Dujon	India	Kingston	1982-83
5 (5c)	P.J.L.Dujon	England	Bridgetown	1985-86
5 (5c)	P.J.L.Dujon	Australia	St John's	1990-91

NEW ZEALAND

7 (7c)	I.D.S.Smith	Sri Lanka	Hamilton	1990-91
5 (5c)	R.I.Harford	India	Wellington	1967-68
5 (5c)	K.J.Wadsworth	Pakistan	Auckland	1972-73
5 (5c)	W.K.Lees	Sri Lanka	Wellington	1982-83
5 (4c, 1s)	I.D.S.Smith	England	Auckland	1983-84
5 (5c)	I.D.S.Smith	Sri Lanka	Auckland	1990-91
5 (5c)	A.C.Parore	England	Auckland	1991-92

INDIA

6 (5c, 1s)	S.M.H.Kirmani	New Zealand	Christchurch	1975-76
5 (3c, 2s)	B.K.Kunderan	England	Bombay[1]	1961-62
5 (5c)	S.M.H.Kirmani	Pakistan	Faisalabad	1982-83
5 (0c, 5s)	K.S.More	West Indies	Madras[1]	1987-88

PAKISTAN

7 (7c)	Wasim Bari	New Zealand	Auckland	1978-79
5 (4c, 1s)	Imtiaz Ahmed	Australia	Lahore[2]	1959-60
5 (5c)	Wasim Bari	England	Leeds	1971
5 (5c)	Saleem Yousuf	Sri Lanka	Karachi	1985-86
5 (5c)	Saleem Yousuf	New Zealand	Faisalabad	1990-91

SRI LANKA

6 (6c)	S.A.R.Silva	India	Colombo (SSC)	1985-86
5 (5c)	S.A.R.Silva	India	Colombo (PSS)	1985-86
5 (5c)	H.P.Tillakaratne	New Zealand	Hamilton	1990-91

MOST STUMPINGS IN A SERIES

9	P.W.Sherwell	South Africa	v	Australia	in Australia	1910-11

MOST STUMPINGS IN A MATCH

6	K.S.More	India	v	West Indies	Madras[1]	1987-88

MOST STUMPINGS IN AN INNINGS

5	K.S.More	India	v	West Indies	Madras[1]	1987-88

WICKET-KEEPERS WITH 30 DISMISSALS IN THE CALENDAR YEAR

Player	Country	Year	Tests	C	S	Dismissals
P.J.L.Dujon	West Indies	1984	15	54	1	55
R.W.Marsh	Australia	1981	13	52	1	53
R.W.Taylor	England	1978	14	43	1	44
R.W.Marsh	Australia	1982	12	42	1	43
R.W.Marsh	Australia	1975	10	38	2	40
R.C.Russell	England	1990	12	39	1	40
P.J.L.Dujon	West Indies	1991	10	40	-	40
A.P.E.Knott	England	1974	14	37	2	39
D.L.Murray	West Indies	1976	12	37	2	39
A.P.E.Knott	England	1971	11	34	4	38
S.M.H.Kirmani	India	1983	18	35	3	38
P.J.L.Dujon	West Indies	1988	12	37	1	38
R.W.Marsh	Australia	1974	9	36	1	37
A.T.W.Grout	Australia	1961	9	33	3	36
K.J.Wright	Australia	1979	10	31	4	35
R.W.Taylor	England	1982	14	35	-	35

P.J.L.Dujon	West Indies	1983	11	34	1	35
Wasim Bari	Pakistan	1983	11	32	3	35
A.T.W.Grout	Australia	1964	10	33	1	34
I.A.Healy	Australia	1991	10	34	-	34
R.W.Marsh	Australia	1977	10	33	-	33
Wasim Bari	Pakistan	1979	9	31	2	33
P.R.Downton	England	1985	9	31	1	32
T.G.Evans	England	1957	9	29	2	31
J.M.Parks	England	1966	10	28	3	31
S.M.H.Kirmani	India	1979	14	27	4	31
A.T.W.Grout	Australia	1959	8	24	6	30
A.P.E.Knott	England	1973	13	30	-	30

NO BYES CONCEDED IN TOTAL OF 500 RUNS

4-671	H.P.Tillakaratne	Sri Lanka	v	India	Wellington	1990-91
8d-659	T.G.Evans	England	v	Australia	Sydney	1946-47
652	S.M.H.Kirmani	India	v	Pakistan	Faisalabad	1982-83
619	J.L.Hendriks	West Indies	v	Australia	Sydney	1968-69
5d-616	I.D.S.Smith	New Zealand	v	Pakistan	Auckland	1988-89
7d-601	R C Russell	England	v	Australia	Leeds	1989
9d-559	W.W.Wade	South Africa	v	England	Cape Town	1938-39
551	J.J.Kelly	Australia	v	England	Sydney	1897-98
9d-551	A.P.E.Knott	England	v	New Zealand	Lord's	1973
5d-544	Imtiaz Ahmed	Pakistan	v	England	Birmingham	1962
3d-543	T.M.Findlay	West Indies	v	New Zealand	Georgetown	1971-72
9d-536	I.A.Healy	Australia	v	West Indies	Bridgetown	1990-91
9d-532	A.P.E.Knott	England	v	Australia	The Oval	1975
531	D.T.Lindsay	South Africa	v	England	Johannesburg[3]	1964-65
528	S.M.H.Kirmani	India	v	Australia	Adelaide	1980-81
528	R.C.Russell	England	v	Australia	Lord's	1989
7d-526	A.P.E.Knott	England	v	West Indies	Port-of-Spain	1967-68
521	W.A.S.Oldfield	Australia	v	England	Brisbane[1]	1928-29
520	J.H.B.Waite	South Africa	v	Australia	Melbourne	1952-53
515	P.J.L.Dujon	West Indies	v	Australia	Adelaide	1988-89
4d-514	R.G.de Alwis	Sri Lanka	v	Australia	Kandy	1982-83
5d-514	C.J.Richards	England	v	Australia	Adelaide	1986-87
6d-512	B.N.French	England	v	New Zealand	Wellington	1987-88
510	J.L.Hendriks	West Indies	v	Australia	Melbourne	1968-69
509	W.B.Phillips	Australia	v	West Indies	Bridgetown	1983-84
6d-507	K.J.Wadsworth	New Zealand	v	Pakistan	Dunedin	1972-73
8d-503	S.M.H.Kirmani	India	v	Pakistan	Faisalabad	1978-79

MOST BYES CONCEDED IN AN INNINGS

37	F.E.Woolley	England	v	Australia	The Oval	1934
(At the age of 47, standing-in for the injured L.E.G.Ames).						
33	J.T.Murray	England	v	India	Bombay[2]	1961-62
33	J.M.Parks	England	v	West Indies	Kingston	1967-68

Fielding

MOST CATCHES IN TESTS

		Tests	C	A	E	SA	WI	NZ	I	P	SL
				Opponents							
A.R.Border	A	133	**137**	-	49	-	19	25	14	22	8
G.S.Chappell	A	87	**122**	-	61	-	16	18	5	22	-
I.V.A.Richards	WI	121	**122**	24	29	-	-	7	39	23	-
I.T.Botham	E	102	**120**	61	-	-	15	14	14	14	2
M.C.Cowdrey	E	114	**120**	40	-	22	21	15	11	11	-
R.B.Simpson	A	62	**110**	-	30	27	29	-	21	3	-
W.R.Hammond	E	85	**110**	43	-	30	22	9	6	-	-
G.S.Sobers	WI	93	**109**	27	40	-	-	11	27	4	-
S.M.Gavaskar	I	125	**108**	19	35	-	17	11	-	19	7
I.M.Chappell	A	75	**105**	-	31	11	24	16	17	6	-

The most successful catchers for the other countries are:

		Tests	C	A	E	SA	WI	NZ	I	P	SL
B.Mitchell	SA	42	**56**	10	43	-	-	3	-	-	-
J.V.Coney	NZ	52	**64**	24	12	-	8	-	1	10	9
Javed Miandad	P	117	**93**	10	22	-	12	20	18	-	11
A.Ranatunga	SL	36	**17**	6	2	-	-	4	2	3	-

MOST CATCHES IN A SERIES

(§ In first Test series)

C	Tests	Player	Against	Season
AUSTRALIA				
15 §	5	J.M.Gregory	England	1920-21
14	6	G.S.Chappell	England	1974-75
13 §	5	R.B.Simpson	South Africa	1957-58
13	5	R.B.Simpson	West Indies	1960-61
12	5	D.F.Whatmore	India	1979-80
12	6	A.R.Border	England	1981
ENGLAND				
12 §	5	L.C.Braund	Australia	1901-02
12	5	W.R.Hammond	Australia	1934
12	3	J.T.Ikin	South Africa	1951
12	6	A.W.Greig	Australia	1974-75
12	6	I.T.Botham	Australia	1981
SOUTH AFRICA				
12	5	A.E.E.Vogler	England	1909-10
12	5	B.Mitchell	England	1930-31
12	5	T.L.Goddard	England	1956-57
WEST INDIES				
12	5	G.S.Sobers	Australia	1960-61
NEW ZEALAND				
8	5	B.Sutcliffe	South Africa	1953-54
8	4	B.A.G.Murray	India	1967-68
8	4	J.J.Crowe	West Indies	1984-85
INDIA				
12	5	E.D.Solkar	England	1972-73
PAKISTAN				
9	5	W.Mathias	West Indies	1957-58
SRI LANKA				
6 §	2	Y.Goonasekera	New Zealand	1982-83
6 §	3	S.M.S.Kaluperuma	New Zealand	1983-84

MOST CATCHES IN A MATCH

(§ In first Test. # In last Test)

AUSTRALIA

7	G.S.Chappell	v	England	Perth	1974-75
6	J.M.Gregory	v	England	Sydney	1920-21
6 #	V.Y.Richardson	v	South Africa	Durban2	1935-36
6 #	R.N.Harvey	v	England	Sydney	1962-63
6	I.M.Chappell	v	New Zealand	Adelaide	1973-74
6	D.F.Whatmore	v	India	Kanpur	1979-80

ENGLAND

6	A.Shrewsbury	v	Australia	Sydney	1887-88
6	F.E.Woolley	v	Australia	Sydney	1911-12
6	M.C.Cowdrey	v	West Indies	Lord's	1963
6	A.W.Greig	v	Pakistan	Leeds	1974
6	A.J.Lamb	v	New Zealand	Lord's	1983
6	G.A.Hick	v	Pakistan	Leeds	1992

SOUTH AFRICA

6	A.E.E.Vogler	v	England	Durban[1]	1909-10
6	B.Mitchell	v	Australia	Melbourne	1931-32

WEST INDIES

6	G.S.Sobers	v	England	Lord's	1973

INDIA

7 §	Yajurvindra Singh	v	England	Bangalore	1976-77
6	E.D.Solkar	v	West Indies	Port-of-Spain	1970-71

PAKISTAN

5	Majid Khan	v	Australia	Karachi	1979-80

SRI LANKA

5	Y.Goonasekera	v	New Zealand	Wellington	1982-83

MOST CATCHES IN AN INNINGS

(§ In first Test. # In last Test)

AUSTRALIA

5	V.Y.Richardson #	v	South Africa	Durban[2]	1935-36

ENGLAND

4	L.C.Braund	v	Australia	Sheffield	1902
4	W.Rhodes	v	Australia	Manchester	1905
4	L.C.Braund	v	Australia	Sydney	1907-08
4	F.E.Woolley	v	Australia	Sydney	1911-12
4	H.Larwood	v	Australia	Brisbane[1]	1928-29
4	J.E.McConnon	v	Pakistan	Manchester	1954
4	P.B.H.May	v	Australia	Adelaide	1954-55
4	P.H.Parfitt	v	Australia	Nottingham	1972
4	A.W.Greig	v	Pakistan	Leeds	1974
4	P.H.Edmonds	v	New Zealand	Christchurch	1977-78
4	A.J.Lamb	v	New Zealand	Lord's	1983
4	G.A.Hick	v	Pakistan	Leeds	1992

SOUTH AFRICA

4	A.E.E.Vogler	v	England	Durban[1]	1909-10
4	A.W.Nourse	v	England	Durban[2]	1922-23
4	B.Mitchell	v	Australia	Melbourne	1931-32
4	T.L.Goddard	v	Australia	Sydney	1963-64
4	A.J.Traicos §	v	Australia	Durban[2]	1969-70

WEST INDIES					
4	E.D.Weekes	v	India	Kingston	1952-53
4	G.S.Sobers	v	England	Port-of-Spain	1959-60
4	G.S.Sobers	v	England	Nottingham	1966
4	R.C.Fredericks	v	Australia	Port-of-Spain	1972-73
4	G.S.Sobers	v	England	Lord's	1973
4	I.V.A.Richards	v	India	Kingston	1988-89
4	A.L.Logie	v	Pakistan	Lahore²	1990-91
NEW ZEALAND					
4	J.J.Crowe	v	West Indies	Bridgetown	1984-85
4	M.D.Crowe	v	West Indies	Kingston	1984-85
INDIA					
5	Yajurvindra Singh §	v	England	Bangalore	197-77
5	M Azharuddin	v	Pakistan	Karachi	1989-90
5	K.Srikkanth	v	Australia	Perth	1991-92
PAKISTAN					
4	W.Mathias	v	West Indies	Bridgetown	1957-58
4	Hanif Mohammad	v	England	Dacca	1968-69
4	Aamer Malik §	v	England	Faisalabad	1987-88
SRI LANKA					
4	Y.Goonasekera	v	New Zealand	Wellington	1982-83

PLAYERS WITH 15 CATCHES IN THE CALENDAR YEAR

Player	Country	Year	Tests	C
J.M.Gregory	Australia	1921	12	27
R.B.Simpson	Australia	1964	14	26
A.W.Greig	England	1974	13	23
I.M.Chappell	Australia	1974	9	21
I.T.Botham	England	1979	9	20
G.S.Chappell	Australia	1974	9	19
G.R.J.Roope	England	1978	9	19
M.D.Crowe	New Zealand	1985	10	19
A.L.Logie	West Indies	1988	12	19
L.C.Braund	England	1902	9	18
W.R.Endean	South Africa	1953	7	18
R.N.Harvey	Australia	1959	9	18
R.B.Simpson	Australia	1961	9	18
G.R.J.Roope	England	1973	8	18
A.R.Border	Australia	1980	10	18
A.R.Border	Australia	1981	10	18
I.M.Chappell	Australia	1969	8	17
J.M.Brearley	England	1977	10	17
A.W.Greig	England	1977	10	17
J.M.Brearley	England	1978	10	17
I.T.Botham	England	1981	13	17
C.H.Lloyd	West Indies	1984	14	17
G.A.Gooch	England	1986	11	17
D.C.Boon	Australia	1989	11	17
G.B.Hole	Australia	1953	7	16
G.S.Chappell	Australia	1975	10	16
I.V.A.Richards	West Indies	1980	11	16
D.B.Vengsarkar	India	1979	18	16
G.S.Chappell	Australia	1980	10	16
I.V.A.Richards	West Indies	1981	11	16

M.E.Waugh	Australia	1991	9	16 #
A.R.Border	Australia	1985	12	16
W.R.Hammond	England	1928	10	15
M.C.Cowdrey	England	1957	9	15
A.L.Wadekar	India	1968	7	15
K.R.Stackpole	Australia	1969	8	15
M.H.Denness	England	1974	14	15
J.J.Crowe	New Zealand	1985	10	15
C.L.Hooper	West Indies	1991	10	15

 # Waugh achieved the feat in his debut calendar year.

MOST SUBSTITUTE CATCHES BY ONE FIELDER IN A MATCH

FOUR					
Gursharan Singh	India	v	West Indies	Ahmedabad	1983-84
THREE					
H.Strudwick	England	v	Australia	Melbourne	1903-04
J.E.D.Sealy	West Indies	v	England	Port-of-Spain	1929-30
W.V.Rodriguez	West Indies	v	India	Port-of-Spain	1961-62
Yajurvindra Singh	India	v	West Indies	Madras[1]	1978-79
Haroon Rashid	Pakistan	v	England	Leeds	1982
M.J.Greatbatch	New Zealand	v	England	Christchurch	1987-88

MOST SUBSTITUTE CATCHES BY ONE FIELDER IN AN INNINGS

THREE					
H.Strudwick	England	v	Australia	Melbourne	1903-04
Haroon Rashid	Pakistan	v	England	Leeds	1982
Gursharan Singh	India	v	West Indies	Ahmedabad	1983-84

All Round

1000 RUNS AND 100 WICKETS

	Tests	Runs	Wkts	Tests for Double
AUSTRALIA				
R.Benaud	63	2201	248	32
A K.Davidson	44	1328	186	34
G Giffen	31	1238	103	30
I.W.Johnson	45	1000	109	45
R.R.Lindwall	61	1502	228	38
K.R.Miller	55	2958	170	33
M.A.Noble	42	1997	121	27
ENGLAND				
T.E.Bailey	61	2290	132	47
I.T.Botham	102	5200	383	21
J.E.Emburey	60	1540	138	46
A.W.Greig	58	3599	141	37
R.Illingworth	61	1836	122	47
W.Rhodes	58	2325	127	44
M W.Tate	39	1198	155	33
F.J.Titmus	53	1449	153	40
SOUTH AFRICA				
T.L.Goddard	41	2516	123	36
WEST INDIES				
M.D.Marshall	81	1810	376	49
G.S.Sobers	93	8032	235	48
NEW ZEALAND				
J.G.Bracewell	41	1001	102	41
R.J.Hadlee	86	3124	431	28
INDIA				
Kapil Dev	115	4690	401	25
M.H.Mankad	44	2109	162	23
R.J.Shastri	76	3760	148	44
PAKISTAN				
Abdul Qadir	67	1029	236	62
Imran Khan	88	3807	362	30
Intikhab Alam	47	1493	125	41
Sarfraz Nawaz	55	1045	177	55

1000 RUNS, 50 WICKETS AND 50 CATCHES

	Tests	Runs	Wkts	Catches
AUSTRALIA				
R.Benaud	63	2201	248	65
R.B.Simpson	62	4869	71	110
ENGLAND				
I.T.Botham	102	5200	383	120
A.W.Greig	58	3599	141	87
W.R.Hammond	85	7249	83	110
W.Rhodes	58	2325	127	60
F.E.Woolley	64	3283	83	64
WEST INDIES				
G.S.Sobers	93	8032	235	109
INDIA				
Kapil Dev	115	4690	401	58

1000 RUNS AND 100 WICKETKEEPING DISMISSALS

	Tests	Runs	Dismissals	Tests for Double
AUSTRALIA				
I.A.Healy	39	1218	117	36
R.W.Marsh	96	3633	355	25
W.A.S.Oldfield	54	1427	130	41
ENGLAND				
T.G.Evans	91	2439	219	42
A.P.E.Knott	95	4389	269	30
J.M.Parks	46	1962	114	41
R.W.Taylor	57	1156	174	47
SOUTH AFRICA				
J.H.B.Waite	50	2405	141	36
WEST INDIES				
P.J.L.Dujon	81	3322	272	30
D.L.Murray	62	1993	189	33
NEW ZEALAND				
I.D.S.Smith	63	1815	177	42
INDIA				
S.M.H.Kirmani	88	2759	198	42
PAKISTAN				
Saleem Yousuf	32	1055	104	32
Wasim Bari	81	1366	228	53

250 RUNS AND 20 WICKETS IN A SERIES *(§ In first Test series)*

	Tests	Runs	Wkts				
G.Giffen	5	475	34	Australia	v	England	1894-95
L.C.Braund §	5	256	21	England	v	Australia	1901-02
G.A.Faulkner	5	545	29	South Africa	v	England	1909-10
G.J.Thompson	5	267	23	England	v	South Africa	1909-10
J.M.Gregory §	5	442	23	Australia	v	England	1920-21
K.R.Miller	5	362	20	Australia	v	West Indies	1951-52
K.R.Miller	5	439	20	Australia	v	West Indies	1954-55
R.Benaud	5	329	30	Australia	v	South Africa	1957-58
G.S.Sobers	5	424	23	West Indies	v	India	1961-62
G.S.Sobers	5	322	20	West Indies	v	England	1963
G.S.Sobers	5	722	20	West Indies	v	England	1966
T.L.Goddard	5	294	26	South Africa	v	Australia	1966-67
A.W.Greig	5	430	24	England	v	West Indies	1973-74
I.T.Botham	6	291	23	England	v	Australia	1978-79
Kapil Dev	6	278	32	India	v	Pakistan	1979-80
I T.Botham	6	399	34	England	v	Australia	1981
Kapil Dev	6	318	22	India	v	England	1981-82
R.J.Hadlee	4	301	21	New Zealand	v	England	1983
I.T.Botham	6	250	31	England	v	Australia	1985

250 RUNS AND 20 WICKETKEEPING DISMISSALS IN A SERIES

	Tests	Runs	Dismissals				
J H.B Waite	5	263	26	South Africa	v	New Zealand	1961-62
D T.Lindsay	5	606	24	South Africa	v	Australia	1966-67
A P.E.Knott	6	364	23	England	v	Australia	1974-75
P.J.L.Dujon	5	305	20	West Indies	v	England	1988

500 RUNS IN A SERIES BY A WICKET-KEEPER

	Tests	Runs	Avge				
B.K.Kunderan	5	525	52.50	India	v	England	1963-64
D.T.Lindsay	5	606	86.57	South Africa	v	Australia	1966-67

MATCH DOUBLE - 100 RUNS AND 10 WICKETS

A.K.Davidson	44 80	5-135) 6-87)	Australia	v	West Indies	Brisbane[2]	1960-61
I.T.Botham	114	6-58) 7-48)	England	v	India	Bombay[3]	1979-80
Imran Khan	117	6-98) 5-82)	Pakistan	v	India	Faisalabad	1982-83

A CENTURY AND 5 WICKETS IN AN INNINGS OF THE SAME MATCH

(§ In first Test)

			Opponents		
AUSTRALIA					
C.Kelleway	114	5-33	South Africa	Manchester	1912
J.M.Gregory	100	7-69	England	Melbourne	1920-21
K.R.Miller	109	6-107	West Indies	Kingston	1954-55
R.Benaud	100	5-84	South Africa	Johannesburg[3]	1957-58
ENGLAND					
A.W.Greig	148	6-164	West Indies	Bridgetown	1973-74
I.T.Botham	103	5-73	New Zealand	Christchurch	1977-78
I.T.Botham	108	8-34	Pakistan	Lord's	1978
I.T.Botham	114	6-58) 7-48)	India	Bombay[3]	1979-80
I.T.Botham	149*	6-95	Australia	Leeds	1981
I.T.Botham	138	5-59	New Zealand	Wellington	1983-84
SOUTH AFRICA					
J.H.Sinclair	106	6-26	England	Cape Town	1898-99
G.A.Faulkner	123	5-120	England	Johannesburg[1]	1909-10
WEST INDIES					
D.S.Atkinson	219	5-56	Australia	Bridgetown	1954-55
O.G.Smith	100	5-90	India	Delhi	1958-59
G.S.Sobers	104	5-63	India	Kingston	1961-62
G.S.Sobers	174	5-41	England	Leeds	1966
NEW ZEALAND					
B.R.Taylor §	105	5-86	India	Calcutta	1964-65
INDIA					
M.H.Mankad	184	5-196	England	Lord's	1952
P.R.Umrigar	172*	5-107	West Indies	Port-of-Spain	1961-62
PAKISTAN					
Mushtaq Mohammad	201	5-49	New Zealand	Dunedin	1972-73
Mushtaq Mohammad	121	5-28	West Indies	Port-of-Spain	1976-77
Imran Khan	117	6-88) 5-82)	India	Faisalabad	1982-83
Wasim Akram	123	5-100	Australia	Adelaide	1989-90

A CENTURY AND FIVE DISMISSALS IN AN INNINGS BY A WICKETKEEPER

D.T.Lindsay	182	6c	South Africa	v	Australia	Johannesburg[3]	1966-67
I.D.S.Smith	113*	4c, 1s	New Zealand	v	England	Auckland	1983-84
S.A.R.Silva	111	5c	Sri Lanka	v	India	Colombo (PSS)	1985-86

The Captains

RESULT SUMMARY

AUSTRALIA (38)	Tests as Captain	Opponents E	SA	WI	NZ	I	P	SL	Results W	L	D	Tie	Toss Won
D.W.Gregory	**3**	3	-	-	-	-	-	-	2	1	-	-	2
W.L.Murdoch	**16**	16	-	-	-	-	-	-	5	7	4	-	7
T.P.Horan	**2**	2	-	-	-	-	-	-	-	2	-	-	1
H.H.Massie	**1**	1	-	-	-	-	-	-	1	-	-	-	1
J.M.Blackham	**8**	8	-	-	-	-	-	-	3	3	2	-	4
H.J.H.Scott	**3**	3	-	-	-	-	-	-	-	3	-	-	1
P.S.McDonnell	**6**	6	-	-	-	-	-	-	1	5	-	-	4
G.Giffen	**4**	4	-	-	-	-	-	-	2	2	-	-	3
G.H.S.Trott	**8**	8	-	-	-	-	-	-	5	3	-	-	5
J.Darling	**21**	18	3	-	-	-	-	-	7	4	10	-	7
H.Trumble	**2**	2	-	-	-	-	-	-	2	-	-	-	1
M.A.Noble	**15**	15	-	-	-	-	-	-	8	5	2	-	11
C.Hill	**10**	5	5	-	-	-	-	-	5	5	-	-	-
S.E.Gregory	**6**	3	3	-	-	-	-	-	2	1	3	-	1
W.W.Armstrong	**10**	10	-	-	-	-	-	-	8	-	2	-	4
H.L.Collins	**11**	8	3	-	-	-	-	-	5	2	4	-	7
W.Bardsley	**2**	2	-	-	-	-	-	-	-	-	2	-	1
J.Ryder	**5**	5	-	-	-	-	-	-	1	4	-	-	2
W.M.Woodfull	**25**	15	5	5	-	-	-	-	14	7	4	-	12
V.Y.Richardson	**5**	-	5	-	-	-	-	-	4	-	1	-	1
D.G.Bradman	**24**	19	-	-	-	5	-	-	15	3	6	-	10
W.A.Brown	**1**	-	-	-	1	-	-	-	1	-	-	-	-
A.L.Hassett	**24**	10	10	4	-	-	-	-	14	4	6	-	18
A.R.Morris	**2**	1	-	-	-	-	-	-	-	2	-	-	2
I.W.Johnson	**17**	9	-	5	-	2	1	-	7	5	5	-	6
R.R.Lindwall	**1**	-	-	-	-	1	-	-	-	-	1	-	-
I.D.Craig	**5**	-	5	-	-	-	-	-	3	-	2	-	3
R.Benaud	**28**	14	1	5	-	5	3	-	12	4	11	1	11
R.N.Harvey	**1**	1	-	-	-	-	-	-	1	-	-	-	-
R.B.Simpson	**39**	8	9	10	-	10	2	-	12	12	15	-	19
B.C.Booth	**2**	2	-	-	-	-	-	-	-	1	1	-	1
W.M.Lawry	**25**	9	4	5	-	7	-	-	9	8	8	-	8
B.N.Jarman	**1**	1	-	-	-	-	-	-	-	-	1	-	1
I.M.Chappell	**30**	16	-	5	6	-	3	-	15	5	10	-	17
G.S.Chappell	**48**	15	-	12	8	3	9	1	21	13	14	-	29
G.N.Yallop	**7**	6	-	-	-	-	1	-	1	6	-	-	6
K.J.Hughes	**28**	6	-	7	-	6	9	-	4	13	11	-	13
A.R.Border	**70**	23	-	13	11	11	6	6	22	16	31	1	35
	516	274	53	72	26	50	34	7	212	146	156	2	259

ENGLAND (69)	Tests as Captain	Opponents A	SA	WI	NZ	I	P	SL	Results W	L	D	Tie	Toss Won
James Lillywhite	**2**	2	-	-	-	-	-	-	1	1	-	-	-
Lord Harris	**4**	4	-	-	-	-	-	-	2	1	1	-	2
A.Shaw	**4**	4	-	-	-	-	-	-	-	2	2	-	4
A.N.Hornby	**2**	2	-	-	-	-	-	-	-	1	1	-	1
Hon.I.F.W.Bligh	**4**	4	-	-	-	-	-	-	2	2	-	-	3
A.Shrewsbury	**7**	7	-	-	-	-	-	-	5	2	-	-	3
A.G.Steel	**4**	4	-	-	-	-	-	-	3	1	-	-	2
W.W.Read	**2**	1	1	-	-	-	-	-	2	-	-	-	-

W.G.Grace	**13**	13	-	-	-	-	-	-	8	3	2	-	4
C.A.Smith	**1**	-	1	-	-	-	-	-	1	-	-	-	-
M.P.Bowden	**1**	-	1	-	-	-	-	-	1	-	-	-	1
A.E.Stoddart	**8**	8	-	-	-	-	-	-	3	4	1	-	2
T.C.O'Brien	**1**	-	1	-	-	-	-	-	1	-	-	-	-
Lord Hawke	**4**	-	4	-	-	-	-	-	4	-	-	-	4
A.C.MacLaren	**22**	22	-	-	-	-	-	-	4	11	7	-	11
P.F.Warner	**10**	5	5	-	-	-	-	-	4	6	-	-	5
Hon F.S.Jackson	**5**	5	-	-	-	-	-	-	2	-	3	-	5
R.E.Foster	**3**	-	3	-	-	-	-	-	-	2	3	-	3
F.L.Fane	**5**	3	2	-	-	-	-	-	2	3	-	-	3
A.O.Jones	**2**	2	-	-	-	-	-	-	2	-	1	-	1
H.D.G.Leveson Gower	**3**	-	3	-	-	-	-	-	1	2	-	-	-
J.W.H.T.Douglas	**18**	12	6	-	-	-	-	-	8	8	2	-	7
C.B Fry	**6**	3	3	-	-	-	-	-	4	-	2	-	1
Hon.L.H.Tennyson	**3**	3	-	-	-	-	-	-	-	1	2	-	2
F.T.Mann	**5**	-	5	-	-	-	-	-	2	1	2	-	3
A.E.R.Gilligan	**9**	5	4	-	-	-	-	-	4	4	1	-	2
A.W Carr	**6**	4	2	-	-	-	-	-	1	-	5	-	3
A.P.F.Chapman	**17**	9	5	3	-	-	-	-	9	2	6	-	9
R.T.Stanyforth	**4**	-	4	-	-	-	-	-	2	1	1	1	-
G.T.S.Stevens	**1**	-	1	-	-	-	-	-	-	1	-	-	-
J.C.White	**4**	1	3	-	-	-	-	-	1	1	2	-	3
A.H.H.Gilligan	**4**	-	-	-	4	-	-	-	1	-	3	-	1
Hon.F.S.G.Calthorpe	**4**	-	-	4	-	-	-	-	1	1	2	-	2
R.E.S.Wyatt	**16**	5	5	5	1	-	-	-	3	5	8	-	12
D.R.Jardine	**15**	5	-	2	4	4	-	-	9	1	5	-	7
C.F.Walters	**1**	1	-	-	-	-	-	-	-	1	-	-	-
G.O.B.Allen	**11**	5	-	3	-	3	-	-	4	5	2	-	6
R.W.V.Robins	**3**	-	-	-	3	-	-	-	1	-	2	-	2
W.R.Hammond	**20**	8	5	3	1	3	-	-	4	3	13	-	12
N.W.D.Yardley	**14**	6	5	3	-	-	-	-	4	7	3	-	9
K.Cranston	**1**		-	-	1		-	-	-	-	1	-	-
F.G.Mann	**7**	-	5	-	2	-	-	-	2	-	5	-	5
F.R.Brown	**15**	5	5	1	4	-	-	-	5	6	4	-	3
N.D.Howard	**4**	-	-	-	-	4	-	-	1	-	3	-	2
D.B.Carr	**1**	-	-	-	-	1	-	-	-	1	-	-	1
L.Hutton	**23**	10	-	5	2	4	2	-	11	4	8	-	7
Rev.D.S.Sheppard	**2**	-	-	-	-	-	2	-	1	-	1	-	1
P.B.H.May	**41**	13	10	8	7	3	-	-	20	10	11	-	26
M.C.Cowdrey	**27**	6	5	10	-	2	4	-	8	4	15	-	17
E.R.Dexter	**30**	10	-	5	3	5	7	-	9	7	14	-	13
M.J.K.Smith	**25**	5	8	1	6	5	-	-	5	3	17	-	10
D.B.Close	**7**	-	-	1	-	3	3	-	6	-	1	-	4
T.W.Graveney	**1**	1	-	-	-	-	-	-	-	-	1	-	-
R.Illingworth	**31**	11	-	6	8	3	3	-	12	5	14	-	15
A R.Lewis	**8**	-	-	-	-	5	3	-	1	2	5	-	3
M.H.Denness	**19**	6	-	5	2	3	3	-	6	5	8	-	9
J.H.Edrich	**1**	1	-	-	-	-	-	-	-	1	-	-	-
A.W.Greig	**14**	4	-	5	-	5	-	-	3	5	6	-	6
J.M.Brearley	**31**	18	-	-	3	5	5	-	18	4	9	-	13
G.Boycott	**4**	-	-	-	3	-	1	-	1	1	2	-	3
I.T.Botham	**12**	3	-	9	-	-	-	-	-	4	8	-	6
K.W.R.Fletcher	**7**	-	-	-	-	6	-	1	1	1	5	-	5
R.G.D.Willis	**18**	5	-	-	7	3	3	-	7	5	6	-	8
D.I.Gower	**32**	12	-	10	-	6	3	1	5	18	9	-	14
M.W.Gatting	**23**	6	-	1	6	2	8	-	2	5	16	-	14
J.E.Emburey	**2**	-	-	2	-	-	-	-	-	2	-	-	1
C.S.Cowdrey	**1**	-	-	1	-	-	-	-	-	1	-	-	-

	Tests as Captain	A	SA	WI	NZ	I	P	SL	W	L	D	Tie	Toss Won
G.A.Gooch	**28**	4	-	8	6	3	5	2	10	7	11	-	13
A.J.Lamb	**3**	1	-	2	-	-	-	-	-	3	-	-	2
	686	274	102	104	72	78	52	4	239	187	260	-	339

SOUTH AFRICA (25)	Tests as Captain	Opponents A	E	WI	NZ	I	P	SL	Results W	L	D	Tie	Toss Won
O.R.Dunell	**1**	-	1	-	-	-	-	-	-	-	-	-	1
W.H.Milton	**2**	-	2	-	-	-	-	-	-	2	-	-	1
E.A.Halliwell	**3**	1	2	-	-	-	-	-	-	3	-	-	1
A.R.Richards	**1**	-	1	-	-	-	-	-	-	1	-	-	-
M.Bisset	**2**	-	2	-	-	-	-	-	-	2	-	-	-
H.M.Taberer	**1**	1	-	-	-	-	-	-	-	-	1	-	1
J.H.Anderson	**1**	1	-	-	-	-	-	-	-	1	-	-	-
P.W.Sherwell	**13**	5	8	-	-	-	-	-	5	6	2	-	5
S.J.Snooke	**5**	-	5	-	-	-	-	-	3	2	-	-	3
F.Mitchell	**3**	2	1	-	-	-	-	-	-	3	-	-	2
L.J.Tancred	**3**	1	2	-	-	-	-	-	-	2	1	-	2
H.W.Taylor	**18**	3	15	-	-	-	-	-	1	10	7	-	11
H.G.Deane	**12**	-	12	-	-	-	-	-	2	4	6	-	9
E.P.Nupen	**1**	-	1	-	-	-	-	-	1	-	-	-	-
H.B.Cameron	**9**	5	2	-	2	-	-	-	2	5	2	-	3
H.F.Wade	**10**	5	5	-	-	-	-	-	1	4	5	-	5
A.Melville	**10**	-	10	-	-	-	-	-	-	4	6	-	4
A.D.Nourse	**15**	5	10	-	-	-	-	-	1	9	5	-	7
J.E.Cheetham	**15**	5	3	-	7	-	-	-	7	5	3	-	6
D.J.McGlew	**14**	1	8	-	5	-	-	-	4	6	4	-	4
C.B.van Ryneveld	**8**	4	4	-	-	-	-	-	2	4	2	-	3
T.L.Goddard	**13**	5	5	-	3	-	-	-	1	2	10	-	4
P.L.van der Merwe	**8**	5	3	-	-	-	-	-	4	1	3	-	4
A Bacher	**4**	4	-	-	-	-	-	-	4	-	-	-	4
K.C.Wessels	**1**	-	-	1	-	-	-	-	-	1	-	-	1
	173	53	102	1	17	-	-	-	38	78	57	-	81

WEST INDIES (22)	Tests as Captain	Opponents A	E	SA	NZ	I	P	SL	Results W	L	D	Tie	Toss Won
R.K.Nunes	**4**	-	4	-	-	-	-	-	-	3	1	-	2
E.L.G.Hoad	**1**	-	1	-	-	-	-	-	-	-	1	-	1
N.Betancourt	**1**	-	1	-	-	-	-	-	-	-	1	-	1
M.P.Fernandes	**1**	-	1	-	-	-	-	-	1	-	-	-	1
G.C.Grant	**12**	5	7	-	-	-	-	-	3	7	2	-	5
R.C.Grant	**3**	-	3	-	-	-	-	-	-	1	2	-	2
G.A.Headley	**1**	-	1	-	-	-	-	-	-	-	1	-	1
J.D.C.Goddard	**22**	4	11	-	2	5	-	-	8	7	7	-	12
J.B.Stollmeyer	**13**	3	5	-	-	5	-	-	3	4	6	-	7
D.S.Atkinson	**7**	3	-	-	4	-	-	-	3	3	1	-	3
F.C.M.Alexander	**18**	-	5	-	-	5	8	-	7	4	7	-	9
F.M.M.Worrell	**15**	5	5	-	-	5	-	-	9	3	2	1	9
G.S.Sobers	**39**	10	13	-	8	8	-	-	9	10	20	-	27
R.B.Kanhai	**13**	5	8	-	-	-	-	-	3	3	7	-	6
C.H.Lloyd	**74**	22	18	-	3	20	1	-	36	12	26	-	35
A.I.Kallicharran	**9**	3	-	-	-	6	-	-	1	2	6	-	4
D.L.Murray	**1**	1	-	-	-	-	-	-	-	-	1	-	1
I.V.A.Richards	**50**	11	19	-	7	8	5	-	27	8	15	-	24
C.G.Greenidge	**1**	-	-	-	-	-	1	-	-	1	-	-	1
D.L.Haynes	**4**	-	1	-	-	-	3	-	1	1	2	-	2
R.B.Richardson	**1**	-	-	1	-	-	-	-	1	-	-	-	-
	291	72	104	1	24	62	28	-	112	70	108	1	152

NEW ZEALAND (21)	Tests as Captain	Opponents A	E	SA	WI	I	P	SL	Results W	L	D	Tie	Toss Won
T.C.Lowry	**7**	7	1	-	-	-	-	-	-	2	5	-	5
M.L.Page	**7**	-	5	2	-	-	-	-	-	3	4	-	4
W.A.Hadlee	**8**	1	7	-	-	-	-	-	-	2	6	-	4
B.Sutcliffe	**4**	-	-	2	2	-	-	-	-	3	1	-	4
W.M.Wallace	**2**	-	-	2	-	-	-	-	-	1	1	-	-
G.O.Rabone	**5**	-	2	3	-	-	-	-	-	4	1	-	2
H.B.Cave	**9**	-	-	-	1	5	3	-	-	5	4	-	5
J.R.Reid	**34**	-	13	8	3	4	6	-	3	18	13	-	17
M.E.Chapple	**1**	-	1	-	-	-	-	-	-	-	1	-	-
B.W.Sinclair	**3**	-	2	-	-	1	-	-	-	1	2	-	3
G.T.Dowling	**19**	-	5	-	5	6	3	-	4	7	8	-	10
B.E.Congdon	**17**	6	5	-	3	-	3	-	1	7	9	-	4
G.M.Turner	**10**	2	-	-	-	6	2	-	1	6	3	-	2
J.M.Parker	**1**	-	-	-	-	-	1	-	-	-	1	-	-
M.G.Burgess	**10**	1	6	-	-	-	3	-	1	6	3	-	4
G.P.Howarth	**30**	5	7	-	7	3	3	5	11	7	12	-	17
J.V.Coney	**15**	6	3	-	3	-	3	-	5	4	6	-	8
J.J.Crowe	**6**	3	2	-	-	-	-	1	-	1	5	-	3
J.G.Wright	**14**	2	4	-	-	6	2	-	3	3	8	-	8
M.D.Crowe	**8**	-	3	-	-	-	3	2	-	5	3	-	4
I.D.S.Smith	**1**	-	-	-	-	-	-	1	-	-	1	-	1
	211	26	72	17	24	28	29	9	29	85	97	-	105

INDIA (25)	Tests as Captain	Opponents A	E	SA	WI	NZ	P	SL	Results W	L	D	Tie	Toss Won
C.K.Nayudu	**4**	-	4	-	-	-	-	-	-	3	1	-	1
Maharajkumar of Vizianagram	**3**	-	3	-	-	-	-	-	-	2	1	-	1
Nawab of Pataudi, sr	**3**	-	3	-	-	-	-	-	-	1	2	-	3
N.B.Amarnath	**15**	5	-	-	5	-	5	-	2	6	7	-	4
V.S.Hazare	**14**	-	9	-	5	-	-	-	1	5	8	-	8
M.H.Mankad	**6**	-	-	-	1	-	5	-	-	1	5	-	1
Ghulam Ahmed	**3**	-	-	-	2	1	-	-	-	2	1	-	1
P.R.Umrigar	**8**	3	-	-	1	4	-	-	2	2	4	-	6
H.R.Adhikari	**1**	-	-	1	-	-	-	-	-	-	1	-	1
D.K.Gaekwad	**4**	-	4	-	-	-	-	-	-	4	-	-	2
Pankaj Roy	**1**	-	1	-	-	-	-	-	-	1	-	-	1
G.S.Ramchand	**5**	5	-	-	-	-	-	-	1	2	2	-	4
N.J.Contractor	**12**	-	5	-	2	-	5	-	2	2	8	-	7
Nawab of Pataudi, jr	**40**	11	8	-	10	1	-	-	9	19	12	-	20
C.G.Borde	**1**	1	-	-	-	-	-	-	-	1	-	-	-
A.L.Wadekar	**16**	-	11	-	5	-	-	-	4	4	8	-	7
S.Venkataraghavan	**5**	-	4	-	1	-	-	-	-	2	3	-	2
S.M.Gavaskar	**47**	9	14	-	6	4	13	1	9	8	30	-	22
B.S.Bedi	**22**	5	5	-	4	5	3	-	6	11	5	-	13
G.R.Viswanath	**2**	-	1	-	-	-	1	-	-	1	1	-	2
Kapil Dev	**34**	6	3	-	11	-	8	6	4	7	22	1	15
D.B.Vengsarkar	**10**	-	-	-	7	3	-	-	2	5	3	-	4
R.J.Shastri	**1**	-	-	-	1	-	-	-	1	-	-	-	1
K.Srikkanth	**4**	-	-	-	-	-	4	-	-	-	4	-	1
M.Azharuddin	**12**	5	3	-	-	3	-	1	1	6	5	-	8
	273	50	78	-	62	31	44	8	44	95	133	1	135

PAKISTAN (14)	Tests as Captain	Opponents A	E	SA	WI	NZ	I	SL	Results W	L	D	Tie	Toss Won
A.H.Kardar	**23**	1	4	-	5	3	10	-	6	6	11	-	10
Fazal Mahmood	**10**	2	-	-	3	-	5	-	2	2	6	-	6
Imtiaz Ahmed	**4**	1	3	-	-	-	-	-	-	2	2	-	4
Javed Burki	**5**	-	5	-	-	-	-	-	-	4	1	-	3
Hanif Mohammad	**11**	2	3	-	-	6	-	-	2	2	7	-	6
Saeed Ahmed	**3**	-	3	-	-	-	-	-	-	-	3	-	1
Intikhab Alam	**17**	3	6	-	2	6	-	-	1	5	11	-	12
Majid Khan	**3**	-	3	-	-	-	-	-	-	-	3	-	1
Mushtaq Mohammad	**19**	5	-	-	5	6	3	-	8	4	7	-	10
Wasim Bari	**6**	-	6	-	-	-	-	-	-	2	4	-	4
Asif Iqbal	**6**	-	-	-	-	-	6	-	-	2	4	-	3
Javed Miandad	**33**	9	8	-	4	6	-	6	13	6	14	-	12
Imran Khan	**48**	8	8	-	9	2	15	6	14	8	26	-	26
Zaheer Abbas	**14**	3	3	-	-	3	5	-	3	1	10	-	6
	202	34	52	-	28	32	44	12	49	44	109	-	104

SRI LANKA (6)	Tests as Captain	Opponents A	E	SA	WI	NZ	I	P	Results W	L	D	Tie	Toss Won
B.Warnapura	**4**	1	1	-	-	-	1	2	-	3	1	-	2
L.R.D.Mendis	**19**	1	1	-	-	4	6	7	2	8	9	-	10
D.S.De Silva	**2**	-	-	-	-	2	-	-	-	2	-	-	1
R.S.Madugalle	**2**	1	1	-	-	-	-	-	-	2	-	-	-
A.Ranatunga	**9**	5	-	-	-	3	1	-	-	3	6	-	6
P.A.de Silva	**4**	-	1	-	-	-	-	3	-	2	2	-	3
	40	7	4	-	-	9	8	12	2	20	18	-	21

MOST CONSECUTIVE MATCHES AS CAPTAIN

			From	To
Australia	70	A.R.Border	1984-85	# 1992-93
England	35	P.B.H.May	1955	1959
South Africa	18	H.W.Taylor	1913-14	1924
West Indies	39	G.S.Sobers	1964-65	1971-72
New Zealand	34	J.R.Reid	1955-56	1965
India	22	B.S.Bedi	1975-76	1978-79
	22	S.M.Gavaskar	1980-81	1982-83
Pakistan	23	A.H.Kardar	1952-53	1957-58
Sri Lanka	18	L.R.D.Mendis	1982-83	1986-87

 # to date.

In addition to those listed above, the following had unbroken captaincy runs of 20 or more matches

29	C.H.Lloyd (WI)
25	W.M.Woodfull (A), R.Illingworth (E), D.I.Gower (E)
23	M.W.Gatting (E)
21	Nawab of Pataudi, jr (I)
20	M.J.K.Smith (E), W.M.Lawry (A), J.M.Brearley (E), Kapil Dev (I)

WINNING ALL FIVE TOSSES IN A SERIES

Captains				Venue	
Hon F.S.Jackson	England	v	Australia	England	1905
M.A.Noble	Australia	v	England	England	1909
H.G.Deane	South Africa	v	England	South Africa	1927-28
J.D.C.Goddard	West Indies	v	India	India	1948-49
A.L.Hassett	Australia	v	England	England	1953
P.B.H.May (3))	England	v	West Indies	West Indies	1959-60
M.C.Cowdrey (2))					

M.C.Cowdrey	England	v	South Africa	England	1960
Nawab of Pataudi , jr	India	v	England	India	1963-64
G.S.Sobers	West Indies	v	England	England	1966
G.S.Sobers	West Indies	v	New Zealand	West Indies	1971-72
C.H.Lloyd	West Indies	v	India	West Indies	1982-83

The following Australian captains won five tosses during six-match series in Australia: I.M.Chappell v England 1974-75; G.S.Chappell v West Indies 1975-76; G.N.Yallop v England 1978-79.
K.W.R.Fletcher (England) won five successive tosses during the six-match series in India in 1981-82.
M.C.Cowdrey won the toss for England in nine consecutive Tests from 1959-60 to 1961.

CAPTAINS WHO SENT THE OPPOSITION IN

(§ In first match as captain. # In last Test as captain. ¶ In only Test as captain.)

AUSTRALIA	Opponents	Result		
P.S.McDonnell §	England	Lost by 13 runs	Sydney	1886-87
P.S.McDonnell	England	Lost by 126 runs	Sydney	1887-88
G.Giffen §	England	Lost by 94 runs	Melbourne	1894-95
M.A.Noble	England	Won by 9 wkts	Lord's	1909
A.L.Hassett	West Indies	Won by 7 wkts	Sydney	1951-52
A.L.Hassett	England	Drawn	Leeds	1953
A.R.Morris #	England	Lost by 38 runs	Sydney	1954-55
I.W.Johnson	England	Drawn	Sydney	1954-55
R.Benaud	England	Won by 9 wkts	Melbourne	1958-59
R.Benaud	Pakistan	Won by 8 wkts	Dacca	1959-60
R.Benaud	West Indies	Won by 2 wkts	Melbourne	1960-61
R.B.Simpson §	South Africa	Won by 8 wkts	Melbourne	1963-64
R.B.Simpson	Pakistan	Drawn	Melbourne	1964-65
R.B.Simpson	West Indies	Drawn	Port-of-Spain	1964-65
R.B.Simpson	South Africa	Lost by 8 wkts	Durban[2]	1966-67
W.M.Lawry	West Indies	Won by Innings + 30 runs	Melbourne	1968-69
W.M.Lawry	India	Won by 10 wkts	Calcutta	1969-70
W.M.Lawry	England	Drawn	Perth	1970-71
I.M.Chappell §	England	Lost by 62 runs	Sydney	1970-71
I.M.Chappell	New Zealand	Drawn	Sydney	1973-74
I.M.Chappell	England	Won by 9 wkts	Perth	1974-75
I.M.Chappell	England	Drawn	Melbourne	1974-75
G.S.Chappell	West Indies	Won by 8 wkts	Melbourne	1975-76
G.S.Chappell	West Indies	Won by 7 wkts	Sydney	1975-76
G.S.Chappell	New Zealand	Won by 10 wkts	Auckland	1976-77
G.S.Chappell	England	Drawn	The Oval	1977
R.B.Simpson	West Indies	Lost by 198 runs	Port-of-Spain	1977-78
G.N.Yallop	England	Lost by 166 runs	Perth	1978-79
G.N.Yallop	England	Lost by 205 runs	Adelaide	1978-79
G.N.Yallop #	Pakistan	Lost by 71 runs	Melbourne	1978-79
K.J.Hughes §	Pakistan	Won by 7 wkts	Perth	1978-79
G.S.Chappell	England	Won by 6 wkts	Sydney	1979-80
G.S.Chappell	West Indies	Lost by 408 runs	Adelaide	1979-80
G.S.Chappell	New Zealand	Won by 10 wkts	Brisbane[2]	1980-81
G.S.Chappell	New Zealand	Won by 8 wkts	Perth	1980-81
G.S.Chappell	India	Lost by 59 runs	Melbourne	1980-81
K.J.Hughes	England	Won by 4 wkts	Nottingham	1981
K.J.Hughes	England	Drawn	Lord's	1981
G.S.Chappell	Pakistan	Won by 10 wkts	Brisbane[2]	1981-82
G.S.Chappell	New Zealand	Drawn	Wellington	1981-82
G.S.Chappell	England	Drawn	Perth	1982-83
G.S.Chappell	England	Won by 7 wkts	Brisbane[2]	1982-83
G.S.Chappell	England	Lost by 3 runs	Melbourne	1982-83
K.J.Hughes	Pakistan	Won by 10 wkts	Sydney	1983-84
K.J.Hughes	West Indies	Lost by Innings + 112 runs	Perth	1984-85
A.R.Border	West Indies	Drawn	Melbourne	1984-85

A.R.Border	England	Won by 4 wkts	Lord's	1985
A.R.Border	New Zealand	Won by 4 wkts	Sydney	1985-86
A.R.Border	England	Lost by 7 wkts	Brisbane[2]	1986-87
A.R.Border	New Zealand	Won by 9 wkts	Brisbane[2]	1987-88
A.R.Border	New Zealand	Drawn	Melbourne	1987-88
A.R.Border	West Indies	Lost by 169 runs	Perth	1988-89
A.R.Border	West Indies	Lost by 285 runs	Melbourne	1988-89
A.R.Border	Pakistan	Drawn	Sydney	1989-90
A.R.Border	England	Won by 10 wkts	Brisbane[2]	1990-91
A.R.Border	West Indies	Lost by 343 runs	Bridgetown	1990-91
A.R.Border	India	Won by 10 wkts	Brisbane[2]	1991-92

ENGLAND	Opponents	Result		
A.E.Stoddart	Australia	Lost by Innings + 147 runs	Sydney	1894-95
Lord Hawke	South Africa	Won by Innings + 33 runs	Cape Town	1895-96
A.C.MacLaren	Australia	Lost by 229 runs	Melbourne	1901-02
A.O.Jones #	Australia	Lost by 49 runs	Sydney	1907-08
J.W.H.T.Douglas	Australia	Won by Innings + 225 runs	Melbourne	1911-12
A.W.Carr	Australia	Drawn	Leeds	1926
A.P.F.Chapman	South Africa	Lost by 28 runs	Johannesburg[1]	1930-31
A.P.F.Chapman #	South Africa	Drawn	Durban[2]	1930-31
R.E.S.Wyatt	West Indies	Won by 4 wkts	Bridgetown	1934-35
R.E.S.Wyatt	West Indies	Lost by 217 runs	Port-of-Spain	1934-35
R.E.S.Wyatt #	South Africa	Drawn	The Oval	1935
G.O.B.Allen §	India	Won by 9 wkts	Lord's	1936
W.R.Hammond #	New Zealand	Drawn	Christchurch	1946-47
F.R.Brown §	New Zealand	Drawn	Manchester	1949
L.Hutton	Pakistan	Drawn	Lord's	1954
L.Hutton	Australia	Lost by Innings + 154 runs	Brisbane[2]	1954-55
L.Hutton #	New Zealand	Won by 8 wkts	Dunedin	1954-55
P.B.H.May	Australia	Lost by 10 wkts	Adelaide	1958-59
E.R.Dexter	New Zealand	Won by Innings + 47 runs	Wellington	1962-63
E.R.Dexter	Australia	Drawn	Lord's	1964
M.J.K.Smith	South Africa	Drawn	Johannesburg[3]	1964-65
M.J.K.Smith	South Africa	Drawn	The Oval	1965
D.B.Close #	Pakistan	Won by 8 wkts	The Oval	1967
R.Illingworth	Australia	Drawn	Nottingham	1972
M.H.Denness	Australia	Lost by 163 runs	Adelaide	1974-75
M.H.Denness	New Zealand	Drawn	Christchurch	1974-75
M.H.Denness #	Australia	Lost by Innings + 85 runs	Birmingham	1975
A.W.Greig #	Australia	Lost by 45 runs	Melbourne	1976-77
G.Boycott	New Zealand	Lost by 72 runs	Wellington	1977-78
J.M.Brearley	Australia	Lost by 138 runs	Perth	1979-80
I.T.Botham	West Indies	Lost by Innings + 79 runs	Port-of-Spain	1980-81
I.T.Botham	West Indies	Lost by 298 runs	Bridgetown	1980-81
J.M.Brearley #	Australia	Drawn	The Oval	1981
K.W.R.Fletcher	India	Drawn	Madras[1]	1981-82
R.G.D.Willis	Australia	Lost by 8 wkts	Adelaide	1982-83
D.I.Gower	Sri Lanka	Drawn	Lord's	1984
D.I.Gower	Australia	Drawn	Manchester	1985
D.I.Gower	Australia	Won by Innings + 118 runs	Birmingham	1985
D.I.Gower	West Indies	Lost by Innings + 30 runs	Bridgetown	1985-86
D.I.Gower	West Indies	Lost by 240 runs	St John's	1985-86
M.W.Gatting	New Zealand	Drawn	The Oval	1986
M.W.Gatting	Australia	Won by Innings + 14 runs	Melbourne	1986-87
M.W.Gatting	Pakistan	Drawn	Birmingham	1987
M.W.Gatting	New Zealand	Drawn	Auckland	1987-88
G.A.Gooch	Sri Lanka	Won by 7 wkts	Lord's	1988
D.I.Gower	Australia	Lost by 210 runs	Leeds	1989
G.A.Gooch	West Indies	Drawn	Port-of-Spain	1989-90

A.J.Lamb §	West Indies	Lost by 164 runs	Bridgetown	1989-90
G.A.Gooch	Pakistan	Drawn	Birmingham	1992

SOUTH AFRICA	Opponents	Result		
E.A.Halliwell §	England	Lost by 288 runs	Port Elizabeth	1895-96
P.W.Sherwell	Australia	Lost by 530 runs	Melbourne	1910-11
P.W.Sherwell #	Australia	Lost by 7 wkts	Sydney	1910-11
H.W.Taylor	England	Lost by Innings + 18 runs	Birmingham	1924
H.G.Deane	England	Lost by 87 runs	Cape Town	1927-28
H.G.Deane	England	Won by 4 wkts	Johannesburg[1]	1927-28
H.G.Deane	England	Won by 8 wkts	Durban[2]	1927-28
H.G Deane	England	Drawn	The Oval	1929
T.L.Goddard	Australia	Drawn	Sydney	1963-64
P.L.van der Merwe #	Australia	Won by 7 wkts	Port Elizabeth	1966-67
K.C.Wessels §	West Indies	Lost by 52 runs	Bridgetown	1991-92

WEST INDIES	Opponents	Result		
R.S.Grant	England	Drawn	Manchester	1939
F.C.M.Alexander	Pakistan	Lost by 41 runs	Dacca	1958-59
F.M.M.Worrell	India	Won by Innings + 30 runs	Bridgetown	1961-62
G.S.Sobers	Australia	Lost by 382 runs	Sydney	1968-69
G.S.Sobers	New Zealand	Won by 5 wkts	Auckland	1968-69
G.S.Sobers	India	Drawn	Kingston	1970-71
G.S.Sobers	New Zealand	Drawn	Port-of-Spain	1971-72
R.B.Kanhai	England	Won by 7 wkts	Port-of-Spain	1973-74
R.B.Kanhai	England	Drawn	Bridgetown	1973-74
C.H.Lloyd	Pakistan	Drawn	Lahore[2]	1974-75
C.H.Lloyd	India	Won by 10 wkts	Kingston	1975-76
C.H.Lloyd	Pakistan	Drawn	Georgetown	1976-77
C.H.Lloyd	Pakistan	Lost by 266 runs	Port-of-Spain	1976-77
C H Lloyd	Australia	Won by Innings + 106 runs	Port-of-Spain	1977-78
C H Lloyd	Australia	Won by 9 wkts	Bridgetown	1977-78
A.I.Kallicharran	India	Drawn	Bombay[3]	1978-79
D.L.Murray ¶	Australia	Drawn	Brisbane[2]	1979-80
C.H.Lloyd	England	Drawn	Manchester	1980
I V A.Richards §	England	Drawn	Kingston	1980
C H Lloyd	Australia	Won by 5 wkts	Adelaide	1981-82
C.H.Lloyd	India	Won by 4 wkts	Kingston	1982-83
C.H.Lloyd	India	Drawn	Port-of-Spain	1982-83
C H Lloyd	India	Won by 10 wkts	Bridgetown	1982-83
C H Lloyd	India	Drawn	St John's	1982-83
I.V.A.Richards	Australia	Drawn	Port-of-Spain	1983-84
C.H.Lloyd	Australia	Won by 10 wkts	Bridgetown	1983-84
C.H.Lloyd	Australia	Won by 10 wkts	Kingston	1983-84
C.H.Lloyd	England	Won by 9 wkts	Lord's	1984
C.H.Lloyd	Australia	Won by 8 wkts	Brisbane[2]	1984-85
I.V.A.Richards	New Zealand	Won by 10 wkts	Bridgetown	1984-85
I.V.A.Richards	England	Won by 7 wkts	Port-of-Spain	1985-86
I.V.A.Richards	England	Won by 10 wkts	Port-of-Spain	1985-86
I.V.A.Richards	New Zealand	Drawn	Wellington	1986-87
I.V.A.Richards	India	Drawn	Bombay[3]	1987-88
I.V.A.Richards	Pakistan	Won by 2 wkts	Bridgetown	1987-88
I.V.A.Richards	England	Won by 10 wkts	Leeds	1988
I.V.A.Richards	India	Won by 8 wkts	Bridgetown	1988-89
I.V.A.Richards	India	Won by 7 wkts	Kingston	1988-89
I.V.A.Richards	Australia	Drawn	Port-of-Spain	1990-91
I.V.A.Richards	England	Lost by 115 runs	Leeds	1991
I.V.A.Richards	England	Won by 7 wkts	Birmingham	1991

NEW ZEALAND	Opponents	Result		
T.C.Lowry	England	Drawn	Auckland	1929-30
T.C.Lowry #	England	Drawn	Manchester	1931
B.Sutcliffe	West Indies	Drawn	Auckland	1951-52
B.Sutcliffe	South Africa	Lost by 9 wkts	Johannesburg[2]	1953-54
J.R.Reid	South Africa	Drawn	Auckland	1963-64
J.R.Reid	Pakistan	Drawn	Lahore[2]	1964-65
G.T.Dowling	India	Lost by 272 runs	Auckland	1967-68
G.T.Dowling	West Indies	Won by 6 wkts	Wellington	1968-69
G.T.Dowling	England	Drawn	Auckland	1970-71
B.E.Congdon	England	Drawn	Lord's	1973
B.E.Congdon	Australia	Won by 5 wkts	Christchurch	1973-74
B.E.Congdon	Australia	Lost by 297 runs	Auckland	1973-74
G.M.Turner	Australia	Drawn	Christchurch	1976-77
M.G.Burgess	Pakistan	Lost by 128 runs	Christchurch	1978-79
G.P.Howarth	West Indies	Drawn	Christchurch	1979-80
G.P.Howarth	West Indies	Drawn	Auckland	1979-80
G.P.Howarth	Australia	Drawn	Melbourne	1980-81
G.P.Howarth	Australia	Won by 5 wkts	Auckland	1981-82
G.P.Howarth	Australia	Lost by 8 wkts	Christchurch	1981-82
G.P.Howarth	Sri Lanka	Won by 6 wkts	Wellington	1982-83
G.P.Howarth	England	Won by 5 wkts	Leeds	1983
G.P Howarth	England	Lost by 127 runs	Lord s	1983
G.P.Howarth	Sri Lanka	Drawn	Colombo (SSC)	1983-84
G.P.Howarth	Pakistan	Won by Innings + 99 runs	Auckland	1984-85
G.P.Howarth	Pakistan	Won by 2 wkts	Dunedin	1984-85
G.P.Howarth #	West Indies	Lost by 10 wkts	Kingston	1984-85
J.V.Coney §	Australia	Won by Innings + 41 runs	Brisbane[2]	1985-86
J.V.Coney	Australia	Won by 6 wkts	Perth	1985-86
J.V.Coney	Australia	Drawn	Wellington	1985-86
J.V.Coney	Australia	Drawn	Christchurch	1985-86
J.V.Coney	England	Won by 8 wkts	Nottingham	1986
J.V.Coney #	West Indies	Won by 5 wkts	Christchurch	1986-87
J.J.Crowe §	Sri Lanka	Drawn	Colombo (CCC)	1986-87
J.J.Crowe	England	Drawn	Christchurch	1987-88
J.G.Wright	Australia	Drawn	Perth	1989-90
J.G.Wright	England	Drawn	Lord's	1990
J.G.Wright #	England	Lost by 114 runs	Birmingham	1990
M.D.Crowe	Pakistan	Lost by 65 runs	Faisalabad	1990-91
I.D.S.Smith ¶	Sri Lanka	Drawn	Auckland	1990-91
M.D.Crowe	England	Lost by Innings + 4 runs	Christchurch	1991-92
M.D.Crowe	England	Lost by 168 runs	Auckland	1991-92

INDIA	Opponents	Result		
Nawab of Pataudi, sr	England	Drawn	Manchester	1946
N.B.Amarnath	Pakistan	Drawn	Calcutta	1952-53
P.R.Umrigar	Australia	Lost by 94 runs	Calcutta	1956-57
Nawab of Pataudi, jr	England	Drawn	Kanpur	1963-64
Nawab of Pataudi, jr	Australia	Drawn	Calcutta	1964-65
Nawab of Pataudi, jr	Australia	Lost by 39 runs	Brisbane[2]	1967-68
Nawab of Pataudi, jr	Australia	Lost by 144 runs	Sydney	1967-68
Nawab of Pataudi, jr	New Zealand	Lost by 6 wkts	Christchurch	1967-68
A.L.Wadekar	West Indies	Drawn	Bridgetown	1970-71
Nawab of Pataudi, jr	West Indies	Lost by 267 runs	Bangalore	1974-75
B.S.Bedi	West Indies	Drawn	Port-of-Spain	1975-76
S.M.Gavaskar	Australia	Drawn	Adelaide	1980-81
S.M.Gavaskar	New Zealand	Lost by 62 runs	Wellington	1980-81
S.M.Gavaskar	Pakistan	Drawn	Lahore[2] (1st)	1982-83
S.M Gavaskar	Pakistan	Drawn	Lahore[2] (5th)	1982-83
Kapil Dev	Pakistan	Drawn	Jullundur	1983-84

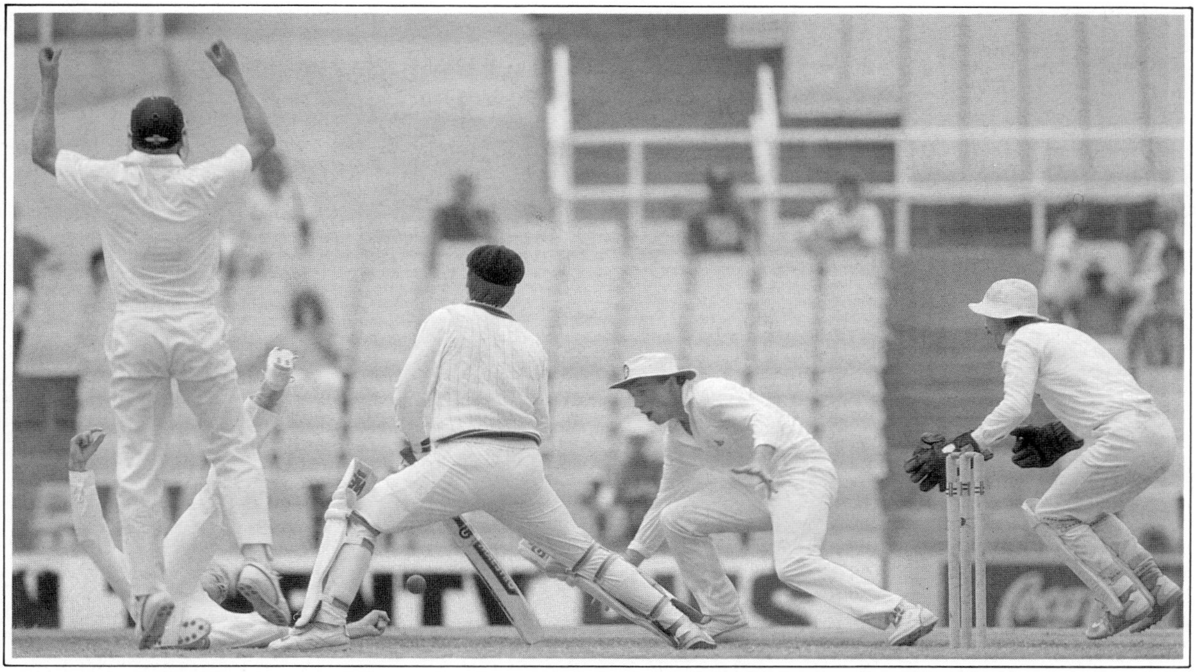

Australian batsman Steve Waugh grimly defending against the England spinners at Sydney during the 1990-91 series. *(Courtesy PBL Marketing.)*

David Boon (Australia) is bowled by the England spinner Phil Tufnell for 121 at the Adelaide Oval during the 1990-91 Ashes series. *(Courtesy PBL Marketing.)*

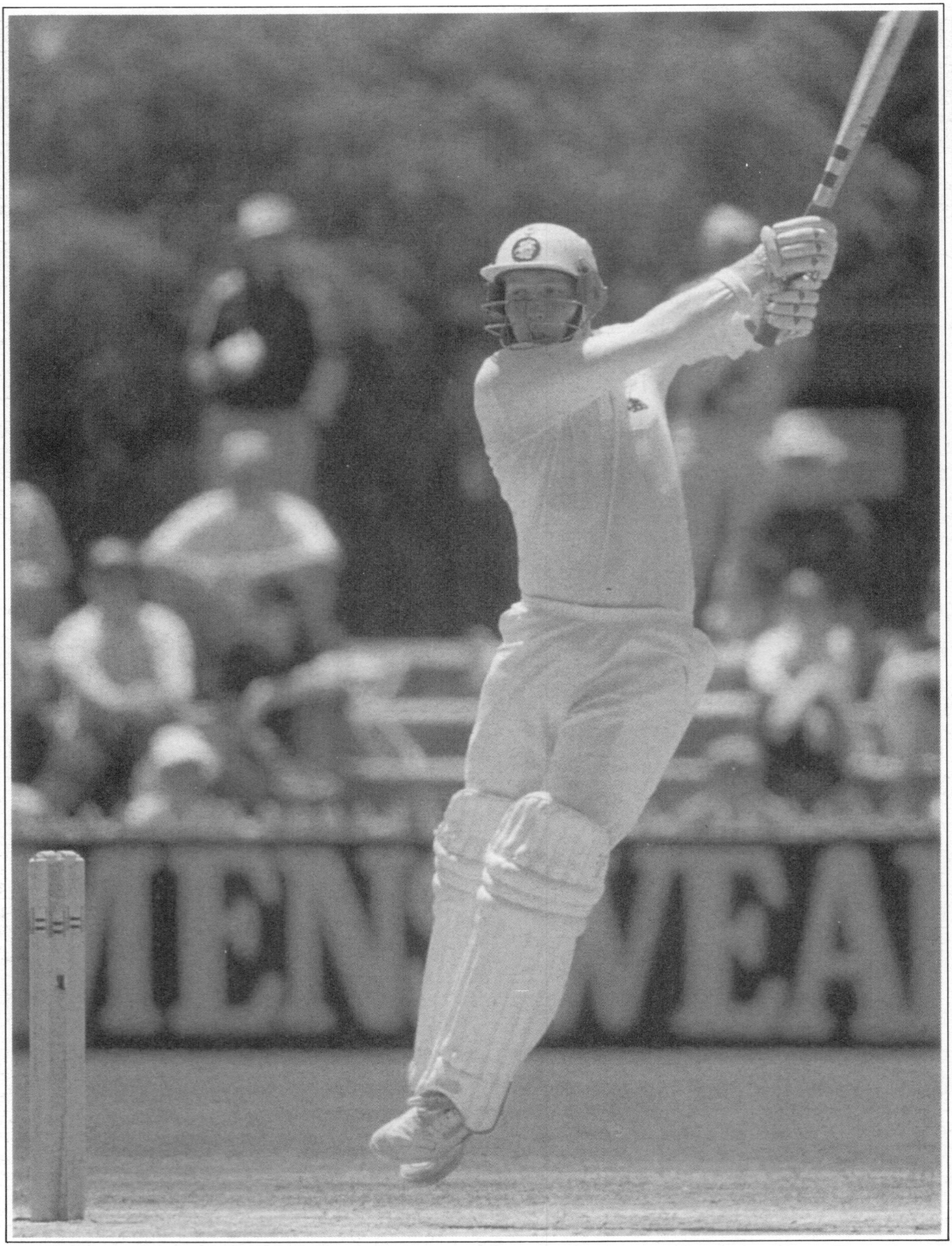

England opening batsman Mike Atherton attempts to square cut the new ball during the Test match against Australia played at Adelaide in the 1990-91 series. *(Courtesy PBL Marketing.)*

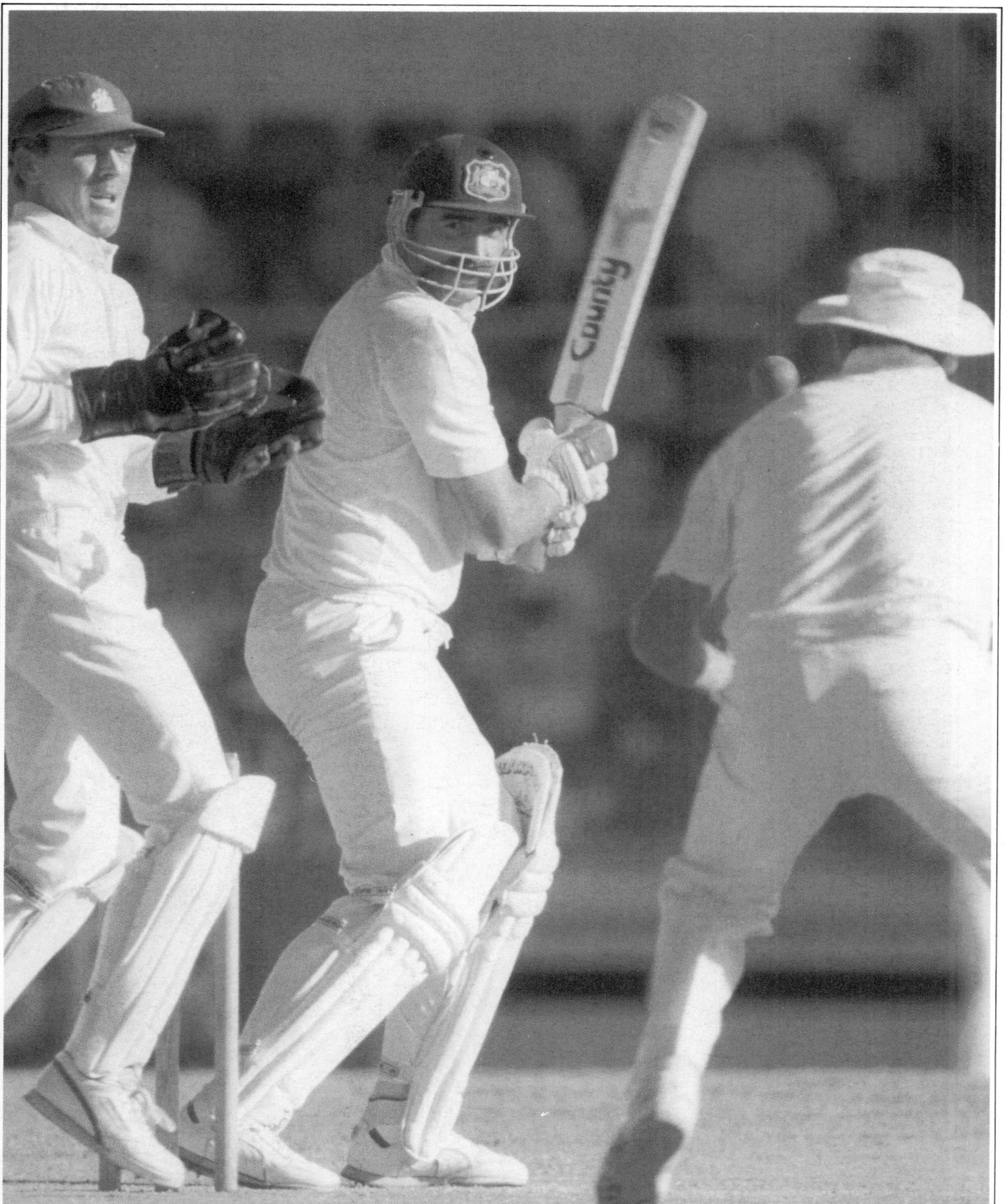

Australia's high-profile fast bowler Merv Hughes is out for a duck after being caught by England captain Graham Gooch in the fifth Test played at Perth in the 1990-91 Ashes series. *(Courtesy PBL Marketing.)*

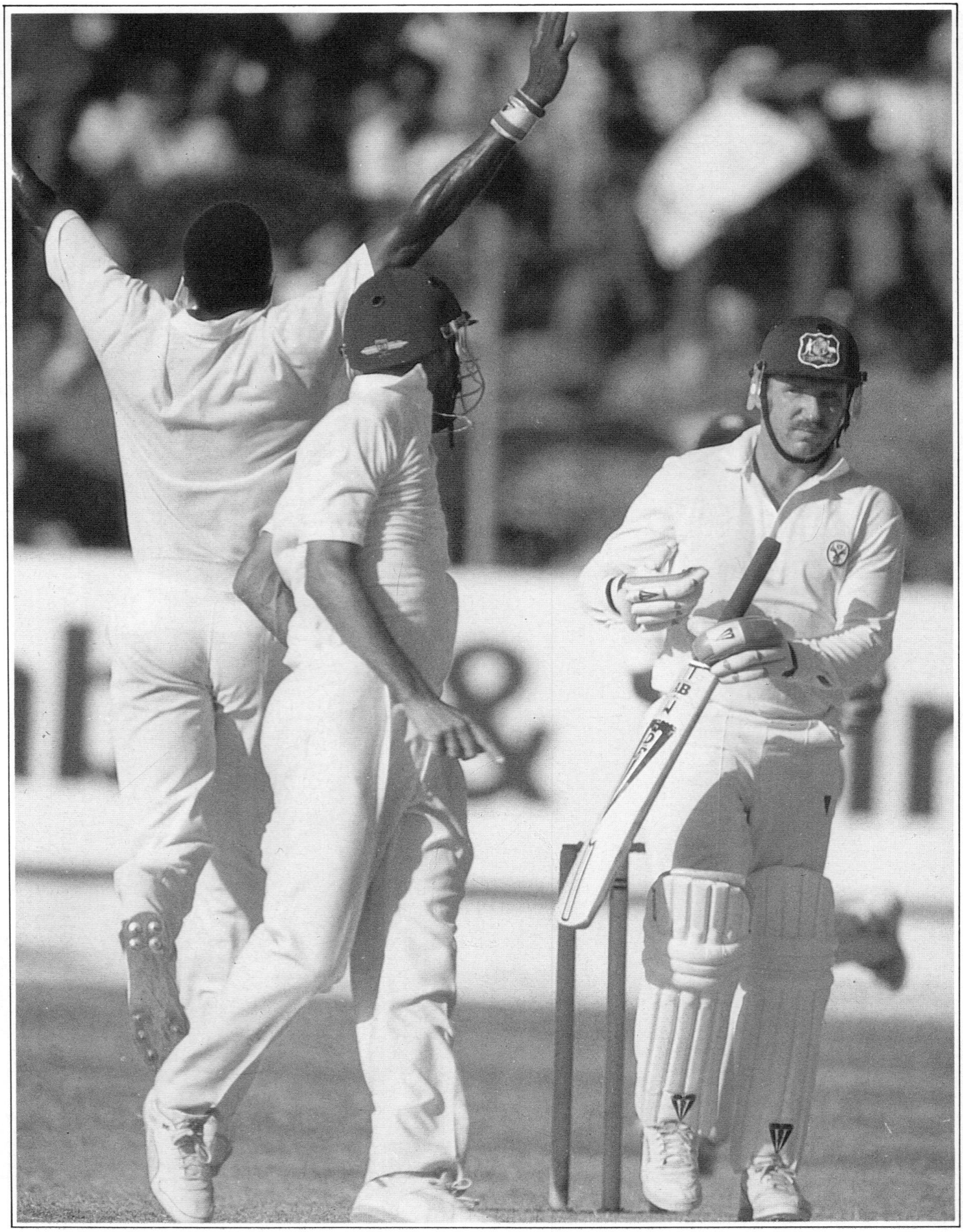

Allan Border (Australia) is sent on his way after edging Curtly Ambrose to the wicketkeeper Jeff Dujon in the first Test against the West Indies played at Sabina Park in 1991.

(Courtesy Australian Picture Library/All Sport/Simon Bruty.)

Kapil Dev	West Indies	Lost by 138 runs	Ahmedabad	1983-84
Kapil Dev	Australia	Drawn	Melbourne	1985-86
Kapil Dev	England	Won by 5 wkts	Lord's	1986
D.B.Vengsarkar	West Indies	Drawn	Georgetown	1988-89
D.B.Vengsarkar	West Indies	Lost by 217 runs	Port-of-Spain	1988-89
K.Srikkanth §	Pakistan	Drawn	Karachi	1989-90
M.Azharuddin	New Zealand	Drawn	Auckland	1990-91
M.Azharuddin	England	Lost by 247 runs	Lord's	1990
M.Azharuddin	Australia	Drawn	Sydney	1991-92
M.Azharuddin	Australia	Lost by 38 runs	Adelaide	1991-92

PAKISTAN	Opponents	Result		
Fazal Mahmood §	West Indies	Won by 10 wkts	Karachi	1958-59
Javed Burki	England	Lost by Innings + 117 runs	Leeds	1962
Javed Burki	England	Drawn	Nottingham	1962
Hanif Mohammad	New Zealand	Drawn	Wellington	1964-65
Hanif Mohammad	New Zealand	Won by Innings + 64 runs	Rawalpindi	1964-65
Intikhab Alam	Australia	Lost by 52 runs	Sydney	1972-73
Mushtaq Mohammad	India	Won by 8 wkts	Lahore²	1978-79
Mushtaq Mohammad	New Zealand	Drawn	Auckland	1978-79
Javed Miandad	Australia	Lost by 286 runs	Perth	1981-82
Javed Miandad	Sri Lanka	Won by Innings + 102 runs	Lahore²	1981-82
Imran Khan	Australia	Won by 9 wkts	Lahore²	1982-83
Imran Khan	India	Won by Innings + 86 runs	Karachi	1982-83
Imran Khan	India	Won by 10 wkts	Faisalabad	1982-83
Zaheer Abbas	Australia	Lost by Innings + 9 runs	Perth	1983-84
Zaheer Abbas	England	Drawn	Lahore²	1983-84
Javed Miandad	Sri Lanka	Won by 8 wkts	Sialkot	1985-86
Imran Khan	India	Drawn	Calcutta	1986-87
Imran Khan	England	Drawn	Manchester	1987
Imran Khan	West Indies	Drawn	Port-of-Spain	1987-88
Imran Khan	New Zealand	Drawn	Wellington	1988-89
Imran Khan	India	Drawn	Faisalabad	1989-90
Imran Khan	India	Drawn	Lahore²	1989-90
Imran Khan	India	Drawn	Sialkot	1989-90
Imran Khan	Australia	Lost by 92 runs	Melbourne	1989-90
Javed Miandad	New Zealand	Won by Innings + 43 runs	Faisalabad	1990-91
Imran Khan	Sri Lanka	Won by 3 wkts	Faisalabad	1991-92

SRI LANKA	Opponents	Result		
D.S.de Silva §	New Zealand	Lost by Innings + 25 runs	Christchurch	1982-83
L.R.D.Mendis	Pakistan	Won by 8 wkts	Colombo (CCC)	1985-86
A.Ranatunga §	Australia	Drawn	Brisbane²	1989-90
A.Ranatunga	Australia	Lost by 173 runs	Hobart	1989-90
A.Ranatunga	New Zealand	Drawn	Wellington	1990-91
A.Ranatunga	New Zealand	Drawn	Hamilton	1990-91
P.A.de Silva	Pakistan	Drawn	Gujranwala	1991-92
A.Ranatunga	Australia	Lost by 16 runs	Colombo (SSC)	1992-93
A.Ranatunga	Australia	Drawn	Colombo (KS)	1992-93

SUMMARY	Captains	Instances	W	L	D
Australia	14	57	25	18	14
England	28	49	10	19	20
South Africa	7	11	3	6	2
West Indies	9	42	21	4	17
New Zealand	12	41	11	11	19
India	11	26	1	10	15
Pakistan	8	26	10	5	11
Sri Lanka	4	9	1	3	5
TOTAL	93	261	82	76	103

HIGHEST INDIVIDUAL INNINGS BY CAPTAINS

333	G.A.Gooch	England	v	India	Lord's	1990
311	R.B.Simpson	Australia	v	England	Manchester	1964
299	M.D.Crowe	New Zealand	v	Sri Lanka	Wellington	1990-91
285*	P.B.H.May	England	v	West Indies	Birmingham	1957
270	D.G.Bradman	Australia	v	England	Melbourne	1936-37
242*	C.H.Lloyd	West Indies	v	India	Bombay[3]	1974-75
240	W.R.Hammond	England	v	Australia	Lord's	1938
239	G.T.Dowling	New Zealand	v	India	Christchurch	1967-68
235	G.S.Chappell	Australia	v	Pakistan	Faisalabad	1979-80

CENTURY IN EACH INNINGS BY A CAPTAIN

189	104*	A.Melville	South Africa	v	England	Nottingham	1947
132	127*	D.G.Bradman	Australia	v	India	Melbourne	1947-48
153	115	R.B.Simpson	Australia	v	Pakistan	Karachi	1964-65
145	121	I.M.Chappell	Australia	v	New Zealand	Wellington	1973-74
123	109*	G.S.Chappell	Australia	v	West Indies	Brisbane[2]	1975-76
107	182*	S.M.Gavaskar	India	v	West Indies	Calcutta	1978-79
140	114*	A.R.Border	Australia	v	New Zealand	Christchurch	1985-86
333	123	G.A.Gooch	England	v	India	Lord's	1990

CENTURY AND A NINETY IN SAME MATCH BY A CAPTAIN

104	93	Hanif Mohammad	Pakistan	v	Australia	Melbourne	1964-65
152	95*	G.S.Sobers	West Indies	v	England	Georgetown	1967-68
119	94	L.R.D.Mendis	Sri Lanka	v	England	Lord's	1984

CENTURIES BY RIVAL CAPTAINS IN THE SAME TEST

H.W.Taylor	South Africa	109	J.W.H.T.Douglas	England	119	Durban[2]	1913-14
A.P.F.Chapman	England	121	W.M.Woodfull	Australia	155	Lord's	1930
W.R.Hammond	England	240	D.G.Bradman	Australia	102*	Lord's	1938
A.Melville	South Africa	103	W.R.Hammond	England	140	Durban[2]	1938-39
L.Hutton	England	145	A.L.Hassett	Australia	104	Lord's	1953
P.B.H.May	England	117	D.J.McGlew	South Africa	104*	Manchester	1955
D.J.McGlew	South Africa	120	J.R.Reid	New Zealand	142	Johannesburg[1]	1961-62
E.R.Dexter	England	174	R.B.Simpson	Australia	311	Manchester	1964
G.S.Sobers	West Indies	113*	M.C.Cowdrey	England	101	Kingston	1967-68
W.M.Lawry	Australia	151	G.S.Sobers	West Indies	113	Sydney	1968-69
G.S.Sobers	West Indies	142	B.E.Congdon	New Zealand	126	Bridgetown	1971-72
R.B.Kanhai	West Indies	105	I.M.Chappell	Australia	106*	Bridgetown	1972-73
B.E.Congdon	New Zealand	132	I.M.Chappell	Australia	145 + 121	Wellington	1973-74
S.M.Gavaskar	India	205	A.I.Kallicharran	West Indies	187	Bombay[3]	1978-79
Javed Miandad	Pakistan	106*	G.S.Chappell	Australia	235	Faisalabad	1979-80
Imran Khan	Pakistan	117	S.M.Gavaskar	India	127*	Faisalabad	1982-83
C.H.Lloyd	West Indies	143	Kapil Dev	India	100*	Port-of-Spain	1982-83
Kapil Dev	India	119	A.R.Border	Australia	106	Madras[1]	1986-87
M.W.Gatting	England	150*	Imran Khan	Pakistan	118	The Oval	1987
D.B.Vengsarkar	India	102	I.V.A.Richards	West Indies	146	Delhi	1987-88
Javed Miandad	Pakistan	107	A.R.Border	Australia	113*	Faisalabad	1988-89
G.A.Gooch	England	333 + 123	M.Azharuddin	India	121	Lord's	1990
G.A.Gooch	England	116	M.Azharuddin	India	179	Manchester	1990

SEVEN WICKETS IN AN INNINGS BY A CAPTAIN

9-83	Kapil Dev	India	v	West Indies	Ahmedabad	1983-84
8-60	Imran Khan	Pakistan	v	India	Karachi	1982-83
8-106	Kapil Dev	India	v	Australia	Adelaide	1985-86
7-40	Imran Khan	Pakistan	v	England	Leeds	1987
7-44	I.W.Johnson	Australia	v	West Indies	Georgetown	1954-55
7-46	A.R.Border	Australia	v	West Indies	Sydney	1988-89
7-52	Intikhab Alam	Pakistan	v	New Zealand	Dunedin	1972-73
7-52	Imran Khan	Pakistan	v	England	Birmingham	1982
7-53	D.S.Atkinson	West Indies	v	New Zealand	Auckland	1955-56
7-80	G.O.B.Allen	England	v	India	The Oval	1936
7-80	Imran Khan	Pakistan	v	West Indies	Georgetown	1987-88
7-100	M.A.Noble	Australia	v	England	Sydney	1903-04

TEN WICKETS IN A MATCH BY A CAPTAIN

12-100	Fazal Mahmood	Pakistan	v	West Indies	Dacca	1958-59
11-79	Imran Khan	Pakistan	v	India	Karachi	1982-83
11-90	A.E.R.Gilligan	England	v	South Africa	Birmingham	1924
11-96	A.R.Border	Australia	v	West Indies	Sydney	1988-89
11-121	Imran Khan	Pakistan	v	West Indies	Georgetown	1987-88
11-130	Intikhab Alam	Pakistan	v	New Zealand	Dunedin	1972-73
11-150	E.P.Nupen	South Africa	v	England	Johannesburg[1]	1930-31
11-180	Imran Khan	Pakistan	v	India	Faisalabad	1982-83
10-77	Imran Khan	Pakistan	v	England	Leeds	1987
10-78	G.O.B.Allen	England	v	India	Lord's	1936
10-135	Kapil Dev	India	v	West Indies	Ahmedabad	1983-84
10-182	Intikhab Alam	Pakistan	v	New Zealand	Dacca	1969-70
10-194	B.S.Bedi	India	v	Australia	Perth	1977-78

A CENTURY AND FIVE WICKETS IN AN INNINGS BY A CAPTAIN

219	5-56	D.S.Atkinson	West Indies	v	Australia	Bridgetown	1954-55
174	5-41	G.S.Sobers	West Indies	v	England	Leeds	1966
121	5-28	Mushtaq Mohammad	Pakistan	v	West Indies	Port-of-Spain	1976-77
117	6-98) 5-82)	Imran Khan	Pakistan	v	India	Faisalabad	1982-83

HUNDRED RUNS AND EIGHT WICKETS IN A MATCH BY A CAPTAIN

121	56	5-28	3-69	Mushtaq Mohammad	Pakistan	v	West Indies	Port-of-Spain	1976-77
174		5-41	3-39	G.S.Sobers	West Indies	v	England	Leeds	1966
117		6-98	5-82	Imran Khan	Pakistan	v	India	Faisalabad	1982-83
67*	46	5-49	3-66	Imran Khan	Pakistan	v	England	Leeds	1982
35	68	3-71	5-36	G.O.B.Allen	England	v	Australia	Brisbane[2]	1936-37

YOUNGEST CAPTAINS

Years	Days						
21	77	Nawab of Pataudi, jr	India	v	West Indies	Bridgetown	1961-62
22	194	I.D.Craig	Australia	v	South Africa	Johannesburg[3]	1957-58
22	260	Javed Miandad	Pakistan	v	Australia	Karachi	1979-80
22	306	M.Bisset	South Africa	v	England	Johannesburg[1]	1898-99
23	144	M.P.Bowden	England	v	South Africa	Cape Town	1888-89
23	217	G.C.Grant	West Indies	v	Australia	Adelaide	1930-31
23	292	Hon I.F.W.Bligh	England	v	Australia	Melbourne	1882-83

OLDEST CAPTAINS

Years	Days						
50	320	W.G.Grace	England	v	Australia	Nottingham	1899
45	245	G.O.B.Allen	England	v	West Indies	Kingston	1947-48

General

MOST TEST MATCH APPEARANCES

			Opponents							
For	Total		A	E	SA	WI	NZ	I	P	SL
Australia	**133**	A.R.Border	-	41	-	26	17	20	22	7
England	**117**	D.I.Gower	42	-	-	19	13	24	17	2
South Africa	**50**	J.H.B.Waite	14	21	-	-	15	-	-	-
West Indies	**121**	I.V.A.Richards	34	36	-	-	7	28	16	-
New Zealand	**86**	R.J.Hadlee	23	21	-	10	-	14	12	6
India	**125**	S.M.Gavaskar	20	38	-	27	9	-	24	7
Pakistan	**117**	Javed Miandad	24	22	-	14	17	28	-	12
Sri Lanka	**36**	A.Ranatunga	7	3	-	-	7	8	11	-

MOST CONSECUTIVE APPEARANCES

		From		To	
130	A.R.Border (Australia)	Melbourne	1978-79	Moratuwa	#1992-93
106	S.M.Gavaskar (India)	Bombay[3]	1974-75	Madras[1]	1986-87
87	G.R.Viswanath (India)	Georgetown	1970-71	Karachi	1982-83
85	G.S.Sobers (West Indies)	Port-of-Spain	1954-55	Port-of-Spain	1971-72
72	D.L.Haynes (West Indies)	Brisbane[2]	1979-80	Lord's	1988
71	I.M.Chappell (Australia)	Adelaide	1965-66	Melbourne	1975-76
66	Kapil Dev (India)	Faisalabad	1978-79	Delhi	1984-85
65	A.P.E.Knott (England)	Auckland	1970-71	The Oval	1977
65	I.T.Botham (England)	Wellington	1977-78	Karachi	1983-84
61	R.B.Kanhai (West Indies)	Birmingham	1957	Sydney	1968-69
61	I.V.A.Richards (West Indies)	Nottingham	1980	Madras[1]	1987-88
58 §	J R.Reid (New Zealand)	Manchester	1949	Leeds	1965
58 §	A.W.Greig (England)	Manchester	1972	The Oval	1977
56	S.M.H.Kirmani (India)	Madras[1]	1979-80	Kanpur	1984-85
53	K.J.Hughes (Australia)	Brisbane[2]	1978-79	Sydney	1982-83
53	Javed Miandad (Pakistan)	Lahore[2]	1977-78	Sydney	1983-84
52	F.E.Woolley (England)	The Oval	1909	The Oval	1926
52	P.B.H.May (England)	The Oval	1953	Leeds	1959
52	R.W.Marsh (Australia)	Brisbane[2]	1970-71	The Oval	1977
51	G.S.Chappell (Australia)	Perth	1970-71	The Oval	1977
51	D.I.Gower (England)	Bombay[3]	1981-82	Lord's	1986

The most for South Africa is 45 § by A.W.Nourse; for Pakistan 45 by Asif Iqbal; and for Sri Lanka 26 by A.Ranatunga.
§ Entire Test career. # To date.

PLAYERS WHO REPRESENTED TWO COUNTRIES

					Total Tests
Amir Elahi	India (1)	1947-48	Pakistan (5)	1952-53	6
J.J.Ferris	Australia (8)	1886-87 to 1890	England (1)	1891-92	9
S.C.Guillen	West Indies (5)	1951-52	New Zealand (3)	1955-56	8
Gul Mahomed	India (8)	1946 to 1952-53	Pakistan (1)	1956-57	9
F.Hearne	England (2)	1888-89	South Africa (4)	1891-92 to 1895-96	6
A.H.Kardar	India (3)	1946 §	Pakistan (23)	1952-53 to 1957-58	26
W.E.Midwinter	Australia (8)	1876-77 to 1886-87	England (4)	1881-82	12
F.Mitchell	England (2)	1898-99	South Africa (3)	1912	5
W.L.Murdoch	Australia (18)	1876-77 to 1890	England (1)	1891-92	19
Nawab of Pataudi, sr	England (3)	1932-33 to 1934	India (3)	1946	6
A.E.Trott	Australia (3)	1894-95	England (2)	1898-99	5
S.M.J.Woods	Australia (3)	1888	England (3)	1895-96	6
K.C.Wessels	Australia (24)	1982-83 to 1985-86	South Africa (1)	1991-92	25

§ As "Abdul Hafeez'.

RELATED TEST PLAYERS

FATHER AND TWO SONS

N.B.Amarnath and his sons M. and S.(India)
W.A.Hadlee and his sons D.R. and R.J.(New Zealand)

FATHERS AND SONS

N.B. and M., S.Amarnath (India)
W.M. and R.W.Anderson (New Zealand)
B.L. and C.L.Cairns (New Zealand)
M.C. and C.S.Cowdrey (England)
D.K. and A.D.Gaekwad (India)
E.J. and S.E.Gregory (Australia)
W.A. and D.R., R.J.Hadlee (New Zealand)
J.Hardstaff, sr and J.Hardstaff, jr (England)
G.A. and R.G.A.Headley (West Indies)
F.Hearne (England and South Africa) and G.A.L.Hearne (South Africa)
L. and R.A.Hutton (England)
M.Jahangir Khan (India) and Majid Khan (Pakistan)
J.D. and D.T.Lindsay (South Africa)
V.L. and S.V.Manjrekar (India)
M.H. and A.V.Mankad (India)
F.T. and F.G.Mann (England)
Hanif Mohammad and Shoaib Mohammad (Pakistan)
Nazar Mohammad and Mudassar Nazar (Pakistan)
A.W. and A.D.Nourse (South Africa)
J.H. and J.M.Parks (England)
Nawab of Pataudi, sr (England and India) and Nawab of Pataudi, jr (India)
Pankaj and Pranab Roy (India)
O.C. and A.P.H.Scott (West Indies)
M.J. and A.J.Stewart (England)
F.W. and M.W.Tate (England)
C.L. and D.C.H.Townsend (England)
L.R. and L.Tuckett (South Africa)
H.G. and G.E.Vivian (New Zealand)
S.Wazir Ali (India) and Khalid Wazir (Pakistan)

FOUR BROTHERS

Hanif, Mushtaq, Sadiq and Wazir Mohammad (Pakistan)
Hanif, Mushtaq and Sadiq all played against New Zealand at Karachi in 1969-70

THREE BROTHERS

G.S., I.M. and T.M.Chappell (Australia)
E.M., G.F. and W.G.Grace (England)
A., F. and G.G.Hearne (England) - F.Hearne also played for South Africa
A.B., L.J. and V.M.Tancred (South Africa)
All three Grace brothers played against Australia at The Oval in 1880.
A. and G.G.Hearne (E) and F.Hearne (SA) all played in the match between South Africa and England at Cape town in 1891-92.

TWO BROTHERS

ENGLAND

A.E.R. and A.H.H.Gilligan
A.W. and I.A.Greig
G. and J.R.Gunn
D.W. and P.E.Richardson
C.L. and R.A.Smith
C.T. and G.B.Studd
G.E. and J.T.Tyldesley
C.E.M. and E.R.Wilson

AUSTRALIA

K.A. and R.G.Archer
A.C. and C.Bannerman
J. and R.Benaud
D.W. and E. Gregory
M.R. and R.N.Harvey
C.E. and R.W.McLeod
A.E, and G.H.S.Trott
H. and J.W.Trumble
M.E. and S.R.Waugh

SOUTH AFRICA

P.A.M. and R.H.M.Hands
A.J. and D.B.Pithey
P.M. and R.G.Pollock
A.R. and W.H.M.Richards
A.M.B. and E.A.B.Rowan
S.D. and S.J.Snooke
G.L. and L.E.Tapscott
D. and H.W.Taylor
H.F. and W.W.Wade

WEST INDIES
D.S. and E.S.Atkinson
F.J. and J.H.Cameron
C.M. and R.J.Christiani
B.A. and C.A.Davis
G.C. and R.S.Grant
N.E. and R.E.Marshall
E.L. and W.H.St Hill
J.B. and V.H.Stollmeyer

SRI LANKA
A. and D.Ranatunga
M.S. and S.Wettimuny

NEW ZEALAND
B.P. and J.G.Bracewell
J.J. and M.D.Crowe
D.R. and R.J.Hadlee
G.P. and H.J.Howarth
J.M. and N. M.Parker

PAKISTAN
Rameez Raja and Wasim Raja
Azmat Rana and Shafqat Rana
Pervez Sajjad and Waqar Hassan
Saeed Ahmed and Younis Ahmed

INDIA
M. and S.Amarnath
L.Amar Singh and L.Ramji
A L. and M.L.Apte
B P. and S.P.Gupte
A G Kripal Singh and
A G Milkha Singh
C.K. and C.S.Nayudu
S Nazir Ali and S.Wazir Ali

YOUNGEST TEST PLAYERS

Years	Days						
15	124	Mushtaq Mohammad	Pakistan	v	West Indies	Lahore[1]	1958-59
16	189	Aaqib Javed	Pakistan	v	New Zealand	Wellington	1988-89
16	205	S.R.Tendulkar	India	v	Pakistan	Karachi	1989-90
16	221	Aftab Baloch	Pakistan	v	New Zealand	Dacca	1969-70
16	248	Nasim-ul-Ghani	Pakistan	v	West Indies	Bridgetown	1957-58
16	352	Khalid Hassan	Pakistan	v	England	Nottingham	1954
17	69	Ataur Rehmann	Pakistan	v	England	Leeds	1992
17	118	L.Sivaramakrishnan	India	v	West Indies	St John	1982-83
17	122	I.E.D.Sealy	West Indies	v	England	Bridgetown	1929-30
17	189	C.D.U.S.Weerasinghe	Sri Lanka	v	India	Colombo (PSS)	1985-86
17	193	Maninder Singh	India	v	Pakistan	Karachi	1932-83
17	239	I.D.Craig	Australia	v	South Africa	Melbourne	1952-53
17	245	G.S.Sobers	West Indies	v	England	Kingston	1953-54
17	265	V.L.Mehra	India	v	New Zealand	Bombay[2]	1955-56
17	300	Hanif Mohammad	Pakistan	v	India	Delhi	1952-53
17	341	Intikhab Alam	Pakistan	v	Australia	Karachi	1959-60
17	364	Waqar Younis	Pakistan	v	India	Karachi	1989-90
18	1	M.S.Atapattu	Sri Lanka	v	India	Chandigarh	1990-91
18	5	Zahid Fazal	Pakistan	v	West Indies	Karachi	1990-91
18	13	A.G.Milkha Singh	India	v	Australia	Madras[2]	1959-60
18	26	Majid Khan	Pakistan	v	Australia	Karachi	1964-65
18	31	M.R.Bynoe	West Indies	v	Pakistan	Lahore[1]	1958-59
18	41	Salahuddin	Pakistan	v	New Zealand	Rawalpindi	1964-65
18	44	Khalid Wazir	Pakistan	v	England	Lord's	1954
18	78	A.Ranatunga	Sri Lanka	v	England	Colombo (PSS)	1981-82
18	81	B.R.Jurangpathy	Sri Lanka	v	India	Kandy	1985-86
18	105	J.B.Stollmeyer	West Indies	v	England	Lord's	1939
18	136	Ijaz Ahmed	Pakistan	v	India	Madras[1]	1986-87
18	149	D.B.Close	England	v	New Zealand	Manchester	1949
18	173	A.T.Roberts	West Indies	v	New Zealand	Auckland	1955-56
18	186	Haseeb Ahsan	Pakistan	v	West Indies	Bridgetown	1957-58
18	190	Imran Khan	Pakistan	v	England	Birmingham	1971
18	197	D.L.Freeman	New Zealand	v	England	Christchurch	1932-33
18	232	T.W.Garrett	Australia	v	England	Melbourne	1876-77
18	236	Wasim Akram	Pakistan	v	New Zealand	Auckland	1984-85
18	242	A.P.H.Scott	West Indies	v	India	Kingston	1952-53
18	249	B.S.Chandrasekhar	India	v	England	Bombay[2]	1963-64
18	260	Mohammad Ilyas	Pakistan	v	Australia	Melbourne	1964-65
18	267	H.G.Vivian	New Zealand	v	England	The Oval	1931
18	270	R.I.Shastri	India	v	New Zealand	Wellington	1980-81
18	288	C.Sharma	India	v	Pakistan	Lahore[2]	1984-85
18	295	R.O.Collinge	New Zealand	v	Pakistan	Wellington	1964-65

18	311	P.A.De Silva	Sri Lanka	v	England	Lord's	1984
18	312	S.Venkataraghavan	India	v	New Zealand	Madras²	1964-65
18	316	B.P.Bracewell	New Zealand	v	England	The Oval	1978
18	323	Saleem Malik	Pakistan	v	Sri Lanka	Karachi	1981-82

The youngest player to represent South Africa was A.E.Ochse who was 19 years 1 day old when he appeared against England at Port Elizabeth in 1888-89.

OLDEST PLAYERS ON TEST DEBUT

Years	Days						
49	119	J.Southerton	England	v	Australia	Melbourne	1876-77
47	284	Miran Bux	Pakistan	v	India	Lahore¹	1954-55
46	253	D.D.Blackie	Australia	v	England	Sydney	1928-29
46	237	H.Ironmonger	Australia	v	England	Brisbane²	1928-29
42	242	N.Betancourt	West Indies	v	England	Port-of-Spain	1929-30
41	337	E.R.Wilson	England	v	Australia	Sydney	1920-21
41	27	R.J.D.Jamshedji	India	v	England	Bombay¹	1933-34
40	345	C.A.Wiles	West Indies	v	England	Manchester	1933
40	216	S.Kinneir	England	v	Australia	Sydney	1911-12
40	110	H.W.Lee	England	v	South Africa	Johannesburg¹	1930-31
40	56	G.W.A.Chubb	South Africa	v	England	Nottingham	1951
40	37	C.Ramaswami	India	v	England	Manchester	1936

The oldest player to make his debut for New Zealand was H.M.McGirr who was 38 years 101 days old when he appeared against England at Auckland in 1929-30; and for Sri Lanka D.S.De Silva who was 39 years 251 days old when he made his debut in his country's inaugural Test against England at Colombo (PSS) in 1981-82.

OLDEST TEST PLAYERS

(Age on final day of their last Test match)

Years	Days						
52	165	W.Rhodes	England	v	West Indies	Kingston	1929-30
50	327	H.Ironmonger	Australia	v	England	Sydney	1932-33
50	320	W.G.Grace	England	v	Australia	Nottingham	1899
50	303	G.Gunn	England	v	West Indies	Kingston	1929-30
49	139	J.Southerton	England	v	Australia	Melbourne	1876-77
47	302	Miran Bux	Pakistan	v	India	Peshawar	1954-55
47	249	J.B.Hobbs	England	v	Australia	The Oval	1930
47	87	F.E.Woolley	England	v	Australia	The Oval	1934
46	309	D.D.Blackie	Australia	v	England	Adelaide	1928-29
46	206	A.W.Nourse	South Africa	v	England	The Oval	1924
46	202	H.Strudwick	England	v	Australia	The Oval	1926
46	41	E.H.Hendren	England	v	West Indies	Kingston	1934-35
45	245	G.O.B.Allen	England	v	West Indies	Kingston	1947-48
45	215	P.Holmes	England	v	India	Lord's	1932
45	140	D.B.Close	England	v	West Indies	Manchester	1976
44	341	E.G.Wynyard	England	v	South Africa	Johannesburg¹	1905-06
44	317	J.M.M.Commaille	South Africa	v	England	Cape Town	1927-28
44	238	R.Abel	England	v	Australia	Manchester	1902
44	236	G.A.Headley	West Indies	v	England	Kingston	1953-54
44	105	Amir Elahi	Pakistan	v	India	Calcutta	1952-53

LONGEST CAREERS

(From debut to final day of last match)

Years	Days			From		To	
30	315	W.Rhodes	England	Nottingham	1899	Kingston	1929-30
26	355	D.B.Close	England	Manchester	1949	Manchester	1976
25	13	F.E.Woolley	England	The Oval	1909	The Oval	1934
24	10	G.A.Headley	West Indies	Bridgetown	1929-30	Kingston	1953-54
22	233	J.B.Hobbs	England	Melbourne	1907-08	The Oval	1930
22	120	G.Gunn	England	Sydney	1907-08	Kingston	1929-30
22	18	S.E.Gregory	Australia	Lord's	1890	The Oval	1912

LONGEST INTERVALS BETWEEN APPEARANCES

Years	Days			From		To	
17	316	G.Gunn	England	Sydney	1911-12	Bridgetown	1929-30
17	111	Younis Ahmed	Pakistan	Lahore[2]	1969-70	Jaipur	1986-87
14	92	J.M.M.Commaille	South Africa	Cape Town	1909-10	Birmingham	1924
14	28	D.C.Cleverley	New Zealand	Christchurch	1931-32	Wellington	1945-46
13	53	F.Mitchell	England/South Africa	Cape Town	1898-99	Manchester	1912
13	32	G.M.Carew	West Indies	Bridgetown	1934-35	Port-of-Spain	1947-48
12	160	N.B.Amarnath	India	Madras[1]	1933-34	Lord's	1946
12	81	W.E.Hollies	England	Kingston	1934-35	Nottingham	1947
12	14	Nawab of Pataudi, sr	England/India	Nottingham	1934	Lord's	1946

The most matches between appearances is 104 by Younis Ahmed (as above).

ON THE FIELD THROUGHOUT A MATCH

						Days
Nazar Mohammad	Pakistan	v	India	Lucknow	1952-53	4
D.J.McGlew	South Africa	v	New Zealand	Wellington	1952-53	4
C.A.Milton	England	v	New Zealand	Leeds	1958	5#
J.H.Edrich	England	v	New Zealand	Leeds	1965	5
D.Lloyd	England	v	India	Birmingham	1974	3
G.Boycott	England	v	Australia	Leeds	1977	4
Taslim Arif	Pakistan	v	Australia	Faisalabad	1979-80	4
S.M.Gavaskar	India	v	West Indies	Georgetown	1982-83	5#
D.S.B.P.Kuruppu	Sri Lanka	v	New Zealand	Colombo (CCC)	1986-87	5†

† In first Test. Rain prevented play on two days.

Umpires

MOST TEST MATCHES

Tests		Venue	From	To
48	F.Chester	England	1924	1955
47	H.D.Bird	England	1973	1992
42	C.S.Elliott	England (41)	1957	1974
		New Zealand (1)	1970-71	
36	D.J.Constant	England	1971	1988
33	J.S.Buller	England	1956	1969
33	A.R.Crafter	Australia	1978-79	1991-92
32	R.W.Crockett	Australia	1901-02	1924-25
31	D.Sang Hue	West Indies	1961-62	1980-81
29	J.Phillips	England (11)	1893	1905
		Australia (13)	1884-85	1897-98
		South Africa (5)	1905-06	
29	F.S.Lee	England	1949	1962
29	C.J.Egar	Australia	1960-61	1968-69
29	Khizer Hayat	Pakistan	1979-80	1991-92
27	R.C.Bailhache	Australia	1974-75	1988-89
27	D.M.Archer	West Indies	1980-81	1991-92
25	R.Gosein	West Indies	1964-65	1977-78
25	L.P.Rowan	Australia	1962-63	1970-71

Most for other countries:

24	F.R.Goodall	New Zealand	1964-65	1987-88
24	S.J.Woodward	New Zealand	1978-79	1990-91
17	B.Satyaji Rao	India	1960-61	1978-79
17	Swaroop Kishen	India	1978-79	1984-85
14	R.G.A.Ashman	South Africa	1935-36	1949-50
6	H.C.Felsinger	Sri Lanka	1981-82	1985-86
6	K.T.Francis	Sri Lanka	1981-82	1992-93

C.J.Egar & L.P.Rowan stood together in 19 Tests, four more than the partnership of R.Gosein & D.Sang Hue.

Individual Career Records

These career records for all players appearing in official Test matches are complete to 14 September 1992. (* not out)

AUSTRALIA

	BATTING AND FIELDING										BOWLING						
	Tests	I	N	Runs	HS	Avge	100	50	Ct	St	Balls	Runs	Wks	Avge	5w	10w	BB
a'Beckett,EL	4	7	0	143	41	20.42	-	-	4	-	1062	317	3	105.66	-	-	1/41
Alderman,TM	41	53	22	203	26*	6.54	-	-	27	-	10181	4616	170	27.15	14	1	6/47
Alexander,G	2	4	0	52	33	13.00	-	-	2	-	168	93	2	46.50	-	-	2/69
Alexander,HH	1	2	1	17	17*	17.00	-	-	-	-	276	154	1	154.00	-	-	1/129
Allan,FE	1	1	0	5	5	5.00	-	-	-	-	180	80	4	20.00	-	-	2/30
Allan,PJ	1	-	-	-	-	-	-	-	-	-	192	83	2	41.50	-	-	2/58
Allen,RC	1	2	0	44	30	22.00	-	-	2	-	-						
Andrews,TJE	16	23	1	592	94	26.90	-	4	12	-	156	116	1	116.00	-	-	1/23
Archer,KA	5	9	0	234	48	26.00	-	-	-	-	-						
Archer,RG	19	30	1	713	128	24.58	1	2	20	-	3576	1318	48	27.45	1	-	5/53
Armstrong,WW	50	84	10	2863	159*	38.68	6	8	44	-	8022	2923	87	33.59	3	-	6/35
Badcock,CL	7	12	1	160	118	14.54	1	-	3	-	-						
Bannerman,AC	28	50	2	1108	94	23.08	-	8	21	-	292	163	4	40.75	-	-	3/111
Bannerman,C	3	6	2	239	165*	59.75	1	-	-	-	-						
Bardsley,W	41	66	5	2469	193*	40.47	6	14	12	-	-						
Barnes,SG	13	19	2	1072	234	63.05	3	5	14	-	594	218	4	54.50	-	-	2/25
Barnett,BA	4	8	1	195	57	27.85	-	1	3	2	-						
Barrett,JE	2	4	1	80	67*	26.66	-	1	1	-	-						
Beard,GR	3	5	0	114	49	22.80	-	-	-	-	259	109	1	109.00	-	-	1/26
Benaud,J	3	5	0	223	142	44.60	1	-	-	-	24	12	2	6.00	-	-	2/12
Benaud,R	63	97	7	2201	122	24.45	3	9	65	-	19108	6704	248	27.03	16	1	7/72
Bennett,MJ	3	5	2	71	23	23.66	-	-	5	-	665	325	6	54.16	-	-	3/79
Blackham,JM	35	62	11	800	74*	15.68	-	4	37	24	-						
Blackie,DD	3	6	3	24	11*	8.00	-	-	2	-	1260	444	14	31.71	1	-	6/94
Bonnor,GJ	17	30	0	512	128	17.06	1	2	16	-	164	84	2	42.00	-	-	1/5
Boon,DC	66	121	12	4699	200	43.11	13	20	65	-	12	5	0	-	-	-	0/5
Booth,BC	29	48	6	1773	169	42.21	5	10	17	-	436	146	3	48.66	-	-	2/33
Border,AR	133	230	42	9775	205	51.99	24	56	137	-	3541	1389	38	36.55	2	1	7/46
Boyle,HF	12	16	4	153	36*	12.75	-	-	10	-	1744	641	32	20.03	1	-	6/42
Bradman,DG	52	80	10	6996	334	99.94	29	13	32	-	160	72	2	36.00	-	-	1/8
Bright,RJ	25	39	8	445	33	14.35	-	-	13	-	5541	2180	53	41.13	4	1	7/87
Bromley,EH	2	4	0	38	26	9.50	-	-	2	-	60	19	0	-	-	-	-
Brown,WA	22	35	1	1592	206*	46.82	4	9	14	-	-						
Bruce,W	14	26	2	702	80	29.25	-	5	12	-	988	440	12	36.66	-	-	3/88
Burge,PJP	42	68	8	2290	181	38.16	4	12	23	-	-						
Burke,JW	24	44	7	1280	189	34.59	3	5	18	-	814	230	8	28.75	-	-	4/37
Burn,EJK	2	4	0	41	19	10.25	-	-	-	-	-						
Burton,FJ	2	4	2	4	2*	2.00	-	-	1	1	-						
Callaway,ST	3	6	1	87	41	17.40	-	-	-	-	471	142	6	23.66	1	-	5/37
Callen,IW	1	2	2	26	22*	-	-	-	1	-	440	191	6	31.83	-	-	3/83
Campbell,GD	4	4	0	10	6	2.50	-	-	1	-	951	503	13	38.69	-	-	3/79
Carkeek,W	6	5	2	16	6*	5.33	-	-	6	-	-						
Carlson,PH	2	4	0	23	21	5.75	-	-	2	-	368	99	2	49.50	-	-	2/41
Carter,H	28	47	9	873	72	22.97	-	4	44	21	-						
Chappell,GS	87	151	19	7110	247*	53.86	24	31	122	-	5327	1913	47	40.70	1	-	5/61
Chappell,IM	75	136	10	5345	196	42.42	14	26	105	-	2873	1316	20	65.80	-	-	2/21
Chappell,TM	3	6	1	79	27	15.80	-	-	2	-	-						

AUSTRALIA (cont.)				**BATTING AND FIELDING**										**BOWLING**			
	Tests	I	N	Runs	HS	Avge	100	50	Ct	St	Balls	Runs	Wks	Avge	5w	10w	BB
Charlton,PC	2	4	0	29	11	7.25	-	-	-	-	45	24	3	8.00	-	-	3/18
Chipperfield,AG	14	20	3	552	109	32.47	1	2	15	-	924	437	5	87.40	-	-	3/91
Clark,WM	10	19	2	98	33	5.76	-	-	6	-	2793	1265	44	28.75	-	-	4/46
Colley,DJ	3	4	0	84	54	21.00	-	1	1	-	729	312	6	52.00	-	-	3/83
Collins,HL	19	31	1	1352	203	45.06	4	6	13	-	654	252	4	63.00	-	-	2/47
Coningham,A	1	2	0	13	10	6.50	-	-	-	-	186	76	2	38.00	-	-	2/17
Connolly,AN	29	45	20	260	37	10.40	-	-	17	-	7818	2981	102	29.22	4	-	6/47
Cooper,BB	1	2	0	18	15	9.00	-	-	2	-	-						
Cooper,WH	2	3	1	13	7	6.50	-	-	1	-	466	226	9	25.11	1	-	6/120
Corling,GE	5	4	1	5	3	1.66	-	-	-	-	1159	447	12	37.25	-	-	4/60
Cosier,GJ	18	32	1	897	168	28.93	2	3	14	-	899	341	5	68.20	-	-	2/26
Cottam,JT	1	2	0	4	3	2.00	-	-	1	-	-						
Cotter,A	21	37	2	457	45	13.05	-	-	8	-	4633	2549	89	28.64	7	-	7/148
Coulthard,G	1	1	1	6	6*	-	-	-	-	-	-						
Cowper,RM	27	46	2	2061	307	46.84	5	10	21	-	3005	1139	36	31.63	-	-	4/48
Craig,ID	11	18	0	358	53	19.88	-	2	2	-	-						
Crawford,WPA	4	5	2	53	34	17.66	-	-	1	-	437	107	7	15.28	-	-	3/28
Darling,J	34	60	2	1657	178	28.56	3	8	27	-	-						
Darling,LS	12	18	1	474	85	27.88	-	3	8	-	162	65	0	-	-	-	-
Darling,WM	14	27	1	697	91	26.80	-	6	5	-	-						
Davidson,AK	44	61	7	1328	80	24.59	-	5	42	-	11587	3819	186	20.53	14	2	7/93
Davis,IC	15	27	1	692	105	26.61	1	4	9	-	-						
Davis,SP	1	1	0	0	0	0.00	-	-	-	-	150	70	0	-	-	-	-
De Courcy,JH	3	6	1	81	41	16.20	-	-	3	-	-						
Dell,AR	2	2	2	6	3*	-	-	-	-	-	559	160	6	26.66	-	-	3/65
Dodemaide,AIC	10	15	6	202	50	22.44	-	1	6	-	2184	963	34	28.32	1	-	6/58
Donnan,H	5	10	1	75	15	8.33	-	-	1	-	54	22	0	-	-	-	-
Dooland,B	3	5	1	76	29	19.00	-	-	3	-	880	419	9	46.55	-	-	4/69
Duff,RA	22	40	3	1317	146	35.59	2	6	14	-	180	85	4	21.25	-	-	2/43
Duncan,JRF	1	1	0	3	3	3.00	-	-	-	-	112	30	0	-	-	-	-
Dyer,GC	6	6	0	131	60	21.83	-	1	22	2	-						
Dymock,G	21	32	7	236	31*	9.44	-	-	1	-	5545	2116	78	27.12	5	1	7/67
Dyson,J	30	58	7	1359	127*	26.64	2	5	10	-	-						
Eady,CJ	2	4	1	20	10*	6.66	-	-	2	-	223	112	7	16.00	-	-	3/30
Eastwood,KH	1	2	0	5	5	2.50	-	-	-	-	40	21	1	21.00	-	-	1/21
Ebeling,HI	1	2	0	43	41	21.50	-	-	-	-	186	89	3	29.66	-	-	3/74
Edwards,JD	3	6	1	48	26	9.60	-	-	1	-	-						
Edwards,R	20	32	3	1171	170*	40.37	2	9	7	-	12	20	0	-	-	-	-
Edwards,WJ	3	6	0	68	30	11.33	-	-	-	-	-						
Emery,SH	4	2	0	6	5	3.00	-	-	2	-	462	249	5	49.80	-	-	2/46
Evans,E	6	10	2	82	33	10.25	-	-	5	-	1247	332	7	47.42	-	-	3/64
Fairfax,AG	10	12	4	410	65	51.25	-	4	15	-	1520	645	21	30.71	-	-	4/31
Favell,LE	19	31	3	757	101	27.03	1	5	9	-	-						
Ferris,JJ	8	16	4	98	20*	8.16	-	-	4	-	2030	684	48	14.25	4	-	5/26
Fingleton,JHW	18	29	1	1189	136	42.46	5	3	13	-	-						
Fleetwood-Smith,LO	10	11	5	54	16*	9.00	-	-	-	-	3093	1570	42	37.38	2	1	6/110
Francis,BC	3	5	0	52	27	10.40	-	-	1	-	-						
Freeman,EW	11	18	0	345	76	19.16	-	2	5	-	2183	1128	34	33.17	-	-	4/52
Freer,FW	1	1	1	28	28*	-	-	-	-	-	160	74	3	24.66	-	-	2/49
Gannon,JB	3	5	4	3	3*	3.00	-	-	3	-	726	361	11	32.81	-	-	4/77
Garrett,TW	19	33	6	339	51*	12.55	-	1	7	-	2708	970	36	26.94	2	-	6/78
Gaunt,RA	3	4	2	6	3	3.00	-	-	1	-	716	310	7	44.28	-	-	3/53
Gehrs,DRA	6	11	0	221	67	20.09	-	2	6	-	6	4	0	-	-	-	-
Giffen,G	31	53	0	1238	161	23.35	1	6	24	-	6391	2791	103	27.09	7	1	7/117
Giffen,WF	3	6	0	11	3	1.83	-	-	1	-	-						
Gilbert,DR	9	12	4	57	15	7.12	-	-	-	-	1647	843	16	52.68	-	-	3/48

AUSTRALIA (cont.)	BATTING AND FIELDING										BOWLING						
	Tests	I	N	Runs	HS	Avge	100	50	Ct	St	Balls	Runs	Wks	Avge	5w	10w	BB
Gilmour,GJ	15	22	1	483	101	23.00	1	3	8	-	2661	1406	54	26.03	3	-	6/85
Gleeson,JW	29	46	8	395	45	10.39	-	-	17	-	8857	3367	93	36.20	3	-	5/61
Graham,H	6	10	0	301	107	30.10	2	-	3	-	-						
Gregory,DW	3	5	2	60	43	20.00	-	-	-	-	20	9	0	-	-	-	-
Gregory,EJ	1	2	0	11	11	5.50	-	-	1	-	-						
Gregory,JM	24	34	3	1146	119	36.96	2	7	37	-	5582	2648	85	31.15	4	-	7/69
Gregory,RG	2	3	0	153	80	51.00	-	2	1	-	24	14	0	-	-	-	-
Gregory,SE	58	100	7	2282	201	24.53	4	8	25	-	30	33	0	-	-	-	-
Grimmett,CV	37	50	10	557	50	13.92	-	1	17	-	14513	5231	216	24.21	21	7	7/40
Groube,TU	1	2	0	11	11	5.50	-	-	-	-	-						
Grout,ATW	51	67	8	890	74	15.08	-	3	163	24	-						
Guest,CEJ	1	1	0	11	11	11.00	-	-	-	-	144	59	0	-	-	-	-
Hamence,RA	3	4	1	81	30*	27.00	-	-	1	-	-						
Hammond,JR	5	5	2	28	19	9.33	-	-	2	-	1031	488	15	32.53	-	-	4/38
Harry,J	1	2	0	8	6	4.00	-	-	1	-	-						
Hartigan,RJ	2	4	0	170	116	42.50	1	-	1	-	12	7	0	-	-	-	-
Hartkopf,AEV	1	2	0	80	80	40.00	-	1	-	-	240	134	1	134.00	-	-	1/120
Harvey,MR	1	2	0	43	31	21.50	-	-	-	-	-						
Harvey,RN	79	137	10	6149	205	48.41	21	24	64	-	414	120	3	40.00	-	-	1/8
Hassett,AL	43	69	3	3073	198*	46.56	10	11	30	-	111	78	0	-	-	-	-
Hawke,NJN	27	37	15	365	45*	16.59	-	-	9	-	6974	2677	91	29.41	6	1	7/105
Hazlitt,GR	9	12	4	89	34*	11.12	-	-	4	-	1563	623	23	27.08	1	-	7/25
Healy,IA	39	58	4	1218	71	22.55	-	6	115	2							
Hendry,HSTL	11	18	2	335	112	20.93	1	-	10	-	1706	640	16	40.00	-	-	3/36
Hibbert,PA	1	2	0	15	13	7.50	-	-	1	-	-						
Higgs,JD	22	36	16	111	16	5.55	-	-	3	-	4752	2057	66	31.16	2	-	7/143
Hilditch,AMJ	18	34	0	1073	119	31.55	2	6	13	-	-						
Hill,C	49	89	2	3412	191	39.21	7	19	33	-	-						
Hill,JC	3	6	3	21	8*	7.00	-	-	2	-	606	273	8	34.12	-	-	3/35
Hoare,DE	1	2	0	35	35	17.50	-	-	2	-	232	156	2	78.00	-	-	2/68
Hodges,JH	2	4	1	10	8	3.33	-	-	-	-	136	84	6	14.00	-	-	2/7
Hogan,TG	7	12	1	205	42*	18.63	-	-	2	-	1436	706	15	47.06	1	-	5/66
Hogg,RM	38	58	13	439	52	9.75	-	1	7	-	7633	3503	123	28.47	6	2	6/74
Hohns,TV	7	7	1	136	40	22.66	-	-	3	-	1528	581	17	34.11	-	-	3/59
Holland,RG	11	15	4	35	10	3.18	-	-	5	-	2889	1352	34	39.76	3	2	6/54
Hookes,DW	23	41	3	1306	143*	34.36	1	8	12	-	96	41	1	41.00	-	-	1/4
Hopkins,AJY	20	33	2	509	43	25.45	-	-	11	-	1327	696	26	26.76	-	-	4/81
Horan,TP	15	27	2	471	124	18.84	1	1	6	-	373	143	11	13.00	1	-	6/40
Hordern,HV	7	13	2	254	50	23.09	-	1	6	-	2148	1075	46	23.36	5	2	7/90
Hornibrook,PM	6	7	1	60	26	10.00	-	-	7	-	1579	664	17	39.05	1	-	7/92
Howell,WP	18	27	6	158	35	7.52	-	-	12	-	3892	1407	49	28.71	1	-	5/81
Hughes,KJ	70	124	6	4415	213	37.41	9	22	50	-	85	28	0	-	-	-	-
Hughes,MG	37	49	5	688	72*	15.63	-	2	17	-	8421	4154	144	28.84	5	1	8/87
Hunt,WA	1	1	0	0	0	0.00	-	-	1	-	96	39	0	-	-	-	-
Hurst,AG	12	20	3	102	26	6.00	-	-	3	-	3054	1200	43	27.90	2	-	5/28
Hurwood,A	2	2	0	5	5	2.50	-	-	2	-	517	170	11	15.45	-	-	4/22
Inverarity,RJ	6	11	1	174	56	17.40	-	1	4	-	372	93	4	23.25	-	-	3/26
Iredale,FA	14	23	1	807	140	36.68	2	4	16	-	12	3	0	-	-	-	-
Ironmonger,H	14	21	5	42	12	2.62	-	-	3	-	4695	1330	74	17.97	4	2	7/23
Iverson,JB	5	7	3	3	1*	0.75	-	-	2	-	1108	320	21	15.23	1	-	6/27
Jackson,A	8	11	1	474	164	47.40	1	2	7	-	-						
Jarman,BN	19	30	3	400	78	14.81	-	2	50	4	-						
Jarvis,AH	11	21	3	303	82	16.83	-	1	9	9	-						
Jenner,TJ	9	14	5	208	74	23.11	-	1	5	-	1881	749	24	31.20	1	-	5/90
Jennings,CB	6	8	2	107	32	17.83	-	-	5	-	-						
Johnson,IW	45	66	12	1000	77	18.51	-	6	30	-	8780	3182	109	29.19	3	-	7/44

AUSTRALIA (cont.)	BATTING AND FIELDING										BOWLING						
	Tests	I	N	Runs	HS	Avge	100	50	Ct	St	Balls	Runs	Wks	Avge	5w	10w	BB
Johnson,LJ	1	1	1	25	25*	-	-	-	2	-	282	74	6	12.33	-	-	3/8
Johnston,WA	40	49	25	273	29	11.37	-	-	16	-	11048	3826	160	23.91	7	-	6/44
Jones,DM	52	89	11	3631	216	46.55	11	14	34	-	198	64	1	64.00	-	-	1/5
Jones,E	19	26	1	126	20	5.04	-	-	21	-	3748	1857	64	29.01	3	1	7/88
Jones,SP	12	24	4	432	87	21.60	-	1	12	-	262	112	6	18.66	-	-	4/47
Joslin,LR	1	2	0	9	7	4.50	-	-	-	-	-						
Kelleway,C	26	42	4	1422	147	37.42	3	6	24	-	4363	1683	52	32.36	1	-	5/33
Kelly,JJ	36	56	17	664	46*	17.02	-	-	43	20	-						
Kelly,TJD	2	3	0	64	35	21.33	-	-	1	-	-						
Kendall,TK	2	4	1	39	17*	13.00	-	-	2	-	563	215	14	15.35	1	-	7/55
Kent,MF	3	6	0	171	54	28.50	-	2	6	-	-						
Kerr,RB	2	4	0	31	17	7.75	-	-	1	-	-						
Kippax,AF	22	34	1	1192	146	36.12	2	8	13	-	72	19	0	-	-	-	-
Kline,LF	13	16	9	58	15*	8.28	-	-	9	-	2373	776	34	22.82	1	-	7/75
Laird,BM	21	40	2	1341	92	35.28	-	11	16	-	18	12	0	-	-	-	-
Langley,GRA	26	37	12	374	53	14.96	-	1	83	15	-						
Laughlin,TJ	3	5	0	87	35	17.40	-	-	3	-	516	262	6	43.66	1	-	5/101
Laver,FJ	15	23	6	196	45	11.52	-	-	8	-	2361	964	37	26.05	2	-	8/31
Lawry,WM	67	123	12	5234	210	47.15	13	27	30	-	14	6	0	-	-	-	-
Lawson,GF	46	68	12	894	74	15.96	-	4	10	-	11118	5501	180	30.56	11	2	8/112
Lee,PK	2	3	0	57	42	19.00	-	-	1	-	436	212	5	42.40	-	-	4/111
Lillee,DK	70	90	24	905	73*	13.71	-	1	23	-	18467	8493	355	23.92	23	7	7/83
Lindwall,RR	61	84	13	1502	118	21.15	2	5	26	-	13650	5251	228	23.03	12	-	7/38
Love,HSB	1	2	0	8	5	4.00	-	-	3	-	-						
Loxton,SJE	12	15	0	554	101	36.93	1	3	7	-	906	349	8	43.62	-	-	3/55
Lyons,JJ	14	27	0	731	134	27.07	1	3	3	-	316	149	6	24.83	1	-	5/30
McAlister,PA	8	16	1	252	41	16.80	-	-	10	-	-						
Macartney,CG	35	55	4	2131	170	41.78	7	9	17	-	3561	1240	45	27.55	2	1	7/58
McCabe,SJ	39	62	5	2748	232	48.21	6	13	41	-	3746	1543	36	42.86	-	-	4/13
McCool,CL	14	17	4	459	104*	35.30	1	1	14	-	2504	958	36	26.61	3	-	5/41
McCormick,EL	12	14	5	54	17*	6.00	-	-	8	-	2107	1079	36	29.97	-	-	4/101
McCosker,RB	25	46	5	1622	127	39.56	4	9	21	-	-						
McDermott,CJ	39	54	5	582	42*	11.87	-	-	9	-	9100	4671	167	27.97	9	2	8/97
McDonald,CC	47	83	4	3107	170	39.32	5	17	14	-	8	3	0	-	-	-	-
McDonald,EA	11	12	5	116	36	16.57	-	-	3	-	2885	1431	43	33.27	2	-	5/32
McDonnell,PS	19	34	1	950	147	28.78	3	2	6	-	52	53	0	-	-	-	-
McIlwraith,J	1	2	0	9	7	4.50	-	-	1	-	-						
Mackay,KD	37	52	7	1507	89	33.48	-	13	16	-	5792	1721	50	34.42	2	-	6/42
McKenzie,GD	60	89	12	945	76	12.27	-	2	34	-	17681	7328	246	29.78	16	3	8/71
McKibbin,TR	5	8	2	88	28*	14.66	-	-	4	-	1032	496	17	29.17	-	-	3/35
McLaren,JW	1	2	2	0	0*	-	-	-	-	-	144	70	1	70.00	-	-	1/23
Maclean,JA	4	8	1	79	33*	11.28	-	-	18	-	-						
McLeod,CE	17	29	5	573	112	23.87	1	4	9	-	3374	1325	33	40.15	2	-	5/65
McLeod,RW	6	11	0	146	31	13.27	-	-	3	-	1089	384	12	32.00	1	-	5/55
McShane,FG	3	6	1	26	12*	5.20	-	-	2	-	108	48	1	48.00	-	-	1/39
Maddocks,LV	7	12	2	177	69	17.70	-	1	18	1	-						
Maguire,JN	3	5	1	28	15*	7.00	-	-	2	-	616	323	10	32.30	-	-	4/57
Mailey,AA	21	29	9	222	46*	11.10	-	-	14	-	6119	3358	99	33.91	6	2	9/121
Mallett,AA	38	50	13	430	43*	11.62	-	-	30	-	9990	3940	132	29.84	6	1	8/59
Malone,MF	1	1	0	46	46	46.00	-	-	-	-	342	77	6	12.83	1	-	5/63
Mann,AL	4	8	0	189	105	23.62	1	-	2	-	552	316	4	79.00	-	-	3/12
Marr,AP	1	2	0	5	5	2.50	-	-	-	-	48	14	0	-	-	-	-
Marsh,GR	50	93	7	2854	138	33.18	4	15	38	-	-						
Marsh,RW	96	150	13	3633	132	26.51	3	16	343	12	72	54	0	-	-	-	-
Martin,JW	8	13	1	214	55	17.83	-	1	5	-	1846	832	17	48.94	-	-	3/56
Massie,HH	9	16	0	249	55	15.56	-	1	5	-	-						

AUSTRALIA (cont.)	Tests	I	N	Runs	HS	Avge	100	50	Ct	St	Balls	Runs	Wks	Avge	5w	10w	BB
				BATTING AND FIELDING										BOWLING			
Massie,RAL	6	8	1	78	42	11.14	-	-	1	-	1739	647	314	20.87	2	1	8/53
Matthews,CD	3	5	0	54	32	10.80	-	-	1	-	570	313	6	52.16	-	-	3/95
Matthews,GRJ	31	50	8	1740	130	41.42	4	11	16	-	5677	2714	57	47.61	2	1	5/103
May,TBA	7	10	4	90	24	15.00	-	-	1	-	1997	895	25	35.80	-	-	4/97
Mayne,LC	6	11	3	76	13	9.50	-	-	3	-	1251	628	19	33.05	-	-	4/33
Mayne,RE	4	4	1	64	25*	21.33	-	-	2	-	6	1	0	-	-	-	-
Meckiff,I	18	20	7	154	45*	11.84	-	-	9	-	3734	1423	45	31.62	2	-	6/38
Meuleman,KD	1	1	0	0	0	0.00	-	-	1	-	-						
Midwinter,WE	8	14	1	174	37	13.38	-	-	5	-	949	333	14	23.78	1	-	5/78
Miller,KR	55	87	7	2958	147	36.97	7	13	38	-	10461	3906	170	22.97	7	1	7/60
Minnett,RB	9	15	0	391	90	26.06	-	3	-	-	589	290	11	26.36	-	-	4/34
Misson,FM	5	5	3	38	25*	19.00	-	-	6	-	1197	616	16	38.50	-	-	4/58
Moody,TM	8	14	0	456	106	32.57	2	3	9	-	432	147	2	73.50	-	-	1/17
Moroney,J	7	12	1	383	118	34.81	2	1	-	-	-						
Morris,AR	46	79	3	3533	206	46.48	12	12	15	-	111	50	2	25.00	-	-	1/5
Morris,S	1	2	1	14	10*	14.00	-	-	-	-	136	73	2	36.50	-	-	2/73
Moses,H	6	10	0	198	33	19.80	-	-	1	-	-						
Moss,JK	1	2	1	60	38*	60.00	-	-	-	-	-						
Moule,WH	1	2	0	40	34	20.00	-	-	1	-	51	23	3	7.66	-	-	3/23
Murdoch,WL	18	33	5	896	211	32.00	2	1	13	1	-						
Musgrove,H	1	2	0	13	9	6.50	-	-	-	-	-						
Nagel,LE	1	2	1	21	21*	21.00	-	-	-	-	262	110	2	55.00	-	-	2/110
Nash,LJ	2	2	0	30	17	15.00	-	-	6	-	311	126	10	12.60	-	-	4/18
Nitschke,HC	2	2	0	53	47	26.50	-	-	3	-	-						
Noble,MA	42	73	7	1997	133	30.25	1	16	26	-	7159	3025	121	25.00	9	2	7/17
Noblet,G	3	4	1	22	13*	7.33	-	-	1	-	774	183	7	26.14	-	-	3/21
Nothling,OE	1	2	0	52	44	26.00	-	-	-	-	276	72	0	-	-	-	-
O'Brien,LPJ	5	8	0	211	61	26.37	-	2	3	-	-						
O'Connor,JDA	4	8	1	86	20	12.28	-	-	3	-	692	340	13	26.15	1	-	5/40
O'Donnell,SP	6	10	3	206	48	29.42	-	-	4	-	940	504	6	84.00	-	-	3/37
Ogilvie,AD	5	10	0	178	47	17.80	-	-	5	-	-						
O'Keeffe,KJ	24	34	9	644	85	25.76	-	1	15	-	5384	2018	53	38.07	1	-	5/101
Oldfield,WAS	54	80	17	1427	65*	22.65	-	4	78	52	-						
O'Neill,NC	42	69	8	2779	181	45.55	6	15	21	-	1392	667	17	39.23	-	-	4/41
O'Reilly,WJ	27	39	7	410	56*	12.81	-	1	7	-	10024	3254	144	22.59	11	3	7/54
Oxenham,RK	7	10	0	151	48	15.10	-	-	4	-	1802	522	14	37.28	-	-	4/39
Palmer,GE	17	25	4	296	48	14.09	-	-	13	-	4517	1678	78	21.51	6	2	7/65
Park,RL	1	1	0	0	0	0.00	-	-	-	-	6	9	0	-	-	-	-
Pascoe,LS	14	19	9	106	30*	10.60	-	-	2	-	3403	1668	64	26.06	1	-	5/59
Pellew,CE	10	14	1	484	116	37.23	2	1	4	-	78	34	0	-	-	-	-
Phillips,WB	27	48	2	1485	159	32.28	2	7	52	-	-						
Phillips,WN	1	2	0	22	14	11.00	-	-	-	-	-						
Philpott,PI	8	10	1	93	22	10.33	-	-	5	-	2262	1000	26	38.46	1	-	5/90
Ponsford,WH	29	48	4	2122	266	48.22	7	6	21	-	-						
Pope,RJ	1	2	0	3	3	1.50	-	-	-	-	-						
Rackemann,CG	11	12	4	43	15*	5.37	-	-	2	-	2546	1028	39	26.35	3	1	6/86
Ransford,VS	20	38	6	1211	143*	37.84	1	7	10	-	43	28	1	28.00	-	-	1/9
Redpath,IR	66	120	11	4737	171	43.45	8	31	83	-	64	41	0	-	-	-	-
Reedman,JC	1	2	0	21	17	10.50	-	-	1	-	57	24	1	24.00	-	-	1/12
Reid,BA	26	32	13	91	13	4.78	-	-	5	-	5926	2633	106	24.83	4	2	7/51
Reiffel,PR	1	1	0	9	9	9.00	-	-	1	-	168	80	2	40.00	-	-	2/34
Renneberg,DA	8	13	7	22	9	3.66	-	-	2	-	1598	830	23	36.08	2	-	5/39
Richardson,AJ	9	13	0	403	100	31.00	1	2	1	-	1812	521	12	43.41	-	-	2/20
Richardson,VY	19	30	0	706	138	23.53	1	1	24	-	-						
Rigg,KE	8	12	0	401	127	33.41	1	1	5	-	-						
Ring,DT	13	21	2	426	67	22.42	-	4	5	-	3024	1305	35	37.28	2	-	6/72

AUSTRALIA (cont.)				**BATTING AND FIELDING**								**BOWLING**					
	Tests	I	N	Runs	HS	Avge	100	50	Ct	St	Balls	Runs	Wks	Avge	5w	10w	BB
Ritchie,GM	30	53	5	1690	146	35.20	3	7	14	-	6	10	0	-	-	-	-
Rixon,SJ	13	24	3	394	54	18.76	-	2	42	5	-						
Robertson,WR	1	2	0	2	2	1.00	-	-	-	-	44	24	0	-	-	-	-
Robinson,RD	3	6	0	100	34	16.66	-	-	4	-	-						
Robinson,RH	1	2	0	5	3	2.50	-	-	1	-	-						
Rorke,GF	4	4	2	9	7	4.50	-	-	1	-	703	203	10	20.30	-	-	3/23
Rutherford,JW	1	1	0	30	30	30.00	-	-	-	-	36	15	1	15.00	-	-	1/11
Ryder,J	20	32	5	1394	201*	51.62	3	9	17	-	1897	743	17	43.70	-	-	2/20
Saggers,RA	6	5	2	30	14	10.00	-	-	16	8	-						
Saunders,JV	14	23	6	39	11*	2.29	-	-	5	-	3565	1796	79	22.73	6	-	7/34
Scott,HJH	8	14	1	359	102	27.61	1	1	8	-	28	26	0	-	-	-	-
Sellers,RHD	1	1	0	0	0	0.00	-	-	1	-	30	17	0	-	-	-	-
Serjeant,CS	12	23	1	522	124	23.72	1	2	13	-	-						
Sheahan,AP	31	53	6	1594	127	33.91	2	7	17	-	-						
Shepherd,BK	9	14	2	502	96	41.93	-	5	2	-	26	9	0	-	-	-	-
Sievers,MW	3	6	1	67	25*	13.40	-	-	4	-	602	161	9	17.88	1	-	5/21
Simpson,RB	62	111	7	4869	311	46.81	10	27	110	-	6881	3001	71	42.26	2	-	5/57
Sincock,DJ	3	4	1	80	29	26.66	-	-	2	-	724	410	8	51.25	-	-	3/67
Slater,KN	1	1	1	1	1*	-	-	-	-	-	256	101	2	50.50	-	-	2/40
Sleep,PR	14	21	1	483	90	24.15	-	3	4	-	2982	1397	31	45.06	1	-	5/72
Slight,J	1	2	0	11	11	5.50	-	-	-	-	-						
Smith,DBM	2	3	1	30	24*	15.00	-	-	-	-	-						
Smith,SB	3	5	0	41	12	8.20	-	-	1	-	-						
Spofforth,FR	18	29	6	217	50	9.43	-	1	11	-	4185	1731	94	18.41	7	4	7/44
Stackpole,KR	43	80	5	2807	207	37.42	7	14	47	-	2321	1001	15	66.73	-	-	2/33
Stevens,GB	4	7	0	112	28	16.00	-	-	2	-							
Taber,HB	16	27	5	353	48	16.04	-	-	56	4	-						
Tallon,D	21	26	3	394	92	17.13	-	2	50	8	-						
Taylor,JM	20	28	0	997	108	35.60	1	8	11	-	114	45	1	45.00	-	-	1/25
Taylor,MA	33	62	4	2842	219	49.00	8	17	39	-							
Taylor,PL	13	19	3	431	87	26.93	-	2	10	-	2227	1068	27	39.55	1	-	6/78
Thomas,G	8	12	1	325	61	29.54	-	3	3	-	-						
Thompson,N	2	4	0	67	41	16.75	-	-	3	-	112	31	1	31.00	-	-	1/14
Thoms,GR	1	2	0	44	28	22.00	-	-	-	-	-						
Thomson,AL	4	5	4	22	12*	22.00	-	-	-	-	1519	654	12	54.50	-	-	3/79
Thomson,JR	51	73	20	679	49	12.81	-	-	20	-	10535	5601	200	28.00	8	-	6/46
Thurlow,HM	1	1	0	0	0	0.00	-	-	-	-	234	86	0	-	-	-	-
Toohey,PM	15	29	1	893	122	31.89	1	7	9	-	2	4	0	-	-	-	-
Toshack,ERH	12	11	6	73	20*	14.60	-	-	4	-	3140	989	47	21.04	4	1	6/29
Travers,JPF	1	2	0	10	9	5.00	-	-	1	-	48	14	1	14.00	-	-	1/14
Tribe,GE	3	3	1	35	25*	17.50	-	-	-	-	760	330	2	165.00	-	-	2/48
Trott,AE	3	5	3	205	85*	102.50	-	2	4	-	474	192	9	21.33	1	-	8/43
Trott,GHS	24	42	0	921	143	21.92	1	4	21	-	1890	1019	29	35.13	-	-	4/71
Trumble,H	32	57	14	851	70	19.79	-	4	45	-	8099	3072	141	21.78	9	3	8/65
Trumble,JW	7	13	1	243	59	20.25	-	1	3	-	600	222	10	22.20	-	-	3/29
Trumper,VT	48	48	8	3163	214*	39.04	8	13	31	-	546	317	8	39.62	-	-	3/60
Turner,A	14	27	1	768	136	29.53	1	3	15	-	-						
Turner,CTB	17	32	4	323	29	11.53	-	-	8	-	5179	1670	101	46.53	11	2	7/43
Veivers,TR	21	30	4	813	88	31.26	-	7	7	-	4191	1375	33	41.66	-	-	4/68
Veletta,MRJ	8	11	0	207	39	18.81	-	-	12	-	-						
Waite,MG	2	3	0	11	8	3.66	-	-	1	-	552	190	1	190.00	-	-	1/150
Walker,MHN	34	43	13	586	78*	19.53	-	1	12	-	10094	3792	138	27.47	6	-	8/143
Wall,TW	18	24	5	121	20	6.36	-	-	11	-	4812	2010	56	35.89	3	-	5/14
Walters,FH	1	2	0	12	7	6.00	-	-	2	-	-						
Walters,KD	74	125	14	5357	250	48.26	15	33	43	-	3295	1425	49	29.08	1	-	5/66
Ward,FA	4	8	5	36	18	6.00	-	-	1	-	1268	574	11	52.18	1	-	6/102

AUSTRALIA (cont.)

	BATTING AND FIELDING										BOWLING						
	Tests	I	N	Runs	HS	Avge	100	50	Ct	St	Balls	Runs	Wks	Avge	5w	10w	BB
Warne,SK	4	7	1	94	35	15.66	-	-	2	-	637	386	4	96.50	-	-	3/11
Watkins,JR	1	2	1	39	36	39.00	-	-	1	-	48	21	0	-	-	-	-
Watson,GD	5	9	0	97	50	10.77	-	1	1	-	552	254	6	42.33	-	-	2/67
Watson,WJ	4	7	1	106	30	17.66	-	-	2	-	6	5	0	-	-	-	-
Waugh,ME	14	21	2	698	139	36.73	2	3	22	-	786	392	11	35.63	-	-	4/80
Waugh,SR	44	67	11	2097	177*	37.44	3	13	15	-	4076	1980	44	45.00	2	-	5/69
Wellham,DM	6	11	0	257	103	23.36	1	-	5	-	-						
Wessels,KC	24	42	1	1761	179	42.95	4	9	18	-	90	42	0	-	-	-	-
Whatmore,DF	7	13	0	293	77	22.53	-	2	13	-	30	11	0	-	-	-	-
Whitney,MR	11	17	8	55	13	6.11	-	-	1	-	2534	1266	37	34.21	2	1	7/27
Whitty,WJ	14	19	7	161	39*	13.41	-	-	4	-	3357	1373	65	21.12	3	-	6/17
Wiener,JM	6	11	0	281	93	25.54	-	2	4	-	78	41	0	-	-	-	-
Wilson,JW	1	-	-	-	-	-	-	-	-	-	216	64	1	64.00	-	-	1/25
Wood,GM	59	112	6	3374	172	31.83	9	13	41	-	-						
Woodcock,AJ	1	1	0	27	27	27.00	-	-	1	-	-						
Woodfull,WM	35	54	4	2300	161	46.00	7	13	7	-	-						
Woods,SMJ	3	6	0	32	18	5.33	-	-	1	-	217	121	5	24.20	-	-	2/35
Woolley,RD	2	2	0	21	13	10.50	-	-	7	-	-						
Worrall,J	11	22	3	478	76	25.15	-	5	13	-	255	127	1	127.00	-	-	1/97
Wright,KJ	10	18	5	219	55*	16.84	-	4	31	4	-						
Yallop,GN	39	70	3	2756	268	41.13	8	9	23	-	192	116	1	116.00	-	-	1/21
Yardley,B	33	54	4	978	74	19.56	-	4	31	-	8909	3986	126	31.63	6	1	7/98
Zoehrer,TJ	10	14	2	246	52*	20.50	-	1	18	1	-						

ENGLAND

	BATTING AND FIELDING										BOWLING						
	Tests	I	N	Runs	HS	Avge	100	50	Ct	St	Balls	Runs	Wks	Avge	5w	10w	BB
Abel,R	13	22	2	744	132*	37.20	2	2	13	-	-						
Absolom,CA	1	2	0	58	52	29.00	-	1	-	-	-						
Agnew,JP	3	4	3	10	5	10.00	-	-	-	-	552	373	4	93.25	-	-	2/51
Allen,DA	39	51	15	918	88	25.50	-	5	10	1	11297	3779	122	30.97	4	-	5/30
Allen,GOB	25	33	2	750	122	24.19	1	3	20	-	4386	2379	81	29.37	5	1	7/80
Allom,MJC	5	3	2	14	8*	14.00	-	-	-	-	817	265	14	18.92	1	-	5/38
Allott,PJW	13	18	3	213	52*	14.20	-	1	4	-	2225	1084	26	41.69	1	-	6/61
Ames,LEG	47	72	12	2434	149	40.56	8	7	74	23	-						
Amiss,DL	50	88	10	3612	262*	46.30	11	11	24	-	-						
Andrew,KV	2	4	1	29	15	9.66	-	-	1	-	-						
Appleyard,R	9	9	6	51	19*	17.00	-	-	4	-	1596	554	31	17.87	1	-	5/51
Archer,AG	1	2	1	31	24*	31.00	-	-	-	-	-						
Armitage,T	2	3	0	33	21	11.00	-	-	-	-	12	15	0	-	-	-	-
Arnold,EG	10	15	3	160	40	13.33	-	-	8	-	1683	788	31	25.41	1	-	5/37
Arnold,GG	34	46	11	421	59	12.02	-	1	9	-	7650	3254	115	28.29	6	-	6/45
Arnold,J	1	2	0	34	34	17.00	-	-	-	-	-						
Astill,WE	9	15	0	190	40	12.66	-	-	7	-	2182	856	25	34.24	-	-	4/58
Atherton,MA	21	39	1	1311	151	34.50	3	9	20	-	366	282	1	282.00	-	-	1/60
Athey,CWJ	23	41	1	919	123	22.97	1	4	13	-	-						
Attewell,W	10	15	6	150	43*	16.66	-	-	9	-	2850	626	28	22.35	-	-	4/42
Bailey,RJ	4	8	0	119	43	14.87	-	-	-	-	-						
Bailey,TE	61	91	14	2290	134*	29.74	1	10	32	-	9712	3856	132	29.21	5	1	7/34
Bairstow,DL	4	7	1	125	59	20.83	-	1	12	1	-						
Bakewell,AH	6	9	0	409	107	45.44	1	3	3	-	18	8	0	-	-	-	-
Balderstone,JC	2	4	0	39	35	9.75	-	-	1	-	96	80	1	80.00	-	-	1/80
Barber,RW	28	45	3	1495	185	35.59	1	9	21	-	3426	1806	42	43.00	-	-	4/132
Barber,W	2	4	0	83	44	20.75	-	-	1	-	2	0	1	0.00	-	-	1/0

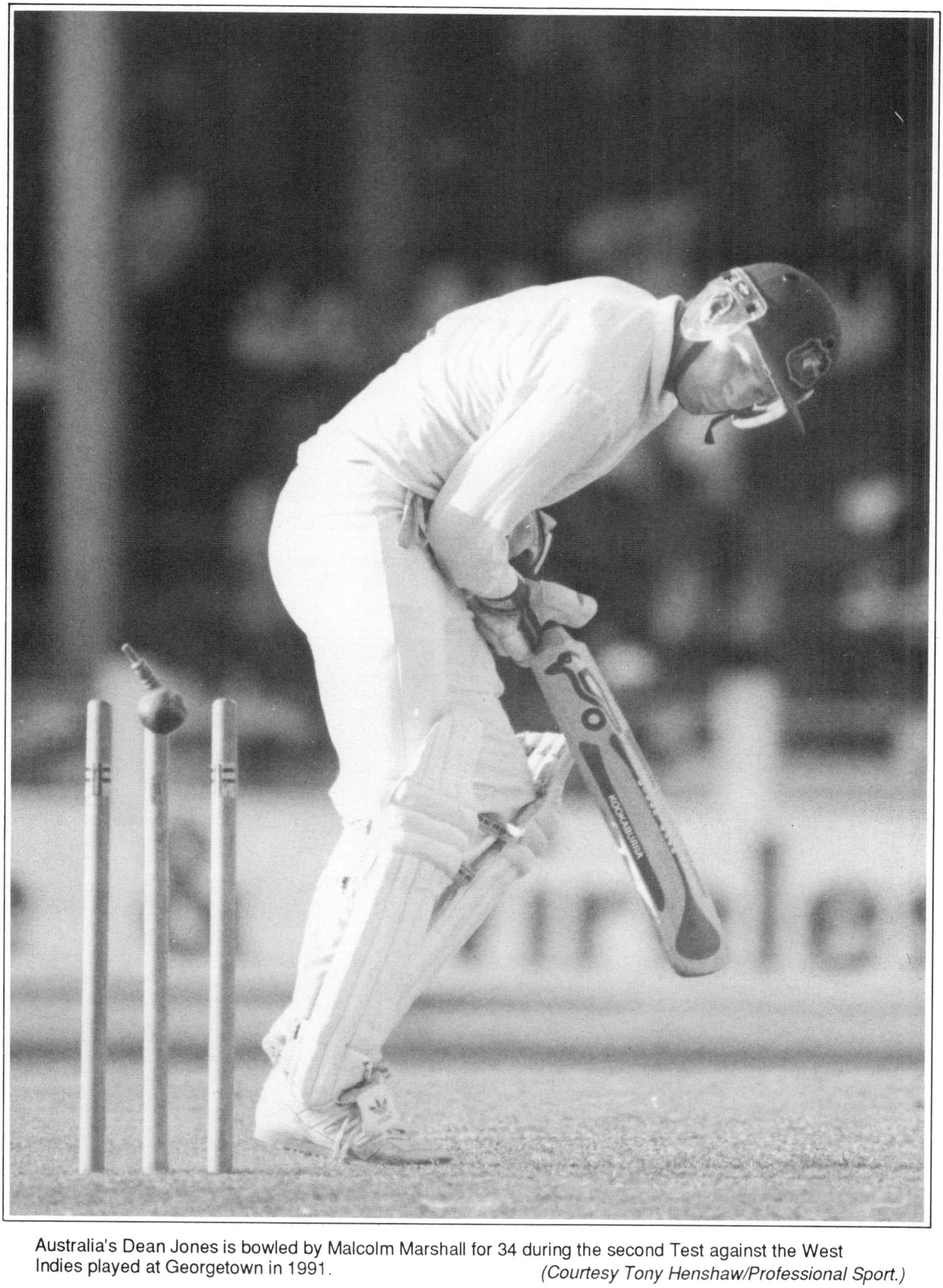

Australia's Dean Jones is bowled by Malcolm Marshall for 34 during the second Test against the West Indies played at Georgetown in 1991. *(Courtesy Tony Henshaw/Professional Sport.)*

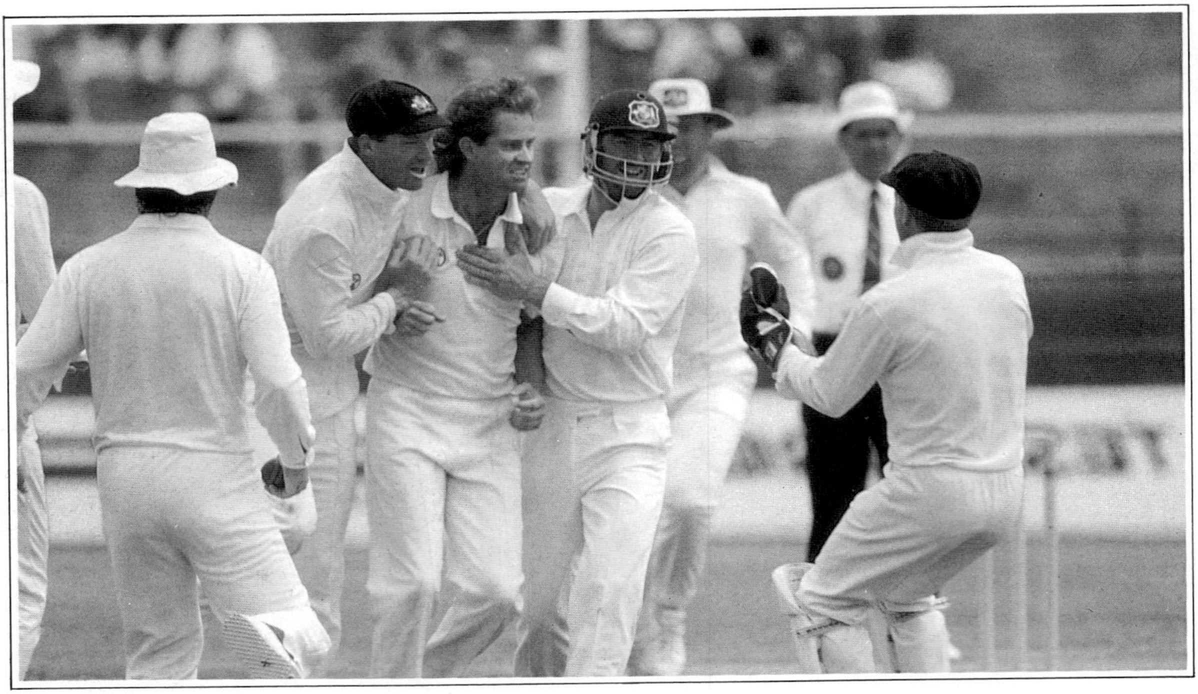

Terry Alderman (centre) is congratulated by fellow Australians Geoff Marsh (left) and Dean Jones (right) after an early bowling success against England at the 'Gabba. (Australia v England, Brisbane, 1990-91.)
(Courtesy PBL Marketing.)

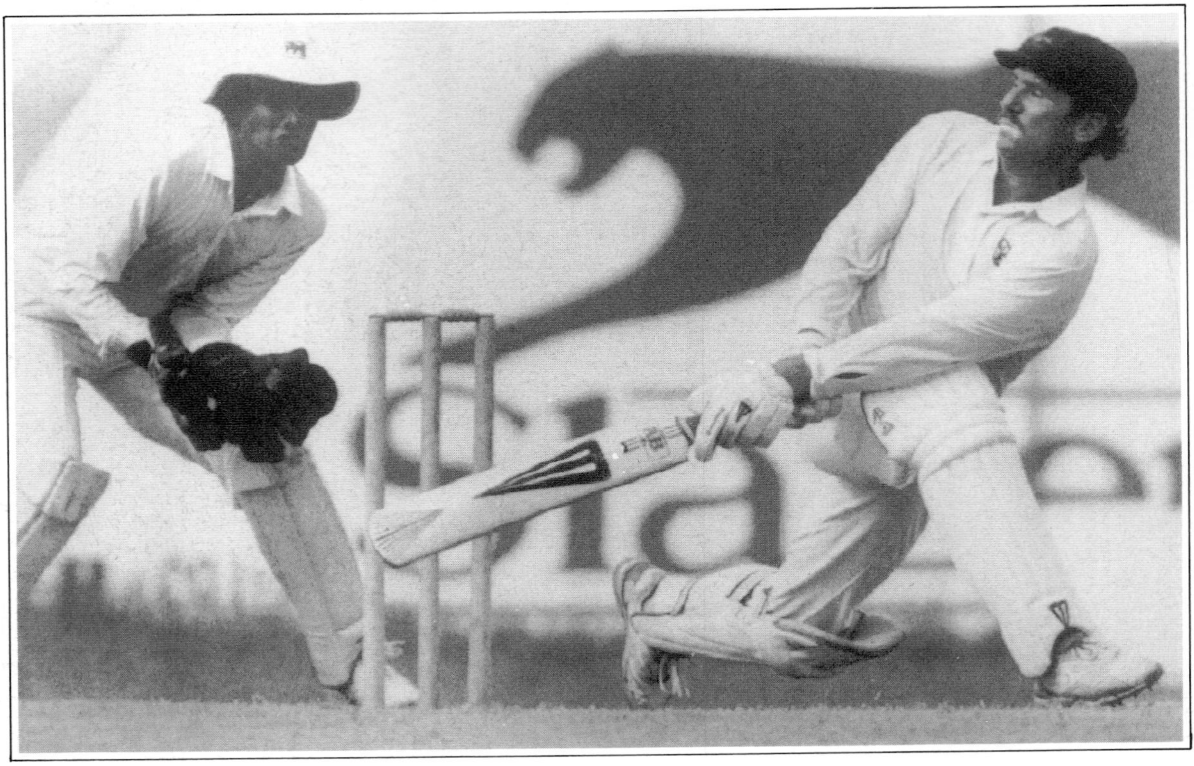

Australian captain Alan Border sweeps Sri Lankan spinner Don Anurasiri to the boundary during the third Test against Sri Lanka played in Colombo in September 1992. *(Courtesy Reuters.)*

ENGLAND (cont.)			**BATTING AND FIELDING**											**BOWLING**			
	Tests	I	N	Runs	HS	Avge	100	50	Ct	St	Balls	Runs	Wks	Avge	5w	10w	BB
Barlow,GD	3	5	1	17	7*	4.25	-	-	-	-	-						
Barlow,RG	17	30	4	591	62	22.73	-	2	14	-	2456	767	34	22.55	3	-	7/40
Barnes,SF	27	39	9	242	38*	8.06	-	-	12	-	7873	3106	189	16.43	24	7	9/103
Barnes,W	21	33	2	725	134	23.38	1	5	19	-	2289	793	51	15.54	3	-	6/28
Barnett,CJ	20	35	4	1098	129	35.41	2	5	14	-	256	93	0	-	-	-	-
Barnett,KJ	4	7	0	207	80	29.57	-	2	1	-	36	32	0	-	-	-	-
Barratt,F	5	4	1	28	17	9.33	-	-	2	-	750	235	5	47.00	-	-	1/8
Barrington,KF	82	131	15	6806	256	58.67	20	35	58	-	2715	1300	29	44.85	-	-	3/4
Barton,VA	1	1	0	23	23	23.00	-	-	-	-							
Bates,W	15	26	2	656	64	27.33	-	5	9	-	2364	821	50	16.42	4	1	7/28
Bean,G	3	5	0	92	50	18.40	-	1	4	-	-						
Bedser,AV	51	71	15	714	79	12.75	-	1	26	-	15918	5876	236	24.89	15	5	7/44
Benson,MR	1	2	0	51	30	25.50	-	-	-	-	-						
Berry,R	2	4	2	6	4*	3.00	-	-	2	-	653	228	9	25.33	1	-	5/63
Binks,JG	2	4	0	91	55	22.75	-	1	8	-	-						
Bird,MC	10	16	1	280	61	18.66	-	2	5	-	264	120	8	15.00	-	-	3/11
Birkenshaw,J	5	7	0	148	64	21.14	-	1	3	-	1017	469	13	36.07	1	-	5/57
Bligh,Hon.IFW	4	7	1	62	19	10.33	-	-	7	-	-						
Blythe,C	19	31	12	183	27	9.63	-	-	6	-	4546	1863	11	18.63	9	4	8/59
Board,JH	6	12	2	108	29	10.80	-	-	8	3	-						
Bolus,JB	7	12	0	496	88	41.33	-	4	2	-	18	16	0	-	-	-	-
Booth,MW	2	2	0	46	32	23.00	-	-	-	-	312	130	7	18.57	-	-	4/49
Bosanquet,BJT	7	14	3	147	27	13.36	-	-	9	-	970	604	25	24.16	2	-	8/107
Botham,IT	102	161	6	5200	208	33.54	14	22	120	-	21815	10878	383	28.40	27	4	8/34
Bowden,MP	2	2	0	25	25	12.50	-	-	1	-	-						
Bowes,WE	15	11	5	28	10*	4.66	-	-	2	-	3655	1519	68	22.33	6	-	6/33
Bowley,EH	5	7	0	252	109	36.00	1	-	2	-	252	116	0	-	-	-	-
Boycott,G	108	193	23	8114	246*	47.72	22	42	33	-	944	382	7	54.57	-	-	3/47
Bradley,WM	2	2	1	23	23*	23.00	-	-	-	-	625	233	6	38.83	1	-	5/67
Braund,LC	23	41	3	987	104	25.97	3	2	39	-	3803	1810	47	38.51	3	-	8/81
Brearley,JM	39	66	3	1442	91	22.88	-	9	52	-	-						
Brearley,W	4	5	2	21	11*	7.00	-	-	-	-	705	359	17	21.11	1	-	5/110
Brennan,DV	2	2	0	16	16	8.00	-	-	-	1	-						
Briggs,J	33	50	5	815	121	18.11	1	2	12	-	5332	2094	118	17.74	9	4	8/11
Broad,BC	25	44	2	1661	162	39.54	6	6	10	-	6	4	0	-	-	-	-
Brockwell,W	7	12	0	202	49	16.83	-	-	6	-	582	309	5	61.80	-	-	3/33
Bromley-Davenport,HR																	
	4	6	0	128	84	21.33	-	1	1	-	155	98	4	24.50	-	-	2/46
Brookes,D	1	2	0	17	10	8.50	-	-	1	-	-						
Brown,A	2	1	1	3	3*	-	-	-	1	-	323	150	3	50.00	-	-	3/27
Brown,DJ	26	34	5	342	44*	11.79	-	-	7	-	5098	2237	79	28.31	2	-	5/42
Brown,FR	22	30	1	734	79	25.31	-	5	22	-	3260	1398	45	31.06	1	-	5/49
Brown,G	7	12	2	229	84	29.90	-	2	9	3	-						
Brown,JT	8	16	3	470	140	36.15	1	1	7	-	35	22	0	-	-	-	-
Buckenham,CP	4	7	0	43	17	6.14	-	-	2	-	1182	593	21	28.23	1	-	5/115
Butcher,AR	1	2	0	34	20	17.00	-	-	-	-	12	9	0	-	-	-	-.
Butcher,RO	3	5	0	71	32	14.20	-	-	3	-							
Butler,HJ	2	2	1	15	15*	15.00	-	-	1	-	552	215	12	17.91	-	-	4/34
Butt,HR	3	4	1	22	13	7.33	-	-	1	1	-						
Calthorpe,Hon.FSG	4	7	0	129	49	18.42	-	-	3	-	204	91	1	91.00	-	-	1/38
Capel,DJ	15	25	1	374	98	15.58	-	2	6	-	2000	1064	21	50.66	-	-	3/88
Carr,AW	11	13	1	237	62	19.75	-	1	3	-	-						
Carr,DB	2	4	0	135	76	33.75	-	1	-	-	210	140	2	70.00	-	-	2/84
Carr,DW	1	1	0	0	0	0.00	-	-	-	-	414	282	7	40.28	1	-	5/146
Cartwright,TW	5	7	2	26	9	5.20	-	-	2	-	1611	544	15	36.26	1	-	6/94
Chapman,APF	26	36	4	925	121	28.90	1	5	32	-	40	20	0	-	-	-	-

ENGLAND (cont.)	**BATTING AND FIELDING**											**BOWLING**					
	Tests	I	N	Runs	HS	Avge	100	50	Ct	St	Balls	Runs	Wks	Avge	5w	10w	BB
Charlwood,HRJ	2	4	0	63	36	15.75	-	-	-	-	-						
Chatterton,W	1	1	0	48	48	48.00	-	-	-	-	-						
Childs,JH	2	4	4	2	2*	-	-	-	1	-	516	183	3	61.00	-	-	1/13
Christopherson,S	1	1	0	17	17	17.00	-	-	-	-	136	69	1	69.00	-	-	1/52
Clark,EW	8	9	5	36	10	9.00	-	-	-	-	1931	899	32	28.09	1	-	5/98
Clay,JC	1	-	-	-	-	-	-	-	1	-	192	75	0	-	-	-	-
Close,DB	22	37	2	887	70	25.34	-	4	24	-	1212	532	18	29.55	-	-	4/35
Coldwell,LJ	7	7	5	9	6*	4.50	-	-	1	-	1668	610	22	27.72	1	-	6/85
Compton,DCS	78	131	15	5807	278	50.06	17	28	49	-	2716	1410	25	56.40	1	-	5/70
Cook,C	1	2	0	4	4	2.00	-	-	-	-	180	127	0	-	-	-	-
Cook,G	7	13	0	203	66	15.61	-	2	9	-	42	27	0	-	-	-	-
Cook,NGB	15	25	4	179	31	8.52	-	-	5	-	4174	1689	52	32.48	4	1	6/65
Cope,GA	3	3	0	40	22	13.33	-	-	1	-	864	277	8	34.62	-	-	3/102
Copson,WH	3	1	0	6	6	6.00	-	-	1	-	762	297	15	19.80	1	-	5/85
Cornford,WL	4	4	0	36	18	9.00	-	-	5	3	-						
Cottam,RMH	4	5	1	27	13	6.75	-	-	2	-	903	327	14	23.35	-	-	4/50
Coventry,Hon.CJ	2	2	1	13	12	13.00	-	-	-	-	-						
Cowans,NG	19	29	7	175	36	7.95	-	-	9	-	3452	2003	51	39.27	2	-	6/77
Cowdrey,CS	6	8	1	101	38	14.42	-	-	5	-	399	309	4	77.25	-	-	2/65
Cowdrey,MC	114	188	15	7624	182	44.06	22	38	120	-	119	104	0	-	-	-	-
Coxon,A	1	2	0	19	19	9.50	-	-	-	-	378	172	3	57.33	-	-	2/90
Cranston,J	1	2	0	31	16	15.50	-	-	1	-	-						
Cranston,K	8	14	0	209	45	14.92	-	-	3	-	1010	461	18	25.61	-	-	4/12
Crapp,JF	7	13	2	319	56	29.00	-	3	7	-	-						
Crawford,JN	12	23	2	469	74	22.33	-	2	13	-	2203	1150	39	29.48	3	-	5/48
Curtis,TS	5	9	0	140	41	15.55	-	-	3	-	18	7	0	-	-	-	-
Cuttell,WR	2	4	0	65	21	16.25	-	-	2	-	285	73	6	12.16	-	-	3/17
Dawson,EW	5	9	0	175	55	19.44	-	1	-	-	-						
Dean,H	3	4	2	10	8	5.00	-	-	2	-	447	153	11	13.90	-	-	4/19
DeFreitas,PAJ	31	46	4	527	55*	12.54	-	1	6	-	6628	3017	93	32.44	3	-	7/70
Denness,MH	28	45	3	1667	188	39.69	4	7	28	-	-						
Denton,D	11	22	1	424	104	20.19	1	1	8	-	-						
Dewes,JG	5	10	0	121	67	12.10	-	1	-	-	-						
Dexter,ER	62	102	8	4502	205	47.89	9	27	29	-	5317	2306	66	34.93	-	-	4/10
Dilley,GR	41	58	19	521	56	13.35	-	2	10	-	8192	4107	138	29.76	6	-	6/38
Dipper,AE	1	2	0	51	40	25.50	-	-	-	-	-						
Doggart,GHG	2	4	0	76	29	19.00	-	-	3	-	-						
D'Oliveira,BL	44	70	8	2484	158	40.06	5	15	29	-	5706	1859	47	39.55	-	-	3/46
Dollery,HE	4	7	0	72	37	10.28	-	-	1	-	-						
Dolphin,A	1	2	0	1	1	0.50	-	-	1	-	-						
Douglas,JWHT	23	35	2	962	119	29.15	1	6	9	-	2812	1496	45	33.02	1	-	5/46
Downton,PR	30	48	8	785	74	19.62	-	4	70	5	-						
Druce,NF	5	9	0	252	64	28.00	-	1	5	-	-						
Ducat,A	1	2	0	5	3	2.50	-	-	1	-	-						
Duckworth,G	24	28	12	234	39*	14.62	-	-	45	15	-						
Duleepsinhji,KS	12	19	2	995	173	58.52	3	5	10	-	6	7	0	-	-	-	-
Durston,FJ	1	2	1	8	6*	8.00	-	-	-	-	202	136	5	27.20	-	-	4/102
Edmonds,PH	51	65	15	875	64	17.50	-	2	42	-	12028	4273	125	34.18	2	-	7/66
Edrich,JH	77	127	9	5138	310*	43.54	12	24	43	-	30	23	0	-	-	-	-
Edrich,WJ	39	63	2	2440	219	40.00	6	13	39	-	3234	1693	41	41.29	-	-	4/68
Elliott,H	4	5	1	61	37*	15.25	-	-	8	3	-						
Ellison,RM	11	16	1	202	41	13.46	-	-	2	-	2264	1048	35	29.94	3	1	6/77
Emburey,JE	60	89	18	1540	75	21.68	-	8	33	-	14227	5105	138	36.99	6	-	7/78
Emmett,GM	1	2	0	10	10	5.00	-	-	-	-	-						
Emmett,T	7	13	1	160	48	13.33	-	-	9	-	728	284	9	31.55	1	-	7/68
Evans,AJ	1	2	0	18	14	9.00	-	-	-	-	-						

ENGLAND (cont.)	**BATTING AND FIELDING**										**BOWLING**						
	Tests	I	N	Runs	HS	Avge	100	50	Ct	St	Balls	Runs	Wks	Avge	5w	10w	BB
Evans,TG	91	133	14	2439	104	20.49	2	8	173	46	-						
Fagg,AE	5	8	0	150	39	18.75	-	-	5	-	-						
Fairbrother,NH	7	9	1	63	33*	7.87	-	-	4	-	-						
Fane,FL	14	27	1	682	143	26.23	1	3	6	-	-						
Farnes,K	15	17	5	58	20	4.83	-	-	1	-	3932	1719	60	28.65	3	1	6/96
Farrimond,W	4	7	0	116	35	16.57	-	-	5	2	-						
Fender,PGH	13	21	1	380	60	19.00	-	2	14	-	2178	1185	29	40.86	2	-	5/90
Ferris,JJ	1	1	0	16	16	16.00	-	-	-	-	272	91	13	7.00	2	1	7/37
Fielder,A	6	12	5	78	20	11.14	-	-	4	-	1491	711	26	27.34	1	-	6/82
Fishlock,LB	4	5	1	47	19*	11.75	-	-	1	-	-						
Flavell,JA	4	6	2	31	14	7.75	-	-	-	-	792	367	7	52.42	-	-	2/65
Fletcher,KWR	59	96	14	3272	216	39.90	7	19	54	-	285	193	2	96.50	-	-	1/6
Flowers,W	8	14	0	254	56	18.14	-	1	2	-	858	296	14	21.14	1	-	5/46
Ford,FGJ	5	9	0	168	48	18.66	-	-	5	-	210	129	1	129.00	-	-	1/47
Foster,FR	11	15	1	71	330	23.57	-	3	11	-	2447	926	45	20.57	4	-	6/91
Foster,NA	28	43	7	410	39	11.38	-	-	7	-	6081	2797	88	31.78	5	1	8/107
Foster,RE	8	14	1	602	287	46.30	1	1	13	-	-						
Fothergill,AJ	2	2	0	33	32	16.50	-	-	-	-	321	90	8	11.25	-	-	4/19
Fowler,G	21	37	0	1307	201	35.32	3	8	10	-	18	11	0	-	-	-	-
Fraser,ARC	11	14	1	88	29	6.76	-	-	1	-	3058	1256	47	26.72	4	-	6/82
Freeman,AP	12	16	5	154	50*	14.00	-	1	4	-	3732	1707	66	25.86	5	3	7/71
French,BN	16	21	4	308	59	18.11	-	1	38	1	-						
Fry,CB	26	41	3	1223	144	32.18	2	7	17	-	10	3	0	-	-	-	-
Gatting,MW	68	117	14	3870	207	37.57	9	18	51	-	752	317	4	79.25	-	-	1/14
Gay,LH	1	2	0	37	33	18.50	-	-	3	1	-						
Geary,G	14	20	4	249	66	15.56	-	2	13	-	3810	1353	46	29.41	4	1	7/70
Gibb,PA	8	13	0	581	120	44.69	2	3	3	1	-						
Gifford,N	15	20	9	179	25*	16.27	-	-	8	-	3084	1026	33	31.09	1	-	5/55
Gilligan,AER	11	16	3	209	39*	16.07	-	-	3	-	2404	1046	36	29.05	2	1	6/7
Gilligan,AHH	4	4	0	71	32	17.75	-	-	-	-	-						
Gimblett,H	3	5	1	129	67*	32.25	-	1	1	-	-						
Gladwin,C	8	11	5	170	51*	28.33	-	1	2	-	2129	571	15	38.06	-	-	3/21
Goddard,TWJ	8	5	3	13	8	6.50	-	-	3	-	1563	588	22	26.72	1	-	6/29
Gooch,GA	99	179	6	7573	333	43.77	17	41	96	-	2295	894	22	40.63	-	-	3/39
Gover,AR	4	1	1	2	2*	-	-	-	1	-	816	359	8	44.87	-	-	3/85
Gower,DI	117	204	18	8231	215	44.25	18	39	74	-	36	20	1	20.00	-	-	1/1
Grace,EM	1	2	0	36	36	18.00	-	-	1	-	-						
Grace,GF	1	2	0	0	0	0.00	-	-	2	-	-						
Grace,WG	22	36	2	1098	170	32.29	2	5	39	-	666	236	9	26.22	-	-	2/12
Graveney,TW	79	123	13	4882	258	44.38	11	20	80	-	260	167	1	167.00	-	-	1/34
Greenhough,T	4	4	1	4	2	1.33	-	-	1	-	1129	357	16	22.31	1	-	5/35
Greenwood,A	2	4	0	77	49	19.25	-	-	2	-	-						
Greig,AW	58	93	4	3599	148	40.43	8	20	87	-	9802	4541	141	32.20	6	2	8/86
Greig,IA	2	4	0	26	14	6.50	-	-	-	-	188	114	4	28.50	-	-	4/53
Grieve,BAF	2	3	2	40	14*	40.00	-	-	-	-	-						
Griffith,SC	3	5	0	157	140	31.40	1	-	5	-	-						
Gunn,G	15	29	1	1120	122*	40.00	2	7	15	-	12	8	0	-	-	-	-
Gunn,JR	6	10	2	85	24	10.62	-	-	3	-	999	387	18	21.50	1	-	5/76
Gunn,W	11	20	2	392	102*	21.77	1	1	5	-	-						
Haig,NE	5	9	0	126	47	14.00	-	-	4	-	1026	448	13	34.46	-	-	3/73
Haigh,S	11	18	3	113	25	7.53	-	-	8	-	1294	622	24	25.91	1	-	6/11
Hallows,C	2	2	1	42	26	42.00	-	-	-	-	-						
Hammond,WR	85	140	16	7249	336*	58.45	22	24	110	-	7969	3138	83	37.80	2	-	5/36
Hampshire,JH	8	16	1	403	107	26.86	1	2	9	-	-						
Hardinge,HTW	1	2	0	30	25	15.00	-	-	-	-	-						
Hardstaff,J sr	5	10	0	311	72	31.10	-	3	1	-	-						

ENGLAND (cont.)	BATTING AND FIELDING										BOWLING						
	Tests	I	N	Runs	HS	Avge	100	50	Ct	St	Balls	Runs	Wks	Avge	5w	10w	BB
Hardstaff,J jr	23	38	3	1636	205*	46.74	4	10	9	-	-						
Harris,Lord	4	6	1	145	52	29.00	-	1	2	-	32	29	0	-	-	-	-
Hartley,JC	2	4	0	15	9	3.75	-	-	2	-	192	115	1	115.00	-	-	1/62
Hawke,Lord	5	8	1	55	30	7.85	-	-	3	-	-						
Hayes,EG	5	9	1	86	35	10.75	-	-	2	-	90	52	1	52.00	-	-	1/28
Hayes,FC	9	17	1	244	106*	15.25	1	-	7	-	-						
Hayward,TW	35	60	2	1999	137	34.46	3	12	19	-	887	514	14	36.71	-	-	4/22
Hearne,A	1	1	0	9	9	9.00	-	-	1	-	-						
Hearne,F	2	2	0	47	27	23.50	-	-	1	-	-						
Hearne,GG	1	1	0	0	0	0.00	-	-	-	-	-						
Hearne,JT	12	18	4	126	40	9.00	-	-	4	-	2976	1082	49	22.08	4	1	6/41
Hearne,JW	24	36	5	806	114	26.00	1	2	13	-	2926	1462	30	48.73	1	-	5/49
Hemmings,EE	16	21	4	383	95	22.52	-	2	5	-	4437	1825	43	42.44	1	-	6/58
Hendren,EH	51	83	9	3525	205*	47.63	7	21	33	-	47	31	1	31.00	-	-	1/27
Hendrick,M	30	35	15	128	15	6.40	-	-	25	-	6208	2248	87	25.83	-	-	4/28
Heseltine,C	2	2	0	18	18	9.00	-	-	3	-	157	84	5	16.80	1	-	5/38
Hick,GA	11	17	0	307	51	18.05	-	1	22	-	774	306	6	51.00	-	-	4/126
Higgs,K	15	19	3	185	63	11.56	-	1	4	-	4112	1473	71	20.74	2	-	6/91
Hill,A	2	4	2	101	49	50.50	-	-	1	-	340	130	7	18.57	-	-	4/27
Hill,AJL	3	4	0	251	124	62.75	1	1	1	-	40	8	4	2.00	-	-	4/8
Hilton,MJ	4	6	1	37	15	7.40	-	-	1	-	1244	477	14	34.07	1	-	5/61
Hirst,GH	24	38	3	790	85	22.57	-	5	18	-	3967	1770	59	30.00	3	-	5/48
Hitch,JW	7	10	3	103	51*	14.71	-	1	4	-	462	325	7	46.42	-	-	2/31
Hobbs,JB	61	102	7	5410	211	56.94	15	28	17	-	376	165	1	165.00	-	-	1/19
Hobbs,RNS	7	8	3	34	15*	6.80	-	-	8	-	1291	481	12	40.08	-	-	3/25
Hollies,WE	13	15	8	37	18*	5.28	-	-	2	-	3554	1332	44	30.27	5	-	7/50
Holmes,ERT	5	9	2	114	85*	16.28	-	1	4	-	108	76	2	38.00	-	-	1/10
Holmes,P	7	14	1	357	88	27.46	-	4	3	-	-						
Hone,L	1	2	0	13	7	6.50	-	-	2	-	-						
Hopwood,JL	2	3	1	12	8	6.00	-	-	-	-	462	155	0	-	-	-	-
Hornby,AN	3	6	0	21	9	3.50	-	-	-	-	28	0	1	0.00	-	-	1/0
Horton,MJ	2	2	0	60	58	30.00	-	1	2	-	238	59	2	29.50	-	-	2/24
Howard,ND	4	6	1	86	23	17.20	-	-	4	-	-						
Howell,H	5	8	6	15	5	7.50	-	-	-	-	918	559	7	79.85	-	-	4/115
Howorth,R	5	10	2	145	45*	18.12	-	-	2	-	1536	635	19	33.42	1	-	6/124
Humphries,J	3	6	1	44	16	8.80	-	-	7	-	-						
Hunter,J	5	7	2	93	39*	18.60	-	-	8	3	-						
Hussain,N	3	5	0	100	35	20.00	-	-	1	-	-						
Hutchings,KL	7	12	0	341	126	28.41	1	1	9	-	90	81	1	81.00	-	-	1/5
Hutton,L	79	138	15	6971	364	56.67	19	33	57	-	260	232	3	77.33	-	-	1/2
Hutton,RA	5	8	2	219	81	36.50	-	2	9	-	738	257	9	28.55	-	-	3/72
Iddon,J	5	7	1	170	73	28.33	-	2	-	-	66	27	0	-	-	-	-
Igglesden,AP	1	1	1	2	2*	-	-	-	1	-	222	146	3	48.66	-	-	2/91
Ikin,JT	18	31	2	606	60	20.89	-	3	31	-	572	354	3	118.00	-	-	1/38
Illingworth,R	61	90	11	1836	113	23.24	2	5	45	-	11934	3807	122	31.20	3	-	6/29
Illingworth,RK	2	4	2	31	13	15.50	-	-	1	-	340	213	4	53.25	-	-	3/110
Insole,DJ	9	17	2	408	110*	27.20	1	1	8	-	-						
Jackman,RD	4	6	0	42	17	7.00	-	-	-	-	1070	445	14	31.78	-	-	4/110
Jackson,Hon.FS	20	33	4	1415	144*	48.79	5	6	10	-	1587	799	24	33.29	1	-	5/52
Jackson,HL	2	2	1	15	8	15.00	-	-	1	-	498	155	7	22.14	-	-	2/26
Jameson,JA	4	8	0	214	82	26.75	-	1	-	-	42	17	1	17.00	-	-	1/17
Jardine,DR	22	33	6	1296	127	48.00	1	10	26	-	6	10	0	-	-	-	-
Jarvis,PW	6	9	2	109	29*	15.57	-	-	-	-	1347	708	14	50.57	-	-	4/107
Jenkins,RO	9	12	1	198	39	18.00	-	-	4	-	2118	1098	32	34.31	1	-	5/116
Jessop,GL	18	26	0	569	104	21.88	1	3	11	-	742	354	10	35.40	-	-	4/68
Jones,AO	12	21	0	291	34	13.85	-	-	15	-	228	133	3	44.33	-	-	3/73

ENGLAND (cont.)	BATTING AND FIELDING										BOWLING						
	Tests	I	N	Runs	HS	Avge	100	50	Ct	St	Balls	Runs	Wks	Avge	5w	10w	BB
Jones,IJ	15	17	9	38	16	4.75	-	-	4	-	3546	1769	44	40.20	1	-	6/118
Jupp,H	2	4	0	68	63	17.00	-	1	2	-	-						
Jupp,VWC	8	13	1	208	38	17.33	-	-	5	-	1301	616	28	22.00	-	-	4/37
Keeton,WW	2	4	0	57	25	14.25	-	-	-	-	-						
Kennedy,AS	5	8	2	93	41*	15.50	-	-	5	-	1683	599	31	19.32	2	-	5/76
Kenyon,D	8	15	0	192	87	12.80	-	1	5	-	-						
Killick,ET	2	4	0	81	31	20.25	-	-	2	-	-						
Kilner,R	9	8	1	233	74	33.28	-	2	6	-	2368	734	24	30.58	-	-	4/51
King,JH	1	2	0	64	60	32.00	-	1	-	-	162	99	1	99.00	-	-	1/99
Kinneir,S	1	2	0	52	30	26.00	-	-	-	-	-						
Knight,AE	3	6	1	81	70*	16.20	-	1	1	-	-						
Knight,BR	29	38	7	812	127	26.19	2	-	14	-	5377	2223	70	31.75	-	-	4/38
Knight,DJ	2	4	0	54	38	13.50	-	-	1	-	-						
Knott,APE	95	149	15	4389	135	32.75	5	30	250	19	-						
Knox,NA	2	4	1	24	8*	8.00	-	-	-	-	126	105	3	35.00	-	-	2/39
Laker,JC	46	63	15	676	63	14.08	-	2	12	-	12027	4101	193	21.24	9	3	10/53
Lamb,AJ	79	139	10	4656	142	36.09	14	18	75	-	30	23	1	23.00	-	-	1/6
Langridge,J	8	9	0	242	70	26.88	-	1	6	-	1074	413	19	21.73	2	-	7/56
Larkins,W	13	25	1	493	64	20.54	-	3	8	-							
Larter,JDF	10	7	2	16	10	3.20	-	-	5	-	2172	941	37	25.43	2	-	5/57
Larwood,H	21	28	3	485	98	19.40	-	2	15	-	4969	2212	78	28.35	4	1	6/32
Lawrence,DV	5	6	0	60	34	10.00	-	-	-	-	1089	676	18	37.55	1	-	5/106
Leadbeater,E	2	2	0	40	38	20.00	-	-	3	-	289	218	2	109.00	-	-	1/38
Lee,HW	1	2	0	19	18	9.50	-	-	-	-	-						
Lees,WS	5	9	3	66	25*	11.00	-	-	2	-	1256	467	26	17.96	2	-	6/78
Legge,GB	5	7	1	299	196	49.83	1	-	1	-	30	34	0	-	-	-	-
Leslie,CFH	4	7	0	106	54	15.14	-	1	1	-	96	44	4	11.00	-	-	3/31
Lever,JK	21	31	5	306	53	11.76	-	1	11	-	4433	1951	73	26.72	3	1	7/46
Lever,P	17	18	2	350	88*	21.87	-	2	11	-	3571	1509	41	36.80	2	-	6/38
Leveson Gower,HDG	3	6	2	95	31	23.75	-	-	1	-	-						
Levett,WHV	1	2	1	7	5	7.00	-	-	3	-	-						
Lewis,AR	9	16	2	457	125	32.64	1	3	-	-	-						
Lewis,CC	14	19	1	446	70	24.77	-	3	13	-	3096	1520	42	36.19	2	-	6/111
Leyland,M	41	65	5	2764	187	46.06	9	10	13	-	1103	585	6	97.50	-	-	3/91
Lilley,AFA	35	52	8	903	84	20.52	-	4	70	22	25	23	1	23.00	-	-	1/23
Lillywhite,J	2	3	1	16	10	8.00	-	-	1	-	340	126	8	15.75	-	-	4/70
Lloyd,D	9	15	2	552	214*	42.46	1	-	11	-	24	17	0	-	-	-	-
Lloyd,TA	1	1	1	10	10*	-	-	-	-	-	-						
Loader,PJ	13	19	6	76	17	5.84	-	-	2	-	2662	878	39	22.51	1	-	6/36
Lock,GAR	49	63	9	742	89	13.74	-	3	59	-	13147	4451	174	25.58	9	3	7/35
Lockwood,WH	12	16	3	231	52*	17.76	-	1	4	-	1970	884	43	20.55	5	1	7/71
Lohmann,GA	18	26	2	213	62*	8.87	-	1	28	-	3821	1205	112	10.75	9	5	9/28
Lowson,FA	7	13	0	245	68	18.84	-	2	5	-	-						
Lucas,AP	5	9	1	157	55	19.62	-	1	1	-	120	54	0	-	-	-	-
Luckhurst,BW	21	41	5	1298	131	36.05	4	5	14	-	57	32	1	32.00	-	-	1/9
Lyttelton,Hon.A	4	7	1	94	31	15.66	-	-	2	-	48	19	4	4.75	-	-	4/19
Macaulay,GG	8	10	4	112	76	18.66	-	1	5	-	1701	662	24	27.58	1	-	5/64
MacBryan,JCW	1	-	-	-	-	-	-	-	-	-	-						
McConnon,JE	2	3	1	18	11	9.00	-	-	4	-	216	74	4	18.50	-	-	3/19
McGahey,CP	2	4	0	38	18	9.50	-	-	1	-	-						
MacGregor,G	8	11	3	96	31	12.00	-	-	14	3	-						
McIntyre,AJW	3	6	0	19	7	3.16	-	-	8	-	-						
MacKinnon,FA	1	2	0	5	5	2.50	-	-	-	-	-						
MacLaren,AC	35	61	4	1931	140	33.87	5	8	29	-	-						
McMaster,JEP	1	1	0	0	0	0.00	-	-	-	-	-						
Makepeace,JWH	4	8	0	279	117	34.87	1	2	-	-	-						

ENGLAND (cont.)	BATTING AND FIELDING										BOWLING						
	Tests	I	N	Runs	HS	Avge	100	50	Ct	St	Balls	Runs	Wks	Avge	5w	10w	BB
Malcolm,DE	21	29	8	105	15*	5.00	-	-	3	-	4881	2673	74	36.12	4	1	6/77
Mallender,NA	2	3	0	8	4	2.66	-	-	-	-	449	215	10	21.50	1	-	5/50
Mann,FG	7	12	2	376	136*	37.60	1	-	3	-	-						
Mann,FT	5	9	1	281	84	35.12	-	2	4	1	1						
Marks,VJ	6	10	1	249	83	27.66	-	3	-	-	1082	484	11	44.00	-	-	3/78
Marriott,CS	1	1	0	0	0	0.00	-	-	1	-	247	96	11	8.72	2	1	6/59
Martin,F	2	2	0	14	13	7.00	-	-	2	-	410	141	14	10.07	2	1	6/50
Martin,JW	1	2	0	26	26	13.00	-	-	-	-	270	129	1	129.00	-	-	1/111
Mason,JR	5	10	0	129	32	12.90	-	-	3	-	324	149	2	74.50	-	-	1/8
Matthews,ADG	1	1	1	2	2*	-	-	-	1	-	180	65	2	32.50	-	-	1/13
May,PBH	66	106	9	4537	285*	46.77	13	22	42	-	-						
Maynard,MP	1	2	0	13	10	6.50	-	-	-	-	-						
Mead,CP	17	26	2	1185	182*	49.37	4	3	4	-	-						
Mead,W	1	2	0	7	7	3.50	-	-	1	-	265	91	1	91.00	-	-	1/91
Midwinter,WE	4	7	0	95	36	13.57	-	-	5	-	776	272	10	27.20	-	-	4/81
Milburn,C	9	16	2	654	139	46.71	2	2	7	-	-						
Miller,AM	1	2	2	24	20*	-	-	-	-	-	-						
Miller,G	34	51	4	1213	98*	25.80	-	7	17	-	5149	1859	60	30.98	1	-	5/44
Milligan,FW	2	4	0	58	38	14.50	-	-	1	-	45	29	0	-	-	-	-
Millman,G	6	7	2	60	32*	12.00	-	-	13	2	-						
Milton,CA	6	9	1	204	104*	25.50	1	-	5	-	24	12	0	-	-	-	-
Mitchell,A	6	10	0	298	72	29.80	-	2	9	-	6	4	0	-	-	-	-
Mitchell,F	2	4	0	88	41	22.00	-	-	2	-	-						
Mitchell,TB	5	6	2	20	9	5.00	-	-	1	-	894	498	8	62.25	-	-	2/49
Mitchell-Innes,NS	1	1	0	5	5	5.00	-	-	-	-	-						
Mold,AW	3	3	1	0	0*	0.00	-	-	1	-	491	234	7	33.42	-	-	3/44
Moon,LJ	4	8	0	182	36	22.75	-	-	4	-	-						
Morley,F	4	6	2	6	2*	1.50	-	-	4	-	972	296	16	18.50	1	-	5/56
Morris,H	3	6	0	115	44	19.16	-	-	3	-	-						
Morris,JE	3	5	2	71	32	23.66	-	-	3	-	-						
Mortimore,JB	9	12	2	243	73*	24.30	-	1	3	-	2162	733	13	56.38	-	-	3/36
Moss,AE	9	7	1	61	26	10.16	-	-	1	-	1657	626	21	29.80	-	-	4/35
Moxon,MD	10	17	1	455	99	28.43	-	3	10	-	48	30	0	-	-	-	-
Munton,TA	2	2	1	25	25*	25.00	-	-	-	-	405	200	4	50.00	-	-	2/22
Murdoch,WL	1	1	0	12	12	12.00	-	-	-	1	-						
Murray,JT	21	28	5	506	112	22.00	1	2	52	3	-						
Newham,W	1	2	0	26	17	13.00	-	-	-	-	-						
Newport,PJ	3	5	1	110	40*	27.50	-	-	1	-	669	417	10	41.70	-	-	4/87
Nichols,MS	14	19	7	355	78*	29.58	-	2	11	-	2565	1152	41	28.09	2	-	6/35
Oakman,ASM	2	2	0	14	10	7.00	-	-	7	-	48	21	0	-	-	-	-
O'Brien,TC	5	8	0	59	20	7.37	-	-	4	-	-						
O'Connor,J	4	7	0	153	51	21.85	-	1	2	-	162	72	1	72.00	-	-	1/31
Old,CM	46	66	9	845	65	14.82	-	2	22	-	8858	4020	143	28.11	4	-	7/50
Oldfield,N	1	2	0	99	80	49.50	-	1	-	-	-						
Padgett,DEV	2	4	0	31	51	12.75	-	-	-	-	12	8	0	-	-	-	-
Paine,GAE	4	7	1	97	49	16.16	-	-	5	-	1044	467	17	27.47	1	-	5/168
Palairet,LCH	2	4	0	49	20	12.25	-	-	2	-	-						
Palmer,CH	1	2	0	22	22	11.00	-	-	-	-	30	15	0	-	-	-	-
Palmer,KE	1	1	0	10	10	10.00	-	-	-	-	378	189	1	189.00	-	-	1/113
Parfitt,PH	37	52	6	1882	131*	40.91	7	6	42	-	1326	574	12	47.83	-	-	2/5
Parker,CWL	1	1	1	3	3*	-	-	-	-	-	168	32	2	16.00	-	-	2/32
Parker,PWG	1	2	0	13	13	6.50	-	-	-	-	-						
Parkhouse,WGA	7	13	0	373	78	28.69	-	2	3	-	-						
Parkin,CH	10	16	3	160	36	12.30	-	-	3	-	2095	1128	32	35.25	2	-	5/38
Parks,JH	1	2	0	29	22	14.50	-	-	-	-	126	36	3	12.00	-	-	2/26
Parks,JM	46	68	7	1962	108*	32.16	2	9	103	11	54	51	1	51.00	-	-	1/43

ENGLAND (cont.)	BATTING AND FIELDING										BOWLING						
	Tests	I	N	Runs	HS	Avge	100	50	Ct	St	Balls	Runs	Wks	Avge	5w	10w	BB
Pataudi,Nawab of, sr	3	5	0	144	102	28.80	1	-	-	-	-						
Paynter,E	20	31	5	1540	243	59.23	4	7	7	-	-						
Peate,E	9	14	8	70	13	11.66	-	-	2	-	2096	682	31	22.00	2	-	6/85
Peebles,IAR	13	17	8	98	26	10.88	-	-	5	-	2882	1391	45	30.91	3	-	6/63
Peel,R	20	33	4	427	83	14.72	-	3	17	-	5216	1715	101	16.98	5	1	7/31
Penn,F	1	2	1	50	27*	50.00	-	-	-	-	12	2	0	-	-	-	-
Perks,RTD	2	2	2	3	2*	-	-	-	1	-	829	355	11	32.27	2	-	5/100
Philipson,H	5	8	1	63	30	9.00	-	-	8	3	-						
Pigott,ACS	1	2	1	12	8*	12.00	-	-	-	-	102	75	2	37.50	-	-	2/75
Pilling,R	8	13	1	91	23	7.58	-	-	10	4	-						
Place,W	3	6	1	144	107	28.80	1	-	-	-	-						
Pocock,PI	25	37	4	206	33	6.24	-	-	15	-	6650	2976	67	44.41	3	-	6/79
Pollard,R	4	3	2	13	10*	13.00	-	-	3	-	1102	378	15	25.20	1	-	5/24
Poole,CJ	3	5	1	161	69*	40.25	-	2	1	-	30	9	0	-	-	-	-
Pope,GH	1	1	1	8	8*	-	-	-	-	-	218	85	1	85.00	-	-	1/49
Pougher,AD	1	1	0	17	17	17.00	-	-	2	-	105	26	3	8.66	-	-	3/26
Price,JSE	15	15	6	66	32	7.33	-	-	7	-	2724	1401	40	35.02	1	-	5/73
Price,WFF	1	2	0	6	6	3.00	-	-	2	-	-						
Prideaux,RM	3	6	1	102	64	20.40	-	1	-	-	12	0	0	-	-	-	-
Pringle,DR	30	50	4	695	63	15.10	-	1	10	-	5287	2518	70	35.97	3	-	5/95
Pullar,G	28	49	4	1974	175	43.86	4	12	2	-	66	37	1	37.00	-	-	1/1
Quaife,WG	7	13	1	228	68	19.00	-	1	4	-	15	6	0	-	-	-	-
Radford,NV	3	4	1	21	12*	7.00	-	-	-	-	678	351	4	87.75	-	-	2/131
Radley,CT	8	10	0	481	158	48.10	2	2	4	-	-						
Ramprakash,MR	9	15	1	241	29	17.21	-	-	5	-	7	8	0	-	-	-	0/3
Randall,DW	47	79	5	2470	174	33.37	7	12	31	-	16	3	0	-	-	-	-
Ranjitsinhji,KS	15	26	4	989	175	44.95	2	6	13	-	97	39	1	39.00	-	-	1/23
Read,HD	1	-	-	-	-	-	-	-	-	-	270	200	6	33.33	-	-	4/136
Read,JM	17	29	2	463	57	17.14	-	2	8	-	-						
Read,WW	18	27	1	720	117	27.69	1	5	16	-	60	63	0	-	-	-	-
Reeve,DA	3	5	0	124	59	24.80	-	1	1	-	149	60	2	30.00	-	-	1/4
Relf,AE	13	21	3	416	63	23.11	-	1	14	-	1764	624	25	24.96	1	-	5/85
Rhodes,HJ	2	1	1	0	0*	-	-	-	-	-	449	244	9	27.11	-	-	4/50
Rhodes,W	58	98	21	2325	179	30.19	2	11	60	-	8231	3425	127	26.96	6	1	8/68
Richards,CJ	8	13	0	285	133	21.92	1	-	20	1	-						
Richardson,DW	1	1	0	33	33	33.00	-	-	1	-	-						
Richardson,PE	34	56	1	2061	126	37.47	5	9	6	-	120	48	3	16.00	-	-	2/10
Richardson,T	14	24	8	177	25*	11.06	-	-	5	-	4497	2220	88	25.22	11	4	8/94
Richmond,TL	1	2	0	6	4	3.00	-	-	-	-	114	86	2	43.00	-	-	2/69
Ridgway,F	5	6	0	49	24	8.16	-	-	3	-	793	379	7	54.14	-	-	4/83
Robertson,JDB	11	21	2	881	133	46.36	2	6	6	-	138	58	2	29.00	-	-	2/17
Robins,RWV	19	27	4	612	108	26.60	1	4	12	-	3318	1758	64	27.46	1	-	6/32
Robinson,RT	29	49	5	1601	175	36.38	4	6	8	-	6	0	0	-	-	-	-
Roope,GRJ	21	32	4	860	77	30.71	-	7	35	-	172	76	0	-	-	-	-
Root,CF	3	-	-	-	-	-	-	-	-	-	642	194	8	24.25	-	-	4/84
Rose,BC	9	16	2	358	70	25.57	-	2	4	-	-						
Royle,VPFA	1	2	0	21	18	10.50	-	-	2	-	16	6	0	-	-	-	-
Rumsey,FE	5	5	3	30	21*	15.00	-	-	-	-	1145	461	17	27.11	-	-	4/25
Russell,CAG	10	18	2	910	140	56.87	5	2	8	-	-						
Russell,RC	31	49	10	1060	128*	27.17	1	3	80	8	-						
Russell,WE	10	18	1	362	70	23.27	-	2	4	-	144	44	0	-	-	-	-
Salisbury,IDK	2	3	0	66	50	22.00	-	1	-	-	421	306	5	61.20	-	-	3/49
Sandham,A	14	23	0	879	325	38.21	2	3	4	-	-						
Schultz,SS	1	2	1	20	20	20.00	-	-	-	-	35	26	1	26.00	-	-	1/16
Scotton,WH	15	25	2	510	90	22.17	-	3	4	-	20	20	0	-	-	-	-
Selby,J	6	12	1	256	70	23.27	-	2	1	-	-						

ENGLAND (cont.)	BATTING AND FIELDING												BOWLING				
	Tests	I	N	Runs	HS	Avge	100	50	Ct	St	Balls	Runs	Wks	Avge	5w	10w	BB
Selvey,MWW	3	5	3	15	5*	7.50	-	-	1	-	492	343	6	57.16	-	-	4/41
Shackleton,D	7	13	7	113	42	18.83	-	-	1	-	2078	768	18	42.66	-	-	4/72
Sharp,J	3	6	2	188	105	47.00	1	1	1	-	183	111	3	37.00	-	-	3/67
Sharpe,JW	3	6	4	44	26	22.00	-	-	-	-	975	305	11	27.72	1	-	6/84
Sharpe,PJ	12	21	4	786	111	46.23	1	4	17	-	-						
Shaw,A	7	12	1	111	40	10.09	-	-	4	-	1099	285	12	23.75	1	-	5/38
Sheppard,Rev.DS	22	33	2	1172	119	37.80	3	6	12	-	-						
Sherwin,M	3	6	4	30	21*	15.00	-	-	5	2	-						
Shrewsbury,A	23	40	4	1277	164	35.47	3	4	29	-	12	2	0	-	-	-	-
Shuter,J	1	1	0	28	28	28.00	-	-	-	-	-						
Shuttleworth,K	5	6	0	46	21	7.66	-	-	1	-	1071	427	12	35.58	1	-	5/47
Sidebottom,A	1	1	0	2	2	2.00	-	-	-	-	112	65	1	65.00	-	-	1/65
Simpson,RT	27	45	3	1401	156*	33.35	4	6	5	-	45	22	2	11.00	-	-	2/4
Simpson-Hayward,GHT	5	8	1	105	29*	15.00	-	-	1	-	898	420	23	18.26	2	-	6/43
Sims,JM	4	4	0	16	12	4.00	-	-	6	-	887	480	11	43.63	1	-	5/73
Sinfield,RA	1	1	0	6	6	6.00	-	-	-	-	378	123	2	61.50	-	-	1/51
Slack,WN	3	6	0	81	52	13.50	-	1	3	-	-						
Smailes,TF	1	1	0	25	25	25.00	-	-	-	-	120	62	3	20.66	-	-	3/44
Small,GC	17	24	7	263	59	15.47	-	1	9	-	3921	1871	55	34.01	2	-	5/48
Smith,AC	6	7	3	118	69*	29.50	-	1	20	-	-						
Smith,CA	1	1	0	3	3	3.00	-	-	-	-	154	61	7	8.71	1	-	5/19
Smith,CIJ	5	10	0	102	27	10.20	-	-	1	-	930	393	15	26.20	1	-	5/16
Smith,CL	8	14	1	392	91	30.15	-	2	5	-	102	39	3	13.00	-	-	2/31
Smith,D	2	4	0	128	57	32.00	-	1	1	-	-						
Smith,DM	2	4	0	80	47	20.00	-	-	-	-	-						
Smith,DR	5	5	1	38	34	9.50	-	-	2	-	972	359	6	59.83	-	-	2/60
Smith,DV	3	4	1	25	16*	8.33	-	-	-	-	270	97	1	97.00	-	-	1/12
Smith,EJ	11	14	1	113	22	8.69	-	-	17	3	-						
Smith,H	1	1	0	7	7	7.00	-	-	1	-	-						
Smith,MJK	50	78	6	2278	121	31.63	3	11	53	-	214	128	1	128.00	-	-	1/10
Smith,RA	36	66	14	2645	148*	50.86	7	18	26	-	24	6	0	-	-	-	0/6
Smith,TPB	4	5	0	33	24	6.60	-	-	1	-	538	319	3	106.33	-	-	2/172
Smithson,GA	2	3	0	70	35	23.33	-	-	-	-	-						
Snow,JA	49	71	14	772	73	13.54	-	2	16	-	12021	5387	202	26.66	8	1	7/40
Southerton,J	2	3	1	7	6	3.50	-	-	2	-	263	107	7	15.28	-	-	4/46
Spooner,RH	10	15	0	481	119	32.06	1	4	4	-	-						
Spooner,RT	7	14	1	354	92	27.23	-	3	10	2	-						
Stanyforth,RT	4	6	1	13	6*	2.60	-	-	7	2	-						
Staples,SJ	3	5	0	65	39	13.00	-	-	-	-	1149	435	15	29.00	-	-	3/50
Statham,JB	70	87	28	675	38	11.44	-	-	28	-	16056	6261	252	24.84	9	1	7/39
Steel,AG	13	20	3	600	148	35.29	2	-	5	-	1364	605	29	20.86	-	-	3/27
Steele,DS	8	16	0	673	106	42.06	1	5	7	-	88	39	2	19.50	-	-	1/1
Stephenson,JP	1	2	0	36	25	18.00	-	-	-	-	-						
Stevens,GTS	10	17	0	263	69	15.47	-	1	9	-	1186	648	20	32.40	2	1	5/90
Stevenson,GB	2	2	1	28	27*	28.00	-	-	-	-	312	183	5	36.60	-	-	3/111
Stewart,AJ	22	40	4	1493	190	41.47	4	6	27	-	-						
Stewart,MJ	8	12	1	385	87	35.00	-	2	6	-	-						
Stoddart,AE	16	30	2	996	173	35.57	2	3	6	-	162	94	2	47.00	-	-	1/10
Storer,W	6	11	0	215	51	19.54	-	1	11	-	168	108	2	54.00	-	-	1/24
Street,GB	1	2	1	11	7*	11.00	-	-	-	1	-						
Strudwick,H	28	42	13	230	24	7.93	-	-	60	12	-						
Studd,CT	5	9	1	160	48	20.00	-	-	5	-	384	98	3	32.66	-	-	2/35
Studd,GB	4	7	0	31	9	4.42	-	-	8	-	-						
Subba Row,R	13	22	1	984	137	46.85	3	4	6	-	6	2	0	-	-	-	-
Sugg,FH	2	2	0	55	31	27.50	-	-	-	-	-						

ENGLAND (cont.)				**BATTING**	**AND**	**FIELDING**								**BOWLING**			
	Tests	I	N	Runs	HS	Avge	100	50	Ct	St	Balls	Runs	Wks	Avge	5w	10w	BB
Sutcliffe,H	54	84	9	4555	194	60.73	16	23	23	-	-						
Swetman,R	11	17	2	254	65	16.93	-	1	24	2	-						
Tate,FW	1	2	1	9	5*	9.00	-	-	2	-	96	51	2	25.50	-	-	2/7
Tate,MW	39	52	5	1198	100*	25.48	1	5	11	-	12523	4055	155	26.16	7	1	6/42
Tattersall,R	16	17	7	50	10*	5.00	-	-	8	-	4228	1513	58	26.08	4	1	7/52
Tavare,CJ	31	56	2	1755	149	32.50	2	12	20	-	30	11	0	-	-	-	-
Taylor,K	3	5	0	57	24	11.40	-	-	1	-	12	6	0	-	-	-	-
Taylor,LB	2	1	1	1	1*	-	-	-	1	-	381	178	4	44.50	-	-	2/34
Taylor,RW	57	83	12	1156	97	16.28	-	3	167	7	12	6	0	-	-	-	-
Tennyson,Hon.LH	9	12	1	345	74*	31.36	-	4	6	-	6	1	0	-	-	-	-
Terry,VP	2	3	0	16	8	5.33	-	-	2	-	-						
Thomas,JG	5	10	4	83	31*	13.83	-	-	-	-	774	504	10	50.40	-	-	4/70
Thompson,GJ	6	10	1	273	63	30.33	-	2	5	-	1367	638	23	27.73	-	-	4/50
Thomson,NI	5	4	1	69	39	23.00	-	-	3	-	1488	568	9	63.11	-	-	2/55
Titmus,FJ	53	76	11	1449	84*	22.29	-	10	35	-	15118	4931	153	32.22	7	-	7/79
Tolchard,RW	4	7	2	129	67	25.80	-	1	5	-	-						
Townsend,CL	2	3	0	51	38	17.00	-	-	-	-	140	75	3	25.00	-	-	3/50
Townsend,DCH	3	6	0	77	36	12.83	-	-	1	-	6	9	0	-	-	-	-
Townsend,LF	4	6	0	97	40	16.16	-	-	2	-	399	205	6	34.16	-	-	2/22
Tremlett,MF	3	5	2	20	18*	6.66	-	-	-	-	492	226	4	56.50	-	-	2/98
Trott,AE	2	4	0	23	16	5.75	-	-	-	-	474	198	17	11.64	1	-	5/49
Trueman,FS	67	85	14	981	39*	13.81	-	-	64	-	15178	6625	307	21.57	17	3	8/31
Tufnell,NC	1	1	0	14	14	14.00	-	-	-	1	-						
Tufnell,PCR	10	13	8	23	8	4.60	-	-	4	-	2773	1091	38	28.71	4	1	7/47
Turnbull,MJL	9	13	2	61	224	20.36	-	1	1	-	-						
Tyldesley,GE	14	20	2	990	122	55.00	3	6	2	-	3	2	0	-	-	-	-
Tyldesley,JT	31	55	1	1661	138	30.75	4	9	16	-	-						
Tyldesley,RK	7	7	1	47	29	7.83	-	-	1	-	1615	619	19	32.57	-	-	3/50
Tylecote,EFS	6	9	1	152	66	19.00	-	1	5	5	-						
Tyler,EJ	1	1	0	0	0	0.00	-	-	-	-	145	65	4	16.25	-	-	3/49
Tyson,FH	17	24	3	230	37*	10.95	-	-	4	-	3452	1411	76	18.56	4	1	7/27
Ulyett,G	25	39	0	949	149	24.33	1	7	19	-	2627	1020	50	20.40	1	-	7/36
Underwood,DL	86	116	35	937	45*	11.56	-	-	44	-	21862	7674	297	25.83	17	6	8/51
Valentine,BH	7	9	2	454	136	64.85	2	1	2	-	-						
Verity,H	40	44	12	669	66*	20.90	-	3	30	-	11173	3510	144	24.37	5	2	8/43
Vernon,GF	1	2	1	14	11*	14.00	-	-	-	-	-						
Vine,J	2	3	2	46	36	46.00	-	-	-	-	-						
Voce,W	27	38	15	308	66	13.39	-	1	15	-	6360	2733	98	27.88	3	2	7/70
Waddington,A	2	4	0	16	7	4.00	-	-	1	-	276	119	1	119.00	-	-	1/35
Wainwright,E	5	9	0	132	49	14.66	-	-	2	-	127	73	0	-	-	-	-
Walker,PM	3	4	0	128	52	32.00	-	1	5	-	78	34	0	-	-	-	-
Walters,CF	11	18	3	784	102	52.26	1	7	6	-	-						
Ward,Alan	5	6	1	40	21	8.00	-	-	3	-	761	453	14	32.35	-	-	4/61
Ward,Albert	7	13	0	487	117	37.46	1	3	1	-	-						
Wardle,JH	28	41	8	653	66	19.78	-	2	12	-	6597	2080	102	20.39	5	1	7/36
Warner,PF	15	28	2	622	132*	23.92	1	3	3	-	-						
Warr,JJ	2	4	0	4	4	1.00	-	-	-	-	584	281	1	281.00	-	-	1/76
Warren,A	1	1	0	7	7	7.00	-	-	1	-	236	113	6	18.83	1	-	5/57
Washbrook,C	37	66	6	2569	195	42.81	6	12	12	-	36	33	1	33.00	-	-	1/25
Watkin,SL	2	3	0	8	6	2.66	-	-	-	-	216	153	5	30.60	-	-	3/38
Watkins,AJ	15	24	4	810	137*	40.50	2	4	17	-	1364	554	11	50.36	-	-	3/20
Watson,W	23	37	3	879	116	25.85	2	3	8	-	-						
Webbe,AJ	1	2	0	4	4	2.00	-	-	2	-	-						
Wellard,AW	2	4	0	47	38	11.75	-	-	2	-	456	237	7	33.85	-	-	4/81
Wharton,A	1	2	0	20	13	10.00	-	-	-	-	-						
Whitaker,JJ	1	1	0	11	11	11.00	-	-	1	-	-						

ENGLAND (cont.)	BATTING AND FIELDING										BOWLING						
	Tests	I	N	Runs	HS	Avge	100	50	Ct	St	Balls	Runs	Wks	Avge	5w	10w	BB
White,DW	2	2	0	0	0	0.00	-	-	-	-	220	119	4	29.75	-	-	3/65
White,JC	15	22	9	239	29	18.38	-	-	6	-	4801	1581	49	32.26	3	1	8/126
Whysall,WW	4	7	0	209	76	29.85	-	2	7	-	16	9	0	-	-	-	-
Wilkinson,LL	3	2	1	3	2	3.00	-	-	-	-	573	271	7	38.71	-	-	2/12
Willey,P	26	50	6	1184	102*	26.90	2	5	3	-	1091	456	7	65.14	-	-	2/73
Williams,NF	1	1	0	38	38	38.00	-	-	-	-	246	148	2	74.00	-	-	2/148
Willis,RGD	90	128	55	840	28*	11.50	-	-	39	-	17357	8190	325	25.20	16	-	8/43
Wilson,CEM	2	4	1	42	18	14.00	-	-	-	-	-						
Wilson,D	6	7	1	75	42	12.50	-	-	1	-	1472	466	11	42.36	-	-	2/17
Wilson,ER	1	2	0	10	5	5.00	-	-	-	-	123	36	3	12.00	-	-	2/28
Wood,A	4	5	1	80	53	20.00	-	1	10	1	-						
Wood,B	12	21	0	454	90	21.61	-	2	6	-	98	50	0	-	-	-	-
Wood,GEC	3	2	0	7	6	3.50	-	-	5	1	-						
Wood,H	4	4	1	204	134*	68.00	1	1	2	1	-						
Wood,R	1	2	0	6	6	3.00	-	-	-	-	-						
Woods,SMJ	3	4	0	122	53	30.50	-	1	4	-	195	129	5	25.80	-	-	3/28
Woolley,FE	64	98	7	3283	154	36.07	5	23	64	-	6495	2815	83	33.91	4	1	7/76
Woolmer,RA	19	34	2	1059	149	33.09	3	2	10	-	546	299	4	74.75	-	-	1/8
Worthington,TS	9	11	0	321	128	29.18	1	1	8	-	633	316	8	39.50	-	-	2/19
Wright,CW	3	4	0	125	71	31.25	-	1	-	-	-						
Wright,DVP	34	39	13	289	45	11.11	-	-	10	-	8135	4224	108	39.11	6	1	7/105
Wyatt,RES	40	64	6	1839	149	31.70	2	12	16	-	1395	642	18	35.66	-	-	3/4
Wynward,EG	3	6	0	72	30	12.00	-	-	-	-	24	17	0	-	-	-	-
Yardley,NWD	20	34	2	812	99	25.37	-	4	14	-	1662	707	21	33.66	-	-	3/67
Young,HI	2	2	0	43	43	21.50	-	-	1	-	556	262	12	21.83	-	-	4/30
Young,JA	8	10	5	28	10*	5.60	-	-	5	-	2368	757	17	44.52	-	-	3/65
Young,RA	2	4	0	27	13	6.75	-	-	6	-	-						

SOUTH AFRICA

	BATTING AND FIELDING										BOWLING						
	Tests	I	N	Runs	HS	Avge	100	50	Ct	St	Balls	Runs	Wks	Avge	5w	10w	BB
Adcock,NAT	26	39	12	146	24	5.40	-	-	4	-	6391	2195	104	21.10	5	-	6/43
Anderson,JH	1	2	0	43	32	21.50	-	-	1	-	-						
Ashley,WH	1	2	0	1	1	0.50	-	-	-	-	173	95	7	13.57	1	-	7/95
Bacher,A	12	22	1	679	73	32.33	-	6	10	-	-						
Balaskas,XC	9	13	1	174	122*	14.50	1	-	5	-	1572	806	22	36.63	1	-	5/49
Barlow,EJ	30	57	2	2516	201	45.74	6	15	35	-	3021	1362	40	34.05	1	-	5/85
Baumgartner,HV	1	2	0	19	16	9.50	-	-	1	-	166	99	2	49.50	-	-	2/99
Beaumont,R	5	9	0	70	31	7.77	-	-	2	-	6	0	0	-	-	-	-
Begbie,DW	5	7	0	138	48	19.71	-	-	2	-	160	130	1	130.00	-	-	1/38
Bell,AJ	16	23	12	69	26*	6.27	-	-	6	-	3342	1567	48	32.64	4	-	6/99
Bisset,M	3	6	2	103	35	25.75	-	-	2	1	-						
Bissett,GF	4	4	2	38	23	19.00	-	-	-	-	989	469	25	18.76	2	-	7/29
Blanckenberg,JM	18	30	7	455	59	19.78	-	2	9	-	3888	1817	60	30.28	4	-	6/76
Bland,KC	21	39	5	1669	144*	49.08	3	9	10	-	394	125	2	62.50	-	-	2/16
Bock,EG	1	2	2	11	9*	-	-	-	-	-	138	91	0	-	-	-	-
Bond,GE	1	1	0	0	0	0.00	-	-	-	-	16	16	0	-	-	-	-
Bosch,T	1	2	2	5	5*	-	-	-	-	-	297	104	3	34.66	-		2/61
Botten,JT	3	6	0	65	33	10.83	-	-	1	-	828	337	8	42.12	-	-	2/56
Brann,WH	3	5	0	71	50	14.20	-	1	2	-	-						
Briscoe,AW	2	3	0	33	16	11.00	-	-	1	-	-						
Bromfield,HD	9	12	7	59	21	11.80	-	-	13	-	1810	599	17	35.23	1	-	5/88
Brown,LS	2	3	0	17	8	5.66	-	-	-	-	318	189	3	63.00	-	-	1/30
Burger,CGD	2	4	1	62	37*	20.66	-	-	1	-	-						

SOUTH AFRICA (cont.)	BATTING AND FIELDING										BOWLING						
	Tests	I	N	Runs	HS	Avge	100	50	Ct	St	Balls	Runs	Wks	Avge	5w	10w	BB
Burke,SF	2	4	1	42	20	14.00	-	-	-	-	660	257	11	23.36	2	1	6/128
Buys,ID	1	2	1	4	4*	4.00	-	-	-	-	144	52	0	-	-	-	-
Cameron,HB	26	45	4	1239	90	30.21	-	10	39	12	-						
Campbell,T	5	9	3	90	48	15.00	-	-	7	1	-						
Carlstein,PR	8	14	1	190	42	14.61	-	-	3	-	-						
Carter,CP	10	15	5	181	45	18.10	-	-	2	-	1475	694	28	24.78	2	-	6/50
Catterall,RH	24	43	2	1555	120	37.92	3	11	12	-	342	162	7	23.14	-	-	3/15
Chapman,HW	2	4	1	39	17	13.00	-	-	1	-	126	104	1	104.00	-	-	1/51
Cheetham,JE	24	43	6	883	89	23.86	-	5	13	-	6	2	0	-	-	-	-
Chevalier,GA	1	2	1	0	0*	0.00	-	-	1	-	253	100	5	20.00	-	-	3/68
Christy,JAJ	10	18	0	618	103	34.33	1	5	3	-	138	92	2	46.00	-	-	1/15
Chubb,GWA	5	9	3	63	15*	10.50	-	-	-	-	1425	577	21	27.47	2	-	6/51
Cochran,JAK	1	1	0	4	4	4.00	-	-	-	-	138	47	0	-	-	-	-
Coen,SK	2	4	2	101	41*	50.50	-	-	1	-	12	7	0	-	-	-	-
Commaille,JMM	12	22	1	355	47	16.90	-	-	1	-	-						
Conyngham,DP	1	2	2	6	3*	-	-	-	1	-	366	103	2	51.50	-	-	1/40
Cook,FJ	1	2	0	7	7	3.50	-	-	-	-	-						
Cooper,AHC	1	2	0	6	6	3.00	-	-	1	-	-						
Cox,JL	3	6	1	17	12*	3.40	-	-	1	-	576	245	4	61.25	-	-	2/74
Cripps,G	1	2	0	21	18	10.50	-	-	-	-	15	23	0	-	-	-	-
Crisp,RJ	9	13	1	123	35	10.25	-	-	3	-	1428	747	20	37.35	1	-	5/99
Cronje,WJ	1	2	0	7	5	3.50	-	-	-	-							
Curnow,SH	7	14	0	168	47	12.00	-	-	5	-	-						
Dalton,EL	15	24	2	698	117	31.72	2	3	5	-	864	490	12	40.83	-	-	4/59
Davies,EQ	5	8	3	9	3	1.80	-	-	-	-	768	481	7	68.71	-	-	4/75
Dawson,OC	9	15	1	293	55	20.92	-	1	10	-	1294	578	10	57.80	-	-	2/57
Deane,HG	17	27	2	628	93	25.12	-	3	8	-	-						
Dixon,CD	1	2	0	0	0	0.00	-	-	1	-	240	118	3	39.33	-	-	2/62
Donald,AA	1	2	0	0	0	0.00	-	-	-	-	270	144	6	24.00	-	-	4/77
Dower,RR	1	2	0	9	9	4.50	-	-	2	-	-						
Draper,RG	2	3	0	25	15	8.33	-	-	-	-	-						
Duckworth,CAR	2	4	0	28	13	7.00	-	-	3	-	-						
Dumbrill,R	5	10	0	153	36	15.30	-	-	3	-	816	336	9	37.33	-	-	4/30
Duminy,JP	3	6	0	30	12	5.00	-	-	2	-	60	39	1	39.00	-	-	1/17
Dunell,OR	2	4	1	42	26*	14.00	-	-	1	-	-						
Du Preez,JH	2	2	0	0	0	0.00	-	-	2	-	144	51	3	17.00	-	-	2/22
Du Toit,JF	1	2	2	2	2*	-	-	-	1	-	85	47	1	47.00	-	-	1/47
Dyer,DV	3	6	0	96	62	16.00	-	1	-	-	-						
Elgie,MK	3	6	0	75	56	12.50	-	1	4	-	66	46	0	-	-	-	-
Endean,WR	28	52	4	1630	162*	33.95	3	8	41	-	-						
Farrer,WS	6	10	2	221	40	27.62	-	-	2	-	-						
Faulkner,GA	25	47	4	1754	204	40.79	4	8	20	-	4227	2180	82	26.58	4	-	7/84
Fellows-Smith,JP	4	8	2	166	35	27.66	-	-	2	-	114	61	0	-	-	-	-
Fichardt,CG	2	4	0	15	10	3.75	-	-	2	-	114	61	0	-	-	-	-
Finlason,CE	1	2	0	6	6	3.00	-	-	-	-	12	7	0	-	-	-	-
Floquet,CE	1	2	1	12	11*	12.00	-	-	-	-	48	24	0	-	-	-	-
Francis,HH	2	4	0	39	29	9.75	-	-	1	-	-						
Francois,CM	5	9	1	252	72	31.50	-	1	5	-	684	225	6	37.50	-	-	3/23
Frank,CN	3	6	0	236	152	39.33	1	-	-	-	-						
Frank,WHB	1	2	0	7	5	3.50	-	-	-	-	58	52	1	52.00	-	-	1/52
Fuller,ERH	7	9	1	64	17	8.00	-	-	3	-	1898	668	22	30.36	1	-	5/66
Fullerton,GM	7	13	0	325	88	25.00	-	3	10	2	-						
Funston,KJ	18	33	1	824	92	25.75	-	5	7	-	-						
Gamsy,D	2	3	1	39	30*	19.50	-	-	5	-	-						
Gleeson,RA	1	2	1	4	3	4.00	-	-	2	-	-						
Glover,GK	1	2	1	21	18*	21.00	-	-	-	-	65	28	1	28.00	-	-	1/28

SOUTH AFRICA (cont.)	BATTING AND FIELDING										BOWLING						
	Tests	I	N	Runs	HS	Avge	100	50	Ct	St	Balls	Runs	Wks	Avge	5w	10w	BB
Goddard,TL	41	78	5	2516	112	34.46	1	18	48	-	11736	3226	123	26.22	5	-	6/53
Gordon,N	5	6	2	8	7*	2.00	-	-	1	-	1966	807	20	40.35	2	-	5/103
Graham,R	2	4	0	6	4	1.50	-	-	2	-	240	127	3	42.33	-	-	2/22
Grieveson,RE	2	2	0	114	75	57.00	-	1	7	3	-						
Griffin,GM	2	4	0	25	14	6.25	-	-	-	-	432	192	8	24.00	-	-	4/87
Hall,AE	7	8	2	11	5	1.83	-	-	4	-	2361	886	40	22.15	3	1	7/63
Hall,GG	1	1	0	0	0	0.00	-	-	-	-	186	94	1	94.00	-	-	1/94
Halliwell,EA	8	15	0	188	57	12.53	-	1	9	2	-						
Halse,CG	3	3	3	30	19*	-	-	-	1	-	587	260	6	43.33	-	-	3/50
Hands,PAM	7	12	0	300	83	25.00	-	2	3	-	37	18	0	-	-	-	-
Hands,RHM	1	2	0	7	7	3.50	-	-	-	-	-						
Hanley,MA	1	1	0	0	0	0.00	-	-	-	-	232	88	1	88.00	-	-	1/57
Harris,TA	3	5	1	100	60	25.00	-	1	1	-	-						
Hartigan,GPD	5	10	0	114	51	11.40	-	1	-	-	252	141	1	141.00	-	-	1/72
Harvey,RL	2	4	0	51	28	12.75	-	-	-	-	-						
Hathorn,CMH	12	20	1	325	102	17.10	1	-	5	-	-						
Hearne,F	4	8	0	121	30	15.12	-	-	2	-	62	40	2	20.00	-	-	2/40
Hearne,GAL	3	5	0	59	28	11.80	-	-	3	-	-						
Heine,PS	14	24	3	209	31	9.95	-	-	8	-	3890	1455	58	25.08	4	-	6/58
Hime,CFW	1	2	0	8	8	4.00	-	-	-	-	55	31	1	31.00	-	-	1/20
Hudson,AC	1	2	0	163	163	81.50	1	-	1	-							
Hutchinson,P	2	4	0	14	11	3.50	-	-	3	-	-						
Ironside,DEJ	3	4	2	37	13	18.50	-	-	1	-	985	275	15	18.33	1	-	5/51
Irvine,BL	4	7	0	353	102	50.42	1	2	2	-	-						
Johnson,CL	1	2	0	10	7	5.00	-	-	1	-	140	57	0	-	-	-	-
Keith,HJ	8	16	1	318	73	21.20	-	2	9	-	108	63	0	-	-	-	-
Kempis,GA	1	2	1	0	0*	0.00	-	-	-	-	168	76	4	19.00	-	-	3/53
Kirsten,PN	1	2	0	63	52	31.50	-	1	2	-							
Kotze,JJ	3	5	0	2	2	0.40	-	-	3	-	413	243	6	40.50	-	-	3/64
Kuiper,AP	1	2	0	34	34	17.00	-	-	1	-							
Kuys,F	1	2	0	26	26	13.00	-	-	-	-	60	31	2	15.50	-	-	2/31
Lance,HR	13	22	1	591	70	28.14	-	5	7	-	948	479	12	39.91	-	-	3/30
Langton,ABC	15	23	4	298	73*	15.68	-	2	8	-	4199	1827	40	45.67	1	-	5/58
Lawrence,GB	5	8	0	141	43	17.62	-	-	2	-	1334	512	28	18.28	2	-	8/53
Le Roux,FL	1	2	0	1	1	0.50	-	-	-	-	54	24	0	-	-	-	-
Lewis,PT	1	2	0	0	0	0.00	-	-	-	-	-						
Lindsay,DT	19	31	1	1130	182	37.66	3	5	57	2	-						
Lindsay,JD	3	5	2	21	9*	7.00	-	-	4	1	-						
Lindsay,NV	1	2	0	35	29	17.50	-	-	1	-	-						
Ling,WVS	6	10	0	168	38	16.80	-	-	1	-	18	20	0	-	-	-	-
Llewellyn,CB	15	28	1	544	90	20.14	-	4	7	-	2292	1421	48	29.60	4	1	6/92
Lundie,EB	1	2	1	1	1	1.00	-	-	-	-	286	107	4	26.75	-	-	4/101
Macaulay,MJ	1	2	0	33	21	16.50	-	-	-	-	276	73	2	36.50	-	-	1/10
McCarthy,CN	15	24	15	28	5	3.11	-	-	6	-	3499	1510	36	41.94	2	-	6/43
McGlew,DJ	34	64	6	2440	255*	42.06	7	10	18	-	32	23	0	-	-	-	-
McKinnon,AH	8	13	7	107	27	17.83	-	-	1	-	2546	925	26	35.57	-	-	4/128
McLean,RA	40	73	3	2120	142	30.28	5	10	23	-	4	1	0	-	-	-	-
McMillan,Q	13	21	4	306	50*	18.00	-	1	8	-	2021	1243	36	34.52	2	-	5/66
Mann,NBF	19	31	1	400	52	13.33	-	1	3	-	5796	1920	58	33.10	1	-	6/59
Mansell,PNF	13	22	2	355	90	17.75	-	2	15	-	1506	736	11	66.90	-	-	3/58
Markham,LA	1	1	0	20	20	20.00	-	-	-	-	104	72	1	72.00	-	-	1/34
Marx,WFE	3	6	0	125	36	20.83	-	-	-	-	228	144	4	36.00	-	-	3/85
Meintjes,DJ	2	3	0	43	21	14.33	-	-	3	-	246	115	6	19.16	-	-	3/38
Melle,MG	7	12	4	68	17	8.50	-	-	4	-	1667	851	26	32.73	2	-	6/71
Melville,A	11	19	2	894	189	52.58	4	3	8	-	-						
Middleton,J	6	12	5	52	22	7.42	-	-	1	-	1064	442	24	18.41	2	-	5/51

SOUTH AFRICA (cont.)	BATTING AND FIELDING										BOWLING						
	Tests	I	N	Runs	HS	Avge	100	50	Ct	St	Balls	Runs	Wks	Avge	5w	10w	BB
Mills,C	1	2	0	25	21	12.50	-	-	2	-	140	83	2	41.50	-	-	2/83
Milton,WH	3	6	0	68	21	11.33	-	-	1	-	79	48	2	24.00	-	-	1/5
Mitchell,B	42	80	9	3471	189*	48.88	8	21	56	-	2519	1380	27	51.11	1	-	5/87
Mitchell,F	3	6	0	28	12	4.66	-	-	-	-	-						
Morkel,DPB	16	28	1	663	88	24.55	-	4	13	-	1704	821	18	45.61	-	-	4/93
Murray,ARA	10	14	1	289	109	22.23	1	1	3	-	2374	710	18	39.44	-	-	4/169
Nel,JD	6	11	0	150	38	13.63	-	-	1	-	-						
Newberry,C	4	8	0	62	16	7.75	-	-	3	-	558	268	11	24.36	-	-	4/72
Newson,ES	3	5	1	30	16	7.50	-	-	3	-	874	265	4	66.25	-	-	2/58
Nicholson,F	4	8	1	76	29	10.85	-	-	3	-	-						
Nicolson,JFW	3	5	0	179	78	35.80	-	1	-	-	24	17	0	-	-	-	-
Norton,NO	1	2	0	9	7	4.50	-	-	-	-	90	47	4	11.75	-	-	4/47
Nourse,AD	34	62	7	2960	231	53.81	9	14	12	-	20	9	0	-	-	-	-
Nourse,AW	45	83	8	2234	111	29.78	1	15	43	-	3234	1553	41	37.87	-	-	4/25
Nupen,EP	17	31	7	348	69	14.50	-	2	9	-	4159	1788	50	35.76	5	1	6/46
Osche,AE	2	4	0	16	8	4.00	-	-	-	-	-						
Osche,AL	3	4	1	11	4*	3.66	-	-	1	-	649	362	10	36.20	-	-	4/79
O'Linn,S	7	12	1	297	98	27.00	-	2	4	-	-						
Owen-Smith,HG	5	8	2	252	129	42.00	1	1	4	-	156	113	0	-	-	-	-
Palm,AW	1	2	0	15	13	7.50	-	-	1	-	-						
Parker,GM	2	4	3	3	2*	1.50	-	-	-	-	366	273	8	34.12	1	-	6/152
Parkin,DC	1	2	0	6	6	3.00	-	-	1	-	130	82	3	270.33	-	-	3/82
Partridge,JT	11	12	5	73	13*	10.42	-	-	6	-	3684	1373	44	31.20	3	-	7/91
Pearse,COC	3	6	0	55	31	9.16	-	-	1	-	144	106	3	35.33	-	-	3/56
Pegler,SJ	16	28	5	356	35*	15.47	-	-	5	-	2989	1572	47	33.44	2	-	7/65
Pithey,AJ	17	27	1	819	154	31.50	1	4	3	-	12	5	0	-	-	-	-
Pithey,DB	8	12	1	138	55	12.54	-	1	6	-	1424	577	12	48.08	1	-	6/58
Plimsoll,JB	1	2	1	16	8*	16.00	-	-	-	-	237	143	3	47.66	-	-	3/128
Pollock,PM	28	41	13	607	75*	21.67	-	2	9	-	6522	2806	116	24.18	9	1	6/38
Pollock,RG	23	41	4	2256	274	60.97	7	11	17	-	414	204	4	51.00	-	-	2/50
Poore,RM	3	6	0	76	20	12.66	-	-	3	-	9	4	1	4.00	-	-	1/4
Pothecray,JE	3	4	0	26	12	6.50	-	-	2	-	828	354	9	39.33	-	-	4/58
Powell,AW	1	2	0	16	11	8.00	-	-	2	-	20	10	1	10.00	-	-	1/10
Prince,CFH	1	2	0	6	5	3.00	-	-	-	-	-						
Pringle,MW	1	2	0	19	15	9.50	-	-	-	-	208	105	2	52.50	-	-	2/62
Procter,MJ	7	10	1	226	48	25.11	-	-	4	-	1514	616	41	15.02	1	-	6/73
Promnitz,HLE	2	4	0	14	5	3.50	-	-	2	-	528	161	8	20.12	1	-	5/58
Quinn,NA	12	18	3	90	28	6.00	-	-	1	-	2922	1145	35	32.71	1	-	6/92
Reid,N	1	2	0	17	11	8.50	-	-	-	-	126	63	2	31.50	-	-	2/63
Richards,AR	1	2	0	6	6	3.00	-	-	-	-	-						
Richards,BA	4	7	0	508	140	72.57	2	2	3	-	72	26	1	26.00	-	-	1/12
Richards,WHM	1	2	0	4	4	2.00	-	-	-	-	-						
Richardson,DJ	1	2	0	10	8	5.00	-	-	6	-							
Robertson,JB	3	6	1	51	17	10.20	-	-	2	-	738	321	6	53.50	-	-	3/143
Rose-Innes,A	2	4	0	14	13	3.50	-	-	2	-	128	89	5	17.80	1	-	5/43
Routledge,TW	4	8	0	72	24	9.00	-	-	2	-	-						
Rowan,AMB	15	23	6	290	41	17.05	-	-	7	-	5193	2084	54	38.59	4	-	5/68
Rowan,EAB	26	50	5	1965	236	43.66	3	12	14	-	19	7	0	-	-	-	-
Rowe,GA	5	9	3	26	13*	4.33	-	-	4	-	998	456	15	30.40	1	-	5/115
Rushmere,MW	1	2	0	6	3	3.00	-	-	-	-							
Samuelson,SV	1	2	0	22	15	11.00	-	-	1	-	108	64	0	-	-	-	-
Schwarz,RO	20	35	8	374	61	13.85	-	1	18	-	2639	1417	55	25.76	2	-	6/47
Seccull,AW	1	2	1	23	17*	23.00	-	-	1	-	60	37	2	18.50	-	-	2/37
Seymour,MA	7	10	3	84	36	12.00	-	-	2	-	1458	588	9	65.33	-	-	3/80
Shalders,WA	12	23	1	355	42	16.13	-	-	3	-	48	6	1	6.00	-	-	1/6
Shepstone,GH	2	4	0	38	21	9.50	-	-	2	-	115	47	0	-	-	-	-

SOUTH AFRICA (cont.)	BATTING AND FIELDING											BOWLING					
	Tests	I	N	Runs	HS	Avge	100	50	Ct	St	Balls	Runs	Wks	Avge	5w	10w	BB
Sherwell,PW	13	22	4	427	115	23.72	1	1	20	16	-						
Siedle,IJ	18	34	0	977	141	28.73	1	5	7	-	19	7	1	7.00	-	-	1/7
Sinclair,JH	25	47	1	1069	106	23.23	3	3	9	-	3598	1996	63	31.68	1	-	6/26
Smith,CJE	3	6	1	106	45	21.20	-	-	2	-	-						
Smith,FW	3	6	1	45	12	9.00	-	-	2	-	-						
Smith,VI	9	16	6	39	11*	3.90	-	-	3	-	1655	769	12	64.08	-	-	4/143
Snell,RP	1	2	0	6	6	3.00	-	-	-	-	204	157	8	19.62	-	-	4/74
Snooke,SD	1	1	0	0	0	0.00	-	-	2	-	-						
Snooke,SJ	26	46	1	1008	103	22.40	1	5	24	-	1620	702	35	20.05	1	1	8/70
Solomon,WRT	1	2	0	4	2	2.00	-	-	1	-	-						
Stewart,RB	1	2	0	13	9	6.50	-	-	2	-	-						
Stricker,LA	13	24	0	342	48	14.25	-	-	3	-	174	105	1	105.00	-	-	1/36
Susskind,MJ	5	8	0	268	65	33.50	-	4	1	-	-						
Taberer,HM	1	1	0	2	2	2.00	-	-	-	-	60	47	1	48.00	-	-	1/25
Tancred,AB	2	4	1	87	29	29.00	-	-	2	-	-						
Tancred,LJ	14	26	1	530	97	21.20	-	2	3	-	-						
Tancred,VM	1	2	0	25	18	12.50	-	-	-	-	-						
Tapscott,GL	1	2	0	5	4	2.50	-	-	1	-	-						
Tapscott,LE	2	3	1	58	50*	29.00	-	1	-	-	12	2	0	-	-	-	-
Tayfield,HJ	37	60	9	862	75	16.90	-	2	26	-	13568	4405	170	25.91	14	2	9/113
Taylor,AI	1	2	0	18	12	9.00	-	-	-	-	-						
Taylor,D	2	4	0	85	36	21.25	-	-	-	-	-						
Taylor,HW	42	76	4	2936	176	40.77	7	17	19	-	342	156	5	31.20	-	-	3/15
Theunissen,NH	1	2	1	2	2*	2.00	-	-	-	-	80	51	0	-	-	-	-
Thornton,PG	1	1	1	1	1*	-	-	-	1	-	24	20	1	20.00	-	-	1/20
Tomlinson,DS	1	1	0	9	9	9.00	-	-	-	-	60	38	0	-	-	-	-
Traicos,AJ	3	4	2	8	5*	4.00	-	-	4	-	470	207	4	51.75	-	-	2/70
Trimborn,PHJ	4	4	2	13	11*	6.50	-	-	7	-	747	257	11	23.36	-	-	3/12
Tuckett,L	9	14	3	131	40*	11.90	-	-	9	-	2104	980	19	51.57	2	-	5/68
Tuckett,LR	1	2	1	0	0*	0.00	-	-	2	-	120	69	0	-	-	-	
Twentyman-Jones,PS	1	2	0	0	0	0.00	-	-	-	-	-						
Van der Bijl,PGV	5	9	0	460	125	41.11	1	2	1	-	-						
Van der Merwe,EA	2	4	1	27	19	9.00	-	-	3	-	-						
Van der Merwe,PL	15	23	2	533	76	25.38	-	3	11	-	79	22	1	22.00	-	-	1/6
Van Ryneveld,CB	19	33	6	724	83	26.81	-	3	14	-	1554	671	17	39.47	-	-	4/67
Varnals,GD	3	6	0	97	23	16.16	-	-	-	-	12	2	0	-	-	-	-
Viljoen,KG	27	50	2	124	1365	28.43	2	9	5	-	48	23	0				
Vincent,CL	25	38	12	526	60	20.23	-	2	27	-	5851	2631	84	31.32	3	-	6/51
Vintcent,CH	3	6	0	26	9	4.33	-	-	1	-	369	193	4	48.25	-	-	3/8
Vogler,AEE	15	26	6	340	65	17.00	-	2	20	-	2764	1455	64	22.73	5	1	7/94
Wade,HF	10	18	2	327	40*	20.43	-	-	4	-	-						
Wade,WW	11	19	1	511	125	28.38	1	3	15	2	-						
Waite,JHB	50	86	7	2405	134	30.44	4	16	124	17	-						
Walker,KA	2	3	0	11	10	3.66	-	-	3	-	495	197	6	32.83	-	-	4/63
Ward,TA	23	42	9	459	64	13.90	-	2	19	13	-						
Watkins,JC	15	27	1	612	92	23.53	-	3	12	-	2805	816	29	28.13	-	-	4/22
Wesley,C	3	5	0	49	35	9.80	-	-	1	-	-						
Wessels,KC	1	2	0	133	74	66.50	-	2	1	-							
Westcott,RJ	5	9	0	166	62	18.44	-	1	-	-	32	22	0	-	-	-	-
White,GC	17	31	2	872	147	30.06	2	4	10	-	498	301	9	33.44	-	-	4/47
Willoughby,JT	2	4	0	8	5	2.00	-	-	-	-	275	159	6	26.50	-	-	2/37
Wimble,CS	1	2	0	0	0	0.00	-	-	-	-	-						
Winslow,PL	5	9	0	186	108	20.66	1	-	1	-	-						
Wynne,OE	6	12	0	219	50	18.25	-	1	3	-	-						
Zulch,JW	16	32	2	985	150	32.83	2	4	4	-	24	28	0	-	-	-	-

WEST INDIES

	BATTING AND FIELDING										BOWLING						
	Tests	I	N	Runs	HS	Avge	100	50	Ct	St	Balls	Runs	Wks	Avge	5w	10w	BB
Achong,EE	6	11	1	81	22	8.10	-	-	6	-	918	378	8	47.25	-	-	2/64
Adams,JC	1	2	1	90	79*	90.00	-	1	2	-	160	59	4	14.75	-	-	4/43
Alexander,FCM	25	38	6	961	108	30.03	1	7	85	5	-						
Ali,Imtiaz	1	1	1	1	1*	-	-	-	-	-	204	89	2	44.50	-	-	2/37
Ali,Inshan	12	18	2	172	25	10.75	-	-	7	-	3718	1621	34	47.67	1	-	5/59
Allan,DW	5	7	1	75	40*	12.50	-	-	15	3	-						
Allen,IBA	2	2	2	5	4*	-	-	-	-	1	282	180	5	36.00	-	-	2/69
Ambrose,CEL	34	51	9	513	43	12.21	-	1	7	-	8219	3320	148	22.43	6	1	8/45
Arthurton,KLT	6	10	2	186	59	23.25	-	1	2	-	102	46	0	-	-	-	-
Asgarali,NR	2	4	0	62	29	15.50	-	-	-	-	-						
Atkinson,DS	22	35	6	922	219	31.79	1	5	11	-	5201	1647	47	35.04	3	-	7/53
Atkinson,ES	8	9	1	126	37	15.75	-	-	2	-	1634	589	25	23.56	1	-	5/42
Austin,RA	2	2	0	22	20	11.00	-	-	2	-	6	5	0	-	-	-	-
Bacchus,SFAF	19	30	0	782	250	26.06	1	3	17	-	6	3	0	-	-	-	-
Baichan,L	3	6	2	184	105*	46.00	1	-	2	-	-						
Baptiste,EAE	10	11	1	233	87*	23.30	-	1	2	-	1362	562	16	35.12	-	-	3/31
Barrett,AG	6	7	1	40	19	6.66	-	-	-	-	1612	603	13	46.38	-	-	3/43
Barrow,I	11	19	2	276	105	16.23	1	-	17	5	-						
Bartlett,EL	5	8	1	131	84	18.71	-	1	2	-	-						
Benjamin,KCG	1	2	0	8	7	4.00	-	-	-	-	204	108	2	54.00	-	-	2/87
Benjamin,WKM	8	10	1	124	40*	13.77	-	-	3	-	1248	564	26	21.69	-	-	4/52
Best,CA	8	13	1	342	164	28.50	1	1	8	-	30	21	0	-	-	-	-
Betancourt,N	1	2	0	52	39	26.00	-	-	-	-	-						
Binns,AP	5	8	1	64	27	9.14	-	-	14	3	-						
Birkett,LS	4	8	0	136	64	17.00	-	1	4	-	126	71	1	71.00	-	-	1/16
Bishop,IR	11	17	7	156	30*	15.60	-	-	1	-	2425	1091	53	20.58	3	-	6/87
Boyce,KD	21	30	3	657	95*	24.33	-	4	5	-	3501	1801	60	30.01	2	1	6/77
Browne,CR	4	8	1	176	70*	25.14	-	1	1	-	840	288	6	48.00	-	-	2/72
Butcher,BF	44	78	6	3104	209*	43.11	7	16	15	-	256	90	5	18.00	1	-	5/34
Butler,LS	1	1	0	16	16	16.00	-	-	-	-	240	151	2	75.50	-	-	2/151
Butts,CG	7	8	1	108	38	15.42	-	-	2	-	1554	595	10	59.50	-	-	4/73
Bynoe,MR	4	6	0	111	48	18.50	-	-	4	-	30	5	1	5.00	-	-	1/5
Camacho,GS	11	22	0	640	87	29.09	-	4	4	-	18	12	0	-	-	-	-
Cameron,FJ	5	7	1	151	75*	25.16	-	1	-	-	786	278	3	92.66	-	-	2/74
Cameron,JH	2	3	0	6	5	2.00	-	-	-	-	232	88	3	29.33	-	-	3/66
Carew,GM	4	7	1	170	107	28.33	1	-	1	-	18	2	0	-	-	-	-
Carew,MC	19	36	3	1127	109	34.15	1	5	13	-	1174	437	8	54.62	-	-	1/11
Challenor,G	3	6	0	101	46	16.83	-	-	-	-	-						
Chang,HS	1	2	0	8	6	4.00	-	-	-	-	-						
Christiani,CM	4	7	2	98	32*	19.60	-	-	6	1	-						
Christiani,RJ	22	37	3	896	107	26.35	1	4	19	2	234	108	3	36.00	-	-	3/52
Clarke,CB	3	4	1	3	2	1.00	-	-	-	-	456	261	6	43.50	-	-	3/59
Clarke,ST	11	16	5	172	35*	15.63	-	-	2	-	2477	1170	42	27.85	1	-	5/126
Constantine,LN	18	33	0	635	90	19.24	-	4	28	-	3583	1746	58	30.10	2	-	5/75
Croft,CEH	27	37	22	158	33	10.53	-	-	8	-	6165	2913	125	23.30	3	-	8/29
Da Costa,OC	5	9	1	153	39	19.12	-	-	5	-	372	175	3	58.33	-	-	1/14
Daniel,WW	10	11	4	46	11	6.57	-	-	4	-	1754	910	36	25.27	1	-	5/39
Davis,BA	4	8	0	245	68	30.62	-	3	1	-	-						
Davis,CA	15	29	5	1301	183	54.20	4	4	4	-	894	330	2	165.00	-	-	1/27
Davis,WW	15	17	4	202	77	15.53	-	1	10	-	2773	1472	45	32.71	-	-	4/19
De Caires,FI	3	6	0	232	80	38.66	-	2	1	-	12	9	0	-	-	-	-
Depeiza,CC	5	8	2	187	122	31.16	1	-	7	4	30	15	0	-	-	-	-
Dewdney,DT	9	12	5	17	5*	2.42	-	-	-	-	1641	807	21	38.42	1	-	5/21

WEST INDIES (cont.)	BATTING AND FIELDING										BOWLING						
	Tests	I	N	Runs	HS	Avge	100	50	Ct	St	Balls	Runs	Wks	Avge	5w	10w	BB
Dowe,UG	4	3	2	8	5*	8.00	-	-	3	-	1014	534	12	44.50	-	-	4/69
Dujon,PJL	81	115	11	3322	139	31.94	5	16	267	5	-						
Edwards,RM	5	8	1	65	22	9.28	-	-	-	-	1311	626	18	34.77	1	-	5/84
Ferguson,W	8	10	3	200	75	28.57	-	2	11	-	2568	1165	34	34.26	3	1	6/92
Fernandes,MP	2	4	0	49	22	12.25	-	-	-	-	-						
Findlay,TM	10	16	3	212	44*	16.30	-	-	19	2	-						
Foster,MLC	14	24	5	580	125	30.52	1	1	3	-	1776	600	9	66.66	-	-	2/41
Francis,GN	10	18	4	81	19*	5.78	-	-	7	-	1619	763	23	33.17	-	-	4/40
Frederick,MC	1	2	0	30	30	15.00	-	-	-	-	-						
Fredericks,RC	59	109	7	4334	169	42.49	8	26	62	-	1187	548	7	78.28	-	-	1/12
Fuller,RL	1	1	0	1	1	1.00	-	-	-	-	48	12	0	-	-	-	-
Furlonge,HA	3	5	0	99	64	19.80	-	1	-	-	-						
Ganteaume,AG	1	1	0	112	112	112.00	1	-	-	-	-						
Garner,J	58	68	14	672	60	12.44	-	1	42	-	13169	5433	259	20.97	7	-	6/56
Gaskin,BBM	2	3	0	17	10	5.66	-	-	1	-	474	158	2	79.00	-	-	1/15
Gibbs,GL	1	2	0	12	12	6.00	-	-	1	-	24	7	0	-	-	-	-
Gibbs,LR	79	109	39	488	25	6.97	-	-	52	-	27115	8989	309	29.09	18	2	8/38
Gilchrist,R	13	14	3	60	12	5.45	-	-	4	-	3227	1521	57	26.68	1	-	6/55
Gladstone,G	1	1	1	12	12*	-	-	-	-	-	300	189	1	189.00	-	-	1/139
Goddard,JDC	27	39	11	859	83*	30.67	-	4	22	-	2931	1050	33	31.81	1	-	5/31
Gomes,HA	60	91	11	3171	143	39.63	9	13	18	-	2401	930	15	62.00	-	-	2/20
Gomez,GE	29	46	5	1243	101	30.31	1	8	18	-	5236	1590	58	27.41	1	1	7/55
Grant,GC	12	21	5	413	71*	25.81	-	3	10	-	24	18	0	-	-	-	-
Grant,RS	7	11	1	220	77	22.00	-	1	13	-	986	353	11	32.06	-	-	3/68
Gray,AH	5	8	2	48	12*	8.00	-	-	6	-	888	377	22	17.13	-	-	4/39
Greenidge,AE	6	10	0	222	69	22.20	-	2	5	-	-						
Greenidge,CG	108	185	16	7558	226	44.72	19	34	96	-	26	4	0	-	-	-	-
Greenidge,GA	5	9	2	209	50	29.85	-	1	3	-	156	75	0	-	-	-	-
Grell,MG	1	2	0	34	21	17.00	-	-	1	-	30	17	0	-	-	-	-
Griffith,CC	28	42	10	530	54	16.56	-	1	16	-	5631	2683	94	28.54	5	-	6/36
Griffith,HC	13	23	5	91	18	5.05	-	-	4	-	2663	1243	44	28.25	2	-	6/103
Guillen,SC	5	6	2	104	54	26.00	-	1	9	2	-						
Hall,WW	48	66	14	818	50*	15.73	-	2	11	-	10421	5066	192	26.38	9	1	7/69
Harper,RA	24	31	3	532	74	19.00	-	3	35	-	3465	1252	45	27.82	1	-	6/57
Haynes,DL	103	180	21	6725	184	42.29	16	37	59	-	18	8	1	8.00	-	-	1/2
Headley,GA	22	40	4	2190	270*	60.83	10	5	14	-	398	230	0	-	-	-	-
Headley,RGA	2	4	0	62	42	15.50	-	-	2	-	-						
Hendriks,JL	20	32	8	447	64	18.62	-	2	42	5	-						
Hoad,ELG	4	8	0	98	36	12.25	-	-	1	-	-						
Holder,VA	40	59	11	682	42	14.20	-	-	16	-	9095	3627	109	33.27	3	-	6/28
Holding,MA	60	76	10	910	73	13.78	-	6	22	-	12680	5898	249	23.68	13	2	8/92
Holford,DAJ	24	39	5	768	105*	22.58	1	3	18	-	4816	2009	51	39.39	1	-	5/23
Holt,JK	17	31	2	1066	166	36.75	2	5	8	-	30	20	1	20.00	-	-	1/20
Hooper,CL	32	54	4	1409	134	28.18	3	7	29	-	2920	1247	15	83.13	-	-	2/28
Howard,AB	1	-	-	-	-	-	-	-	-	-	372	140	2	70.00	-	-	2/140
Hunte,CC	44	78	6	3245	260	45.06	8	13	16	-	270	110	2	55.00	-	-	1/17
Hunte,EAC	3	6	1	166	58	33.20	-	2	5	-	-						
Hylton,LG	6	8	2	70	19	11.66	-	-	1	-	965	418	16	26.12	-	-	4/27
Johnson,HHH	3	4	0	38	22	9.50	-	-	-	-	789	238	13	18.30	2	1	5/41
Johnson,TF	1	1	1	9	9*	-	-	-	1	-	240	129	3	43.00	-	-	2/53
Jones,CEL	4	7	0	63	19	9.00	-	-	3	-	102	11	0	-	-	-	-
Jones,PE	9	11	2	47	10*	5.22	-	-	4	-	1842	751	25	30.04	1	-	5/85
Julien,BD	24	34	6	866	121	30.92	2	3	14	-	4542	1868	50	37.36	1	-	5/57
Jumadeen,RR	12	14	10	84	56	21.00	-	1	4	-	3140	1141	29	39.34	-	-	4/72
Kallicharran,AI	66	109	10	4399	187	44.43	12	21	51	-	406	158	4	39.50	-	-	2/16
Kanhai,RB	79	137	6	6227	256	47.53	15	28	50	-	183	85	0	-	-	-	-

WEST INDIES (cont.)	**BATTING AND FIELDING**													**BOWLING**			
	Tests	I	N	Runs	HS	Avge	100	50	Ct	St	Balls	Runs	Wks	Avge	5w	10w	BB
Kentish,ESM	2	2	1	1	1*	-	-	-	1	-	540	178	8	22.25	1	-	5/49
King,CL	9	16	3	418	100*	32.15	1	2	5	-	582	282	3	94.00	-	-	1/30
King,FM	14	17	3	116	21	8.28	-	-	5	-	2869	1159	29	39.96	-	-	5/74
King,LA	2	4	0	41	20	10.25	-	-	2	-	476	154	9	17.11	1	-	5/46
Lambert,CB	1	2	0	53	39	26.50	-	-	2	-	4	4	1	4.00	-	-	1/4
Lara,BC	2	4	0	130	64	32.50	-	1	5	-	-						
Lashley,PD	4	7	0	159	49	22.71	-	-	4	-	18	1	1	1.00	-	-	1/1
Legall,RA	4	5	0	50	23	10.00	-	-	8	1	-						
Lewis,DM	3	5	2	259	88	86.33	-	3	8	-	-						
Lloyd,CH	110	175	14	7515	242*	46.67	19	39	90	-	1716	622	10	62.20	-	-	2/13
Logie,AL	52	78	9	2470	130	35.79	2	16	57	-	7	4	0	-	-	-	-
McMorris,EDAS	13	21	0	564	125	26.85	1	3	5	-	-						
McWatt,CA	6	9	2	202	54	28.85	-	2	9	1	24	16	1	16.00	-	-	1/16
Madray,IS	2	3	0	3	2	1.00	-	-	2	-	210	108	0	-	-	-	-
Marshall,MD	81	107	11	1810	92	18.85	-	10	25	-	17585	7876	376	20.94	22	4	7/22
Marshall,NE	1	2	0	8	8	4.00	-	-	-	-	279	62	2	31.00	-	-	1/22
Marshall,RE	4	7	0	143	30	20.42	-	-	1	-	52	15	0	-	-	-	-
Martin,FR	9	18	1	486	123*	28.58	1	-	2	-	1346	619	8	77.37	-	-	3/91
Martindale,EA	10	14	3	58	22	5.27	-	-	5	-	1605	804	37	21.72	3	-	5/22
Mattis,EH	4	5	0	145	71	29.00	-	1	3	-	36	14	0	-	-	-	-
Mendonça,IL	2	2	0	81	78	40.50	-	1	8	2	-						
Merry,CA	2	4	0	34	13	8.50	-	-	1	-	-						
Miller,R	1	1	0	23	23	23.00	-	-	-	-	96	28	0	-	-	-	-
Moseley,EA	2	4	0	36	26	9.00	-	-	1	-	522	261	6	43.50	-	-	2/70
Mudie,GH	1	1	0	5	5	5.00	-	-	-	-	174	40	3	13.33	-	-	3/23
Murray,DA	19	31	3	601	84	21.46	-	3	57	5	-						
Murray,DL	62	96	9	1993	91	22.90	-	11	181	8	-						
Nanan,R	1	2	0	16	8	8.00	-	-	2	-	216	91	4	22.75	-	-	2/37
Neblett,JM	1	2	1	16	11*	16.00	-	-	-	-	216	75	1	75.00	-	-	1/44
Noreiga,JM	4	5	2	11	9	30.62	-	-	2	-	1322	493	17	29.00	2	-	9/95
Nunes,RK	4	8	0	245	92	30.62	-	2	2	-	-						
Nurse,SM	29	54	1	2523	258	47.60	6	10	2	1	-	42	7	0	-	-	-
Padmore,AL	2	2	1	8	8*	8.00	-	-	-	-	474	135	1	135.00	-	-	1/36
Pairaudeau,BH	13	21	0	454	115	21.61	1	3	6	-	6	3	0	-	-	-	-
Parry,DR	12	20	3	381	65	22.41	-	3	4	-	1909	936	23	40.69	1	-	5/15
Passailaigue,CC	1	2	1	46	44	46.00	-	-	3	-	12	15	0	-	-	-	-
Patterson,BP	27	37	16	145	21*	6.90	-	-	5	-	4673	2748	92	29.87	5	-	5/39
Payne,TRO	1	1	0	5	5	5.00	-	-	5	-	-						
Philip,N	9	15	5	297	47	29.70	-	-	5	-	1820	1041	28	37.17	-	-	4/48
Pierre,LR	1	-	-	-	-	-	-	-	-	-	42	28	0	-	-	-	-
Rae,AF	15	24	2	1016	109	46.18	4	4	10	-	-						
Ramadhin,S	43	58	14	361	44	8.20	-	-	9	-	13939	4579	158	28.98	10	1	7/49
Richards,IVA	121	182	12	8540	291	50.23	24	45	122	-	5170	1964	32	61.37	-	-	2/17
Richardson,RB	63	109	10	4693	194	47.40	14	18	70	-	60	14	0	-	-	-	-
Rickards,KR	2	3	0	104	67	34.66	-	1	-	-	-						
Roach,CA	16	32	1	952	209	30.70	2	6	5	-	222	103	2	51.50	-	-	1/18
Roberts,AME	47	62	11	762	68	14.94	-	3	9	-	111355	5174	202	25.61	11	2	7/54
Roberts,AT	1	2	0	28	28	14.00	-	-	-	-	-						
Rodriguez,WV	5	7	0	96	50	13.71	-	1	3	-	573	374	7	53.42	-	-	3/51
Rowe,LG	30	49	2	2047	302	43.55	7	7	17	-	86	44	0	-	-	-	-
St Hill,EL	2	4	0	18	12	4.50	-	-	-	-	558	221	3	73.66	-	-	2/110
St Hill,WH	3	6	0	117	38	19.50	-	-	1	-	12	9	0	-	-	-	-
Scarlett,RO	3	4	1	54	29*	18.00	-	-	2	-	804	209	2	104.50	-	-	1/46
Scott,APH	1	1	0	5	5	5.00	-	-	-	-	264	140	0	-	-	-	-
Scott,OC	8	13	3	171	35	17.10	-	-	-	-	1405	925	22	42.04	1	-	5/266
Sealey,BJ	1	2	0	41	29	20.50	-	-	-	-	30	10	1	10.00	-	-	1/10

WEST INDIES (cont.)	Tests	I	N	Runs	HS	Avge	100	50	Ct	St	Balls	Runs	Wks	Avge	5w	10w	BB
	BATTING AND FIELDING											BOWLING					
Sealy,JED	11	19	2	478	92	28.11	-	3	6	1	156	94	3	31.33	-	-	2/7
Shepherd,JN	5	8	0	77	32	9.62	-	-	4	-	1445	479	19	25.21	1	-	5/104
Shillingford,GC	7	8	1	57	25	8.14	-	-	2	-	1181	537	15	35.80	-	-	3/63
Shillingford,IT	4	7	0	218	120	31.14	1	-	1	-	-						
Shivnarine,S	8	14	1	379	63	29.15	-	4	6	-	336	167	1	167.00	-	-	1/13
Simmons,PV	8	16	0	268	38	16.75	-	-	5	-	48	20	0	-	-	-	-
Singh,CK	2	3	0	11	11	3.66	-	-	2	-	506	166	5	33.20	-	-	2/28
Small,JA	3	6	0	79	52	13.16	-	1	3	-	366	184	3	61.33	-	-	2/67
Small,MA	2	1	1	3	3*	-	-	-	-	-	270	153	4	38.25	-	-	3/40
Smith,CW	5	10	1	222	55	24.66	-	1	4	1	-						
Smith,OG	26	42	0	1331	168	31.69	4	6	9	-	4431	1625	48	33.85	1	-	5/90
Sobers,GS	93	160	21	8032	365*	57.78	26	30	109	-	21599	7999	235	34.03	6	-	6/73
Solomon,JS	27	46	7	1326	100*	34.00	1	9	13	-	702	268	4	67.00	-	-	1/20
Stayers,SC	4	4	1	58	35*	19.33	-	-	-	-	636	364	9	40.44	-	-	3/65
Stollmeyer,JB	32	56	5	2159	160	42.33	4	12	20	-	990	507	13	39.00	-	-	3/32
Stollmeyer,VH	1	1	0	96	96	96.00	-	1	-	-	-						
Taylor,J	3	5	3	4	4*	2.00	-	-	-	-	672	273	10	27.30	1	-	5/109
Trim,J	4	5	1	21	12	5.25	-	-	2	-	794	291	18	16.16	1	-	5/34
Valentine,AL	36	51	21	141	14	4.70	-	-	13	-	12953	4215	139	30.32	8	2	8/104
Valentine,VA	2	4	1	35	19*	11.66	-	-	-	-	288	104	1	104.00	-	-	1/55
Walcott,CL	44	74	7	3798	220	56.68	15	14	53	11	1194	408	11	37.09	-	-	3/50
Walcott,LA	1	2	1	40	24	40.00	-	-	-	-	48	32	1	32.00	-	-	1/17
Walsh,CA	51	69	22	456	30*	9.70	-	-	7	-	10114	4444	178	24.96	5	1	6/62
Watson,CD	7	6	1	12	5	2.40	-	-	1	-	1458	724	19	38.10	-	-	4/62
Weekes,ED	48	81	5	4455	207	58.61	15	19	49	-	122	77	1	77.00	-	-	1/8
Weekes,KH	2	3	0	173	137	57.66	1	-	-	-	-						
White,AW	2	4	1	71	57*	23.66	-	1	1	-	491	152	3	50.66	-	-	2/34
Wight,CV	2	4	1	67	23	22.33	-	-	-	-	30	6	0	-	-	-	-
Wight,GL	1	1	0	21	21	21.00	-	-	-	-	-						
Wiles,CA	1	2	0	2	2	1.00	-	-	-	-	-						
Willett,ET	5	8	3	74	26	14.80	-	-	-	-	1326	482	11	43.81	-	-	3/33
Williams,AB	7	12	0	469	111	39.08	2	1	5	-	-						
Williams,D	1	2	0	6	5	3.00	-	-	4	1	-						
Williams,EAV	4	6	0	113	72	18.83	-	1	2	-	796	241	9	26.77	-	-	3/51
Wishart,KL	1	2	0	52	52	26.00	-	1	-	-	-						
Worrell,FMM	51	87	9	3860	261	49.48	9	22	43	-	7141	2672	69	38.72	2	-	7/70

NEW ZEALAND

	Tests	I	N	Runs	HS	Avge	100	50	Ct	St	Balls	Runs	Wks	Avge	5w	10w	BB
	BATTING AND FIELDING											BOWLING					
Alabaster,JC	21	34	6	272	34	9.71	-	-	7	-	3992	1863	49	38.02	-	-	4/46
Alcott,CFW	6	7	2	113	33	22.60	-	-	3	-	1206	541	6	90.16	-	-	2/102
Anderson,RW	9	18	0	423	92	23.50	-	3	1	-	-						
Anderson,WM	1	2	0	5	4	2.50	-	-	1	-	-						
Andrews,B	2	3	2	22	17	22.00	-	-	1	-	256	154	2	77.00	-	-	2/40
Badcock,FT	7	9	2	137	64	19.57	-	2	1	-	1608	610	16	38.12	-	-	4/80
Barber,RT	1	2	0	17	12	8.50	-	-	1	-	-						
Bartlett,GA	10	18	1	263	40	15.47	-	-	8	-	1768	792	24	33.00	1	-	6/38
Barton,PT	7	14	0	285	109	20.35	1	1	4	-	-						
Beard,DD	4	7	2	101	31	20.20	-	-	2	-	806	302	9	33.55	-	-	3/22
Beck,JEF	8	15	0	394	99	26.26	-	3	-	-	-						
Bell,W	2	3	3	21	21*	-	-	-	1	-	491	235	2	117.50	-	-	1/54
Bilby,GP	2	4	0	55	28	13.75	-	-	3	-	-						
Blain,TE	3	5	0	73	37	14.60	-	-	1	-	-						

NEW ZEALAND (cont.)	**BATTING AND FIELDING**										**BOWLING**						
	Tests	I	N	Runs	HS	Avge	100	50	Ct	St	Balls	Runs	Wks	Avge	5w	10w	BB
Blair,RW	19	34	6	189	64*	6.75	-	1	5	-	3525	1515	43	35.23	-	-	4/85
Blunt,RC	9	13	1	330	96	27.50	-	1	5	-	936	472	12	39.33	-	-	3/17
Bolton,BA	2	3	0	59	33	19.66	-	-	1	-	-						
Boock,SL	30	41	8	207	37	6.27	-	-	14	-	6598	2564	74	34.64	4	-	7/87
Bracewell,BP	6	12	2	24	8	2.40	-	-	1	-	1036	585	14	41.78	-	-	3/110
Bracewell,JG	41	60	11	1001	110	20.42	1	4	31	-	8403	3653	102	35.81	4	1	6/32
Bradburn,GE	4	7	2	97	30*	19.40	-	-	3	-	372	194	2	97.00	-	-	1/32
Bradburn,WP	2	4	0	62	32	15.50	-	-	2	-	-						
Brown,VR	2	3	1	51	36*	25.50	-	-	3	-	342	176	1	176.00	-	-	1/17
Burgess,MG	50	92	6	2684	119*	31.20	5	14	34	-	498	212	6	35.33	-	-	3/23
Burke,C	1	2	0	4	3	2.00	-	-	-	-	66	30	2	15.00	-	-	2/30
Burtt,TB	10	15	3	252	42	21.00	-	-	2	-	2593	1170	33	35.45	3	-	6/162
Butterfield,LA	1	2	0	0	0	0.00	-	-	-	-	78	24	0	-	-	-	-
Cairns,BL	43	65	8	928	64	16.28	-	2	30	-	10628	4279	130	32.91	6	1	7/74
Cairns,CL	5	8	0	165	61	20.62	-	1	4	-	1128	700	20	35.00	2	-	6/52
Cameron,FJ	19	30	20	116	27*	11.60	-	-	2	-	4570	1849	62	29.82	3	-	5/34
Cave,HB	19	31	5	229	22*	8.80	-	-	8	-	4074	1467	34	43.14	-	-	4/21
Chapple,ME	14	27	1	497	76	19.11	-	3	10	-	248	84	1	84.00	-	-	1/24
Chatfield,EJ	43	54	33	180	21*	8.57	-	-	7	-	10360	3958	123	32.17	3	1	6/73
Cleverley,DC	2	4	3	19	10*	19.00	-	-	-	-	222	130	0				
Collinge,RO	35	50	13	533	68*	14.40	-	2	10	-	7689	3393	116	29.25	3	-	6/63
Colquhoun,IA	2	4	2	1	1*	0.50	-	-	4	-	-						
Coney,JV	52	85	14	2668	174*	37.57	3	16	64	-	2835	966	27	35.77	-	-	3/28
Congdon,BE	61	114	7	3448	176	32.22	7	19	44	-	5620	2154	59	36.50	1	-	5/65
Cowie,J	9	13	4	90	45	10.00	-	-	3	-	2028	969	45	21.53	4	1	6/40
Cresswell,GF	3	5	3	14	12*	7.00	-	-	-	-	650	292	13	22.46	1	-	6/168
Cromb,IB	5	8	2	123	51*	20.50	-	1	1	-	960	442	8	55.25	-	-	3/113
Crowe,JJ	39	65	4	1601	128	26.24	3	6	41	-	18	3	0		-	-	
Crowe,MD	59	98	10	4205	299	47.78	13	14	58	-	1341	651	14	46.50	-	-	2/25
Cunis,RS	20	31	8	295	51	12.82	-	1	1	-	4250	1887	51	37.00	1	-	6/76
D'Arcy,JW	5	10	0	136	33	13.60	-	-	-	-	-						
Dempster,CS	10	15	4	723	136	65.72	2	5	2	-	5	10	0	-	-	-	
Dempster,EW	5	8	2	106	47	17.66	-	-	1	-	544	219	2	109.50	-	-	1/24
Dick,AE	17	30	4	370	50*	14.23	-	1	47	4	-						
Dickinson,GR	3	5	0	31	11	6.20	-	-	3	-	451	245	8	30.62	-	-	3/66
Donnelly,MP	7	12	1	582	206	52.90	1	4	7	-	30	20	0	-	-	-	-
Dowling,GT	39	77	3	2306	239	31.16	3	11	23	-	36	19	1	19.00	-	-	1/19
Dunning,JA	4	6	1	38	19	7.60	-	-	2	-	830	493	5	98.60	-	-	2/35
Edgar,BA	39	68	4	1958	161	30.59	3	12	14	-	18	3	0	-	-	-	-
Edwards,GN	8	15	0	377	55	25.13	-	3	7	-	-						
Emery,RWG	2	4	0	46	28	11.50	-	-	-	-	46	52	2	26.00	-	-	2/52
Fisher,FE	1	2	0	23	14	11.50	-	-	-	-	204	78	1	78.00	-	-	1/78
Foley,H	1	2	0	4	2	2.00	-	-	-	-	-						
Franklin,TJ	21	37	1	828	101	23.00	1	4	8	-	-						
Freeman,DL	2	2	0	2	1	1.00	-	-	-	-	240	169	1	169.00	-	-	1/91
Gallichan,N	1	2	0	32	30	16.00	-	-	-	-	264	113	3	37.66	-	-	3/99
Gedye,SG	4	8	0	193	55	24.12	-	2	-	-	-						
Gillespie,SR	1	1	0	28	28	28.00	-	-	-	-	162	79	1	79.00	-	-	1/79
Gray,EJ	10	16	0	248	50	15.50	-	1	6	-	2076	886	17	52.11	-	-	3/73
Greatbatch,MJ	20	33	5	1116	146*	39.85	2	5	14	-	6	0	0	-	-	-	-
Guillen,SC	3	6	0	98	41	16.33	-	-	4	1	-						
Guy,JW	12	23	2	440	102	20.95	1	3	2	-	-						
Hadlee,DR	26	42	5	530	56	14.32	-	1	8	-	4883	2389	71	33.64	-	-	4/30
Hadlee,RJ	86	134	19	3124	151*	27.16	2	15	39	-	21918	9611	431	22.29	36	9	9/52
Hadlee,WA	11	19	1	543	116	30.16	1	2	6	-	-						
Harford,NS	8	15	0	229	93	15.26	-	2	-	-	-						

NEW ZEALAND (cont.)	BATTING AND FIELDING										BOWLING						
	Tests	I	N	Runs	HS	Avge	100	50	Ct	St	Balls	Runs	Wks	Avge	5w	10w	BB
Harford,RI	3	5	2	7	6	2.33	-	-	11	-	-						
Harris,PGZ	9	18	1	378	101	22.23	1	1	6	-	42	14	0	-	-	-	-
Harris,RM	2	3	0	31	13	10.33	-	-	-	-	-						
Hartland,BR	3	6	0	88	45	14.66	-	-	1	-	-						
Hastings,BF	31	56	6	1510	117*	30.20	4	7	23	-	22	9	0	-	-	-	-
Hayes,JA	15	22	7	73	19	4.86	-	-	3	-	2675	1217	30	40.56	-	-	4/36
Henderson,M	1	2	1	8	6	8.00	-	-	1	-	90	64	2	32.00	-	-	2/38
Horne,PA	4	7	0	71	27	10.14	-	-	3	-	-						
Hough,KW	2	3	2	62	31*	62.00	-	-	1	-	462	175	6	29.16	-	-	3/79
Howarth,GP	47	83	5	2531	147	32.44	6	11	29	-	614	271	3	90.33	-	-	1/13
Howarth,HJ	30	42	18	291	61	12.12	-	1	33	-	8833	3178	86	36.95	2	-	5/34
James,KC	11	13	2	52	14	4.72	-	-	11	5	-						
Jarvis,TW	13	22	1	625	182	29.76	1	2	3	-	12	3	0	-	-	-	-
Jones,AH	23	42	5	1929	186	52.13	6	6	15	-	216	126	1	126.00	-	-	1/40
Kerr,JL	7	12	1	212	59	19.27	-	1	4	-	-						
Kuggeleijn,CM	2	4	0	7	7	1.75	-	-	1	-	97	67	1	67.00	-	-	1/50
Latham,RT	1	1	0	25	25	25.00	-	-	2	-	-						
Lees,WK	21	37	4	778	152	23.57	1	1	52	7	5	4	0	-	-	-	-
Leggatt,IB	1	1	0	0	0	0.00	-	-	2	-	24	6	0	-	-	-	-
Leggatt,JG	9	18	2	351	61	21.93	-	2	-	-	-						
Lissette,AF	2	4	2	2	1*	1.00	-	-	1	-	288	124	3	41.33	-	-	2/73
Lowry,TC	7	8	0	223	80	27.87	-	2	8	-	12	5	0	-	-	-	-
McEwan,PE	4	7	1	96	40*	16.00	-	-	5	-	36	13	0	-	-	-	-
MacGibbon,AR	26	46	5	814	66	19.85	-	3	13	-	5659	2160	70	30.85	1	-	5/64
McGirr,HM	2	1	0	51	51	51.00	-	1	-	-	180	115	1	115.00	-	-	1/65
McGregor,SN	25	47	2	892	111	19.82	1	3	9	-	-						
McLeod,EG	1	2	1	18	16	18.00	-	-	-	-	12	5	0	-	-	-	-
McMahon,TG	5	7	4	7	4*	2.33	-	-	7	1	-						
McRae,DAN	1	2	0	8	8	4.00	-	-	-	-	84	44	0	-	-	-	-
Matheson,AM	2	1	0	7	7	7.00	-	-	2	-	282	136	2	68.00	-	-	2/7
Meale,T	2	4	0	21	10	5.25	-	-	-	-	-						
Merritt,WE	6	8	1	73	19	10.42	-	-	2	-	936	617	12	51.41	-	-	4/104
Meuli,EM	1	2	0	38	23	19.00	-	-	-	-	-						
Milburn,BD	3	3	2	8	4*	8.00	-	-	6	2	-						
Miller,LSM	13	25	0	346	47	13.84	-	-	1	-	2	1	0	-	-	-	-
Mills,JE	7	10	1	241	117	26.77	1	-	1	-	-						
Moir,AM	17	30	8	327	41*	14.86	-	-	2	-	2650	1418	28	50.64	2	-	6/155
Moloney,DAR	3	6	0	156	64	26.00	-	1	3	-	12	9	0	-	-	-	-
Mooney,FLH	14	22	2	343	46	17.15	-	-	22	8	8	0	0	-	-	-	-
Morgan,RW	20	34	1	734	97	22.24	-	5	12	-	1114	609	5	121.80	-	-	1/16
Morrison,BD	1	2	0	10	10	5.00	-	-	1	-	186	129	2	64.50	-	-	2/129
Morrison,DK	25	35	10	146	27*	5.84	-	-	7	-	5196	3011	78	38.60	5	-	5/69
Morrison,JFM	17	29	0	656	117	22.62	1	3	9	-	264	71	2	35.50	-	-	2/52
Motz,RC	32	56	3	612	60	11.54	-	3	9	-	7034	3148	100	31.48	5	-	6/63
Murray,BAG	13	26	1	598	90	23.92	-	5	21	-	6	0	1	0.00	-	-	1/0
O'Sullivan,DR	11	21	4	158	23*	9.29	-	-	2	-	2744	1221	18	67.83	1	-	5/148
Overton,GWF	3	6	1	8	3*	1.60	-	-	1	-	729	258	9	28.66	-	-	3/65
Page,ML	14	20	0	492	104	24.60	1	2	6	-	379	231	5	46.20	-	-	2/21
Parker,JM	36	63	2	1498	121	24.55	3	5	30	-	40	24	1	24.00	-	-	1/24
Parker,NM	3	6	0	89	40	14.83	-	-	2	-							
Parore,AC	2	4	1	47	20	15.66	-	-	10	1	-						
Patel,DN	16	31	2	598	99	20.62	-	2	3	-	2092	961	15	64.06	-	-	4/87
Petherick,PJ	6	11	4	34	13	4.85	-	-	4	-	1305	685	16	42.81	-	-	3/90
Petrie,EC	14	25	5	258	55	12.90	-	1	25	-	-						
Playle,WR	8	15	0	151	65	10.06	-	1	4	-	-						
Pollard,V	32	59	7	1266	116	24.34	2	7	19	-	4421	1853	40	46.32	-	-	3/3

NEW ZEALAND (cont.)	**BATTING AND FIELDING**										**BOWLING**						
	Tests	I	N	Runs	HS	Avge	100	50	Ct	St	Balls	Runs	Wks	Avge	5w	10w	BB
Poore,MB	14	24	1	355	45	15.43	-	-	1	-	788	367	9	40.77	-	-	2/28
Priest,MW	1	1	0	26	26	26.00	-	-	-	-	72	26	1	26.00	-	-	1/26
Pringle,C	6	10	2	80	24*	10.00	-	-	-	-	1326	695	18	38.61	1	1	7/52
Puna,N	3	5	3	31	18*	15.50	-	-	1	-	480	240	4	60.00	-	-	2/40
Rabone,GO	12	20	2	562	107	31.22	1	2	5	-	1385	635	16	39.68	1	-	6/68
Redmond,RE	1	2	0	163	107	81.50	1	1	-	-	-						
Reid,JF	19	31	3	1296	180	46.28	6	2	9	-	18	7	0	-	-	-	-
Reid,JR	58	108	5	3428	142	33.28	6	22	43	1	7725	2835	85	33.35	1	-	6/60
Roberts,ADG	7	12	1	254	84*	23.09	-	1	4	-	440	182	4	45.50	-	-	1/12
Roberts,AW	5	10	1	248	66*	27.55	-	3	4	-	459	209	7	29.85	-	-	4/101
Robertson,GK	1	1	0	12	12	12.00	-	-	-	-	144	91	1	91.00	-	-	1/91
Rowe,CG	1	2	0	0	0	0.00	-	-	1	-	-						
Rutherford,KR	30	49	4	831	107*	18.46	1	5	21	-	256	161	1	161.00	-	-	1/38
Scott,RH	1	1	0	18	18	18.00	-	-	-	-	138	74	1	74.00	-	-	1/74
Scott,VJ	10	17	1	458	84	28.62	-	3	7	-	18	14	0	-	-	-	-
Shrimpton,MJF	10	19	0	265	46	13.94	-	-	2	-	257	158	5	31.60	-	-	3/35
Sinclair,BW	21	40	1	1148	138	29.43	3	3	8	-	60	32	2	16.00	-	-	2/32
Sinclair,IM	2	4	1	25	18*	8.33	-	-	1	-	233	120	1	120.00	-	-	1/79
Smith,FB	4	6	1	237	96	47.40	-	2	1	-							
Smith,HD	1	1	0	4	4	4.00	-	-	-	-	120	113	1	113.00	-	-	1/113
Smith,IDS	63	88	17	1815	173	25.56	2	6	168	8	18	5	0	-	-	-	-
Snedden,CA	1	-	-	-	-	-	-	-	-	-	96	46	0	-	-	-	-
Snedden,MC	25	30	8	327	33*	14.86	-	-	7	-	4775	2199	58	37.91	1	-	5/68
Sparling,JT	11	20	2	229	50	12.72	-	1	3	-	708	327	5	65.40	-	-	1/9
Stirling,DA	6	9	2	108	26	15.42	-	-	1	-	902	601	13	46.23	-	-	4/88
Su'a,ML	2	3	2	56	36	56.00	-	-	1	-	600	236	8	29.50	-	-	3/87
Sutcliffe,B	42	76	8	2727	230*	40.10	5	15	20	-	538	344	4	86.00	-	-	2/38
Taylor,BR	30	50	6	898	124	20.40	2	2	10	-	6334	2953	111	26.60	4	-	7/74
Taylor,DD	3	5	0	159	77	31.80	-	1	2	-	-						
Thomson,K	2	4	1	94	69	31.33	-	1	-	-	21	9	1	9.00	-	-	1/9
Thomson,SA	4	8	2	242	80*	40.33	-	2	3	-	526	282	6	47.00	-	-	3/63
Tindill,EWT	5	9	1	73	37*	9.12	-	-	6	1	-						
Troup,GB	15	18	6	55	13*	4.58	-	-	2	-	3183	1454	39	37.28	1	1	6/95
Truscott,PB	1	2	0	29	26	14.50	-	-	1	-	-						
Turner,GM	41	73	6	2991	259	44.64	7	14	42	-	12	5	0	-	-	-	-
Vance,RH	4	7	0	207	68	29.57	-	1	-	-	-						
Vivian,GE	5	6	0	110	43	18.33	-	-	3	-	198	107	1	107.00	-	-	1/14
Vivian,HG	7	10	0	421	100	42.10	1	5	4	-	1311	633	17	37.23	-	-	4/85
Wadsworth,KJ	33	51	4	1010	80	21.48	-	5	92	4	-						
Wallace,WM	13	21	0	439	66	20.90	-	5	5	-	6	5	0	-	-	-	-
Ward,JT	8	12	6	75	35*	12.50	-	-	16	1	-						
Watson,W	10	14	5	54	11	6.00	-	-	3	-	2688	1100	30	36.66	1	-	6/78
Watt,L	1	2	0	2	2	1.00	-	-	-	-							
Webb,MG	3	2	0	12	12	6.00	-	-	-	-	732	471	4	117.75	-	-	2/114
Webb,PN	2	3	0	11	5	3.66	-	-	2	-	-						
Weir,GL	11	16	2	416	74*	29.71	-	3	3	-	342	209	7	29.85	-	-	3/38
White,DJ	2	4	0	31	18	7.75	-	-	-	-	3	5	0	-	-	-	-
Whitelaw,PE	2	4	2	64	30	32.00	-	-	-	-	-						
Wright,JG	77	138	6	4964	185	37.60	12	21	36	-	30	5	0	-	-	-	-
Yuile,BW	17	33	6	481	64	17.81	-	1	12	-	2897	1213	34	35.67	-	-	4/43

INDIA

	BATTING AND FIELDING										BOWLING						
	Tests	I	N	Runs	HS	Avge	100	50	Ct	St	Balls	Runs	Wks	Avge	5w	10w	BB
Abid Ali,S	29	53	3	1018	81	20.36	-	6	32	-	4164	1980	47	42.12	1	-	6/55
Adhikari,HR	21	36	8	872	114*	31.14	1	4	8	-	170	82	3	27.33	-	-	3/68
Amarnath,M	69	113	10	4378	138	42.50	11	24	47	-	3676	1782	32	55.68	-	-	4/63
Amarnath,NB	24	40	4	878	118	24.38	1	4	13	-	4241	1481	45	32.91	2	-	5/96
Amarnath,S	10	18	0	550	124	30.55	1	3	4	-	11	5	1	5.00	-	-	1/5
Amar Singh,L	7	14	1	292	51	22.46	-	1	3	-	2182	858	28	30.64	2	-	7/86
Amir Elahi	1	2	0	17	13	8.50	-	-	-	-	-						
Ankola,SA	1	1	0	6	6	6.00	-	-	-	-	180	128	2	64.00	-	-	1/35
Apte,AL	1	2	0	15	8	7.50	-	-	-	-	-						
Apte,ML	7	13	2	542	163*	49.27	1	3	2	-	6	3	0	-	-	-	-
Arshad Ayub	13	19	4	257	57	17.13	-	1	2	-	3662	1438	41	35.07	3	-	5/50
Arun,B	2	2	1	4	2*	4.00	-	-	2	-	252	116	4	29.00	-	-	3/76
Arun Lal	16	29	1	729	93	26.03	-	6	13	-	16	7	0	-	-	-	-
Azad,K	7	12	0	135	24	11.25	-	-	3	-	750	373	3	124.33	-	-	2/84
Azharuddin,M	46	70	3	3168	199	47.28	11	10	35	-	6	8	0	-	-	-	-
Baig,AA	10	18	0	428	112	23.77	1	2	6	-	18	15	0	-	-	-	-
Banerjee,S	1	1	0	3	3	3.00	-	-	-	-	108	47	3	15.66	-	-	3/47
Banerjee,SA	1	1	0	0	0	0.00	-	-	3	-	306	181	5	36.20	-	-	4/120
Banerjee,SN	1	2	0	13	8	6.50	-	-	-	-	273	127	5	25.40	-	-	4/54
Baqa Jilani,M	1	2	1	16	12	16.00	-	-	-	-	90	55	0	-	-	-	-
Bedi,BS	67	101	28	656	50*	8.98	-	1	26	-	21367	7637	266	28.71	14	1	7/98
Bhandari,P	3	4	0	77	39	19.25	-	-	1	-	78	39	0	-	-	-	-
Bhat,AR	2	3	1	6	6	3.00	-	-	-	-	438	151	4	37.75	-	-	2/65
Binny,RMH	27	41	5	830	83*	23.05	-	5	11	-	2870	1534	47	32.63	2	-	6/65
Borde,CG	55	97	11	3061	177*	35.59	5	18	37	-	5695	2417	52	46.48	1	-	5/88
Chandrasekhar,BS	58	80	39	167	22	4.07	-	-	25	-	15963	7199	242	29.74	16	2	8/79
Chauhan,CPS	40	68	2	2084	97	31.57	-	16	38	-	174	106	2	53.00	-	-	1/4
Chowdhury,NR	2	2	1	3	3*	3.00	-	-	-	-	516	205	1	205.00	-	-	1/130
Colah,SHM	2	4	0	69	31	17.25	-	-	2	-	-						
Contractor,NJ	31	52	1	1611	108	31.58	1	11	18	-	186	80	1	80.00	-	-	1/9
Dani,HT	1	-	-	-	-	-	-	-	1	-	60	19	1	19.00	-	-	1/9
Desai,RB	28	44	13	418	85	13.48	-	1	9	-	5597	2761	74	37.31	2	-	6/56
Dilawar Hussain	3	6	0	254	59	42.33	-	3	6	1	-						
Divecha,RV	5	5	0	60	26	12.00	-	-	5	-	1044	361	11	32.81	-	-	3/102
Doshi,DR	33	38	10	129	20	4.60	-	-	10	-	9322	3502	114	30.71	6	-	6/102
Durani,SA	29	50	2	1202	104	25.04	1	7	14	-	6446	2657	75	35.42	3	1	6/73
Engineer,FM	46	87	3	2611	121	31.08	2	16	66	16	-						
Gadkari,CV	6	10	4	129	50*	21.50	-	1	6	-	102	45	0	-	-	-	-
Gaekwad,AD	40	70	4	1985	201	30.07	2	10	15	-	334	187	2	93.50	-	-	1/4
Gaekwad,DK	11	20	1	350	52	18.42	-	1	5	-	12	12	0	-	-	-	-
Gaekwad,HG	1	2	0	22	14	11.00	-	-	-	-	222	47	0	-	-	-	-
Gandotra,A	2	4	0	54	18	13.50	-	-	1	-	6	5	0	-	-	-	-
Gavaskar,SM	125	214	16	10122	236*	51.12	34	45	108	-	380	206	1	206.00	-	-	1/34
Ghavri,KD	39	57	14	913	86	21.23	-	2	16	-	7042	3656	109	33.54	4	-	5/33
Ghorpade,JM	8	15	0	229	41	15.26	-	-	4	-	150	131	0	-	-	-	-
Ghulam Ahmed	22	31	9	192	50	8.72	-	1	11	-	5650	2052	68	30.17	4	1	7/49
Gopalan,MJ	1	2	1	18	11*	18.00	-	-	3	-	114	39	1	39.00	-	-	1/39
Gopinath,CD	8	12	1	242	50*	22.00	-	1	2	-	48	11	1	11.00	-	-	1/11
Guard,GM	2	2	0	11	7	5.50	-	-	2	-	396	182	3	60.66	-	-	2/69
Guha,S	4	7	2	17	6	3.40	-	-	2	-	674	311	3	103.66	-	-	2/66
Gul Mahomed	8	15	0	166	34	11.06	-	-	3	-	77	24	2	12.00	-	-	2/21
Gupte,BP	3	3	2	28	17*	28.00	-	-	-	-	678	349	3	116.33	-	-	1/54
Gupte,SP	36	42	13	183	21	6.31	-	-	14	-	11284	4403	149	29.55	12	1	9/102

INDIA (cont.)	**BATTING AND FIELDING**										**BOWLING**						
	Tests	I	N	Runs	HS	Avge	100	50	Ct	St	Balls	Runs	Wks	Avge	5w	10w	BB
Gursharan Singh	1	1	0	18	18	18.00	-	-	2	-	-						
Hanumant Singh	14	24	2	686	105	31.18	1	5	11	-	66	51	0	-	-	-	-
Hardikar,MS	2	4	1	56	32*	18.66	-	-	3	-	108	55	1	55.00	-	-	1/9
Hazare,VS	30	52	6	2192	164*	47.65	7	9	11	-	2840	1220	20	61.00	-	-	4/29
Hindelkar,DD	4	7	2	71	26	14.20	-	-	3	-	-						
Hirwani,ND	14	18	10	45	17	5.62	-	-	5	-	3978	1799	58	31.01	3	1	8/61
Ibrahim,KC	4	8	0	169	85	21.12	-	1	-	-							
Indrajitsinhji,KS	4	7	1	51	23	8.50	-	-	6	3	-						
Irani,JK	2	3	2	3	2*	3.00	-	-	2	1	-						
Jahingir Khan,M	4	7	0	39	13	5.57	-	-	4	-	606	255	4	63.75	-	-	4/60
Jai,LP	1	2	0	19	19	9.50	-	-	-	-	-						
Jaisimha,ML	39	71	4	2056	129	30.68	3	12	17	-	2097	829	9	92.11	-	-	2/54
Jamshedji,RJD	1	2	2	5	4*	-	-	-	2	-	210	137	3	45.66	-	-	3/137
Jayantilal,K	1	1	0	5	5	5.00	-	-	-	-	-						
Joshi,PG	12	20	1	207	52*	10.89	-	1	18	9	-						
Kanitkar,HS	2	4	0	111	65	27.75	-	1	-	-	-						
Kapil Dev	115	168	13	4690	163	30.25	7	24	58	-	24967	11894	401	29.66	23	2	9/83
Kardar,AH	3	5	0	80	43	16.00	-	-	1	-	-						
Kenny,RB	5	10	1	245	62	27.72	-	3	1	-	-						
Kirmani,SMH	88	124	22	2759	102	27.04	2	12	160	38	18	13	1	13.00	-	-	1/9
Kishenchand,G	5	10	0	89	44	8.90	-	-	1	-	-						
Kripal Singh,AG	14	20	5	422	100*	28.13	1	2	4	-	1518	584	10	58.40	-	-	3/43
Krishnamurthy,P	5	6	0	33	20	5.50	-	-	7	1	-						
Kulkarni,RR	3	2	0	2	2	1.00	-	-	1	-	366	227	5	45.40	-	-	3/85
Kulkarni,UN	4	8	5	13	7	4.33	-	-	-	-	448	238	5	47.60	-	-	2/37
Kumar,VV	2	2	0	6	6	3.00	-	-	2	-	605	202	7	28.85	1	-	5/64
Kumble,AR	1	1	0	2	2	2.00	-	-	-	-	360	170	3	56.66	-	-	3/105
Kunderan,BK	18	34	4	981	192	32.70	2	3	23	7	24	13	0	-	-	-	-
Lall Singh	1	2	0	44	29	22.00	-	-	1	-	-						
Lamba,R	4	5	0	102	53	20.40	-	1	5	-	-						
Madan Lal,S	39	62	16	1042	74	22.65	-	5	15	-	5997	2846	71	40.08	4	-	5/23
Maka,ES	2	1	1	2	2*	-	-	-	2	1	-						
Malhotra,A	7	10	1	226	72*	25.11	-	1	2	-	18	3	0	-	-	-	-
Maninder Singh	34	38	12	99	15	3.80	-	-	9	-	7816	3143	81	38.80	3	2	7/27
Manjrekar,SV	21	34	2	1303	218	40.71	3	5	12	-	11	11	0	-	-	-	-
Manjrekar,VL	55	92	10	3208	189*	39.12	7	15	19	2	204	44	1	44.00	-	-	1/16
Mankad,AV	22	42	3	991	97	25.41	-	6	12	-	41	43	0	-	-	-	-
Mankad,MH	44	72	5	2109	231	31.47	5	6	33	-	14686	5236	162	32.32	8	2	8/52
Mantri,MK	4	8	1	67	39	9.57	-	-	8	1	-						
Meherhomji,KR	1	1	1	0	0*	-	-	-	1	-	-						
Mehra,VL	8	14	1	329	62	25.30	-	2	1	-	36	6	0	-	-	-	-
Merchant,VM	10	18	0	859	154	47.72	3	3	7	-	54	40	0	-	-	-	-
Milka Singh,AG	4	6	0	92	35	15.33	-	-	2	-	6	2	0	-	-	-	-
Modi,RS	10	17	1	736	112	46.00	1	6	3	-	30	14	0	-	-	-	-
More,KS	38	53	12	1104	73	26.92	-	6	82	16	12	12	0	-	-	-	-
Muddiah,VM	2	3	1	11	11	5.50	-	-	-	-	318	134	3	44.66	-	-	2/40
Mushtaq Ali,S	11	20	1	612	112	32.21	2	3	7	-	378	202	3	67.33	-	-	1/45
Nadkarni,RG	41	67	12	1414	122*	25.70	1	7	22	-	9165	2559	88	29.07	4	1	6/43
Naik,SS	3	6	0	141	77	23.50	-	1	-	-							
Naoomal Jeoomal	3	5	1	108	43	27.00	-	-	-	-	108	68	2	34.00	-	-	1/4
Narasimha Rao,MV	4	6	1	46	20*	9.20	-	-	8	-	463	227	3	75.66	-	-	2/46
Navle,JG	2	4	0	42	13	10.50	-	-	1	-	-						
Nayak,SV	2	3	1	19	11	9.50	-	-	1	-	231	132	1	132.00	-	-	1/16
Nayudu,CK	7	14	0	350	81	25.00	-	2	4	-	858	386	9	42.88	-	-	3/40
Nayudu,CS	11	19	3	147	36	9.18	-	-	3	-	522	359	2	179.50	-	-	1/19
Nazir Ali,S	2	4	0	30	13	7.50	-	-	-	-	138	83	4	20.75	-	-	4/83

INDIA (cont.)	BATTING AND FIELDING										BOWLING						
	Tests	I	N	Runs	HS	Avge	100	50	Ct	St	Balls	Runs	Wks	Avge	5w	10w	BB
Nissar,Mahomed	6	11	3	55	14	6.87	-	-	2	-	1211	707	25	28.28	3	-	5/90
Nyalchand,S	1	2	1	7	6*	7.00	-	-	-	-	384	97	3	32.33	-	-	3/97
Pai,AM	1	2	0	10	9	5.00	-	-	-	-	114	31	2	15.50	-	-	2/29
Palia,PE	2	4	1	29	16	9.66	-	-	-	-	42	13	0	-	-	-	-
Pandit,CS	5	8	1	171	39	24.42	-	-	14	2	-						
Parkar,GA	1	2	0	7	6	3.50	-	-	1	-	-						
Parkar,RD	2	4	0	80	35	20.00	-	-	-	-	-						
Parsana,DD	2	2	0	1	1	0.50	-	-	-	-	120	50	1	50.00	-	-	1/32
Patankar,CT	1	2	1	14	13	14.00	-	-	3	-	-						
Pataudi,Nawab of, sr	3	5	0	55	22	11.00	-	-	-	-	-						
Pataudi,Nawab of, jr	46	83	3	2793	203*	34.91	6	16	27	-	132	88	1	88.00	-	-	1/10
Patel,BP	21	38	5	972	115*	29.45	1	5	17	-	-						
Patel,JM	7	10	1	25	12	2.77	-	-	2	-	1725	637	29	21.96	2	1	9/69
Patel,RG	1	2	0	0	0	0.00	-	-	1	-	84	51	0	-	-	-	-
Patiala,Yuvaraj of	1	2	0	84	60	42.00	-	1	-	-	-						
Patil,SM	29	47	4	1588	174	36.93	4	7	12	-	645	240	9	26.66	-	-	2/28
Patil,SR	1	1	1	14	14*	-	-	-	1	-	138	51	2	25.50	-	-	1/15
Phadkar,DG	31	45	7	1229	123	32.34	2	8	21	-	5994	2285	62	36.85	3	-	7/159
Prabhakar,M	18	30	7	876	95	38.08	-	6	6	-	4562	2331	53	43.98	3	-	6/132
Prasanna,EAS	49	84	20	735	37	11.48	-	-	18	-	14353	5742	189	30.38	10	2	8/76
Punjabi,PH	5	10	0	164	33	16.40	-	-	5	-	-						
Rai Singh,K	1	2	0	26	24	13.00	-	-	-	-	-						
Rajinder Pal	1	2	1	6	3*	6.00	-	-	-	-	78	22	0	-	-	-	-
Rajindernath,V	1	-	-	-	-	-	-	-	-	4	-						
Rajput,LS	2	4	0	105	61	26.25	-	1	1	-	-						
Raman,WV	6	10	1	303	96	33.66	-	3	3	-	258	66	2	33.00	-	-	1/7
Ramaswami,C	2	4	1	170	60	56.66	-	1	-	-	-						
Ramchand,GS	33	53	5	1180	109	24.58	2	5	20	-	4976	1899	41	46.31	1	-	6/49
Ramji,L	1	2	0	1	1	0.50	-	-	1	-	138	64	0	-	-	-	-
Rangachari,CR	4	6	3	8	8*	2.66	-	-	-	-	846	493	9	54.77	1	-	5/107
Rangnekar,KM	3	6	0	33	18	5.50	-	-	1	-	-						
Ranjane,VB	7	9	3	40	16	6.66	-	-	1	-	1265	649	19	34.15	-	-	4/72
Razdan,V	2	2	1	6	6*	6.00	-	-	-	-	240	141	5	28.20	1	-	5/79
Reddy,B	4	5	1	38	21	9.50	-	-	9	2	-						
Rege,MR	1	2	0	15	15	7.50	-	-	1	-	-						
Roy,A	4	7	0	91	48	13.00	-	-	-	-	-						
Roy,Pankaj	43	79	4	2442	173	32.56	5	9	13	-	104	66	1	66.00	-	-	1/6
Roy,Pranab	2	3	1	71	60*	35.50	-	1	1	-	-						
Sandhu,BS	8	11	4	214	71	30.57	-	2	1	-	1020	557	10	55.70	-	-	3/87
Sardesai,DN	30	55	4	2001	212	39.23	5	9	4	-	59	45	0	-	-	-	-
Sarwate,CT	9	17	1	208	37	13.00	-	-	-	-	658	374	3	124.66	-	-	1/16
Saxena,RC	1	2	0	25	16	12.50	-	-	-	-	12	11	0	-	-	-	-
Sekhar,TA	2	1	1	0	0*	-	-	-	-	-	216	129	0	-	-	-	-
Sen,P	14	18	4	165	25	11.78	-	-	20	11	-						
Sengupta,AK	1	2	0	9	8	4.50	-	-	-	-	-						
Sharma,AK	1	2	0	53	30	26.50	-	-	1	-	24	9	0	-	-	-	-
Sharma,C	23	27	9	396	54	22.00	-	1	7	-	3470	2163	61	35.45	4	1	6/58
Sharma,G	5	4	1	11	10*	3.66	-	-	2	-	1307	418	10	41.80	-	-	4/88
Sharma,PH	5	10	0	187	54	18.70	-	1	1	-	24	8	0	-	-	-	-
Sharma,SK	2	3	1	56	38	28.00	-	-	1	-	414	247	6	41.16	-	-	3/37
Shastri,RJ	76	115	14	3760	206	37.22	11	12	36	-	15391	6028	148	40.72	2	-	5/75
Shinde,SG	7	11	5	85	14	14.16	-	-	-	-	1515	717	12	59.75	1	-	6/91
Shodhan,RH	3	4	1	181	110	60.33	1	-	1	-	60	26	0	-	-	-	-
Shukla,RC	1	-	-	-	-	-	-	-	-	-	294	152	2	76.00	-	-	2/82
Sidhu,NS	20	33	2	894	116	28.83	2	4	3	-	6	9	0	-	-	-	-
Sivaramakrishnan,L	9	9	1	130	25	16.25	-	-	9	-	2367	1145	26	44.03	3	1	6/64

INDIA (cont.)	BATTING AND FIELDING										BOWLING						
	Tests	I	N	Runs	HS	Avge	100	50	Ct	St	Balls	Runs	Wks	Avge	5w	10w	BB
Sohoni,SW	4	7	2	83	29*	16.60	-	-	2	-	532	202	2	101.00	-	-	1/16
Solkar,ED	27	48	6	1068	102	25.42	1	6	53	-	2265	1070	18	59.44	-	-	3/28
Sood,MM	1	2	0	3	3	1.50	-	-	-	-	-						
Srikkanth,K	43	72	3	2062	123	29.88	2	12	40	-	216	113	0	-	-	-	-
Srinath,J	5	9	4	78	21	15.60	-	-	1	-	1207	553	10	55.30	-	-	3/59
Srinivasan,TE	1	2	0	48	29	24.00	-	-	-	-	-						
Subramanya,V	9	15	1	263	75	18.78	-	2	9	-	444	201	3	67.00	-	-	2/32
Sunderam,G	2	1	1	3	3*	-	-	-	-	-	396	166	3	55.33	-	-	2/46
Surendranath,R	11	20	7	136	27	10.46	-	-	4	-	2602	1053	26	40.50	2	-	5/75
Surti,RF	26	48	4	1263	99	28.70	-	9	26	-	3870	1962	42	46.71	1	-	5/74
Swamy,VN	1	-	-	-	-	-	-	-	-	-	108	45	0	-	-	-	-
Tamhane,NS	21	27	5	225	54*	10.22	-	1	35	16	-						
Tarapore,KK	1	1	0	2	2	2.00	-	-	-	-	114	72	0	-	-	-	-
Tendulkar,SR	16	25	2	956	148*	41.56	3	4	10	-	246	119	3	39.66	-	-	2/10
Umrigar,PR	59	94	8	3631	223	42.22	12	14	33	-	4725	1473	35	42.08	2	-	6/74
Vengsarkar,DB	116	185	22	6868	166	42.13	17	35	78	-	47	36	0	-	-	-	-
Venkatapathy Raju,SL	8	12	3	151	31	16.77	-	-	3	-	1629	588	20	29.40	1	-	6/12
Venkataraghavan,S	57	76	12	748	64	11.68	-	2	44	-	14877	5634	156	36.11	3	1	8/72
Venkataramana,M	1	2	2	0	0*	-	-	-	1	-	70	58	1	58.00	-	-	1/10
Viswanath,GR	91	155	10	6080	222	41.93	14	35	63	-	70	46	1	46.00	-	-	1/11
Viswanath,S	3	5	0	31	20	6.20	-	-	11	-	-						
Vizianagaram, Maharajkumar of	3	6	2	33	19*	8.25	-	-	1	-	-						
Wadekar,AL	37	71	3	2113	143	31.07	1	14	46	-	61	55	0	-	-	-	-
Wassan,AS	4	5	1	94	53	23.50	-	1	1	-	712	504	10	50.40	-	-	4/108
Wazir Ali,S	7	14	0	237	42	12.92	-	-	1	-	30	25	0	-	-	-	-
Yadav,NS	35	40	12	404	43	14.42	-	-	10	-	8349	3580	102	35.09	3	-	5/76
Yajurvindra Singh	4	7	1	109	43*	7.16	-	-	11	-	120	50	0	-	-	-	-
Yashpal Sharma	37	59	11	1606	140	33.45	2	9	16	-	30	17	1	17.00	-	-	1/6
Yograj Singh	1	2	0	10	6	5.00	-	-	-	-	90	63	1	63.00	-	-	1/63

PAKISTAN

	BATTING AND FIELDING										BOWLING						
	Tests	I	N	Runs	HS	Avge	100	50	Ct	St	Balls	Runs	Wks	Avge	5w	10w	BB
Aamer Malik	13	17	3	489	117	34.92	2	2	15	1	126	73	1	73.00	-	-	1/0
Aamer Sohail	5	9	1	413	205	51.62	1	1	3	-	30	14	0	-	-	-	0/0
Aaqib Javed	13	10	3	26	10	3.71	-	-	1	-	2004	1013	25	40.52	-	-	4/100
Abdul Kadir	4	8	0	272	95	34.00	-	2	-	1	-						
Abdul Qadir	67	77	10	1029	61	15.35	-	3	15	-	17126	7742	236	32.80	15	5	9/56
Afaq Hussain	2	4	4	66	35*	-	-	-	2	-	240	106	1	106.00	-	-	1/40
Aftab Baloch	2	3	1	97	69*	48.50	-	1	-	-	44	17	0	-	-	-	-
Aftab Gul	6	8	0	182	33	22.75	-	-	3	-	6	4	0	-	-	-	-
Agha Saadat Ali	1	1	1	8	8*	-	-	-	3	-	-						
Agha Zahid	1	2	0	15	14	7.50	-	-	-	-	-						
Akram Raza	3	2	0	5	5	2.50	-	-	4	-	476	218	5	43.60	-	-	2/37
Alimuddin	25	45	2	1091	109	25.37	2	7	8	-	84	75	1	75.00	-	-	1/17
Amir Elahi	5	7	1	65	47	10.83	-	-	-	-	400	248	7	35.42	-	-	4/134
Anil Dalpat	9	12	1	167	52	15.18	-	1	23	3	-						
Anwar Hussain	4	6	0	42	17	7.00	-	-	-	-	36	29	1	29.00	-	-	1/25
Anwar Khan	1	2	1	15	12	15.00	-	1	-	-	32	12	0	-	-	-	-
Arif Butt	3	5	0	59	20	11.80	-	-	-	-	666	288	14	20.57	1	-	6/89
Ashraf Ali	8	8	3	229	65	45.80	-	2	17	5	-						
Asif Iqbal	58	99	7	3575	175	38.85	11	12	36	-	3864	1502	53	28.33	2	-	5/48

PAKISTAN (cont.)	BATTING AND FIELDING										BOWLING						
	Tests	I	N	Runs	HS	Avge	100	50	Ct	St	Balls	Runs	Wks	Avge	5w	10w	BB
Asif Masood	16	19	10	93	30*	10.33	-	-	5	-	3038	1568	38	41.26	1	-	5/111
Asif Mujtaba	8	13	0	292	59	22.46	-	3	7	-	96	32	1	32.00	-	-	1/0
Ataur Rehman	1	-	-	-	-	-	-	-	-	-	108	69	3	23.00	-	-	3/69
Azeem Hafeez	18	21	5	134	24	8.37	-	-	1	-	4291	2202	63	34.95	4	-	6/46
Azhar Khan	1	1	0	14	14	14.00	-	-	-	-	18	2	1	2.00	-	-	1/2
Azmat Rana	1	1	0	49	49	49.00	-	-	-	-	-						
D'Souza,A	6	10	8	76	23*	38.00	-	-	3	-	1587	745	17	43.82	1	-	5/112
Ehteshamuddin	5	3	1	2	2	1.00	-	-	2	-	940	375	16	23.43	1	-	5/47
Farooq Hamid	1	2	0	3	3	1.50	-	-	-	-	184	107	1	107.00	-	-	1/82
Farrukh Zaman	1	-	-	-	-	-	-	-	-	-	80	15	0	-	-	-	-
Fazal Mahmood	34	50	6	620	60	14.09	-	1	11	-	9834	3434	139	24.70	13	4	7/42
Ghazali,MEZ	2	4	0	32	18	8.00	-	-	-	-	48	18	0	-	-	-	-
Ghulam Abbas	1	2	0	12	12	6.00	-	-	-	-	-						
Gul Mahomed	1	2	1	39	27*	39.00	-	-	-	-	-						
Hanif Mohammad	55	97	8	3915	337	43.98	12	15	40	-	206	95	1	95.00	-	-	1/1
Haroon Rashid	23	36	1	1217	153	34.77	3	5	16	-	8	3	0	-	-	-	-
Haseeb Ahsan	12	16	7	61	14	6.77	-	-	1	-	2835	1330	27	49.25	2	-	6/202
Ijaz Ahmed	19	25	0	743	122	29.72	2	3	6	-	54	18	1	18.00	-	-	1/9
Ijaz Butt	8	16	2	279	58	19.92	-	1	5	-	-						
Ijaz Faqih	5	8	1	183	105	26.14	1	-	-	-	534	299	4	74.75	-	-	1/38
Imran Khan	88	126	25	3807	136	37.69	6	18	28	-	19458	8258	362	22.81	23	6	8/58
Imtiaz Ahmed	41	72	1	2079	209	29.28	3	11	77	16	6	0	0	-	-	-	-
Intikhab Alam	47	77	10	1493	138	22.28	1	8	20	-	10474	4494	125	35.92	5	2	7/52
Inzamamul Haq	4	6	1	66	26	13.20	-	-	4	-	-						
Iqbal Qasim	50	57	15	549	56	13.07	-	1	42	-	13019	4807	171	28.11	8	2	7/49
Israr Ali	4	8	1	33	10	4.71	-	-	1	-	318	165	6	27.50	-	-	2/29
Jalaluddin	6	3	2	3	2	3.00	-	-	-	-	1200	538	11	48.90	-	-	3/77
Javed Akhtar	1	2	1	4	2*	4.00	-	-	-	-	96	52	0	-	-	-	-
Javed Burki	25	48	4	1341	140	30.47	3	4	7	-	42	23	0	-	-	-	-
Javed Miandad	117	177	21	8465	280*	54.26	23	41	93	1	1470	682	17	40.11	-	-	3/74
Kardar,AH	23	37	3	847	93	24.91	-	5	15	-	2712	954	21	45.42	-	-	3/35
Khalid Hassan	1	2	1	17	10	17.00	-	-	-	-	126	116	2	58.00	-	-	2/116
Khalid Ibadulla	4	8	0	253	166	31.62	1	-	3	-	336	99	1	99.00	-	-	1/42
Khalid Wazir	2	3	1	14	9*	7.00	-	-	-	-	-						
Khan Mohammad	13	17	7	100	26*	10.00	-	-	4	-	3157	1292	54	23.92	4	-	6/21
Liaquat Ali	5	7	3	28	12	7.00	-	-	1	-	808	359	6	59.83	-	-	3/80
Mahmood Hussain	27	39	6	336	35	10.18	-	-	5	-	5910	2628	68	38.64	2	-	6/67
Majid Khan	63	106	5	3930	167	38.91	8	19	70	-	3584	1456	27	53.92	-	-	4/45
Mansoor Akhtar	19	29	3	655	111	25.19	1	3	9	-	-						
Manzoor Elahi	4	6	1	109	52	21.80	-	1	4	-	180	84	2	42.00	-	-	1/8
Maqsood Ahmed	16	27	1	507	99	19.50	-	2	13	-	462	191	3	63.66	-	-	2/12
Masood Anwar	1	2	0	39	37	19.50	-	-	0	-	161	102	3	34.00	-	-	2/59
Mathias,W	21	36	3	783	77	23.72	-	3	22	-	24	20	0	-	-	-	-
Miran Bux	2	3	2	1	1*	1.00	-	-	-	-	348	115	2	57.50	-	-	2/82
Mohammad Aslam	1	2	0	34	18	17.00	-	-	-	-	-						
Mohammad Farooq	7	9	4	85	47	17.00	-	-	1	-	1427	682	21	32.47	-	-	4/70
Mohammad Ilyas	10	19	0	441	126	23.21	1	1	6	-	84	63	0	-	-	-	-
Mohammad Munaf	4	7	2	63	19	12.60	-	-	-	-	769	341	11	31.00	-	-	4/42
Mohammad Nazir	14	18	10	144	29*	18.00	-	-	4	-	3262	1124	34	33.05	3	-	7/99
Mohsin Kamal	7	7	5	31	13*	15.50	-	-	2	-	1024	597	17	35.11	-	-	4/127
Mohsin Khan	48	79	6	2709	200	37.10	7	9	34	-	86	30	0	-	-	-	-
Moin Khan	9	11	2	134	32	14.88	-	-	17	1							
Mudassar Nazar	76	116	8	4114	231	38.09	10	17	48	-	5967	2532	66	38.36	1	-	6/32
Mufasir-ul-Haq	1	1	1	8	8*	-	-	-	1	-	222	84	3	28.00	-	-	2/50
Munir Malik	3	4	1	7	4	2.33	-	-	1	-	684	358	9	39.77	1	-	5/128
Mushtaq Ahmed	8	11	3	45	11*	5.62	-	-	1	-	1584	716	19	37.68	-	-	3/32

PAKISTAN (cont.)	**BATTING AND FIELDING**										**BOWLING**						
	Tests	I	N	Runs	HS	Avge	100	50	Ct	St	Balls	Runs	Wks	Avge	5w	10w	BB
Mushtaq Mohammad	57	100	7	3643	201	39.17	10	19	42	-	5260	2309	79	29.22	3	-	5/28
Nadeem Abbasi	3	2	0	46	36	23.00	-	-	6	-	-						
Nadeem Ghauri	1	1	0	0	0	0.00	-	-	0	-	48	20	0	-	-	-	-
Nasim-ul-Ghani	29	50	5	747	101	16.60	1	2	11	-	4406	1959	52	37.67	2	-	6/76
Naushad Ali	6	11	0	156	39	14.18	-	-	9	-	-						
Naved Anjum	2	3	0	44	22	14.66	-	-	0	-	342	162	4	40.50	-	-	2/57
Nazar Mohammad	5	8	1	277	124*	39.57	1	1	7	-	12	4	0	-	-	-	-
Niaz Ahmed	2	3	3	17	16*	-	-	-	1	-	294	94	3	31.33	-	-	2/72
Pervez Sajjad	19	20	11	123	24	13.66	-	-	9	-	4145	1410	59	23.89	3	-	7/74
Qasim Omar	26	43	2	1502	210	36.63	3	5	15	-	6	0	0	-	-	-	-
Rameez Raja	44	71	5	2149	122	32.56	2	16	26	-							
Rashid Khan	4	6	3	155	59	51.66	-	1	2	-	738	360	8	45.00	-	-	3/129
Rehman,SF	1	2	0	10	8	5.00	-	-	1	-	204	99	1	99.00	-	-	1/43
Rashid Latif	1	1	0	50	50	50.00	-	1	2	1	-						
Rizwan-uz-Zaman	11	19	1	345	60	19.16	-	3	4	-	132	46	4	11.50	-	-	3/26
Sadiq Mohammad	41	74	2	2579	166	35.81	5	10	28	-	200	98	0	-	-	-	-
Saeed Ahmed	41	78	4	2991	172	40.41	5	16	13	-	1980	802	22	36.45	-	-	4/64
Saeed Anwar	1	2	-	-	-	-.00	-	-	1	-	-						
Salahuddin	5	8	2	117	34*	19.50	-	-	3	-	546	187	7	26.71	-	-	2/36
Saleem Jaffer	14	14	6	42	10*	5.25	-	-	2	-	2531	1139	36	31.63	1	-	5/40
Saleem Malik	71	101	18	3743	165	45.09	10	21	48	-	272	118	5	23.60	-	-	1/3
Saleem Yousuf	32	44	5	1055	91*	27.05	-	5	91	13	-						
Salim Altaf	21	31	12	276	53*	14.52	-	1	3	-	4001	1710	46	37.17	-	-	4/11
Sarfraz Nawaz	55	72	13	1045	90	17.71	-	4	26	-	13926	5798	177	32.75	4	1	9/86
Shafiq Ahmed	6	10	1	99	27*	11.00	-	-	-	-	8	1	0	-	-	-	-
Shafqat Rana	5	7	0	221	95	31.57	-	2	5	-	36	9	1	9.00	-	-	1/2
Shahid Israr	1	1	1	7	7*	-	-	-	2	-	-						
Shahid Mahboob	1	-	-	-	-	-	-	-	-	-	294	131	2	65.50	-	-	2/131
Shahid Mahmood	1	2	0	25	16	12.50	-	-	-	-	36	23	0	-	-	-	-
Shahid Saeed	1	1	0	12	12	12.00	-	-	-	-	90	43	0	-	-	-	-
Sharpe,D	3	6	0	134	56	22.33	-	1	2	-	-						
Shoaib Mohammad	39	58	6	2443	203*	46.98	7	10	20	-	252	113	5	22.60	-	-	2/8
Shujauddin	19	32	6	395	47	15.19	-	-	8	-	2313	801	20	40.05	-	-	3/18
Sikander Bakht	26	35	12	146	22*	6.34	-	-	7	-	4873	2412	67	36.00	3	1	8/69
Tahir Naqqash	15	19	5	300	57	21.42	-	1	3	-	2800	1398	34	41.11	2	-	5/40
Talat Ali	10	18	2	370	61	23.12	-	2	4	-	20	7	0	-	-	-	-
Taslim Arif	6	10	2	501	201*	62.62	1	2	7	2	30	28	1	28.00	-	-	1/28
Tauseef Ahmed	33	37	19	297	35*	16.50	-	-	9	-	7604	2888	93	31.05	3	-	6/45
Waqar Hassan	21	35	1	1071	189	31.50	1	6	10	-	6	10	0	-	-	-	-
Waqar Younis	19	21	4	131	20*	7.70	-	-	1	-	3746	1908	93	20.51	10	2	7/76
Wasim Akram	44	56	9	971	123	20.66	1	4	12	-	9648	4100	169	24.26	11	2	6/62
Wasim Bari	81	112	26	1366	85	15.88	-	6	201	27	8	2	0	-	-	-	-
Wasim Raja	57	92	14	2821	125	36.16	4	18	20	-	4092	1826	51	35.80	-	-	4/50
Wazir Mohammad	20	33	4	801	189	27.62	2	3	5	-	24	15	0	-	-	-	-
Younis Ahmed	4	7	1	177	62	29.50	-	1	-	-	6	6	0	-	-	-	-
Zaheer Abbas	78	124	11	5062	274	44.79	12	20	34	-	370	132	3	44.00	-	-	2/21
Zahid Fazal	6	10	0	223	78	22.30	-	1	4	-	-						
Zakir Khan	2	2	2	9	9*	-	-	-	1	-	444	259	5	51.80	-	-	3/80
Zulfiqar Ahmed	9	10	4	200	63*	33.33	-	1	5	-	1285	366	20	18.30	2	1	6/42
Zulqarnain	3	4	0	24	13	6.00	-	-	8	2							

SRI LANKA

	BATTING AND FIELDING										BOWLING						
	Tests	I	N	Runs	HS	Avge	100	50	Ct	St	Balls	Runs	Wks	Avge	5w	10w	BB
Ahangama,FS	3	3	1	11	11	5.50	-	-	1	-	804	348	18	19.33	1	-	5/52
Amalean,KN	2	3	2	9	7*	9.00	-	-	1	-	244	156	7	22.28	-	-	4/97
Amerasinghe,MJG	2	4	1	54	34	18.00	-	-	3	-	300	150	3	50.00	-	-	2/73
Anurasiri,SD	12	15	4	36	16	3.27	-	-	3	-	2173	831	23	36.13	-	-	4/71
Atapattu,MS	2	4	0	1	1	0.25	-	-	-	-							
De Alwis,RG	11	19	0	152	28	8.00	-	-	21	2	-						
De Mel,ALF	17	28	5	326	34	14.17	-	-	9	-	3518	2180	59	36.94	3	-	6/109
De Silva,DS	12	22	3	406	61	21.36	-	2	5	-	3031	1424	38	37.47	1	-	5/59
De Silva,EAR	10	16	4	185	50	15.41	-	1	4	-	2388	1032	8	129.00	-	-	2/67
De Silva,GRA	4	7	2	41	14	8.20	-	-	-	-	956	385	7	55.00	-	-	2/38
de Silva,PA	27	48	2	1825	267	39.67	5	6	16	-	318	220	3	73.33	-	-	2/65
Dias,RL	20	36	1	1285	109	36.71	3	8	9	-	24	16	0	-	-	-	-
Fernando,ERNS	5	10	0	112	46	11.20	-	-	-	-	-						
Goonasekera,Y	2	4	0	48	23	12.00	-	-	6	-	-						
Goonatillake,HM	5	10	2	191	56	23.87	-	1	11	2	-						
Guneratne,RPW	1	2	2	0	0*	-	-	-	-	-	102	84	0	-	-	-	-
Gurusinha,AP	20	33	5	1152	137	41.14	4	3	16	-	718	354	13	27.23	-	-	2/18
Hathurusingha,UC	9	15	0	547	81	36.46	-	4	1	-	714	304	9	33.77	-	-	4/66
Jayasekera,RSA	1	2	0	2	2	1.00	-	-	-	-							
Jayasuriya,ST	8	12	2	402	81	40.20	-	3	7	-	96	45	0	-	-	-	0/1
Jeganathan,S	2	4	0	19	8	4.75	-	-	-	-	32	12	0	-	-	-	-
John,VB	6	10	5	53	27*	10.60	-	-	2	-	1281	614	28	21.92	2	-	5/60
Jurangpathy,BR	2	4	0	1	1	0.25	-	-	2	-	150	93	1	93.00	-	-	1/69
Kaluperuma,LW	2	4	1	12	11*	4.00	-	-	2	-	162	93	0	-	-	-	-
Kaluperuma,SMS	4	8	0	88	23	11.00	-	-	6	-	240	124	3	41.33	-	-	2/17
Kaluwitharana,RS	2	3	1	137	132*	68.50	1	-	4	-							
Kuruppu,DSBP	4	7	2	320	201*	64.00	1	-	1	-	-						
Kuruppuarachchi,AK	2	2	2	0	0*	-	-	-	-	-	272	152	8	19.00	1	-	5/44
Labrooy,GF	9	14	3	158	70*	14.36	-	1	3	-	2158	1194	27	44.22	1	-	5/133
Liyanage,DK	2	2	0	5	4	2.50	-	-	-	-	455	223	8	27.75	-	-	4/56
Madugalle,RS	21	39	4	1029	103	29.40	1	7	9	-	84	38	0	-	-	-	-
Madurasinghe,MAWR	3	6	1	24	11	4.80	-	-	-	-	396	172	3	57.33	-	-	3/60
Mahanama,RS	14	21	0	625	85	29.76	-	5	9	-	36	30	0	-	-	-	0/3
Mendis,LRD	24	43	1	1329	124	31.64	4	8	9	-	-						
Muralidharan,M	2	1	1	0	0*	-	-	-	1	-	397	199	4	49.75	-	-	2/109
Ramanayake,CPH	13	19	6	129	34*	9.92	-	-	4	-	2964	1550	36	43.05	1	-	5/82
Ranasinghe,AN	2	4	0	88	77	22.00	-	1	-	-	114	69	1	69.00	-	-	1/23
Ranatunga,A	36	61	3	2023	135*	34.87	3	13	17	-	1862	820	14	58.57	-	-	2/17
Ranatunga,D	2	3	0	87	44	29.00	-	-	-	-							
Ratnayake,RJ	23	36	6	433	56	14.43	-	2	9	-	4955	2563	73	35.11	5	-	6/66
Ratnayeke,JR	22	38	6	807	93	25.21	-	5	1	-	3833	1972	56	35.21	4	-	8/83
Samarasekera,MAR	4	7	0	118	57	16.85	-	1	3	-	192	104	3	34.66	-	-	2/38
Senanayake,CP	3	5	0	97	64	19.40	-	1	2								
Silva,SAR	9	16	2	353	111	25.21	2	-	33	1	-						
Tillakaratne,HP	10	16	1	388	82	25.86	-	2	28	-							
Warnapura,B	4	8	0	96	38	12.00	-	-	2	-	90	46	0	-	-	-	-
Warnaweera,KPJ	3	5	1	6	3	1.50	-	-	-	-	567	205	4	51.25	-	-	3/90
Weerasinghe,CDUS	1	1	0	3	3	3.00	-	-	-	-	114	36	0	-	-	-	-
Wettimuny,MD	2	4	0	28	17	7.00	-	-	2	-	-						
Wettimuny,S	23	43	1	1221	190	29.07	2	6	10	-	24	37	0	-	-	-	-
Wickramasinghe,GP	4	5	1	24	21	6.00	-	-	2	-	774	420	11	38.18	1	-	5/73
Wickremasinghe,ADG	1	1	0	2	2	2.00	-	-	3	-							

SRI LANKA (cont.)

	BATTING AND FIELDING											BOWLING					
	Tests	I	N	Runs	HS	Avge	100	50	Ct	St	Balls	Runs	Wks	Avge	5w	10w	BB
Wijegunawardene,KIW	2	4	1	14	6*	4.66	-	-	-	-	364	148	7	21.14	-	-	4/52
Wijesuriya,RGCE	4	7	2	22	8	4.40	-	-	1	-	586	294	1	294.00	-	-	1/68

COMPLETE TEST RECORD FOR PLAYERS REPRESENTING TWO COUNTRIES

	BATTING AND FIELDING											BOWLING					
	Tests	I	N	Runs	HS	Avge	100	50	Ct	St	Balls	Runs	Wks	Avge	5w	10w	BB
Amir Elahi (I/P)	6	9	1	82	47	10.25	-	-	-	-	400	248	7	35.42	-	-	4/134
Ferris,JJ (A/E)	9	17	4	114	20*	8.76	-	-	4	-	2302	775	61	12.70	6	1	7/37
Guillen,SC (W/N)	8	12	2	202	54	20.20	-	1	13	3	-						
Gul Mahomed (I/P)	9	17	1	205	34	12.81	-	-	3	-	77	24	2	12.00	-	-	2/21
Hearne,F (E/SA)	6	10	0	168	30	16.80	-	-	3	-	62	40	2	20.00	-	-	2/40
Kardar,AH (I/P)	26	42	3	927	93	23.76	-	5	16	-	2712	954	21	45.42	-	-	3/35
Midwinter,WE (A/E)	12	21	1	269	37	13.45	-	-	10	-	1725	605	24	25.20	1	-	5/78
Mitchell,F (E/SA)	5	10	0	116	41	11.60	-	-	2	-	-						
Murdoch,WL (A/E)	19	34	5	908	211	31.31	2	1	13	2	-						
Pataudi, Nawab of, sr (E/I)	6	10	0	199	102	19.90	1	-	-	-	-						
Trott,AE (A/E)	5	9	3	228	85*	38.00	-	2	4	-	948	390	26	15.00	2	-	8/43
Wessels,KC (A/SA)	25	44	1	1894	179	44.04	4	11	19	-	90	42	0	-	-	-	-
Woods,SMJ (A/E)	6	10	0	154	53	15.40	-	1	5	-	412	250	10	25.00	-	-	3/28

NOTES

ACKNOWLEDGEMENTS

The Publishers express their gratitude to the following for permission to reproduce material in copyright:

Australian Picture Library, Sydney
Bryan Charlton, Adelaide
David Syme & Co. Limited, Melbourne
The *Dominion,* Wellington
The *Herald and Weekly Times,* Melbourne
PBL Marketing, Sydney
Professional Sport, London
Reuters Australia Pty Limited, Sydney

Every effort has been made to contact the copyright owners of copyright material included in this collection. The Publishers apologise for any unwitting oversights.